THE HUMAN SPECIES

THIRD EDITION

THE HUMAN SPECIES

An Introduction to Biological Anthropology

John H. Relethford

State University of New York
College at Oneonta

Mayfield Publishing Company

Mountain View, California
London • Toronto

Library of Congress Cataloging-in-Publication Data
Relethford, John H.
    The human species : an introduction to biological anthropology /
John H. Relethford—3rd ed.
        p. cm.
    Includes bibliographical references and index.
    ISBN 1-55934-664-7
        1. Physical anthropology.   I. Title.
GN60.R392 1996
573—dc20   96-11412
                                                                            CIP

Manufactured in the United States of America

10   9   8   7   6   5   4   3

Mayfield Publishing Company
1280 Villa Street
Mountain View, California 94041

Sponsoring editor, Janet M. Beatty; production editor, Melissa Kreischer; manuscript
editor, Carol Dondrea; text and cover designer, Anna George; art director, Jeanne M.
Schreiber; art manager, Susan Breitbard; photo researcher, Brian Pecko; illustrators,
John and Judy Waller; manufacturing manager, Amy Folden. Cover photos, (inset) ©
Kevin O'Farrell: CONCEPTS; (background) © Philippe Plailly/Science Photo
Library/Photo Researchers, Inc. The text was in 10/12 Goudy Old Style (Monotype)
by American Composition and Graphics and printed on acid-free 50# Somerset
Matte by Quebecor Printing Book Group, Hawkins.

Preface

This text introduces the field of biological anthropology (also known as physical anthropology), the science concerned with human biological origins, evolution, and variation. The text addresses the major questions that concern biological anthropologists: "What are humans?", "How are we similar to and different from other animals?", "Where are our origins?", "How did we evolve?", "Are we still evolving?", "How are we different from one another?", and "What does the future hold for the human species?"

Organization

The book is divided into four parts. Part One, "Evolutionary Background," gives readers the grounding they will need in genetics and evolutionary theory to better understand the remainder of the text. Chapter 1 begins with an overview of anthropology and biological anthropology and discusses the scientific method as it relates to evolution. A brief history of evolutionary science and a discussion of the "creation-evolution" debate conclude the chapter.

Chapter 2 reviews molecular and Mendelian genetics as applied to humans in order to provide genetic background for later chapters. It includes a basic review of cell biology. The next two chapters review evolutionary theory—Chapter 3 focuses on microevolution and Chapter 4 looks at macroevolution. Chapter 5 examines the fossil record for evolution, first looking at dating methods and other techniques of fossil analysis and concluding with a brief summary of the evolution of life prior to the origin of primates.

Part Two addresses "Our Place in Nature," specifically the biology, behavior, and evolution of primates. A main focus of this section are the questions "What are humans?" and "How are we related to other living creatures?" Chapter 6 examines issues in classification and looks at the basic biology and behavior of mammals in general, and primates in particular. Chapter 7 evaluates the different types of primates in terms of classification, biology, and behavior, with particular attention given to our close relatives, the apes. Chapter 8 looks specifically at the human species and includes a comparison of human traits with those of apes. Chapter 9 summarizes the major events of primate origins and evolution, from the time of the disappearance of the dinosaurs 65 million years ago to the split of ape and human lines 5–7 million years ago.

Part Three devotes three chapters to "Human Evolution." Chapter 10 begins with a brief review of human evolutionary history and follows with a detailed summary of the first hominids, the australopithecines, and with the emergence of the genus *Homo* characterized by a larger brain and the advent of stone tool technology. Chapter 11 examines the continued biological and cultural evolution of the genus *Homo*. Chapter 12 looks at the fossil and archaeological evidence for the origin of modern humans and includes a discussion of current controversies (Did modern humans evolve throughout the world, or are our recent ancestors exclusively from Africa?).

Part Four focuses on "Human Variation," with an emphasis on understanding how modern peoples differ from one another and why. This section also looks at the way the human species continues to evolve, both biologically and culturally. Chapter 13 examines different ways we measure human variation and contrasts racial and evolutionary approaches to variation. Chapter 14 provides a number of case studies of evolution in modern and recent human populations. Chapter 15 looks at how humans adapt to different environments—both genetically and culturally. Chapter 16 explores the evolution of patterns of human health and disease in our evolutionary past and in today's world. Chapter 17 looks at changes in the demographic structure of human populations.

Not all instructors will use the same sequence of chapters. Some may prefer a different arrangement of topics. I have attempted to write chapters in such a way as to accommodate such changes whenever possible. For example, some instructors may prefer to cover human variation before the sections on primates and human evolution. In that case, a sequence of Parts One, Four, Two and Three would work well.

Features

Throughout the text, I have attempted to provide new material relevant to the field and fresh treatments of traditional material. Key features include:

- *All areas of contemporary biological anthropology are covered.* In addition to traditional coverage of areas such as genetics, evolutionary theory, primate behavior, and the fossil record, the text includes material often neglected in introductory texts. There are separate chapters on adaptation, human health and disease, and demography, and the study of human growth is incorporated into several chapters.

- *The relationship between biology and culture is a major focus.* The biocultural framework is introduced in the first chapter and integrated throughout the text.
- *Behavior is discussed in an evolutionary context.* The evolutionary nature of primate and human behavior is emphasized in a number of chapters, including those on primate biology and behavior (6–8) and the fossil record of human evolution (10–12).
- *The emphasis is on the human species in its context within the primate order.* Discussions of mammals and nonhuman primates continually refer back to their potential relevance for understanding the human species. In fact, a separate chapter on the biology and behavior of the human species written from a comparative perspective has been added to this edition.
- *Hypothesis testing is emphasized.* From the first chapter, where students are introduced to the scientific method, I emphasize how various hypotheses are tested. Rather than provide a dogmatic approach with all the "right" answers, the text examines evidence in the context of hypothesis testing. With this emphasis, readers can see how new data can lead to changes in basic models and can better understand the "big picture" of biological anthropology.

New to This Edition

Every chapter has been carefully revised in light of new findings in the field and comments from users of the second edition. In fact, a number of chapters have been re-ordered, added, and merged or deleted based on the helpful feedback I received from colleagues. To make the text as clear, accessible, and up - to - date as possible, I've made the following specific changes:

- Each chapter now includes a box that focuses on a "Special Topic." Some of the topics focus on contemporary issues (for example, "The Coming Plague?"), some on historical issues (for example, "The Piltdown Hoax"), and some on a wide range of other subjects (for example, "Science Fiction and Orthogenesis").
- The chapter on the fossil record (5) has been moved earlier in the text to form a bridge between the chapter on macroevolutionary theory (4) and the chapters on the primates (6—9).
- The chapters on primate biology and behavior have been completely rewritten to form two new chapters. The first of these (Chapter 6) provides a general summary of the biology and behavior of mammals and primates and discusses alternate models of primate behavior. The section on sociobiology has been moved here and a new section on socioecology has been added.
- Chapter 7 is devoted to the variation in the biology and behavior of primates and reviews the entire order, from prosimians to the great apes.

Several case studies on primate behavior have been added and treatment of the bonobo has been expanded.

- A new chapter (8) has been added that focuses exclusively on the human species. Material on the patterns of human growth and their evolutionary significance has been moved here.
- The chapter on primate evolution (9) has been streamlined and revised to emphasize the major evolutionary trends in primate evolution, underlining the issue of Miocene ape diversity and the way it precludes drawing specific family trees.
- The chapter on the first hominids (10) has been revised to begin with a brief summary of human evolution in order to provide a conceptual framework for the student. Information on new species (*Ardipithecus ramidus* and *Australopithecus anamensis*) has been added, as has new information on dating and anatomy. The section on evolutionary trends has been rewritten to minimize phylogenetic arguments and to emphasize basic questions (for example, "Why did we become bipedal?").
- The chapter on the evolution of the genus *Homo* has been split into two chapters (11 and 12). Chapter 11 now covers *Homo erectus* and "archaic" *Homo sapiens*. New data have been incorporated, including the finding of a possible earlier date for the arrival of *Homo erectus* in Asia. A new Chapter 12 focuses on the origin of modern humans. In addition to a complete revision of the modern human origins debate, this chapter adds new material on modern human archaeology and questions of language origins.
- The chapters on human variation (13–17) have all been placed in a single unit (Part Four). New case studies have been used in Chapter 14 to illustrate human microevolution. The chapters on health and disease (16) and demography (17) have been rewritten to focus on evolutionary issues, and case studies have been revised, added, or deleted to relate to this main point. Material on the secular change in human growth and protein-calorie malnutrition has been moved into Chapter 16.
- The appendix on primate classification has been revised and simplified. Two new appendixes have been added: one on comparative skeletal anatomy and one on metric conversion factors.

Study Helps

To make the text more accessible and interesting, I have included frequent examples and illustrations of basic ideas as well as abundant maps to help orient students. I have kept the technical jargon to a minimum, yet every introductory text contains a number of specialized terms that students must learn. The first mention of these terms in the text appears in **boldface** type and accompanying short definitions appear in the text margins. A glossary is provided at the end of the book, often with more detailed definitions.

Each chapter ends with a summary and a list of supplemental readings. A list of references appears at the end of the book, providing the complete reference for studies cited in the text.

Ancillaries

The *Instructor's Manual* includes a test bank of more than 700 questions, as well as chapter overviews and outlines, topics for class discussion, and sources for laboratory equipment.

A *Computerized Test Bank* is available free of charge to qualifying adopters. Also available to qualifying adopters is a package of 68 color and black-and-white transparency acetates.

Acknowledgments

My thanks go to the dedicated and hardworking people at Mayfield, both those I have dealt with personally and the others behind the scenes. I give special thanks to Jan Beatty, sponsoring editor, for continued encouragement and support. I am also extremely grateful to Melissa Kreischer, production editor, for her excellence, dedication, and patience. Pam Trainer, permissions editor, and Carol Dondrea, manuscript editor, were also very helpful.

I also thank my colleagues who served as reviewers: Mark N. Cohen, SUNY at Plattsburg; Lynne E. Christenson, San Diego State University; Katherine A. Dettwyler, Texas A & M University; Susan J. Haun, University of Memphis; Janis Faye Hutchinson, University of Houston; Lynnette Leidy, University of Massachusetts at Amherst; Jonathan Marks, Yale University; Jim Mielke, University of Kansas; Deborah Overdorff, University of Texas at Austin; Renee L. Pennington, Pennsylvania State University; and Jane Underwood, University of Arizona. Having been a reviewer myself, I appreciate the extensive time and effort these individuals have taken. I also thank other colleagues who have spent time discussing the second edition with me and who have offered many valuable suggestions: Barry Bogin, University of Michigan at Dearborn; Kenneth Kennedy, Cornell University; Lorena Madrigal, University of South Florida; Carol Raemsch, SUNY at Albany; Linda Taylor, University of Miami; and David Tracer, University of Washington.

Last, but not least, I dedicate this to my family: to my wife and best friend, Hollie Jaffe, and to my wonderful sons, David, Benjamin, and Zane. You make it all worthwhile.

Contents

**PART TWO
OUR PLACE IN NATURE   *133***

**PART THREE
HUMAN EVOLUTION   257**

**PART FOUR
HUMAN VARIATION**   *351*

PART ONE

Evolutionary Background

The Study of Biological Anthropology

CHAPTER **1**

What is anthropology? To many people, it is the study of the exotic extremes of human nature. To others, it is the study of ancient ruins and lost civilizations. The study of anthropology seems strange to many, and the practitioners of this field, the anthropologists, seem even stranger. The stereotype of an anthropologist is a pith-helmeted, pipe-smoking eccentric, tracking chimpanzees through the forest, digging up the bones of million-year-old ancestors, interviewing lost tribes about their sexual customs, and recording the words of the last speakers of a language. Another popular image presented in the media is Indiana Jones, the intrepid archaeologist of the film *Raiders of the Lost Ark*. Here is a man who is versed in the customs and languages of many societies past and present, feels at home anywhere in the world, and makes a living teaching, finding lost treasures, rescuing beautiful women in distress, and fighting Nazis (Figure 1.1).

Of course, Indiana Jones is a fictional character. Some real-life anthropologists are almost as well known: Jane Goodall, Margaret Mead, Donald Johanson, and the late Dian Fossey. These anthropologists have studied chimpanzees, Samoan culture, the fossils of human ancestors, and gorillas.

Their research conjures up images of anthropology every bit as varied as the imaginary adventures of Indiana Jones. Anthropologists do study all these things, and more. The sheer diversity of topics investigated by anthropologists seems almost to defy any sort of logic. In one department of anthropology, for example, the research interests of the faculty include modern human origins, Caribbean music, Iroquois history, comparative religion, and tourism. The methods of data collection and analysis are almost as diverse. What pulls these different subjects together?

In one obvious sense, they all share an interest in the same subject—human beings. In fact, the traditional textbook definition of anthropology is the "study of humans." Though this definition is easy to remember, it is not terribly useful. After all, scientists in other fields, such as researchers in anatomy and biochemistry, also study humans. And there are many fields within the social sciences whose sole interest is humans. History, geography, political science, economics, sociology, and psychology are all devoted to the study of human beings, and no one would argue that these fields are merely branches of anthropology.

WHAT IS ANTHROPOLOGY?

What, then, is a suitable definition of anthropology? **Anthropology** could be described as the science of human cultural and biological variation and evolution. The first part of this definition includes both human culture and biology. **Culture** is learned behavior. Culture includes social and economic systems, marriage customs, religion, philosophy, and all other behaviors that are acquired through the process of learning rather than through instinct. The joint emphasis on culture and biology is an important feature of anthropology, and one that sets it apart from many other fields. A biochemist may be interested in specific aspects of human biology and consider the study of human cultural behaviors less important. To a sociologist, cultural behaviors and not human biology are the main focus of attention. Anthropology, however, is characterized by a concern with *both* culture and biology as vital in understanding the human condition.

Biology and Culture

To the anthropologist, humans must be understood in terms of learned behavior as well as biology. We rely extensively on learned behaviors in virtually all aspects of our life. Even the expression of our sexual drives must be understood in light of human cultural systems. Although the actual basis of our sex drive is biological, the ways in which we express it are shaped by behaviors we have learned. The very inventiveness of humans, with our vast technology, is testimony to the powerful effect of learning. However, we are not purely cultural creatures. We are also biological organisms. We need to

eat and breathe, and we are affected by our external environment. In addition, our biology sets certain limits on our potential behaviors. For example,
all human cultures have some type of social structure that provides for the
care of children until they are old enough to fend for themselves. This is not
simply kindness to children; our biological position as mammals requires
such attentiveness to children for survival. In contrast with other animal
species, whose infants need little or no care, human infants are physically
incapable of taking care of themselves.

Anthropology is concerned not only with culture and biology, but also
with their interaction. Just as humans are not solely cultural or solely biological, we are not simply the sum of these two, either. Humans are biocultural
organisms, which means that our culture and biology influence each other.
The **biocultural approach** to studying human beings is a main theme of this
book, and you will examine many examples of biocultural interaction. For
now, however, consider one—population growth (which will be covered in
greater detail in Chapter 17). The growth of a population depends, in part,
on how many people are born relative to how many die. If more people are
born than die in a given period of time, then the population will grow. Obviously, population growth is in part caused by biological factors affecting the
birth and death rates. A variety of cultural factors, such as economic system
and marriage patterns, also affect population growth.

A variety of cultural factors, including technological changes and ideological outlooks, affect the birth rate. Developments in medicine and medical care change the death rate. Further, changes in biological factors can lead
to cultural changes. For example, the slowing of the birth rate has led to a
reduction in the number of college students during the past decade. This
change will further affect aspects of our society such as college admissions
standards, availability of federal funds for education, and competition for
jobs among graduates.

The entire process of population growth and its biological and cultural
implications is considerably more complicated than described here. The
basic point, however, should be clear: by studying the process of population
growth, we can see how cultural factors affect biological factors and vice
versa.

The biocultural perspective of anthropology points to one of the
unique strengths of anthropology as a science: it is **holistic,** meaning that it
takes into consideration all aspects of human existence. Population growth
again provides an example. Where the sociologist may be concerned with

▲▲▲

anthropology The
science that investigates
human biological and
cultural variation and
evolution.

culture Behavior that is
learned and socially
transmitted.

biocultural approach
Studying humans in
terms of the interaction
between biology and
culture in evolutionary
adaptation.

holistic Integrating all
aspects of existence in
understanding human
variation and evolution.

■ **FIGURE 1.2**
Biological variation in a group
of children. (© Peter Menzel/
Stock Boston)

effects of population growth on social structure and the psychologist may be
concerned with effects of population growth on psychological stress, the
anthropologist is interested potentially in all aspects of population growth.
In a given study, this analysis may include the relationship among diet, fertility, religion, disease, social systems, and political systems, to name but a few
factors.

The biocultural nature of anthropology makes it a difficult subject to
classify in college catalogs. By now you are aware that different academic
departments are grouped under the arts, humanities, natural sciences, mathematics, and social sciences. Where does anthropology, with its interest in
both human culture and biology, fit in? Is it a natural science or a social science? Most college and universities place departments of anthropology with
the social sciences, primarily because historically most anthropologists have
been concerned with cultural anthropology. Many schools, however, allow
completion of a biological anthropology course to fulfill a natural science
requirement. The distinctions drawn between different branches of learning
should not prevent you from seeing that anthropology has strong ties with
both the natural and social sciences.

Variation

A major characteristic of anthropology is its concern with **variation.** In a general sense, variation refers to differences among individuals or populations. The anthropologist is interested in differences and similarities among human groups, in terms of both biology and culture. Anthropologists use the **comparative approach** to attempt to generalize about those aspects of human behavior and biology that are similar in all populations and those that are unique to specific environments and cultures. How do groups of people differ from one another? *Why* do they differ? These are questions about variation, and they apply equally to cultural and biological traits (Figure 1.2). For example, do all human cultures practice the same marriage customs? (They don't.) Are there discernible reasons why one group has a certain type of marriage system? An example of a biological trait that raises questions about variation is skin color. Can groups be characterized by a certain skin color, or does skin color vary within groups? Is there any pattern in the distribution of skin color that makes sense in terms of environmental differences?

Evolution

Evolution is change in living organisms over generations. Both cultural and biological evolution interest anthropologists. How and why do human culture and biology change? For example, anthropologists may be interested in the origin of marriage systems. When, how, and why did certain marriage systems evolve? For that matter, when did the custom of marriage first originate, and why? As for skin color, an anthropologist would be interested in what skin color the first humans may have had, and where, when, how, and why other skin colors may have evolved.

Adaptation

In addition to the concepts of variation and evolution, the anthropologist is interested in the process of **adaptation.** At the broadest level, adaptations are advantageous changes. Any aspect of biology or behavior that confers some advantage on an individual or population can be considered an adaptation. Cultural adaptations include technological devices such as clothing,

variation The differences that exist among individuals or populations.

comparative approach Comparing human populations to determine common and unique behaviors or biological traits.

evolution Change in populations of organisms from one generation to the next.

adaptation The process of successful interaction between a population and an environment.

shelter, and methods of food production. Such technologies can improve the well-being of humans. Cultural adaptations also include social systems and rules for behaviors. For example, the belief in certain societies that sexual relations with a woman must be avoided for some time after she gives birth can be adaptive in the sense that these behaviors influence the rate of population growth.

Cultural adaptations may vary in their effect on different members of a population. What is adaptive for some people may not be adaptive for others. For example, changes in certain tax laws may be advantageous for certain income groups and disadvantageous for others. Beliefs that reduce population growth can be adaptive in certain environments but nonadaptive in others.

Adaptations can also be biological. Some biological adaptations are physiological in nature and involve metabolic changes. For example, when you are too hot, you will sweat. Sweating is a short-term physiological response that removes excess heat through the process of evaporation. Within limits, it aids in maintaining a constant body temperature. Likewise, shivering is an adaptive response to cold. The act of shivering increases metabolic rate and provides more heat.

Biological adaptations can also be genetic in nature. Here, changes in genes over many generations produce variation in biological traits. The darker skin color of many humans native to regions near the equator is one example of a long-term genetic adaptation. The darker skin provides protection from the harmful effects of ultraviolet radiation (see Chapter 14 for more information on skin color and variation).

Anthropologists look at patterns of human variation and evolution in order to understand the nature of cultural and biological adaptations. In some cases, explanations are relatively clear, whereas in others we still seek explanations for the adaptive value of any given behavior or trait. In such a quest, we must always remember two important rules about adaptation. First, adaptations are often specific to a particular environment. What is adaptive in one environment may not be in another environment. Second, we must keep in mind that not all aspects of behavior or biology are adaptive. The forward-jutting human chin, for example, seems not to reflect any adaptive "value" or "function." Instead, it is caused by different rates of growth within the jaw.

The Subfields of Anthropology

In a general sense, anthropology is concerned with determining what humans are, how they evolved, and how they differ from one another. Where other disciplines focus on specific issues of humanity, anthropology is unique in dealing simultaneously with questions of origins, evolution, variation, and adaptation.

Even though anthropology has a wide scope and appears to encompass anything and everything pertaining to humans, the study of anthropology in the United States is often characterized by four separate subfields, each with a specific focus. These four subfields are cultural anthropology, anthropological archaeology, linguistic anthropology, and biological anthropology. Some anthropologists add a fifth subfield—applied anthropology, which is concerned with the application of anthropological findings to contemporary matters and issues. Whether one characterizes applied anthropology as a separate subfield or as the practical extension of research in the four subfields, there is growing interest (and employment) in areas in which anthropological ideas and methods can add value. Some examples include public health, economic policy, agricultural and industrial development, and population control, to name a few.

CULTURAL ANTHROPOLOGY   **Cultural anthropology** deals primarily with variation in the cultures of populations in the present or recent past. Its subjects include social, political, economic, and ideological aspects of human cultures. Cultural anthropologists look at all aspects of behavior within a society. Even when they are interested in a specific aspect of a culture, such as marriage systems, they look at how these behaviors relate to all other aspects of culture. Marriage systems, for example, may have an effect on the system of inheritance and may also be closely related to religious views. Comparison of cultures is used to determine common and unique features among different cultures. Information from this subfield will be presented later in the book to aid in the interpretation of the relationship between human culture and biology.

ANTHROPOLOGICAL ARCHAEOLOGY   Archaeology is the study of cultural behaviors in the historic and prehistoric past. **Anthropological archaeology** uses the methods of archaeology to infer the behaviors of past societies. The archaeologist deals with such remains of past societies as tools, shelters, remains of animals eaten for food, and other objects that have survived. These remains, termed *artifacts*, are used to reconstruct past behavior. To help fill in the gaps, the archaeologist makes use of the findings of cultural anthropologists who have studied similar societies. Archaeological findings are critical in understanding the behavior of early humans and their evolution. Some of these findings for the earliest humans are presented later in this text.

▲▲

cultural anthropology Focuses on variations in cultural behaviors among human populations.

anthropological archaeology Focuses on cultural variation in prehistoric (and some historic) populations by analyzing the culture's remains.

LINGUISTIC ANTHROPOLOGY   **Linguistic anthropology** is the study of language. Spoken language is a behavior that appears to be uniquely human. This subfield of anthropology deals with the analysis of languages usually in nonliterate societies and with general trends in the evolution of languages. A major question raised by linguistic anthropology concerns the extent to which language shapes culture. Is language necessary for the transmission of culture? Does a language provide information about the beliefs and practices of a human culture?

Biological anthropology must consider many of the findings of linguistic anthropology in the analysis of human variation and evolution. When comparing humans and apes, we must ask whether language is a unique human characteristic. If it is, then what biological and behavioral differences exist between apes and humans that lead to the fact that one species has language and the other lacks it? Linguistics is also important in considering human evolution. When did language begin? Why?

BIOLOGICAL ANTHROPOLOGY   The subject of this book is the subfield of **biological anthropology,** which is concerned with the biological evolution and variation of the human species, past and present. Biological anthropology is often referred to by another name—*physical anthropology.* The course you are currently enrolled in might be known by either name. Actually, the two names refer to the same field. Early in the twentieth century the field was first known as physical anthropology, reflecting its then primary interest in the *physical* variation of past and present humans and our primate relatives. Much of the research in the field focused on descriptive studies of physical variations, with little theoretical background. Starting in the 1950s, physical anthropologists became more familiar with the rapidly growing fields of genetics and evolutionary science. As a result, the field of physical anthropology became more concerned with biological processes, particularly with genetics. After a while, many in the field began using the term *biological anthropology* to emphasize the new focus on biological processes. In most circles today, the two terms are used more or less interchangeably.

It is useful to consider the field of biological anthropology in terms of four major questions it seeks to answer. First, *What are humans?* That is, How are we related to other living creatures? Who are our closest living relatives? What makes us similar to other living creatures? How are we unique? A second major question concerns our past. *What is the fossil record for human evolution?* Where have we come from? What does the history of our species look like? A third question concerns variation among modern humans. *How are humans around the world like, or unlike, each other?* What causes the patterns of human variation that we see? The fourth question relates back to the biocultural nature of human beings: *How does culture affect biology, and vice versa?* What impact have the rapid and amazing cultural changes in our species' recent past had on our biology? Are our biological and cultural adaptations out of synch?

There are several traditionally defined areas within biological anthropology, such as primate studies, paleoanthropology, and human variation. Primate studies are concerned with defining humans in the natural world, specifically in terms of the primates (a group of mammals that includes prosimians, monkeys, apes, and humans). Primate studies look at the anatomy, behavior, and evolution of the other primates as a standard of comparison with those aspects of humans. In this way, we can learn something about what it is to be human.

Paleoanthropology is the study of the fossil remains of human evolution. Researchers in this field are interested in determining who our ancestors were, and when, how, and why they evolved. Paleoanthropologists work closely with archaeologists to reconstruct the behaviors of our ancestors.

The study of human variation is concerned with how and why humans differ from each other in their biological makeup. This subfield considers the ways in which culture and biology interact in the modern world, including such topics as the genetics of populations, demography (the study of population size and composition), physical growth and development, and human health and disease. Several decades ago, human variation was the concern of only a few biological anthropologists. Today it is perhaps the largest research area within biological anthropology.

SCIENCE AND EVOLUTION

Biological anthropology is an evolutionary science. All the major questions just presented may be addressed using modern evolutionary theory. Biological evolution simply refers to change in the genetic makeup of populations over time.

Characteristics of Science

Before we consider how evolution works, it is important to understand exactly what a science is.

FACTS   At one time or another, you have probably heard someone make the statement that evolution is a theory, not a fact. Or you might have heard

▲▲

linguistic anthropology
Focuses on the nature of human language, the relationship of language to culture, and the languages of nonliterate peoples.

biological anthropology
Focuses on the biological evolution of humans and human ancestors, the relationship of humans to other organisms, and

patterns of biological variation within and among human populations. Also referred to as physical anthropology.

Biological Anthropologists at Work

The research interests of biological anthropologists are quite varied. This photo essay provides some examples.

Dr. Barry Bogin is a professor of anthropology in the Department of Behavioral Sciences at the University of Michigan at Dearborn. His area of specialization is the study of human growth, including studies of seasonal variation in growth rates, the evolution of human growth patterns, and the relationship between social and cultural factors and child growth. Much of his recent research has focused on an analysis of the cultural correlates of differences in growth patterns of Ladinos and Mayans in Guatemala and the United States. He is shown here measuring the height of a Mayan woman who has immigrated to the United States.

Dr. Michael Crawford is a professor of anthropology at the University of Kansas. He specializes in anthropological genetics, the study of the forces affecting genetic variation between and within human populations. Dr. Crawford's research includes studies of genetic markers, DNA, body and cranial measures, fingerprints, and dental

measurements from human populations across the globe. His research has taken him to Mexico, Belize, Ireland, Italy, Alaska, and Siberia, among other places. Currently, he is studying the Evenki reindeer herders of Siberia (shown here), specifically their genetic relationship to the first inhabitants of the New World and their adaptation to extremely cold climates.

Dr. Katherine Dettwyler is an associate professor of anthropology at Texas A&M University. Her research interests include child growth and health and biocultural studies of breast feeding. Her book *Dancing Skeletons* (Waveland Press, 1994) describes her recent research on infant and child growth as it relates to health and nutrition in Mali, West Africa. Dr. Dettwyler is actively involved in a number of organizations to promote improved nutrition in Mali.

Dr. Dean Falk is a professor of anthropology at the State University of New York at Albany. Her primary research interest is the evolution and comparative anatomy of primate brains, including the human brain. Dr. Falk is an expert in the field of paleoneurology, which involves the reconstruction of brain anatomy from fossil evidence. Her recent

Barry Bogin

Michael Crawford

Katherine Dettwyler

Dean Falk

research deals with how the brain cools itself, including implications for human evolution and the origin of an enlarged brain in our early ancestors. Her model of brain evolution is described in *Braindance* (1992).

Dr. Lyle Konigsberg, an associate professor of anthropology at the University of Tennessee, is particularly interested in integrating the study of prehistoric human skeletal remains with genetic and demographic theory. Dr. Konigsberg investigates patterns of prehistoric biological variation across space and time. His current work involves an analysis of prehistoric Native American populations, dating between 500 and 6,000 years ago.

Dr. Henry McHenry is a professor of anthropology at the University of California at Davis. His primary research interest is paleoanthropology, the study of the fossil remains of human ancestors. Dr. McHenry's current research focuses specifically on estimating the body size of early humans from their skeletal remains. He uses these estimates to make inferences regarding a variety of topics, including gender-based differences in body size, variations in relative brain size, and other aspects of ecology and social behavior.

Dr. Lorena Madrigal, an associate professor of anthropology at the University of South Florida, studies the biology and microevolution of human populations in Costa Rica, particularly demography and genetics. Her earlier work focused on the relationship among fertility, genetic change, and the sickle cell gene. Recently, her work has expanded to include aspects of maturation, miscarriage, frequency of twinning, and seasonal variation in demographic rates, among other topics. Most recently, Dr. Madrigal has been involved in the historical demography of Escazú, a small rural population in Costa Rica.

Dr. Barbara Smuts is a professor at the University of Michigan at Ann Arbor. Her work examines the behavior of baboons, particularly the social relationships between mothers and daughters. Her current research focuses on olive baboons in Kenya, Africa, and she also studies mother–infant relationships among bottle-nosed dolphins.

Henry McHenry

Lyle Konigsberg

Barbara Smuts

Lorena Madrigal

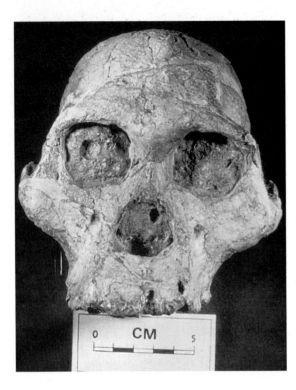

■ FIGURE 1.3
A skull of *Australopithecus africanus*, a human ancestor that lived two to three million years ago. (© K. Cannon-Bonventre/Anthro-Photo)

that it is a fact, not a theory. Which is it, theory or fact? The truth of the matter is that someone who makes either of these statements does not understand what a theory or a fact is. Evolution is both fact and theory. A fact is simply a verifiable truth. It is a fact that the earth is round. It is a fact that when you drop something, it falls to the ground (assuming you are in the presence of a gravitational field and you are not dropping something that floats or flies away!). Evolution is a fact. Living organisms have changed in the past and they continue to change today. There are forms of life living today that did not exist millions of years ago. There are also forms of life that did live in the past but are not around today, such as our ancestors (Figure 1.3). Certain organisms have shown definite changes in their biological makeup. Horses, for example, used to have five toes, then three, and today they have one. Human beings have larger brains and smaller teeth today than they did a million years ago. Some changes are even apparent over shorter intervals of time. For example, human teeth are on average smaller today than they were only 10,000 years ago. All of these statements and many others are verifiable truths. They are facts.

HYPOTHESES   What is a hypothesis? A **hypothesis** is simply an explanation of observed facts. For example, consider gravity. Gravity is a fact. It is observable. Many hypotheses could be generated to explain gravity. You could hypothesize that gravity is caused by a giant living in the core of our planet drawing in air, thus causing a pull on all objects on the earth's surface. Bizarre as it sounds, this is a scientific hypothesis because it can be tested. It is, however, easily shown to be incorrect (air movement can be measured and it does not flow in the postulated direction).

TESTABILITY   To be scientific, a hypothesis must be testable. The potential must exist for a hypothesis to be rejected. Just as the presence of the hypothetical giant in the earth can be tested (it doesn't exist!), predictions made about gravitational strength can also be tested. Not all hypotheses can be tested, however, and for this reason they are not scientific hypotheses. That doesn't necessarily mean they are true or false, but only that they cannot be tested. For example, you might come up with a hypothesis that all the fossils we have ever found were put in the ground by God to confuse us. This is not a scientific hypothesis because we have no objective way of testing the statement.

Many evolutionary hypotheses, however, are testable. For example, specific predictions about the fossil record can be made based on our knowledge of evolution. One such prediction is that humans evolved after the extinction of the dinosaurs. The potential exists for this statement to be rejected; all we need is evidence that humans existed before, or at the same time as, the dinosaurs. Because we have found no such evidence, we cannot reject the hypothesis. We can, however, imagine a situation in which the hypothesis could be rejected. If we cannot imagine such a situation, then the hypothesis cannot be tested. For example, imagine that someone tells you that all the people on the earth were created 5 minutes ago, complete with memories! Any evidence you muster against this idea could be explained away. Therefore, this hypothesis is not scientific because there is no possible way to reject it.

THEORIES   What is the difference between a theory and a hypothesis? In some disciplines the two terms are sometimes used to mean the same thing. In the natural and physical sciences, however, theory means something different from hypothesis. A **theory** is a set of hypotheses that have been tested repeatedly and that have not been rejected. Evolution falls into this category. Evidence from many sources has confirmed the basic hypotheses making up evolutionary theory (discussed later in the chapter).

▲▲

hypothesis An explanation of observed facts.

theory A set of hypotheses that have been tested repeatedly and that have not been rejected. This term is sometimes used in a different sense in social science literature.

■ **FIGURE 1.4**
Charles Darwin.
(Neg. no. 326697. Courtesy
Department of Library Services,
American Museum of Natural
History)

The Development of Evolutionary Theory

As with all general theories, modern evolutionary theory is not static. Scientific research is a dynamic process, with new evidence being used to support, clarify, and, most important, reject previous ideas. There will always be continual refinements in specific aspects of the theory and its applications. Because science is a dynamic process, evolutionary theory did not come about overnight. Charles Darwin (1809–1882) is most often credited as the "father of evolutionary thought" (Figure 1.4). It is true that Darwin provided a powerful idea that forms the center of modern evolutionary thought. He did not work in an intellectual vacuum, however, but rather built on the ideas of earlier scholars. Darwin's model was not the first evolutionary theory; it forms, rather, the basis of the one that has stood the test of time.

PRE-DARWINIAN THOUGHT   To understand Darwin's contribution and evolution in general, it is necessary to take a look at earlier ideas. For many centuries the concept of change, biological or otherwise, was rather unusual in Western thought. Much of Greek philosophy, for example, posits a static, unchanging view of the world. In later Western thought, the universe, earth, and all living creatures were regarded as having been created by God in their present form, showing little if any change over many generations. Many biologists (then called natural historians) shared this view, and their science consisted mainly of description and categorization. A good example is Carolus Linnaeus (1707–1778), a Swedish naturalist who compiled the first formal classification of all known living creatures. Such a classification is called a **taxonomy,** and it serves to help organize information. Linnaeus's taxonomy organized all known living creatures into meaningful groups. For example, humans, dogs, cats, and many other animals are mammals, characterized primarily by the presence of mammary glands to feed offspring. Linnaeus used a variety of traits to place all then-known creatures into various categories. A taxonomy helps clarify relationships between different organisms. For example, bats are classified as mammals because they possess mammary glands—and not as birds simply because they have wings.

Linnaeus also gave organisms a name reflecting their genus and species. A **species** is a group of populations whose members can interbreed and produce fertile offspring. A **genus** is a group of similar species, often sharing certain common forms of adaptation. Modern humans, for example, are known by the name *Homo sapiens.* The first word is the genus and the second word is the species (more detail on genus and species is given in Chapter 4).

The reason for the relationships among organisms, however, was not often addressed by early natural historians. The living world was felt to be the product of God's work, and the task of the natural historian was description and classification. This static view of the world began to change in the eighteenth and nineteenth centuries. One important reason for this change was that excavations began to produce many fossils that did not fit neatly into the classification system. For example, imagine that you found the remains of a modern horse. This would pose no problem in interpretation; the bones are those of a dead horse, perhaps belonging to a farmer several years ago. Now suppose you found what at first glance appeared to be a horse but was somewhat smaller and had five toes instead of the single hoof of a modern horse. If you found more and more of these five-toed horses, you would ask what creature the toes belonged to. Because horses do not have five toes today, your only conclusion would be that there once existed horses with five toes and that they do not exist any more. This conclusion, though hardly startling now, was a real thunderbolt to those who believed the world was created as it is today, with no change.

Apart from finding fossil remains of creatures that were somewhat similar to modern-day forms, excavations also uncovered fossil remnants of truly unusual creatures, such as the dinosaurs. Discovery of the fossil record began to chip away at the view that the world is as it always had been, and the concept of change began to be incorporated into explanations of the origin of life. Not all scholars, however, came up with the same hypotheses.

One French anatomist, Georges Cuvier (1769–1832), analyzed many of the fossil remains found in quarries. He showed that many of these belonged to animals that no longer existed; that is, they had become extinct. Cuvier used a hypothesis called **catastrophism** to explain these extinctions. The hypothesis posited a series of catastrophes in the planet's past, during which many living creatures were destroyed. Following these catastrophes, organisms from unaffected areas moved in. The changes over time observed in the fossil record could therefore be explained as a continual process of catastrophes followed by repopulation from other regions (Mayr 1982).

Another hypothesis was put forth by the French scientist Jean-Baptiste Lamarck (1744–1829). He believed that evolution occurred through a natural process of organisms adjusting to their environment. One of his ideas was that an organism could change during its lifetime and then pass these changes on to its offspring. According to Lamarck's idea of **acquired characteristics,** a jungle cat that developed stronger leg muscles through constant running and jumping would pass along stronger muscles to its offspring. Of course, it is easy now to reject the concept of acquired characteristics. For example, someone who loses a finger in an accident will still have

---

taxonomy A formal classification of organisms.

species A group of populations whose members can interbreed

naturally and produce fertile offspring.

genus Groups of species with similar adaptations.

catastrophism The hypothesis that explains evolutionary change in terms of repeated natural catastrophes.

acquired characteristics Lamarck's hypothesis that traits change in response to environmental demands and are passed on to offspring.

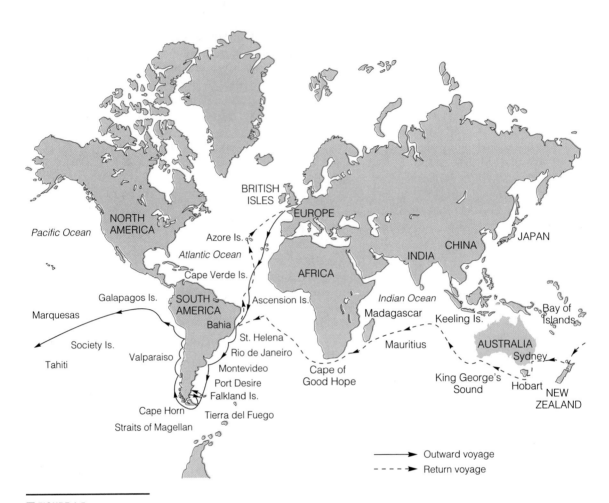

Pacific Ocean

NORTH
AMERICA

BRITISH
ISLES

EUROPE

Azore Is.

Atlantic Ocean

Cape Verde Is.

Galapagos Is.

Marquesas

SOUTH
AMERICA

Bahia

Ascension Is.

AFRICA

INDIA

CHINA

JAPAN

Indian Ocean

Madagascar   Keeling Is.

Bay of
Islands

Society Is.

Tahiti

Valparaiso

St. Helena

Rio de Janeiro

Montevideo

Port Desire

Mauritius

AUSTRALIA
Sydney

Cape Horn

Falkland Is.

Tierra del Fuego

Straits of Magellan

Cape of
Good Hope

King George's
Sound

Hobart
NEW
ZEALAND

⟶ Outward voyage

- - - ➤ Return voyage

■ FIGURE 1.5

Darwin's observations of variation in the different regions he visited aboard the H.M.S. *Beagle* shaped his theory of natural selection.

children with the correct number of fingers. Instead of looking back and ridiculing Lamarck for his ideas, however, we must realize that he was actually quite astute in noting the intimate relationship among organisms, their environments, and evolution.

CHARLES DARWIN AND NATURAL SELECTION Cuvier and Lamarck are perhaps the best-known examples of what many have called "pre-Darwinian" theorists. Evolution was well accepted, and various models were being developed to explain this fact, before Darwin. Charles Darwin developed the theory of natural selection that has since been supported by testing. His major contribution was to combine information from a variety of different fields, such as geology and economics, to form his theory.

With this background in mind, let us look at Darwin and his accomplishment. Charles Darwin had been interested in biology and geology since he was a small child. Born to well-to-do parents, Darwin attended college and had planned to enter the ministry, although he was not as enthusiastic about this career as he was about his studies of natural history. Because of his scientific and social connections, Darwin was able to accompany the scientific survey ship *Beagle* as an unpaid naturalist. The *Beagle* conducted a five-year journey around the world collecting plant and animal specimens in South America and the Galapagos Islands (in the Pacific Ocean near Ecuador), among other places (Figure 1.5).

During these travels, Darwin came to several basic conclusions about variation in living organisms. First, he found a tremendous amount of observable variation in most living species. Instead of looking at the world in terms of fixed, rigid categories (as did mainstream biology in his time), Darwin saw that individuals within species varied considerably from place to place. With careful attention, you can see the world in much the same way that Darwin did. You will see, for example, that people around you vary to an incredible degree. Some are tall, some are short, some are dark, and some are light. Facial features, musculature, hair color, and many other characteristics come in many different forms even in a single classroom. Remember, too, that what you see are only those visible characteristics. With the right type of equipment, you could look at genetic and biochemical variation within your classroom and find even more evidence of tremendous diversity.

Darwin also noted that the variations he saw made sense in terms of the environment (Figure 1.6). Creatures in cold climates often have fur for protection. Birds in areas where insects live deep inside tree branches have long beaks to allow them to extract these insects and eat them. In other words, organisms appear well adapted to specific environments. Darwin believed that the environment acted to change organisms over time. But how?

To help answer this question, Darwin turned to the writings of the economist Thomas Malthus (1766–1834), who had noted that more individuals are born in most species than can possibly survive. In other words, many organisms die before reaching maturity and reproducing. If it were not for this mortality, populations would grow too large for their environments to support them. Certain fish, for example, can produce as many as 8,000 eggs in a single year. Assume for the moment that half of these eggs are female. Now assume that each of these females then also lays 8,000 eggs in a single year. To make things simple, let us further assume that a female fish breeds only once in her life. If you start with two fish (one male and one female), in the next generation you have 8,000 fish. Half of these are females, and each produces 8,000 more fish, for a total of 32 million fish. If the fish continue reproducing in this way, there will be roughly 2.1×10^{36} fish (that is, 2.1 followed by 36 zeroes) after only 10 generations! Suppose these are relatively small fish, each one weighing only 100 grams (a little less than a quarter of a pound). The total weight of all fish after 10 generations would be roughly 2.1×10^{38} grams (or roughly 2.3×10^{32} tons!).

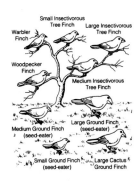

■ **FIGURE 1.6**
The sizes, beak shapes, and diets of this sample of Darwin's finches show differences in adaptation among closely related species. (From E. Peter Volpe, *Understanding Evolution*, 5th ed. Copyright © 1985 Wm. C. Brown Communication, Inc., Dubuque, Iowa. All Rights Reserved. Reprinted by permission)

■ FIGURE 1.7
Adaptation in the peppered moth. The dark-colored moth is more visible on light-colored tree trunks and therefore at greater risk of being seen and eaten by a bird (*top*). The light-colored moth is at greater risk of being eaten on dark-colored tree trunks (*bottom*). (© Michael Tweedie/Photo Researchers, Inc.)

To give you an idea of exactly how large these numbers are, consider the fact that the total weight of our sun is 1.99×10^{33} grams (Pasachoff 1979). If the cycle begins with two fish, after 10 generations the total weight of the fish will be greater than the weight of the sun! Because we are not all currently smothered in fish, something is wrong with this simple model.

Malthus provided the answer. Most of the fish will die before they reproduce. Some eggs will become diseased and die, and others will be eaten by predators. Only a small number of the eggs will actually survive long enough to reproduce. Malthus is best known for extrapolating the principle of population growth into human terms; his lesson is that unless we control our growth there will soon be too many of us to feed.

To Charles Darwin, the ideas of Malthus provided the needed information to solve the problem of adaptation and evolution. Not all individuals in a species survive and reproduce. Some failure to reproduce may be random, but some is related to specific characteristics of an individual. If there are two birds, one with a short beak and one with a long beak, in an environment that requires reaching inside branches to feed, it stands to reason that the bird with the longer beak is more likely to feed itself, survive, and reproduce. In certain environments, some individuals possess traits that enhance their probability of survival and reproduction. If these traits are due, in part or whole, to inherited characteristics, then they will be passed on to the next generation.

In some ways, Darwin's idea was not new. Animal and plant breeders had used this principle for centuries. Controlled breeding and artificial selection had resulted in many traits in domesticated plants and animals, such as livestock size, milk production in cows, and a variety of other traits. The same principle is used in producing pedigreed dogs and many forms of tropical fish. The difference is that Darwin saw that nature (the environment) could select those individuals that survived and reproduced. Hence, he called his concept **natural selection.**

Although the theory of evolution by natural selection is most often associated with Charles Darwin, another English natural historian, Alfred Russel Wallace (1823–1913), came up with essentially the same idea. In fact, Darwin and Wallace communicated their ideas to each other and first presented the theory of natural selection in a joint paper in 1858. Many scholars feel that Wallace's independent work urged Darwin finally to put forward the ideas he had developed years earlier but had not published. To ensure timely publication, Darwin condensed his many years of work into a 490-page "abstract" entitled *On the Origin of Species by Means of Natural Selection*, published in 1859 (Futuyma 1983).

EXAMPLES OF NATURAL SELECTION   One excellent example of how natural selection works is the story of populations of the peppered moth in England over the last few centuries (Figure 1.7). These moths come in two distinct colors, dark and light. Early observations found that most of these moths were light-colored, thus allowing them to camouflage themselves on tree trunks. By blending in, they had a better chance of avoiding the birds that tried to eat them. Roughly 1 percent of the moths, however, were dark-colored and thus at an obvious disadvantage. Naturalists noted that the frequency of dark-colored moths increased to almost 90 percent in the century following the beginning of the Industrial Revolution in England (Grant 1985). The reason for this change was the fact that industrialization brought about massive pollution in the surrounding countryside. The trees became darker in color after being covered with soot. The light moths were at a disadvantage, and the dark moths, now better camouflaged, were better off. Proportionately, more dark moths survived and passed their dark color to the next generation. In evolutionary terminology, the dark moths were *selected for* and the light moths were *selected against*. After antipollution laws were passed and the environment began to recover, the situation reversed: once again light moths survived better, and were selected for, whereas dark moths were selected against.

This well-known study shows us more than just the workings of natural selection. It also illustrates several important principles of evolution. First, we cannot always state with absolute certainty which traits are "good" and which are "bad." It depends on the specific environment. When the trees were light in color, the light-colored moths were at an advantage, but when the situation changed, the dark-colored moths gained the advantage. Second, evolution does not proceed unopposed in one direction. Under certain situations, biological traits can change in a different direction. In the case of the moths, evolution produced a change from light to dark to light again. Third, evolution does not occur in a vacuum. It is affected by changes in the environment and by changes in other species. In this example, changes in the cultural evolution of humans led to a change in the environment, which further affected the evolution of the moths. Finally, the moth study shows us the critical importance of variation to the evolutionary process. If the original population of moths did not possess the dark-colored variation, they might have been wiped out after the trees turned darker in color. Variation must exist for natural selection to operate effectively.

Another example of natural selection is found in P. R. Grant's (1991) continuing work on the variation and evolution of Galapagos finches. Grant found that average beak size changed over time in direct response to changes in the environment. In drought years, the average beak is larger. Why? The simplest explanation is that drought conditions make those finches with larger beaks better able to crack the larger seeds that are more common under drought conditions. In wetter years, seeds are smaller and finches with small beaks are favored. Grant has observed these changes over several decades. The changes in beak size over time shows that the changing environment affects the probability of survival and reproduction.

MODERN EVOLUTIONARY THOUGHT   Darwin provided part of the answer of how evolution worked, but he did not have all the answers. Many early critics of Darwin's work focused on certain questions that Darwin could not answer.

natural selection
A mechanism for evolutionary change favoring the survival and reproduction of some organisms over others because of their biological characteristics.

One important question concerns the origins of variation: Given that natural selection operates on existing variation, then where do those variations come from? Why, at the outset, were some moths light and others dark? Natural selection can act only on preexisting variation; it cannot create new variations. Another question is: How are traits inherited? The theory of natural selection states that certain traits are selected for and passed on to future generations. How are these traits passed on? Darwin knew that traits were inherited, but he did not know the mechanism. Still another question involves how new forms and structures come into being.

Darwin is to be remembered and praised for his work in providing the critical base from which evolutionary science developed. He did not, however, have all the answers, as no scientist does. Even today people tend to equate evolutionary science with Darwin to the exclusion of all work since that time. Some critics of evolutionary theory point to a single aspect of Darwin's work, show it to be in error, and then proceed to claim all of evolutionary thought suspect. In reality, a scientific theory will continue to change as new evidence is gathered and as further tests are constructed.

Modern evolutionary theory relies not only on the work of Darwin and Wallace but also on developments in genetics, zoology, embryology, physiology, and mathematics, to name but a few fields. The basic concept of natural selection as stated by Darwin has been tested and found to be valid. Refinements have been added, and some aspects of the original idea have been changed. We now have answers to many of Darwin's questions.

Biological evolution consists of changes in the genetic composition of populations. As shown in Chapter 3, the relative frequencies of genes change over time because of four mechanisms, or evolutionary forces. Natural selection is one of these mechanisms. Those individuals with genetic characteristics that improve their relative survival or reproduction pass their genetic material on to the next generation. In the peppered moth example discussed earlier, the dark moths were more likely to survive in an environment where pollution made the trunks of trees darker in color. Thus, the relative frequency of genes for dark moth color increased over time (at least until the environment changed again).

Evolutionary change from one generation to the next, or over many generations, is the product of the joint effect of the four evolutionary forces. Our discussion here simplifies a complex idea, but it does suggest that evolution is more than simply natural selection. Modern evolutionary theory encompasses all four evolutionary forces and will be discussed in greater detail in the next three chapters.

Evidence for Evolution

Because this book is concerned with human variation and evolution, you will be provided with numerous examples of how evolution works in human populations, past and present. It is important to understand from the start that biological evolution is a documented fact and that the modern theory of evolution has stood up under many scientific tests.

The fossil record provides evidence of evolution. The story the fossils tell is one of change. Creatures existed in the past that are no longer with us. Sequential changes are found in many fossils showing the change of certain features over time from a common ancestor, as in the case of the horse. Apart from demonstrating that evolution did occur, the fossil record also provides tests of the predictions made from evolutionary theory. For example, the theory predicts that single-celled organisms evolved before multi-celled organisms. The fossil record supports this prediction—multicelled organisms are found in layers of earth millions of years after the first appearance of single-celled organisms. Note that the possibility always remains that the opposite could be found! If multicelled organisms were indeed found to have evolved before single-celled organisms, then the theory of evolution would be rejected. A good scientific theory always allows for the possibility that it may be rejected. The fact that we have not found such a case in countless examinations of the fossil record strengthens the case for evolutionary theory. Remember, in science you do not prove a theory; rather, you fail to reject it.

The fossil record is not the only evidence we have that evolution has occurred. Comparison of living organisms provides further confirmation. For example, the African apes are the closest living relatives of humans. We see this in a number of characteristics. African apes and humans share the same type of dental pattern, have a similar shoulder structure, and have DNA (the genetic code) that is over 98 percent identical. Even though any one of these traits, or others, could be explained as coincidental, why do so many independent traits show the same pattern? One possibility, of course, is that they were designed that way by an ultimate Creator. The problem with this idea is that it cannot be tested. It is a matter of faith and not of science. Another problem is that we must then ask ourselves why a Creator would use the same basic pattern for so many traits in different creatures. Evolution, on the other hand, offers an explanation. Apes and humans share many characteristics because they evolved from a common ancestor (Figure 1.8).

Another example of shared characteristics is the python, a large snake. Like many vertebrates, the python has a pelvis, the skeletal structure that connects the lower legs to the upper body (Futuyma 1983). From a structural standpoint, of what possible use is a pelvis to a creature that has no legs? If the python was created, then what purpose would there have been to give it a pelvis? We can of course argue that no one can understand the motivations of a Creator, but that is hardly a scientific explanation. Evolutionary reasoning provides an answer: the python has retained the pelvis from an earlier ancestor that did have legs.

Further, fascinating evidence of shared characteristics is the discovery of fossils of early whales with reduced hind limbs (Gingerich et al. 1990). Whales are aquatic mammals that have lost hind limbs and pelvic bones since their evolutionary separation from other mammals over 50 million

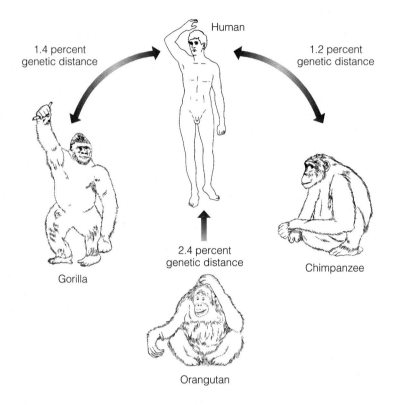

Human

1.4 percent
genetic distance

1.2 percent
genetic distance

Gorilla

2.4 percent
genetic distance

Chimpanzee

Orangutan

years ago. The discovery of fossil whales with small, and perhaps somewhat functional, hind limbs provides another example of shared characteristics that can be explained only through evolution. This discovery also provides an excellent illustration of a transitional form—a fossil that links both early and modern forms.

Another line of evidence supporting evolution is the laboratory and field studies of living organisms. Ongoing evolutionary change has been documented in many organisms, including humans. Specific predictions of the effect of evolutionary mechanisms have been tested and verified in controlled experiments and observational studies. The study of moth color is but one of many examples of this kind of analysis.

Science and Religion

The subject of evolution has always been controversial, and the implications of evolution have sometimes frightened people. For example, the fact that humans and apes evolved from a common ancestor has always upset some people who feel that their humanity is somehow degraded by having ancestors supposedly less worthy than ourselves. Another conflict lies in the implications evolution has for religious views. In the United States a number of laws have prohibited the teaching of evolution in public schools. Many of these laws stayed on the books until the late 1960s.

Numerous legal battles have been fought over these anti-evolution laws. Perhaps the most famous of these was the "Scopes Monkey Trial" in 1925. John Scopes, a high school teacher in Dayton, Tennessee, was arrested for violating the state law prohibiting the teaching of evolution. The town and trial quickly became the center of national attention, primarily because of the two celebrities in the case—William Jennings Bryan, a former U.S. Secretary of State, who represented the state of Tennessee, and Clarence Darrow, one of the most famous American trial lawyers ever, who represented Scopes. The battle between these two eloquent speakers captured the attention of the country (Figure 1.9). In the end, Scopes was found guilty of violating the law, and he was fined $100. The fine was later suspended on a legal technicality. The story of this trial, which has been dramatized in play and movie versions as *Inherit the Wind*, is a powerful story portraying the fight of those who feel strongly about academic freedom and freedom of speech against ignorance and oppression. In reality, the original arrest of Scopes appears to have been planned by several local people, including Scopes, to put the town on the map (Gould 1983).

In retrospect, the Scopes trial may seem amusing. We laugh at early attempts to control subject matter in classrooms and often feel that we have gone beyond such battles. Nothing could be further from the truth, however. For many people, evolution represents a threat to their beliefs in the sudden creation of all life by a creator. Attempts to legislate the teaching of the Biblical view of creation in science classes, however, violate the First Amendment of the Constitution as an establishment of religion. To circumvent this problem, opponents of evolution have devised a new strategy by calling their teachings "creation science," supposedly the scientific study of special creation. The word *God* does not always appear in definitions of creation science, but the word *creator* often does.

In March 1981, the Arkansas state legislature passed a law (Act 590) requiring that creation science be taught in public schools for equal amounts of time as evolution. The American Civil Liberties Union challenged this law, and it was overturned in a federal district court in 1982. A similar law passed in Louisiana in 1981 was later overturned. The Louisiana case has since been appealed and brought to the U.S. Supreme Court, which upheld the ruling of the lower court in 1987. Among other legal problems they raise, both the Arkansas and Louisiana laws have been found to be unconstitutional under the First Amendment.

What is "creation science"? Why shouldn't it be taught in science classes? Shouldn't science be open to new ideas? These questions all center on the issue of whether creation science is a science or not. As typically applied, creation science is not a science; at best, it is a grab bag of ideas spruced up with scientific jargon. One of the original definitions is found in Act 590 of the Arkansas law, which defines creation science as

■ **FIGURE 1.9**
The Scopes Trial. William Jennings Bryan (*right*) represented the state of Tennessee and Clarence Darrow (*left*) represented John Scopes.
(© AP/Wide World Photos)

the scientific evidence for creation and inferences from these scientific evidences. Creation-science includes the scientific evidences and related inferences that indicate: (1) Sudden creation of the universe, energy, and life from nothing; (2) The insufficiency of mutation and natural selection in bringing about development of all living kinds from a single organism; (3) Changes only within fixed limits of originally created kinds of plants and animals; (4) Separate ancestry for man and apes; (5) Explanation of the earth's geology by catastrophism, including the occurrence of a worldwide flood; and (6) A relatively recent inception of the earth and living kinds. (Montagu 1984:376–377)

None of these statements is supported by scientific evidence, and creationist writers generally use very little actual evidence to support their views. Some have written that the Biblical Flood can be supported by the fossil record. Earth's past is essentially recorded by the order in which different levels of earth and fossils are found. In general, that is, the deeper a fossil is found, the older it is. Creationists explain this order as being caused by the flight of animals from the Flood. As the waters rose, they say, birds flew and small mammals ran up mountains to escape drowning; these creatures were therefore drowned at higher elevations.

According to creationists, then, you will find fish at lower levels and birds and mammals at higher levels. The fossil record does show this phenomenon. Isn't this proof for "creation science"? No. Think about the Flood scenario for a moment and you will see that it just doesn't make sense. Why didn't the winged reptiles fly away like the birds did? Why are single-celled organisms found earlier than multicelled organisms of similar size and overall shape? Why did large, heavy creatures such as giant tortoises and hippopotami survive instead of sinking? Why didn't the small, fast dinosaurs survive? Why did certain fish die before others, when they were just as swift and just as good at swimming? Many challenges can be raised to the idea of a single gigantic flood causing the order found in the fossil record (Kitcher 1982; Futuyma 1983). The fossil record, in short, provides ample evidence to reject the Flood hypothesis.

Another example cited by creationists as "proof" of special creation is the "fact" that dinosaur and human footprints have been found at the same geological level along the Paluxy River in Texas. Closer examination has shown that the footprints were not distinguishable and that a number of tracks had been carved to attract tourists and their money (Kitcher 1982).

The main "scientific" work of the creationists consists of attempting to find fault with evolutionary theory. The reasoning is that if evolution can be rejected, then special creation must be true. This strategy actually uses an important feature of scientific research by attempting to reject a given hypothesis. The problem is that none of the creationists' attacks on evolution has been supported by scientific evidence. Certainly some predictions of evolutionary theory have been proven incorrect, but that is to be expected because science is a dynamic process. The basic finds of evolution, however, have been supported time and time again.

Another problem is that this method works only when the hypothesis and its alternative cover all possible cases. Are evolution and special creation by a single creator the only possible explanations? Perhaps the universe was created by several creators. Perhaps the universe and natural law were created by a creator, but life evolved from natural law. You might try to think up other alternatives. Remember, however, that to be scientific a hypothesis must be testable.

On an emotional level, the doctrines of "creation science" attract many people. Given the concept of free speech, why shouldn't creation science be given equal time? The problem with equal time is that it assumes that both ideas have equal merit. Consider that some people still believe the earth is flat. They are certainly entitled to their opinion, but it would be absurd to mandate "equal time" in geography and geology classes for this idea. Also, the concept of equal time is not really that fairminded after all. The specific story many creationists refer to is the Biblical story of Genesis. Many other cultures have their own creation stories. Shouldn't they receive equal time as well? In one sense, they should, though the proper forum for such discussions is probably a course in comparative religions, not a science class.

Perhaps the biggest problem advocates of "creation science" have introduced is that they appear to place religion and science at odds with each other. Religion and science both represent ways of looking at the world and, though they work on different levels, they are not contradictory. You can be religious and believe in God and still accept the fact of evolution and evolutionary theory. Only if you take the story of Genesis as a literal, historical account does a conflict exist. Most major religions in the world accept the findings of evolution. Many people, including some scientists, look to the evolutionary process as evidence of God's work.

Many creationists fear that science has eroded our faith in God and has therefore led to a decline in morals and values. They imply that science (and evolution in particular) makes statements about human morality. It does not. Science has nothing to say about right and wrong; that is the function of social ethics, philosophies, and religion. Religion and science are important to many people. To put them at odds with each other does both a disservice. It is no surprise that many ministers, priests, and rabbis have joined in the fight against the laws of "creation science."

SUMMARY

Anthropology is the study of human biological and cultural variation and evolution. Anthropology asks questions that focus on what humans are and the origins, evolution, and variation of our biology and behaviors, because humans are both biological and cultural organisms. In the United States, anthropology is characterized by four subfields with specific concerns: cultural anthropology (the study of cultural behavior), anthropological archaeology (the study of past cultures), linguistic anthropology (the study of language as a human characteristic), and biological anthropology (the study of human biological evolution and variation).

As a science, anthropology has certain requirements and characteristics. Hypotheses must be testable and verifiable. The main theoretical base of biological anthropology is the theory of evolution. A major feature of evolutionary theory is Darwin's idea of natural selection. In any environment in which resources are necessarily limited, some organisms are more likely to survive and reproduce than others because of their biological characteristics. Those who survive pass these traits on to the next generation.

A current controversy involves the efforts of certain people to pass laws requiring that "creation science" be taught in public schools. Examination of this field shows that it is not a science at all. Apart from these debates, it should be noted that today there is little conflict between religion and science in the United States. Each perspective addresses different questions in different ways.

SUPPLEMENTAL READINGS

Futuyma, D. J. 1983. *Science on Trial: The Case for Evolution.* New York: Pantheon Books. An excellent review of evolution and a detailed critique of "creation science," particularly strong in its discussion of scientific method and evidence for evolution.

Gould, S. J. 1977. *Ever Since Darwin.* New York: W. W. Norton. The first of several books of essays, most written originally for *Natural History*, on evolutionary biology. Essays deal with evolutionary theory, the history of evolutionary science, and the evolution–creation debate, among other topics. Other books by the same author, also published by W. W. Norton, are *The Panda's Thumb* (1980), *Hen's Teeth and Horse's Toes* (1983), *The Flamingo's Smile* (1985), *Bully for Brontosaurus* (1991), and *Eight Little Piggies* (1993).

For further information on the current status of the scientific, legal, and educational aspects of the evolution–creation debate, contact: National Center for Science Education, P. O. Box 9477, Berkeley, Calif. 94709-0477.

Human Genetics

Is human behavior the result of biology *or* culture? This question has been asked countless times in human history, often with serious cultural and political consequences. To anthropologists, the question is somewhat meaningless; we recognize *both* biological and cultural factors as important and look at the relative potential contributions of both. It is hard to untangle these effects.

To understand human biological variation and evolution, we must consider the science of genetics. The study of genetics actually encompasses a number of different areas, depending on the level of analysis. Genetics can be studied on the molecular level, with the focus on what genes are and how they act to produce biological structures.

Genetics also involves the process of inheritance. To what extent are we a reflection of our parents? How are traits inherited? This branch of the field is called **Mendelian genetics,** after the scientist Gregor Mendel, who first worked out many of the principles of inheritance.

Finally, genetics can be studied at the level of a population. Here we are interested in describing the patterns of genetic variation within and among

▲▲▲▲▲▲▲▲▲▲▲▲▲▲▲▲▲▲▲▲▲▲▲▲▲▲▲▲▲▲

Mendelian genetics
The branch of genetics concerned with pattern and processes of inheritance. This field was named after Gregor Mendel, the first scientist to work out of these principles.

29

different populations. The changes that take place in the frequency of genes within a population constitute the process of **microevolution.** At the level of the population, we seek the reasons for evolutionary change from one generation to the next. Projection of these findings allows us to understand better the long-term pattern of evolution over thousands and millions of years and the origin of new species (**macroevolution**).

MOLECULAR GENETICS

DNA: The Genetic Code

The study of genetics at the molecular level concerns the amazing properties of a molecule known as deoxyribonucleic acid, or **DNA** for short. The DNA molecule provides the codes for biological structures and the means to translate this code. It is perhaps best to think of DNA as a set of instructions for determining the makeup of biological organisms. Quite simply, DNA provides information for building, operating, and repairing organisms. In this context, the process of genetic inheritance is seen as the transmission of this information, or the passing on of the instructions needed for biological structures. Evolution can be viewed in this context as the transfer of information from one generation to the next, along with the possibility that this information will change.

An understanding of both the structure and function of DNA is necessary to understand the processes of genetic inheritance and evolution. The exact biochemistry of DNA is beyond the scope of this text, but its basic nature can be discussed in the context of information transfer.

THE STRUCTURE OF DNA The physical appearance of the DNA molecule resembles a ladder that has been twisted into the shape of a helix (Figure 2.1). In biochemical terms, the rungs of the ladder are of major importance. These rungs are made up of chemical units called **bases.** There are four possible types of bases, identified by the first letter of their longer chemical names: A (adenine), T (thymine), G (guanine), and C (cytosine). These bases form the "alphabet" used in specifying and carrying out genetic instructions.

All biological structures, from nerve cells to blood cells to bone cells, are made up predominantly of proteins. Proteins in turn are made up of amino acids, whose chemical properties allow them to bond together to form proteins. Each amino acid is coded for by three of the four chemical bases just discussed. For example, the base sequence CGA provides the code for the amino acid alanine, and the base sequence TTT codes for the amino acid lysine. There are 64 possible codes that can be specified, using some combination of three bases. This might not seem like a lot, except for the fact that only 20 amino acids need to be specified by the genetic code. The

■ FIGURE 2.1
The structure of the DNA molecule. DNA consists of two strands arranged in a helix joined together by chemical bases (see text).

■ TABLE 2.1
DNA Base Sequences for Amino Acids

FIRST BASE	SECOND BASE							
	A		T		C		G	
A	AAA	Phenylalanine	ATA	Tyrosine	ACA	Cysteine	AGA	Serine
	AAT	Leucine	ATT	Stop	ACT	Stop	AGT	Serine
	AAC	Leucine	ATC	Stop	ACC	Tryptophan	AGC	Serine
	AAG	Phenylalanine	ATG	Tyrosine	ACG	Cysteine	AGG	Serine
T	TAA	Isoleucine	TTA	Asparagine	TCA	Serine	TGA	Threonine
	TAT	Isoleucine	TTT	Lysine	TCT	Arginine	TGT	Threonine
	TAC	Methionine	TTC	Lysine	TCC	Arginine	TGC	Threonine
	TAG	Isoleucine	TTG	Asparagine	TCG	Serine	TGG	Threonine
C	CAA	Valine	CTA	Aspartic acid	CCA	Glycine	CGA	Alanine
	CAT	Valine	CTT	Glutamic acid	CCT	Glycine	CGT	Alanine
	CAC	Valine	CTC	Glutamic acid	CCC	Glycine	CGC	Alanine
	CAG	Valine	CTG	Aspartic acid	CCG	Glycine	CGG	Alanine
G	GAA	Leucine	GTA	Histidine	GCA	Arginine	GGA	Proline
	GAT	Leucine	GTT	Glutamine	GCT	Arginine	GGT	Proline
	GAC	Leucine	GTC	Glutamine	GCC	Arginine	GGC	Proline
	GAG	Leucine	GTG	Histidine	GCG	Arginine	GGG	Proline

Rows refer to the first of the three bases and columns refer to the second of the three bases. These base sequences are for the DNA molecule. The 64 different combinations code for 20 amino acids and one termination sequence ("Stop"). To convert to messenger RNA, substitute U for A, A for T, G for C, and C for G. To convert to transfer RNA, substitute U for A.

three-base code provides more than enough possibilities to code for these amino acids. In fact, some amino acids have several different codes; alanine, for example, can be specified by the base sequences CGA, CGG, CGT, and CGC. Some of the base sequences, such as ATT, act to form "punctuation" for the genetic instructions; that is, they provide the code to start or stop "messages." A list of the different DNA sequences is shown in Table 2.1.

The ability of four different bases, taken three at a time, to specify all the information needed for the synthesis of proteins is astounding. It boggles the mind that the diverse structure of complex protein molecules can be specified with only a four-letter "alphabet." As an analogy, consider the way

microevolution Short-term evolutionary change.

macroevolution Long-term evolutionary change.

DNA The molecule that provides the genetic code for biological structures and the means to translate this code.

base Chemical unit that makes up part of the DNA molecule whose sequence specifies genetic instructions.

in which computers work. All computer operations, from word processing to complex mathematical simulations, ultimately are translated to a set of computer instructions that use only a simple two-letter alphabet—on or off! These two instructions make up a larger set of codes that provide information on computer operations. These operations are combined to generate computer languages that can be used to write a variety of programs.

The ability of the DNA molecule to use the different amino acid codes lies in a simple property of the chemical bases. The base A bonds with the base T, and the base G bonds with the base C. This chemical property allows the DNA molecule to carry out a number of functions, including the ability to make copies of itself and to direct the synthesis of proteins.

■ FIGURE 2.2
Replication of the DNA molecule.

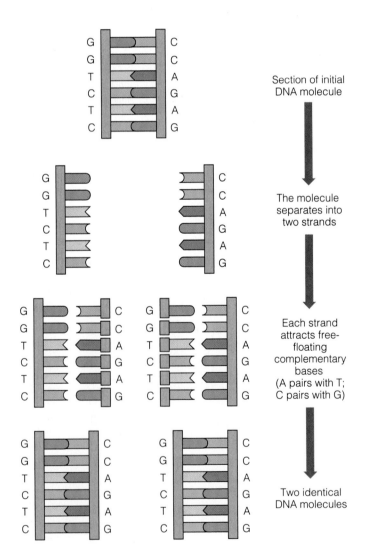

Section of initial DNA molecule

The molecule separates into two strands

Each strand attracts free-floating complementary bases (A pairs with T; C pairs with G)

Two identical DNA molecules

FUNCTIONS OF DNA The DNA molecule can make copies of itself. Remember that the DNA molecule is made up of two strands that form the long arms of the ladder. Each rung of the ladder consists of two bases. If one part of the rung contains the base A, then the other part of the rung will contain the base T because A and T bond together.

To understand how DNA can make copies of itself, consider the following sequence of bases on one strand of the DNA molecule—GGTCTC. Because A and T bond together and G and C bond together, the corresponding sequence of bases on the other strand of the DNA molecule is CCAGAG. The DNA molecule can separate into two distinct strands. Once separate, each strand attracts free-floating bases. The strand GGTCTC attracts the bases CCAGAG, and the strand CCAGAG attracts the bases GGTCTC. When the new bases have attached themselves to the original strands, the result is two identical DNA molecules. This process is diagrammed in Figure 2.2. Keep in mind that this description is somewhat oversimplified—in reality, the process is biochemically much more complex.

The ability of the DNA molecule (Figure 2.3) to control protein synthesis also involves the attraction of complementary bases, but with the help of another molecule—ribonucleic acid, or **RNA** for short. In simple terms, RNA serves as the messenger for the information coded by the DNA molecule. One major difference between DNA and RNA is that in RNA the base A attracts a base called U (uracil) instead of T.

Consider the DNA base sequence GGT. In protein synthesis, the DNA molecule separates into two strands, and one strand (containing CCA) becomes inactive. The active strand, GGT, attracts free-floating bases to form a strand of **messenger RNA.** Because A bonds with T and G bonds with C, this strand consists of the sequence CCA. The strand then travels to the site of protein synthesis. Once there, the strand of messenger RNA transfers its information by attracting **transfer RNA,** which is a free-floating molecule. The sequence of messenger RNA containing the sequence CCA attracts a transfer RNA molecule with a complementary sequence—GGU. The result is that the amino acid proline (specified by the RNA sequence GGU or the DNA sequence GGT) is included in the chain of amino acids making up a particular protein. To summarize, one strand of the DNA molecule produces the complementary strand of messenger RNA, which then travels to the site of protein synthesis and attracts a complementary strand of transfer RNA, which carries the specified amino acid. This process is illustrated for the DNA sequence GGTCTC in Figure 2.4.

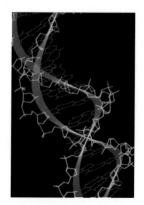

■ FIGURE 2.3
Computer representation of the DNA molecule.
(© Will & Demi McIntyre/Photo Researchers, Inc.)

▲▲▲

RNA The molecule that functions to carry out the instructions for protein synthesis specified by the DNA molecule.

messenger RNA The form of RNA that transports the genetic instructions from the DNA molecule to the site of protein synthesis.

transfer RNA A free-floating molecule that is attracted to a strand of messenger RNA, resulting in the synthesis of a protein chain.

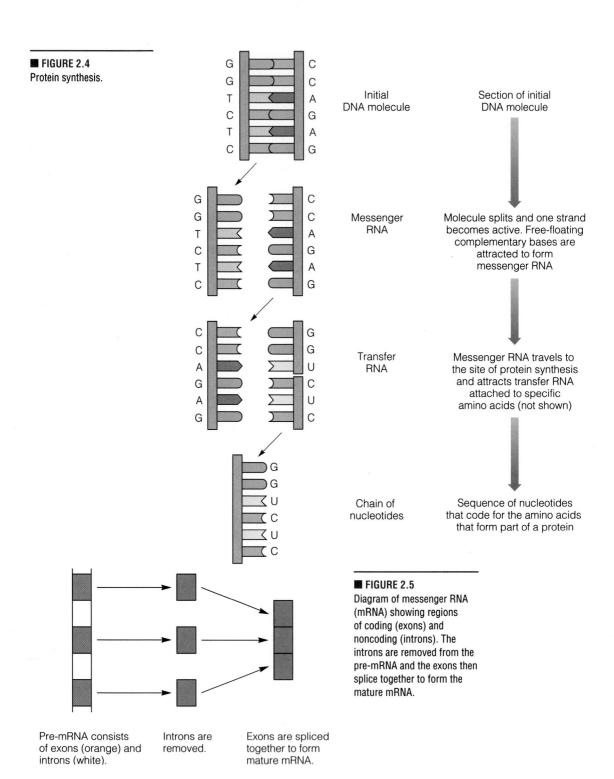

■ FIGURE 2.4
Protein synthesis.

Initial
DNA molecule

Section of initial
DNA molecule

Messenger
RNA

Molecule splits and one strand
becomes active. Free-floating
complementary bases are
attracted to form
messenger RNA

Transfer
RNA

Messenger RNA travels to
the site of protein synthesis
and attracts transfer RNA
attached to specific
amino acids (not shown)

Chain of
nucleotides

Sequence of nucleotides
that code for the amino acids
that form part of a protein

■ FIGURE 2.5
Diagram of messenger RNA
(mRNA) showing regions
of coding (exons) and
noncoding (introns). The
introns are removed from the
pre-mRNA and the exons then
splice together to form the
mature mRNA.

Pre-mRNA consists
of exons (orange) and
introns (white).

Introns are
removed.

Exons are spliced
together to form
mature mRNA.

In many organisms (including humans) in which the DNA is contained in a separate part of the cell (the nucleus), the entire process is a bit more complicated. Not all of the DNA sequence is translated into amino acids. During the final stage of messenger RNA creation, sections are "cut out" and are not included in the mature messenger RNA. Thus, a sequence of DNA can contain both sections that code for amino acids that make up proteins (called **exons**) and sections that do not code for amino acids that make up proteins (called **introns**) (Figure 2.5). The evolutionary significance of the noncoding regions is not known at present.

This simplified discussion shows the basic nature of the structure and functions of the DNA molecule. More advanced discussion can be found in most genetics textbooks. For our purposes, however, the broad view will suffice. If we consider DNA as a "code," we can then look at the processes of transmission and change of information without actually having to consider the exact biochemical mechanisms.

Chromosomes and Genes

DNA is contained within the nucleus of each cell. Another form of DNA, contained in a part of the cell called the mitochondrion, is discussed later in Chapter 12. The DNA sequences are bound together by proteins in long strands called **chromosomes** that are found within the nucleus of each cell. With the exception of those in the sex cells (egg and sperm), chromosomes occur in pairs. Most body cells contain both members of these pairs. Different species have different numbers of chromosomes. For example, humans have 23 pairs, chimpanzees have 24 pairs, fruit flies have 4 pairs, and certain plant species have thousands of pairs. There is no relationship between the number of chromosome pairs a species has and its intelligence or biological complexity.

With certain exceptions, each cell in the human body contains a complete set of chromosomes and DNA. Nerve cells contain the DNA for bone cells, for example, and vice versa. Some type of regulation takes place within different cells to ensure that only certain genes are expressed in the right places, but the exact nature of this regulation is not known completely at present.

▲▲▲

exon A section of DNA that codes for the amino acids that make up proteins. It is contrasted with an intron.

intron A section of DNA that does not code for the amino acids that make up proteins. It is contrasted with an exon.

chromosome A long strand of DNA sequences.

PCR and Ancient DNA

In the summer of 1994, film goers were thrilled by the movie *Jurassic Park*, based on the novel of the same name by Michael Crichton (who studied anthropology as an undergraduate). The plot revolves around the construction of a dinosaur theme park—with live dinosaurs! In *Jurassic Park*, scientists recover amber dating back to the time of the dinosaurs. Trapped in the amber are mosquitoes who, prior to being trapped in the tree sap that becomes amber, had drunk the blood of dinosaurs. Using this blood, the fictional scientists reconstruct the DNA of the original dinosaurs and bring a number of extinct species back to life.

A fascinating story, but how accurate is it? Could we reconstruct sufficient DNA sequences of ancient creatures to bring them back to life? At present, we lack the technology to do so. However, we *can* reconstruct some ancient DNA sequences (although not well enough to recreate a dinosaur). Fragments of ancient DNA *have* been reconstructed, including some from amber many millions of years old. We have also been able to obtain DNA fragments from human populations many thousands of years old (Stone and Stoneking 1993; Hagelberg 1994).

The heart of these achievements is a relatively new technique called the *polymerase chain reaction* (PCR).

This technique involves the laboratory synthesis of millions of copies of DNA fragments from very small initial amounts (Erlich et al. 1991). The process is essentially cyclical—the DNA strands are separated and form the template for new strands, thus resulting in a doubling of the DNA each time through the cycle (see adjoining figure). This method is very efficient in extracting DNA sequences from very small samples. In fact, it is so efficient that one of the technical problems is that it often picks up DNA from people's cells floating around the lab as dust! (Hagelberg 1994). The PCR method is also useful to anthropologists working on living human populations. Samples can be collected and transported easily—such as single plucked hairs!

The PCR method has also proven valuable in the field of forensics. Very small samples can yield sufficient DNA to help identify skeletal remains of murder victims. One notorious case involved the skeletal remains that were attributed to the infamous Nazi doctor Joseph Mengele. Extracts of bone were taken, and the DNA was amplified using PCR and then compared to the known surviving relatives of Mengele. Based on this comparison, the skeletal remains were definitely identified as having been Mengele (Hagelberg 1994).

Simplified diagram of the polymerase chain reaction (PCR) used to amplify small amounts of DNA. Each time through the cycle the amount of DNA doubles.

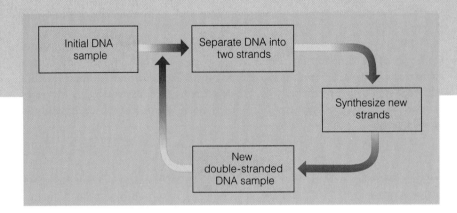

Initial DNA sample → Separate DNA into two strands → Synthesize new strands → New double-stranded DNA sample →

GENES The term *gene*, although used frequently, actually encompasses a variety of definitions. In the most general sense, a **gene** can be defined as a section of DNA that has an identifiable structure or function (Marks and

Lyles 1994). In the past, the gene tended to be defined most often on the basis of its function, such as a gene that controls for a particular blood group. Today, we use a broader definition because we realize that large sections of DNA do not have a specific function. In terms of genes that have a given function, many code for the production of a specific protein. For example, the **hemoglobin** molecule in your blood (which transports oxygen) is made up of four protein chains. For each chain, there is a section of the DNA that contains the genetic code for the proteins in that chain.

Aside from manufacture of proteins, another function of genes is the regulation of biological processes. For example, consider the fact that in many humans the enzyme needed to digest milk sugar stops being produced several years after birth. Or consider the fact that sexual maturation in humans occurs during adolescence and not in infancy. Many biological characteristics are subject to regulation in terms of when they take effect or are expressed. Genes that are responsible for this regulation are known as **regulatory genes,** and they act by turning other genes on or off at the appropriate time.

Regulatory genes may have great evolutionary significance. For example, regulatory genes may help explain the great physical differences between chimpanzees and humans even though over 98 percent of their structural genes are identical. The major genetic difference between humans and chimpanzees may be caused by regulatory genes, which act on the timing of growth and development, and could lead to differences in brain size, facial structures, and other physical features.

A possible example of regulatory genes is the absence of teeth in birds. Evolutionary analysis has concluded that modern birds evolved from primitive reptiles. One major change in this evolution is that birds have no teeth (other than the egg tooth they use in hatching). In 1980, however, scientists were able to induce the tissue of a hen to grow teeth! Teeth are produced by certain outer embryonic tissues forming the enamel and other inner tissues forming the dentin underneath. In what appears at first to be a bizarre experiment, Kollar and Fisher (1980) combined the outer tissues of a hen with the inner tissues of a mouse. These grafts produced dentin and teeth. Modern birds lack the necessary type of tissue to form dentin but still have the capacity to form it when we combine their tissue in the laboratory with the appropriate tissue from another animal (the mouse, in this case). This experiment shows that the genetic code for teeth still exists in birds, but it is turned off, most likely by some combination of regulatory genes.

Another example suggesting the action of regulatory genes is the lack of five toes in horses. Modern horses have one single toe, although occasionally horses are born with two or three toes (Gould 1983). It appears that horses

gene A section of DNA that has an identifiable structure or function.	**hemoglobin** The molecule in blood cells that transports oxygen.	**regulatory genes** Genes that code for the regulation of such	biological processes as growth and development.

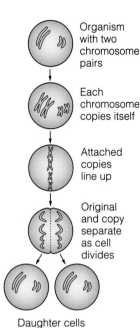

Organism with two chromosome pairs

Each chromosome copies itself

Attached copies line up

Original and copy separate as cell divides

Daughter cells are copies of parent cell

■ **FIGURE 2.6**

The process of mitosis, the formation of body cells. Each chromosome copies itself, the attached copies line up in the cell, and the original and copy split when the cell divides. The result is two identical cells. (From *Human Antiquity: An Introduction to Physical Anthropology and Archaeology*, 2d ed., by Kenneth Feder and Michael Park, Fig 4.2. Copyright © 1993 by Mayfield Publishing Company)

still have the genetic code for additional toes, but these instructions are turned off.

During the 1980s a group of regulatory genes known as **homeobox genes** was discovered. These genes encode a sequence of 60 amino acids that regulate embryonic development. Specifically, they subdivide a developing embryo into different regions from head to tail that then form limbs and other structures. One fascinating aspect of this discovery is that these genes are similar in many organisms, such as insects, mice, and humans. Preliminary research suggests that the process of embryonic development into head, trunk, and tail may have occurred only once in evolution (De Robertis et al. 1990). Another example of homeobox genes was found in a study of the development of wings in insects. Some insects have wings and some do not. Recent analyses suggest that wings developed *once* in the common ancestor of all insects, but in some later forms homeobox genes repressed their development (Carroll et al. 1995). In other words, even wingless insects may carry the genetic code for wings—it has simply been "switched off."

MITOSIS AND MEIOSIS   The DNA molecule provides for the transmission of genetic information. Production of proteins and regulation are only two aspects of information transfer. Because organisms start life as a single cell that subsequently multiplies, it is essential that the genetic information within the initial cell be transferred to all future cells. The ability of DNA to replicate itself is involved in the process of cell replication, known as **mitosis** (Figure 2.6). When a cell divides, each chromosome duplicates and then splits. Each chromosome has replicated itself, so that when the cell finishes dividing, the result is two cells with the full set of chromosomes.

The process is different when information is passed on from one generation to the next. The genetic code is passed on from parents to offspring through the sex cells—the sperm in males and the egg in females. The sex cells, however, do not contain the full set of chromosomes but only one chromosome from each pair (i.e., only one-half of the set). Whereas your other body cells have a total of 46 chromosomes (2 each for 23 pairs), your sex cells contain only 23 chromosomes (1 from each pair). When you have a child, you contribute 23 chromosomes, and your mate contributes 23 chromosomes. Your child then has the normal complement of 46 chromosomes in 23 pairs. If both chromosomes in each pair were passed on, your children would have 23 pairs from both you and your mate, for a total of 46 pairs. Your children's children would receive 46 pairs from each parent, for a total of 92 pairs. If this process continued, there would soon not be enough room in a cell for all of the chromosome pairs!

Sex cells are created through the process of **meiosis** (Figure 2.7). Basically, this involves the replication of chromosomes followed by cell division, followed by another cell division without an intervening round of replication. In sperm, the result is that four sex cells are produced from the initial set of 23 pairs of chromosomes. The process is similar in egg cells except that only one of the four cells is functional.

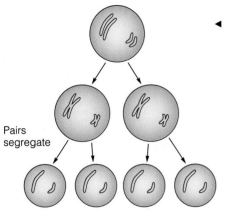

Pairs
segregate

Each sex cell has half the normal
number of chromosomes

◀ ■ FIGURE 2.7
The process of meiosis, the
formation of sex cells.
Meiosis begins in the same
way as mitosis: each
chromosome makes a copy
of itself. The pairs of
chromosomes then segregate,
forming four sex cells, each
with one chromosome rather
than a pair of chromosomes.
(Adapted from *Human Antiquity:
An Introduction to Physical
Anthropology and Archaeology*, 2d
ed., by Kenneth Feder and Michael
Park, Fig. 4.2. Copyright © 1993
by Mayfield Publishing Company)

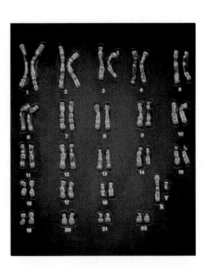

■ FIGURE 2.8
All 23 pairs of chromosomes
typically found in a
human being. This set of
chromosomes came from
a man—note the 23rd pair
has an X chromosome and
a Y chromosome. (© CNRI/
Science Photo Library/Photo
Researchers, Inc.)

The process of meiosis is extremely important in understanding genetic inheritance. Because only one of each pair of chromosomes is found in a functional sex cell, this means that a person contributes half of his or her offspring's genes. The other half comes from the other parent. Usually, each human child has a full set of 23 chromosome pairs, one of each pair from each parent (Figure 2.8).

MENDELIAN GENETICS

Many of the facts known about genetic inheritance were discovered over a century before the structure of DNA was known. Although people knew where babies came from and noted the close resemblance of parents and children, the mechanisms of inheritance were unknown until the nineteenth century. An Austrian priest, Gregor Mendel (1822–1884), carried out an extensive series of experiments in plant breeding. His carefully tabulated results provided the basis of what we know about the mechanisms of genetic inheritance.

Before Mendel's research, it was commonly assumed that inheritance involved the blending together of genetic information in the egg and sperm. The genetic material was thought to mix together in the same way that different color paints mix together. Mendel's experiments showed a different

---

homeobox genes A group of regulatory genes that encode a sequence of 60 amino

acids regulating embryonic development.

mitosis The process of replication of chromosomes in body cells.

meiosis The creation of sex cells by replication of chromosomes followed by two cell divisions.

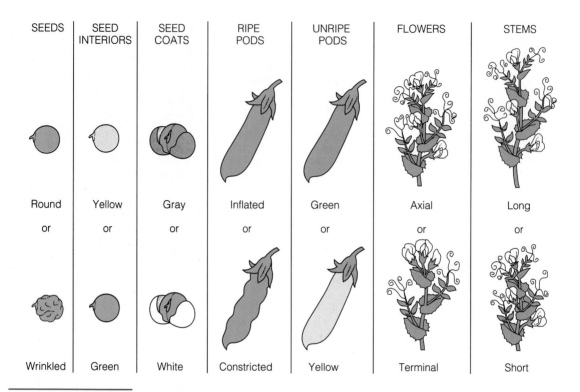

SEEDS	SEED INTERIORS	SEED COATS	RIPE PODS	UNRIPE PODS	FLOWERS	STEMS
Round	Yellow	Gray	Inflated	Green	Axial	Long
or	or	or	or	or	or	or
Wrinkled	Green	White	Constricted	Yellow	Terminal	Short

■ **FIGURE 2.9**
The seven phenotypic characteristics investigated by Gregor Mendel in his experiments on breeding in pea plants. Each of the seven traits has two distinct phenotypes.

pattern of inheritance—the genetic information is inherited in discrete units (genes). These genes do not blend together in an offspring.

In one experiment, Mendel crossed pea plants whose seeds were yellow with pea plants whose seeds were green (Figure 2.9). Under the idea of blending, one might expect all offspring to have mustard-colored seeds—a mixture of the yellow and green. In reality, Mendel found that all the offspring plants had yellow seeds. This discovery suggested that somehow one trait (yellow seed color) dominated in its effects.

When Mendel crossed the plants in this new generation together, he found that some of their offspring had yellow seeds and some had green seeds. Somehow the genetic information for green seeds had been hidden for a generation and then appeared again. Mendel counted how many there were of each color. The ratio of plants with yellow seeds to those with green seeds was very close to a 3:1 ratio. This finding suggested to Mendel that a regular process occurred during inheritance that could be explained in terms of simple mathematical principles. With these and other results, Mendel formulated several principles of inheritance. Though Mendel's work remained virtually unknown during his lifetime, his work was rediscovered in 1900. In recognition of his accomplishments, the science of genetic inheritance is called Mendelian genetics.

Genotypes and Phenotypes

The specific position of a gene on a chromosome is called a **locus** (plural **loci**). The alternative forms of a gene at a locus are called **alleles.** For example, a number of different genetic systems control the types of molecules present on the surface of red blood cells. One of these blood groups, known as the MN system, determines whether or not you have M molecules, N molecules, or both on the surface of your red blood cells. The MN system has two forms, or alleles—M and N. Another blood group system, the ABO system, has three alleles—A, B, and O. Even though three different forms of this gene are found in the human species, each individual only has two genes at the ABO locus. Some genetic loci have only one allele, some have two, and some have three or more.

MENDEL'S LAW OF SEGREGATION   The genetic basis of any trait is determined by an allele from each parent. At any given locus there are two alleles, one on each member of the chromosome pair. One allele came from the mother and one allele came from the father. Alleles occur in pairs, and when sex cells are formed, only one of each pair is passed on (**Mendel's Law of Segregation**).

The two alleles at a locus in an individual specify the **genotype,** the genetic endowment of an individual. The two alleles might be the same form or might be different. If the alleles from both parents are the same, the genotype is **homozygous.** If the alleles from the parents are different, the genotype is **heterozygous.**

The actual observable trait is known as the **phenotype.** The relationship between genotype and phenotype is affected by the relationship between the two alleles present at any locus. If the genotype is homozygous, both alleles contain the same genetic information. What happens in heterozygotes, where the two alleles are different?

DOMINANT AND RECESSIVE ALLELES   In a heterozygote, an allele is **dominant** when it masks the effect of the other allele at a given locus. The opposite of a

---

locus The specific location of a gene on a chromosome.

allele The alternative form of a gene that occurs at a given locus. Some genes have only one allele, some have two, and some have many alternative forms.

Alleles occur in pairs, one on each chromosome.

Mendel's Law of Segregation Sex cells contain one of each pair of alleles.

genotype The genetic endowment of an individual from the two alleles present at a given locus.

homozygous Both alleles at a given locus are identical.

heterozygous The two alleles at a given locus are different.

phenotype The observable appearance of a given genotype in the organism.

dominant allele An allele that masks the effect of the other allele (which is recessive) in a heterozygous genotype.

■ TABLE 2.2
Genotypes and Phenotypes for PTC Tasting

GENOTYPE	PHENOTYPE
TT	Taster
Tt	Taster
tt	Nontaster

Because *T* is dominant, the genotypes *TT* and *Tt* both produce the taster phenotype. This example is somewhat oversimplified, because in reality the phenotype can also be affected by diet.

dominant allele is a **recessive** allele, whose effect may be masked. A simple example helps make these concepts clearer. One genetic trait in human beings is the ability to taste certain substances, including a chemical known as PTC. The ability to taste PTC appears to be controlled by a single locus and is also affected to some extent by environmental factors such as diet. There are two alleles for the PTC-tasting trait: the allele *T*, which is also called the "taster" allele, and the allele *t*, which is also called the "non-taster" allele. Given these two alleles, three combinations of alleles can be present in an individual. A person could have the *T* allele from both parents, which would give the genotype *TT*. A person could have a *t* allele from both parents, giving the genotype *tt*. Both *TT* and *tt* are homozygous genotypes because both alleles are the same. The third possible genotype occurs when the allele from one parent is *T* and the allele from the other parent is *t*. This gives the heterozygous genotype of *Tt*. It does not matter which parent provided the *T* allele and which provided the *t* allele; the genotype is the same in both cases.

What phenotype is associated with each genotype? The phenotype is affected by both the relationship of the two alleles and by the environment. For the moment, let us ignore possible environmental effects. Consider the *T* allele as providing instructions that allow tasting and the *t* allele as providing instructions for nontasting. If the genotype is *TT*, then both alleles code for tasting and the phenotype is obviously "taster." Likewise, if the genotype is *tt*, then both alleles code for nontasting and the phenotype is "nontaster." What of the heterozygote *Tt*? One allele codes for tasting and one codes for nontasting. Does this mean that both will be expressed and that a person will have the tasting ability but not to as great a degree as a person with genotype *TT*? Or does it mean that only one of the alleles is expressed? If so, which one?

There is no way you can answer this question using only the data provided so far. You must know if either the *T* or *t* allele is dominant, and this can be determined only through experimentation. For this trait, it turns out that the *T* allele is dominant and the *t* allele is recessive. When both alleles are present in a genotype, the *T* allele masks the effect of the *t* allele. Therefore, a person with the genotype *Tt* has the "taster" phenotype (Table 2.2). The relationship between genotype and phenotype does not take into consideration known environmental effects on PTC tasting. Under certain types of diet, some "tasters" will show less ability to taste weaker concentrations of the PTC chemical.

The action of dominant and recessive alleles explains why Mendel's second-generation pea plants all had yellow seeds. The allele for yellow seed color is dominant, and the allele for green seed color is recessive.

Dominance and recessiveness refer only to the effect an allele has in producing a phenotype. These terms say nothing about the frequency or value of an allele. Dominant alleles can be common or rare, harmful or helpful.

■ TABLE 2.3
Genotypes and Phenotypes of the MN Blood Group System

GENOTYPE	PHENOTYPE
MM	M molecules
MN	M and N molecules
NN	N molecules

The *M* and *N* alleles are codominant, so they are both expressed in the heterozygote.

■ TABLE 2.4
Genotypes and Phenotypes of the ABO System

The ABO system has three alleles *(A, B, O)* that code for the type of molecule on the surface of the red blood cells (A, B, and O molecules). The *A* and *B* alleles are codominant, and the *O* allele is recessive to both *A* and *B*.

GENOTYPE	PHENOTYPE
AA	A
AO	A
BB	B
BO	B
AB	AB
OO	O

Note: There are also different forms of the *A* allele not shown here (A_1, A_2, etc.).

CODOMINANT ALLELES   Some alleles are **codominant,** meaning that when two different alleles are present in a genotype, then both are expressed. That is, neither allele is dominant or recessive. One example of a codominant genetic system in humans is the MN blood group, mentioned before. There are two alleles—M, which codes for the production of M molecules, and N, which codes for the production of N molecules. Therefore, there are three possible genotypes: MM, MN, and NN.

The phenotypes for the homozygous genotypes are easy to determine. Individuals with genotype MM have two alleles coding for the production of M molecules and will have the M molecule phenotype. Likewise, individuals with the genotype NN will have two N alleles and will have the N molecule phenotype. But what of the heterozygote genotype MN? Again, there is no way to answer this question without knowing the pattern of dominance. Experimentation has shown that the M and N alleles are codominant. When both are present (genotype MN), then both are expressed. Therefore, an individual with genotype MN will produce both M and N molecules. Their phenotype is MN, indicating the presence of both molecules (Table 2.3).

In complex genetic systems with more than two alleles some alleles may be dominant and some may be codominant. A good example of dominance and codominance in the same system is the ABO blood group. The alleles, genotypes, and phenotypes of this system are described in Table 2.4.

▲▲

recessive allele An allele whose effect is masked by the other allele (which is dominant) in a heterozygous genotype.

codominant When both alleles affect the phenotype of a heterozygous genotype and neither is dominant over the other.

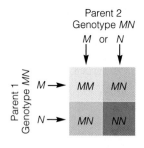

Parent 2
Genotype *MN*

M or N

Parent 1
Genotype *MN*

M → MM   MN

N → MN   NN

■ FIGURE 2.10
Inheritance of MN blood group phenotypes for two parents, both with *MN* genotype.

Predicting Offspring Distributions

When parents each contribute a sex cell, they are passing on only one allele at each locus to their offspring. The possible genotypes and phenotypes of the offspring reflect a 50 percent chance of transmittal for any given allele of a parent. This simple statement of probability allows prediction of the likely distribution of genotypes and phenotypes among the offspring.

Figure 2.10 illustrates this method using the MN blood group system for two hypothetical parents, each with the genotype MN. Each parent has a 50 percent chance of passing on an M allele and a 50 percent chance of passing on an N allele. Given these probabilities, we expect one out of four offspring (25 percent) to have genotype MM, and therefore phenotype M. In two out of four cases (50 percent), we expect the offspring to have genotype MN, and therefore phenotype MN. Finally, in one out of four cases (25 percent), we expect the offspring to have genotype NN, and therefore phenotype N. Of course, different parental genotypes will give a different set of offspring probabilities.

Remember that these distributions give the expected probabilities. The exact distributions will not always occur because each offspring is an independent event. If the hypothetical couple first has a child with the genotype MN, this will not influence the genotype of their next child. The distributions give the proportions expected for a very large number of offspring.

To help understand the difference between expected and actual distribution, consider coin flipping. If you flip a coin, you expect to get heads 50 percent of the time and tails 50 percent of the time. If you flip 10 coins one after another, you expect to get five heads and five tails. You may, however, get four heads and six tails.

■ FIGURE 2.11
Inheritance of PTC-tasting genotypes and phenotypes for two parents, both with the *Tt* genotype. Phenotypes are shown in parentheses.

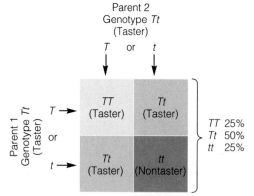

Parent 2
Genotype *Tt*
(Taster)

T   or   t

Parent 1
Genotype *Tt*
(Taster)

T →

t →

TT
(Taster)   Tt
(Taster)

Tt
(Taster)   tt
(Nontaster)

TT 25%
Tt 50%
tt 25%

■ FIGURE 2.12
Inheritance of PTC-tasting genotypes and phenotypes for two parents, one with the *Tt* genotype and one with the *tt* genotype. Phenotypes are shown in parentheses.

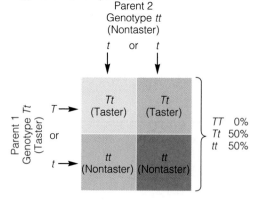

Parent 2
Genotype *tt*
(Nontaster)

t   or   t

Parent 1
Genotype *Tt*
(Taster)

T →

t →

Tt
(Taster)   Tt
(Taster)

tt
(Nontaster)   tt
(Nontaster)

TT 0%
Tt 50%
tt 50%

Analysis of possible offspring shows that recessive alleles can produce an interesting effect; it is possible for children to have a different phenotype from either of the parents. For example, consider two parents, both with the genotype *Tt* for the PTC-tasting locus. Both parents have the "taster" phenotype. What genotypes and phenotypes will their children be likely to have? The expected genotype distribution is 25 percent *TT*, 50 percent *Tt*, and 25 percent *tt* (Figure 2.11).

Given this distribution of genotypes, what is the probable distribution of phenotypes? Genotypes *TT* and *Tt* are both "tasters," and therefore 75 percent of the children are expected to also be "tasters." Twenty-five percent of the children, however, are expected to have the genotype *tt* and will therefore have the "nontaster" phenotype. These children would have a different phenotype from either parent. An additional example, also using the PTC-tasting locus, is shown in Figure 2.12, which looks at the genotype and phenotype offspring distributions in the case where one parent has the *Tt* genotype and the other has the *tt* genotype.

A recessive trait, then, can remain hidden in one generation. This fact has great implications for genetic disease. For example, the disease cystic fibrosis occurs when a person is homozygous for a recessive allele. Therefore, two parents who have the heterozygous genotype do not manifest the disease, but they have a 25 percent chance of giving birth to a child who has the recessive homozygous condition, and therefore the disease.

Chromosomes and Inheritance

Alleles occur in pairs. Mendel showed that when alleles are passed on from parents to offspring, only one of each pair is contributed by each parent. The specific chromosome at any pair that is passed on is random. There is a 50 percent chance of either chromosome being passed on each time a sex cell is created.

MENDEL'S LAW OF INDEPENDENT ASSORTMENT Mendel's experiments revealed another aspect of probability in inheritance and the creation of sex cells. **Mendel's Law of Independent Assortment** states that the segregation of any pair of chromosomes does not influence the segregation of any other pair of chromosomes. In other words, chromosomes from separate pairs are inherited independently.

For example, imagine an organism with three chromosome pairs that we will label A, B, and C. To keep the members of each pair straight in our minds, label the chromosome of each pair as 1 or 2. This hypothetical organism has six chromosomes: A1, A2, B1, B2, C1, and C2. During the creation of a sex cell the A1 chromosome has a 50 percent chance of occurring, and so does the A2 chromosome. This same logic extends to the B and C chromosome pairs. Mendel's Law of Independent Assortment states that the seg-

▲▲▲▲▲▲▲▲▲▲▲▲▲▲▲▲▲▲▲▲▲▲▲▲▲▲▲▲▲

Mendel's Law of Independent Assortment The segregation of any pair of chromosomes does not affect the probability of segregation for other pairs of chromosomes.

regation of one pair of chromosomes does not affect the segregation of any other pair of chromosomes. It is just as likely to have a sex cell containing A1, B1, and C1 as it is to have a sex cell containing A1, B1, and C2. There are eight possible and equally likely outcomes for the sex cells: A1B1C1, A1B1C2, A1B2C1, A1B2C2, A2B1C1, A2B1C2, A2B2C1, A2B2C2. Given that any individual could have any one of the eight possible sex cells from both parents, the total number of combinations of offspring in this hypothetical organism is $8 \times 8 = 64$.

Independent assortment provides a powerful mechanism for shuffling different combinations of chromosomes and thus introduces great potential for genetic diversity. In humans, who have 23 chromosome pairs, the number are even more impressive. From any given individual, there are $2^{23} = 8,388,608$ possible combinations of sex cells. This means that two parents could produce a maximum of 70,368,744,177,664 genetically unique offspring!

LINKAGE   A major implication of Mendel's Law of Independent Assortment is that genes are inherited independently. This is true only to the extent that genes are on different chromosomes. Remember, it is the pairs of chromosomes that separate during meiosis, not each individual pair of alleles. When alleles are on the same chromosome, they are inherited together. This is called **linkage.** Linked alleles are not inherited independently because they are, by definition, on the same chromosome.

CROSSING OVER   An exception to the rule of linkage is **crossing over,** the switching of segments of DNA between the chromosome pairs during meiosis. Suppose, for example, that there are two genetic loci on the same chromosome, the first having alleles A or a and the second having alleles B or b. Suppose that you have the genotypes Aa and Bb, with one chromosome containing the A allele and the B allele, and the other chromosome having the a allele and the b allele. Because these two loci are both on the same chromosome, you would expect linkage to cause the two systems to be inherited together. That is, your possible sex cells would have A and B, or a and b. Any offspring inheriting the A allele would also be expected to inherit the B allele. Likewise, any offspring inheriting the a allele would also inherit the b allele. During meiosis, chromosome pairs sometimes exchange pieces, a process known as crossing over. For example, the segment of DNA containing the a allele could switch with the segment of DNA containing the A allele on the other chromosome. Therefore, you could have a sex cell with a and B, or a sex cell with A and b (Figure 2.13). Crossing over does not change the genetic material. The alleles are still the same, but they can occur in different combinations. Crossing over provides yet another mechanism for increasing genetic variation by providing new combinations of alleles.

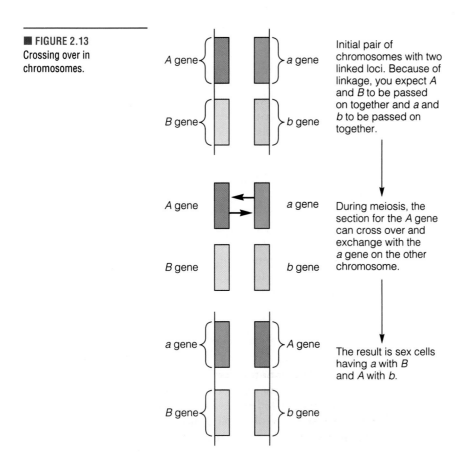

■ FIGURE 2.13
Crossing over in
chromosomes.

A gene — *a* gene

Initial pair of
chromosomes with two
linked loci. Because of
linkage, you expect *A*
and *B* to be passed
on together and *a* and
b to be passed on
together.

B gene — *b* gene

A gene — *a* gene

During meiosis, the
section for the *A* gene
can cross over and
exchange with the
a gene on the other
chromosome.

B gene — *b* gene

a gene — *A* gene

The result is sex cells
having *a* with *B*
and *A* with *b*.

B gene — *b* gene

SEX CHROMOSOMES AND SEX DETERMINATION   One of the 23 pairs of human chromosomes is called the sex chromosome pair because these chromosomes contain the genetic information determining the individual's sex. There are two forms of sex chromosomes, X and Y. Females have two X chromosomes (XX), and males have one X and one Y chromosome (XY).

The Y chromosome is much smaller than the X chromosome. Almost all genes found on X are therefore not found on Y. This means that males possess only one allele for certain traits because their Y chromosome lacks the corresponding section of DNA. Therefore, males will manifest a trait given only one allele, whereas females require the same allele from both parents to show the trait. An example of this sex difference is hemophilia, a

linkage When alleles on the same chromosome are inherited together.

crossing over When segments of DNA

switch between pairs of chromosomes.

genetic disorder that interferes with the normal process of blood clotting. The allele for hemophilia is recessive and is found on the segment of the X chromosome that has no corresponding portion on the Y chromosome. For females to be hemophiliac, they must inherit two copies of this allele, one from each parent. This is unlikely because the hemophilia allele is rare. Males, however, need only inherit one copy of the X chromosome from the mother. As a result, hemophilia is more common in males than females.

The Genetics of Complex Physical Traits

The discussion of genetics thus far has focused on simple discrete genetic traits. Traits such as the MN blood group are genetically "simple" because they result from the action of a single locus with a clear-cut mode of inheritance. These traits are also discrete, meaning that they produce a finite number of phenotypes. For example, you have the M or the N or the MN phenotype for the MN blood group system; you cannot have an intermediate phenotype. Your MN phenotype is also produced entirely from genetic factors. It is not influenced by the environment. Except for a complete blood transfusion, your MN blood group phenotype is the same all of your life.

These simple discrete traits are very useful for demonstrating the basic principles of Mendelian inheritance. It is not wise, however, to think of all biological traits as resulting from a single locus, exhibiting a finite number of phenotypes, or not being affected by the environment. Many of the characteristics of interest in human evolution, such as skin color, body size, brain size, and intelligence, do not fall into this simple category. Such traits have a complex mode of inheritance in that one or more genes may contribute to the phenotype and they may be affected by the environment. The combined action of genetics and environment produces traits with a continuous distribution. An example is human height. People do not come in three different heights (short, medium, and tall), nor five, nor twenty. Height can take on an infinite number of phenotypes. People can be 1,700 mm tall, 1701 mm tall, and any value in between, such as 1,700.3 mm or 1,700.65 mm.

Complex traits tend to produce more individuals with average values than extreme values. It is not uncommon to find human males between 1,676 and 1,981 mm (5.5 and 6.5 feet) tall. It is much rarer to find someone taller than 2,134 mm (7 feet). A typical distribution of a complex trait, human height, is shown in Figure 2.14.

POLYGENIC TRAITS AND PLEIOTROPY   Many complex traits are **polygenic,** the result of two or more loci. When several loci act to control a trait, many different genotypes and phenotypes can result. A number of physical characteristics, such as human skin color and height, may be polygenic. A single allele can also have multiple effects on an organism. When an allele has effects on multiple traits, this is referred to as **pleiotropy.** In chickens, one of the

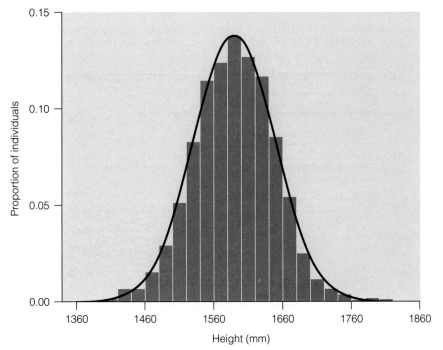

■ FIGURE 2.14
The distribution of a normally distributed continuous trait. This figure is based on the actual distribution of height (mm) of 1,986 Irish women (author's unpublished data). The height of the curve represents the proportion of women with any given height. Most individuals have a value close to the average for the population (the highest point on the curve, which corresponds to a height of 1,589 mm). The solid line is the fit of the normal distribution.

alleles that causes white feather color also acts to slow down overall body growth (Lerner and Libby 1976). In humans, the sickle cell allele affects the structure of the blood's hemoglobin and also leads to changes in overall body growth and health.

The concepts of polygenic traits and pleiotropy are important in considering the interrelated nature of biological systems. Analysis of simple discrete traits on a gene-by-gene basis is useful in understanding genetics, but it should not lead you to think that any organism is simply a collection of single, independent loci.

Figure 2.15 shows several different models of genetic interaction. Figure 2.15a represents the nature of some simple genetic traits, whereby each cause has a single effect. Figure 2.15b represents a polygenic trait, whereby many loci contribute to a single effect. Pleiotropic effects are shown in Figure 2.15c, whereby a single allele has multiple effects. Figure 2.15d is the most realistic model for many complex traits; each allele has multiple effects, and each effect has multiple causes. In this case, the trait is caused by polygenic and pleiotropic effects. To complicate matters, consider variations of this model in which not all alleles have the same effect, some alleles are dominant

▲▲

polygenic Refers to a genetic trait affected by two or more loci.

pleiotropy When a single allele can have

multiple effects on an organism.

■ FIGURE 2.15
The relationship between a
gene and a biological effect.
(a) Single gene, single
effect. (b) Polygenic trait.
(c) Pleiotropy. (d) A polygenic
trait and pleiotropy.

a. Each gene has a distinct biological effect.

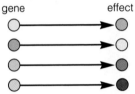

b. Polygenic trait: many genes contribute to a single effect.

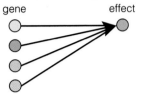

c. Pleiotropy: a gene has multiple effects.

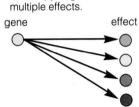

d. Polygenic traits and pleiotropy.

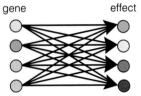

■ FIGURE 2.15
The relationship between a gene and a biological effect. (a) Single gene, single effect. (b) Polygenic trait. (c) Pleiotropy. (d) A polygenic trait and pleiotropy.

and some are not, and environmental factors act to obscure what we actually observe. It is no wonder that the study of the genetics of complex traits is extremely difficult, requiring sophisticated mathematical methods.

HERITABILITY   Complex traits reflect the joint effect of genetics and the environment. A common measure in studies of complex traits is **heritability,** which is the proportion of total variance in a trait that is attributable to genetic variation in a specific population (the value can be different in different populations). Complex traits show variation; for example, some people are taller than others, and some people have longer heads than others. The variation that we see is the total phenotypic variation. Some of this variation is due to genetic factors; some people may have a genetic potential for being taller, for example. The variation caused by genetic factors is called the *genetic variation.* Some of the total variation is also due to differences in environmental factors. For example, some people may have different diets, which would affect their height. We call this the *environmental variation.* Thus, total variation is made up of two components: genetic variation and environmental variation (or, in mathematical terms, total variation = genetic variation + environmental variation). Heritability is simply the *proportion* of total variation that is due to genetic variation. That is,

$$\text{Heritability} = \frac{\text{Genetic variation}}{\text{Total variation}} = \frac{\text{Genetic variation}}{\text{Genetic} + \text{Environmental}\atop \text{variation} \quad\quad \text{variation}}$$

Heritability is computed with this formula using complex methods of comparing relatives and environmental factors to estimate the genetic and environmental components. Heritability can range from 0 (no genetic variation) to 1 (no environmental variation). A high heritability, say greater than 0.5, indicates that the majority of variation is caused by genetic variation.

Although useful, the concept of heritability can be misleading. When we hear of a trait that has a high heritability, we are tempted to conclude that the trait is controlled almost exclusively by genetic factors and that environmental factors have little effect. The problem with reading too much into the concept of heritability is that it is a *relative* measure of the degree of genetic variation in a *specific* environment. Consider, for example, an estimate of heritability for human height. If the specific population we are looking at has little variation in diet, disease, and other environmental factors that can affect height, then the environmental variation will be low. As a result, the heritability will be high. If, however, the environmental variation changes, resulting in greater differences within the population in terms of diet and other factors, then the environmental variation increases, and heritability will be lower. Heritability, then, is a relative measure that can vary from one population to the next. It is not a measure of the extent to which genetics controls a trait; it is only a relative measure of variation.

MAJOR GENES   Recently, more attention has been given to **major genes.** In a major gene model the majority of genetic variation is due to a single locus. The continuous distribution of the trait is the result of environmental effects and can be enhanced by the smaller effect of other loci. In contrast to certain polygenic models whereby all loci contribute equally, a major gene model postulates that a single locus has the greatest effect. A trait controlled by a major gene often shows the same type of distribution as a polygenic trait (see Figure 2.14). Developments in statistical analysis have allowed tests for major genes.

MUTATIONS

As shown earlier, the process of genetic inheritance produces new combinations of genes in offspring. The independent assortment of chromosomes during meiosis and the action of crossing over both act to create new genetic combinations. They do not act to create any new genetic material, however. In order to explain past evolution, we need a mechanism for introducing new alleles and variation. The origin of new genetic variation was a problem to Darwin, but we now know new alleles are brought about through the process of mutation.

▲▲

heritability   The proportion of total variation of a trait that is due to genetic variation.

major genes   Genes that have the primary effect on the phenotypic distribution of a complex trait.

Evolutionary Significance of Mutations

A **mutation** is a change in the genetic code. Mutations are the ultimate source of all genetic variation. Mutations are caused by a number of environmental factors such as background radiation, which includes radiation from the earth's crust and cosmic rays. Such background radiation is all around us, in the air we breathe and the food we eat. Mutations may also be caused by heat and ingested substances such as caffeine.

A growing concern is the effect of environmental changes on mutation rates. Human-made radiation, as from certain industries, not only might be dangerous to exposed individuals but might also affect their future offspring by creating mutational effects in sex cells. Numerous studies of laboratory animals, such as fruit flies, have shown clearly that the mutation rate increases with exposure to radiation. Less is known about the effect of increased radiation on mutations in humans and other mammals. Studies of the children of survivors of the atomic bomb attacks in Japan at the end of World War II have so far failed to show definite evidence of any increase in the rate of mutations in sex cells (although mutations in body cells in the exposed parents were frequent). Given the definite evidence of radiation effects from experimental animals, this failure may reflect an inadequate sample size or other methodological difficulties in the human studies. Another possibility is that mammalian cells have a high capacity for DNA repair.

Mutations can take place in any cell of the body. To have evolutionary importance, however, the mutation must occur in a sex cell. A mutation in a skin cell on the end of your finger has no evolutionary significance because it will not be passed on to your offspring.

Mutations are random. That is, there is no way of predicting when a specific mutation will take place or what, if any, phenotypic effect it will have. All we can do is estimate the probability of a mutation occurring at a given locus over a given amount of time. The randomness of mutations also means that mutations do not appear when they might be needed. Many mosquitoes have adapted to insecticides because a mutation was present in the population that acted to confer some resistance to the insecticide. If that mutation had not been present, the mosquitoes would have died. The mosquitoes' need for a certain genetic variant had no effect on whether or not the mutation appeared.

Mutations can have different effects depending on the specific type of mutation and the environment. The conventional view of mutations has long been that they are mostly harmful. A classic analogy is the comparison of the genetic code with the engine of an automobile. If an engine part is changed at random, the most likely result is that the car will not operate, or at least not as well as it did before the change.

Some mutations, however, are advantageous. They lead to change that improves the survival and reproduction of organisms. In recent decades, we have also discovered that some mutations are neutral. That is, the genetic change has no detectable effect on survival or reproduction. There is continued controversy among geneticists about the relative frequency of neutral mutations. Some claim that many mutations are neutral in their effect. Others note the difficulties in detecting the effects of many mutations.

Whether or not a mutation is neutral, advantageous, or disadvantageous depends in large part on the environment. Genetic variants that are harmful in certain environments might actually be helpful in other environments.

Types of Mutations

We now recognize that there are a variety of ways in which mutations occur (Marks 1995). Mutations can involve changes in a single DNA base, in larger sections of DNA, and in entire chromosomes. One example is the substitution of one DNA base for another, such as the widely studied **sickle cell allele.** The red blood cells produced in individuals with two copies of this allele (one from each parent) are misshapen and do not transport oxygen efficiently. The result is a severe form of anemia (sickle cell anemia) that leads to sickness and death. The specific cause of this allele is a mutation in the sixth amino acid (out of 146 amino acids) of the beta chain of hemoglobin. The DNA for the normal beta hemoglobin allele contains instructions for the amino acid, glutamic acid at this position (CTC). The sickle cell mutation occurs when the base T is changed to an A, which specifies the amino acid valine (CAC). This small change affects the entire structure of the red blood cells and, in turn, the well-being of the individual.

Substitution of one base for another is only one type of mutation. Mutations can also involve the addition or deletion of a base, or of large sections of DNA. In these cases, the genetic message is changed. Also, sections of DNA can be duplicated or moved from one place to another, and sections of DNA can be added or lost when crossing over is not equal.

The genetic information contained in the chromosomes can also be altered by the deletion or duplication of part or all of the chromosome. For example, an entire chromosome from a pair can be lost (**monosomy** = one chromosome) or can occur in duplicate, giving three chromosomes (**trisomy**). One result of the latter is Down syndrome, a condition characterized by certain cranial features (Figure 2.16), poor physical growth, and mental retardation (usually mild). Down syndrome is caused by the duplication of

■ **FIGURE 2.16**
Facial appearance of a child with Down syndrome.
(Courtesy March of Dimes Birth Defects Foundation)

---

mutation A mechanism for evolutionary change resulting from a random change in the genetic code; the ultimate source of all genetic variation.

sickle cell allele An allele of the hemoglobin locus. Individuals homozygous for the sickle cell allele have sickle cell anemia.

monosymy When only one chromosome rather than a pair is present in body cells.

trisomy When three chromosomes rather than a pair occur in body cells.

one of the 21st chromosome pair. Affected individuals have a total of 47 chromosomes, one more than the normal 46. Down syndrome can also be caused by mutations of the 21st chromosome. In some individuals the change involves the exchange of parts of the 21st chromosome with other chromosomes.

Several chromosomal mutations involve the sex chromosomes. One, known as Turner's syndrome, occurs when an individual has only one X chromosome instead of two. These individuals thus have only 45 chromosomes and develop as females. Those with Turner's syndrome are generally short, have undeveloped ovaries, and are sterile. Another condition, known as Klinefelter's syndrome, occurs in males with an extra X chromosome. Instead of the normal XY combination, these males have an XXY combination for a total of 47 chromosomes. They are characterized by small testes and reduced fertility.

Rates of Mutations

Specific mutations are relatively rare events, although the *exact* rate of mutations is difficult to determine in many cases. Part of the problem in determining the rate of mutations is the fact that several different base sequences can specify the same amino acid. For example, the amino acid glycine is specified by the sequence CCA. If a mutation occurs in which the third base changes from an A to a G, the net result is the sequence CCG, which also specifies glycine. This hypothetical mutation leads to no biochemical change and is considered neutral. If there is no observable change, then the mutation will usually go unnoticed.

A mutation is also more apparent if it involves a dominant allele because a heterozygote receiving one copy of the mutant allele will show the mutant phenotype. If a mutant allele is recessive, then phenotypic expression will require two copies of the mutant allele, which is a less common event. Recessive mutant alleles go unnoticed under these circumstances.

Another problem in identifying mutations is that harmful mutations may result in spontaneous abortion (miscarriage) before pregnancy has been detected. Roughly 15 percent of all recognized conceptions result in spontaneous abortion, of which 50 percent can be traced to specific chromosomal mutations (Sutton and Wagner 1985). For such an event to be recorded, however, a woman must be aware that she is pregnant, which she usually doesn't know until a month or more after conception. Some researchers feel that a large number of unrecognized conceptions are expelled spontaneously during the first few weeks after conception. If so, any prediction of mutation rates based on recognized conceptions will be an underestimate.

Despite these problems, research has provided estimates of a range in the rates of mutation. For single-base mutations in humans, this range is from 1 to 100 mutations per million sex cells (Lerner and Libby 1976). This translates to a probability between 0.000001 and 0.0001 of a mutation occurring at a given locus for a given sex cell.

Regardless of the specific mutation rates for a given gene or chromosome, one thing is clear—mutation rates are generally low. Given these low probabilities, it may be tempting to regard mutation as so rare that it has no special evolutionary significance. The problem with this reasoning is that the estimated rates refer to a *single* specific locus. Human chromosomes have many loci. The exact number is not known, but it has been estimated at roughly 100,000 (Woodward 1992). The probability that a specific locus will show a mutation in any individual is low, but the probability of *any* locus showing a mutation is much higher.

As an example, assume a mutation rate of 1 in 100,000 (0.00001) for 100,000 loci. Statistically there is a 63 percent chance of a person having at least one mutation. Now assume a small population of 25 people. Given the same mutation rate, the probability of finding at least one mutation in this population is over 99.999 percent.

Even though mutation is a rare event for any given locus, there is a high probability of at least one new mutation in each individual. When we consider the genetics of an entire population or species, the net result is that mutation is common within a single generation. In fact, many studies estimate that all of us carry at least one lethal recessive mutant allele.

GENETICS AND BEHAVIOR

Perhaps the most controversial topic in genetics is the question of the extent to which behavior is governed by genetic factors. The controversy arises not so much from academic debate but from the social implications, real and imagined, of this question. Problems arise out of a misunderstanding of the basic concepts of genetics or are produced by those seeking any "scientific" fact, regardless of truth, to support and further their own social or political agenda. Much of this controversy revolves around the concept of race, which is discussed in Chapter 13. The present section focuses on basic strategies involved in relating genes and behavior.

Is a behavior, such as intelligence or shyness, caused by genes ("nature") or the physical and cultural environment ("nurture")? The debate of nature versus nurture has a long history in Western civilization. The prevalent view among scientists reflects not only current research but also the social and cultural climate of the times. Scientists are people, too, as susceptible to biases and prejudices as everyone else. A major lesson of the history of science is that cultural beliefs influence the methodology and interpretation of scientific results.

At the beginning of the twentieth century, the prevalent view was that "nature" was the more important determinant of many behaviors, particularly intelligence. This emphasis shifted to "nurture" during the period from the 1930s to the 1960s, when environmental factors were seen as being the most, if not the only, important factor.

Much of the debate over nature versus nurture is nonsense, however. Any attempt to relegate human behaviors to either genetics *or* environment is fruitless. Genes and environment are both important in their effect on human behaviors. The proper question is not which is more important, but rather how they interact.

For example, consider the nature of maternal behaviors. The studies of primate behavior discussed in Chapters 6 and 7 show clearly that maternal behaviors are in part the result of learning within a social context. Females with good mothers tend to be good mothers themselves. Chimpanzee females learn, and practice, maternal behaviors as part of socialization. Experiments with monkeys have shown that maternally deprived infants tend to grow up to be poor parents. Learning clearly has an effect on maternal behaviors. Does this mean that there is no genetic component?

Consider the differences in parental care between fish and mammals. On average, fish provide much less care to offspring than mammals. The whole structure of mammalian biology is a reflection of the close bonds between mother and infant (see Chapter 6). Regardless of environment, fish cannot provide as much parental care as mammals. A genetic component is at work, then, if only in terms of the entire group. Regardless of our mammalian heritage of intensive care, however, our own species unfortunately provides many examples of poor parenting. Clearly, both genetic and environmental factors are important in maternal behaviors. It is not "nature" *or* "nurture," but both.

What are the implications of the joint interaction of genetics and environment? If a behavior is affected to some extent by genetics, is there then an innate difference between people with different alleles? In terms of the fish example, this question asks whether or not certain females will automatically be better mothers because of genetic differences. Even if genetic differences in a behavior exist, this does not mean that those differences will override environmental factors. We cannot ignore the interaction between genetics and environment. Certain forms of human nearsightedness are due entirely to inheritance, but they can nonetheless be corrected for by glasses (Gould 1987).

Another problem is that the focus is often on extrapolating from large-scale differences (e.g., species) to small-scale differences (e.g., individuals within a species). The fact that, on average, mammals show more parental care than fish does not necessarily mean that some humans will manifest differences in parenting behavior because of genetic factors. It is quite possible that no genetic variation exists within our species for many behaviors. That is, we all have the same alleles (Harpending et al. 1987).

SUMMARY

The DNA molecule specifies the genetic code or set of instructions needed to produce biological structures. DNA acts along with a related molecule, RNA, to translate these instructions into proteins. The DNA is contained along structures within the cell called chromosomes. Chromosomes come in pairs. A segment of DNA that codes for a certain product is called a gene. The different forms of genes present at a locus are called alleles. The DNA molecule has the ability to make copies of itself, allowing transmission of genetic information from cell to cell, and from generation to generation.

Meiosis is the process of sex cell formation that results in one of each chromosome pair being transmitted from parent to offspring. Each individual receives half of his or her alleles from each parent. The two alleles together specify the genetic constitution of an individual—the genotype. The physical manifestation of the genotype is known as the phenotype. The relationship between genotype and phenotype depends on whether an allele is dominant, recessive, or codominant. In complex physical traits, the phenotype is the result of the combined effect of genetics and environment.

The ultimate source of all genetic variation is mutation—a random change in the genetic code. Some mutations are neutral in effect; others are helpful or harmful. The effect of any mutation often depends on the specific environmental conditions. Mutations for any given allele are relatively rare events, but given the large number of loci in many organisms, it is highly probable that each individual has at least one mutant allele.

Genetic factors have been linked to human behaviors. Such behaviors appear to be influenced by both genetics and environment. Given the biocultural nature of human beings, it should be no surprise that both genes and environment have an effect on both biology and behavior.

SUPPLEMENTAL READINGS

Marks, J. 1995. *Human Biodiversity: Genes, Race, and History*. New York: Aldine de Gruyter. A historically oriented review of different approaches to human biological variation, with many discussions of the nature of genes and the mechanisms of human genetics.

Woodward, V. 1992. *Human Heredity and Society*. St. Paul, Minn.: West. A well-written introduction to molecular and Mendelian genetics that focuses on humans.

CELL BIOLOGY:
A Review

This section, which focuses on the structure of the cell and on the processes of mitosis and meiosis, can be used as a supplement for students wishing to review the basic biology necessary for an understanding of the fundamental principles of Mendelian genetics.

THE CELL

All living creatures are made up of cells. Humans, like many organisms, are multicelled. Figure 2.17 shows some of the components of a typical cell. Two major structures are the *nucleus* and the *cytoplasm;* the latter contains a number of other structures. The entire body of the cell is enclosed by a *cell membrane*.

Within the cytoplasm, *mitochondria* convert some cellular material into energy that is then used for cellular activity (see Chapter 12 for further discussion). *Ribosomes* are small particles that are frequently attached to a larger structure known as the *endoplasmic reticulum*. Composed of RNA and proteins, ribosomes serve as sites for the manufacture of proteins.

As discussed in Chapter 2, the DNA sequences that make up the genetic code are bound together by proteins in long strands known as *chromosomes*. In body cells, chromosomes come in pairs and humans have 23 pairs of chromosomes. The chromosomes within the nucleus of the cell contain all of the DNA, with the exception of something called mitochondrial DNA (see Chapter 12).

MITOSIS

DNA has the ability to make copies of itself. This ability is vital for transmitting genetic information from cell to cell and for transmitting genetic information from generation to generation. The replication of DNA is part of the process of cell replication. We will examine two basic processes: mitosis, the replication of body cells, and meiosis, the replication of sex cells.

Mitosis produces two identical body cells from one original. Between cell divisions, each chromosome produces an exact copy of itself, resulting in two

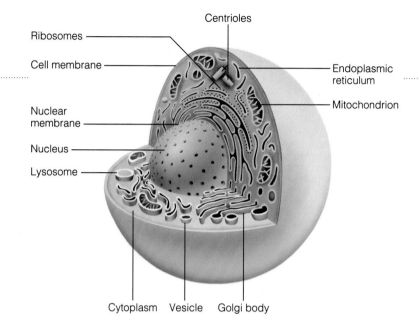

Ribosomes

Cell membrane

Nuclear
membrane

Nucleus

Lysosome

Centrioles

Endoplasmic
reticulum

Mitochondrion

Cytoplasm   Vesicle   Golgi body

■ FIGURE 2.17
Schematic diagram of a cell.

the spindle fibers attach to the centromeres. During *anaphase*, the centromere divides and the two strands of chromatids (original and duplicate) split and move toward opposite ends of the cell. During *telophase*, new nuclear membranes form around each of the two clusters of chromosomes. Finally, the cell membrane pinches in the middle, creating two identical cells.

MEIOSIS

pairs with two chromosomes each. When a cell divides, each part contains one of each of the pairs of chromosomes. Thus, two identical body cells, each with the full number of chromosome pairs, is produced. As outlined in Figure 2.18, five stages compose the process of mitosis: interphase, prophase, metaphase, anaphase, and telophase. (Some people do not refer to interphase as a stage.)

During *interphase*, the chromosomes that are dispersed throughout the nucleus duplicate. During *prophase*, the chromosomes, each of which

is attached to its copy, become tightly coiled and move toward one another in the nucleus. Each of the two copies is called a *chromatid* and their point of attachment is called the *centromere*. Small structures located outside the nuclear membrane, known as *centrioles* (see Figure 2.17), move toward opposite ends of the cell and *spindle fibers* form between the centrioles. The nuclear membrane then dissolves.

During *metaphase*, the duplicated chromosomes line up along the middle of the cell and

Meiosis, the production of sex cells (gametes), differs from mitosis in several ways. The main difference is that sex cells contain only half of an organism's DNA—one chromosome from each pair. Thus, when a new zygote, or fertilized egg, is formed from the joining of egg and sperm, the offspring will have 23 chromosome pairs. One of each pair comes from the mother and one of each pair comes from the father.

Meiosis involves two cycles of cell division (see Figure 2.19). The total sequence of events following the initial duplication of

Original cell with two
pairs of chromosomes.

Interphase
Replication of
chromosomes.

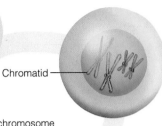

Chromosome
pair

Nucleus

Nuclear
membrane

Chromatid

■ FIGURE 2.18
The five phases of mitosis. In
this example, the original
body cell contains two pairs
of chromosomes. Mitosis
produces two identical body
cells, each containing two
chromosome pairs (a total of
four chromosomes each).

Prophase
Chromosomes come together. Each chromosome
and its copy (chromatid) are connected at a point
known as the centromere. Centrioles move to
opposite ends of cell. Spindle fibers are
formed. Nuclear membrane dissolves.

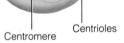

Metaphase
Chromosomes
line up. Spindle
fibers attach to
centromeres.

Spindle
fiber

Centromere

Centrioles

Anaphase
Centromeres split.
Chromatids separate.
Chromatids move to
opposite ends of cell.

Telophase
Nuclear membranes reform.
Cell membrane begins to pinch
to start formation of two cells.

Two identical cells
now exist, each with
two chromosome pairs.

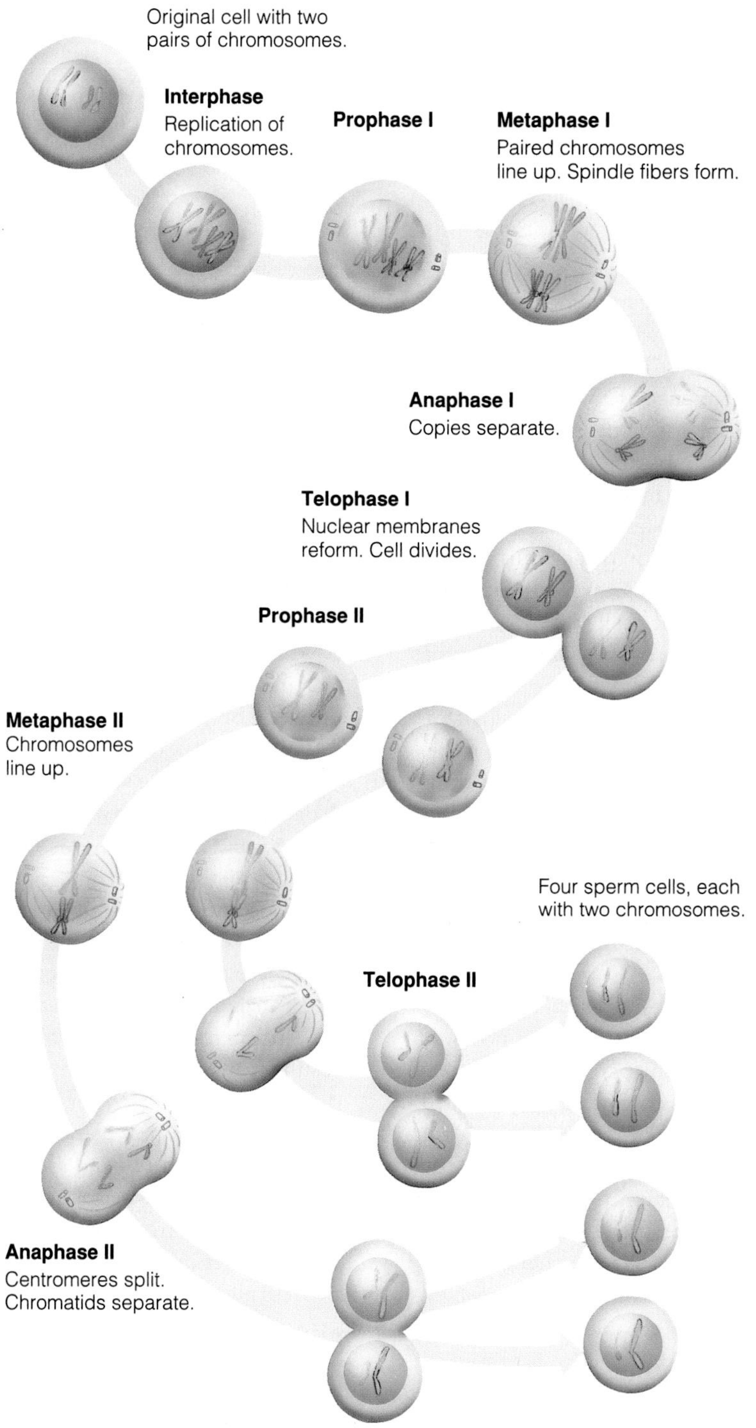

Original cell with two pairs of chromosomes.

Interphase
Replication of chromosomes.

Prophase I

Metaphase I
Paired chromosomes line up. Spindle fibers form.

Anaphase I
Copies separate.

Telophase I
Nuclear membranes reform. Cell divides.

Prophase II

Metaphase II
Chromosomes line up.

Four sperm cells, each with two chromosomes.

Telophase II

Anaphase II
Centromeres split. Chromatids separate.

■ FIGURE 2.19
The phases of meiosis for a sperm cell. In this example, the original cell contained two chromosome pairs. As a result of meiosis, four sperm cells were produced, each with two chromosomes. The process is similar for egg cells, except that one egg cell and three polar bodies are produced.

chromosomes (interphase) involves eight stages: prophase I, metaphase I, anaphase I, telophase I, prophase II, metaphase II, anaphase II, and telophase II. Figure 2.19 presents a diagram of this process for the production of sperm cells, for a hypothetical organism with two chromosome pairs. Each of the two pairs of chromosomes has replicated itself by the start of prophase I, leading to eight chromatids: the two chromosomes of each pair duplicate, giving a total of $2 \times 2 \times 2 = 8$ chromatids, each pair of which attaches to one of the centromeres through a process known as *synapsis*. At the end of prophase I the nuclear mem brane dissolves. Then, during metaphase I, the paired chromosomes line up and spindle fibers form. The copies separate during anaphase I. During telophase I, the nuclear membranes reform and the cell divides. The realization of two cells, each containing eight chromatids, constitutes prophase II. During metaphase II, the chromosomes line up, after which the centromeres split and the chromatids sepa-

rate, completing anaphase II. The nuclear membranes reform during telophase II, and the cell divides. The net result of this sequence of two cell divisions is four sperm cells, each with two chromosomes—half of the genetic material of the father. The process is similar for the production of egg cells from the female, except that the net result is one egg cell and three structures known as *polar bodies* that do not function as sex cells.

Meiosis thus allows half of a parent's genetic material to be passed on to the next generation. When a sperm cell fertilizes an egg cell, the total number of chromosomes is restored. For humans, the resulting zygote contains $23 + 23 = 46$ chromosomes, or 23 chromosome pairs.

Sex cells may also contain genetic combinations not present in the parent. When synapsis occurs during prophase I, and the chromosomes pair with their copies, becoming attached to one another at several places, the potential exists for genetic material to be exchanged, a process known as *crossing over*.

The resulting genetic combinations allow for variation in each sex cell from its source.

Independent assortment also enhances genetic variability. As discussed in Chapter 2, according to this principle, the segregation of any pair of chromosomes does not affect the probability of segregation of any other pair of chromosomes. If you had two chromosome pairs, A and B, with two chromosomes each (A1 and A2, and B1 and B2), only one of each pair will be found in any sex cell. However, you might have one sex cell with A1 and B1 and another sex cell with A1 and B2. Whichever member of the first pair of chromosomes is found in any given sex cell has no bearing on whichever member of the second pair is also found in that sex cell. Independent assortment results from processes occurring during metaphase I. When the paired chromosomes line up, they do so at random and are not influenced by whether they originally came from the person's mother or father. This process allows for tremendous genetic variability in potential offspring.

Microevolution

Biological evolution is genetic change through time and can be studied at two different levels. Microevolution consists of changes in the frequency of alleles in a population from one generation to the next. Macroevolution comprises long-term patterns of genetic change over thousands and millions of generations as well as the process of species formation. This chapter deals with the general principles of microevolution. Macroevolution is discussed in Chapter 4.

POPULATION GENETICS

Microevolution takes into account changes in the frequency of alleles from one generation to the next. The focus is generally not on the specific genotypes or phenotypes of individuals, but rather on the total pattern of an entire biological population. We are interested in defining the relative frequencies of different alleles, genotypes, and phenotypes for the entire population being studied. We then seek to determine if any apparent change in these frequencies has occurred over time. If changes have occurred, we try to explain them.

Definitions of Population

The term **breeding population** is used frequently in evolutionary theory. In an abstract sense, a breeding population is a group of organisms that tends to choose mates from within the group. This definition is a bit tricky because it is not clear what proportion of mating within a group defines a breeding population.

For example, suppose you travel to a village in a remote mountain region. You find that 99 percent of all the people in the village are married to others who were born in the same village. In this case, the village would appear to fit our ideal definition. But, what if only 80 percent of the people choose their mates from within the village? What if the number were 50 percent? At what point do you stop referring to the population as a "breeding population"? There is no quick and ready answer to this question.

On a practical level, human populations are initially most often defined on the basis of geographic and political boundaries. A small isolated island, for example, easily fits the requirements of a defined population. In most cases, the local geographic unit (such as town or village) is used. Because many human populations have distinct geographic boundaries, this solution often provides the best approach. Care must be taken, however, to ensure that a local geographic unit, such as a town, is not composed of distinct subpopulations, such as groups belonging to different religious sects. A rural Irish village fits this criterion because most of its residents belong to the same religion, social class, and occupational group. New York City, on the other hand, clearly contains a number of subpopulations defined in terms of ethnicity, religion, social class, and other factors. In this case, subpopulations defined on the basis of these factors would serve as our units of analysis.

In many cases, the definition of a population depends on the specific research question asked. For example, if the goal of a study is to look at spatial variation in biological variation, populations defined on the basis of geography are most suitable. If, however, the goal of a study is to look at genetic variation among ethnic groups, then ethnicity should be used to define the populations.

Another potential problem in defining populations is determining the difference between the total census population and the breeding population. Microevolutionary theory specifically concerns those individuals who contribute to the next generation. The total population refers to everybody, whether or not they are likely to breed. The breeding population is smaller than the total population because of a number of factors. First, some individuals in the total population will be too young or too old to mate. Second, cultural factors and geographic distribution may act to limit an individual's choice of mate, and as a consequence some individuals will not breed. If, for example, you live in an isolated area, there may not be enough individuals of the opposite sex from which to choose a mate. Such factors must be taken into consideration in defining a breeding population.

Once a population has been defined, the next step in microevolutionary analysis is to determine the frequencies of genotypes and alleles within the population.

Genotype and Allele Frequencies

The genotype frequency is a measure of the relative proportions of different genotypes within a population. Likewise, an allele frequency is simply a measure of the relative proportion of alleles within a population. Genotype frequencies are obtained by dividing the number of individuals with each genotype by the total number of individuals. For example, consider a hypothetical population of 200 people for the MN blood group system where there are 98 people with genotype MM, 84 people with genotype MN, and 18 people with genotype NN. The genotype frequencies are therefore:

Frequency of MM = 98/200 = 0.49

Frequency of MN = 84/200 = 0.42

Frequency of NN = 18/200 = 0.09

Note that the total frequency of all genotypes adds up to 1 (0.49 + 0.42 + 0.09 = 1).

Allele frequencies are computed by counting the number of each allele and dividing that number by the total number of alleles. In the example here, the total number of alleles is 400 because there are 200 people, each with two alleles. To find out the number of M alleles for each genotype, count up the number of alleles for each genotype and multiply that number by the number of people with that genotype. Finally, add up the number for all genotypes. In the example, 98 people have the MM genotype, and therefore 98 people each have two M alleles. The total number of M alleles for people with the MM genotype is 98 × 2 = 196. For the MN genotype, 84 people have one M allele, giving a total of 84 × 1 = 84 M alleles. For the NN genotype, 18 people have no M alleles, for a total of 18 × 0 = 0 M alleles. Adding the number of M alleles for all genotypes gives a total of 196 + 84 + 0 = 280 M alleles. The frequency of the M allele is therefore 280/400 = 0.7. The frequency of the N allele can be computed in the same way, giving an allele frequency of 0.3. Note that the frequencies of all alleles must add up to 1. Another example of allele frequency computation is given in Table 3.1.

The method of counting alleles to determine allele frequencies can be used only when the number of individuals with each genotype can be determined. If one of the alleles is dominant, this may not be possible, and other

breeding population A group of organisms that tend to choose mates from within the group.

■ TABLE 3.1
Example of Allele Frequency Computation

Imagine you have just collected information on *MN* blood group genotypes for 250 humans in a given population. Your data are:

Number of *MM* genotype = 40
Number of *MN* genotype = 120
Number of *NN* genotype = 90

The allele frequencies are computed as follows:

GENOTYPE	NUMBER OF PEOPLE	TOTAL NUMBER OF ALLELES	NUMBER OF M ALLELES	NUMBER OF N ALLELES
MM	40	80	80	0
MN	120	240	120	120
NN	90	180	0	180
Total	250	500	200	300

The relative frequency of the *M* allele is computed as the number of *M* alleles divided by the total number of alleles: 200/500 = 0.4.

The relative frequency of the *N* allele is computed as the number of *N* alleles divided by the total number of alleles: 300/500 = 0.6.

As a check, note that the relative frequencies of the alleles must add up to 1.0 (0.4 + 0.6 = 1.0).

methods must be used. The computation of allele frequencies when more than two alleles are present at a given locus also may require special methods. Such methods are beyond the scope of this text but may be found in any comprehensive text on population genetics (e.g., Cavalli-Sforza and Bodmer 1971).

Hardy-Weinberg Equilibrium

The mathematical basis of microevolutionary theory rests upon Mendel's principles and the use of a model known as **Hardy-Weinberg equilibrium.** This model, developed independently by G. H. Hardy and W. Weinberg, provides a method of predicting genotype frequencies in future generations under the assumption that mating is at random and that no evolution takes place.

The Hardy-Weinberg equilibrium model is a mathematical statement using symbols to represent allele frequencies. Many microevolutionary models assume a single locus with two alleles (e.g., A and a). By convention, the symbols p and q are used to represent the frequencies of the A allele and the a allele, respectively. These symbols are a form of shorthand because it is easier to say p than "the frequency of the A allele."

The Hardy-Weinberg equilibrium model states that given allele frequencies of p and q, the expected genotype frequencies are:

Frequency of $AA = p^2$

Frequency of $Aa = 2pq$

Frequency of $aa = q^2$

The mathematical proof of this relationship is given in Appendix 1, which also provides a brief mathematical discussion of population genetics. Assume a population with two alleles (A and a) with allele frequencies of $p = 0.6$ and $q = 0.4$. Using the Hardy-Weinberg equilibrium model, the predicted genotype frequencies are:

$AA = (0.6)^2 = (0.6)(0.6) = 0.36$

$Aa = 2(0.6)(0.4) \qquad = 0.48$

$aa = (0.4)^2 = (0.4)(0.4) = 0.16$

The Hardy-Weinberg equilibrium model can also be used to show that, given certain assumptions, there will be no change in allele frequency from one generation to the next (see Appendix 1).

The Hardy-Weinberg equilibrium model makes several assumptions. It assumes random mating within the population (with respect to the locus or loci of interest). That is, every individual has an equal chance of mating with any individual of the opposite sex (both sexes are also assumed to have equal allele frequencies). The Hardy-Weinberg equilibrium model also assumes that the population is large enough that there is no variation in allele frequencies caused by sampling (no genetic drift); there is no movement into or out of the population (no gene flow); there are no new alleles (no mutation); and there is no difference in the fertility or mortality of different genotypes (no natural selection). If we compare the expected genotype frequencies with those actually observed and find no difference, then we can conclude that the population is in Hardy-Weinberg equilibrium. If the predicted and observed genotype frequencies are not the same, then the population is not in Hardy-Weinberg equilibrium, and we know that at least one of the assumptions must be incorrect. Further analysis would then be needed to determine which of these assumptions was incorrect.

There are two basic reasons a population might not be in a state of Hardy-Weinberg equilibrium. Observed and predicted genotype frequencies may differ because of the effects of evolutionary forces and/or nonrandom mating. **Evolutionary forces** are those mechanisms that actually lead to a change in allele frequency over time. The evolutionary forces are mutation,

Hardy-Weinberg equilibrium In the absence of evolutionary forces, allele frequencies remain constant from one generation to the next.

evolutionary forces Four mechanisms that can cause changes in allele frequencies from one generation to the next.

■ **FIGURE 3.1**
Inbreeding is used with many domesticated animals to produce certain types of characteristics. (Courtesy of Kenneth Feder, Central Connecticut State University)

natural selection, genetic drift, and gene flow (described in detail in the following section). These four forces are the only mechanisms that can cause the frequency of an allele to change over time. For example, if you observe an allele frequency of 0.5 for a population in one generation and then return a generation later to find a frequency of 0.4, then evolution has occurred. This change can be due only to mutation, natural selection, drift, and/or gene flow. Given such a large change, mutation could be ruled out as a major force, for mutation leads to only small changes in any single generation for any given locus. In this case, natural selection, gene flow, and/or genetic drift would be considered more likely forces acting to change allele frequencies. Examination of factors such as migration rates, population size, environmental variation, and differential survival would then be needed to further pinpoint the most likely explanation for the change.

Random mating is one form of mating system. **Nonrandom mating,** however, refers to the patterns of mate choice within a population and to its genetic consequences. Nonrandom mating includes **inbreeding,** the mating of biologically related individuals (Figure 3.1), and **assortative mating,** mating on the basis of phenotypic similarity or dissimilarity. Mating systems do not change allele frequencies, but they do have an effect on the *rate* of allele frequency change.

EVOLUTIONARY FORCES

Mutation

Mutation introduces new alleles into a population. Therefore, the frequency of different alleles will change over time. For example, consider a genetic locus with a single allele, A, for a population of 100 people (and therefore 200 alleles, because each person has two alleles). Everyone in the population will have genotype AA, and the frequency of the A allele is 1.0 (100 percent). Now, assume that one of the A alleles being passed on to the next generation changes into a new form, *a*. Assuming the population stays the same size (to make the mathematics a bit easier), there will be 199 A alleles and 1 *a* allele in the next generation. The frequency of A will have changed from 1.0 to 0.995 (199/200), and the frequency of *a* will have changed from 0.0 to 0.005 (1/200).

If there is no further evolutionary change, the allele frequencies will remain the same in future generations. If this mutation continues to recur, the frequency of the *a* allele will slowly increase, assuming no other evolutionary forces are operating. For typical mutation rates, such a process would take a very long time.

Mutations can also occur in the reverse direction; that is, an *a* allele could mutate back to the original form A. Not much information is available on back mutation rates in human populations, but they do appear to be much rarer than the usual mutation rate.

Although mutations are vital to evolution because they provide new variations, mutation rates are low and do not lead, by themselves, to major changes in allele frequency. The other evolutionary forces increase or decrease the frequencies of mutant alleles. If you visited a population over two generations and noted that the frequency of a given allele changed from 0.30 to 0.40, it would be extremely unlikely that this magnitude of change would be due solely to mutation. The other evolutionary forces would be responsible for such large changes.

Many discrete genetic traits are **polymorphisms** (many forms). A genetic polymorphism is a locus with two or more alleles having frequencies too large to be a result of mutation alone. The usual, somewhat arbitrary, cutoff point for these allele frequencies is 0.01. If an allele has a frequency greater than 0.01, we can safely assume this relatively high frequency is caused by factors other than mutation. For example, a locus with allele frequencies of $A = 1.0$ and $a = 0.0$ would not be polymorphic because only one allele (A) is present in the population. Likewise, a locus with frequencies of $A = 0.999$ and $a = 0.001$ would also not be a genetic polymorphism because only one allele has a frequency greater than 0.01. If the allele frequencies were $A = 0.2$ and $a = 0.8$, this would be evidence of genetic polymorphism. Both alleles have frequencies greater than 0.01. Such frequencies are explained by natural selection, genetic drift, and/or gene flow.

Natural Selection

As discussed in Chapter 1, natural selection filters genetic variation. Individuals with certain biological characteristics that allow them to survive to reproduce, pass on the alleles for such characteristics to the next generation. Natural selection does not create new genetic variation (only mutation can do that), but it does change the relative frequencies of different alleles.

The analysis of natural selection focuses on **fitness,** the probability of survival and reproduction of an organism. For any locus, fitness is measured as the relative genetic contribution of a genotype to the next generation. Imagine a locus with two alleles, A and a, and the genotypes AA, Aa, and aa. If all individuals with genotypes AA and Aa survive and reproduce but

▲▲

nonrandom mating
Patterns of mate choice that influence the distributions of genotype and phenotype frequencies.

inbreeding Mating between biologically related individuals.

assortative mating Mating between

phenotypically similar or dissimilar individuals.

polymorphism A discrete genetic trait in which there are at least two alleles at a locus

having frequencies greater than 0.01.

fitness An organism's probability of survival and reproduction.

■ **TABLE 3.2**
Example of Natural Selection against a Recessive Homozygote

This example uses an initial population size before selection of 200 people. The locus has two alleles, *A* and *a*. Initially there are 50 people with genotype *AA*, 100 people with genotype *Aa*, and 50 people with genotype *aa*. The allele frequencies before selection are therefore 0.5 for *A* and 0.5 for *a*. The fitness values have been chosen to illustrate total selection against the recessive homozygote.

	GENOTYPE			
	AA	*Aa*	*aa*	TOTAL
Number of people *before selection*	50	100	50	200
Fitness (percentage *that survives)*	100%	100%	0%	
Number of people *after selection*	50	100	0	150

There are 150 people after selection. Using the method of allele frequency computation shown in Table 3.1 and in the text, the allele frequencies after selection are 200/300 = 0.667 for the *A* allele and 100/300 = 0.333 for the *a* allele.

---

only half of those with genotypes *aa* survive and reproduce, then the fitness of genotype *aa* is half of that of genotypes *AA* and *Aa*. Fitness refers to the proportion of individuals with a given phenotype who survive and reproduce.

Depending on the fitness of each genotype, natural selection can have different effects. Some of the more common forms of natural selection are discussed here, along with a few examples from human populations. Additional examples will be presented in Chapter 14.

SELECTION AGAINST RECESSIVE ALLELES   Consider what happens when one allele is dominant and one is recessive. Let A be the dominant allele and *a* be the recessive allele. Based on what you learned in Chapter 2, the genotypes AA and Aa will both give rise to the same phenotype because A is dominant. Because AA and Aa specify the same phenotype, they have the same fitness. For this hypothetical example, let us assume that the fitness of AA and Aa is 100 percent. That is, all individuals with these genotypes survive and reproduce in equal numbers. Now, let us further assume that the fitness of people with the recessive phenotype (those with the genotype *aa*) have a fitness of 0 percent. That is, no one with this genotype will survive and reproduce. This hypothetical example corresponds to a situation where a recessive allele (*a*) is fatal for those who have two copies (*aa*). Now, assume a population of 200 people before selection with the following distribution of genotypes: AA = 50, Aa = 100, *aa* = 50. Using the methods discussed

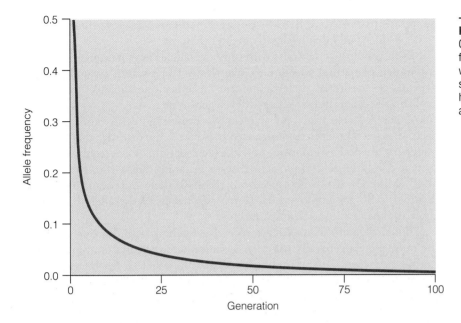

■ **FIGURE 3.2**
Change over time in the frequency of a recessive allele when there is complete selection against the recessive homozygote, and the initial allele frequency is 0.5.

earlier, the allele frequencies can be found: the frequency of A is 0.5, and the frequency of a is 0.5.

Table 3.2 shows the process of natural selection using these hypothetical numbers. After selection, the number of individuals in each genotype is: AA = 50, Aa = 100, aa = 0. All individuals with genotypes AA and Aa survive, and none of those with genotype aa survive. After selection, there are 150 individuals, and the allele frequencies are A = 0.6667 and a = 0.3333.

This example shows the effect of selection against a recessive allele. The frequency of the a allele drops from 0.5 to 0.3333. Because a is a harmful allele, however, you might expect that the a allele would be totally eliminated. This does not occur. Because the heterozygote (Aa) is not eliminated through selection, these individuals continue to pass the a allele on to the next generation. The recessive allele a cannot be eliminated in a single generation.

This simple example illustrates another feature of natural selection. Figure 3.2 shows the frequency of the a allele for 100 generations of natural selection. The allele frequencies in subsequent generations can be determined by finding out the expected genotype frequencies after selection (using the Hardy-Weinberg model) and examining the expected effects of another generation of selection. Note that the frequency of a does not decrease at the same rate over time. The amount of reduction in a actually slows down over time. As the frequency of a slowly approaches zero, an increasingly lower percentage of the population will be recessive homozygotes; consequently, fewer will be eliminated every generation. Ultimately, a balance will be reached as the reduction in the a allele due to selection is offset by new mutations from A to a. Because mutation rates are very low, this frequency of the a allele will be only slightly greater than zero.

Even simple genetic traits with only two alleles have a number of different models of natural selection to investigate. The result of natural selection depends on the initial allele frequencies, whether one allele is dominant or not, and the exact fitness values for each genotype.

A case of selection against recessive homozygotes in humans is Tay-Sachs disease. This affliction is caused by a metabolic disorder that results in blindness, mental retardation, and the destruction of the central nervous system. Children with Tay-Sachs disease generally die within the first few years of life. The disease is caused by a recessive allele and occurs in those individuals who are homozygous. Heterozygotes carry the allele but do not show any major biological impairments.

When deleterious alleles are recessive, such as with Tay-Sachs disease, the frequency is generally not zero, because heterozygotes continue to pass the allele on from generation to generation. Nonetheless, the frequency of a harmful recessive allele will still be very low. This low frequency is maintained by mutation but is kept from increasing by natural selection.

SELECTION AGAINST DOMINANT ALLELES   What if a dominant allele is selected against? As an example, consider the same starting point, as in the previous example: $AA = 50$, $Aa = 100$, and $aa = 50$, giving initial allele frequencies of $A = 0.5$ and $a = 0.5$. Complete selection against the dominant allele (A) will mean a fitness of 0 percent for genotypes AA and Aa and a fitness of 100 percent for the genotype aa. After selection, there are no AA individuals, no Aa individuals, and 50 aa individuals (Table 3.3). The allele frequencies after selection are $A = 0.0$ and $a = 1.0$. The dominant allele has been completely eliminated after one generation of selection. There will be no further change unless the allele is reintroduced into the population by mutation or migration from an area where fitness is not zero. If the fitness values of AA and Aa were greater than zero but less than 100 percent, then the A allele would not be eliminated because some individuals with this allele would survive.

An example of a dominant allele in human beings is achondroplastic dwarfism. This type of dwarfism (small body size and abnormal body proportions) is caused by a dominant allele found in very low frequencies in human populations—roughly 0.00005 (Figure 3.3). Because the achondroplastic allele is dominant, individuals with one or two of the alleles will show the disease. Virtually all achondroplastic dwarfs are heterozygotes. The condition is usually caused by a mutation occurring in the sex cells of one parent. We know that a mutation is involved in a majority of these cases because roughly 80 percent of dwarfs have two normal parents. Because the condition is caused by a dominant allele, the only way a child could receive the allele would be from a parent or through mutation. If the parent had the allele, he or she would also be a dwarf. Therefore, when both parents of a dwarf are not dwarfs, we know the offspring's dwarfism is the result of a

■ FIGURE 3.3
Achondroplastic dwarfism is a genetic disorder caused by a dominant allele. This toddler has very short arms and legs. (Courtesy March of Dimes Birth Defects Foundation)

■ TABLE 3.3
Example of Natural Selection against the Dominant Allele

This example uses an initial population size before selection of 200 people. The locus has two alleles, *A* and *a*. Initially there are 50 people with genotype *AA,* 100 people with genotype *Aa,* and 50 people with genotype *aa*. The allele frequencies before selection are therefore 0.5 for *A* and 0.5 for *a*. The fitness values have been chosen to illustrate total selection against the dominant homozygote and the heterozygote.

	GENOTYPE			
	AA	*Aa*	*aa*	*TOTAL*
Number of people before selection	50	100	50	200
Fitness (percentage that survives)	0%	0%	100%	
Number of people after selection	0	0	50	50

There are 50 people after selection. Based on the method of allele frequency computation shown in Table 3.1 and in the text, the allele frequencies after selection are 0/100 = 0.0 for the *A* allele and 100/100 = 1.0 for the *a* allele. The dominant allele *A* has been eliminated in one generation of natural selection.

mutation. In cases where two dwarfs mate, the offspring can be homozygous for the disease and such offspring generally die before, or shortly after, birth.

The low frequency of achondroplastic dwarfs is the result of natural selection acting to remove the harmful allele from the population. Although there is no major risk of mortality for a heterozygous achondroplastic dwarf, selection acts on differential reproduction. Given their physical appearance, these dwarfs have few opportunities to mate. The most likely mating is between two dwarfs. In these cases, there is additional selection because they have an increased risk of having children with two copies of the achondroplastic allele; these children generally die early in life. Thus, both differences in mortality and fertility can affect the degree of selection against an allele.

SELECTION FOR THE HETEROZYGOTE   The previous examples discussed selection against recessive and dominant homozygotes, which act to increase the frequency of one allele and decrease the frequency of another. Selection could also occur *for* recessive or dominant homozygotes, which would act to increase the frequency of an allele. With time, the allele frequencies will approach 0 or 1, depending on which allele is selected against.

These models might lead us to expect patterns of genetic variation whereby most populations have allele frequencies close to either 0 or 1 and few populations have intermediate values. However, studies of human

---

■ TABLE 3.4
Example of Natural Selection for the Heterozygote

This example uses an initial population size before selection of 200 people. The locus has two alleles, *A* and *a*. Initially there are 50 people with genotype *AA*, 100 people with genotype *Aa*, and 50 people with genotype *aa*. The allele frequencies before selection are therefore 0.5 for *A* and 0.5 for *a*. The fitness values have been chosen to illustrate selection for the heterozygote and partial selection against both homozygotes. Note that because this is a codominant system, each genotype specifies a different phenotype.

	GENOTYPE			
	AA	*Aa*	*aa*	*TOTAL*
Number of people before selection	50	100	50	200
Fitness (percentage that survives)	70%	100%	20%	
Number of people after selection	35	100	10	145

There are 145 people after selection. Using the method of allele frequency computation shown in Table 3.1 and in the text, the allele frequencies after selection are 170/290 = 0.586 for the *A* allele and 120/290 = 0.414 for the *a* allele.

---

genetic variation have found that for many loci the allele frequencies are intermediate, with values such as 0.3, 0.5, or 0.8. We could argue that selection is not yet complete and that given enough time all allele frequencies would be close to 0 or 1, but the wealth of information regarding allele frequencies in human groups makes this very unlikely. Why, then, do many loci show intermediate frequencies? Is there a way that natural selection can produce such values?

A classic example of an intermediate allele frequency in human populations is the sickle cell allele, discussed briefly in the last chapter. Because people homozygous for this allele have sickle cell anemia and are likely to die early in life, this appears to be a classic situation of selection against a homozygote. If this were the case, we might expect most human populations to have frequencies of the sickle cell allele close to 0 and, in fact, many do. However, a number of populations in parts of Africa, India, and the Mediterranean show higher frequencies. In some African groups, the frequency of the sickle cell allele is greater than 20 percent (Roychoudhury and Nei 1988). How can a harmful allele exist at such a high frequency?

The answer is a form of selection known as selection for the heterozygote (and therefore against the homozygotes). Consider fitness values of: *AA* = 70 percent, *Aa* = 100 percent, and *aa* = 20 percent. Here, only 70 percent of those with genotype *AA* and 20 percent of those with genotype *aa*

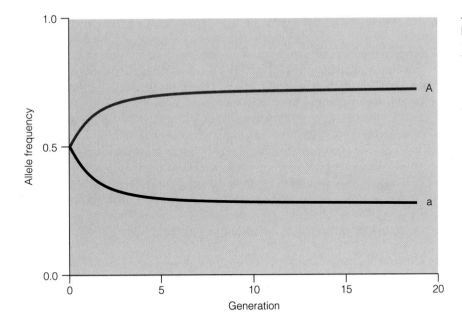

■ FIGURE 3.4
Change over time in allele frequencies when there is selection for the heterozygote (*Aa*). The initial allele frequencies are both 0.5. The fitness of each genotype (the relative frequency of survival) is: *AA* = 70%, *Aa* = 100%, and *aa* = 20%.

survive for every 100 people with genotype *Aa* (the heterozygote). Selection is for the heterozygote and against the homozygotes. Let the frequency of both the *A* and *a* alleles equal 0.5. In a population of 200 people, this means we start with 50 *AA* people, 100 *Aa* people, and 50 *aa* people before selection. Given these fitness values, there will be 35 people with *AA*, 100 with *Aa*, and 10 with *aa* after selection. The allele frequencies after selection are *A* = 0.586 and *a* = 0.414 (Table 3.4).

Why would the frequency of the *A* allele increase and the frequency of the *a* allele decrease? In selection for the heterozygote, both alleles are being selected for, because every *Aa* person can contribute both alleles to the next generation. Also, both alleles are being selected against. When *AA* people die or fail to reproduce, then two *A* alleles are lost from the population. When *aa* people die or fail to reproduce, two *a* alleles are lost from the population. Selection for the heterozygote involves selection for and against both alleles. Because the fitness of *AA* is greater in this example than the fitness of *aa* (70 percent versus 20 percent), proportionately more individuals with genotype *AA* will survive and reproduce. Hence, proportionately more *A* alleles will appear in the next generation.

Figure 3.4 shows the pattern of allele frequency change over 20 generations using the initial values and fitness values in this example. Note that the frequency of *A* continues to increase for the first few generations but soon levels off. There is no change in the allele frequency after approximately eight generations. This is the expected pattern when there is selection for the heterozygote. A balance is reached between selection for and against the two alleles A and *a*. The exact value of this balancing point will depend on the fitness values of the homozygous genotypes. Selection for the heterozygote is also called **balancing selection.**

Given this model, the distribution of sickle cell allele frequencies in humans make sense. In many environments there is selection against the sickle cell homozygote and the frequency is low. In environments where malaria is common, the heterozygotes have an advantage because they are less susceptible to malaria. People homozygous for the sickle cell allele are likely to suffer from sickle cell anemia and die. People homozygous for the normal allele are more likely to suffer from malaria. Thus, there is selection against both homozygotes (although more selection against those with sickle cell anemia) and selection for the heterozygote. A balance of allele frequencies is predicted and has been found in many human populations. A more complete discussion of the sickle cell example is given in Chapter 14.

SELECTION AND COMPLEX TRAITS   The previous examples used simple genetic traits to illustrate basic principles of natural selection. Selection also affects complex traits, however, such as those discussed in Chapter 2. For complex traits, we focus on measures of the average value and variation around this average. Because complex traits are continuous, we look at the effects of selection on the average value of a trait and on the lower and higher extremes.

There are several forms of selection on complex traits. **Stabilizing selection** refers to selection against both extremes of a trait's range in values. Individuals with extreme high or low values of a trait are less likely to survive and reproduce, and those with values closer to the average are more likely to survive and reproduce. The effect of stabilizing selection is to maintain the population at the same average value over time. Extreme values are selected against each generation, but the average value in the population does not change.

Human birth weight is a good example of stabilizing selection. The weight of a newborn child is the result of a number of environmental factors, such as mother's age, weight, and history of smoking, among many others. There is also a genetic component to birth weight. Newborns who are very small (less than 2.5 kg) are less likely to survive than newborns who are heavier. Very small babies are more prone to disease and have weaker systems, making their survival more difficult. Newborns who are too large are also likely to be selected against, because a very large child may create complications during childbirth and both mother and child may die. Thus, there is selection against both extremes, small and large.

Stabilizing selection on birth weight has been documented for a number of human populations. These studies show a definite relationship between birth weight and mortality. The results of one study based on 13,730 newborns (Karn and Penrose 1951) are shown in Figure 3.5. Mortality rates are highest for those newborns with low (less than 2.7 kg) and high (greater than 4.5 kg) birth weights.

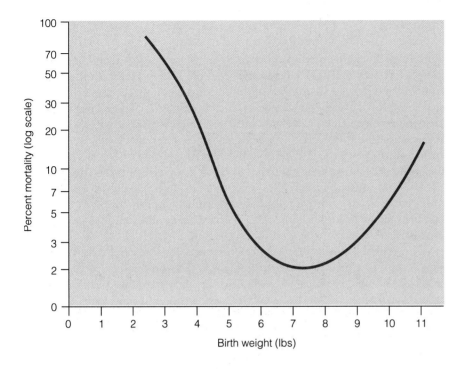

■ FIGURE 3.5
Stabilizing selection for human birth weight based on data from Karn and Penrose (1951). Babies born smaller or larger than the optimum birth weight have increased mortality. (From E. Peter Volpe, *Understanding Evolution*, 5th ed. Copyright © 1985 Wm. C. Brown Communications, Inc., Dubuque, Iowa. All Rights Reserved. Reprinted by permission)

Another type of selection for complex traits is known as **directional selection,** selection against one extreme and/or for the other extreme. In other words, a direct relationship exists between survival and reproduction on one hand and the value of a trait on the other. The result is a change over time in one direction. The average value for a trait moves in one direction or the other. Perhaps the most dramatic example of directional selection in human evolution has been the threefold increase in brain size over the last four million years. Another example is the lighter skin that probably evolved in prehistoric humans as they moved north out of Africa (see Chapter 14).

A third type of selection for complex traits is **diversifying selection,** where selection is *for* the extremes and *against* the average value. Although this type of selection is theoretically interesting, there is no evidence of its action at present in human populations. (Which of course could mean we just haven't found it!)

▲▲

balancing selection	**stabilizing selection**	**directional selection**	**diversifying selection**
Selection for the heterozygote and against the homozygotes (the heterozygote is most fit).	Selection against both extreme values in a continuous trait.	Selection against one extreme in a continuous trait and/or selection for the other extreme.	Selection for the extremes in a continuous trait and against the average value.

Genetic Drift

Genetic drift is the random change in allele frequency from one generation to the next. These random changes are the result of the nature of probability. Think for a moment about flipping a coin in the air. What is the probability of its landing with the head facing up? It is 50 percent. The coin has two possible values, heads and tails, and when you flip it you will get one or the other. Suppose you flip a coin 10 times. How many heads and how many tails do you expect to get? Because the probability of getting a head or a tail is 50 percent, you expect to get five heads and five tails. Try this experiment several times. Did you always get five tails and five heads? Sometimes you get five heads and five tails, but sometimes you get different numbers. You may get six heads and four tails, or three heads and seven tails, or, much less likely, all heads.

The probability for different combinations of heads and tails from flipping a coin 10 times is shown in Table 3.5. The probability of getting all heads (or all tails) is rather low—0.001. Note, however, that the probability of getting four heads and six tails (or six heads and four tails) is much higher—0.205. Also note that the probability of getting exactly five heads and five tails is 0.246. This means that there is roughly a 75 percent chance of *not* getting exactly five heads and five tails.

The probability of 50 percent heads and 50 percent tails is the expected distribution. If you flip 10 coins enough times, you will find that the number of heads and tails grows closer to a 50:50 ratio. Often we hear about the "law of averages." The idea here is that if you flip a coin and get heads several times in a row, then you are very likely to get a tail the next time. This is wrong, and using this "law" is an easy way to lose money if you gamble. Each flip of the coin is an independent event. Whatever happened the time before cannot affect the next flip. *Each* time you flip the coin you have a 50 percent chance of getting a head and a 50 percent chance of getting a tail.

What does this have to do with genetics? The reproductive process in this way is like a coin toss. During the process of sex cell replication (meiosis), only one allele out of two at a given locus is used. The probability of either allele being passed on is 50 percent, just like a coin toss. Imagine a locus with two alleles, A and a. Now imagine a man and a woman, each with genotype Aa, who have a child. The man can pass on either an A allele or an a allele. Likewise, a woman can pass on either an A allele or an a allele. As we saw in the last chapter, the probable distribution of genotypes among the children is 25 percent AA, 50 percent Aa, and 25 percent aa. If the couple has four children, you would expect one with AA, two with Aa, and one with aa. Thanks to random chance, however, the couple may get a different distribution of genotypes. You can model such a simple example by flipping a coin to simulate a child receiving an A allele or an a allele from either parent. Let "heads" represent the A allele and "tails" represent the a allele.

This author performed the experiment four times to simulate four children born to these parents. Two of the children had genotype AA and two

■ **TABLE 3.5**
Probability of Getting Different Numbers of Heads and Tails from 10 Coin Flips

Number of Heads	Number of Tails	Probability
0	10	0.001
1	9	0.010
2	8	0.044
3	7	0.117
4	6	0.205
5	5	0.246
6	4	0.205
7	3	0.117
8	2	0.044
9	1	0.010
10	0	0.001

These probabilities refer only to the case where 10 coins are flipped. Other numbers of coins will give different probabilities. To see how these probabilities are computed, see Thomas (1986).

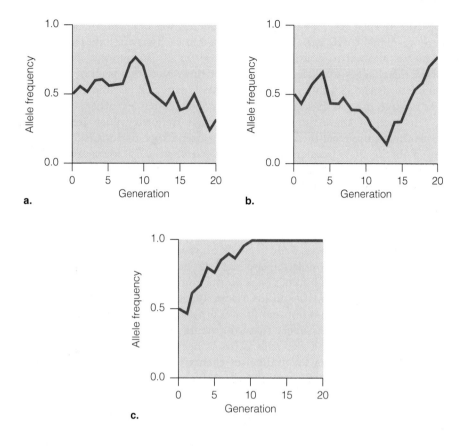

a.

b.

c.

■ **FIGURE 3.6**
Three computer simulations
of 20 generations of genetic
drift for populations of 10
individuals. Each simulation
started with an initial allele
frequency of 0.5.

had genotype *Aa*. Note that the allele frequencies have changed from the parent's generation to the children's generation. The allele frequencies of the parents were *A* = 0.5 and *a* = 0.5. The four children have a total of eight alleles, of which six are *A* and two are *a*. The frequency of *A* in the children is 6/8 = 0.75 and the frequency of *a* is 2/8 = 0.25. You might want to try this experiment several times to see the range of allele frequencies that can result.

When genetic drift occurs in populations, the same principle applies. Allele frequencies can change because of random chance. Sometimes the allele frequency will increase, and sometimes it will decrease. The direction of allele frequency change caused by genetic drift is random. The only time drift will not produce a change in allele frequency is when only one allele is present at a given locus. For example, if each parent passed on an *A* allele to each of the four children, the frequency of the *A* allele would be 1.0 among the children. The *a* allele would have been lost.

Genetic drift occurs in each generation. Such a process is too complicated to simulate using coins, but computers or random number tables can be used to model the effects of drift over time (see Cavalli-Sforza and Bodmer 1971:389). Figure 3.6 shows the results of three computer simulations

▲▲▲▲▲▲▲▲▲▲▲▲▲▲▲▲▲▲▲▲▲▲▲▲▲▲▲▲▲

genetic drift A
mechanism for
evolutionary change
resulting from the
random fluctuations of
gene frequencies from
one generation to the
next.

of drift. In each case, the initial allele frequency was 0.5, and the population size was equal to 10 individuals (20 alleles) in each generation. The simulation was allowed to continue in each case for 20 generations. The graphs show the changes in allele frequency over time. Note that each of the three simulations shows a different pattern. This is expected because genetic drift is a random process. Each simulation is an independent event.

In each of these three graphs, the allele frequency fluctuates up and down. In Figure 3.6a, the allele frequency after 20 generations is 0.3. In Figure 3.6b, the allele frequency after 20 generations is 0.75. In Figure 3.6c, the allele frequency is equal to 1.0 after 10 generations, and it does not change any further. Given enough time, and assuming no other evolutionary forces affect allele frequencies, genetic drift will ultimately lead to an allele's becoming fixed at a value of 0.0 or 1.0. Thus, genetic drift leads to the reduction of variation within a population, given enough time.

The effect of genetic drift depends on the size of the breeding population. The larger the population size, the less change will occur from one generation to the next. Thinking back to the coin toss analogy will show you that this makes sense. If you flip a coin 10 times and get three heads and seven tails, it is not that unusual. If you flip a coin 1 million times, however, it would be much less likely that you would get the same proportions— 300,000 heads and 700,000 tails. This is because of a basic principle of probability: the greater the number of events, the fewer deviations from the expected frequencies (50 percent heads and 50 percent tails).

The effect of population size on genetic drift is shown in Figure 3.7. These graphs show the results of 1,000 simulations of genetic drift for four different values of breeding population size: $N = 10, 50, 100, 1,000$. In each computer run the initial allele frequency was set to 0.5, and the simulation was allowed to continue for 20 generations. The four graphs show the distribution of allele frequency values after 20 generations of genetic drift. Figure 3.7a shows this distribution for a population size of $N = 10$. Note that the majority of the 1,000 simulations resulted in final allele frequencies of less than 0.1 or greater than 0.9. In small populations, genetic drift more often results in a quick loss of one allele or another. Figure 3.7b shows the distribution of final allele frequencies for a population size of $N = 50$. Here there are fewer extreme values and more values falling between 0.3 and 0.7. Figures 3.7c and 3.7d show the distributions for population sizes of $N = 100$ and $N = 1,000$. It is clear from these graphs that the larger the population size, the fewer deviations in allele frequency caused by genetic drift. The main point here is that genetic drift has the greatest evolutionary effect in relatively small breeding populations.

EXAMPLES OF GENETIC DRIFT   Genetic drift in human populations is shown in a case study of a group known as the Dunkers, a religious sect that emigrated from Germany to the United States in the early 1700s. Approximately 50 families composed the initial group. Glass (1953) studied the genetic

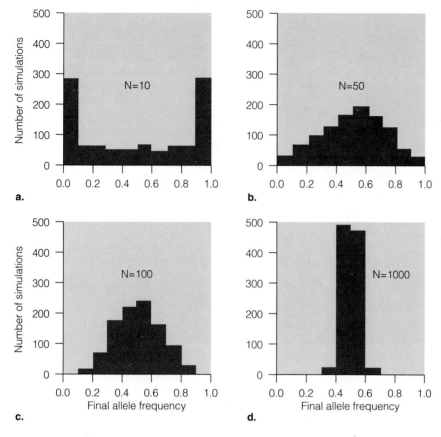

FIGURE 3.7
Allele frequency distributions for 1,000 computer simulations of 20 generations of genetic drift. The distributions show the number of times a given allele frequency was reached after 20 generations of drift. In all cases, the initial allele frequency was 0.5. Each graph represents a different value of population size: (a) = 10, (b) = 50, (c) = 100, (d) = 1,000.

characteristics of the descendants of the original founding group living in Pennsylvania. These populations have never been greater than several hundred people and thus provide a unique opportunity to study genetic drift in a small human group. Glass found that the Dunker population differed in a number of genetic traits from both the modern German and U.S. populations. Furthermore, the allele frequencies of Germany and the United States were almost identical, suggesting that other factors such as natural selection were unlikely. For example, the allele frequencies for the MN blood group were roughly M = 0.55 and N = 0.45 for both the United States and German samples. In the Dunker population, however, the allele frequencies were M = 0.655 and N = 0.345. Based on these and additional data, Glass concluded that the genetics of the Dunker population were shaped to a large extent by genetic drift over two centuries. Although 200 years seems like a long time to you and me, it is a fraction of an instant in evolutionary time. Genetic drift can clearly produce rapid changes under the proper circumstances.

Genetic drift in human populations has also been found on Tristan da Cunha, a small island in the south Atlantic Ocean. In 1816, the English

Tay-Sachs Disease: Genetic Drift or Natural Selection?

Earlier in this chapter, Tay-Sachs disease was presented as an example of a lethal recessive allele—people with two Tay-Sachs alleles generally die very early in life. As expected, the frequency of this disease tends to be rather low around the world, affecting roughly 1 in every 500,000 births. What is unusual about Tay-Sachs disease is the fact that among Jews of Eastern European ancestry (Ashkenazi Jews) the rate is much higher: Tay-Sachs affects roughly 1 in every 6,000 births in some of these populations (Molnar 1992). The occurrence of Tay-Sachs is also high in some other human populations.

What would be responsible for higher frequencies of a lethal allele in certain populations? Is it something related to their history, their environment, or some complex set of factors? One suggestion is genetic drift. Jewish populations have tended to be rather small and isolated, factors that increase the likelihood of genetic drift. Although selection acts to reduce the frequency of the allele, the random nature of genetic drift might have caused an increase relative to larger populations, which experienced less genetic drift.

Closer examination, however, argues against the genetic drift hypothesis. The Tay-Sachs disease is not due to a specific mutant allele, but actually can arise from several different mutations. All of these mutant alleles have elevated frequencies in Ashkenazi populations. It seems unlikely that all of these mutant forms would drift to higher frequencies (Marks 1995).

What else could be responsible for the elevated frequency of Tay-Sachs disease? There is some evidence suggesting that people who carry one Tay-Sachs allele (heterozygotes) have increased resistance to tuberculosis. If so, then the heterozygotes would have greater fitness than either the normal homozygote (who would be more susceptible to tuberculosis) or those homozygous for the Tay-Sachs allele (who have zero fitness). This is a case of balancing selection and, as discussed in the text, would lead to a balance in allele frequencies.

However, why would this type of selection take place only among the Ashkenazi? Cultural and historical data provide a possible answer. Due to discrimination, the Jewish populations of Eastern Europe were frequently isolated into overcrowded ghettos under conditions that would increase the threat of tuberculosis (Marks 1995).

The tuberculosis hypothesis is just that—a possible explanation that remains to be fully tested. If correct, it provides us with yet another example of the compromises that occur during evolution. There is no "perfect" genotype. Everything has a price in terms of fitness, and natural selection often reflects this balance between cost and benefit.

established a small garrison on the island. When they left, one man and his wife remained, to be joined later by a handful of other settlers. Given such a small number of original settlers, what do you suppose is the probability that the families represented all the genetic variation present in the population they came from? The probability would be very low. Genetic drift is often caused when a small number of founders form a new population: this type of genetic drift is known as **founder effect.** An analogy would be a barrel containing thousands of red and blue beads, mixed in equal proportions. If you reached into the barrel and randomly pulled out a handful of beads, you might not get 50 percent red and 50 percent blue. Because of random chance, founders are not likely to be an exact genetic representation of the original population. The smaller the number of founders, the greater the deviation will be.

Over time, the population of Tristan da Cunha remained small. The population size was further reduced twice because of emigration and disaster. Given its initial small population, combined with two further reductions and a maximum population size less than 300, the island had the opportunity to experience considerable genetic drift. This effect is seen dramatically through analysis of historical records for the island; for example, it was found that two of the original founders contributed genetically to more than 29 percent of the 1961 population (Roberts 1968; Underwood 1979).

Gene Flow

The fourth evolutionary force is **gene flow,** the movement of alleles from one population to another. The term *migration* is often used to mean the same thing as gene flow. From a conservative standpoint, however, this is not completely accurate. Migration refers to the more or less permanent movement of individuals from one place to another. Why the confusion? After all, excepting artificial insemination, your alleles do not move unless you do. You can migrate, though, without passing on any alleles. You can also be involved in gene flow without actually making a permanent move to a new place. In many texts on microevolution the terms *gene flow* and *migration* are used interchangeably. Keep in mind, however, that there are certain distinctions in the real world.

Gene flow involves the movement of alleles between at least two populations. When gene flow occurs, the two populations mix genetically and tend to become more similar. Under most conditions, the more the two populations mix, the more similar they will become genetically (assuming that the two environments are not different enough to produce different effects of natural selection).

Consider a genetic locus with two alleles, A and a. Assume two populations, 1 and 2. Now, assume that all the alleles in population 1 are A and all the alleles in population 2 are a. The allele frequencies of these two imaginary populations are:

Population 1	*Population 2*
Frequency of A = 1.0	Frequency of A = 0.0
Frequency of a = 0.0	Frequency of a = 1.0

Now imagine a situation where 10 percent of the people in population 1 move to population 2, and vice versa. This movement constitutes gene flow. What effect will the gene flow have? After gene flow has taken place, population 1 is made up of 90 percent A alleles and 10 percent a alleles. Population

---

founder effect A type of genetic drift caused by the formation of a new population by a small number of individuals.

gene flow A mechanism for evolutionary change resulting from the movement of genes from one population to another.

■ **FIGURE 3.8**
Effects of gene flow over time. Population 1 started with an allele frequency of 1.0, and population 2 started with an allele frequency of 0.0. The two populations exchange 10 percent of their genes with each generation. Over time, the continued gene flow acts to make the two populations more similar genetically.

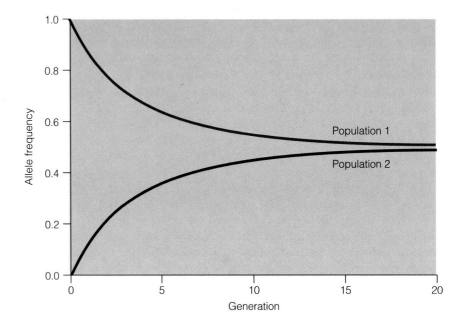

■ **FIGURE 3.8**
Effects of gene flow over time. Population 1 started with an allele frequency of 1.0, and population 2 started with an allele frequency of 0.0. The two populations exchange 10 percent of their genes with each generation. Over time, the continued gene flow acts to make the two populations more similar genetically.

2 is made up of 10 percent *A* alleles and 90 percent *a* alleles. The allele frequencies of the two populations, though still different, have become more similar as the consequence of gene flow. If the same rate of gene flow (10 percent) continues generation after generation, the two populations will become more and more similar genetically. After 20 generations of gene flow, the two populations will be almost identical. The accumulated effects of gene flow over time are shown for this hypothetical example in Figure 3.8.

Apart from making populations more similar, gene flow can also introduce new variation within a population. In the example, a new allele (*a*) was introduced into population 1 as the result of gene flow. A new mutation arising in one population can be spread throughout the rest of a species by gene flow.

Compared to many other organisms, humans are relatively mobile creatures. Human populations show a great deal of variation in degree of migration. Even today, many humans live and work within a small area and choose mates from nearby. Some people are more mobile than others, the extent of their mobility depending on a number of factors such as available technology, occupation, income, and other social factors.

In spite of local and regional differences, humans today all belong to the same species. Even though genetic variation exists among populations, they are in fact characterized more by their similarity. A critical factor in the cohesiveness of the human species, gene flow acts to reduce differences among groups.

The amount of gene flow between human populations depends on a variety of environmental and cultural factors. Geographic distance is a major

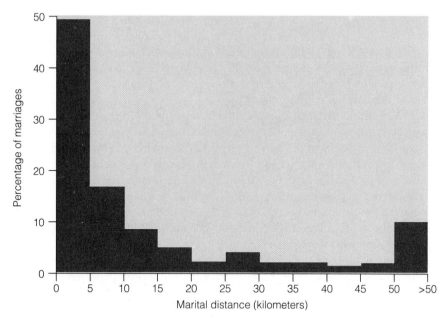

■ FIGURE 3.9
Percentage of marriages
taking place at various marital
distances (the distance
between the premarital
residences of bride and
groom) for the town of
Leominster, Massachusetts,
1800–1850. (*Source*: author's
unpublished data)

determinant of migration and gene flow. The farther two populations are apart geographically, the less likely they are to exchange mates. Even in today's modern world, with access to jet airplanes and other devices, you are still more likely to choose a spouse from nearby than from across the country. Exceptions to the rule do occur, of course, but the influence of geographic distance is still very strong.

Studies of migration and gene flow often look at distance between birthplaces or premarital residences of married couples. If you had been born in New York City and your spouse had been born in Chicago, the distance between your birthplaces would be approximately 1,300 km (roughly 800 miles). If both you and your spouse had come from the same neighborhood in the same city, your marital distance would be close to zero. The relationship between migration and geographic distance is similar in most human populations (Relethford 1992). Most marriages take place within a few kilometers, and the number of marriages quickly decreases as the distance between populations increases. This indicates that the majority of genes flowing into human populations comes from a local area and a small proportion from farther distances.

The relationship between the frequency of marriages and geographic distance is shown in Figure 3.9. This graph presents the results of a historical study of migration into the town of Leominster, Massachusetts, using marriage records from the year 1800 through 1849. A total of 1,602 marriages took place in the population over the 50-year period. Of these, almost half (49.2 percent) were between a bride and groom who were both native to Leominster. An additional 16.5 percent of the marriages took place between couples whose premarital residences were between 5 and 10 km (roughly 8 to 16 miles) apart. Note that the percentage of marriages diminishes quickly after a distance of 5 km. Also note that almost 10 percent of the couples come from distances greater than 50 km. This type of long-range migration (and gene flow) acts to keep populations from diverging too much from the rest of the species.

Geographic distance is a major determinant of human migration and gene flow, but it is not the only one. Ethnic differences also act to limit them. Most large cities have distinct neighborhoods that correspond to different ethnic communities. A large proportion of marriages takes place within these groups because of the common human preference for marrying within one's own social and cultural group. Likewise, religious differences also act as barriers to gene flow because many, though not all, people prefer to marry within the same religion. Further, social class and educational differences can also limit gene flow.

In other parts of the world we see other cultural differences that restrict gene flow. In many Pacific islands, for example, several different language groups coexist within a small geographic area. Differences in language enhance the cultural distances among populations and act to limit the number of marriages across language groups. Friedlaender's (1975) study of migration on Bougainville Island in Melanesia shows the effect of language differences on marriage frequency. He looked at marriages within and among small villages belonging to eight different language groups within roughly a 100-km range. The percentage of marriages within each language group are listed in Table 3.6. For the entire island, 90 percent of all marriages took place within the same language group (the percentage varies from 70 to 98 percent for the eight groups).

■ TABLE 3.6
Rates of Marriage within Language Groups on Bougainville Island

LANGUAGE GROUP	PERCENTAGE OF MARRIAGES OCCURRING WITHIN LANGUAGE GROUP
Aita	95
Eivo	85
Nasioi	95
Rotokas	98
Simeku	90
Siwai	94
Torau	96
Uruava	70

Source: Friedlaender (1975:76).

Interaction of the Evolutionary Forces

It is convenient to discuss each of the four evolutionary forces separately, but in reality they act together to produce allele frequency change. Mutation acts to introduce new genetic variants; natural selection, genetic drift, and gene flow act to change the frequency of the mutant allele. Sometimes the evolutionary forces act together, and sometimes they act in opposition. Their exact interaction depends on a wide variety of factors, such as the biochemical and physical effects of different alleles, presence or absence of dominance, population size, population distribution, and the environment, to name but a few. Many biological anthropologists attempt to unravel some of these factors in human population studies.

In general, we look at how natural selection, genetic drift, and gene flow act to increase or decrease genetic variation within and between groups. (Mutation gets less attention because, even though it introduces new genetic variants, the change in allele frequency in one generation is low.) An increase in variation within a population means that individuals within the population will be more genetically different from one another. A decrease in variation within a population means the reverse; individuals will become more similar to one another genetically. An increase in variation among populations means that two or more populations will become more different from one another genetically, and a decrease in variation within populations means the reverse.

Let us first consider the effects of genetic drift, gene flow, and natural selection on allele frequency variation. Genetic drift tends to remove alleles from a population and therefore acts to reduce variation within a population. On the other hand, because genetic drift is a random event and occurs independently in different populations, the pattern of genetic drift will tend to be different on average in different populations. On average, then, genetic drift will act to increase variation among populations. Gene flow acts to introduce new alleles into a population and can have the effect of increasing variation within a population. Gene flow also acts to reduce variation among populations in most cases.

Natural selection can either increase or decrease variation within a population, depending on the specific type of selection and the initial allele frequencies. Selection against recessive homozygotes, for example, will lead to the gradual decrease of one allele and consequently reduce variation. Selection for an advantageous mutation, however, will result in an increase in the frequency of the mutant and act to increase variation within the population. Selection can also either increase or decrease variation among populations, depending on environmental variation. If two populations have similar environments, then natural selection will take place in the same way in both groups and therefore will act to reduce genetic differences between them. On the other hand, if the two populations are in different enough environments that natural selection operates in different ways, then variation between the populations may be increased. Table 3.7 summarizes the effects of different evolutionary forces on variation within and among populations.

Different evolutionary forces can produce the same, or opposite, effects. Different forces can also act in opposition to one another. Genetic drift and gene flow, for example, have opposite effects on variation within and among populations. If both of these forces operate at the same time, they can counteract each other.

Several examples help illustrate the ways in which different evolutionary forces can interact. Consider the forces of mutation and genetic drift. How might these two forces interact? Mutation acts to change allele frequency by the introduction of a new allele, whereas genetic drift causes random fluctuations in allele frequency from one generation to the next. If both operate at the same time, drift may act to increase or decrease the frequency of the new mutation. Consider what happens where everyone in a population has two A alleles and there is then a mutation from A to a in one individual. The person with the mutation can either pass on the A allele or the a allele, each

■ TABLE 3.7
Summary of the Effects of Selection, Drift, and Gene Flow on Variation within and among Populations

EVOLUTIONARY FORCE	VARIATION WITHIN POPULATIONS	VARIATION AMONG POPULATIONS
Selection	Increase or decrease	Increase or decrease
Genetic drift	Decrease	Increase
Gene flow	Increase	Decrease

A decrease in variation within a population makes individuals more similar to one another, whereas an increase in variation within a population makes individuals less similar to one another. A decrease in variation among populations makes the populations more similar to one another, whereas an increase in variation among populations makes the populations less similar to one another. Note that natural selection can either increase or decrease variation; the exact effect depends on the type of selection and differences in environment (see text).

with a 50 percent probability. It is possible that the new mutant allele will be lost from the population because of random chance. It is also possible that the frequency of the mutant allele will increase because of random chance. The person with the mutation may pass the mutant form on to all of his or her children, and each of them might continue to pass it on to their children.

To give you an idea of how mutation and genetic drift can interact, this author performed a simple computer simulation that allowed for a single mutation followed by genetic drift. In this simulation, a population size of 10 was used in which all individuals initially had the same allele. A single mutation event was then allowed, which meant that the frequency of the mutant allele was $1/20 = 0.05$ (1 mutant allele out of all 20 alleles in the population). Genetic drift was then simulated for 20 generations. This entire simulation experiment was repeated 1,000 times and the results are shown in Table 3.8.

As expected, genetic drift leads to the loss of the mutant allele most of the time (in this case, 889 out of 1,000 times). In most of the remaining cases, however, the frequency of the mutant allele actually increased. In 45 cases, the frequency of the mutant allele was greater than 0.5 after 20 generations. In 5 cases, the mutant allele had become fixed within the population! Such computer simulations are a bit simplistic and somewhat unrealistic, but they do show how two evolutionary forces can interact.

Many other possibilities for interaction also exist. For example, natural selection reduces the frequency of a harmful recessive mutant allele. Gene flow tends to counter the effects of genetic drift on variation among populations. Genetic drift can increase the frequency of a harmful allele even if it is being selected against.

■ TABLE 3.8
Results of Computer Simulation of Mutation and Genetic Drift

A total of 1,000 independent computer simulations were performed using a population size of 10 individuals with a single initial mutation (1 mutant allele out of 20 in the population, giving an initial allele frequency of 1/20 = 0.05). Following mutation, the computer simulated genetic drift for 20 generations. The following shows the distribution of the frequencies of the mutant allele after 20 generations (see text).

FINAL FREQUENCY OF THE MUTANT ALLELE	NUMBER OF CASES
0.0	889
0.01–0.09	2
0.10–0.19	22
0.20–0.29	11
0.30–0.39	16
0.40–0.49	15
0.50–0.59	9
0.60–0.69	11
0.70–0.79	9
0.80–0.89	9
0.90–0.99	2
1.0	5

Much of microevolutionary theory deals with the mathematics describing such interactions. Studies of actual populations must take these interactions into account and try to control for them in analysis. There are some basic rules for interpreting genetic variation. If populations are large, then drift is unlikely to have much of an effect. Gene flow can be measured to some extent by looking at migration rates to determine how powerful an effect it would have. Natural selection can be investigated by looking at patterns of fertility and mortality among different classes of genotypes.

Imagine that you have visited a population over two generations. You note that the frequency of a certain allele has changed from 0.4 to 0.5. Furthermore, assume that the population has been totally isolated during the last generation and that the size of the breeding population has stayed at roughly 50 people. What could have caused the allele frequency change? Because mutation occurs at much lower rates, it could not be responsible. Given that the population was totally isolated, gene flow could not be responsible. Drift may have caused the change in allele frequency, for the size of the breeding population is rather low. Natural selection could also have produced the change. You would have to know more about the specific alleles and genotypes involved, environmental factors, and patterns of mortality and fertility to determine whether selection had an effect. Even given this rather limited information, you can rule out mutation and gene flow and proceed to develop tests to determine the relative influence of drift and selection.

The study of any natural population is much more complex. With laboratory animals, you can control for a variety of factors to help your analysis. In dealing with human populations, however, you must rely on observations as they occur in nature.

Nonrandom Mating

Recall that one of the assumptions of the Hardy-Weinberg equilibrium model is random mating. Populations often show deviations from random mating, such as inbreeding, where mates are closely related. Actually, we are all inbred to some extent, but we generally reserve the term for "close" biological relatedness, such as between first cousins or closer. What is the genetic effect of inbreeding? Closely related individuals are more likely to have similar alleles inherited from a common ancestor. Thus, inbreeding increases the probability of having a homozygous genotype. For example, if two first cousins mate, the probability that their offspring will have a homozygous genotype is 6.25 percent greater than that for a non-inbred mating (this number is called the inbreeding coefficient, and is discussed further in Appendix 1).

The genetic effects of inbreeding are often harmful. Studies have shown that the incidence of congenital birth defects and mortality during the first year of life is higher among inbred offspring than among the offspring of others (Bittles et al. 1991). Some studies have suggested higher rates of mental retardation among inbred children, but others have not confirmed this. For the most part, overall rates of inbreeding in human populations tend to be low compared to rates among other organisms. These lower rates appear in part due to the high mobility of the human species (more gene flow) and in part reflect the fact that most societies have cultural rules discouraging, or prohibiting, mating with close relatives.

At a broader level, the evolutionary effect of inbreeding is to change *genotype* frequencies, but not *allele* frequencies. Inbreeding results in more homozygotes and fewer heterozygotes, but does not change the frequency of the alleles (only their distribution into genotypes). As such, inbreeding does not change allele frequencies over time. Inbreeding can, however, affect the *rate* of allele frequency change. If, for example, there is selection against a homozygote, then inbreeding will produce more homozygotes to be selected against, and the rate of selection will change.

Assortative mating is another form of nonrandom mating. With this type of mating, individuals choose mates that are biologically similar to themselves. Humans typically choose mates similar to themselves for a variety of social and biological traits (Buss 1985). A typical example is assortative mating for skin color; on average, people tend to choose mates with similar skin color. Evolutionarily, the effect is the same as for inbreeding—genotype frequencies are changed but not allele frequencies.

SUMMARY

The study of microevolution looks at changes in the frequencies of alleles from one generation to the next. Such analyses allow detailed examination of the factors that can alter allele frequencies in the short term and also provide us with inferences about long-term patterns of evolution. Changes in allele frequencies stem from four evolutionary forces: mutation, natural selection, genetic drift, and gene flow.

Mutation is the ultimate source of all genetic variation but occurs at low enough rates that additional factors are needed to explain polymorphic frequencies (whereby two or more alleles have frequencies greater than 0.01). The other three evolutionary forces are responsible for increasing or decreasing the frequency of a mutant allele. Natural selection changes allele frequencies through the process of differential survival and reproduction of individuals having certain genotypes. Genetic drift is the random change in allele frequencies from one generation to the next and has the greatest effect in small populations. Gene flow, the movement of alleles between populations, acts to reduce genetic differences between different groups.

The rate of allele frequency change is affected by nonrandom mating patterns, such as inbreeding and assortative mating. The allele frequencies do not change, but the genotype frequencies are affected. More homozygotes occur than expected from random mating, which can result in more rapid change in allele frequencies because of natural selection.

SUPPLEMENTAL READINGS

Christiansen, F. B. 1986. *Population Genetics*. Palo Alto, Ca.: Blackwell.

Hartl, D. L. 1988. *A Primer of Population Genetics*. 2d ed. Sunderland, Mass.: Sinauer. These two texts provide greater focus on the mathematical aspects of population genetics.

Underwood, J. H. 1979. *Human Variation and Human Microevolution*. Englewood Cliffs, N. J.: Prentice-Hall. A basic treatment of human microevolution with some, but not extensive, mathematics, clearly written, with many excellent examples of case studies from human populations. This is a recommended starting place for those interested in additional information on human microevolution.

CHAPTER 4   *Macroevolution*

Chapters 2 and 3 dealt with evolution from the perspectives of molecular, Mendelian, and population genetics. Whereas microevolution is relatively easy to observe and understand in living populations, the long-term nature of evolutionary change is somewhat more difficult to grasp. Part of the problem is that extremely long periods of time, ranging from thousands to millions of years, are involved in macroevolution.

When so-called "creation scientists" dispute evolution, they generally mean macroevolution. Few doubt the existence of short-term, microevolutionary changes when we can see such changes in our daily lives, from changing patterns of disease to the kinds of alterations brought about by animal and plant breeding. The long-term pattern of evolution, however, is generally more difficult to grasp. Creationism argues that we cannot directly observe changes over millions of years and therefore cannot make scientific tests. It is true that we cannot undertake laboratory tests lasting for millions of years, but we still can make scientific predictions. Many sciences, including geology and astronomy, are historical in nature. That is, we rely on some record (geologic strata or stellar configurations, for example) to note what has happened. We can establish the facts of change. The same is true of macroevolution. The fossil record provides us with information about what *has* happened. We must then utilize other information available to us to determine *why* such change has occurred. A geologist makes use of the fact that geologic processes occur in a regular manner and therefore occurred in the same way in ancient times. Geologists use available information about current geologic processes to explain patterns of change in the past. In much the same way, evolutionary science takes what we know about microevolution and extends it to explain the long-term pattern of macroevolution.

To many, but not all, evolutionary biologists, macroevolution is merely the net effect of microevolutionary change over long periods of time. Some, however, believe that additional forces must be considered in explaining macroevolution.

Perhaps the single largest task of macroevolutionary theory is to explain the origin of new species. Along with this goes the task of explaining the major changes in the fossil record. For example, what evolutionary factors were responsible for the development of flight in birds? What species lived in the past but are not alive today? Why have some species died out while others continued to the present? Why have some organisms, such as our ancestors, changed so much in relatively short periods of time, whereas other organisms, such as cockroaches, have scarcely changed at all over many millions of years?

The origin of new species has been observed in historical times and in the present. Some new species have been brought about by human intervention and controlled breeding, as with many species of tropical fish. There are also examples of new species having arisen naturally in the recent past, such as certain types of fruit flies. In addition, we have information on populations in the process of forming new species, such as certain groups of snails. Most of what we observe about new species formation, however, comes from analysis of the fossil record.

How do new species come into being? It is ironic that even though the title of Darwin's book is *On the Origin of Species*, it did not focus much on this question. Instead, Darwin sought to explain the basic nature of evolutionary change, believing that extension of these principles could explain the formation of new species. Indeed, even though there are different models of species formation, all essentially use the processes of microevolution for explanation.

TAXONOMY AND EVOLUTION

An understanding of the origin of species begins with consideration of the definition of the term *species*. There is considerable controversy regarding its definition and how it relates to models of evolutionary change (Ereshefsky 1992). Therefore, any discussion of macroevolution and the origin of species must begin with an understanding of certain principles of biological classification.

In Chapter 1, you read about Linnaeus's attempt to construct a system of classification for all living creatures. Instead of simply making up a list of all known organisms, Linnaeus developed a scheme by which creatures could be grouped together according to certain shared characteristics. The system of biological classification is called a taxonomy. Even though we now make use of Linnaeus's scheme to describe patterns of evolution, Linnaeus himself did not have this objective in mind. Rather, he sought to understand the nature of God's design in living organisms.

We use systems of classification every day, often without being aware that we do so. We all have the tendency to label objects and people according to certain characteristics. We often use terms such as "liberal" and "conservative" to describe people's political views, and terms such as "white" and "black" to describe people's skin color. Movies are classified into different groups by a rating, such as PG, R, and X.

If you think for a moment, you will realize that a great deal of your daily life revolves around your use and understanding of different systems of classification. In biology, a taxonomy is a system of classification that shows relationships between different groups of organisms. This may sound simple enough but can actually be rather difficult. For example, consider the following list of organisms: flounder, bat, shark, canary, lizard, horse, and whale. How would you classify these creatures? One way might be to put certain animals together according to size: the flounder, bat, canary, and lizard in a "small" category; the shark and horse in a "medium" category; and the whale in a "large" category. Another method would be to put the animals in groups according to where they live: the flounder, shark, and whale in the water; the bat and canary in the air; and the lizard and horse on the land. Still another method would be to put the shark in a separate category from all the others because the shark's skeleton is made of cartilage instead of bone.

The problem with this example is that none of these three ways of classification agrees with the other two. There is no consistency. Biologists actually classify these animals into the following groups: fish (flounder and shark), reptiles (lizard), birds (canary), and mammals (bat, horse, whale). These groups reflect certain common characteristics, such as mammary glands for the mammals. But what makes this system of classification any better than those based on size or habitat? For our purposes, we require taxonomies that reflect evolutionary patterns. As we will see, organisms can have similar traits because they inherited these traits from a common ancestor. Thus, the presence of mammary glands in the bat, horse, and whale represents a trait that has been inherited from a common ancestral species.

Taxonomies are useful in trying to understand evolutionary relationships. In order to reflect the evolutionary process, the taxonomy must reflect evolutionary changes. The groups of mammals, birds, reptiles, and fish are based on characteristics that reflect evolutionary relationships. The bat and the whale are placed in the same group because they have a more recent common ancestor than either does with the lizard, as reflected by certain shared characteristics such as mammary glands. Biological classification should reflect evolutionary processes, but only careful analysis of both living and extinct life forms allows us to discover what characteristics reflect evolutionary relationships.

Taxonomic Categories

The Linnaean taxonomy is a hierarchical classification. That is, each category contains a number of subcategories, which contain further subcategories, and so on. Biological classification uses a number of categories. The more commonly used categories are: kingdom, phylum (plural *phyla*), class, order, family, genus (plural *genera*), and species. In addition, prefixes are often added to distinguish further breakdowns within a particular category, such as subphylum or infraorder. The scientific name given to an organism consists of the genus and species names in Latin. The scientific name for the common house mouse is *Mus musculus*. Modern human beings are known as *Homo sapiens*, translated roughly as "wise humans."

Any given genus may contain a number of different species. The genus *Homo*, for example, contains modern humans (*Homo sapiens*) as well as extinct human species (*Homo erectus* and *Homo habilis*). These three species are placed in the same genus because of certain common characteristics, such as large brain size.

The categories of classification are often vaguely defined. Genus, for example, refers to a group of species that shares similar environments, patterns of adaptation, and physical structures. An example is the horse and the zebra, different species that are placed in the genus *Equus* (there are several species of zebra). These species are four-legged, hoofed grazers. The basis for assigning a given species to one genus or another is often unclear. This uncertainty is even more problematic when fossil remains are assigned to different categories. The only category with a precise meaning is the species, and even that has certain problems in application.

Definitions of Species

The concept of species is a shifting one that can be defined in terms of various contexts.

THE BIOLOGICAL SPECIES CONCEPT Species may be defined on the basis of reproduction. If organisms from two populations are capable of breeding naturally and can produce fertile offspring, then they belong to the same

The horse and donkey can mate and produce offspring (a mule), but two mules cannot produce offspring. Therefore, the horse and donkey belong to two separate species although they are closely related.

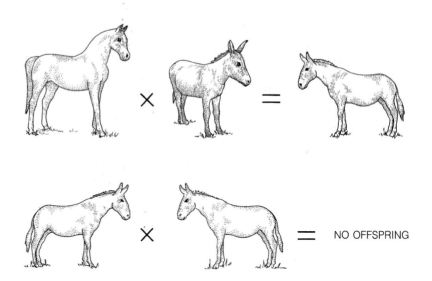

NO OFFSPRING

species. Note that this definition has several parts. First, organisms from two populations must be capable of interbreeding. Second, these matings must occur in nature. Recent advances in biology have allowed individuals usually considered to be separate species to produce offspring under laboratory conditions. In understanding who we are and how we evolved, we are interested in breeding that takes place naturally. Third and finally, the offspring must be *fertile*—that is, capable of producing further offspring.

Perhaps the best known example of an application of the species concept is the mule. Mules are farm animals produced as the offspring of a horse bred with a donkey. The horse and the donkey interbreed naturally, which satisfies the first and second parts of the species definition. The offspring (mules) are sterile, however, and cannot produce further offspring. The only way to get a mule is to mate a horse and a donkey. Because the offspring are not fertile, the horse and the donkey are considered separate species (see Figure 4.1). On the other hand, all human populations around the world belong to the same species because members can interbreed and produce fertile offspring.

The concept of biological species appears to provide a useful test for the purposes of classification. One of its problems, however, is that it only provides a simple yes or no answer to the question of similarity. It does not reflect any degree of similarity among organisms that belong to different species. For example, horses and donkeys are obviously more similar to each other than either is to an ant. The different species names show only that all are different species, but not which species are more similar to each other. The fact that horses and donkeys can interbreed shows us that they are closely related species.

The idea of species, moreover, flatly assumes that two organisms either belong or do not belong to the same species. It does not allow for any kind of intermediate state. Why should this be a problem? Consider as an example two modern species that had a common ancestor at some point in the past. We usually draw an evolutionary "tree," showing the point at which a new "branch," or species, comes into being. If some populations of species A evolved into species B, then at what point did those populations stop being species A and start being species B? The species concept suggests that this change was instantaneous because a creature either belongs to one species or the other. Any system of classification tends to ignore variation within groups. In the real world, however, evolution and variation work to break down rigid systems of classification. Organisms become difficult to classify when they are constantly changing.

As an example of this problem, consider the populations of gypsy moths in Asia. When moths from the populations farthest apart are bred, their offspring are sterile. According to the biological species concept, these populations of moths belong to separate species. Populations that are closer together, however, are capable of producing fertile offspring, which suggests that they belong to the same species (Futuyma 1986).

MODES OF SPECIES CHANGE The biological species concept is useful when comparing two or more populations living at a single point in time. In theory, reproductive isolation can be tested to determine if these populations belong to the same species. How can the biological species concept be applied when comparing groups of organisms over a period of time? This question requires looking at two different modes of the evolutionary change of species.

First, a species can change over time. According to this mode of evolutionary change, a single species exists at any given point in time but evolves over a period of time. An example is the evolution of humans. The most likely scenario of human evolution over the past two million years (see Chapters 10–12) is a change from a species known as *Homo habilis* into a species known as *Homo erectus* into our own species *Homo sapiens*. Although a single species exists within the genus *Homo* at any point in time, there is continued evolutionary change such that the most recent forms (ourselves) are quite different from the earliest forms. For example, our brains are roughly twice as large. The suggestion here is of a single species evolving over time.

This mode of species change is known as **anagenesis,** or straight-line evolution. It is illustrated as a straight line, as shown in Figure 4.2 where form A evolves into form B and then into form C. Although this mode of evolutionary change is fairly straightforward, complications arise when considering the naming of species. Should form A be called a different species from form B? In the case of human evolution, should *Homo erectus* actually be given a different species name from *Homo sapiens*? The problem is that the

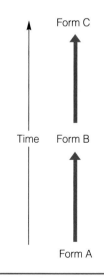

■ FIGURE 4.2
Anagenesis, the linear evolution of a species over time. Form A changes over time into form B and then further changes into form C.

▲▲▲▲▲▲▲▲▲▲▲▲▲▲▲▲▲▲▲▲▲▲▲▲▲▲▲▲▲

anagenesis The transformation of a single species over time.

traditional biological species concept doesn't really apply. Form A and form B are by necessity isolated from each other reproductively because they lived at different times. There is no way they could interbreed any more than you could mate with an early human who lived 1.5 million years B.P. (we'll leave out science fiction and time machines here).

Many researchers modify the species concept to deal with this type of situation. Different physical forms along a single lineage (an evolutionary line such as that shown in Figure 4.2) are given different species names out of convenience, and as a label to represent the types of physical change shown over time. Such forms are referred to as **paleospecies** and are used more as labels than as units representing the species concept. In recent years there has been a tendency to move away from the use of paleospecies, at least among some evolutionary biologists.

Anagenesis is not the only mode of species change. If you think about it, anagenesis is not completely sufficient as an explanation of macroevolution. Where do new species come from? The other mode of species change is **cladogenesis,** or branching evolution. Cladogenesis involves the formation of new species (speciation) whereby one or more new species branch off from an original species. In Figure 4.3, a portion of species A first branches off to produce species B (living at the same time), then a portion of species B branches to produce species C. This example starts with one species and ends up with three. The factors responsible for speciation will be discussed later in this chapter.

The problem of species naming is complicated by the fact that evolutionary relationships among fossil forms are not always clear. Some of these

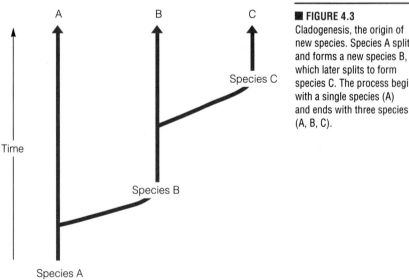

■ FIGURE 4.3
Cladogenesis, the origin of new species. Species A splits and forms a new species B, which later splits to form species C. The process begins with a single species (A) and ends with three species (A, B, C).

problems will be addressed later. For now, keep in mind that species names often mean different things to different people. The naming of species might adhere to an evolutionary model or might serve only as convenient labels of physical variation.

PATTERNS OF MACROEVOLUTION

Evolutionary forces interact to change populations over time (anagenesis) and lead to the formation of new species (cladogenesis). In addition to these processes, the study of macroevolution is concerned with the rate of evolutionary change and the failure of species to adapt over time.

Speciation

The fossil record shows many examples of new species arising. How? You know that genetic differences between populations come about as a result of evolutionary forces. For a population to become a new species, these generic differences must be great enough to prevent successful interbreeding with the original parent species. For this to occur, the population must become reproductively isolated from the original parent species.

REPRODUCTIVE ISOLATION   **Reproductive isolation** is genetic change that can lead to an inability to produce fertile offspring. How does this happen? Evolutionary forces can produce such a situation. The first step in **speciation** (the formation of a new species from a parent species) is the elimination or reduction of gene flow between populations. Because gene flow acts to reduce differences between populations, its continued action tends to keep all populations in the same species. Gene flow does not need to be eliminated altogether, but it must be reduced sufficiently to allow the other evolutionary forces to make the populations genetically different. Populations must become genetically isolated from one another for speciation to occur.

The most common form of isolation in animal species is geographic isolation. When two populations are separated by a physical barrier, such as a river or mountain range, or by great distances, gene flow is cut off between

paleospecies Species identified from fossil remains based on their physical similarities and differences to other species.

cladogenesis The formation of one or more new species from another over time.

reproductive isolation The genetic isolation of populations that may render them incapable of producing offspring.

speciation The origin of a new species.

the populations. As long as the populations remain isolated, genetic changes occurring in one group will not spread to other groups. As we saw in Chapter 3, geographic distance limits gene flow even in our own highly mobile species. The effects of geographic distance in causing reproductive isolation are even more dramatic in other species.

Geographic separation is the most common means of producing reproductive isolation among animal populations, but other mechanisms may also cause isolation. Some of these can operate within a single geographic region. Populations may be isolated by behavioral differences such as feeding habits. Some groups may eat during the day and others at dusk. Because the groups are not in frequent contact with one another, there is opportunity for isolation to develop. Although geographic isolation is in theory not required, the actual probability of speciation occurring in geographically adjacent groups remains highly controversial. One review notes that there is little evidence to date of speciation occurring without geographic isolation (Coyne 1992).

GENETIC DIVERGENCE   Isolation is the first step in the speciation process. By itself, this isolation does not guarantee speciation. Elimination of gene flow provides the opportunity for speciation. Other evolutionary forces must then act upon this isolation to produce a situation in which the isolated groups have changed sufficiently to make fertile interbreeding no longer possible. Isolation, however, does not always lead to speciation.

How can the evolutionary forces lead to speciation? Mutation might act to increase variation among populations because it occurs independently in the genetic composition of separate groups. Without gene flow to spread them, individual mutations will accumulate in each group, making isolated populations genetically divergent. Genetic drift also contributes to differences in allele frequencies among small populations. In addition, if the two populations are in separate environments, then natural selection will lead to genetic differences. Once gene flow has been eliminated, the other evolutionary forces will act to make the populations genetically divergent. When this process continues to the point where the two populations can no longer interbreed and produce fertile offspring, they have become separate species.

There is continued debate over the role of the various evolutionary forces in producing genetic divergence. For many years, speciation was felt to be solely the by-product of natural selection. That is, as two populations came to occupy separate environments, the action of natural selection would cause these groups to become different. Speciation has been viewed as a consequence of this differential adaptation. In recent years, however, more attention has been given to the contributions to speciation of mutation and genetic drift in small populations. In the former view, the old species gradually formed two or more species, with natural selection operating on large populations. The more recent view is that new species often form from small populations and, as such, are affected extensively by mutation and genetic drift.

Adaptive Radiation

The process of speciation minimally results in two species: the original parent species and the new offspring species. Under certain circumstances, many new species can come into being in a short period of time. This rapid diversification of species is associated with changing environmental conditions. When new environments open up, or when new adaptations to a specific environment develop, many new species can form—a process known as **adaptive radiation.**

New environments often open up following the demise of other species. One example, discussed in greater detail in Chapter 5, is the rise of mammals following the extinction of the dinosaurs. Once the dinosaurs were gone, there were vacant environments for mammals to adapt to. The rise of flowering plants at about the same time also provided many new habitats. The result was an adaptive radiation of mammalian species.

The Tempo and Mode of Macroevolution

During the past 25 years, considerable attention has been given to the tempo (how fast?) and mode (the mechanism) of macroevolutionary change. How quickly do new species form? Does speciation occur in large or small populations? What are the effects of natural selection and the other evolutionary forces in producing new species? These are all questions about the tempo and mode of macroevolution.

GRADUALISM   Charles Darwin saw speciation as a slow and gradual process, taking thousands or millions of years. To Darwin, natural selection acted on populations ultimately to produce new species. The view that macroevolution is a slow and gradual process is called **gradualism.** According to this view, small changes in each generation over time result in major biological changes.

Gradualism, then, regards speciation as a slow process that takes a long time to occur. New species form from large portions of an original species. In such large populations, genetic drift and mutation have little impact in each generation. Natural selection, slowly operating on some initial mutation(s), is primarily responsible for speciation.

The gradualistic model predicts that, given a suitable fossil record, we will see a smooth and gradual transition from one species into another.

▲▲▲

adaptive radiation The formation of many new species following the availability of new environments or the development of a new adaptation.

gradualism A model of macroevolutionary change whereby evolutionary changes occur at a slow, steady rate over time.

Although there are examples of such change in the fossil record, it is not always apparent. In some cases we lack transitional forms. Does this lack of evidence indicate problems in the fossil record or in the theory of gradualism itself?

PUNCTUATED EQUILIBRIUM   An alternative theory has been suggested by Niles Eldredge and Stephen Jay Gould in the form of a model known as **punctuated equilibrium** (Eldredge and Gould 1972; Gould and Eldredge 1977). This theory suggests that the pattern of macroevolution consists of long periods of time when little evolutionary change occurs (**stasis**) and short periods of time when rapid evolutionary change occurs. To Eldredge and Gould, the tempo of macroevolution is not gradual; rather, it is static at times and rapid at other times. Long periods of stasis are punctuated by short periods of rapid evolutionary change. Examples of gradualism and punctuated equilibrium are given in Figure 4.4.

Eldredge and Gould also view speciation as a rapid event occurring within small, isolated populations on the periphery of a species range. Mutations can spread quickly in small populations as a consequence of inbreeding and genetic drift. If such genetic changes are adaptive and if the newly formed species gains access to the parental species' range it may then spread throughout an area, replacing the original parent species. According to this model, most biological change occurs during speciation. Once a species has been established, it changes little throughout time. Eldredge and Gould argue that stabilizing selection and other factors act to keep a species the same over time. This view contrasts with the gradualistic model, which sees biological change occurring at a slow rate, ultimately leading to separate species.

Punctuated equilibrium makes a prediction about how the fossil record should look. Given stasis, we should see long periods of time when little evolutionary change takes place. Certain organisms, such as the cockroach and coelacanth, seem to follow this pattern—they have not changed much over many millions of years. The punctuated equilibrium model also predicts that new species will appear rather quickly, often without any evidence of a transitional state. Because the model predicts that speciation occurs within small isolated populations, there is little chance that we will have fos-

◼ FIGURE 4.4
The tempo of macroevolution: gradualism and punctuated equilibrium. Each portion of this figure has a line showing the change in value of a physical trait over time. (a) Gradualism: the change over time is linear and constant. (b) A geometric, gradual pattern. The rate of change increases with time, but the curve is still smooth; there are no discontinuities. (c) Punctuated equilibrium: there are periods of no change (stasis) punctuated by periods of rapid change; the net result is a "staircase" pattern.

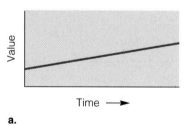
a.

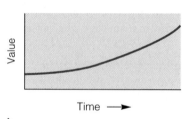
b.

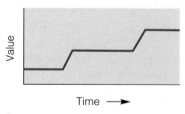
c.

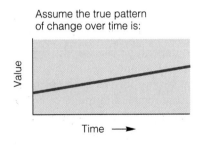

Assume the true pattern of change over time is:

Value

Time →

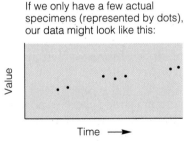

If we only have a few actual specimens (represented by dots), our data might look like this:

Value

Time →

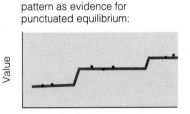

We could interpret such a pattern as evidence for punctuated equilibrium:

Value

Time →

■ FIGURE 4.5
Problems in interpreting the tempo of macroevolutionary change. In this example, gradual change could be interpreted as evidence for punctuated equilibrium because of small sample sizes.

sil evidence actually documenting the initial stages of the origin of a new species.

THE FOSSIL EVIDENCE Gradualism and punctuated equilibrium both make specific predictions of what the fossil record should look like. It should therefore be easy to examine the fossil evidence to determine which model best fits the available data. The fossil record, however, is not always complete enough to allow us to choose between these models. One major problem is that we do not have fossils of every organism that ever lived. Most often, we sample only a small fraction of all these organisms. When we have a "gap" in the fossil record, we cannot always tell whether it is caused by an incomplete record or punctuated equilibrium. It is possible to misinterpret a gradual process as punctuated equilibrium if we do not have a complete sample (Figure 4.5). A gradual change that occurs over 50,000 years could seem "rapid" in the geologic record.

Some organisms are preserved better than others, and thus it is possible in some cases to distinguish between gradualism and punctuated equilibrium. In the case of marine invertebrates, for example, the fossil record is often complete enough to choose between the models. Numerous examples of punctuated equilibrium have been noted using marine invertebrates and other organisms (e.g., Gould and Eldredge 1977; Eldredge 1985).

There is little doubt among evolutionary biologists that stasis and rapid speciation have occurred in some organisms in the fossil record. It is also clear that the fossil record shows many examples of gradualism. Neither model is entirely correct in all cases, however, nor was it meant to be. Both represent different extremes of thinking about the tempo and mode of evo-

punctuated equilibrium
A model of macro-evolutionary change in which long periods of little evolutionary

change (stasis) are followed by relatively short periods of rapid evolutionary change.

stasis Little or no evolutionary change occurring over a long period of time.

lution. Though there is some debate over the genetic mechanisms of punctuated equilibrium, there is less debate on the facts of stasis and rapid speciation (Futuyma 1988). Whether gradualism or punctuated equilibrium is the
dominant mode of macroevolution seems to depend on the specific type of
organism and certain environmental conditions. In some cases gradualism is
more prevalent, and in other cases punctuated equilibrium is more prevalent. Determining the factors responsible for the tempo and mode of evolution under different conditions is a major research objective of evolutionary
biology.

Extinctions and Mass Extinctions

In considering macroevolutionary trends, we must not forget the most common pattern of them all—extinction. It is estimated that over 99 percent of
all species that ever existed have become extinct (Futuyma 1986). In historic
times, humans have witnessed (and helped cause) the extinction of a number
of organisms, such as the passenger pigeon.

What causes extinction? When a species is no longer adapted to a
changed environment, it may die. The exact causes of a species' death vary
from situation to situation. Rapid ecological change may render an environment hostile to a species. For example, temperatures may change and a
species may not be able to adapt. Food resources may be affected by environmental changes, which will then cause problems for a species requiring
these resources. Other species may become better adapted to an environment, resulting in competition and ultimately the death of a species.

Extinction seems, in fact, to be the ultimate fate of all species. Natural
selection is a remarkable mechanism for providing a species with the ability
to adapt to change, but it does not always work. When the environment
changes too rapidly or when the appropriate genetic variations do not exist,
a species can become extinct.

The fossil record shows that extinction has occurred throughout the history of the planet. Recent analyses have also revealed that on some occa-
sions a large number of species became extinct at the same time—a **mass
extinction.** One of the best-known examples of mass extinction occurred
65 million years ago with the demise of dinosaurs and many other forms of
life. Perhaps the largest mass extinction was the one that occurred roughly
225 million years ago, when approximately 95 percent of all species were
wiped out (Gould 1991). Mass extinctions can be caused by a relatively rapid
change in the environment, compounded by the close interrelationship of
many species. If, for example, something were to happen to destroy much of
the plankton in the oceans, then the oxygen content of our planet would
drop, affecting even organisms not living in the oceans. Such a change would
probably lead to a mass extinction.

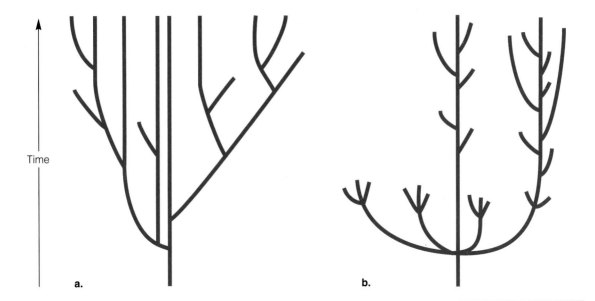

Time

a.   b.

■ FIGURE 4.6
Different views of evolutionary
history and the role of
extinction. (a) Increasing
diversity. (b) Decimation
followed by diversification of
surviving species.
(After Gould [1989])

One interesting, and controversial, finding is that extinctions during the past 250 million years tended to be more intense every 26 million years (Raup and Sepkoski 1986). This periodic extinction might be due to intersection of the earth's orbit with a cloud of comets, although this notion must be considered speculative until further evidence is uncovered.

Recent work has suggested that extinctions may often be random in their effect. That is, certain species may be wiped out and others may survive for no particular reason. A species' survival may have nothing to do with its ability or inability to adapt—it may just be lucky! If so, some of evolutionary history may reflect a sequence of essentially random events. Gould (1989) has suggested that evolutionary history is not the pattern of increasing diversity of species over time traditionally shown in textbooks, but rather a pattern of decimation of existing species (through extinction) followed by diversification of the surviving species (Figure 4.6). All future patterns of evolution are constrained by variation present in survivors. On the basis of his analysis of early invertebrates, Gould suggests that much of later vertebrate evolution (including mammals and humans) may be contingent on the random survival of a particular lineage. If we somehow could observe the history of life from the start, Gould further suggests, random extinction might lead to a totally different pattern of present-day variation. Humans might not have evolved! Although such speculation is not testable, it is interesting.

▲▲▲

mass extinction Many species becoming extinct at roughly the same time.

Species Selection

The concept of extinction has been tied to that of natural selection. **Species selection** refers to the differential survival and reproduction of species. Even though natural selection is often discussed at the level of the individual genotype or phenotype, we may also apply the concept to larger groups, such as populations or species. If some species are better able to survive in a given situation, we have a case of differential mortality of species. It also appears that under certain circumstances some species are more likely to give rise to new species—in essence, a form of differential fertility of species (see Stanley 1979, 1981, for an extensive review of species selection).

Although species selection may be an additional evolutionary mechanism, not all evolutionary biologists support it (Ruse 1987). In many cases, it is difficult to determine whether species are truly a unit of selection or whether differences in survival are just reflections of the aggregate effects of selection upon individuals within a species.

MISCONCEPTIONS ABOUT EVOLUTION

Evolution is a frequently misunderstood subject. Many of our basic ideas regarding evolution are misconceptions that have become part of the general culture. The often used phrase "survival of the fittest" conjures up images that are sometimes at odds with the actual findings of evolutionary science. It is common for such misconceptions to continue even after initial exposure to evolutionary theory.

The Nature of Selection

Many people have a basic understanding of the general principles of natural selection. The problem lies in our misinterpretation of the nature of natural selection.

MISCONCEPTION: *BIGGER IS BETTER*   A common misconception is that natural selection will *always* lead to larger structures. According to this idea, the bigger the brain, the better, and the bigger the body, the better. At first, this idea seems reasonable. After all, larger individuals may be more likely to survive because they can compete more successfully for food and sexual partners. Therefore, larger individuals are more likely to survive and pass their genes on to the next generation. Natural selection is expected to lead to an increase in the size of the body, brain, and other structures. However, this isn't always true. There are numerous examples of species in which *smaller* body size or structures were more adaptive and selected for. Keep in mind that in evolution nothing is free! A larger body may be more adaptive because of sheer size, but a larger body also has greater energy needs. Any advantage gained by a larger body may be offset by the disadvantage of needing more food. What we have to focus on is a *balance* between the adaptive and nonadaptive aspects of any biological characteristic. By walking upright, humans have their hands free, which is rather advantageous. However, we pay the price with varicose veins, back pain, fallen arches, and other nonadaptive consequences of walking on two legs. Again, we need to focus on the relative costs and benefits of any evolutionary change. Of course, this balance will obviously vary in different environments.

MISCONCEPTION: *NEWER IS BETTER* There is a tendency to believe that traits more recent in origin are superior because they are newer. Humans walk on two legs, a trait that appeared more than four million years ago. We also have five digits (fingers and toes) that date back many hundreds of millions of years. Is upright walking better because it is newer? Of course not. Both features are essential to our tool-making way of life. The age of a structure has no bearing on its usefulness.

MISCONCEPTION: *NATURAL SELECTION ALWAYS WORKS* The idea that natural selection will always provide an opportunity for some members of a species to survive is not accurate. Occasionally this author has heard statements such as "we will evolve to tolerate air pollution." Such statements are absurdities. Natural selection only operates on variations that are present. If no genetic variation occurs to aid in breathing polluted air, natural selection will not help us. Even in cases where genetic variation is present, the environment may change too quickly for us to respond through natural selection. All we have to do is to examine the fossil record to see how inaccurate this misconception is—that 99 percent of all past species are extinct shows us that natural selection obviously doesn't always work!

MISCONCEPTION: *THERE IS AN INEVITABLE DIRECTION IN EVOLUTION* An idea popular in the nineteenth century was **orthogenesis,** the notion that evolution would continue in a given direction because of a vaguely defined nonphysical "force" (Mayr 1982). As an alternative to the theory of natural selection, orthogenesis suggested that evolutionary change would continue in the same direction either until a perfect structure was attained or a species became extinct. Apart from the problems of dealing with metaphysical "forces," orthogenesis has long been rejected by analysis of the fossil record

▲▲

species selection A process of selection in which some species are favored to survive and/or develop into new species.

orthogenesis A discredited idea that evolution would continue in a given direction because of some vaguely defined "force."

Science Fiction and Orthogenesis

Evolution, especially human evolution, is a common theme in science fiction. Although a good many science fiction stories have a strong scientific base, others—most likely due to plot needs—do not. Even these stories, though, are valuable in terms of what they tell us about misconceptions about evolution, one of the themes of this chapter.

A personal favorite of mine is an episode of the 1960s science fiction television show, *The Outer Limits*. The episode entitled "The Sixth Finger" is an entertaining treatment of a popular science fiction question: What will humans evolve into? The story, aired in 1963, begins with a young coal miner, Gwyllm Griffiths, who yearns for something more than a life of manual labor. Through his girlfriend Cathy, he meets a local scientist, Professor Mathers, who had once worked on an atomic bomb project. Because of guilt, the scientist is seeking an end to violence and war—through evolution. Reasoning that humans will someday evolve beyond the need for violence, and tormented by the "slow pace of evolution," Mathers invents a machine that will move an organism into its own predestined evolutionary future.

Gwyllm volunteers as a human subject, and the results are predictable. With each exposure to the machine, his head and brain increase in size, as does his intelligence. Additionally, he "evolves" a sixth finger (for "increased dexterity") and assorted mental powers (the sixth finger is particularly interesting because some people today are born with a sixth finger, and there does not appear to be any evolutionary advantage). Gwyllm also develops a dislike for the people around him and eventually decides to destroy them. On his way to demolish the town with his mental powers, he suddenly "evolves beyond the need for violence." He returns to the professor's laboratory and enlists the help of Cathy to operate the machinery while he evolves into "the man of the future." Once Gwyllm is in the machine's chamber, Cathy cannot bear to lose him forever, and pushes the machine's lever to "Backward" rather than "Forward." For a brief moment she pushes too much and the viewer sees Gwyllm evolve back to some sort of subhuman ape, but she quickly corrects the lever and they live happily ever after (in one alternate ending, the script called for Gwyllm to continue evolving back to protoplasm) (Schow and Frentzen 1986).

This episode is quite entertaining, and also provides some good examples of evolutionary misconceptions. For example, the doctrine of orthogenesis, the notion that evolution follows a particular path, is central to the entire plot. This message is not subtle—at one point, Gwyllm speaks about "the goal of evolution." The professor's machine embodies the idea of orthogenesis, with its lever marked "Forward" and "Backward," implying that all of life evolves along a fixed path from past to present. Orthogenesis is also apparent in the continued expansion of the brain and mental powers as Gwyllm evolves "forward," enabling him to read massive volumes at a glance and become a concert pianist overnight.

Despite the scientific inaccuracies, "The Sixth Finger" remains a captivating story. It was also somewhat controversial in that it dealt, on television, with evolution, a theme that had drawn criticism from the network's censor.

and the triumph of natural selection as an explanatory mechanism for evolutionary change. Some of its basic notions, however, are still perpetuated. A common belief is that humans will evolve larger and larger brains, as a continuation of earlier trends (Figure 4.7). The view of orthogenesis is tied in with notions of "progress" and with the misconception that bigger is better. There are many examples from the fossil record of nonlinear change, and many examples of reversals in sizes of structures. In the case of human evolution, brains actually stopped getting larger 50,000 years ago. In fact, the average brain size of humans since that time has decreased slightly as a consequence of a general decrease in skeletal size and ruggedness (Henneberg 1988).

Is it possible for a trend to continue to change in a given direction under the right circumstances? Of course, but change comes through the action of natural selection, not some mysterious internal force. Continuation of any trend depends on the environment, present genetic variation, and basic biological limits. (A 50-foot spider can't exist because it wouldn't be able to absorb enough oxygen for its volume.) Such change also depends on the relative cost and benefits of change. Suppose that an increase in human brain size was combined somehow with an increase in pelvic size (assuming genetic variation was present for both features). A larger pelvis would make walking difficult or even impossible. Evolution works on the entire organism and not one trait at a time. Any change can have both positive and negative effects, but it is the net balance that is critical to the operation of natural selection.

Structure, Function, and Evolution

A number of misconceptions about evolution focus on the relationship between biological structures and their adaptive (or nonadaptive) functions.

MISCONCEPTION: *NATURAL SELECTION ALWAYS PRODUCES PERFECT STRUCTURES*   There is a tendency to view nature as the product of perfect natural engineering. Granted, there are many marvelous and wondrous phenomena in the natural world, but a closer examination shows that biological structures are often far from perfect. Consider human beings. Is the human body perfect? Hardly. Just to note one aspect, consider your skeleton when you stand upright. What is holding in your internal organs? Skin and muscles. Your rib cage provides little support for lower internal organs because it reflects ancestry from a four-legged form. When humans stood up (adaptive), the rib cage offered less support. The result—a variety of complaints and complications, such as hernias. The human skeleton is not perfect, but rather the result of natural selection operating on the variation that was present.

MISCONCEPTION: *ALL STRUCTURES ARE ADAPTIVE*   Natural selection is such a powerful model that it is tempting to apply it to all biological structures. Indeed, many anthropologists and biologists have done so. They examine a structure and explain its function in terms of natural selection. Are all structures adaptive? Many structures simply reflect a by-product of other biological changes and have no adaptive value of their own (Gould and Lewontin 1979). Other structures, such as the human appendix, may have served a function in the past but appear to have no present function.

■ FIGURE 4.7
The theory of orthogenesis predicts continued change in a given direction. Illustrated here is the popular but incorrect notion that humans in the future will have progressively larger brains.

A classic example of a presumably nonadaptive trait is the chin of modern human beings. The jutting chin is relatively modern (see Chapter 12). Earlier forms of *Homo sapiens* lacked the jutting chin in most cases. According to a strict adaptationist perspective, we would become concerned with the function of the jutting chin and attempt to explain it in terms of natural selection. Actually, the jutting chin is simply a by-product of different growth patterns in the human face and jaw. When the face receded, the lower jaw, under a different pattern of growth, stayed at its previous size. The result—a jutting chin that has nothing to do with adaptive value, except as a by-product of adaptive changes in the rest of the face.

Another example deals with an old question: "Why do human men have nipples?" Earlier explanations suggesting that in ancient times men could assist women in breast feeding are ludicrous. The true explanation is simple. Both male and female develop from the same basic body plan during the embryonic stage of prenatal life. Under the influence of sex hormones, various structures develop in different ways (just as the same structure develops into a penis in men and a clitoris in women). The basic body plan for nipples is present in both sexes; for women, these structures develop into breasts capable of lactation. In men, nipples serve no functional purpose. Thus, male nipples are a by-product of the fact that males and females share a similar developmental path, and not the result of some adaptive value (Gould 1991).

MISCONCEPTION: CURRENT STRUCTURES ALWAYS REFLECT INITIAL ADAPTATIONS The idea here is that any given structure, with an associated function, originally evolved specifically for that function. Human beings, for example, walk on two legs; this allows them to hold tools and other objects that are constructed with the aid of an enlarged brain. Although it is tempting to say that both upright walking and a larger brain evolved at the same time because of the adaptive value of having both structures, this is not what happened. Upright walking evolved at least 1.5 million years before the use of stone tools and the expansion of the brain (Chapter 10).

As another example, consider your fingers. You have five of these digits on each hand, which allow you to perform a variety of manipulative tasks. Humans use their hands to manipulate both natural and human-made objects. Manipulative digits are essential to our nature as tool-using creatures. We might therefore suggest that our grasping hands *first* evolved to meet this need; this is not the case. Grasping hands *first* developed in early primate ancestors to meet the needs of living in the trees (Chapter 9). Even though we don't live in trees, we have retained this trait and use it *for a different purpose*. Natural selection operates on the variation that is present. Structures are frequently modified for different uses.

SUMMARY

Macroevolution, the process of long-term evolution, can occur in two ways: anagenesis, the evolution of a single species over time, or cladogenesis, the splitting off of one or more new species from the original parent species. In cladogenesis, new species form through the process of reproductive isolation followed by genetic divergence. Both steps are understood in terms of evolutionary forces. Reduction or elimination of gene flow provides for the beginning of reproductive isolation. Mutation, genetic drift, and selection can then act on this isolation to produce a new species. The relative importance of the evolutionary forces in speciation is still debated.

Two models of macroevolutionary change can be applied to the fossil record. Gradualism states that most evolutionary change is the result of slow but constant change over many generations. New species are believed to form as a by-product of natural selection operating over time. Punctuated equilibrium states that there are long periods of time with little evolutionary change (stasis), punctuated by rapid evolutionary events. New species are seen as forming in small, isolated populations. Analysis of the fossil record shows both models apply under certain situations although it is still not clear which model represents the more common mode of evolution.

The most common evolutionary pattern is extinction. Some scientists have argued that the evolutionary record is best understood as the process of new species forming from old, with many species becoming extinct. The evolutionary trends we observe in the fossil record may reflect the differential survival of species with certain adaptations.

There are many misconceptions regarding natural selection and evolution. Some of the more common of these are: that bigger is better, that newer is better, that natural selection always works, and that there is an inevitable direction to natural selection. There are also misconceptions regarding the relationship of biological structures, their functions, and their evolutionary origin.

SUPPLEMENTAL READINGS

Eldredge, N. 1985. *Time Frames: The Rethinking of Darwinian Evolution and the Theory of Punctuated Equilibria*. New York: Simon & Schuster. A clear review of the punctuated equilibrium model with many examples, primarily from the author's research on fossil marine invertebrates.

Futuyma, D. J. 1986. *Evolutionary Biology*. 2d ed. Sunderland, Mass.: Sinauer. An excellent text on the evolutionary process with extensive coverage of macroevolution and the fossil record.

In addition, the books by Gould listed at the end of Chapter 1 provide many interesting and relevant essays on macroevolution.

CHAPTER **5**

The Fossil Record

 This chapter deals with the fossil record, first discussing methods of analysis, primarily those used to date fossils. Without dates, sequences in evolution cannot be understood. The second part of this chapter provides background on the evolution of life *before* the first primates or humans appeared. Remember that evolution works on preexisting variation. Much of what we are today is related to constraints established in even earlier times.

METHODS OF ANALYSIS

How do we infer macroevolution from the fossil record? The first step in such an analysis is determining the ages of different fossil specimens. At the very least, we must know which fossils are older. Because evolution is a process occurring over time, it is essential that we have a way of determining the time sequence of fossils. If we do not know which fossils are older, then we cannot make any inferences about the nature of evolutionary change.

Two basic classes of methods are used to date fossil remains. **Relative dating** determines which fossils are older but not their exact date. **Chronometric dating** determines an "exact" age (subject to some measurement of possible error and statistical fluctuation).

When we refer to exact dates in the fossil record, we conventionally use the term B.P., which means "Before Present." "Present" has been set arbitrarily as the year 1950. Some people use the term B.C., meaning "Before Christ," but because not all peoples share the belief in Christ, the term B.P. is preferable and has been agreed on internationally. A date of 800,000 years B.P. would mean 800,000 years before the year 1950.

Relative Dating Methods

If we have two sites containing fossil material, relative dating methods can tell us which is older, but not by how much. It is preferable to have exact dates, but this is not possible for all sites. Relative dating methods can tell us the basic time sequence of fossil sites.

STRATIGRAPHY   **Stratigraphy** makes use of the geological process of superposition, which refers to the cumulative buildup over time of the earth's surface. When an organism dies or a tool is discarded on the ground, it will ultimately be buried by dirt, sand, mud, and other materials. Winds move sand over the site, and water can deposit mud over the site. In most cases, the older a site is, the deeper it is. If you stand on the ground and dig down through the earth, the lower layers are older. If you find one fossil 3 ft deep and another 6 ft deep, the principle of stratification allows you to infer that the latter fossil is older. You still do not know how old the fossil is or the exact amount of time between the two fossils, but you have established which is older in geologic time.

In some situations stratigraphy is more difficult to use. Where the earth's crust has folded and broken through the surface of the ground, the usual stratigraphic order is disturbed. This does not invalidate the method, however, for careful geological analysis can reconstruct the patterns of disturbance and allow relative dates to be determined.

▲▲

relative dating The method of estimating the older of two or more fossils or sites but not a specific date.

chronometric dating The method of estimating the specific date of fossils or sites.

B.P. Before Present (1950), the internationally accepted form of designating past dates.

stratigraphy A relative dating method based on the fact that older remains are found deeper in the earth because of cumulative buildup of the earth's surface over time.

OTHER RELATIVE DATING METHODS   A number of other methods provide relative dates for fossils. One such method is **faunal correlation,** which involves comparison of animal remains found at different sites to determine any similarity in time levels. Imagine that you have discovered a site that contains a certain species of fossil pig. Suppose that you know from previous studies that this species of pig has always been found between 2.0 and 1.5 million years B.P. Logically, this suggests that your newly discovered site is also between 1.5 and 2.0 million years old. The only other possibility would be that patterns of evolution occurred in the same way, but at different rates in different areas—an unlikely proposition. Plant pollens sometimes can be used in a similar manner.

Chemical methods also provide relative dates. Fluorine dating, for example, is a method that looks at the accumulation of fluorine in bones. When an organism dies, its bones lose nitrogen and gain fluorine. The rate at which this process occurs varies, so we cannot tell exactly how old a bone is by using the method. The method does, however, allow us to determine if two bones found at the same site are the same age. Other relative dating methods can be applied to human cultural remains. Much like faunal correlation, these methods assign a range of dates based on a comparison with similar sites with known dates.

Chronometric Dating Methods

Chronometric dating methods provide an "exact" date, subject to statistical variation. Chronometric dating relies on constant physical and chemical processes in the universe. Many of these methods utilize the fact that the average rate of radioactive decay is constant for a given radioactive atom no matter what chemical reaction it might be involved in. If we know that a certain element decays into another at a constant rate, and if we can measure the relative proportions of the original and new elements in some object, then we can mathematically determine the age of the object. Radioactive decay is a probabilistic phenomenon, meaning that we know the average time for decay over many atoms. Such processes allow us to specify an average date within the limits of statistical certainty.

CARBON-14 DATING   Living organisms take in the element carbon throughout their lives. Ordinary carbon, carbon-12 (^{12}C), is absorbed by plants, which take in the gas carbon dioxide from the air, and by animals, which eat the plants (or animals that eat the animals that ate the plants). Because of cosmic radiation, some of the carbon in the atmosphere is a radioactive isotope known as carbon-14 (^{14}C). An organism takes in both ^{14}C and ^{12}C, and the proportion of ^{12}C to ^{14}C is constant during the organism's life because the proportion is constant in the atmosphere. When an organism dies, no additional ^{14}C is ingested, and the accumulated ^{14}C begins to decay. The rate at which ^{14}C decays is constant; it takes 5,730 years for one-half of the ^{14}C to decay into ^{14}N (nitrogen-14). Carbon-14 is therefore said to have a **half-life** of 5,730 years. The half-life is the time it takes for half of a radioactive substance to decay.

Carbon-14 dating uses this constant rate of decay to determine the age of materials containing carbon. The process of the radioactive decay of ^{14}C results in the emission of radioactive particles that can be measured. We look at the rate of radioactive emissions for a sample and compare it to the rate of emissions expected in a living organism (a rate of 15 particles per minute per gram of carbon). For example, suppose a sample is analyzed and is found to emit 3.75 particles per minute per gram of carbon. Compared to a living organism, two half-lives have elapsed (one half-life results in 7.5 particles, and a second half-life results in half of this number = 7.5/2 = 3.75). Because the half-life of ^{14}C is 5,730 years, the age of our sample is 5,730 × 2 = 11,460 years ago. If the sample were analyzed in 1996, its date would be 11,414 B.P. (Because 46 years have passed since 1950, the date is 11,460 − 46 = 11,414.)

In theory, any sample containing carbon can be used. In practice, however, bone tends not to be reliable in all cases because of the chemical changes during fossilization, in which carbon is replaced. In most circumstances, charcoal is the best material to use. If we find that a fire occurred at a certain site, either naturally or human-made, we can use the charcoal for carbon-14 dating. Careful attention must be given to possible contaminants at any given site. Another problem is that there has been a certain amount of variability in the proportions of atmospheric carbon over the last few centuries because of industrial pollution. Techniques exist for partial controlling of this factor.

Carbon-14 dating is only useful for sites dating back over the past 50,000 years at most. Any older samples would contain too little ^{14}C to be detected. Though carbon-14 dating is extremely valuable in studies of recent hominid evolution, it is not useful for dating most of earth's geological history.

POTASSIUM-ARGON DATING   Another chronometric dating method that utilizes the process of radioactive decay is **potassium-argon dating.** Here, an

---

faunal correlation
Assigning an approximate age to sites based on the similarity of animal remains with other dated sites.

half-life The average length of time it takes for half of a radioactive substance to decay into another form.

carbon-14 dating A chronometric dating method based on the half-life of carbon-14 that can be applied to organic remains, such as charcoal, dating back over the past 50,000 years.

potassium-argon dating A chronometric dating method based on the half-life of radioactive potassium that can be used to date volcanic rock older than 100,000 years.

■ **FIGURE 5.1**
Hypothetical example of the use of potassium-argon dating. Hominid remains are found between two layers of volcanic ash, one dating to 3.8 million years B.P. and the other dating to 3.2 million years B.P. The hominid can therefore be dated at between 3.8 and 3.2 million years B.P. (From *Human Antiquity: An Introduction to Physical Anthropology and Archaeology*, 2d ed., by Kenneth Feder and Michael Park, Fig. 7.7 Copyright © 1993 by Mayfield Publishing Company)

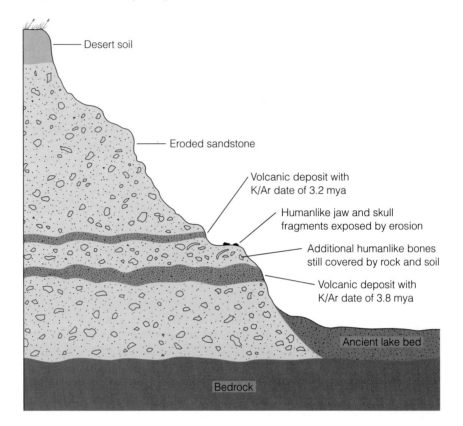

Desert soil

Eroded sandstone

Volcanic deposit with K/Ar date of 3.2 mya

Humanlike jaw and skull fragments exposed by erosion

Additional humanlike bones still covered by rock and soil

Volcanic deposit with K/Ar date of 3.8 mya

Ancient lake bed

Bedrock

isotope of potassium (^{40}K) decays into argon gas (^{40}Ar) with a half-life of approximately 1.31 billion years. This rate of radioactive decay means that this method is best used on samples older than 100,000 years (Figure 5.1).

Potassium-argon dating requires rocks that did not possess any argon gas to begin with. The best material for this method is volcanic rock, for the heat generated by volcanic eruptions removes any initial argon gas. Thus, we are sure that any argon gas we find in a sample of volcanic rock is the result of radioactive decay. By looking at the proportions of ^{40}K and ^{40}Ar, we can determine the number of elapsed half-lives and therefore the age of the volcanic rock.

Though we cannot date a fossil directly with this method, we can assign a date based on the relationship of a fossil find to different levels of volcanic ash. If we find a fossil halfway between two layers of volcanic rock with dates of 4.6 million years B.P. and 4.5 million years B.P., we can then assign the fossil an age of roughly 4.55 million years B.P. Potassium-argon dating is best applied in areas with frequent volcanic eruptions. Fortunately, much of hominid evolution in East Africa took place under such conditions, allowing us to date many fossil sites. A newer and related method, **argon-argon dating,** involves looking at the decay of an argon isotope (^{39}Ar) into argon gas (^{40}Ar). Laser technology allows this method to be applied to very small samples—as small as a single crystal.

■ FIGURE 5.2
Tree rings can be dated by the method of dendrochronology (see text). (Courtesy of Kenneth Feder and Michael Park, Central Connecticut State University)

PALEOMAGNETIC REVERSAL   Another method of dating involves paleomagnetism. When we use a compass to find direction, we rely on the fact that the needle points north. During many times in the past, this was not the case. The magnetic pole has at times shifted to the southern end of the planet. These **paleomagnetic reversals** provide a means by which to date certain rocks. When rocks initially form, they retain the magnetic orientation at the time they came into being—either "normal" (north) or "reversed" (south). By using other dating methods, such as potassium-argon, a chart of the reversals over the last eight million years has been developed. Because these reversals last for different amounts of time, they form a varying pattern. A section of rock can then be compared to the chart to determine the age.

OTHER CHRONOMETRIC DATING METHODS   Many other types of chronometric dating methods can be used in certain circumstances. Some utilize radioactive decay and some use other constant effects for determining age. Archaeologists working on the relatively recent past (within the last 10,000 years) often use a method known as **dendrochronology,** or tree ring counting (Figure 5.2). We know that a tree will accumulate a new ring for every period of

▲▲▲

argon-argon dating A chronometric dating method based on the half-life of radioactive argon that can be used with very small samples.

paleomagnetic reversal A method of dating sites based on the fact that the earth's magnetic pole has shifted back and forth from the north to the south in the past at irregular intervals.

dendrochronology A chronometric dating method based on the fact that trees in dry climates tend to accumulate one growth ring per year.

growth. The width of each ring depends on available moisture and other factors during that specific period. In dry areas there is usually only one growth period in a year. By looking at the width of tree rings, archaeologists have constructed a master chart of tree ring changes. Any new sample, such as a log from a prehistoric dwelling, can be compared to this chart to determine its age.

In addition to radioactive decay, other physical constants allow an estimate of age to be assigned to a sample. **Fission-track dating** relies on the fact that when uranium decays into lead in volcanic glass (obsidian), it leaves small "tracks" across the surface of the glass. We can count the number of tracks and determine the age of the obsidian from the fact that these tracks occur at a constant rate.

Thermoluminescence is a dating method that relies on the fact that certain heated objects accumulate trapped electrons over time, thus allowing us to determine, in some cases, when the object was initially heated. This method has been applied to pottery, bronze, and burned flints. Thermoluminescence can be used to date objects as far back as one million years.

Electron spin resonance is a fairly new method that provides an estimate of dating from observation of radioactive atoms trapped in the calcite crystals present in a number of materials, such as bones and shells. Although this method can be used for sites over a million years old, it works best for dates less than 300,000 years (Grün 1993).

Reconstructing the Past

In addition to dating fossil and archaeological sites, we also need to consider other sources of evidence when putting together a sequence of evolutionary events, and for interpreting them.

TAPHONOMY   When describing the behavior of early hominids, or other organisms, we rely on a wide variety of data to reconstruct their environment and to provide information on population size, diet, presence or absence of predators, and other ecological aspects. Quite often, we rely on what else is found at a given site other than the fossil. For example, the presence of animal bones, particularly those that are fractured, might indicate hunting. The distribution of animal bones might also give us a clue regarding behavior. The types of animal bones found at human hunting sites are different from those found at carnivore sites. A major problem is figuring out how animal bones and other objects got there and what happened to them. Imagine finding the leg bone of a fossil antelope and the leg bone of a fossil hominid at the same site. How did these bones wind up in the same place? Did the hominid hunt and kill the antelope? Did a predator hunt and kill both the antelope and the hominid? Did both bones wash down a river and land at the same place even though they might have originally been separate in time and space?

Some of these questions can be answered by methods developed within the field of **taphonomy,** the study of what happens to plants and animals after they die. This field provides us with valuable information about which bones are more likely to fossilize, which bones are more likely to wash away, the distribution of bones left over by a predator, the likely route of pollen dispersal in the air, and many other similar topics. Taphonomic studies also provide us with ways of finding out whether objects or fossils have been disturbed or whether they have stayed where they were first deposited. Such studies can also help us distinguish between human and natural actions. A fractured leg bone of a deer might result from normal wear and tear on a fossil, or might reflect the action of a prehistoric hunter. By understanding what happens to fossils in general, we are in a better position to infer what happened to *specific* fossils.

PALEOECOLOGY   When reconstructing the past, we need to know more than just what early organisms looked like. We also need to know about the environment in which they lived. What did they eat? Were they predators, or prey? What types of vegetation were available? Where were water sources? These questions, and many others, involve **paleoecology,** the study of ancient environments.

One example of the many methods used in reconstructing ancient environments is **palynology,** the study of fossil pollen. By looking at the types of pollen found at a given site, experts can identify the specific types of plants that existed at that time. They can then make inferences about yearly and seasonal changes in temperature and rainfall based on the relative proportion of plant species. Further information on vegetation can be extracted from analysis of fossil teeth. Microscopic analysis of scratch patterns on teeth can tell us whether an organism relied more heavily on leaves, fruits, or meat. Chemical analysis of teeth can also tell us something about diet. For example, the ratio of the element strontium to the element calcium can reveal whether an organism primarily ate plants or meat. Strontium ratios are higher in plant eaters.

Additional examples of the numerous methods for investigating past environments will be given in the following chapters, where applicable.

▲▲▲

fission-track dating A chronometric dating method based on the number of tracks made across volcanic rock as uranium decays into lead.

thermoluminescence A chronometric dating method based on the capacity of certain heated objects to accumulate trapped electrons over time, which allows the date when the object was initially heated to be determined.

electron spin resonance A chronometric dating method that estimates dates from observation of radioactive atoms trapped in the calcite crystals present in a number of materials, such as bones and shells.

taphonomy The study of what happens to plants and animals after they die.

paleoecology The study of ancient environments.

palynology The study of fossil pollen.

IDENTIFYING SPECIES   Assuming we have good dates for a sample of fossils, and we know as much as possible about their biology and environment, what do we do next? How do we know which organisms are related to one another? Which species became extinct and which evolved into other species? Some of these issues will be dealt with in the next chapter. For now, we concentrate on certain problems in the analysis of fossil remains.

As noted earlier, assignment of fossil specimens into species groups is difficult because we have no direct evidence on which forms were capable of interbreeding. Instead, we have to rely on inferences made from the physical appearance, or morphology, of the fossils. Briefly, we examine physical structure and compare it with other fossils and living organisms, keeping in mind the ranges of variation. When we find two specimens that exceed the normal range of variation for similar organisms, we can make a stronger case for assigning the two specimens into different species.

This approach has problems. Individuals within a species can be mistakenly assigned to different species if care is not taken to consider range of variation. For example, the skulls of adult male and female gorillas are quite different in size and other features. (Figure 5.3). When we encounter such differences among fossil specimens, we must rely on a knowledge of variation in similar living organisms to determine whether sexual dimorphism is likely to be the cause.

Species identification is further complicated by philosophical differences among scientists. Some feel that the range of variation within species is often rather large and suggest that it is simpler to assign fossils to species already known and described rather than create new categories. A scientist with this view is often called a "lumper" because of the preference for lumping new fossils into preexisting categories. Others take a different approach, seeing the evolutionary record as one of frequent speciation. In this case, they anticipate numerous species and tend to call any new fossil that is

■ FIGURE 5.3
Sexual dimorphism in gorilla skulls. The skull of a male gorilla (*left*) is larger than that of the female gorilla (*right*) and also shows heavy crests of bones on top of the skull and at the rear of the skull for muscle attachment. Such sexual differences must be taken into account in analyzing fossil remains and assigning such remains to paleospecies.

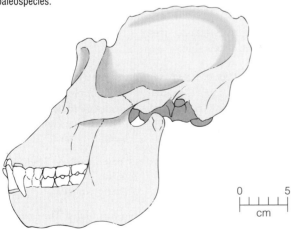
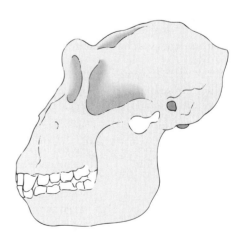

0   5
cm

somewhat different a new species. Scientists with this view are often referred to as "splitters." Identification of species is also complicated by scientists' view as to whether species should be used as convenient labels or whether species should represent new evolutionary lines.

EVOLUTION BEFORE THE PRIMATES

Looking at the early beginnings of life also helps us realize the short length of time humans have been in existence. The genus *Homo* is over 2 million years old. Hominids are over 4 million years old. We think of these dates as representing immense periods of time because of our own relatively short lifetimes. In geologic time, however, hominids have only been around a brief instant. Astronomers estimate the age of our universe to be roughly 15 billion years old. Geological evidence shows the earth to be roughly 4.6 billion years old. Compared to these numbers, 4 millions years is a short time.

Perspectives on Geologic Time

We lose sight of the immense age of the universe and earth because we are not used to dealing with such large numbers. To many people, the difference between a million and a billion does not seem great because both numbers are so extremely large. The astronomer Carl Sagan (1977) has used an analogy he calls the "Cosmic Calendar" to help put these dates into perspective. Imagine the entire history of the universe, from its beginning to the present, as taking a single year. That is, the universe came into being at midnight on January 1 of the year, and the present time is midnight on January 1 a year later. Our own galaxy, the Milky Way, comes into being on May 1, the solar system on September 9, and the earth on September 14. Life on earth begins approximately on September 25, and the oldest known fossils (algae) on October 9. It is not until November 12 that photosynthetic plants come into being. Eukaryotes (cells with nuclei) begin on November 15. Almost 11 complete months pass and nothing resembling a human being has yet evolved!

By December 1, a significant oxygen atmosphere has developed on earth. By December 17, the invertebrates have come into being. The first fish and vertebrates appear on December 19, and colonization of land by early insects and amphibians takes place on December 22. Reptiles appear on the 23rd, dinosaurs on the 24th, and the first mammals on the 25th. By December 28, the dinosaurs have become extinct, and the first primates appear the next day. It is not until the final day of the year, December 31, that apes and humans appear!

The first humans appear at 10:30 P.M. on the final day. Fire is used by 11:00 P.M., and it is not until 11:59:20 that agriculture is invented. The

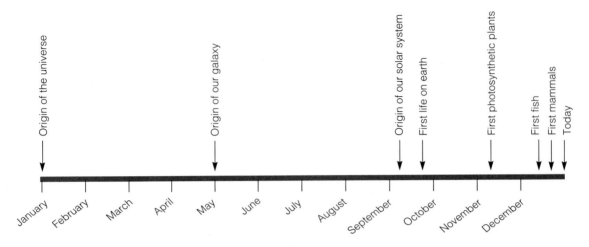

■ FIGURE 5.4
Carl Sagan's "Cosmic Calendar." The history of the universe is compressed into a single year, with the origin of the universe happening on January 1, and the present day occurring at midnight on the following January 1. See the text for additional dates. (*Source:* Sagan [1977])

Roman Empire occurs around 11:59:56. The European Renaissance takes place at one second before midnight. Everything that has occurred since then takes place in the final second (Figure 5.4).

The Origin of Life

Geologists and paleontologists divide the history of the earth into two **eons,** each of which is broken into **eras,** which are further broken into **periods.** The **Precambrian eon** dates from the beginning of the planet 4.6 billion years B.P. until 545 million years B.P. (thus covering almost 90 percent of earth's history). Major events of the Precambrian eon are the origin of life (obviously a major event!), the development of single-celled organisms, and the first appearance of multicelled organisms. Although the fossil record preserves some of the earliest life, we lack direct fossil evidence for the first signs of life. We must rely instead on a knowledge of the early conditions of the planet and combine these observations with laboratory evidence suggesting possible origins of life.

Our evidence to date suggests that life first began through a process of chemical evolution. Laboratory experiments in the 1950s demonstrated that amino acids could be produced under conditions thought similar to those of the early earth. Some scientists suggest that a process of chemical selection took place in which certain chemical forms and reactions may have been favored. These models rely on chemical analogies to variation and natural selection in what we might term a "prebiotic" world (Stebbins 1982). The different hypotheses for the initial origin of life are too detailed to cover here, but are reviewed by Cowen (1995).

In terms of the fossil record, fossilized microscopic cells have been found dating back 3.5 billion years B.P., and suggest considerable biological diversity, including the origin of photosynthesis (Schopf 1993). Fossils that indicate cell division have been found in deposits dating back to 850 million

■ **TABLE 5.1**
Geological Eras and Periods of the Phanerozoic Eon

ERA	PERIOD	MILLIONS OF YEARS B.P.	SOME MAJOR EVOLUTIONARY EVENTS
Cenozoic	Quaternary	1.8–today	Evolution of the genus *Homo*
	Tertiary	65–1.8	Origin and evolution of the primates; origin of hominids
Mesozoic	Cretaceous	145–65	Extinction of the dinosaurs; first birds and placental mammals
	Jurassic	210–145	Dinosaurs dominate; first birdlike reptiles
	Triassic	245–210	First dinosaurs; egg-laying mammals
Paleozoic	Permian	290–245	Radiation of reptiles; mammallike reptiles
	Carboniferous	360–290	Radiation of amphibians; first reptiles and insects
	Devonian	410–360	Many fish; first amphibians; first forests
	Silurian	440–410	First fish with jaws; land plants
	Ordovician	505–440	Early vertebrates, including jawless fish; trilobites and many other invertebrates
	Cambrian	545–505	"Explosion" of life; marine invertebrates

Sources: Cowen (1995), Schopf (1992)

years B.P., and evidence for multicelled organisms goes back to at least 750 million years B.P. (Reader 1986). The last 545 million years of earth's history lies in the **Phanerozoic eon,** which is broken down into three geological eras: Paleozoic, Mesozoic, and Cenozoic. Table 5.1 lists the eras and periods of the Phanerozoic eon and the major evolutionary events that occurred during each.

The Paleozoic Era

The **Paleozoic era** lasted from 545 million to 245 million years B.P. The first geological period of the Paleozoic era is the Cambrian, which was a time of rapid evolution of many life forms. In fact, the term *Cambrian explosion* is

eon The major subdivision of geologic time.

era Subdivision of a geologic eon.

period Subdivision of a geologic era.

Precambrian eon The eon from the earth's beginning (4.6 billion years B.P.) until 545

million years B.P. During this eon, single-celled and simple multicelled organisms first evolved.

Phanerozoic eon The last 545 million years.

Paleozoic era The first geologic era of the Phanerozoic eon, dating roughly between 545 and 245 million years B.P., when the first vertebrates appeared.

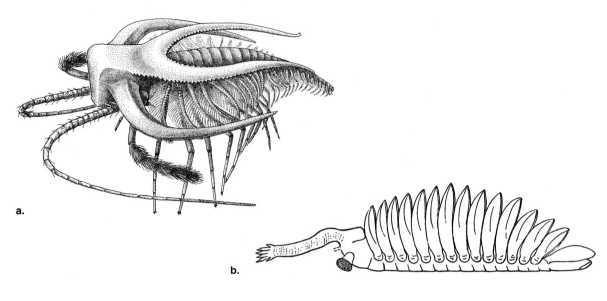

a.

b.

c.

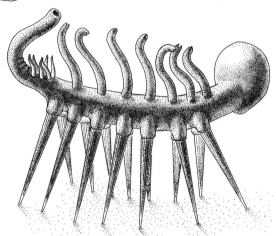

■ FIGURE 5.5

Reconstruction of some early invertebrates from the Cambrian
period: (a) *Marella,* (b) *Opabinia,* (c) *Odontogriphus,*
(d) *Hallucigenia*, (e) *Canadaspis.* Recent studies of *Hallucigenia*
have suggested an alternative reconstruction. (a, c, d, e: The
illustrations by Marianne Collins from *Wonderful Life: The Burgess Shale
and the Nature of History,* by Stephen Jay Gould, are reproduced by
permission of W. W. Norton & Company, Inc. Copyright © 1989 by Stephen
Jay Gould; b: reprinted with permission from Cambridge University Press)

d.

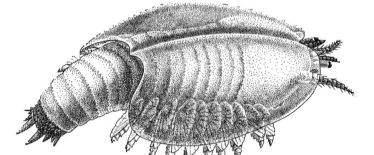

e.

often used to describe the beginning of this period. Creationists like to suggest that the rapid appearance of life forms is proof of an instantaneous creation. As you read earlier, this is not correct. Life forms existed before the Cambrian period and we have fossil evidence of them. The "explosion" actually took place over millions of years.

Early life forms included organisms similar to modern sponges and jellyfish, as well as a wide variety of marine invertebrates that have no living counterpart (Figure 5.5). Such diversity shows us that many species have become extinct, and only a few have living descendants. This recurrent pattern of diversification and extinction was discussed in Chapter 4.

Of particular interest to us are some of the early vertebrates, which first appear at the beginning of the Paleozoic, especially the jawless fish. These creatures possessed the internal segmented vertebral column common to all vertebrates but lacked jaws and teeth. The jawless fish came in many forms and were quite successful several hundred million years ago. Today, only two specialized descendants of this once successful group survive: the hagfish and the lamprey.

Some of these jawless fish developed armor plating around their heads from a hard material known as dentin. The first teeth were nothing more than spikes of dentin folded inward. This new feature may have been a powerful adaptation, allowing them to eat a greater variety of food. Later, the teeth developed further and jaws evolved.

Where did jaws come from? If we look at the embryological development of birds and mammals, we can see how the bones and blood vessels that once served the gill arches of fish have been elaborated to form structures that do other things in higher vertebrates. For example, the first gill arch of jawless fish forms the jaws of descendant vertebrates. The bones of the ears of mammals come from the second gill arch. Evolution does not build structures from scratch, but rather modifies and revises what is already there, frequently adapting old structures for new functions.

One of the next major evolutionary events was the invasion of land by early amphibians. Creationists fault the fossil record for not showing intermediate forms. A typical question is: What is intermediate between a creature that lives in the water and one that lives on land? The answer is simple. Amphibians are such an intermediate form for which we have fossil evidence, and many amphibian species are still alive today.

We are used to thinking that fish have gills that allow oxygen to be absorbed from water, and land animals have lungs that allow oxygen to be absorbed from the air. Actually, many fish, such as the lungfish, have lunglike structures. If you observe tropical fish, you will soon learn that some must periodically swim to the surface of the water to get air. Examples are the gourami and the Siamese fighting fish.

Looking at tropical fish in a store also can give you clues about the origin of movement on land, another important feature of land colonization. Many fish, such as catfish, are bottom dwellers. They rest on the bottom of the fish tank on strongly developed fins. In the Paleozoic era a group of fish called lobe-fins evolved this ability. Some of these adaptations survive in a fish commonly called the "walking catfish," which often moves on land to get from one stream to another, obtaining oxygen from the air as well.

Recent evidence suggests a different, and very interesting, possibility for the origin of legs. A creature that has been named *Acanthostega* lived 360 million years ago, and appears to be a fish with legs! Current thinking suggests that legs evolved in some early fish well before movement onto the land, perhaps as an adaptation for moving through underwater thickets (Zimmer 1995). If so, then some species of early fish had an adaptation that was well suited for further development into structures capable of movement on land. As with the evolution of lungs, the evolution of legs may represent the modification of preexisting adaptations (developed in the water) to meet a new challenge—living on land.

The fossil evidence suggests that such creatures next spent at least some time on land, perhaps for laying eggs. Amphibians represent a transitional form of vertebrate that lives both in water and on land. The early amphibians were successful and many of these forms evolved into modern amphibians. Some early amphibians became highly successful on the land and evolved into early reptiles during the Carboniferous period. This was facilitated by the development of eggs with leathery shells that did not dry out, thus freeing reproduction from the need for a watery environment. The Permian period witnessed an adaptive radiation of reptiles. Reptiles were the dominant form of animal life on the land surface of the planet for more than the next 200 million years.

Mammals and birds eventually evolved from the reptiles. The evolution of mammals from reptiles suggests that an intermediate form of animal intervened. To many, an intermediate form implies some sort of strange-looking creature with a mixture of *modern* reptilian and mammalian features. This is an incorrect view of evolution. Modern reptiles and mammals represent millions of years of evolution from a common ancestor. The first reptiles did not look exactly like modern-day reptiles. In fact, some of the earliest primitive reptiles included a group referred to as the **therapsids,** or mammallike reptiles. The classification of creatures into categories such as mammals or reptiles is a problem when we try to apply these categories to the fossil record. Our definitions of these groups are based on observations of modern-day forms representing millions of years of separate evolution. The further and further we go back in time, the more these groups blur together, and the harder it is to absolutely assign a specific form to one category or the other.

The therapsids are classified as reptiles because they have more features that we would call reptilian. However, they also possessed certain mammalian features, such as different types of teeth (see Chapter 6). We therefore call them, for lack of a better term, mammallike reptiles. Therapsids

■ **FIGURE 5.6**
Dimetrodon, a form of reptile ancestral to mammallike reptiles.

underwent an adaptive radiation during the Permian period of the Paleozoic era, with a wide variety of shapes and sizes. If you have ever played with toy dinosaurs as a child, you will recognize a form known as *Dimetrodon* (Figure 5.6), which is not classified as a dinosaur but as an ancestor of the mammallike reptiles.

The dental adaptations of the therapsids were well suited to life on land, allowing them to forage plants effectively. Although this group was highly successful, it ultimately declined following an adaptive radiation of what we might term "true reptiles" during the Mesozoic. Although it was once thought that all of the therapsids became extinct following the emergence of "true reptiles," recent fossil evidence shows that some of the mammallike reptiles survived at least until 60 million years ago (Fox et al. 1992).

therapsid An early group of reptiles also known as the mammallike reptiles.

Therapsids were the ancestors of later mammals.

■ FIGURE 5.7
Two well-known dinosaurs:
Triceratops (*top*) and
Tyrannosaurus (*bottom*).

Killer From the Sky?

A large asteroid traveling through space hits our planet. The energy released is astounding. The asteroid collides with rock containing large amounts of sulfur. As a consequence, highly acidic rain falls, killing many animals and plants, and further altering the balance of oxygen and carbon dioxide in the atmosphere. In addition, dust and smoke caused by the impact cut down on the available sunlight for perhaps several months. Photosynthesis is affected, and many plants and algae die. Animals dependent on the plants and algae starve, as do animals that prey on the plant eaters. And as if this weren't bad enough, the lack of sunlight also leads to freezing temperatures around the planet.

The above sounds very much like a science fiction plot. Indeed, the ecological and social implications of asteroid impact are a favorite science fiction theme, such as in *Lucifer's Hammer* by Larry Niven and Jerry Pournelle. In this case, however, the scenario is one of several hypotheses regarding the evolutionary effect of asteroid impact (Cowen 1995). Why is so much attention given to the possible effects of an asteroid hitting the earth? To many (but not all) paleontologists, the extinction of the dinosaurs (and other life forms) 65 million years ago was due to such an event. Many characterize events like these as "bad luck" for the species affected. After all, there is no way to evolve to protect against an asteroid impact!

The extinction of the dinosaurs is a well-documented fact. In addition to dinosaurs, other large vertebrates, marine invertebrates, and much of the world's plankton also became extinct. This mass extinction occurred at 65 million years B.P., the agreed-upon boundary between the Cretaceous period of the Mesozoic era and the Tertiary period of the Cenozoic era (the Cretaceous-Tertiary boundary is abbreviated as the K-T boundary).

The idea of an asteroid impact being responsible is fairly new. In 1980, Alvarez and colleagues introduced evidence that such an impact had taken place. Their key finding was large amounts of the metal iridium at the K-T boundary. Normally scarce on earth, iridium is found in higher quantities in meteorites and asteroids. According to Alvarez et al. (1980), the high amount of iridium at the K-T boundary worldwide is best explained by an asteroid hitting the earth at this time. Since initial publication, more and more evidence has accumulated to support the asteroid impact hypothesis (although it is not accepted by all). For example, the finding of quartz crystals altered by sudden pressure at the K-T boundary supports the hypothesis, as does evidence of the crater left by an asteroid (estimated to have been 6 miles in diameter) off the Yucatán Peninsula of Mexico.

What does this all mean for the study of human evolution? As shown in this chapter, mammals had been restricted to a relatively narrow range of environments during the time of the dinosaurs. The expansion of mammals during the past 65 million years has in part been due to the elimination of competition. When the dinosaurs became extinct, new environments became available to mammals. Viewed in this way, all of mammalian evolution (including human evolution) can be seen as contingent upon the extinction of the dinosaurs. What was bad luck for the dinosaurs was good luck for the mammals.

The Mesozoic Era

The **Mesozoic era,** lasting from 245 million to 65 million years B.P., is often called the "Age of Reptiles" because it was the time when reptiles became the dominant form of life on the earth's surface. One of the most successful groups of reptiles were the dinosaurs (Figure 5.7). The major characteristic of the dinosaurs was the modification of the leg and pelvic structures. Many

Mesozoic era The second geologic era of the Phanerozoic eon, dating roughly between 245 and 65 million years B.P., when the first mammals and birds appeared.

dinosaurs were bipedal, and some appear to have been extremely quick movers and efficient walkers and runners (Wilford 1985). The therapsids, on the other hand, did not change much beyond the earliest land vertebrates except for modifications in their teeth. Therapsids were not fast movers and had few defensive or offensive abilities. In the Permian period they did not need such adaptations. The world lay open for them to colonize.

Unfortunately for the therapsids, the ancestors of the dinosaurs developed quicker and more efficient locomotion, and many species further developed powerful hands and teeth to capture prey. Ultimately, the dinosaurs emerged as the dominant form of animal life on land and the therapsids declined in number. Eventually the therapsids became extinct, but before this happened some of the therapsids evolved into what we call "true mammals."

During the Triassic period the monotremes, or egg-laying mammals, evolved. Some, such as the platypus, have survived until the present day. The first placental mammals evolved during the Jurassic period, which was the heyday of the dinosaurs. Birdlike reptiles also evolved during this time period. At the end of the Cretaceous period the dinosaurs became extinct, and mammals became the dominant animal life.

The paragraph you have just finished reading is a rough summary of many complex events taking place over a long time. It is widely thought that the emergence of mammals led to the disappearance of the dinosaurs. After all, mammals have more efficient systems of reproduction, temperature regulation, and an emphasis on social learning, among other adaptations. However, the story is not that simple. There is growing evidence that at least some of the dinosaurs possessed a measure of temperature regulation (see Chapter 6) and had a complex form of social organization (Wilford 1985, Bakker 1986). Also, mammals and dinosaurs coexisted for tens of millions of years. Regardless of the adaptations of the earliest mammals, they were limited in their expansion by the success of the dinosaurs. The mammals were confined to a few small environmental niches. Most were small and probably nocturnal, existing on insects and living in the trees. Only when the dinosaurs became extinct and flowering plants evolved did the mammals undergo an adaptive radiation. Until that time they remained in the shadow of the dinosaurs. Evolution requires opportunities.

Why did the dinosaurs (and many other organisms) become extinct? Some of the more fanciful suggestions include excessive constipation because of changes in plant life. Most theories of dinosaur extinction rely on environmental change, such as the cooling of the earth. If the temperature dropped, then the warm-blooded mammals would seem to be better adapted than the cold-blooded reptiles. A problem with this idea is that there is evidence that at least some of the dinosaurs were warmblooded. Recent explanations of dinosaur extinction have relied on the idea that an asteroid or comet hit the earth with tremendous force, kicking up clouds of dust and blocking the sun. Temperatures dropped and many plant forms became ex-

tinct. As plants died, so did the plant eaters and those who ate the plant
eaters. In other words, the entire ecology of the planet was altered. There is
growing geologic evidence for such a catastrophic event (e.g., Sheehan et al.
1991), although many researchers suggest other factors may have also played
a part.

In any case, the fossil record shows clearly that dinosaurs died out and
mammals took their place during the last of the Cretaceous period. New opportunities opened up for the mammals, and they begin an adaptive radiation, filling vacant environmental niches. The last 65 million years of the
earth's history is the **Cenozoic era,** often called the "Age of Mammals."
Some mammals ultimately evolved to exploit the grasslands. Others developed adaptations that allowed them to become sea creatures, such as the
whale and dolphin. The important event for our purposes was the continued
adaptation to life in the trees by certain mammals. This new group of mammals, the primates, is discussed in the next chapter.

SUMMARY

A variety of methods exist for reconstructing past environments and interpreting the fossil record. Dating methods are particularly important because
they allow fossils to be placed in a sequence through time, from which evolutionary trends can be inferred. Collectively, the methods of paleontology
allow us to understand the history of life.

Life on earth began following a period of chemical evolution. The earliest life forms evolved in ancient oceans. The first vertebrates were the jawless
fish, which evolved into fish with jaws. One group of jawed fish, the lobe-
fins, were the ancestors of all later land vertebrates. After the amphibians
conquered the land, an adaptive radiation of reptiles fully adapted to land
conditions began. One of the first sort of reptiles was the therapsids, or
mammallike reptiles. These forms possessed certain dental traits that allowed them to exploit new types of food. The later adaptive radiation of the
dinosaurs ultimately led to the extinction of the therapsids. Before they disappeared, however, some therapsids evolved into the first true mammals. For
millions of years, the dinosaurs were the dominant land animals and the
mammals existed in the fringe environmental niche of arboreal nocturnal

Cenozoic era The third,
and most recent, geologic
era of the Phanerozoic
eon, dating roughly to

the last 65 million years.
The first primates
appeared during the
Cenozoic era.

life. When the dinosaurs disappeared during the mass extinction at the end of the Mesozoic era, the mammals had the opportunity to expand into newly available niches.

SUPPLEMENTAL READINGS

Cowen, R. 1995. *History of Life.* 2d ed. Boston: Blackwell Scientific Publications. An up-to-date and very thorough review of the fossil record from the origins of life to the present.

Lewin, R. 1982. *Thread of Life: The Smithsonian Looks at Evolution.* New York: W. W. Norton.

Reader, J. 1986. *The Rise of Life: The First 3.5 Billion Years.* New York: Alfred A. Knopf. Well-written, superbly illustrated introduction to evolution from the origin of life to the present.

PART TWO

Our Place in Nature

Primates in Nature

In order to understand the place of humans in nature, it is first necessary to understand the group of mammals to which humans belong—the **primates.** Humans are primates, as are other creatures such as the apes, the monkeys, and the primitive primates known as prosimians. The basic nature of primate biology and behavior is discussed in this chapter. However, because primates belong to a group known as mammals, who in turn belong to a larger group known as vertebrates, it is first necessary to understand the basic characteristics of these larger taxonomic groups. We begin, therefore, by first discussing vertebrates and then mammals, and then go on to discuss the special characteristics of primates.

TAXONOMY

Taxonomy was discussed briefly in Chapters 1 and 4. Here, we turn to a more detailed examination of the philosophies and methods used in constructing biological classifications.

▲▲▲▲▲▲▲▲▲▲▲▲▲▲▲▲▲▲▲▲▲▲▲▲▲▲▲▲

primates The order of mammals that has a complex of characteristics related to an initial adaptation to life in the trees.

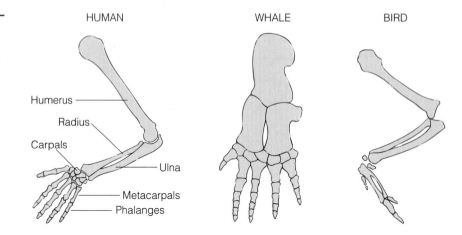

■ **FIGURE 6.1**
Homologous structures: the forelimbs of a human, whale, and bird. Note that the same bones are found in all three vertebrates. Even though the limbs are used differently by all three organisms, the bones show a structural correspondence, reflecting common ancestry. (Adapted with permission from T. Dobzhansky, F. J. Ayala, G. L. Stebbins, and U. W. Valentine, *Evolution*, 1977, page 264, publisher W. H. Freeman)

Methods of Classification

Two species may have the same characteristic for several reasons. First, they both may have inherited the trait from a common ancestor. Humans and monkeys, for example, both have five digits on each limb because they both inherited this trait from a distant common ancestor. Second, the two species may have developed the same trait independently in their evolution. The canary and bat are both small animals capable of flight. The shared characteristic of flight, however, is not due to a common ancestor; rather, both species evolved flight independently. The independent evolution of the same trait can be due to **parallel evolution,** whereby similar traits arise independently in closely related species, or to **convergent evolution,** whereby similar traits arise independently in more distantly related species. To reconstruct evolutionary relations, we are more interested in traits that are similar because of common ancestry rather than parallel or convergent evolution.

HOMOLOGOUS AND ANALOGOUS TRAITS   One of our first steps is to look at a biological trait and determine its structure (how it is put together) and its function (how it is used). **Homologous traits** are traits that show similar structure but may or may not show the same function. For example, each of your arms or legs is composed of a single upper bone and two lower bones. These bones are found in many other organisms, including creatures that use their limbs in quite different ways. Figure 6.1 illustrates the arm bones of a human, a bird, and a whale. Note that each of these has an upper arm bone (humerus) and two lower arm bones (radius and ulna). Furthermore, note that the "hand" of each has five digits made up of carpal and metacarpal bones. These three animals use their limbs for different purposes, but the basic structure is the same; they are the same bones, but they differ in size, shape,

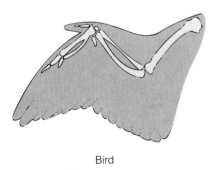

Bird

Fly

■ FIGURE 6.2
Analogous structures: the wings of a bird and a fly. Even though both structures provide the same function (flight), they are structurally different, reflecting independent evolutionary origin. (Adapted with permission from T. Dobzhansky, F. J. Ayala, G. L. Stebbins, and U. W. Valentine, *Evolution*, 1977, page 264, publisher W. H. Freeman)

and function. The correspondence of the arm and hand bones of the animals in Figure 6.1 indicates these bones are homologous structures. The reason for this correspondence is that these traits have been inherited from a common ancestor.

Traits that have the same function but not the same structure are called **analogous traits.** Figure 6.2 illustrates the wings of a bird and a flying insect. The two structures are quite different, but they serve the same function—flight. In this case, evolution has led to the same function from two different starting points. Because the bird and the insect have different structures that do not reflect evolutionary relationship, they are placed in different taxonomic categories. In this case, the development of wings in both birds and insects reflects a case of convergent evolution.

PRIMITIVE AND DERIVED TRAITS   Biological traits can also be characterized as primitive or derived. When a trait has been inherited from an earlier form, we refer to that trait as **primitive.** Traits that have changed from an ancestral state are referred to as **derived.** As an example, consider the number of digits in humans and horses. Both humans and horses are mammals. From fossil evidence we know that the first mammals had five digits on each hand and foot (as did other early land vertebrates). Humans have retained this condition, and we refer to the five digits of the human hand and foot as primitive

parallel evolution
Independent evolution of similar adaptations in closely related species.

convergent evolution
Independent evolution of similar adaptations in rather distinct evolutionary lines.

homologous trait
Physical trait in two species that has a similar structure but may or may not show a similar function.

analogous trait Physical trait that has a similar function in two species but a different structure.

primitive trait A trait that has not changed from an ancestral state. The five digits of the human hand and foot

are primitive traits inherited from earlier vertebrate ancestors.

derived trait A trait that has changed from an ancestral state.

traits. The horse's single digit (a toe), however, is a derived trait relative to the first mammals.

The concept of primitive and derived traits is relative. What is considered primitive at one level of comparison might be considered derived at another level. For example, neither modern apes nor modern humans have a tail. If apes are compared to humans, the absence of a tail is a primitive characteristic—they share this absence because they inherited this characteristic from a common ancestor. Monkeys, however, do have tails. If modern monkeys are compared to modern apes, the lack of a tail in the modern apes is a derived condition—it has changed since the common ancestor of monkeys and apes. The relative nature of primitive and derived traits must always be kept in mind.

To make any comparison, we must have information on modern and fossil forms so that we can determine whether a trait is primitive or derived. We cannot assume that any given organism will be primitive or derived for a given trait without knowing something about the ancestral condition. In other words, we cannot equate the terms *primitive* and *derived* with biased notions of "higher" or "lower" forms. In the past, there was a tendency to regard all traits of modern humans as derived relative to the apes. For some traits, such as increased brain size and upright walking, this holds true. For other traits, such as certain features of the teeth, the opposite is true.

Approaches to Classification

The problem of biological classification may be approached in many different ways. Though most agree that such classification should reflect evolutionary history, opinions differ about how this should be accomplished.

PHENETICS   The classification of organisms on the basis of overall similarity is termed **phenetics.** According to this method, it doesn't matter whether such similarity is the result of common ancestry or parallel evolution. If parallel evolution is fairly common, phenetic classification may suggest a closer evolutionary relationship than actually exists. As a result, species that do not share a common ancestor may be grouped together in a taxonomic group. For example, a phenetic approach places crocodiles and lizards in the same taxonomic class—Reptilia (reptiles). Birds are usually placed in the Aves class. Although this classification fits traditional views of overall similarity, the problem is that birds and crocodiles are more closely related to each other than either is to lizards (Harvey and Pagel 1991).

CLADISTICS   An alternative approach, known as **cladistics,** attempts to focus on evolutionary relationships. A cladist would place birds and crocodiles in the same taxonomic group, and lizards in another. The guiding principle of cladistics is that only shared derived traits should be used to construct taxonomies; shared primitive traits should not. The fact that both humans and monkeys have five digits would not be used to judge their relationship, because comparative and fossil data have shown us that five digits are a primitive trait. Nor are all derived traits applicable. The large brain of humans cannot be used to determine an evolutionary relationship with monkeys or apes because it is *unique* to humans. In cladistics, only homologous traits that are both shared and derived can be used to evaluate the evolutionary relationship of two species. For example, both humans and apes share certain features of their shoulder anatomy (see Chapter 7) that are not shared with monkeys or other primates. Comparative anatomy and the fossil record show that both humans and apes have these traits in common because they inherited them from a common ancestor that had changed from an ancestral state. That is, humans and apes are similar because of shared derived characteristics.

The cladistic school does face some problems. For example, cladists consider parallel evolution to be minimal. However, examples of parallel evolution abound in the fossil record (Cartmill 1982). Another problem with the cladistic method is that it uses traits that occur in one state or the other, primitive or derived. The method fails somewhat when considering continuous traits (Trinkhaus 1990). At what level of measurement do you classify tooth size as "small" or "large"? If we state that large teeth are primitive, we are left with the problem of determining exactly what size should be considered "large." In spite of these and other problems, however, cladistics has become increasingly popular among biological anthropologists. Some of the current debates on classification involving the cladistic approach will be discussed in the next two chapters.

The Vertebrates

As with all living creatures, human beings can be classified according to the different levels of Linnaean taxonomy—kingdom, phylum, class, and so on. The complete taxonomic description of modern humans is given in Table 6.1.

THE ANIMAL KINGDOM   Kingdom is the most inclusive taxonomic category. All living organisms can be placed into one of five kingdoms: plants, animals, fungi, nucleated single-celled organisms, and bacteria. Major differences among these kingdoms are their source of food and their mobility. Whereas

■ TABLE 6.1
Taxonomic Classification of Human Beings

TAXONOMIC CATEGORY	PLACEMENT OF HUMANS
Kingdom	Animals
Phylum	Chordates
Subphylum	Vertebrates
Class	Mammals
Subclass	Placental mammals
Order	Primates
Suborder	Anthropoids
Superfamily	Hominoids
Family	Hominids
Genus/Species	*Homo sapiens*

phenetics A school of thought that stresses the overall physical similarities among organisms in forming biological classifications.

cladistics A school of thought that stresses evolutionary relationships between organisms in forming biological classifications.

plants produce their own food through photosynthesis, animals must ingest food. Humans belong to the animal kingdom. Given that animals must ingest food, it is no surprise to see that most animals have well-developed nervous, sensory, and movement systems to allow them to sense and acquire food.

VERTEBRATE CHARACTERISTICS   Humans belong to the phylum **Chordata** (the chordates, animals with a spinal cord). Perhaps the most important characteristic of chordates is that they possess at some point in their life a **notochord,** a flexible internal rod that runs along the back of the animal. This rod acts to strengthen and support the body. In humans, it is present early in gestation and is later reabsorbed.

Humans belong to the subphylum **Vertebrata** (the vertebrates, animals with backbones). One characteristic of vertebrates is that they have **bilateral symmetry,** which means that the left and right sides of their bodies are approximately mirror images. Imagine a line running down a human being from the top of the head to a spot between the feet. This line divides the body into two mirror images. This pattern contrasts with other phyla of animals such as starfish.

Another characteristic of vertebrates is an internal spinal cord covered by a series of bones known as vertebrae. The nerve tissue is surrounded by these bones and has an enlarged area of nerve tissue at the front end of the cord—the brain.

The general biological structure of human beings can be found in many other vertebrates. Figure 6.1 showed the limb bones of three vertebrates—human, bird, and whale. It is important to note the similarity among these three different organisms. Like most vertebrates, all have the same basic skeletal pattern: a single upper bone and two lower bones in each limb, and five digits. Some vertebrates have changed considerably from this basic pattern. For example, a modern horse has one digit (a toe) on the end of each limb. Humans may seem to be rather specialized and sophisticated creatures, but actually they have retained much of the earliest basic vertebrate skeletal structure.

The subphylum of vertebrates also includes several classes of fish along with the amphibians, reptiles, birds, and mammals. Humans belong to the class of mammals, and much of our biology and behavior can be understood in terms of what it is to be a mammal.

CHARACTERISTICS OF MAMMALS

The first primitive mammals evolved from early reptiles approximately 200 million years B.P. The distinctive features of modern mammals and modern reptiles are the result of that long period of separate evolution in the two classes. It is important to realize that the further back in time we look, the more difficult it is to tell one form from another. Keep in mind that the definition and characteristics of any modern form reflect continued evolution from an earlier ancestor.

Because mammals and reptiles are related through evolution, it is logical and useful to compare these two classes to determine the unique features of each. Modern mammals differ from modern reptiles in reproduction, temperature regulation, diet, skeletal structure, and behavior. As we look at each of these factors separately, do not forget that they are interrelated.

Reproduction

Mammals are often identified as animals that give birth to live offspring, whereas other vertebrates lay eggs. This is not completely accurate. Some fish, such as guppies, give birth to live infants. Also, some mammals, such as the platypus, lay eggs. Others, such as kangaroos, give birth to an extremely immature fetus that completes development inside a pouch in the mother. The most common mammal found today belongs to the subclass of placental mammals, characterized by the development of the fetus inside of the mother's body. Humans are placental mammals.

PLACENTAL MAMMALS   The **placenta** is an organ that develops inside the female during pregnancy. It functions as a link between the circulatory systems of the mother and child, acting to transport food, oxygen, and antibodies as well as to filter out waste products. The efficiency of the placenta means that the developing offspring of placental mammals have a much greater chance of survival than does a reptile developing in an egg or in a nonplacental mammal (both egg layers and marsupials, Figures 6.3 and 6.4). Development inside the mother provides warmth and protection along with proper nutrition. Although placental mammals appear at first glance to be superior to egg-laying reptiles, the presence of a placenta has a cost as well as a benefit. Pregnant mammals consume a great deal of energy, making ample food resources vital to successful birth. Also, the demand on energy sets a limit on the number of offspring any female mammal can have at one time.

Chordata A vertebrate phylum consisting of organisms that possess a notochord at some period during their life.

notochord A flexible internal rod that runs along the back of an animal.

Vertebrata A subphylum of the phylum Chordata, defined by the presence of an internal, segmented spinal column and bilateral symmetry.

bilateral symmetry Symmetry in which the right and left sides of the body are approximately mirror images.

placenta An organ that develops inside a pregnant placental mammal that provides the fetus with oxygen and food and helps filter out harmful substances.

■ FIGURE 6.3
The spiny anteater, an egg-laying mammal. (© Zoological Society of San Diego)

■ FIGURE 6.4
The wallaby, a marsupial mammal. (© Wildlife Conservation Society)

A main feature of mammals is the female mammary glands, which provide food for the newborn infant. Important immunities are also provided in mother's milk. The ready availability of food increases the child's chance of survival. Although advantageous, nursing also has a price; energy is expended by the mother during this process, and only a limited number of offspring can be taken care of at one time.

PARENTAL CARE The **prenatal** (before birth) and **postnatal** (after birth) patterns of parental care in mammals contrast with those of reptiles, which expend less energy during reproduction and care of offspring. Pregnancy and raising offspring take energy; the more offspring an organism has, the less care a parent can give each of them. Consequently, some animals have many offspring but provide little care to them while other animals have few offspring and provide much more care to each.

Species vary in terms of the balance between number of offspring and degree of parental care. One extreme example is the oyster, which produces roughly half a billion eggs a year and provides no parental care. Fish can produce 8,000 eggs a year with a slight amount of parental care. Frogs can lay 200 eggs a year with slightly more parental care.

Compared to other animals, mammals have relatively few offspring but provide much more parental care. The development of the placenta and the mammary glands are biological features that maximize the amount of care given to an offspring. A female lion, for example, has only two offspring per year and provides a great deal of care to them. An extreme example among mammals is the orangutan, an ape that has roughly one child every eight years (Galdikas and Wood 1990).

From an evolutionary viewpoint, which strategy is better: Having many offspring but providing little care, or having fewer offspring and providing greater care? Each strategy has its advantages and disadvantages. In general, those species that have many offspring tend to be at an advantage in rapidly changing environments, whereas those that provide greater care are at an advantage in more stable environments (Pianka 1983).

HUMAN REPRODUCTION AND CHILD CARE As mammals, humans beings have few offspring and provide a great deal of care to each. However, we also differ from the general pattern in that we have more offspring than our closest relatives, the apes, and still provide a great deal of parental care. Our pattern of reproduction is different from that of apes in that we do not wait until a child is fully mature before having another. We most often have one child at a time,

▲▲▲

prenatal The period of life from conception until birth.

postnatal The period of life from birth until death.

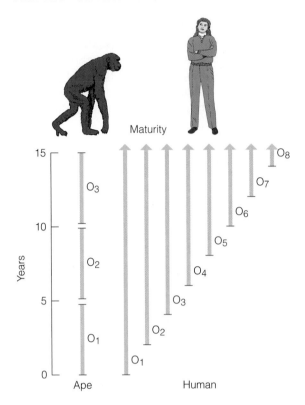

■ **FIGURE 6.5**
Birth spacing in apes and humans over a 15-year period. The letter *O* refers to different offspring born during this time period. In apes, the female gives birth to an offspring roughly every five years: the time required for the offspring to reach maturity. Modern humans do not wait for a child to reach maturity (roughly 15 years) before having another child. Instead, births overlap one another (in this example the overlap is two years). This overlap is possibly a consequence of cultural adaptations that allow the care of more than one child at a time. The result is that humans can have more offspring in a given period of time without sacrificing parental care.

but their periods of dependency on us overlap (Figure 6.5). For example, a woman may give birth to a child and then two years later have another baby, when the first child is not anywhere near maturity. Compared to apes, human females can have more children in a given period of time. We do not, however, sacrifice the amount of parental care given to each child.

Temperature Regulation

Modern mammals are **homoiotherms;** they are able to maintain a constant body temperature under most circumstances. Modern reptiles are cold-blooded and cannot keep their body temperature constant; they need to use the heat of the sun's rays to keep them warm and their metabolism active. Mammals maintain a constant body temperature in several ways. Mammals are covered with fur or hair that insulates the body, preventing heat loss in cold weather and reducing overheating in hot weather. Temporary changes in the size of blood vessels also aid in temperature regulation. When blood vessels contract (vasoconstriction), blood flow is reduced and less heat is lost from the mammal's extremities. When blood vessels dilate (vasodilation), blood flow is increased to the extremities, thus allowing greater heat loss.

Mammals also maintain a constant body temperature by ingesting large quantities of food and converting the food to energy in the form of heat. When you feel hot, your body is not losing the produced heat quickly enough. When you feel cold, you are losing heat too quickly. The ability to convert food energy to heat allows mammals to live comfortably in many environments where reptiles would slow down or even die.

Mammals are thus able to exploit a large number of environments. Heat production and temperature regulation, however, though obviously useful adaptations in certain environments, are not without a price. To obtain energy, mammals need to consume far greater quantities of food than reptiles. In environments where food resources are limited, mammals may be worse off than reptiles. Again, the evolutionary benefit of any trait must be looked at in terms of its cost.

Humans, of course, have gone beyond the basic temperature-regulating abilities of other mammals. We have developed a variety of technologies that help keep us warm or cool. Fire and clothes were the earliest inventions of this sort. Today we have all sorts of heating and cooling devices that enable us to live in virtually any environment on the earth, as well as in outer space. Our culture has allowed us to go beyond our biological limits.

Teeth

The saying, "You are what you eat," is not usually made literally, but in fact it embodies an important truth of ecology and evolution. The nutritional requirements of organisms dictate, in part, their environmental needs. Also, diet is reflected in the physical structure of organisms, particularly the teeth and jaws. Because mammals maintain a constant body temperature by converting food energy to heat, they require a considerable amount of food. The physical features of mammalian teeth reflect this need.

The teeth of modern reptiles are all the same; they all have sharp sides and continue to grow throughout life. The function of reptilian teeth is to hold and kill prey. The food is then most often eaten whole. Mammals, on the other hand, have different types of teeth in their jaws. Mammals only have two sets of teeth during their lives: a set of deciduous ("baby") teeth and a set of permanent teeth. As a mammal grows and matures, the baby teeth fall out and are replaced with the adult teeth. In modern humans this replacement normally starts around age 6 and takes the first 18 or 20 years of life to complete.

homoiotherm
Organism capable of maintaining a constant body temperature under most circumstances.

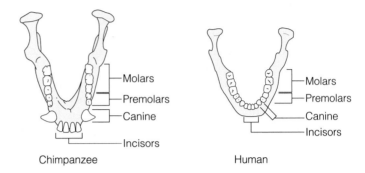

Chimpanzee   Human

TYPES OF TEETH   Mammals have four types of teeth: **incisors, canines, premolars,** and **molars.** These teeth are shown for a chimpanzee and a human in
Figure 6.6. The incisor teeth are flat and located in the front of the jaw. Both
the human and the chimpanzee (and other higher primates) have a total of
four incisors in each jaw. These teeth are used for cutting and slicing of food.
You use your incisors when you eat an apple or corn on the cob. Behind the
incisors are the canine teeth, which are often long and sharp, resembling
fangs or tusks. Apes and humans have two canine teeth in each jaw. In many
mammals the canine teeth are used as weapons or to kill prey. Although the
canine teeth of most mammals are rather large and project beyond the level
of the rest of the teeth, human canines are usually small and nonprojecting.
The explanation of small canine teeth in humans has been a major source of
controversy among anthropologists and will be discussed in later chapters
on human evolution.

The premolar and molar teeth are also known collectively as the back
teeth. Both of these types of teeth are often large in surface area and are
used for grinding and chewing food. When you chew food between your
back teeth, you do not simply move your lower jaw up and down. Instead,
your upper and lower back teeth grind together in a circular motion as your
jaw moves up and down and sideways as well. The structure of the premolar
and molar teeth are different, and in some mammals they have different
functions as well.

DENTAL FORMULAE   Mammals can be characterized by the number of each type
of tooth they have. The usual method of counting teeth is to consider the
number of each type of tooth in one half of one jaw, upper or lower. Only
one half of the jaw is considered because both right and left sides of the jaw
contain the same number of teeth. These numbers are expressed using a
dental formula, which lists the number of incisors, canines, premolars, and
molars in one half of a jaw. A dental formula looks like this: I-C-PM-M.
Here I = number of incisors, C = number of canines, PM = number of
premolars, and M = number of molars. For example, the typical dental for-

mula of humans (as well as apes and some monkeys) is 2-1-2-3. This means that in one half of either jaw there are two incisors, one canine, two premolars, and three molars. Each half of each jaw therefore contains $2 + 1 + 2 + 3 = 8$ teeth. The typical number of teeth in humans is therefore $8 \times 4 = 32$ (two sides of each of two jaws). Some mammals have different numbers of teeth in the top and bottom jaws. In these cases, we use two dental formulae. For example, a dental formula of $\frac{2\text{-}1\text{-}2\text{-}3}{2\text{-}1\text{-}2\text{-}2}$ would indicate two fewer molars in the lower jaw.

DIET AND TEETH   The basic description of the types of teeth is somewhat simplistic. Many mammals have evolved specialized uses of one or more of these tooth types. As noted earlier, human canines are rather different in form and function from those of many other mammals. The general description is useful, however, in showing the importance of differentiated teeth in mammals. By having different types of teeth capable of slicing, cutting, and grinding, mammals are able to eat a wide variety of different foods in an efficient way. The sharp fanglike teeth of reptiles are good for catching and killing prey, but useless for eating plants, fruits, and nuts. Mammals can eat all these different types of food. In addition, the ability to chew the food rather than swallow it whole allows greater efficiency in eating. By chewing, mammals break down the food into smaller pieces that can be digested more easily and efficiently. Also, saliva released in the mouth during chewing begins the process of digestion.

The nature of mammalian diet and teeth relates to their warm-bloodedness. Mammals need more food than reptiles, and their teeth allow them to utilize a wider range of food and to process it more productively. The benefits of differentiated teeth lie in these abilities. The cost is the fact that the teeth tend to wear out over time. When a mammal's adult teeth are worn down, it may not be able to eat or may develop serious dental problems, which could lead to death. As far as recent humans are concerned, we can circumvent these potential problems to a certain extent with dental technology, hygiene, and processed foods. Even so, dental problems continue to pose serious difficulties to human health.

incisor The flat front teeth used for cutting, slicing, and gnawing food.

canine The teeth located in front of the jaw behind the incisors

that are normally used by mammals for puncturing and defense.

premolar One of the types of back teeth

used for crushing and grinding food.

molar The teeth furthest back in the jaw used for crushing and grinding food.

dental formula A shorthand method of describing the number of each type of tooth in one half of one jaw on a mammal.

■ FIGURE 6.7
The orientation of the limbs
to the body in reptiles and in
mammals.

Reptile   Mammal

Skeletal Structure

Both mammals and reptiles share the basic skeletal structure of all vertebrates, but there are some differences, especially in movement. In reptiles,
the four limbs come out from the side of the body for support and movement (Figure 6.7). In four-legged mammals, the limbs slope downward from
the shoulders and hips. Having the limbs tucked in under the body allows
more efficient and quicker movement. The weight of the body is supported
better. Humans differ from the pattern of many mammals by using only two
limbs for movement. Even so, the configuration of the legs follows the basic
pattern; the legs slope inward from the hips and are not splayed out to the
sides.

Behavior

The brains of all vertebrates have similar structures but differ in size, relative
proportions, and functions. All vertebrates have a hindbrain, a midbrain,
and a forebrain. In most vertebrates, the hindbrain is associated with hearing, balance, reflexive behaviors, and control of the autonomic functions of

the body, such as breathing. The midbrain is associated with vision, and the forebrain is associated with chemical sensing such as smelling ability. Compared to fish, reptiles have a relatively larger midbrain and hindbrain because they rely more extensively on vision and hearing. The midbrain of a reptile is particularly enlarged because it functions to coordinate sensory information and body movements.

The brain of a mammal reveals several important shifts in structure and function. The mammalian brain has a greatly enlarged forebrain that is responsible for the processing of sensory information and coordination. In particular, the forebrain contains the **cerebrum,** the outermost layer of brain cells, which is associated with learning, memory, and intelligence. The cerebrum becomes increasingly convoluted, which allows huge numbers of interconnections between brain cells. It accounts for the largest proportion of the mammalian brain.

The overall functions of a brain include basic body maintenance as well as the ability to process information and respond accordingly. Mammals rely more on learning and flexible responses than do reptiles. Behaviors are less instinctual and rigid. Previous experiences (learning) become more important in responding to stimuli. As a consequence, mammals are more capable of developing new responses to different situations and are capable of learning from past mistakes. New behaviors are more likely to develop and can be passed on to offspring through the process of learning. Humans have taken this process even further; our very existence depends on flexible behaviors that must be learned. Although our behavior is to a large extent cultural, our ability to transfer information through learning relies on a biological trait: the mammalian brain.

The behavioral flexibility of mammals ties in with their pattern of reproduction. In general, the more a species relies on parental care, the more intelligent it is and the more it relies on learning rather than instinct. Extensive parental care requires increased intelligence and the ability to learn new behaviors in order to provide maximum care for infants. The increased emphasis on learning requires, in turn, an extended period of childhood during which to absorb the information needed for the adult life. Furthermore, the extension of childhood requires more extensive child care, so that offspring are protected during the time they need to complete their growth and learning.

The major characteristics of mammals are all interrelated. Reproductive behaviors are associated with learning, intelligence, and social behaviors. The ability to maintain body temperature is related to diet and teeth; warm-bloodedness requires vast amounts of energy that in turn is made available from differentiated teeth and a wide dietary base. Also, the reproductive pattern of placental mammals requires great amounts of energy, which in turn relates to diet. In fact, the major characteristics of any group of animals are not merely a list of independent traits; they represent an integrated complex of traits.

▲▲▲▲▲▲▲▲▲▲▲▲▲▲▲▲▲▲▲▲▲▲▲▲▲▲▲▲▲▲

cerebrum The area of the forebrain that consists of the outermost layer of brain cells, associated with memory, learning, and intelligence.

PRIMATE CHARACTERISTICS

There are many different forms of mammals—they are as diverse as mice, whales, giraffes, cats, dogs, and apes. Patterns of biology and behavior vary considerably, although all mammals share to some extent the basic characteristics outlined in the last section.

Recall that the mammalian class is broken down into a number of orders. Humans, as noted, are primates, as are the apes, such as the chimpanzee and gorilla, which are our closest living relatives. Monkeys are also primates, as are more biologically primitive forms known as prosimians. The basic characteristics of primates are discussed in this section, along with a brief survey of the prosimians and monkeys. The next chapter describes variation in the biology and behavior of primates, including a discussion of different types of primates.

No single characteristic identifies primates; rather, they share a set of features. Many of these features relate to living in the trees. Though it is clear that humans, as well as other modern primates, do not live in the trees, they still retain certain features inherited from ancestors who did.

An **arboreal** (tree-living) environment presents different challenges than a **terrestrial** (ground-living) environment. Living in the trees requires an orientation to a three-dimensional environment. Animals that live on the ground generally contend with only two dimensions: length and width. Arboreal animals must also deal with the third dimension, height. Perception of distance and depth is vital to a tree-living form, which moves quickly from one branch to the next, and from one level of the forest to another. Agility is also important, as is the ability to anchor oneself in space.

Many forms of animals, such as squirrels and birds, have adapted to living in the trees. Primates, however, are capable of extensive rapid movement through the trees and are able to move to all areas of a tree, including small terminal branches. A squirrel can climb up and down the trunk of a tree and even large branches, but primates are better equipped to move out to feed on even the smallest of branches. The two major characteristics of primates that account for their success in the trees are the ability to use hands and feet to grasp branches (rather than digging in with claws), and the ability to perceive distance and depth.

Although many primate characteristics relate to living in the trees, some controversy has arisen over whether the *initial* evolution of these traits was the result of arboreal adaptations. Noting that other mammals, such as squirrels, have adapted to the trees without having grasping hands or depth perception, Cartmill (1974) has suggested an alternative for the origin of primate characteristics. He suggests that grasping hands and depth perception first evolved as adaptations for insect hunting in low branches. Later, these features were adapted for life in the trees. In this section, we examine both the arboreal adaptation and insect predation models. The fossil evidence bearing on these models is discussed in Chapter 9.

Not all modern primates have kept the original adaptations of the first primates. For example, humans can still use their hands to grasp objects but cannot do so with their feet. We do not normally use our hands to grasp and hang onto branches. We have taken our inherited ability to grasp and put it to work in another arena: we hold tools, weapons, food, and children. The grasping hands of a human and a tree-living monkey are homologous—that is, they are similar structures because of common descent. The different functions of the hands of humans and tree-living monkeys reflect adaptive changes from the original primate ancestors. Even though humans do things differently, we are still primates and have the basic set of primate characteristics.

The Skeleton

First let us consider some general characteristics in the primate skeletal structure.

GRASPING HANDS A characteristic of the earliest known mammals (and reptiles) is five digits on each hand or foot. Certain mammals, such as the horse, have changed from this ancestral condition and only have a single toe on each limb. Other mammals, such as the primates, have kept the ancestral condition.

Primates, including humans, are primitive in the number of digits on the hands and feet. This statement is confusing because it is hard to reconcile the possession of a primitive trait with the idea that primates, especially humans, represent advanced forms. The problem with such an interpretation is that the term *primitive* is often taken as a sign of being inferior or less "advanced." However, in a biological sense, it simply means that certain traits have not greatly changed since some earlier ancestor. Whether a primitive or derived trait is adaptive or not depends on the specific set of environmental circumstances, not on how old or new a trait is. New is not necessarily better.

In the case of primates, the retention of the primitive characteristics of five digits on the hands and feet turned out to be an important adaptation. The hands and feet of primates are **prehensile,** meaning that they are capable of being used to grasp objects. The ability to grasp involves the movement of the fingers to the palm, thus allowing the fingers to wrap around an object. In many primates, the toes can also wrap around an object. This grasping ability is a remarkable adaptation to living in the trees. Primates can

▲▲▲

arboreal Living in trees.

terrestrial Living on the ground.

prehensile Capable of grasping.

grab onto branches to move about, to provide support while eating, and in general to allow for a high degree of flexibility in moving about their environment. More specialized structures, such as the horse's single hoof, would be useless in the trees because there would be no way to grasp branches.

Another feature of primate hands and feet is their expanded tactile pads (such as the ball of your thumb) and nails instead of claws. Nails serve to protect the sensitive skin at the ends of the fingers and the toes. The numerous nerve endings in the tips of fingers and toes of primates provide an enhanced sense of touch that is useful in manipulating objects.

As mentioned earlier, the characteristics possessed by primates are not the only possible solution to the challenge of living in the trees. Squirrels, for example, use their claws to dig into the bark of limbs and branches when they climb in the trees. The grasping ability of primate hands, however, provides much greater flexibility. Food can be reached at the end of small branches by grasping surrounding branches for support, using a free arm to reach out and grab the food, and then bringing it to the mouth. A small branch might not provide enough surface area for a squirrel to dig its claws into, but a primate can use its grasping hands and feet to hold onto it.

Variations on these themes occur even within primates. Some of the more biologically primitive primates, for example, have a single claw on each hand and foot that they use for specialized purposes. Humans also differ from the general primate conditions. We have lost the ability to use our feet for grasping as a result of anatomical changes relating to our ability to walk on two legs. We also have an enhanced ability for fine manipulation of our fingers in addition to the basic grasping ability.

GENERALIZED STRUCTURE   Biological structures are often classified as specialized or generalized. **Specialized structures** are used in a highly specific way, whereas **generalized structures** can be used in a variety of ways. The hooves of a horse, for example, are a specialization that allows rapid running over land surfaces. The basic skeletal structure of primates is generalized because it allows movement flexibility in a wide variety of circumstances.

The arm and leg bones of primates follow the basic pattern of many vertebrates: each limb consists of an upper bone and two lower bones (refer back to Figure 6.1). This structure allows limbs to bend at the elbows or knees. In climbing or jumping in a tree, you must have this flexibility or you would not be able to move about (imagine trying to jump from one branch to another with your arms and legs made up of one long bone). That the lower part of the limb is made up of two bones provides even greater flexibility. Hold your arm out straight in front of you with your palm down. Now turn your hand so that the palm side is up. This is easy to do, but only because we have two lower arm bones. When turning the hand over, one lower arm bone crosses over the other. Imagine trying to climb in a tree without the ability to move your hand into different positions. This flexibility is obtained by the retention of a generalized skeletal structure.

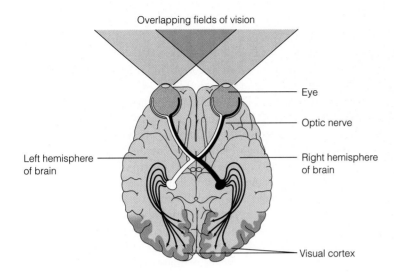
Overlapping fields of vision

Eye

Optic nerve

Left hemisphere
of brain

Right hemisphere
of brain

Visual cortex

■ FIGURE 6.8
Binocular stereoscopic vision
in primates. The fields of
vision for each eye overlap,
and the optic nerve from each
eye is connected to both
hemispheres of the brain.
(From *Human Antiquity: An
Introduction to Physical
Anthropology and Archaeology*, 2d
ed., by Kenneth Feder and Michael
Park. Fig. 5.1. Copyright © 1993
by Mayfield Publishing Company)

Although the grasping hands and generalized skeletons of primates can
be interpreted as arboreal adaptations, Cartmill (1974) raises the possibility
that they first arose as adaptations to insect predation. Grasping hands and
feet would be valuable for running along the ground and on small branches
in search of insects. Once these traits evolved, they could then have been
valuable for further use in arboreal environments.

Vision

The three-dimensional nature of arboreal life requires keen eyesight, particularly depth perception. This feature has evolved from the need to judge distances successfully. (Jumping through the air from branch to branch
demands the ability to judge distances. After all, it is not very adaptive to fall
short of your target and plunge to the ground!)

Depth perception involves **binocular stereoscopic vision.** *Binocular*
refers to overlapping fields of vision. The eyes of many animals are located
at the sides of the skull so that each eye receives a different image with no
overlap (Figure 6.8). The eyes of primates are located in the front of the

▲▲

specialized structure
A biological structure
adapted to a narrow
range of conditions and
used in very specific
ways.

generalized structure
A biological structure
adapted to a wide range
of conditions and used
in very general ways.

**binocular stereoscopic
vision** Overlapping
fields of vision with
both sides of the brain
receiving images from
both eyes, thereby

providing depth
perception.

skull so that the fields of vision overlap. Primates see objects in front of them with both eyes. The *stereoscopic* nature of primate vision refers to the way in which the brain processes visual signals. In nonstereoscopic animals, the information from one eye is received in only one hemisphere of the brain. In primates, the visual signals from both eyes are received in both hemispheres of the brain. The result is an image that has depth. Moving quickly and safely in three dimensions makes use of depth perception.

Many primates also have the ability to perceive colors. Color vision is extremely useful in detecting objects in moderate-contrast environments. In fact, color vision is found in other animals for this reason, including whales, fish, bumblebees, and certain birds. Color vision is also important in primate species that use color as a visual signal of various emotional states, such as anger, or receptivity to sexual relations.

Primates are vision-oriented. On average, their sense of smell is less keen. As a result, the areas of the face devoted to smelling are reduced in primates. Compared to other mammals, primates have short snouts.

The Brain and Behavior

Primates have expanded on the basic pattern of mammalian brains. Their brains are even larger relative to body size. Primate brains have larger visual areas and smaller areas for smelling, corresponding to their increased emphasis of vision over smell as the main sense. Also, primate brains are even more complex than those of most other mammals. Primates have larger proportions of the brain associated with learning and intelligence. Areas of the brain associated with body control and coordination are also proportionately larger, as expected from the demands of arboreal life. Hand–eye coordination, for example, is crucial for moving about in the trees.

LEARNING   The greater size and complexity of primate brains are reflected in their behaviors. Primates rely even more extensively than other mammals on learned behaviors. As a result, it is often difficult to assign specific behaviors to a given species of primate because the increased emphasis on learning allows a great deal of flexibility in behavior patterns.

The increased emphasis on learning means that primates spend a greater proportion of their lives growing up, both biologically and socially, than other animals. The more an animal needs to learn, the longer the period of time needed for learning. An increase in the amount of time spent as an infant or child further means that greater amounts of attention and care are required from parents. Again, we see the intimate relationship among reproduction, care of offspring, learning, and intelligence.

The basic pattern of primate learning provides a means by which new behaviors can be passed on from one generation to the next. If we define culture simply as learned behavior, it is obvious that all primates can be said

■ FIGURE 6.9
A macaque washing food in water. (Steve Gaulin/Anthro-Photo)

to have culture. Most of the time, however, the distinctive nature of human culture is identified as its reliance on language for transmission. Within this framework, the cultural behaviors and social organization of nonhuman primates are often referred to as *protoculture*. No matter what terms we use, however, or how we define human and nonhuman culture, the fact remains that social learning provides a means by which behaviors are passed on from one generation to the next in all primates (and, indeed, in many other mammals).

AN EXAMPLE OF LEARNING IN PRIMATES   Primate studies have provided many good examples of the introduction of new behaviors to a group by one or more individuals that are then learned by other individuals. Studies of the Japanese macaque monkeys on the island of Koshima during the 1950s revealed a number of cases of cultural transmission of new behaviors. The Koshima troop has been provisioned (provided with food) since the early 1950s to keep all the monkeys out in the open for observation purposes (Figure 6.9).

   In 1953, a young female macaque named Imo began washing sweet potatoes in a stream before eating them. Within three years, this behavior had been learned by almost half of the troop. Two years later, only two adults continued this practice. Of the 19 younger monkeys, 15 had adopted this behavior, however, and thereafter almost all newborn infants acquired it by observing their mothers (Bramblett 1976).

Another food-related behavior developed among the troop in 1956 when scientists began feeding the monkeys grains of wheat. The wheat was scattered on a sandy beach to slow down the monkeys' eating so that researchers would have more time to study them. Imo developed a new method of eating the grains of wheat. She took handfuls of sand and wheat down to the water and threw them in. The sand sank while the wheat floated, thus letting her skim the grains off the surface of the water. This new behavior provided a much quicker way of getting the wheat than picking out grains from the sand. The young female's method of wheat washing spread quickly through most of the rest of the troop (Bramblett 1976).

The studies of cultural transmission among the Japanese macaques show the importance of learning in primate societies. The washing of sweet potatoes and the separation of wheat and sand are not innate behaviors in Japanese macaques. These behaviors are transmitted through learning, not genetic inheritance. The studies also show the importance of individual behavior: in both cases, the same monkey introduced the behaviors. If that monkey were not present in that troop, these behaviors might not have developed.

Reproduction and Care of Offspring

As with all mammals, primates are characterized by a small number of offspring and a great deal of parental care. Almost all primates have a reproductive pattern of having one offspring at a time. The next offspring is not born until the previous one is mature enough, biologically and socially, to survive on its own. In some primates, such as the apes, there may be as much as five or more years between offspring. As mentioned earlier, humans are an exception to this rule because we can have overlapping births without sacrificing the quality of parental care.

THE MOTHER–INFANT BOND   Primates have a strong and long-lasting bond between mother and infant. Unlike some mammals, infant primates are entirely helpless. They depend on their mothers for food, warmth, protection, affection, and knowledge, and they remain dependent for a long time. Of all the different types of social bonds in primate societies, the mother–infant bond is the strongest. In many primate species this bond continues well past childhood. Chimpanzees, for example, regularly associate with their mothers through their adult lives (Goodall 1986).

The biological importance of the mother–infant bond is easy to see: the infants are dependent on mother's milk for nourishment. Is that all there is to it? Earlier in this century, some researchers suggested that the entire basis of "mother love" seen in primate infants arose from the infant's need for

food. Laboratory experiments and field observations soon showed that this is not the case; the social aspects of the mother–infant bond are also crucial for survival.

One of the most famous of these experiments was performed by psychologist Harry Harlow, who isolated infant rhesus monkeys from their mothers. He raised them in cages in which he placed two "surrogate mothers," the first a wire framework in the approximate shape of an adult monkey and the second the same structure covered with terry cloth. He then attached a bottle of milk to the "wire mother" (Figure 6.10). Harlow reasoned that if the need for food were stronger than the need for warmth and comfort, the infant monkeys would spend most or all of their time clinging to the "wire mother." If the need for warmth and comfort were more important, the infant would spend most or all of the time clinging to the "cloth mother." The monkeys invariably preferred the warmth and security of the "cloth mothers" to the food provided by the "wire mothers." Even when the infants needed to eat, they often kept part of their body in contact with the "cloth mother." Additional experiments showed that under the stimulus of stress or fear, the monkeys would go to the "cloth mothers" for security (Harlow 1959).

These experiments showed that motherhood was not merely important in terms of nutrition; warmth and comfort were also necessary in an infant's development. But do these experiments mean that natural mothers can be replaced by a bottle and a blanket? Definitely not. As Harlow's monkeys grew up, they showed a wide range of abnormal behaviors. They were often incapable of sexual reproduction, they could not interact normally with other monkeys, and they often were extremely aggressive. The motherless females who later had children did not know how to take care of them and often rejected and mistreated them.

What Will Happen to the Primates?

There are over 230 species of living primates in the world today. Among them, they show a great deal of biological and behavioral variation. Some of these primates, however, such as the mountain gorilla, are currently endangered species. In fact, it is estimated that more than half of the living primate species have small and decreasing populations, and perhaps as much as 20 percent will be extinct by sometime in the next century (Mittermeier and Sterling 1992).

What has caused this danger to living primates? One major factor is the destruction of native habitats. This is a particular danger for primates that live in tropical rain forests, which are being destroyed through forest clearing at a high rate (Wright 1992). Other environments and species, such as the mountain gorilla, whose habitat has been reduced through farming to meet the demands for food of a growing human population, are also in danger. Today, there may be fewer than 400 surviving mountain gorillas (Mittermeier and Sterling 1992).

Hunting by humans is another threat to primate survival. In addition to being a food resource, primates are hunted in many parts of the world for use as bait for other animals, for sale of their body parts as ornaments, and because they are considered agricultural pests. Another threat to primates is the capture of live animals for sale, although international efforts have reduced this demand to some extent. Live capture is particularly a problem when infants are sought after, because the mothers are shot during the capture (Mittermeier and Sterling 1992).

What can be done? There is no single solution—a series of conservation efforts must be applied at an international level. To date, such efforts have led to protected parks and reserves, greater education, development of less harmful agricultural alternatives (thus preserving the environments), and the breeding of endangered primates in captivity (Mittermeier and Sterling 1992; Wright 1992). All of these approaches must continue and be expanded if we are to save the diversity of this remarkable group of our relatives.

These findings have powerful implications. We often speak of "maternal instincts," suggesting that the behaviors associated with successful mothering are somehow innate. Although the basic bond between mother and infant is part of the biological basis of mammals, and maternal feelings are to some extent innate, the specific behaviors that are part of this bond are learned. Mammals, and especially primates, rely extensively on learned behaviors. As a result, variation in behavior is often great and can be influenced by a variety of other factors. Observations of the behavior of primates in their natural environments confirm the fact that maternal behaviors are to a large extent learned. Studies of chimpanzee mothers have shown that young females tend to model their own later parental behaviors after those of their mothers. Similar patterns are seen in humans. For example, the children of abusive parents often tend to be abusive parents themselves. Such research shows us that the study of animal behavior, especially that of other primates, is not an esoteric subject but rather helps us in understanding ourselves.

PATERNAL CARE Maternal care is found throughout the primate order. The mother–infant bond is the strongest social tie within primate groups. What role does the father play in child care among primates? Paternal care is highly variable among primate species. In general, primates that are **monogamous**

(characterized by a more or less permanent bond forming between a single male and female) are most likely to show high levels of paternal care. For example, gibbons (an Asian ape) and many South American monkey species are monogamous and also show frequent participation of fathers in child care. In fact, in some species the fathers do most of the carrying of infants (Jolly 1985). By contrast, species that are polygamous tend, on average, to show less paternal involvement with offspring. This difference may relate to the fact that in monogamous species it is easy for the male to tell he is the father! In a **polygamous** species, paternal behaviors may be less appropriate from a genetic perspective because a male can never be sure if he is the father.

As with many primate behaviors, there is a great deal of variation from one situation to the next. In the a recent study of baboons (an African monkey), Connie Anderson (1992) found regularity in the degree of paternal behaviors. In cases where females mated with a single male more than 70 percent of the time, that male was much more likely to help by carrying the infant. This finding shows that it is often difficult, if not impossible, to ascribe a given behavior to an entire species, because there is often a great deal of variation even within single populations. These results also suggest that adult males are aware of the frequency of mating, thus providing them with some idea of the likely paternity of a child. From an evolutionary perspective, we would expect males to invest time and effort in their own infants, at least infants with a high probability of having been sired by them.

GROWING UP   The importance of the extended period of infant and child growth in primates cannot be overstated. The long period of growth is necessary for learning motor skills and social behaviors. The close bond between mother and infant provides the first important means by which an infant primate learns. It is not the only important social contact for a growing primate, however. The process of socialization in most primates depends to a large extent on close contact with peers. Interaction with other individuals of the same age provides the opportunity to learn specific types of social behaviors as well as how to interact socially in general.

Experiments by Harlow clearly demonstrate the importance of social contact with peers. Monkeys raised by their mothers but kept apart from other infants often grew up showing a range of abnormal behaviors. They would stare at their cages for long periods of time, were often self-destructive, and did not show normal patterns of sexual behavior (Harlow and Harlow 1962). Although some primate species are basically solitary

monogamy An exclusive sexual bond between an adult male and an adult female for a long period of time.

polygamy A sexual bond between an adult male and an adult female in which either individual may have more than one mate at the same time.

apart from the mother–infant bond, most belong to larger social groups and require contact with peers during their growth.

Growing up and learning as a primate also requires that infants and children play a great deal of the time. Play behaviors have often been ignored in studies of human and nonhuman behavior because they are regarded as nonproductive behavior. In truth, play behaviors are essential to the proper biological and social development of primates.

Play behavior can serve several functions. First, physical play allows an infant to develop and practice necessary motor skills. Second, social play provides the opportunity to learn how to behave with others. Needed social skills are learned through play. The importance of play becomes very obvious when we consider what happened to the monkeys that Harlow had separated from their peers. Without normal contact and the opportunity to develop socially, these monkeys become sociopathic.

Social Structure

Primates are essentially social creatures. The close bond between mother and infant, the importance of learning, and the great flexibility in behaviors all point to this fact. Apart from this general need, primates show an amazing amount of variation in the ways in which their societies are structured. The main social group of primates can range in size from two individuals up to several hundred and can have different proportions of males, females, young, and old.

A social group is generally defined as a group within which there is frequent communication or interaction among members. This definition is a big arbitrary, but it provides us with a starting point for looking at variation in primate societies. **Social structure** consists of the composition of the social group and the way in which it is organized. There are five basic types of primate social structure, with variations on most of these.

SOCIAL GROUPS   The smallest social group is the **solitary group,** which consists of the mother and dependent offspring. Adult males and adult females have infrequent contact, generally for mating. A slightly larger social group is the **monogamous family group,** consisting of an adult male, an adult female, and their immature offspring. The adult male and female form a long-term pair bond, and are sexually active only with each other. Although this corresponds to a typical Western notion of "family," it is not that common among primates. The social unit of a few primate species is the **polyandrous group,** a small group of adult males and one or more adult females and their offspring. Although there may be more than one adult female in the group, only one is reproductively active. A **uni-male group** consists of one adult male, several adult females, and their offspring. The most common social structure in nonhuman primate societies is the **multimale/multifemale**

■ **FIGURE 6.11**
Two adult male baboons
engaged in a dominance
dispute. Though physical
violence does occur in
such encounters, much of
the display is bluff. (Irven
Devore/Anthro-Photo)

group, which consists of more than one adult of each sex and the offspring. Given multiple adult males and adult females, these are complex social groups that are often quite large. Given multiple adults, mating tends to be promiscuous. There is considerable variation in this type of social structure, in terms of size, composition, and distribution (Wolfe 1995).

SOCIAL ORGANIZATION AND DOMINANCE   Nonhuman primate societies rank individuals in terms of their relative dominance in the group. A **dominance hierarchy** is the ranking system within the society and reflects which individuals are most and least dominant (Figure 6.11). Dominance hierarchies are found

social structure The composition of a social group and the way it is organized, including size, age structure, and number of each sex in the group.

solitary group The smallest primate social group, consisting of the mother and her dependent offspring.

monogamous family group Social structure in which the primary social group consists of an adult male, an adult female, and their immature offspring.

polyandrous group A rare type of primate social structure, consisting of a small number of adult males, one reproductively active adult female, and

their offspring. Other adult females may belong to the group but are not reproductively active.

uni-male group Social structure in which the primary social group consists of a single adult male, several adult females, and their offspring.

multimale/multifemale group A type of social structure in which the primary social group is made up of several adult males, several adult females, and their offspring.

dominance hierarchy The ranking system within a society that indicates which individuals are dominant in social behaviors.

in most nonhuman primate societies, but they vary widely in their overall importance in everyday life. The dominance hierarchy provides stability in social life. All individuals know their place within the society, eliminating to some extent uncertainty about what to do or whom to follow.

The dominance hierarchy in nonhuman primates is usually ruled by those individuals with the greatest access to food or sex or those that control social behaviors to the greatest extent. Societies with strong male dominance hierarchies are likely to show a moderate to large difference in the sizes of adult males and adult females. The **sexual dimorphism** in body size has often been considered the result of competition among males for breeding females. The males that are larger and stronger are considered more likely to gain access to females and hence pass on their genetic potential for larger size and greater strength.

This pattern does not always hold, however. The adult male most likely to attract mates may not be the male most likely to have access to food. Fedigan (1983) has reviewed the literature on the relationship between dominance rank of males and access to breeding females for a number of primate species and has found that this expected relationship is not always present.

We also see that dominance may reflect additional factors. In the Japanese macaque monkeys, for example, the rank of a male's mother has an influence on the male's dominance rank (Eaton 1976). Males born to high-ranking mothers have a greater chance of achieving high dominance themselves, all other factors being equal.

In a number of primate societies, the dominance hierarchy of females is more stable over time than that of the males. Whereas the position of most dominant male can change quickly, the hierarchy among females remains more constant over time. Even in cases where all males are dominant over females, the female dominance hierarchy exerts an effect on social behaviors within the group, such as the case discussed earlier of mother's rank affecting the rank of male offspring.

MODELS OF PRIMATE BEHAVIOR

In terms of both biology and behavior, primates are an extremely variable group of mammals. The exact nature of this variability is explored in the next chapter, which reviews the different subgroups of living primates. For now, however, it is useful to consider the types of evolutionary models that we use to make some sense of this variation. Two different approaches to the subject are discussed briefly here, along with some examples. Additional examples of primate behavior are covered in the next chapter.

The two explanatory models discussed here are socioecology and sociobiology. It is important to understand that these approaches are *not* mutually exclusive; they tend to overlap considerably. The ultimate objective is to provide explanations of primate behavior from an evolutionary perspective, particularly the complex interaction of nature and nurture.

Socioecology

The study of **socioecology** focuses on relating aspects of social structure and organization to environmental factors, including habitat, diet, presence of predators, and other aspects of the ecology within which primate groups live. One basic question is: To what extent are differences in the type and size of a social group related to environmental factors, as opposed to genetic ancestry? Although some related species often have similar social structures, many of the types of social groups discussed earlier are found in species that are not closely related. Finding similar social groups (e.g., multimale/multife-male groups) in evolutionarily different species of primates argues that such behaviors have arisen independently in different species, suggesting further that the answer might lie in similar environments.

Early studies in socioecology focused on the contrast between species that live in the trees and those that live on the ground (DeVore 1963). This arboreal–terrestrial contrast suggested some basic relationships between habitat and aspects of social organization, territoriality, group size, and **home range** (the size of the geographic area normally occupied by a group). Additional study showed that this simple contrast in habitats did not fully explain variation in primate behavior. Crook and Gartlan (1966) later expanded on this idea by breaking down primate species into five groups defined primarily by habitat and diet. Jolly (1972) later modified this approach, and defined six groups: (1) nocturnal insect eaters, (2) arboreal life eaters, (3) arboreal omnivores, (4) semi-terrestrial leaf eaters, (5) semi-terrestrial omnivores, and (6) primates living in arid environments.

As additional data accumulated on primate behavior and ecology, more effort was devoted to closer examination of the correlation between specific ecological variables and specific primate behaviors. One example of this approach is a paper by Denham (1971), who started with the basic assumption that the key factors to be examined are how a primate group acquires food, defends itself against predators, and reproduces. He then focused on energy density (how much food is available), energy predictability (how the food resources are distributed), and anti-predator strategy (fighting, running, or hiding). As an example of his model, consider his interpretation of the relationship between food resource distribution, primate population distribution, and the extent to which primate groups actively defend a territory. Denham first notes that food resources can range from being evenly distributed over an entire area, or can be found in smaller clumps that are separated by areas with less available food. When the food resources are clumped, we expect to see primate groups in clumps as well because the groups will

---

sexual dimorphism
The average difference in body size between adult males and adult females.

socioecology The study of social structure and organization

in relationship to environmental factors.

home range The size of the geographic area that is normally occupied and used by a social group.

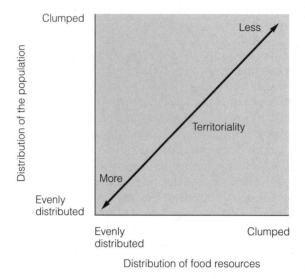

■ FIGURE 6.12

Expected relationship of food resource distribution according to Denham (1971). In general, the clumping of populations follows the clumping of food resources; that is, when food occurs in clumps, so do the primate populations. When food resources are clumped, there is less territorial behavior, perhaps because the spacing of food has already spaced groups apart from one another. When food resources are more evenly distributed, there is a tendency for greater territoriality.

distribute themselves according to the amount of available food. If food is found in small clumps, it doesn't make much sense for the group to be spread out over a large area—the group goes where there is food. Denham predicts that primates that live in environments where the food resources (and the social groups) are more evenly distributed about a region will be more likely to actively defend their territory. If the reverse is true, and both food resources and social groups are found in distinct clumps, then the groups are already separated by distance, and there is less need for an active defense of a territory (Figure 6.12).

Although many of these early studies did find the expected relationships in some species, there was always variation, sometimes within the same species. Studies of primate socioecology found some general trends (e.g., terrestrial social groups tend to be larger than arboreal social groups), but there were always exceptions to these trends (Wrangham 1987). More focused studies have since emerged, looking at more specific ecological relationships, such as between food distribution and patterns of foraging (e.g., Oates 1987) and the relationship between predator pressure and social structure (e.g., Cheney and Wrangham 1987).

Sociobiology

The study of **sociobiology** focuses on evolutionary explanations for behavior. According to one of its main proponents, sociobiology is defined as "the systematic study of the biological basis of all social behavior" (Wilson 1980:322). Most of the work done in sociobiology focuses on natural selec-

■ FIGURE 6.13
Female chimpanzee and her
offspring. The great amount
of care and attention given by
the mother can be interpreted
as maximizing reproductive
success by increasing
parental investment.
(© Marine World Africa USA,
Vallejo, CA)

tion. We assume that a given behavior has at least a partial genetic basis. Given this genetic basis, it is easy to see how certain behaviors could be selected for. If they increase an individual's chance of survival and/or reproduction, then the alleles influencing these behaviors will be passed on to the next generation. Behaviors that seem nonadaptive at first may also be explained by sociobiological hypotheses.

PRINCIPLES OF SOCIOBIOLOGY   Central to much sociobiological theory is the concept of maximizing fitness. This refers to behaviors that increase the probability that an individual's alleles will be passed on to the next generation. If such behaviors are determined even partially by genes, then natural selection will cause those behaviors to increase in frequency. A related concept is the idea of **parental investment,** which refers to parental behaviors that increase the probability that the offspring will survive. According to sociobiological theory, mammalian (and especially primate) females invest a great deal of time and energy in reproduction and care of offspring (Figure 6.13). Even though this investment reduces the number of offspring a female can have, the benefits outweigh the costs.

▲▲▲

sociobiology The study of behavior from an evolutionary perspective, particularly the role of natural selection.

parental investment Parental behaviors that increase the probability that offspring will survive.

Mammalian males, however, often contribute only sperm. From the male standpoint of maximizing fitness, it would seem more advantageous to impregnate many females rather than just one. This argument may explain the large number of primate species in which the fathers contribute little to offspring and are not bonded permanently to any one female. However, a number of primate species are monogamous, showing that this relationship is not as simple as it first appears. In certain environments, it may be more adaptive for a primate male to be monogamous and be involved in child care, so as to maximize his fitness. Obviously, we should not expect to see a universal pattern, but rather one that varies according to environmental circumstances. Thus, an emphasis on sociobiology cannot exclude the study of socioecology.

One area of particular interest in sociobiology is the evolution of altruism. At first glance, such behaviors do not appear to make evolutionary sense. If, for example, you die in an attempt to rescue a child from an oncoming car, then your alleles, including any hypothetical alleles responsible for your altruistic action, will not be passed on. Natural selection would be expected to eliminate any tendencies in future generations.

Is there any evolutionary benefit in sacrificing oneself? Sociobiology has proposed an answer in the form of **kin selection.** Altruistic behaviors may be selected for when they are directed toward one's biological relatives. If you die saving your own child, this act will have two genetic consequences. First, because you die, you will no longer pass alleles on to the next generation. Second, your child will live and have the opportunity to pass on his or her alleles, of which 50 percent came from you. Thus, by saving your child you actually contribute to the survival of some of your own alleles. If your altruistic action was at least partially affected by genetic factors, this behavior will be also passed on through the survival of your child. Sociobiological theory has developed a number of mathematical models that deal with the cost and benefit of altruistic behaviors in terms of the degree of biological relationship between the altruist and the recipient of the action. For example, it is more advantageous to you to save the life of your nephew than your first cousin, because you share more alleles with your nephew.

Although the models of sociobiology are often intuitively correct and logical, there remains great difficulty in testing many of their predictions. Perhaps the greatest problem is in demonstrating the genetic predisposition of behaviors. Further, we often lack sufficient information over enough generations to actually demonstrate a direct relationship between fitness and the behavior in question.

AN EXAMPLE OF PRIMATE SOCIOBIOLOGY   Some of the most interesting issues in sociobiology focus on behaviors that do not at first seem to be adaptive. One classic example of this problem is from Sarah Hrdy's (1977) study of **infanticide** in a particular group of primates—a species of monkey known as langurs. Langurs typically live in uni-male groups. There is frequently

■ FIGURE 6.14
Adult female langurs
attempting to rescue an infant
from an adult male langur.
(Sarah Blaffer Hrdy/Anthro-Photo)

competition between adult males, where a challenger seeks to displace an adult male in such a group. When a new male successfully takes over the group, he often then attempts to kill all the infants fathered by the previous male (Figure 6.14). At first, such behavior seems abnormal and contrary to the survival of the group. The sociobiological explanation, however, is that the new male is increasing his own fitness. First, killing the infants from other males can increase the proportion of one's offspring in the next generation. The competition has been eliminated. Second, females who are still nursing infants are not yet able to become pregnant by the new male, and he has to wait. By killing the infants, the new male ensures that the females are more quickly able to have children with him. The bottom line is that *if* infanticide has some genetic basis, then this act would be selected for because it maximizes the fitness of the killer.

kin selection A concept used in sociobiological explanations of altruism. Sacrificial behaviors, for example, can be selected for if they increase the probability of survival of close relatives.

infanticide The killing of infants.

This interpretation poses a number of problems. First, we do not know how widespread this behavior is and whether it occurs under different environmental conditions. Second, we do not know the extent to which such behaviors are affected by genetic factors. Finally, the hypothesis that differences in fitness are associated with infanticide needs to be tested. To do this, we need to know something about relative survival and differential reproduction, which requires detailed observations over many groups and generations.

The infanticide hypothesis has been controversial and challenged. One of the most recent critiques focused on problems with both the data and hypothesis (Sussman et al. 1995). First, there have been few direct observations of infanticide by langurs—only 21 (and 27 other cases of infanticide in other primate species). Further, few of these observations involved the expected attack of an incoming male directly on an infant. In many cases, the infant's death was accidental, often the result of clinging to a mother who was being attacked. In terms of the sociobiological hypothesis, Sussman and colleagues (1995) noted that there is no evidence for genetic inheritance of this behavior or for increased fitness following the act. Although acknowledging that the data are scanty, Hrdy and her colleagues (1995) argue that there is sufficient evidence to date to make the infanticide hypothesis viable.

Although sociobiological hypotheses can be constructed that are logical and consistent, this does not make them correct. Clearly, more data need to be collected from primate societies to verify or support such hypotheses.

SUMMARY

Taxonomic classification imposes order on the diversity of living creatures. The biological and behavioral nature of human beings is revealed in the different levels of classification to which humans belong. Humans are animals, chordates, and vertebrates. We share certain characteristics, such as a more developed nervous system, with other creatures in these categories.

Humans are mammals, which means we rely a great deal on a reproductive strategy of few births and extensive parental care. This reproductive pattern is associated with higher intelligence and a greater capacity for learned behaviors. Other adaptations of mammals include differentiated teeth, a skeletal structure capable of swift movement, and the ability to maintain a constant body temperature.

Humans belong to a specific order of mammals known as primates. The primates have certain characteristics, such as skeletal flexibility, grasping hands, and keen eyesight, that evolved in order to meet the demands of life in the trees. Though many primate species no longer live in the trees, they have retained these basic characteristics and use them in new ways to adapt to the environment. Most humans no longer use their grasping hands to move about in trees but use them instead for tool manufacture and use.

Primates show a great deal of variation in the size and structure of their social groups, ranging from solitary groups consisting of a female and her offspring to large communities with many adults and offspring. Several different approaches are used to understand the variety of primate social organization. Socioecology focuses on the relationship of group size and structure to the environment, particularly the amount and distribution of food and the presence or absence of predators. Sociobiology focuses on evolutionary explanations for behavior, including concepts that can be used to explain what at first appear to be nonadaptive behaviors, such as altruism.

SUPPLEMENTAL READINGS

Jolly, A. 1985. *The Evolution of Primate Behavior.* 2d ed. New York: Macmillan. An introduction to primate biology and behavior with particular emphasis on studies of social structure and primate psychology.

Passingham, R. 1982. *The Human Primate.* San Francisco: W. H. Freeman. A detailed account of human biology compared with that of other mammals.

Richard, A. F. 1985. *Primates in Nature.* New York: W. H. Freeman. An introduction to primate biology and behavior that emphasizes primate ecology.

Sussman, R. W., ed. 1979. *Primate Ecology: Problem-Oriented Field Studies.* New York: John Wiley & Sons. A collection of research articles dealing with an analysis of primate ecology, including theoretical and field studies.

CHAPTER 7

The Biology and Behavior of the Living Primates

This chapter looks more closely at the biology and behavior of the living primates, with particular attention to the apes, our closest living relatives.

PRIMATE SUBORDERS

The two major subgroups of the living primates are the suborder **Prosimii** and the suborder **Anthropoidea.** These are the official scientific names (in Latin) for the two suborders, although here we will use the more common terms prosimians and anthropoids. Each of these suborders is broken down into smaller taxonomic units, such as infraorders, superfamilies, families, and so on. Figure 7.1 shows the traditional primate taxonomy used throughout most of this chapter. Keep in mind that the cladistic approach (Chapter 6) has challenged parts of this classification; some of the controversies are discussed later.

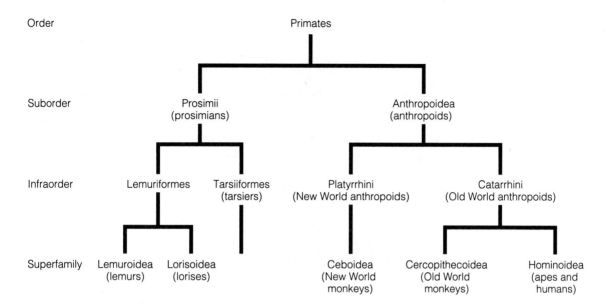

Order		Primates				
Suborder		Prosimii (prosimians)			Anthropoidea (anthropoids)	
Infraorder	Lemuriformes		Tarsiiformes (tarsiers)	Platyrrhini (New World anthropoids)	Catarrhini (Old World anthropoids)	
Superfamily	Lemuroidea (lemurs)	Lorisoidea (lorises)		Ceboidea (New World monkeys)	Cercopithecoidea (Old World monkeys)	Hominoidea (apes and humans)

■ FIGURE 7.1
Summary of traditional primate taxonomy. Names within parentheses are common names. A more detailed taxonomy is provided in Appendix 2.

Prosimians

The word *prosimian* means literally "before simians" (monkeys and apes). In biological terms, prosimians are more primitive, or more like early primate ancestors, than are monkeys and apes.

PROSIMIAN CHARACTERISTICS   The prosimians often lack one or more of the general characteristics of primates. For example, some prosimians lack color vision, and some have a single claw on each hand or foot.

Another primitive characteristic of prosimians is that they rely to a much greater extent on the sense of smell than do the anthropoids. Prosimian brains are also generally smaller relative to body size than are the brains of anthropoids. Prosimians are usually small in size, tend to be solitary, and many are **nocturnal** (active at night). These characteristics and others point to the basic primitive nature of most prosimians. Many prosimians are vertical clingers and leapers. That is, they cling to tree trunks until they're ready to move and then they propel themselves through the air.

▲▲▲

Prosimii (prosimians) The suborder of primates that are biologically primitive

compared to anthropoids.

Anthropoidea (anthropoids) The suborder of primates consisting of monkeys, apes, and humans.

nocturnal Active during the night.

Prosimians themselves show considerable variation. Some prosimians have larger body sizes, some have larger social groups, and some are **diurnal** (active in daylight). This variation makes classification difficult, but it does show us both the general trends of the prosimians as well as specific differences among them.

TYPES OF PROSIMIANS   There are three different groups of prosimians in the world today, each with a number of different species. One group, the **lorises,** are small, solitary, nocturnal prosimians found in Asia and Africa (Figure 7.2). Another group, the **tarsiers,** also small, solitary, and nocturnal, are found in Indonesia. The nocturnal nature of tarsiers is evidenced by their large eyes, the size of which serves to gather available light (Figure 7.3).

The most biologically diverse group of prosimians is the **lemurs,** which are found only on the island of Madagascar off the southeast coast of Africa (Figure 7.4). Some species of lemurs are nocturnal and some are diurnal. Social structure is highly variable among the lemurs: some have the family group structure, some have the uni-male group structure, and some have the multimale/multifemale group structure. Other characteristics, such as body size, diet, and group size, are also variable among lemur species.

The lemurs depart from the typical pattern of prosimians as nocturnal, solitary primates. Their wide range of biological and behavioral characteristics probably reflects their isolation on the island of Madagascar. Because the island has no competing monkey or ape species, and not many other mammals either, the lemurs have expanded into a variety of ecological niches. Apart from these variations, the lemurs are still definitely prosimians—having, among other primitive features, the characteristic reliance on smell.

Note that in Figure 7.1, lemurs and lorises are placed in the same infraorder (Lemuriformes) and tarsiers are placed in a different one. This placement shows the closer biological relationship between lemurs and lorises than between either of these and tarsiers.

Anthropoids

The anthropoids are the higher primates and consist of monkeys and hominoids (apes and humans). Anthropoids are generally larger in overall body size, have larger and more complex brains, rely more on visual abilities, and show more complex social structures than other primates. Except for one

▲▲

| **diurnal** Active during the day. | **loris** Nocturnal prosimian found today in Asia and Africa. | **tarsier** Nocturnal prosimian found today in Indonesia. | **lemur** A prosimian found today on the island of Madagascar. |

monkey species, all anthropoids are diurnal. The anthropoids include both arboreal and terrestrial species.

All living prosimians are found in the Old World, but anthropoids are found in both the New World and the Old World. (The Old World consists of the continents of Africa, Asia, and Europe; the New World is the Americas.) New World anthropoids are found today in Central and South America. Old World anthropoids are found today in Africa and Asia (and one monkey species in Europe). The only New World anthropoids are monkeys, whereas Old World anthropoids include monkeys, apes, and humans.

Alternative Classifications

The traditional division of primates into prosimians and anthropoids is being challenged by a number of scientists. The problem with the traditional classification is that tarsiers, usually classified as prosimians, show several biological characteristics of anthropoids. Lorises and lemurs have moist noses, a trait related to their keen sense of smell. Tarsiers, like anthropoids, lack the moist nose. In addition, recent biochemical investigations have supported the idea that tarsiers are more like anthropoids than prosimians.

Many researchers now advocate placing the lemurs and lorises in one suborder, **Strepsirhini,** characterized by moist noses, and the tarsiers and anthropoids in another suborder, **Haplorhini,** which lacks the moist nose. This text will continue to use the traditional division between prosimians and anthropoids because it provides a useful contrast when discussing primate evolution. However, the alternative classification shows that there is considerable debate regarding the taxonomic placement of the tarsiers. The suborders Strepsirhini and Haplorhini are shown in the alternative primate taxonomy in Figure 7.5, and can be contrasted with the traditional scheme of

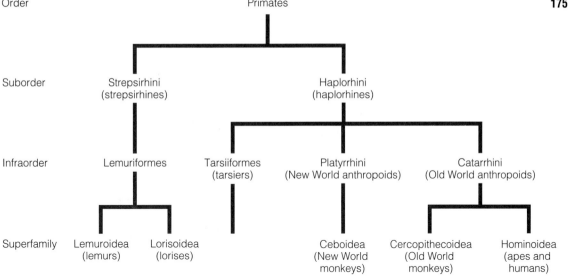

Order	Primates			
Suborder	Strepsirhini (strepsirhines)	Haplorhini (haplorhines)		
Infraorder	Lemuriformes	Tarsiiformes (tarsiers)	Platyrrhini (New World anthropoids)	Catarrhini (Old World anthropoids)
Superfamily	Lemuroidea (lemurs) · Lorisoidea (lorises)		Ceboidea (New World monkeys)	Cercopithecoidea (Old World monkeys) · Hominoidea (apes and humans)

■ **FIGURE 7.5**
An alternative primate taxonomy using the suborders Strepsirhini and Haplorhini. Compare this to Figure 7.1, which uses the traditional breakdown into the suborders Prosimii and Anthropoidea. The difference is that the present chart groups tarsiers with monkeys and hominoids in the suborder Haplorhini rather than with lemurs and lorises. According to this view, tarsiers are more closely related to monkeys and hominoids because they lack the moist nose (associated with greater ability to smell) found in lemurs and lorises. There is debate over which approach is the most appropriate.

Figure 7.1. The major difference is the placement of the tarsiers. Are they more similar evolutionarily to lemurs and lorises, or to monkeys and apes?

What is the relevance of alternative classifications? Once again, this controversy demonstrates the difficulty of taxonomic classification. It is not always possible to place living creatures unambiguously in certain categories. Such problems actually provide us with strong evidence of the evolutionary process. The tarsiers, for example, suggest what a transitional form between prosimians and anthropoids might have looked like.

THE MONKEYS

Anthropoids include monkeys and hominoids (apes and humans). Monkeys and apes are often confused in the popular imagination. In reality, they are easy to tell apart. Monkeys have tails, apes and humans do not. Monkeys also have smaller brains relative to body size than apes or humans. The typical pattern of monkey movement is on all fours (**quadrupedal**), and their

---

Strepsirhini (strepsirhines) One of two suborders of primates suggested to replace the prosimian/anthropoid suborders (the other is the haplorhines). Strepsirhines are primates that have a moist nose (lemurs and lorises).

Haplorhini (haplorhines) One of two suborders of primates suggested to replace the prosimian/anthropoid suborders (the other is the strepsirhines). Haplorhines are primates without a moist nose (tarsiers, monkeys, apes, and humans).

quadrupedal A form of movement in which all four limbs are of equal size and make contact with the ground, and the spine is roughly parallel to the ground.

arms and legs are generally of similar length so that their spines are parallel to the ground. By contrast, apes have longer arms than legs and humans have longer legs than arms.

New World Monkeys

The only form of anthropoids found native to the New World are the New World monkeys (there are no New World apes). Although they share many similarities with Old World monkeys, several important differences reflect separate lines of evolution over the past 30 million years or so.

CHARACTERISTICS   Some of the differences between the New World and Old World monkeys are useful in reconstructing evolutionary relationships. For example, New World monkeys have four more premolar teeth than Old World monkeys. The dental formulae for many New World monkeys is 2-1-3-3, compared to the 2-1-2-3 dental formula of all Old World monkeys. Other differences relate to the way in which the monkeys live; for example, many New World monkeys have prehensile tails.

Because the tail of many New World monkeys is capable of grasping, it is highly useful in moving about and feeding in the trees (Figure 7.6). Typi-

■ **FIGURE 7.6**
A spider monkey, capable of using its tail as a "fifth limb." (© Zoological Society of San Diego)

■ **FIGURE 7.7**
A Bolivian red howler monkey, one of the New World monkeys with a prehensile tail. (© Zoological Society of San Diego)

cally, the monkey uses this "fifth limb" to anchor itself while feeding on the ends of small branches. Old World monkeys have tails, but none of them have prehensile tails. Those New World monkeys with prehensile tails are thus more proficient in terms of acrobatic agility. This difference probably relates to the fact that all New World monkeys are arboreal, whereas some Old World monkeys are terrestrial. The prehensile tail of many New World monkeys appears to be a biological specialization that either did not develop in the Old World monkeys or was lost in that line's evolution from some earlier common ancestor of all monkeys. So, we do not yet know if the prehensile tail is a primitive or derived trait.

CASE STUDY: HOWLER MONKEYS One interesting group of New World monkeys are the howler monkeys, consisting of six species in the genus *Alouatta*. Howler monkeys are found in Mexico and in South America (Figure 7.7). Their name reflects their most unusual characteristic—an enlarged hyoid bone (the bone in the throat), which creates a large resonating chamber capable of making loud sounds that can be heard at a considerable distance. Howlers have prehensile tails and are quite at home in the trees, where they eat primarily fruit and leaves. Adult howlers weigh about 6 to 8 kilograms (13 to 18 pounds), with males larger than females. Males are capable of making deeper and louder howls. Howlers live in multimale/multifemale groups of between 6 and 20 individuals, with more adult females than adult males

(Bramblett 1994). Some groups have been observed to have only one adult male and could rightly be called uni-male groups (Crockett and Eisenberg 1987). Again, variation is typical of primate social structure.

The loud howling of howler monkeys serves many purposes, including warning and defense. These howls often serve to warn away competitors for food and space, and it has been suggested that these vocalizations are a substitute for active fighting (Carpenter 1965; Crockett and Eisenberg 1987). Because groups are widely separated, fighting may be avoided, and thus the spacing may be a group defense. This spacing has also often been interpreted as evidence that howlers have specific territories, which they defend. A strict definition of **territory** is a home range that is actively defended and does not overlap with another group's home range. Actually, few primates are territorial in this sense. Carpenter (1965) noted that howlers do not defend specific and constant boundaries, but rather defend wherever they are at a given time. Crockett and Eisenberg (1987) suggest that howlers cannot actually be considered territorial because the overlap in home ranges is often quite large, but they also note that others interpret the data as showing some territoriality. (Perhaps the most telling observation is the variation that howlers [and many primates] show from study to study.) Although much is still unknown about howler monkeys, it is clear that they are not easily pigeonholed into different categories such as uni-male versus multimale, or territorial versus nonterritorial (Crockett and Eisenberg 1987).

Old World Monkeys

CHARACTERISTICS Old World monkeys are biochemically and physically more similar to humans than are New World monkeys. For example, Old World monkeys have the same number of teeth as apes and humans (a dental formula of 2-1-2-3). Old World monkeys inhabit a wide range of environments. Many species live in tropical rain forests, but other species have adapted to the **savanna** (open grasslands). One species has even learned to survive in the snowy environment of the Japanese mountains (Figure 7.8).

The Old World monkeys, like the New World monkeys, are quadrupedal, running on the ground and branches on all fours. Though Old World monkeys are agile in the trees, many species have adapted to spending more time on the ground in search of food. Most Old World species eat a mixed diet of fruits and leaves (Figure 7.9), although some show dental and digestive specializations for leaf eating. Some Old World species occasionally supplement their primarily vegetarian diet with insects or small animals that they hunt.

■ **FIGURE 7.8**
Japanese macaques, adapted to living in the snow.
(© Steven Kaufman/Peter Arnold, Inc.)

▲▲

territory A home range that is actively defended.

savanna An environment consisting of open grasslands in which food resources tend to be spread out over large areas.

■ FIGURE 7.9
A mandrill, an Old World
monkey. (© Zoological Society
of San Diego)

Social structure is highly variable among Old World monkeys. Most known species have been characterized as having either multimale/multifemale or uni-male social groups. However, a large proportion of Old World monkey species has been observed with more than one social structure, depending on the specific group, once again showing behavioral variation (Figure 7.10). One contributing factor to this variation is the availability of food. In species that have less available food, the uni-male structure is more common, perhaps because additional males would consume food without adding much to group survival.

CASE STUDY: BABOONS   Baboons are one of the most widely studied and interesting of the Old World monkeys (technically, several different monkeys are given the general label of "baboon"; here we refer to the "savanna baboon.") Baboons live in relatively large (20–200) multimale/multifemale groups on the African savanna (Figure 7.11). The savanna is composed primarily of open grasslands, in which food resources tend to be spread out over large areas. Clusters of trees in the savanna provide additional opportunities for food, as well as for protection. Even though baboons are essentially terrestrial, they still have the basic primate adaptations that allow them to climb effectively, which proves useful in hiding from predators, and for shelter when sleeping. Because food resources are spread out over large areas of the savanna, baboons tend to have rather large home ranges, and they cover this

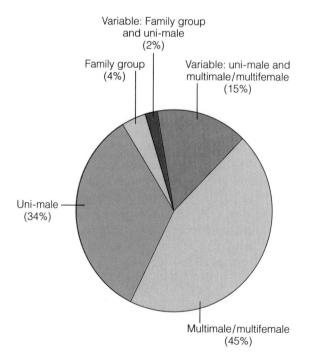

■ FIGURE 7.10
Variation in social structure among Old World monkeys. Numbers represent the percentage of species that have a particular social structure (species for which this information is not known have been excluded). Note that 17 percent of Old World monkey species have been observed with more than one type of social structure. (*Source of data:* Jolly 1985:129, Table 6.5a)

■ FIGURE 7.11
Baboons on the savanna.
(Shirley C. Strum, © 1987
National Geographic Society)

area by foraging as a group. The baboon diet is quite diverse, including grass, leaves, fruit, and occasionally meat that has been obtained from hunting small mammals and birds.

A primary reason why baboons are so widely studied is that they live on the savanna. Our analysis of the first humans shows that they too lived in or near a savanna environment (Chapter 10), and thus many scientists have advocated using the baboon as a possible model for the evolution of human behavior. Today, we recognize many problems with this simple approach, and "baboon models" are seldom used (Strum and Mitchell 1987). Still, the baboon makes an interesting species to study in its own right, and the more we find out about their society, the more we again see the variable nature of primate behavior.

Much of the focus in baboon studies has been on social organization. Adult males are dominant over adult females, and there is a constant shift in the relative position of the most dominant males. Aggressive actions play a role in this continual struggle (Figure 7.12, also refer back to Figure 6.11). Adult males are considerably larger than adult females, and the largest and strongest males often have a greater chance of being the most dominant.

Size and strength are not, however, the only factors affecting male dominance in baboon society. Coalitions of two or more lower-ranking males have often been observed to displace a more dominant male who was actually larger and stronger than either of the lower-ranking males. The ability to aid others is an important determinant of dominance rank.

Environmental factors also affect the pattern of dominance within baboon society. For example, Rowell (1966) found that forest-living baboons

■ **FIGURE 7.12**
An adult male baboon "yawning"—an expression that is interpreted by others as an aggressive display and a warning. Such threat gestures are used in disputes over dominance. (Irven deVore, Anthro-Photo)

have less rigid dominance hierarchies than groups living on the savanna. In addition, the daily life of the forest baboons was more relaxed, as the level of aggression was lower. In forest environments food is generally more available, and there is less threat from predators. Quite simply, a rigid social organization is not needed in this environment.

In the initial years of baboon research, most of the attention was on the dominance hierarchies of the adult males, and less attention was given to the behaviors of adult females. We now realize that the continuity of baboon society revolves around the females, and adult males quite frequently move from one social group to another. The dominance hierarchy of the adult females is generally more stable over time. The importance of female continuity in baboon society must be acknowledged because they are responsible for the care of infants, and they provide the needed socialization prior to maturity.

THE HOMINOIDS

In addition to the monkeys, the other major group of living anthropoids are the **hominoids,** which is a group composed of apes and humans. The similarity of apes and humans (hence their placement in the same superfamily) has long been a source of interest and fascination. Perhaps one of our most memorable images of this relatedness comes from the classic 1933 movie *King Kong.* The giant gorilla discovered on "Skull Island" is captured and brought to New York City for display as the eighth wonder of the world. Ignoring the fantastic nature of some of the plot elements (gorillas could not be that large and still walk), the film draws close comparisons between Kong's behavior and that of the humans in the film. Kong shows love, curiosity, and anger, among other emotions and behaviors. Kong is a mirror for the humans, and the humans are a mirror for Kong. We see ourselves in the beast, and the beast in ourselves.

Hominoid Characteristics

Whether we choose to look at apes as humanlike, or humans as apelike, the fact remains that of all living creatures, the apes are the most similar to humans in both biology and behavior. Before considering the biology and behavior of living apes (the remainder of this chapter) and humans (next chapter), it is necessary to examine some of the general characteristics of all living hominoids.

Unlike monkeys, hominoids do not have tails. Another hominoid characteristic is size: in general, apes and humans are larger than monkeys. Hominoid brains as a rule are larger than monkey brains, both in terms of absolute size and in relationship to body size. Their brains are also more complex, which correlates with the hominoid characteristics of greater intelligence and learning abilities. Hominoids also invest the most time and effort in raising their young.

Hominoids share with Old World monkeys the 2-1-2-3 dental formula (two incisors, one canine, two premolars, and three molars in each half of the upper and lower jaws). The structure of the molar teeth, however, is different in monkeys and hominoids. The most noticeable difference is that the lower molar teeth of hominoids tend to have five **cusps** (raised areas) as compared to the four cusps in the lower molars of monkeys. The deeper grooves between these five cusps form the shape of the letter Y. As such, this characteristic shape is called the "Y-5" pattern (Figure 7.13). This difference may seem trivial, but it does help us in identifying fossils because we can often tell whether a form is a monkey or a hominoid on the basis of the molar teeth.

Perhaps one of the most important characteristics of hominoids is their upper body and shoulder anatomy. Hominoids can raise their arms above their heads with little trouble, whereas a monkey would find this difficult. This ability of hominoids to raise their arms above their heads is based on three basic anatomical features. First, hominoids have a larger and stronger collarbone than monkeys. Second, the hominoid shoulder joint is very flexible and capable of a wide angle of movement. Third, hominoid shoulder blades are located more toward the back. By contrast, monkeys' shoulder blades are located more toward the sides of the chest (Figure 7.14). Hominoid shoulder joints face outward, compared to the shoulder joints of monkeys, which are downward-facing.

Most hominoids have longer front limbs than back limbs. Modern humans are an exception to this rule, with longer legs than arms. This trait facilitates upright walking (discussed later). In apes, the longer front limbs

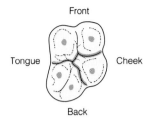

■ FIGURE 7.13
The Y-5 lower molar pattern of hominoids. Circles represent cusps. The heavier line resembles the letter Y on its side.

---

hominoid A superfamily of anthropoids consisting of apes and humans.

cusp A raised area on the chewing surface of a tooth.

■ **FIGURE 7.14**
Top view of the shoulder complex of a monkey (*top*) and a human (*bottom*) drawn to the same scale top to bottom. In hominoids (apes and humans), the clavicle is larger and the scapula is located more toward the rear of the body.

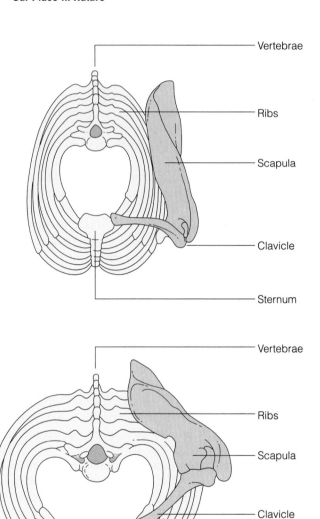

represent an adaptation to hanging from tree limbs. In addition, hominoids generally have long fingers that help them hang suspended from branches. The wrist joint of hominoids contains a disc of cartilage (called a meniscus) between the lower arm bones and the wrist bones. This disc cuts down on contact between bones. As a result, the wrist joints of hominoids are more flexible than those of monkeys, allowing greater hanging ability.

Hominoid anatomy allows them a different type of movement from that of monkeys. Hominoids are adept at climbing and hanging from branches. They are **suspensory climbers.** As hominoids, humans have retained this

TABLE 7.1
Traditional Taxonomy of Living Hominoids

Family	*Genus*	*Species*	*Common name*
Hylobatidae (lesser apes)	*Hylobates*	*agilis*	Agile gibbon
	Hylobates	*concolor*	Crested gibbon
	Hylobates	*hoolock*	Hoolock gibbon
	Hylobates	*klossi*	Kloss's gibbon
	Hylobates	*lar*	White-handed gibbon
	Hylobates	*moloch*	Silver gibbon
	Symphalangus	*syndactylus*	Siamang
Pongidae (great apes)	*Gorilla*	*gorilla*	Gorilla
	Pan	*paniscus*	Bonobo (pygmy chimpanzee)
	Pan	*troglodytes*	Chimpanzee (common chimpanzee)
	Pongo	*pygmaeus*	Orangutan
Hominidae (humans)	*Homo*	*sapiens*	Human

Source: Bramblett (1994)

ability, although we seldom use it in our daily lives. One exception is children playing on so-called "monkey bars" at playgrounds (which should more properly be called "hominoid bars"). The ability to suspend by the arms and then swing from one rung of the bars to the next is a basic hominoid trait.

Living hominoids all share this basic ability but vary quite a bit in terms of their normal patterns of movement. Some apes, for example, are proficient arm swingers, whereas others are expert climbers. Humans have evolved a totally different pattern in which the arms are not used for movement; this allows us to carry things while walking on two legs. These differences in locomotion are discussed later in the chapter. In spite of these differences in function, the close relationship between apes and humans is seen in their shared characteristics of the upper body and shoulder.

Classification of the Hominoids

Between 20 and 8 million years B.P. there were many different types of hominoids. Today we have only the representatives of a few surviving species from this once diverse, widespread group. Living hominoids are divided into three categories: the lesser apes, the great apes, and humans. The lesser apes are the gibbon (six species) and the siamang (one species), and are the least related to humans. The great apes are the Asian orangutan and the African ape, the gorilla, chimpanzee, and bonobo. A list of the scientific and common names of all living hominoids is given in Table 7.1.

That all of these species have certain shared characteristics allows us to classify them as hominoids and to infer that they are related through

▲▲▲▲▲▲▲▲▲▲▲▲▲▲▲▲▲▲▲▲▲▲▲▲▲▲▲▲▲

suspensory climbing
The ability to raise the arms above the head and hang on branches and to climb in this position.

evolution. The specific evolutionary relationship of the different hominoids is more difficult to establish. To uncover our own origins, we are interested in determining which ape species is the most similar to us. In this way we are able to compare the anatomy of living and fossil hominoids to determine what changed in our line, what changed in the ape line, and what stayed the same.

METHODS OF ANALYSIS   For many years, the standard approach has been to compare the physical structure (**morphology**) of these living forms in order to come up with some measure of relatedness. This approach is essentially the phenetic method described in Chapter 6. Such comparison is not as simple as it seems. Remember that two species may share a trait because of common ancestry or because of parallel evolution. When we try to unravel evolutionary relationships, we are interested in finding traits shared by ancestry. Also, all species tend to show evolution from the common ancestor, which means that sometimes an initially shared trait may be lost through time.

Scientists are now relying on a different type of comparison by looking directly at the biochemistry and genetics of the various hominoid species. Similarities and differences between species are revealed by a number of methods that compare proteins and even the genetic code. Constructing taxonomies from biochemical and genetic data has a definite advantage. If we focus on proteins or sections of DNA not affected by natural selection (or at least those we assume not to be affected), then any degree of similarity should reflect relative evolutionary relationships.

One biochemical method consists of looking at immunological reactions. When foreign molecules are introduced into an animal's blood, the animal's immune system provides a defense by producing antibodies to attack the foreign molecules (antigens). If you mix the antibodies from one species with proteins from the blood serum of another species, this reaction will not be as strong. The strength of this reaction relates to the degree of similarity between the two species being compared. Stronger reactions indicate closer molecular similarity. Because molecular structure reflects genetic factors, the stronger the reaction, the more similar genetically the two species being compared.

Comparison of immunological reactions can be used to assess evolutionary relationships and to construct taxonomies. In the case of the hominoids, such research has shown that the orangutan is distinct from the African apes and humans. In other words, the African apes and humans resemble each other more than either resembles the orangutan.

The structure of proteins for two or more species can also be compared. As discussed in Chapter 2, the biochemical structure of proteins can be represented by a sequence of smaller biochemical units called amino acids. The amino acid sequence for a given protein is compared between two or more species to determine the minimum number of genetic differences between one form and another. The smaller the number of differences, the more closely related the two species.

When applied to many proteins, this method produces the same result as that obtained from looking at immunological reactions. Chimpanzees, bonobos, gorillas, and humans form a closely related group; orangutans are set apart from this group. Gibbons and siamangs are even less similar to African apes and humans. This finding supports the idea that the African apes and humans shared a more recent common ancestor than any of them shared with the orangutan. In terms of a family tree, orangutans split off the main branch earlier than the African apes and humans. Put another way, the African apes are the closest living relatives of humans.

In recent years, even more sophisticated methods have been developed to make biochemical and genetic comparisons between living species. For example, newer methods have allowed the comparison of the individual chemical bases that make up DNA. As even more advanced biotechnological methods continue to develop, more and more techniques will become available with which we will be able to provide direct comparisons of the genetic codes of different species.

MODELS OF RELATIONSHIP What conclusions about hominoid classification can we draw based on these different methods? Anatomical, biochemical, and genetic analyses all support classifications in which the lesser apes (gibbons and siamangs) are distinct from the great apes and humans. In other words, all great apes and humans are more similar to one another than any are to the lesser apes.

The *exact* nature of the relationship among the great apes and humans has long been debated. The oldest of these ideas places all the great apes in a group separate from humans (humans were classified as hominids and all great apes were classified as pongids), implying that all great apes are equally similar to one another and that humans are quite distinct. This model, which had its roots in the then-prevailing concept of human uniqueness, is now rejected. Anatomical and genetic data show that humans and the African apes are more similar to one another than any are to the Asian great ape, the orangutan.

Biochemical and genetic comparisons clearly demonstrate that the African apes and humans are most similar to one another. In a classic study of protein differences and DNA sequences between chimpanzees and humans, King and Wilson (1975) found that the two species are over 98 percent identical. Subsequent research confirmed this finding and extended it to the bonobo and the gorilla. The finding implies that humans and African apes all split from a common ancestor at roughly the same time.

The traditional view of humans as separate from all apes is shown in Figure 7.15, which illustrates the traditional taxonomy of hominoids. This perspective is still widespread, in part because it necessitates a separate family (hominids) for human beings and their immediate ancestors. Although many question humans' uniqueness, it is still useful to separate us from the great apes for certain discussions of anatomy, behavior, and evolution. Figure 7.15 represents a phenetic view, emphasizing overall physical (and behavioral)

▲▲▲▲▲▲▲▲▲▲▲▲▲▲▲▲▲▲▲▲▲▲▲▲▲▲▲▲▲

morphology The physical structure of organisms.

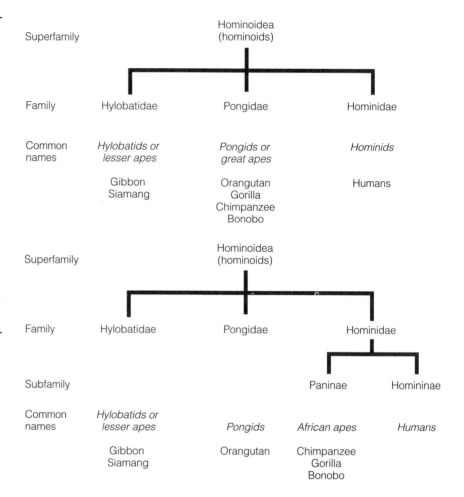

■ FIGURE 7.15
Traditional taxonomic classification of hominoids. Names within parentheses refer to common names. To emphasize certain aspects of behavior and physical characteristics, the orangutan, gorilla, chimpanzee, and bonobo are all placed in a separate category from humans. Although useful for some purposes (such as classifying by behaviors), this classification does not reflect the fact that humans and the African apes are more genetically similar to each other than any are to the orangutan. Compare this classification with Figure 7.16.

■ FIGURE 7.16
Revised taxonomic classification of hominoids to emphasize genetic and evolutionary relationships. The African apes and humans form a group separate from the Asian apes. This classification does not fit our usual informal notion of "ape" versus "human." Although useful, the classification does not reflect common aspects of behavior or physical appearance. Compare this classification with Figure 7.15.

similarity but does not, however, reflect what we know about overall evolutionary similarity.

A different view, based on the cladistic approach, is shown in Figure 7.16, where the term *hominids* is considered to apply to a family made up of two subfamilies: the African apes and humans. This figure correctly shows the finding of many genetic and anatomical studies that African apes and humans form a group separate from that of the Asian apes. Thus, the general term *ape* has little meaning because it refers to species in two distinct groups. Despite the accuracy gained in clarifying evolutionary relationships, for some purposes it is confusing to classify the African apes and humans in one group and the Asian apes in another. For example, in discussions of human evolution, we often wish to contrast and compare our phenetic views on "humans" and "apes," in which case we might prefer the traditional classification in Figure 7.15. Thus, both classifications can be considered correct—depending on the purpose of the classification.

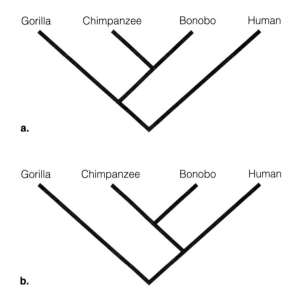

a.

b.

■ **FIGURE 7.17**
Alternative evolutionary relationships between humans and the African apes. (a) The African apes are more similar to one another than any are to humans. (b) Chimpanzees/bonobos and humans are more similar to each other than any is to the gorilla. To date, there has been some evidence supporting both views; the final answer awaits further analysis.

Part of the confusion (especially for introductory students) lies in the different uses of the same names. The term *hominid*, for example, is used to refer only to humans in Figure 7.15, whereas it refers to both humans *and* African apes in Figure 7.16. In order to make things somewhat less confusing in later chapters, we use the traditional classification given in Figure 7.15. Keep in mind, however, that such a phenetic classification does not reflect the evolutionary relationships in terms of common ancestors.

Another problem in hominoid classification is determining the exact relationships between the three African apes and humans. Are the three apes more similar to each other than any is to humans? Figure 7.17 shows the two major interpretations of this problem. Note that in both cases the chimpanzee and bonobo are placed together in one group (their relationship will be discussed later in this chapter). The first view, shown in Figure 7.17a, places all three African apes in one group separate from that of humans. This model conforms to our traditional use of a separation of African apes from humans. An alternative model, shown in Figure 7.17b, suggests that the chimpanzees, bonobos, and humans form one group separate from that of gorillas. There continues to be controversy over which model correctly shows the evolutionary relationships of these four species. Despite growing genetic evidence linking the African apes and humans (Figure 7.18), we are not at present able to resolve this conflict. The four species in Figure 7.17 are *all* so similar genetically that we are not able to judge definitively which are the most similar.

Despite the continuing debate over the exact relationships among the great apes, it is clear that the African apes are the closest living relatives of humans. An exact description of the relationships among these three groups awaits further analysis. Enough evidence has accumulated, however, to suggest that regardless of the exact relationship, the common ancestor of all three groups evolved in a relatively short period of time. This subject is considered further in Chapter 9.

■ **FIGURE 7.18**
The genetic structure of apes is very similar to that of humans. In this picture, a small piece of human DNA from a gene called "U2" is fluorescently labeled (greenish-yellow dots) and hybridized to chromosomes from a gorilla (blue). Because of the similarity of base pairs of humans and apes, the human DNA binds to its complementary sequence in the gorilla, revealing the location of the gene in that species. (© Jon Marks from the *Journal of Human Evolution*, March 1993; with permission of the Academic Press, London)

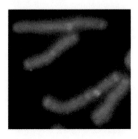

THE LIVING APES

To provide a better comparison of the biology and behavior of the apes and humans, it is necessary to consider briefly the physical characteristics, distribution, environment, and social structure of all of the hominoids. Although the living hominoids all share a number of features, they also show a great deal of biological and behavioral variation.

Gibbons and Siamangs

PHYSICAL CHARACTERISTICS   The gibbon and closely related siamang are the smallest of the living apes. There are six recognized species of gibbon and one species of siamang. For the purpose of this discussion, the term *gibbon* applies to all these forms.

The physical characteristics of gibbons reflect adaptation to life in the trees. The climbing and hanging adaptations of hominoids have evolved in the gibbon to allow highly agile movement through trees. The gibbon's usual form of movement, known as **brachiation,** consists of hand-over-hand swinging from branch to branch. Many primates are often portrayed as arm swingers, but only the gibbon can perform this movement quickly and efficiently (Figure 7.19).

A number of anatomical adaptations allow gibbons efficient arm swinging. They have small body sizes, weighing 5.5 kg on average (12 lb) (Richard 1985). Their arms are extremely long relative to their trunks and legs. Gibbon fingers are elongated and their thumbs are relatively short. The long fingers allow gibbons to form a hook with their hands while swinging from branch to branch. The thumb is short enough to prevent its getting in the way while swinging, but still long enough to allow manipulation.

On the ground, gibbons walk on two legs, though their arms are so long they look awkward to us. These long arms they use for balance. Gibbons also walk on two legs when they move along a branch, often using their arms to grab onto overhead branches for support.

Gibbons show almost no sexual dimorphism in body size. Males and females are the same body size, and both have large canine teeth, with male canines slightly larger on average than females. Gibbons are also monogamous (one male pairs exclusively—usually for life—with a single female). In primates generally, monogamy and lack of sexual dimorphism in body size tend to go together.

DISTRIBUTION AND ENVIRONMENT   Gibbons and siamangs are found in the tropical rain forests of Southeast Asia, specifically Thailand, Vietnam, Burma, and the Malay Peninsula. The rain forest environment is characterized by heavy rainfall that is relatively constant throughout the year. Rain forests have incredibly rich and diverse vegetation. The gibbons' diet consists primarily of fruits supplemented by leaves.

■ FIGURE 7.19
A gibbon brachiating. Gibbons and siamangs are the most acrobatic of the apes and can swing by their arms easily.
(Kenneth Feder)

SOCIAL STRUCTURE   The social group of gibbons is a monogamous structure: an adult male, an adult female, and their offspring. The male and female form a mating pair for their entire lives. For the most part, neither males nor females are dominant over the other. Both exhibit equal levels of aggression.

Gibbons actively defend territories. They do this by making loud vocalizations and putting on aggressive displays to warn off other groups. When groups come into contact in overlapping areas, the males often fight to drive the other group away. Females often aid in these fights.

Though it may be interesting to speculate on the nature of gibbon aggression and territorial behavior as it relates to primate behavior, in reality territorial behavior is rather rare among primates, including the hominoids. Territorial behavior is most often a function of the environment. In tropical rain forests, food is abundant and spread throughout the region. Because food resources are not clumped together, neither are the animal populations. Food is spread out over a large area, so family groups come into frequent contact with one another, necessitating territorial boundaries to establish group boundaries (Denham 1971). In environments where food resources are clustered, social groups tend to cluster as well and are spaced apart from one another at the outset.

▲▲▲▲▲▲▲▲▲▲▲▲▲▲▲▲▲▲▲▲▲▲▲▲▲▲▲▲▲

brachiation A method of movement that uses the arms to swing from branch to branch.

■ FIGURE 7.20
Mother and baby orangutans. (© Zoological Society of San Diego)

■ FIGURE 7.21
An orangutan foraging. (Animals Animals © Mickey Gibson)

Orangutans

The orangutan is a large ape found only in certain areas of Southeast Asia. The word *orangutan* translates from Malay as "man of the forest."

PHYSICAL CHARACTERISTICS   One of the orangutan's most obvious physical features is its reddish brown hair (Figure 7.20). Males are roughly twice the size of females; an average adult male weighs between 80 and 90 kg (roughly 175 to 200 lb), and an average adult female weighs between 33 and 45 kg (roughly 73 to 99 lb) (Markham and Groves 1990). Males also have large pads of fat on their faces. The high degree of sexual dimorphism in orangutans has often been thought surprising because this trait occurs most often in terrestrial species. More recent evidence, however, suggests that orangutans spend more time on the ground than we had once thought. The orangutan is responsible, with the gorilla and chimpanzee, for many reports by early explorers of "wild men," "monsters," and "subhumans."

Orangutans are agile climbers and hangers. In the trees, they use both arms and legs to climb in a slow, cautious manner. They will use one or more limbs to anchor themselves to branches while using the other limbs to feed (Figure 7.21). Younger orangutans occasionally brachiate, but the larger adults generally move through the trees in a different manner. A large orangutan will not swing from one tree to the next; rather, it will rock the tree it is on slowly in the direction of the next tree and then move over when the two trees are close together. The orangutan's great agility in climbing is due, in part, to its basic hominoid shoulder structure.

Orangutans are largely arboreal. Males, however, frequently come to the ground and travel along the forest floor for long distances. On the ground, orangutans walk on all fours but with their fists partially closed. Unlike monkeys, who rest their weight on their palms, orangutans rest on their fists: a form of movement often called fist walking.

Recent data suggest that orangutans produce offspring more slowly than the other great apes (Galdikas and Wood 1990). The average birth interval (the time between successive births) for orangutans is 7.7 years, compared to birth intervals of 3.8 years for gorillas and 5.6 years for chimpanzees (human birth intervals are highly variable but, as discussed in Chapter 6, they can be and often are shorter than that of apes).

In some ways orangutans are very similar to humans. Schwartz (1987) has drawn attention to a number of dental and skeletal traits humans and orangutans share that are not found in the African apes. Humans and orangutans also share certain aspects of their reproductive physiology. For example, both humans and orangutans have the same gestation length (270 days), which is longer than that of the African apes. Also, neither humans nor orangutans have a distinct mating cycle. Most primates have a definite time during the month (**estrus**) when the female is in "heat"—that is, sexually responsive. Neither humans nor orangutans have an estrus cycle. Orangutans are also genetically very similar to humans; the DNA of humans and orangutans differs by slightly more than 2 percent.

DISTRIBUTION AND ENVIRONMENT   The orangutan is found today only in Sumatra and Borneo in Southeast Asia. Orangutans are vegetarians, with over 60 percent of their diet consisting of fruit (Jolly 1985). As does the gibbon, the orangutan lives in tropical rain forests.

The natural range of the orangutan was probably greater in the past, judging from the fact that fossil apes similar to orangutans have been found in Asia dating from 12 million years B.P. (see Chapter 9). Some of the reduced distribution is the result of climatic change in the past. The limited range of orangutans—and of the other apes—today is also due in part to human intervention. As its natural habitats continue to be destroyed, the orangutan is an endangered species and faces extinction (Jolly 1985).

SOCIAL STRUCTURE   Orangutans have the solitary social group structure, consisting of a mother and infant. Males are not needed for protection because there is little danger from predators (Horr 1972). Adult males generally live

estrus A time during the month when females are sexually receptive.

■ FIGURE 7.22
An adult male gorilla knuckle walking. Note the angle of the spine relative to the ground because of the longer front limbs. (© Zoological Society of San Diego)

by themselves, interacting only during times of mating. Orangutans are polygamous; they do not form long-term bonds with any one partner. The small group size of orangutans appears to be related to the nature of the environment; when food resources are widely scattered, there is not enough food in any one place for large groups (Denham 1971).

Gorillas

Gorillas, the largest living primates, are found only in equatorial Africa.

PHYSICAL CHARACTERISTICS An adult male gorilla weighs 160 kg (roughly 350 lb) on average. Adult females weigh less but are still very large for primates (70 kg/155 lb) (Leutenegger 1982). Besides a much larger body size, the adult males also have larger canine teeth and often large crests of bone on top of their skulls for anchoring their large jaw muscles. Gorillas usually have blackish hair; fully mature adult males have silvery gray hair on their backs. These adult males are called "silverbacks."

Their large size makes gorillas predominantly terrestrial. Their typical means of movement is called **knuckle walking:** they move about on all fours, resting their weight on the knuckles of their front limbs. This form of movement is different from the fist walking of orangutans. Gorilla hands

■ FIGURE 7.23
A gorilla social group.
(© Michael K. Nichols/Magnum
Photos Inc.)

have well-developed muscles and strengthened joints to handle the stress of resting on their knuckles. Because their arms are longer than their legs, gorilla spines are at an angle to the ground (Figure 7.22). In contrast, the spine of a typical quadrupedal animal, such as a monkey, is roughly parallel to the ground when walking.

DISTRIBUTION AND ENVIRONMENT Gorillas are found only in certain forested areas in Africa. Their range is disappearing rapidly, primarily as the result of the replacement of forests by human farming land and human poaching (Fossey 1983). Gorillas live in humid rain forests in both the lowlands and in the mountain regions. Compared to the rain forests of the orangutans, the gorilla's environment is characterized by greater clumping of food resources (Denham 1971).

Many myths have circulated about the gorilla's lust for human and non-human flesh, but the truth of the matter is that gorillas are exclusively vegetarian. Over 85 percent of their diet consists of leaves (Jolly 1985). In fact, the intestinal tracts of gorillas are somewhat specialized for the digestion of leaves.

SOCIAL STRUCTURE Gorillas live in small social groups of about a dozen individuals. The social group consists of an adult male (the silverback), several adult females, and their immature offspring (Figure 7.23). Occasionally, one

knuckle walking A form of movement used by chimpanzees and gorillas that is characterized by all four limbs touching the ground, with the weight of the arms resting on the knuckles of the hands.

or more younger adult males are part of the group, but they tend not to mate with the females. Though dominance rank varies among the females and subadult males, the adult silverback male is the most dominant individual in the group and is the leader. The silverback sets the pace for the rest of the group, determining when and how far to move in search of food.

A typical day for a gorilla group consists of eating and resting. Given their large body size and the limited nutritional value of leaves, it is no wonder that gorillas spend most of their day eating. Because of their size, gorillas have few problems with predators (except for humans with weapons). The life of a gorilla is for the most part peaceful, a dramatic contrast to their stereotypical image as aggressive, evil creatures.

Because gorillas are rather peaceful and slow-moving, we have a tendency to think they are "slow" in a mental sense as well. This is another myth of gorilla behavior. Laboratory and field studies of gorillas have shown them to be extremely intelligent creatures. As discussed later, they have even learned sign language.

Chimpanzees

The chimpanzee is perhaps the best known of all the nonhuman primates. Most of our experience with chimpanzees, however, is with captive or trained animals. We like to watch chimpanzees perform "just like humans" and delight in a chimpanzee's smile (which actually signals tension, not pleasure).

From a scientific perspective, chimpanzees are equally fascinating. Genetic studies during the last 20 years have shown that humans and chimpanzees are even more similar than they were previously thought to be. Laboratory and field studies have shown that chimpanzees are capable of behaviors we once thought of as unique to humans, such as toolmaking and language acquisition. Any examination of the human condition must take these remarkable creatures' accomplishments into account.

PHYSICAL CHARACTERISTICS   Chimpanzees are found in Africa. They are smaller than gorillas and show only slight sexual dimorphism. Adult males weigh about 45 kg (99 lb) on average and adult females weigh about 37 kg (82 lb) on average (Leutenegger 1982). Chimpanzees have extremely powerful shoulders and arms. Like humans, chimpanzees show great variation in facial features and overall physical appearance (Figure 7.24).

Chimpanzees, like gorillas, are knuckle walkers, with longer arms than legs. Chimpanzees, however, are more active and agile than gorillas. Chimpanzees are both terrestrial and arboreal. They spend considerable time in the trees, either sleeping or looking for food. They often hang by their arms in the trees. On the ground, they sometimes stand on two legs to carry food or sticks.

■ FIGURE 7.24
Variation in chimpanzee faces.
(© Mike Birkhead/Oxford
Scientific Films/Animals Animals)

DISTRIBUTION AND ENVIRONMENT   Most chimpanzees are found in the African rain forests, although some groups are also found in the mixed forest–savanna environments on the fringe of the rain forests. The chimpanzee diet consists mainly of fruit (almost 70 percent), although they also eat leaves, seeds, nuts, insects, and meat. Chimpanzees have been observed hunting small animals, such as monkeys, and sharing the meat. Though some of the hunting occurs spontaneously when chimpanzees encounter small animals, other hunting behavior appears to be planned and coordinated.

SOCIAL STRUCTURE   Chimpanzees live in large communities of 50 or more individuals. Their social structure constantly changes, with individuals and groups fragmenting and later rejoining the main group. All chimpanzees recognize and interact with others in the group. Chimpanzee groups are less rigid than other multimale primate societies such as baboons. Although all members of the group do interact to some extent, it is common for smaller subgroups to form much of the time. The actual composition of these subgroups also changes frequently.

Social Structure and Testes Size in Primates

Bizarre as it might sound at first, scientists have collected information on the size of the testes, the male reproductive organ that produces sperm, in different primate species, and have made some interesting observations. For example, the size of the testes ranges from roughly 1.2 grams (0.04 oz) in one New World monkey species to 119 grams (over 4 oz, or 1/4 lb) in chimpanzees. However, not all hominoids have such large testes. The average testes size is roughly 30 grams (1 oz) in gorillas, 35 grams (1.25 oz) in orangutans, and 41 grams (1.4 oz) in humans.

A quick look at the testes size of all primate species for which we have data shows that part of the reason for so much variation is differences in body size. In general, the larger the body, the larger the testes. The graph shows the overall relationship between average body size and average testes size for 33 primate species, including prosimians, monkeys, apes, and humans. For technical reasons, we plot the logarithms of both body weight and testes weight. The straight line shows the best fit between the logarithm of body weight and the logarithm of testes weight and clearly shows that the larger the body, the larger the testes. (The relationship is actually curved somewhat,

Source of data: Harcourt et al. (1981).

which is why we use logarithms. This means that the increase is not linear.)

Nevertheless, when we look at the actual data points on the curve, we can see that, although there is an average relationship between body weight and testes weight, it is not perfect. Some species are above the line, meaning they have larger testes than expected, and some species are below the line, meaning they have smaller testes than expected. For example, humans have testes that are about two-thirds the size expected on the basis of our body weight. Chimpanzees, however, have testes that are 2.5 times that expected! Both orangutans and gorillas have smaller testes than expected on the basis of body weight.

Are these deviations random, or do they reflect that some factor other than body weight might be responsible for testes size? Harcourt and colleagues (1981) investigated this question and came to the conclusion that an important factor was the type of social structure associated with each primate species. The graph shows their results. Species that have a single male (either family structure or uni-male structure) are indicated by the filled-in squares. There is a definite tendency for those species to fall below the predicted line—that is, to have smaller testes than

Most social behaviors revolve around the bond between mother and infant (Figure 7.25). Chimpanzees tend to associate with their mothers and other siblings throughout their lives, even after they are fully grown. As with other primates, young females watch and observe their own mothers taking care of children and learn mothering behaviors. There is no close bond between adult males and infants except for associations through the mother. Overall, chimpanzee society can be seen as a collection of smaller groups, defined in terms of mothers and siblings, forming a larger community. Other associations are also common, such as temporary all-male groups. Some chimpanzees are even solitary for periods of time.

Adult males are generally dominant over adult females, although there is much more overlap than found in baboon societies. Some females, for example, are dominant over the lower-ranking males. As with other primates, dominance is influenced by a variety of factors such as size, strength, and the ability to form alliances. Individual intelligence also appears to affect dominance, as was revealed in Jane Goodall's study of the chimpanzees in the Gombe Stream National Park near Lake Tanganyika. In 1964 the commu-

expected. Species with a multimale social structure, indicated by filled-in circles, tend to fall above the predicted line, showing that they have larger testes than expected. The bottom line is that once we control for body size, males in multimale societies have larger testes.

What is the reason for differences according to social structure? Harcourt and colleagues suggest that larger testes are needed in primate societies where mating is frequent and where many males mate with a female during estrus. Chimpanzees are a good example of this. They suggest that natural selection favored males with larger testes, and hence a greater amount of sperm, so they could compete genetically with other males. In primate societies with less frequent mating, and where females generally mate with only one male, larger testes would not be selected for. Examples here include orangutans and gorillas.

Of course, testes size is not only a function of body size and social structure. Harcourt and colleagues note other potential influences, such as seasonality of mating. However, the strong relationship observed in their study suggests that there is often a link between biology and behavior that is best interpreted in an evolutionary context.

Relationship between body weight (logarithm) and testes weight (logarithm) in 33 primate species. The solid line is the predicted relationship between body weight and testes weight. Individual points correspond to the different species. Species with a uni-male society in breeding are indicated by a filled-in square. Species with multimale societies are indicated by a filled-in circle. Species with an unknown social structure are indicated by a filled-in diamond.

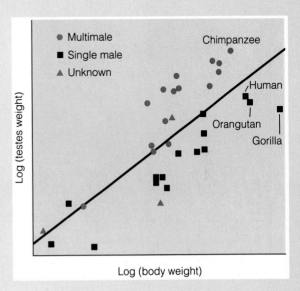

nity studied by Goodall had 14 adult males. The lowest-ranking male (Mike) replaced the most dominant male (Goliath) after inventing a particularly innovative display of dominance. There were a number of empty kerosene cans lying around Goodall's camp that the chimpanzees generally ignored. Mike would charge other males while hitting the cans in front of him, creating an unusual and very noisy display. This behavior was so intimidating to other males that Mike rose from the lowest to the highest rank at once (Goodall 1986). This study shows not only the changing nature of dominance hierarchy but also the role of individual intelligence and initiative; all the males had access to the cans, but only Mike used them.

Studies of the Gombe Stream chimpanzee community have also revealed a number of other interesting features of chimpanzee social behaviors and intelligence. The chimpanzees have been observed making and using tools (discussed at length in Chapter 8), hunting in cooperative groups, and sometimes engaging in widespread aggression against other groups. We examine some of these findings when we consider what behaviors may be considered uniquely human.

■ FIGURE 7.25
Mother and infant
chimpanzees. (Richard
Wrangham/Anthro-Photo)

Bonobos

The **bonobo** is the third and least well known of the African apes. The
bonobo is closely related to the chimpanzee and is commonly considered a
separate species of chimpanzee known as the "pygmy chimpanzee" (compared to what is often termed the "common chimpanzee"). Although the
bonobo is somewhat smaller than the chimpanzee (about 85 percent of the
weight), the term "pygmy chimpanzee" is not really accurate; hence, we use
the name "bonobo" here). The close similarity of chimpanzees and bonobos
is reflected in their assignment to the same genus—*Pan* (the scientific names
are *Pan troglodytes* for the chimpanzee and *Pan paniscus* for the bonobo).

PHYSICAL CHARACTERISTICS At first glance, bonobos seem quite similar to chimpanzees (Figure 7.26). On closer examination, however, we see that the
bonobo has relatively longer legs, a higher center of gravity, and a narrower

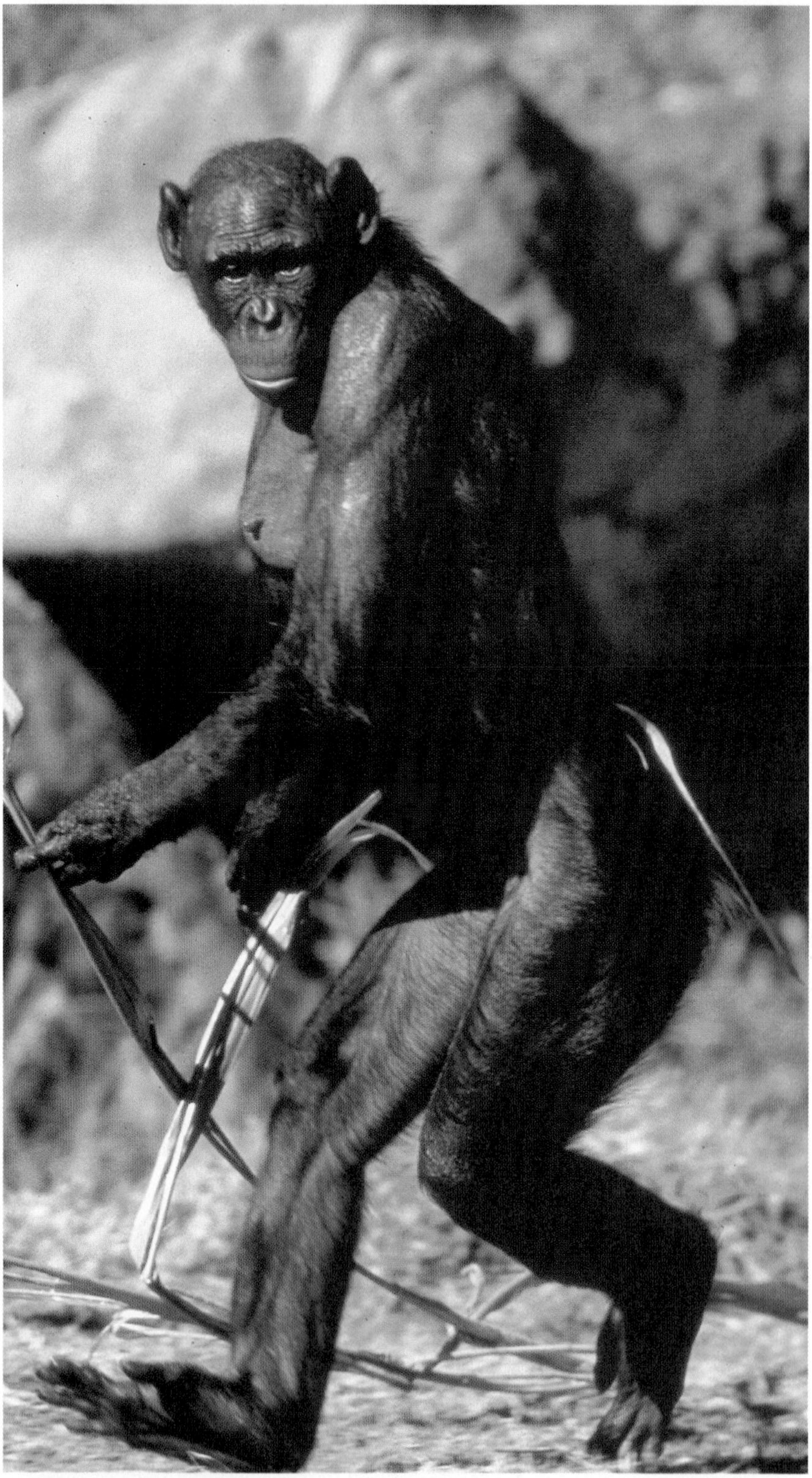

■ FIGURE 7.27
A bonobo. (© Frans Lanting/Minden Pictures)

chest. It tends to have a higher forehead and differently shaped face (Savage-Rumbaugh and Lewin 1994). Like gorillas and chimpanzees, bonobos are frequent knuckle walkers. Of particular interest is the fact that bonobos can walk upright more easily than other apes (Figure 7.27). This observation, combined with other evidence, suggests that the first hominids may have been quite similar in many ways to bonobos. There is some sexual dimorphism—adult males average 43 kg (95 lb) compared to adult females, which average 33 kg (73 lb) (de Waal 1995).

DISTRIBUTION AND ENVIRONMENT Bonobos are found only in a restricted rain forest region in Zaire in central Africa. It is estimated that there are fewer than 10,000 bonobos alive today. Their diet consists primarily of fruit, supplemented with plants. Unlike chimpanzees, bonobos consume little animal protein, and do not hunt monkeys (de Waal 1995).

SOCIAL STRUCTURE As with chimpanzees, bonobos live in multimale/multifemale groups. However, there are important differences in the social organization of these two species. In chimpanzee society, males are dominant over females, and some of the strongest bonds in the social order are between adult males. In bonobo society, things are quite different. Here, the strongest social bonds are between adult females, and even though they are physically smaller, it is the females who are most dominant. In addition, the dominance status of a male depends in large part on the dominance of his mother (de Waal 1995).

Some of the most interesting observations of bonobo behavior have to do with the function of sexual activity in their social interactions. In addition to sexual intercourse, bonobos also engage in a variety of sex play, including rubbing of genitals and oral sex. Continued observation of bonobo groups has revealed that such sex play is frequently used to reduce tension and avoid conflict. Researchers have shown repeatedly that bonobos will engage in a brief period of sex play in a tense social situation. In bonobo society, sexual play is a method of peacemaking (de Waal 1995).

SUMMARY

There is a great deal of biological and behavioral variation among the living primates. The order Primates is composed of the more biologically primitive prosimians and the anthropoids, which consist of monkeys (New World and Old World), apes, and humans. Monkeys are quadrupedal (four-footed) and have a tail. Although New World monkeys are exclusively arboreal, some species of Old World monkeys are arboreal and others are terrestrial.

The hominoids (apes and humans) are a group of anthropoids that share certain characteristics, such as the lack of a tail, similar dental features, larger brains, and a shoulder complex suitable for climbing and hanging. Hominoids consist of the "lesser apes" (gibbons and siamang) and the "great apes." The great apes consist of an Asian species (orangutan) and three African species (gorilla, chimpanzee, bonobo). The African apes are the most similar to humans, although it is not clear which of these three is the *most* similar.

The living apes show a great deal of environmental and anatomical variation. Some are arm swingers (gibbon, siamang), others are knuckle walkers (gorilla, chimpanzee, bonobo), and one is primarily a climber (orangutan). Although the great apes are all similar genetically and have a fairly recent common ancestor (roughly 20 million years ago), they show a great deal of social variation. The orangutan is solitary, the gibbon and siamang live in family groups, the gorilla lives in uni-male groups, and the chimpanzee and bonobo live in larger, complex multimale/multifemale societies.

SUPPLEMENTAL READINGS

In addition to the Jolly and Richard texts listed in Chapter 6, some other useful sources include:

Fossey, D. 1983. *Gorillas in the Mist*. Boston: Houghton Mifflin. A popular and well-written account of the late Dian Fossey's researches on the behavior of the mountain gorilla. Deals specifically with the problem of human intervention and the likely extinction of the mountain gorilla.

Goodall, J. 1986. *The Chimpanzees of Gombe: Patterns of Behavior*. Cambridge, Mass.: Harvard University Press. A comprehensive review of Jane Goodall's research since the early 1960s, this is a well-written and superbly illustrated description of chimpanzee behavior.

Smuts, B. B., Cheney, D. L., Seyfarth, R. M., Wrangham, R. W., and Struhsaker, T. T. 1987. *Primate Societies*. Chicago: University of Chicago Press. A collection of 40 review articles focusing on both individual species and selected topics of behavior.

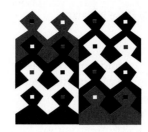

The Human Species

CHAPTER **8**

What are humans? This question has been a focus of science, art, and literature. Many different fields, from theology to psychology, have addressed its ultimate significance. Our perspective on ourselves is not abstract; the way we define what we are affects the way we treat others and the rest of the world.

One of the earliest written definitions of humanity is found in Psalm 8:4–6 of the Bible, where the question is put to God:

> What is man, that thou art mindful of him? and the son of man, that thou visitest him? For thou hath made him a little lower than the angels, and hast crowned him with glory and honor. Thou hast madest him to have dominion over the works of thy hands; thou hast put all things under his feet.

This brief statement reflects a long-standing belief of Western civilization that humans are inherently superior to all other life forms on the planet, ranking far above animals yet "lower than the angels." The view that humans are the supreme creatures in the natural world is also apparent in the works of many Greek philosophers. Aristotle, for example, constructed an arrangement of all things with inanimate matter at the "bottom" and humans at the "top" (Kennedy 1976).

What is the scientific definition of humans? Many sciences attempt to answer this question—zoology, biochemistry, and even computer science among them. In addition, a wide range of disciplines, such as history, geography, economics, political science, sociology, psychology, and anthropology, deal almost exclusively with human beings and their behaviors. From a scientific standpoint, we are interested in a definition of humans that incorporates differences and similarities with other living creatures. This is not always as simple as it sounds. For example, are humans the same as fish? Of course not, but can you explain why? Suppose you answer that humans walk on two legs. Certainly that definition separates fish and humans, but it does not separate humans and kangaroos, which also move about on two legs (albeit quite differently).

This chapter examines modern humans from the same perspective as the last two chapters, focusing on the biologic and behavioral uniqueness assigned to human beings. The final part of this chapter examines the question of how unique we are by comparing certain human behaviors (tool use, language) with similar behaviors seen in some living apes.

CHARACTERISTICS OF LIVING HUMANS

This section focuses on certain key features of modern humans, particularly our brains, upright walking, teeth, reproductive patterns, physical growth, and social structure. Some of these characteristics are also used to identify humanlike ancestors that lie along our evolutionary line since the split of apes and humans some 5 to 7 million years ago (discussed in Chapter 9). Humans and humanlike ancestors are also known by the term **hominid.**

Distribution and Environment

Humans are the most widely distributed living primate species. As later chapters will outline, humans originally evolved in a tropical environment. In fact, much of our present-day biology reflects the fact that we are tropical mammals. During the course of human evolution, however, we have expanded into many different environments. Biological adaptations have aided humans in new environments, such as cold weather and high altitude. The cultural adaptations of humans have allowed even greater expansion. Today there is no place on the planet where we cannot live, given the appropriate technology. Humans can live in the frozen wastes of Antarctica, deep beneath the sea, and in the vacuum of outer space. Our cultural adaptations have allowed us to range far beyond our biological limitations. These adapta-

TABLE 8.1
Brain Volume of Selected Living Primates (in Cubic Centimeters)

PRIMATE SPECIES	RANGE	AVERAGE
Macaque monkey		100
Baboon		200
White-handed gibbon	82–125	102
Siamang	100–152	124
Orangutan	276–540	404
Gorilla	340–752	495
Common chimpanzee	282–500	385
Modern human	900–2000	1345

Averages for macaque and baboon from Campbell (1985:233). Hominoid data from Tobias (1971:34–40), where the averages were taken as the means of males and females.

tions have also permitted incredible population growth. In the past, the planet supported no more than roughly 1 to 6 million people at a hunting-and-gathering level of existence (Weiss 1984). Today the population of the world is over five billion and continuing to grow. It is easily argued that the quality of life is still low for much of the world's human population, but there is no doubting that our ability to learn and develop technology has led to immense potential for population expansion.

Brain Size and Structure

One very obvious biological characteristic of the human species is the large brain. Our bulging and rounded skulls and flat faces contrast with these features in other animals, including the rest of the hominoids. Whereas an ape's skull is characterized by a relatively small brain and large face, modern humans have relatively large brains and small faces.

Table 8.1 lists the brain size (in cubic centimeters) for a number of primate species. There is a clear relationship between taxonomic status and brain size: monkeys have the smallest brains, followed by the lesser apes, great apes, and humans. Absolute brain size is not as useful a measure of intellectual ability because larger animals tend to have larger brains. Elephants and whales, for example, have brains that are four to five times the size of the average human brain.

An alternative way of looking at brain size is to express the weight of the brain as a ratio of body weight. The larger this ratio, the larger the brain is relative to body size. For humans, this ratio is $1/49 = 0.020$. However, this ratio is not very useful: many other primates have larger ratios, but we tend not to think of them as more intelligent (for example, the ratio for the squirrel monkey is $1/31 = 0.032$) (Passingham 1982).

hominid Humans and humanlike ancestors.

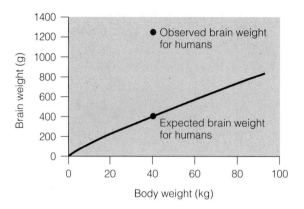

■ **FIGURE 8.1**
Relationship between body weight and brain weight in primates. The line indicates the average relationship among various primate species excluding humans. The two dots show expected and observed brain weight for humans. Our brains are three times the weight expected if we followed the typical primate curve. (*Source:* Harvey et al. 1987)

Among mammals, however, the relationship of brain and body weight is not linear. That is, as the body size increases, the brain size increases—but not at the same rate. Differences in size because of disparate growth rates among various parts of the body (known as **allometry**) are common. Parts of the body grow at different rates. Brain size increases at a nonlinear rate with body size. For example, consider two species of primates in which one species is twice the body weight of the other. If the ratio of brain size to body size were linear, we would expect the brain size of the species with the larger body size to be twice that of the smaller species. Actually, the brain size of the larger-bodied species is on average only 1.6 times as large. Because of this relationship, larger species appear to have smaller brain/body size ratios.

This allometric relationship between brain size and body size is quite regular among almost all primates. The most notable exception is humans. We have brains that are three times the size we would expect for a primate of our body size (Figure 8.1). In addition, our brains have proportionately more cerebral cortex than other primate brains. The cerebral cortex is the part of the brain involved in forming complex associations.

What exactly is the relationship between brain size, relative to body size, and intelligence? This question has been long debated, but with little resolution. Most texts state there is no relationship between relative brain size and intelligence within the human species, although only a few studies were without methodological flaws. It is problematic, however, whether the fossil record of human evolution shows an increase in absolute and relative brain size that corresponds to an increase in mental abilities. Could there be a relationship between relative brain size and intelligence between species, but not within species? A recent study by Willerman and colleagues (1991) helps resolve some of the conflict. They measured the brain size of 40 adults using magnetic resonance imaging and compared these values, adjusted for body size, with IQ test scores. Adjusting their results to the general population, they found a correlation of 0.35 between relative brain size and IQ scores (a positive correlation can take on a value from 0 to 1; the higher the value, the closer the correspondence). Several other studies have shown similar results, with an average correlation between relative brain size and IQ of roughly 0.4. In statistical terms, this means that roughly 16 percent of the observed variation in IQ is related to variation in relative brain size (without getting into the technical details, this number is derived by squaring the correlation coefficient and multiplying by 100—consult most any introductory statistics book for an explanation).

If 16 percent of the observed variation in IQ is related to brain size, then 84 percent of the observed variation is *not* related to such variation. Overall, the results show that relative brain size is a contributing factor, but not the only one. In terms of evolution, the correlation is sufficient to show that natural selection has had an impact. However, the correlation is also low enough that one could not predict accurately a person's IQ from his or her relative brain size. Even the observed correlation might be an overestimate of the relationship between relative brain size and IQ scores. The correlation, for example, may reflect other factors known to affect both growth and IQ, such as nutrition. Also, although we are interested in the general issue of "intelligence," IQ tests measure much more specific aptitudes, such as test-taking ability, and general knowledge, and are also generally acknowledged as having cultural bias. Taking such problems into account, the relatively small brain size–IQ correlation has even less significance among modern humans.

Recent studies have also looked at the relationship among brain size, body size, and metabolism. Larger mammals have larger brain sizes and produce greater amounts of metabolic energy. Mammals show a great deal of variation, however, in the amount of energy used by the brain. The brains of many mammals, such as dogs and cats, use 4 to 6 percent of their body metabolism. Primate brains use a considerably greater proportion of energy; the Old World macaque uses 9 percent and modern humans use 20 percent (Armstrong 1983).

What does all this mean? The human brain is not merely large; it also has a different structure than other primates, with the cortex being disproportionately larger. This difference in structure is also probably related to the higher proportion of metabolic energy used by the human brain. The bottom line is that brain size does not tell the whole story. Thus, the human brain is not only larger than the brain of a chimpanzee; it is also structurally different. The increased convolution of the human cerebral cortex (the folding of brain tissue) means that the brain of a human child with the same volume of that of a chimpanzee has more cerebral cortex.

Discussion of brain size and its relationship to intellectual prowess has historically been part of debates about relative differences in the mental abilities of male and female humans. When *absolute* brain size is used to assess these differences, male brains tend on *average* to be larger. This finding has been used in the past to support ill-conceived beliefs in the mental superiority of males. However, as pointed out by Gould (1981), researchers did not take into account the fact that body size is on average larger in human males and that absolute brain size is closely related to body size. That is, men often

▲▲▲▲▲▲▲▲▲▲▲▲▲▲▲▲▲▲▲▲▲▲▲▲▲▲▲▲▲

allometry The change in proportion of various body parts as a consequence of different growth rates.

have larger brains because they tend to be larger overall. This fact, combined with an understanding of some of the methodological problems of earlier studies, has led Gould to conclude there is no gender difference in relative brain size or overall intellectual ability.

Certain studies, however, do indicate that average gender differences may influence *specific* mental abilities. Falk (1992) has reviewed evidence that females tend on average to score higher on tests of verbal ability and males to score higher on tests of spatial and mathematical abilities. Falk suggests that these findings may be due to gender differences in patterns of brain lateralization. Of course, these tests and measures must be replicated cross-culturally to ensure that various forms of bias are not responsible for such observed differences (such as the fact that females in many cultures are actively discouraged from mathematics). Also, we must never forget that these results focus on *average* test scores and not on total distribution. Both male and female test score distributions overlap each other. For example, some males score higher in verbal skills than some females. As with many comparisons of biology and behavior between the sexes, we do not find exclusively separate distributions, but instead a great deal of overlap.

Bipedalism

Another striking difference between humans and apes is the fact that humans walk on two legs. We are **bipedal** (meaning "two legs"). This does not mean that apes cannot walk on two legs. They can, but not as well and not as often. The physical structure of human beings shows adaptations for upright walking as the normal mode of movement.

Humans are not the only animal that is routinely bipedal. The kangaroo also moves about on two legs, but in a totally different manner than humans. The human form of bipedal movement is best characterized as a "striding gait." Consider walking in slow motion. What happens? First, you stand balanced on two legs. Then you move one leg forward. You shift your body weight so that your weight is transferred to the moving leg. As that leg touches the ground on its heel, all your body weight has been shifted. Your other leg is then free to swing forward. As it does so, you push off with your other foot.

Human walking is more graceful than a slow-motion description sounds. The act of walking consists of alternating legs from swinging free to standing still. We balance on one leg while the other leg moves forward to continue our striding motion. We tend to take these acts for granted, but they are actually quite complicated, requiring both balance and coordination. For example, when you pick one leg up to move it forward, what keeps your body from falling over?

Human bipedalism is made possible by anatomical changes involving the toes, legs, spine, pelvis, and muscles. In terms of actual anatomy, these

■ **FIGURE 8.2**
The skeletal structure of the feet of a chimpanzee (*left*) and a modern human (*right*). Note how the big toe of the human lies parallel to the other toes.

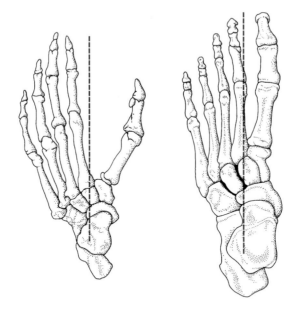

changes are not major: after all, no bones are added or deleted; the same bones can be found in humans and in apes. The changes involve shape, positioning, and function. The net effect of these changes, however, is dramatic. Humans can move about effectively on two legs, allowing the other limbs to be free for other activities.

The feet of human beings reflect adaptation to bipedalism. The feet of a human and a chimp are shown in Figure 8.2. The big toe of the chimp sticks out in the same way that the thumb of all hominoids sticks out from the other fingers. The divergent big toe allows chimps to grasp with their feet. The big toe of the human is tucked in next to the other toes. When we walk, we use the nondivergent big toe to push off during our strides.

Our balance while we stand and walk is partly the result of changes in our legs. Figure 8.3 shows a human skeleton from the frontal view. Note that the width of the body at the knees is less than the width of the body at the hips. Humans are literally "knock-kneed." Our upper leg bones (the femurs) slope inward from the hips. When we stand on one leg, the angle of the femur transmits our weight directly underneath us. The result is that we continue to be balanced while one leg is moving. In contrast, the angle of an ape femur is very slight. The legs of an ape are almost parallel from hips to feet. When an ape stands on two legs and moves one of them, the ape is off balance and tends to fall toward one side. When an ape walks on two legs, it must shift its whole body weight over the supporting leg to stay on balance. This shifting explains the characteristic waddling when apes walk on two legs.

▲▲▲▲▲▲▲▲▲▲▲▲▲▲▲▲▲▲▲▲▲▲▲▲▲▲▲▲

bipedal Moving about on two legs. Unlike the movement of other bipedal animals such as kangaroos, human bipedalism is further characterized by a striding motion.

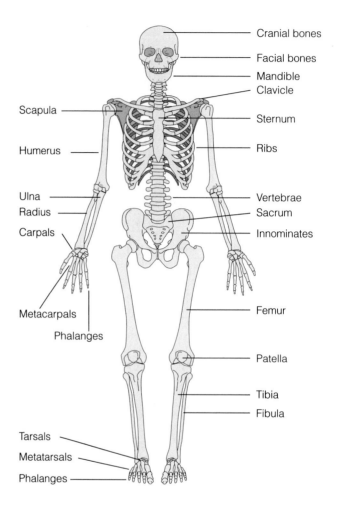

Cranial bones
Facial bones
Mandible
Clavicle
Scapula
Sternum
Humerus
Ribs
Ulna
Vertebrae
Radius
Sacrum
Carpals
Innominates
Metacarpals
Femur
Phalanges
Patella
Tibia
Fibula
Tarsals
Metatarsals
Phalanges

The human spine also allows balance when we walk upright (Figure 8.4). The spinal column of humans is vertical, allowing weight to be transmitted down through the center of the body. In knuckle-walking apes, the spine is bent in an arc so that when the apes stand on two legs, the center of gravity is shifted in front of the body. The ape is off balance and must compensate greatly to stay upright. What is difficult for apes is easy for humans. The human spine is vertical but not straight. It curves in several places, allowing it to absorb the shocks occurring while we walk.

The human pelvis is shaped differently than an ape pelvis (Figure 8.5). It is shorter top to bottom, and wider side to side. The sides of the pelvis are broader and flair out more to the sides, providing changes in muscle attachment that permit striding bipedalism. The shortness of the human pelvis allows greater stability when we stand upright.

The changes in the human pelvis also involve changes in the positioning of various muscles. For example, certain leg muscles attach more on the

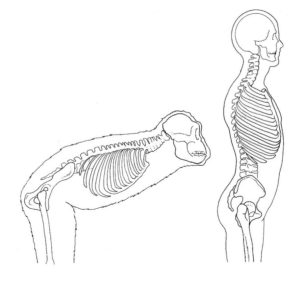

■ FIGURE 8.4
Side view of the skeletons of a chimpanzee (*left*) and a modern human (*right*), illustrating the shape and orientation of the spine.
(Adapted with permission from: Bernard Campbell, *Human Evolution*, Third Edition [New York: Aldine de Gruyter].s Copyright © 1985 Bernard Campbell)

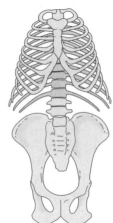
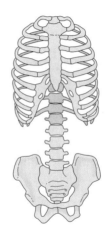

■ FIGURE 8.5
The trunk skeletons of a *chimpanzee (left) and a modern human (right)* drawn to the same size. Note the proportionately shorter and wider pelvis of the human being, reflecting adaptations to upright walking (see text).
(Adapted with permission from: Bernard Campbell, *Human Evolution*, Third Edition [New York: Aldine de Gruyter]. Copyright © 1985 Bernard Campbell)

sides of the pelvis. This change allows humans to maintain their balance while standing without having to bend their knees. Other muscles, such as the gluteus maximus (the large buttock muscle), are larger in humans than in apes. This muscle helps in standing up and in climbing over uneven terrain. The gluteus minimus and gluteus medius muscles have also shifted position relative to apes, allowing the pelvis to remain stable when one leg is lifted during walking.

Canine Teeth

As we saw in the last chapter, human canine teeth are different from canine teeth in many other mammals. Human canines are small and do not project beyond the level of the other teeth. Human canine teeth serve much the same function as the incisor teeth.

That we have small nonprojecting canines has led to much speculation concerning causes and effects of human evolution. Given that canine teeth serve as weapons in many primate species, the lack of large canine teeth in humans seems to imply that we do not need them for weapons anymore. One scenario is that when human ancestors began using tools, they no longer required large canines. As you will see in later chapters, the uniqueness of human canine teeth is a more complex topic than we once thought.

Sex and Reproduction

We humans consider ourselves the sexiest primates. That is, we are more concerned with sex than is any other primate. The fact that humans do not have the estrus cycle has often been cited as a unique aspect of human sexuality. For the most part, temperate-zone domestic animals breed only during certain seasons and mate around the time of ovulation. Human females, in contrast, cycle throughout the year and often mate at any time during the cycle. This may be a primitive characteristic, however. Some mice and rats cycle continuously. Also, as noted in Chapter 7, it now appears that orangutans also lack the estrus cycle. In addition, recent field studies on other primates suggest that many individuals, such as bonobos, mate outside the usual cycle to some extent (Jolly 1985).

Much has been made of the fact that humans have sexual relations while facing each other (the so-called "missionary position"), whereas other primates typically engage in sex with the male behind the female. One explanation is that there is some social benefit to facing each other during sexual intercourse; it is said to increase emotional bonds between male and female. A problem with this suggestion is that most studies of human sexual behavior have found that humans engage in a wide variety of sexual positions. Though the missionary position has been cited as the most common sexual position for certain societies at certain times, it is not the most common everywhere. Human bipedal anatomy may influence the fact that humans use the missionary position while other primates rarely use it. The changes in the human pelvis have shifted the position of the vagina so that the missionary position is easier to attain. Apes rarely have sex in this manner simply because it is not comfortable for them. An exception is the bonobo, which has been observed to have sexual intercourse face to face.

Some authors claim that female orgasm is unique in human beings and have constructed a number of explanations for this fact. There is growing evidence, however, that nonhuman primate females also experience orgasm (Jolly 1985, de Waal 1995).

Human females have relatively large breasts, whereas other primate females do not. One hypothesis is that large breasts developed to resemble buttocks. Given that face-to-face sex is desirable in reinforcing emotional bonds and that males prefer the buttocks (both questionable assumptions), large breasts would serve to attract human males to the female's front. Another suggestion is that large breasts in human females is a by-product of the evolution of fat in human females. Fat reserves are important for females in hunting-and-gathering societies because fat is stored energy that can be used for reproduction in times of food shortage. It has been hypothesized that hormonal changes accompanying increased fat reserves led to increased breast size in human females (Mascia-Lees et al. 1986). This hypothesis, though interesting, still needs to be tested.

The human pattern of reproduction is basically the same as that of most primates: single births. Unlike apes, humans have additional children before the previous children have grown up socially or physically. Because of cultural adaptations, humans have increased reproduction without sacrificing parental care. Compared to apes, a greater proportion of the human life cycle is taken up by physical and social growth prior to maturity. Consider, for example, that a chimpanzee is sexually mature at about 10 years and lives roughly 40 years (Jolly 1985). This means that roughly 25 percent of the chimp's life is spent growing up. Further consider that a human matures at roughly 15 years and that throughout most of history and prehistory, we estimate that humans had an average length of life of roughly 30 years. Compared to other primates, we mature more slowly and require a greater amount of our life for growing and learning. This logic may seem strange since the average length of life today in the United States is roughly 75 years, not 30. However, keep in mind that our relatively long life is neither universal nor very old. Most of the increase in our average length of life has come only in the past century or so (see Chapter 16).

Human Growth

The human life cycle includes changes in physical growth. The major stages of growth are prenatal (before birth) and postnatal (after birth). The general nature of these two stages is reviewed briefly, followed by consideration of what is unique about human growth.

PRENATAL GROWTH   Prenatal life is the period from fertilization through childbirth. After fertilization, the fertilized egg (**zygote**) develops into a cluster of identical cells deriving from the initial fertilized egg. During the first week, the fertilized egg multiplies as it travels into the uterus. By this time, there are roughly 150 cells arranged in a hollow ball that implants itself into the wall of the uterus. Cell differentiation begins. During the second week, the outer layer of this ball forms the beginning of the placenta. Some early differentiation of cells can be seen in the remainder of the ball.

▲▲

zygote A fertilized egg.

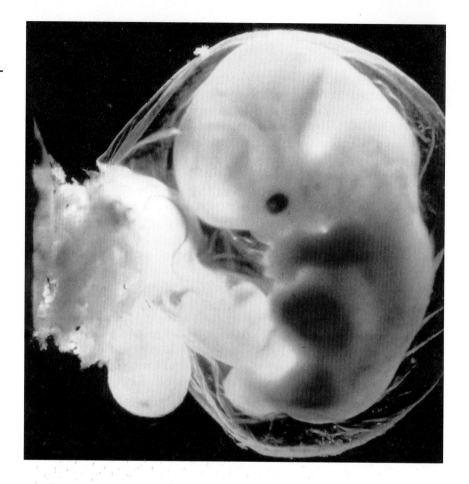

The embryonic stage stretches from roughly two to eight weeks after conception. The **embryo** is very small during this time, reaching an average length of 25 mm (1 in.) by the eighth week. During this time the basic body structure is completed and many of the different organ systems have developed; the embryo has a recognizably human appearance although it is still not complete (Figure 8.6). The fetal stage lasts from this point until birth. Development of body parts and organ systems continues, along with a tremendous amount of body growth and changes in proportions. During the second trimester of pregnancy, the **fetus** shows rapid growth in overall length. During the third trimester, the fetus shows rapid growth in body weight, head size, and brain growth.

THE PATTERN OF HUMAN POSTNATAL GROWTH   We can identify five basic stages in the growth from birth until adulthood (Bogin 1995). The first stage, *infancy*, refers to the time from birth until weaning (typically up to three years in nonindustrialized societies), and is characterized by rapid growth. The second stage, *childhood*, refers to the time from weaning until the end of growth in brain weight, which takes place at about seven years (Cabana et al. 1993). The *juvenile* stage is from this point until the beginning of the fourth stage,

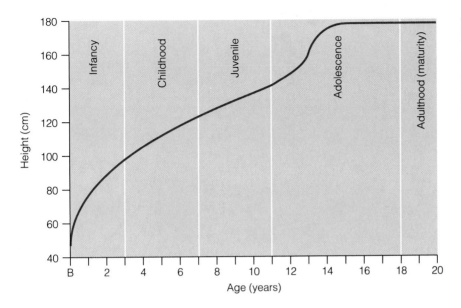

FIGURE 8.7
Typical distance curve for human height. (From *Growth and Development* by Robert M. Malina © 1975, publisher Burgess Publishing Company, Minneapolis, MN; modified as per Bogin 1995)

adolescence, which is the time of sexual maturation and a spurt in body growth. Adolescence begins at about age 10 in females and 12 in males, although there is considerable variation across people and populations. The fifth stage is labeled *adulthood.*

Human growth is usually studied by looking at growth curves. One type of growth curve, the **distance curve,** is a measure of size over time—it shows how big someone is at any given age. Figure 8.7 is a typical distance curve for human height. As we all know, until you reach adulthood, the older you get, the taller you get. However, note that this is not a straight line—you do not grow the same amount each year. This shows that the *rate* of body growth is not the same from year to year. Changes in the rate of growth are best illustrated by a **velocity curve,** which plots the *rate* of change over time. The difference between a distance curve and velocity curve can be illustrated by a simple analogy—driving a car. Imagine driving a car on a highway between two cities. How *far* you have come is your distance, and how *fast* you are going is your velocity.

embryo The stage of human prenatal life lasting from roughly two to eight weeks following conception; characterized by structural development.

fetus The stage of prenatal growth from roughly 8 weeks following conception until birth; characterized by further development and rapid growth.

distance curve A measure of size over time. For example, a distance curve would show how tall someone is at different ages.

velocity curve A measure of the rates of change in growth over time.

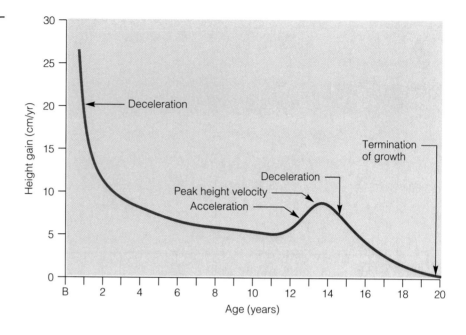

■ FIGURE 8.8
Typical velocity curve for
human height.
(From *Growth and Development*
by Robert M. Malina © 1975,
publisher Burgess Publishing
Company, Minneapolis, MN)

A typical velocity curve for human height is shown in Figure 8.8. The *rate* of growth is greatest immediately after birth, followed by a rapid deceleration during infancy. Even though the rate of growth decreases, we still continue to grow. Referring again to the car analogy, if you decelerate from 50 miles per hour to 30 miles per hour, you are still going forward, although not as fast. During childhood and the juvenile stage, height velocity decreases slightly, but then increases rapidly for a short time during adolescence. At adulthood, the rate of growth again decreases until there is no further significant growth.

Comparing distance and velocity curves for human body size with other organisms has revealed two basic differences: humans have an extended childhood and an adolescent period (Bogin 1988, 1995). In most mammals, the rate of growth decreases from childbirth, and adulthood occurs without any intervening stages. In other mammals, there is a stage of juvenile growth. Only in humans, however, do we see childhood, adolescence, and a long post-reproductive period (Bogin 1995).

This discussion thus far has centered on body size. In order to understand the unique aspects of the human growth pattern, it is also necessary to look at changes in growth for other parts of the body, such as the head and brain tissue. Quite simply, not everything grows at the same rate. Figure 8.9 compares human distance curves for body size, brain size, and the reproductive system. All three are drawn to illustrate the percentage of total adult size attained at any given age. Note the differences in these curves—our brains and reproductive systems obviously do not grow at the same rate as our bodies. In particular, our brain grows most rapidly at first, reaching adult weight

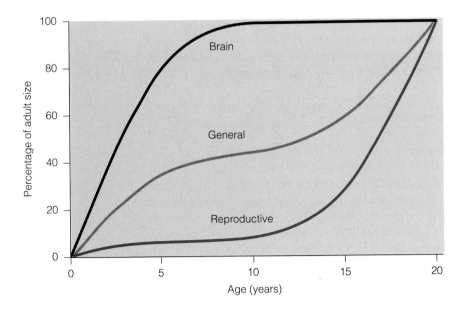

FIGURE 8.9
Distance curves for different body tissues, showing the percentage of total adult size reached at different ages. The general curve represents overall body size (height or weight). The brain curve represents brain weight. The reproductive curve represents the weight of sex organs and tissues. From Bogin (1995), based on Scammon (1930) and updated to include new data on brain growth (Cabana et al. 1993). (Barry Bogin)

by roughly seven years of age (Cabana et al. 1993). The reproductive system grows most slowly, showing hardly any growth until adolescence.

THE EVOLUTION OF HUMAN GROWTH   If you think about it for a moment, these differences in timing of growth make sense. Because humans are dependent on learning as a means of survival, it makes sense to have as large a brain in place as soon as possible. The physical limits to the rate of brain growth while in the womb mean that the best time for extended brain growth to occur is during the first few years of life. Likewise, it makes sense to have sexual maturity postponed until later in life so that we have time to develop physically and socially enough to provide adequately for offspring.

The evolutionary advantage to delayed maturation and an extended childhood is clear—a longer childhood allows more time for brain development, growth, and learning (see Bogin 1995 for additional details and benefits). But why do we have the adolescent growth spurt? Although there is some argument about whether nonhuman primates show any such growth spurt (e.g., Watts 1986, Bogin 1988), there is none about whether humans do—the growth spurt in humans is quite noticeable. Traditional explanations see it as a means of "catching up." If our childhood has been extended, then we have proportionately less time in our lives as reproductive adults (remember that our best estimates suggest that until very recently in human history, people lived an average of 20 to 40 years). The rapid growth during adolescence allows us to reach sexual maturity and adult body size more quickly, thus allowing us to have our extended childhood and an adequate reproductive period as well (Bogin 1988). Without this growth spurt, we would reach adulthood later and possibly not have enough time to adequately care for any offspring. Bogin (1995) has recently questioned this traditional interpretation, and points to additional benefits of the growth spurt, such as providing time for learning adult skills prior to reproduction.

Social Structure

Human social structure is a topic of almost infinite complexity that is thoroughly explored in cultural anthropology textbooks. One observation is obvious—there is extensive variation. Because variation in social structure is great even among the apes, it should come as no surprise that humans, with an even greater emphasis on learned behavior, show greater variation.

A common Western assumption is that the "normal" social structure of human beings is the nuclear monogamous family group: mother, father, and children. Actually, the majority (almost 90 percent) of human societies studied have a stated preference for **polygyny**—a pattern in which one husband has several wives (Harris 1987). A few cultures also practice **polyandry,** in which one woman has several husbands. Because of this, anthropologists have often argued that the basic human pattern is polygyny. However, it must be noted that although many societies state a *preference* for polygyny, it is still much more common for men to have a single wife. In many cases, only the most wealthy or powerful have multiple wives. Fisher (1992) has reviewed the evidence and concludes that for all practical purposes, monogamy is the predominant marriage pattern for humans. This is not to deny the exceptions, but rather it points to our need to contrast stated cultural preferences with actual cultural practices.

Humans show a great deal of variation as well in other aspects of their culture, such as economic systems, political systems, and legal systems. There are also some biological limitations on human cultural behavior, however. Humans are social animals and do not survive well when isolated. Apart from the occasional hermit, humans thrive best in groups. Humans have biological needs, such as food and sex, that structure our behaviors.

ARE HUMANS UNIQUE?

Humans and apes show a great many similarities as well as a great many differences. When we ask whether humans are unique, we do not suggest that we cannot tell an ape and a human apart. Rather, we ask what the extent of these differences is. Are the behaviors of apes and human completely different, or are differences present only in the expression of specific behaviors? Can we say, for example, that humans make tools and apes do not? Or should we say instead that there are differences in the way in which these two groups make and use tools?

According to the view that apes and humans show distinct and major differences, humans possess culture and apes do not. Any cultural behaviors found in apes are labeled as fundamentally different from human cultural behaviors. According to the view that ape–human differences are variations on something that is fundamentally similar, both humans and apes possess culture—the only difference being that humans rely more on culture or that humans have a more developed culture. This debate is semantic to a large extent. A more worthwhile approach is to examine some of the suggested differences between apes and humans in an effort to determine what is truly different.

Tool Use and Manufacture

Tool use has often been cited as a unique human behavior. As defined here, a tool is an object that is not part of the animal. Human tools include pencils, clothes, eating utensils, books, and houses. All of these are objects that are not part of the biological organism (humans) but are used for a specific purpose. Tool use, however, does not seem to be even a unique primate characteristic. Birds use sticks for nests and beavers use dirt in their dams. Both sticks and dirt can be considered tools by this definition.

A more common definition of modern humans focuses on humans as toolmakers (this definition is complicated by the fact that the earliest hominids may not have made tools—see Chapter 10). The key element of this definition is that some object is taken from the environment and modified to meet a new function. Humans take trees to make lumber to build houses. It can be argued that birds modify sticks and beavers modify dirt, but tool manufacture implies something different. Birds, for example, use sticks for building nests but they do not use these sticks for defensive or offensive weapons. Humans, however, can take sticks and use them to make shelters, defend themselves, hunt, dig up roots, and draw pictures in the sand. When we discuss tool manufacture, we mean the new and different ways to modify an object for a task. Humans can apply the same raw materials to a variety of tasks.

polygyny A form of marriage in which a husband has several wives.

polyandry A form of marriage in which a wife has several husbands.

Can Apes Make Stone Tools?

Toolmaking had long been one of the cited unique characteristics of humans, a behavior that set them apart from other animals. The pioneering work of Jane Goodall in the 1960s totally revised how anthropologists defined humankind. Her observations of toolmaking, including the use of fashioned sticks to "fish" for termites and ants, led to the realization that "toolmaking" in and of itself could not be claimed as a unique human trait. Instead, the definition of toolmaking had to be modified, focusing on how *human* toolmaking differed from *ape* toolmaking.

One such qualification dealt with the raw material and type of tool. The archaeological record shows that hominids have been fashioning stone tools for at least 2.5 million years (see Chapter 10). Living apes, however, do not fashion stone tools. (They *do* use stones to crack nuts, but we are talking here about striking one stone against another to fashion a cutting

edge or sharp flake.) This seems to be a reasonable distinction. The problem, however, is figuring out exactly what this distinction means. Does the fact that apes do not make stone tools mean that they *can't* make stone tools? Not necessarily.

Sue Savage-Rumbaugh, an ape language researcher, and Nick Toth, an archaeologist, joined forces to look at these questions (Savage-Rumbaugh and Lewin 1994). Their basic question was, Could an ape be motivated to learn how to make stone tools? For their research, they worked with the bonobo Kanzi (discussed in this chapter as part of the ape language experiments). Rather than condition Kanzi to make tools, they chose a strategy where Kanzi could learn through observation. They placed a reward in a box with a transparent lid and secured the box with string. Nick then showed Kanzi how to hit stones together to produce a sharp flake which could be used to open the box.

In this sense, tool manufacture has long been considered a unique human activity. But research on apes, particularly Goodall's work on chimpanzees, has since shown that this is not true. Apes make and use tools. Though their tools are extremely simple by modern human standards, it is clear that the difference between apes and humans cannot be reduced to humans making tools and apes not making tools. Differences exist in the method and use of manufactured tools, but not the presence or absence of toolmaking.

CHIMPANZEE TERMITE FISHING   In the early 1960s, Jane Goodall reported a remarkable finding—chimpanzees were making and using tools! Though chimpanzees are predominantly fruit eaters, they also enjoy a variety of other foods, including termites. One group of chimpanzees demonstrated a method for capturing termites. They took a grass stem or a stick, went up to a termite mound, and uncovered one of the entrance holes left by the termites. They inserted the stick into the hole, twirled the stick a bit to attract termites down in the mound, and then withdrew the stick. Termites had attached themselves to the stick, and the chimpanzees ate them directly off the stick.

Close analysis of this "termite fishing" behavior shows it to be true tool manufacture along with rather complex tool use. Chimpanzees often spent a great deal of time selecting the appropriate stick. When a suitable stick was

Through observation, Kanzi eventually began attempting to make his own flakes. At first, he was very tentative about striking the stones together with sufficient force, but ultimately developed the appropriate level of force. Kanzi's flaking was still somewhat crude when he invented a different technique: throwing the stones against the hard tile floor. Because Savage-Rumbaugh and Toth were interested in Kanzi's flaking ability, they carpeted the floor to keep him from making flakes with his newly invented, and easier, method. Kanzi was not easily deterred; he pulled up a corner of the carpet to expose part of the hard floor. Even when taken outside, Kanzi would attempt to make flakes by throwing one stone against another.

When prevented from using his own method, Kanzi became increasingly better at flaking stone tools. His blows became harder and more precise. Eventually, Savage-Rumbaugh and Toth were able to conclude that apes *can* make stone tools. The next question is, How do these tools compare with those found with our early ancestors? Although Kanzi had progressed considerably, his tools were still not as sophisticated as the earliest known stone tools. There may be some basic difference here between the toolmaking capabilities of humans and apes—a finding that implies that the abilities of the earliest hominid toolmakers had already progressed beyond those of the apes.

There is still a question as to the significance of the difference between Kanzi's tools and those of our early ancestors. Are the differences a reflection of mental ability? Of manipulative ability? Or experience? Although much remains to be answered by such research, we again see the gap between human and ape to be less than once thought.

not available, they pulled a branch out of the ground or off a bush and stripped away the leaves. This is deliberate manipulation of an object in the environment—toolmaking. The act also reflects a conscious decision-making process.

Termite fishing is not easy. One anthropologist who tried found that it was a difficult process that required a great deal of skill and practice. Even finding the right kind of stick is tricky. If a stick is too flexible or too rigid, it cannot be inserted into the termite tunnel. Taking the stick out without knocking the termites off also calls for careful handling.

Termite fishing is not an innate chimpanzee behavior. It is passed on to others in the group by means of learning. Young chimpanzees watch their elders and imitate them, thus learning the methods and also developing practice. As Goodall has documented, termite fishing has become part of the local group's culture.

OTHER EXAMPLES OF TOOLMAKING   Termite fishing is only one of many types of tool manufacture reported among chimpanzees. Sticks are also used to hunt for ants (Figure 8.10). A chimpanzee will dig up an underground nest with its hands and then insert a long stick into the nest. The ants begin swarming up the stick and the chimpanzee withdraws it to eat the ants. Sticks have also been used to probe holes in dead wood and to break into bee nests (Goodall 1986).

In addition, chimpanzees have been observed making sponges out of leaves. After a rainfall, a chimpanzee often drinks out of pools of water that collect in the holes of tree branches. Often the holes are too small for the chimp to fit its head into, so the chimp creates a tool to soak up the water: he takes a leaf, puts it into his mouth, and chews it slightly. (Chewing increases the ability of the leaf to absorb water.) The chimp inserts this "sponge" into the hole in the branch to soak up the water.

Other examples of chimpanzee toolmaking and tool use include using leaves as napkins and toilet paper, using sticks as weapons, and using rocks to break open nuts and hard fruits (Goodall 1986).

In recent years, researchers have observed that toolmaking and tool use are not specieswide characteristics among chimpanzees. Not all groups have shown the same behaviors. Some use sticks for ant or termite fishing or sponges for drinking; others do not (McGrew 1992). This variation may reflect the importance of individual discoveries. It might also relate to environmental differences, with tool use being more frequent in areas with less immediately available food.

An interesting finding is that bonobos do not engage in tool use in their native environments to any great extent. Although a captive bonobo has been taught to make stone tools (Savage-Rumbaugh and Lewin 1994), the only observation of bonobo tool use in the wild has been the use of leafy twigs as shelter from the rain (McGrew 1992).

HUMAN AND CHIMPANZEE TOOLMAKING   It is obvious that chimpanzees make and use tools in a systematic manner. It is also clear that they use genuine problem-solving abilities in their toolmaking. They see a problem (e.g., termites in the mounds) and create a tool to solve the problem. The implication of these studies is that we can no longer define humans as the only toolmakers. Our definition must be modified, and we must focus on differences in toolmaking between apes and humans.

There are several important differences between chimpanzee and human toolmaking and tool use. First, humans depend on tools; chimpanzees do not. Termite fishing provides a tasty treat for the chimpanzees, but it is not essential for their survival. Chimpanzees survive without tools in many places. Humans, on the other hand, depend on tools for survival. Toolmaking and tool use are not an option for humans; they are an imperative.

A second difference is that humans save their tools. Chimpanzees start over each time they make a tool (one exception is saving the rocks used to crack open nuts). Chimpanzees who fish termites do not save the sticks they have made. Humans save their tools, presumably because of the greater importance tools have for human survival.

Third, humans use tools to make other tools. This allows for the construction of a complex technological system. Thus far, no one has seen chimpanzees do this. A further key distinction of modern humans is that we accumulate our knowledge of toolmaking, building on it generation after generation.

In any case, it is clear that we cannot define modern humans solely in terms of having the ability to make tools. The observations made by Goodall and others regarding chimpanzee tool manufacture have caused us to redefine human behavior and to reconsider our relationship with the apes. We now acknowledge much closer similarities than we did several decades ago. The methods, goals, and complexities of human toolmaking are clearly quite different from those of apes. However, we must acknowledge that we are not as dissimilar as was once thought.

Language Capabilities

Language has long been considered a unique human property. Language is not merely communication but rather a symbolic form of communication. The nonhuman primates communicate basic emotions in a variety of ways. Chimpanzees, for example, have a large number of vocalizations that they use to convey emotional states such as anger, fear, or stress (Figure 8.11). Many primates also use their sense of touch to communicate some emotions by **grooming,** the handling and cleaning of another individual's fur (Figure 8.12). Grooming helps keep the animal clean and also acts to soothe and reassure tense or frightened individuals. Grooming is a common form of social communication among primates.

grooming The handling and cleaning of another individual's fur or hair. In primates, grooming serves as a form of communication that soothes and provides reassurance.

■ FIGURE 8.11
A chimpanzee hooting.
(© Marine World Africa USA,
Vallejo, CA)

■ FIGURE 8.12
Two chimpanzees grooming.
(© Marine World Africa USA,
Vallejo, CA)

WHAT IS LANGUAGE?   Primate communication through vocalizations, grooming, or other methods does not constitute language. Language, as a symbolic form of communication, has certain characteristics that distinguish it from simple communication. Language is an *open system*; that is, new ideas can be expressed that have never been expressed before. Chimpanzee vocalizations, on the other hand, form a closed system capable of conveying only a few basic concepts or emotions. Human language can use a finite number of sounds and create an infinite number of words, sentences, and ideas from these sounds.

Another important characteristic of language is *displacement*. Language allows discussion of objects and events that are displaced—that is, not present—in time and/or space. For example, you can say, "Tomorrow I am going to another country." This sentence conveys an idea that is displaced in both time ("tomorrow") and space ("another country"). We can discuss the past, the future, and faraway places. Displacement is very important for our ability to plan future events—imagine the difficulty in planning a hunt several days from now without the ability to speak of future events!

Language is also arbitrary. The actual sounds we use in our languages need not bear any relationship to reality. Our word for "book" could just as easily be "gurmf" or some other sound. The important point is that we understand the relationship of sounds to objects and ideas. This in turn shows yet another important feature of language—it is learned.

APES AND AMERICAN SIGN LANGUAGE   Early efforts to teach English to apes were failures. One classic experiment was conducted on a young female chimpanzee named Vicki. After years of extensive work Vicki could speak only four words: "Mama," "Papa," "up," and "cup." Later researchers noted that the failure of this experiment might mean only that apes cannot speak English; it said nothing about their ability to understand. Looking back at this study, it is no surprise that Vicki could not speak very well, because the vocal anatomy of chimpanzees makes speaking a human language next to impossible.

In the 1960s, two scientists, Allen and Beatrice Garner, began teaching the American Sign Language to a young female chimpanzee named Washoe. Devised for the deaf, American Sign Language (ASL) is a true symbolic language that does not require vocalization but instead uses hand and finger gestures. Because chimpanzees are capable of making such signs, ASL was considered the most suitable medium to determine whether or not they were capable of using language (Figure 8.13). Washoe quickly learned many signs and soon developed an extensive vocabulary.

Washoe also demonstrated the ability to generalize: to take a concept learned in one context and apply it to another. For example, she would use the sign meaning *open* to refer to boxes as well as doors. This suggests that Washoe truly understood the general concept of *open* and not just the use of the sign in one specific context. Washoe also invented new signs and

"talked" to herself while playing alone, an act human children perform when learning language. Washoe was even observed to swear!

One of the most intriguing findings of the Gardners' research was that Washoe would form simple two- and three-word sentences (for example, "You tickle me"). Early observations suggested that Washoe was not only capable of symbolism but also of grammar and sentence construction.

Washoe was the first ape taught American Sign Language. Since then there have been many experiments into the nature of the language capabilities of apes. Gorillas, as well as chimpanzees, have been taught ASL. Other languages were also invented, including one based on plastic tiles and another using a computer keyboard. Experiments were devised that required two chimpanzees to interact with each other using language. These experiments confirmed the ability to generalize signs and to create new ones. For example, one chimpanzee named Lucy combined the signs *drink* and *fruit* to refer to a watermelon for which she had not been taught a sign. She also invented the phrase "cry hurt food" to refer to radishes, which presumably she found bitter.

HUMAN AND APE LANGUAGE ABILITIES   The purpose of the original research with Washoe was to determine what was unique about the way in which a human child learns language. It was suggested that a comparison of human and chimpanzee language acquisition would reveal at what point human abilities surpassed those of the ape. Washoe's abilities exceeded early expectations, and soon the research focus shifted to the language capabilities of the apes themselves. The ability of Washoe and other apes to learn a symbolic language suggested that language acquisition could no longer be regarded as a unique human feature.

There is considerable debate about the meaning of these studies. Some claim that many of the positive results are the result of unconscious cues given to the apes by humans. Also, there is the problem of interpreting the data and seeing what one wants to see. For example, Washoe signed "water bird" the first time she saw a swan. Some researchers have interpreted this as a true invention. Others have suggested that Washoe simply saw the water and then the bird, and responded with the two signs in sequence. Obviously, much of this research is fraught with the danger of speculation and excessive interpretations for the simple reason that we cannot get inside the chimpanzee's mind.

In spite of the debates, however, there is little doubt that apes can learn and understand the meaning of many signs. Chimpanzees, gorillas, and orangutans have all mastered a certain number. Some chimps have learned over 150 signs by the time they were 7 years old (Snowden 1990). Carefully controlled experiments have shown that the basic vocabulary of apes is not a reflection of unconscious cues given by the scientists. The behavior of signing correctly while playing alone strongly suggests that the apes actually do understand, *in some manner*, the meaning of signs.

Much of the controversy over language acquisition in apes revolves around two different training approaches. Many studies, including the Washoe project, attempted to teach language in an environment similar to that in which human children develop linguistic skills, one offering continued exposure in an unstructured environment with many opportunities for creativity and expression. Other ape studies used controlled, less flexible environments. The controlled experiments were of course designed to minimize cues from humans and to provide more definitive measurements. The problem is that this type of sterile approach is not the most conducive to learning language.

One of the most interesting observations came about by accident during a study conducted by Savage-Rumbaugh, in which researchers were attempting to teach a female bonobo a keyboard-based language. At the time, the bonobo was caring for an infant, Kanzi, who frequently interrupted his mother. Later, when the mother was returned to the breeding colony, Kanzi began to use the keyboard to make requests. Over time, he performed well on a variety of measures (Savage-Rumbaugh and Lewin 1994). Significantly, he learned language by observation, and not through direct training. (After all, the experiment was not designed to teach him; he was simply there to be nursed.) In other words, Kanzi learned elements of language in the same way that human children do.

The suggested ability of apes to understand grammar and to construct sentences is also controversial. Though apes do create correct two- and three-word sentences, the few longer sentences they create are often grammatically incorrect. There has also been evidence that the apes respond to unconscious cues in constructing sentences (as opposed to simple vocabulary identification). Though some see definite evidence of grammar (e.g., Linden 1981), others see little evidence (e.g., Terrace 1979). The debate continues.

Regardless of the outcome, it is clear that the difference between human and ape is not as great as we once thought. We can no longer define modern humans in terms of the capability to learn certain aspects of symbolic language. Apes are certainly capable of symbolic behavior, even if we can debate over exactly how much. Both humans and apes can learn symbols, though humans are clearly better at it. Perhaps one of the major differences is the fact that humans rely on language and apes do not. In their natural habitat, apes do not use sign language. The fact that they are capable of learning language to a certain extent should not detract from the point that they do not use language in their natural environment. As with tool manufacture, we see evidence of capabilities in the apes for behaviors that are optional for them but mandatory for modern humans.

The question of human uniqueness becomes more complicated when we consider possible behaviors of our fossil ancestors. Given a common ancestry with the African apes, at what point did our own patterns of tool-making and language acquisition begin? Studies of modern apes help answer such questions because we can see the *potential* for such behaviors in the modern apes. Using these potentials as a guide to the behavior of the common ancestor of African apes and humans, we can attempt to determine what changes were necessary to arrive at the modern human condition.

SUMMARY

Humans share many features with the other hominoids but also show a number of differences. The main biological characteristics of humans are a large and complex brain, three times its expected value; bipedalism; and small canine teeth. In addition, humans have a growth pattern that is different from other primates in its extended childhood and adolescent growth spurt. Behaviorally, humans are quite variable.

Past behavioral definitions of humans have often focused on humans as toolmakers. However, studies of apes in their native habitat show that they also make and use simple tools. Another oft-cited human characteristic is the use of symbolic language. Although apes are unable physically to speak a human language, studies of American Sign Language and other symbolic, visually-oriented languages show that apes have some language acquisition capabilities. Studies of toolmaking and language acquisition show that the difference between apes and humans may be more a matter of degree than kind. Modern humans remain unique in the specific ways they use tools and language and in their reliance on these behaviors for survival. What is mandatory for humans is optional for apes. Still, the capabilities shown by apes provide us with possible clues regarding human origins.

SUPPLEMENTAL READINGS

In addition to Passingham's book (listed in Chapter 7), other useful sources are:

Fisher, H. 1992. *Anatomy of Love: A Natural History of Mating, Marriage, and Why We Stray.* New York: Ballantine. A well-written and fascinating account of evolutionary explanations of human marriage and mating.

Linden, E. 1986. *Silent Partners: The Legacy of the Ape Language Experiments.* New York: Ballantine.

Patterson, F. and Linden, E. 1981. *The Education of Koko.* New York: Holt, Rinehart and Winston.

Savage-Rumbaugh, S., and Lewin, R. 1994. *Kanzi: The Ape at the Brink of the Human Mind.* New York: John Wiley & Sons.

These last three books are excellent popular accounts of the studies of ape language acquisition.

CHAPTER **9**

Primate Origins and Evolution

As discussed in Chapter 5, the dinosaurs became extinct at the end of the Mesozoic era 65 million years ago. Their demise opened up numerous opportunities for other animals, particularly the mammals, to expand into new environments. This adaptive radiation of mammals included the ancestors of modern-day primates.

Modern primates did not appear instantaneously 65 million years ago. There were no monkeys, apes, or humans at that time. Rather, a group of mammals began adapting to life in the trees. This change provided a base for further evolution, leading ultimately to modern-day primates. It is important to realize that the definitions of modern forms discussed in Chapters 6 and 7 do not always apply to early fossil forms. Any classification based on *modern* characteristics reflects many millions of years of evolution. The further back in time we go, the harder it is to distinguish between different forms of primates.

Also, primate and primatelike forms in the past exhibited an amazing diversity. In the past few decades, we have realized it is not a simple matter to

■ TABLE 9.1
Epochs of the Cenozoic

Epoch	Millions of Years b.p.	Major events in primate evolution
Holocene	0.01–Present	Humans develop agriculture and industry, explore outer space
Pleistocene	1.8–0.01	Evolution of the genus *Homo* (*Homo erectus* and *Homo sapiens*)
Pliocene	5–1.8	First hominids and origin of the genus *Homo*
Miocene	22–5	Radiation of early apes, divergence of apes and hominids
Oligocene	38–22	Radiation of anthropoids
Eocene	55–38	First primates (primitive prosimians); first anthropoids?
Paleocene	65–55	Primatelike mammals

draw family trees connecting earlier forms with modern forms. We now know there were many species of prosimians, monkeys, and apes that have no living counterpart.

EARLY PRIMATE EVOLUTION

Primates evolved during the Cenozoic era, which is the past 65 million years. (The **epochs** of this era are listed in Table 9.1). Primate evolution should not be thought of as a simple evolutionary "tree" with a few branches. A better analogy would be a series of "bushes" with many different branches at each stage of primate evolution. One or more adaptive radiations of primate forms occurred during each epoch. Many of the new forms became extinct, some evolved to become present-day representatives, and some evolved into the next phase of primate evolution.

Overview of Early Primate Evolution

Before getting into the details of primate origins and evolution, it is useful to summarize some of the major events that took place. An adaptive radiation of primatelike mammals led to the origin of what we would call "true primates." The primatelike mammals showed evidence of an initial adaptation to life in the trees. Most of these species died out, but some evolved into primitive prosimians, which were fully adapted to living in the trees. These

epoch Subdivision of a geologic period.

■ **FIGURE 9.1**
A tree shrew, an insectivore
similar in certain respects to
primates. (© Zoological Society
of San Diego)

early prosimians then underwent another adaptive radiation. Although many of these early prosimian species became extinct, some species survived to ultimately evolve into the different lines of modern prosimians. Some of the early prosimians evolved into early anthropoids. A subsequent adaptive radiation led to separate groups of New World monkeys, Old World monkeys, and the first primitive apes.

Primate Origins

At the end of the Mesozoic era there existed a number of mammals called **insectivores** that were arboreal, nocturnal, and ate insects. A modern-day representative of this group is the tree shrew (Figure 9.1), which illustrates the probable morphology of the ancestor of primates. Of all living mammals, the insectivores are most similar to the primates, suggesting that they are ancestral to primates. Paleoanthropologists look at the variation in this early group to try to identify forms that show the transition to the order Primates.

CONTINENTAL DRIFT AND PRIMATE EVOLUTION   Most of the fossil evidence on primate origins comes from deposits over 55 million years ago in North America and Europe of a group of insectivores known as the primatelike mammals. This widespread distribution may seem strange, given the fact that North America and Europe are now separated by the Atlantic Ocean. This was not, however, the configuration at that time. The continents continually move about on large crusted plates on top of a partially molten layer of the earth's mantle—a process known as **continental drift.** This process continues today: North America is slowly drifting away from Europe, toward Asia. The expansion of the South Atlantic has even been measured from satellites. The placement of the different continents at various times in the past is shown in Figure 9.2.

An understanding of past continental drift is crucial in interpreting the fossil evidence for primate evolution. As continents move, their environments change. When continents separate, populations become isolated; when continents join, there is an opportunity for large-scale migrations of populations. Roughly 230 million years ago, all the continents were joined together as one large land mass. By 180 million years B.P., this large mass had split in two: one containing North America, Europe, and Asia, and the other containing South America, Africa, Australia, and Antarctica. By the time of the primatelike mammals, South America had split off from Africa, but North America and Europe were still joined. Thus, it is no surprise to find fossils of primatelike mammals on both continents—they represent part of the group's range on a single land mass.

THE PRIMATELIKE MAMMALS   During the **Paleocene epoch** (65–55 million years B.P.), we find evidence of what are referred to as "primatelike mammals,"

■ **FIGURE 9.2**
Continental drift. Over 200 million years B.P., all of the continents formed a single land mass (called Pangea). By 180 million years B.P., two major land masses had formed (Laurasia and Gondowana). By 65 million years B.P. (the beginning of primate evolution), South America had split from Africa, but North America and Europe were still joined. (From *Human Antiquity: An Introduction to Physical Anthropology and Archaeology,* 2d ed., by Kenneth Feder and Michael Park. Copyright 1993 by Mayfield Publishing Company)

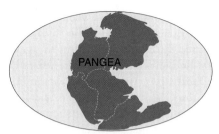

More than 200 million years ago

180 million years ago

65 million years ago

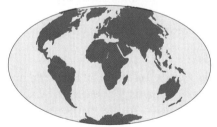

Present

insectivore An order of mammals adapted to insect eating.

continental drift The movement of continental land masses on top of a partially molten layer of the earth's mantle that has altered the relative location of the continents over time.

Paleocene epoch The first epoch of the Cenozoic era, dating roughly between 65 and 55 million years B.P., when the primatelike mammals appeared.

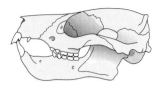

Side view of a skull of a Paleocene primatelike mammal. (Redrawn from Fleagle, *Primate Adaptation and Evolution,* 1988, with permission, Academic Press, Inc.)

which were small creatures, usually no larger than a cat and often smaller. They were quadrupedal (four-footed) mammals whose arms and legs were well adapted for climbing. Within this general group there was considerable diversity. Remains have been assigned to 27 different genera (Conroy 1990). Most of this extensive variation was in body size and dental specializations. Some of the primatelike mammals had large incisors for heavy gnawing, others had teeth better adapted for slicing, and still others had teeth adapted for eating nectar and insects. Such variation is expected from an adaptive radiation. These small insectivores had some ability to climb and thus were able to exploit many different types of food.

In spite of their arboreal adaptations, these creatures are not considered true primates. A picture of the skull of one of these creatures (Figure 9.3) shows why. The front teeth are far apart from the rest of the teeth, a feature not found in primates. The eyes are located more toward the sides of the skull, unlike the forward-facing eyes of primates. In addition, the primatelike mammals lack a **postorbital bar,** a bony ring separating the orbit of the eye from the back of the skull. Primates have a postorbital bar. Also, the hands and feet of these animals did not have the grasping ability of primates, and they had claws instead of nails.

If these forms are not primates, then how can we say they are related to primates? You should not expect to examine the fossil record and see some point at which modern-day primate structure immediately appears. Evolution is **mosaic,** meaning that not all new structures appear at the same time. Examination of the primatelike mammals shows a number of primate features, such as changes in the teeth and development of climbing abilities. In particular, the molar teeth are primatelike, as are the base of the skull and the structure of the ankle (Gingerich 1986). Not enough changes have occurred that we would call them primates, but enough have taken place that we call them primatelike mammals. They are another example of transitional forms in the fossil record.

MODELS OF PRIMATE ORIGINS   The first true primates evolved from a population of primatelike mammals. The general scenario for this change involves continuing adaptation to life in the trees. The primatelike mammals had the beginnings of arboreal adaptations, and many also possessed the more generalized teeth capable of exploiting different types of foods and environments. In an arboreal environment, natural selection would favor those individuals better able to cope with the demands of life in the trees. As discussed in Chapter 6, living in the trees is quite a different experience from living on the ground. First, a three-dimensional orientation is needed. Leaping from branch to branch requires depth perception, which involves forward rotation of the eyes so that the visual fields overlap. Vision, particularly depth perception, becomes a more important sense than smell. The sense of smell is less important in the trees, where constant breezes and winds act to dissipate any smells.

Second, living in the trees also requires an agile body capable of bending and twisting in midair. The early insectivores retained the early generalized vertebrate skeletal structure, and the first primates made use of this flexibility in the trees. The retention of the primitive trait of five digits was also important because having five digits on hands and feet allows the grasping of limbs and branches. Finally, good hand-eye coordination and a brain capable of rapidly processing a large volume of visual information are essential.

The early primatelike mammals already had traits on which natural selection could act. They had a generalized skeletal structure and five digits. Individuals possessing certain variations such as more forward-facing eyes and grasping abilities would be selected for. Over time, the primatelike mammals adapted to life in the trees and became the first true primates.

Primates were not the only animals to adapt to life in the trees. Other mammals, such as squirrels, also adapted to this environment. In considering evolutionary trends, you must remember that there is not necessarily only one set of adaptations to a specific environment. Squirrels use claws to anchor themselves while climbing and do not have the grasping hands and feet of primates. Primates represent only one possible direction, shaped in part by the demands of the environment and the variation present in the original populations. Again, remember that evolution is opportunistic.

Another scenario is the **visual predation model,** developed by Matthew Cartmill (1974), who sees the initial changes in grasping ability and vision as adaptations for hunting insects. Other animals besides primates have stereoscopic vision; it is also found in cats, owls, and hawks, among others. These animals are all active hunters, an activity for which the ability to gauge distance is invaluable. Could insect hunting be the reason for the initial origin of several primate characteristics? Cartmill suggests that the early insectivores hunted out their prey on the ground and on low-lying slender branches in the forest. The development of grasping hands allowed more successful hunting of prey along small branches. The development of stereoscopic vision made it easier for the insectivores to locate prey. In particular, stereoscopic vision allowed them to judge the distance to potential prey without moving their head (which could alert the prey). Cartmill notes that a similar development of stereoscopic vision occurred in cats. According to Cartmill's model, primate adaptations first arose as adaptations to more successful insect predation. Once these traits were established, these adaptations later allowed further exploitation of the trees. As is often the case in evolution,

postorbital bar The bony ring that separates the eye orbit from the back of the skull in primates.

mosaic evolution The concept that major evolutionary changes tend to take place in stages, not all at once.

visual predation model The view of primate origins that hypothesizes that stereoscopic vision and grasping hands first evolved as adaptations for hunting insects along branches.

■ FIGURE 9.4
Side view of the skull of an
Eocene primate. (Redrawn from
Fleagle, *Primate Adaptation and
Evolution*, 1988, with permission,
Academic Press, Inc.)

preexisting structures can be used for different purposes. The fossil record is not complete enough to test fully Cartmill's model, but the dental evidence does show that many of the early primatelike mammals were insect eaters. This observation is consistent with the insect predation idea, but it is not conclusive.

Yet another alternative has been proposed by Sussman (1991), who suggests that primate origins might be related to eating fruit, rather than insects. In Sussman's model, grasping hands are seen as an adaptation for efficiently eating the fruit that grows at the ends of long branches. Other mammals, such as squirrels, take food back to the main trunk of a tree to eat in safety. Grasping hands could have allowed early primates to eat more fruit in less time, and to do so more safely. A problem with this model, however, is that it does not explain binocular stereoscopic vision (Cartmill 1992).

Primates became extremely successful in adapting to an arboreal environment because of their biological and behavioral flexibility. This flexibility is even more important when considering the subsequent evolution of the primates.

THE FIRST PRIMATES   The first "true" primates appeared roughly 50 to 55 million years ago at the beginning of the **Eocene epoch** (55–38 million years B.P.). The climate during this time was warm and humid, and the predominant land environment was tropical and subtropical. Initially, the continents of Europe and North America were still joined, resulting in migration and similarity among the fossils we find in this region. Many orders of modern-day mammals first appeared during this time, including aquatic mammals (whales, porpoises, and dolphins), rodents, and horses.

Fossil primates from the Eocene epoch have been found both in North America and in Europe. During the Eocene, there was an adaptive radiation of the first true primates—the early prosimians. This adaptive radiation was part of the general increase in the diversity of mammals associated with the warming of the climate and related environmental changes. Five families of primates containing as many as 67 new genera evolved during the Eocene (Fleagle 1988).

The Eocene forms possessed stereoscopic vision, grasping hands, and other anatomical features characteristic of primates. A picture of the skull of an Eocene primate (Figure 9.4) shows many of these changes. Compared to the Paleocene primatelike mammals, the snout is reduced and the teeth are closer together. These forms possessed a postorbital bar and had larger brain cases and features of cerebral blood supply similar to that of modern primates (Fleagle 1988). The large size of the eyes of some of the Eocene primates suggests they were still nocturnal.

These early primitive primates were similar, in a *general* sense, to living prosimians. In a rough sense, there are two basic groups of early Eocene primates. One group, primarily diurnal leaf and fruit eaters, is broadly similar to modern lemurs and lorises. The other group, primarily smaller, nocturnal fruit and insect eaters, is broadly similar to modern tarsiers.

What became of these early primates? Many different species ultimately became extinct, leaving no descendants. Others evolved into the present-day prosimians. We lack sufficient data, however, to identify individual species as the ancestors of present-day prosimians. Only in a general sense can we link these two groups of early primates to living prosimians.

Anthropoid Origins

What of the anthropoids? Although living anthropoids are more similar to tarsiers than to lemurs or lorises, identification of the first anthropoids and their relationship to other fossil primates is not as clear. Recent fossil discoveries have suggested that anthropoids first evolved fairly early in primate evolution, perhaps as much as 50 million years ago (Godinot and Mahboubi 1992; Simons and Rasmussen 1994). It is possible that anthropoids developed not from the lemur-loris group or the tarsier group, but from a third, independent line in early primate evolution. It is too soon to determine which of these ideas (if any) is correct. The major lesson we have learned from recent fossil discoveries is that past diversity was much greater than we once thought, and even given our recent accumulation of data, we are unlikely to have sampled more than a fraction of early primate diversity.

OLD WORLD ANTHROPOIDS We have evidence of anthropoid fossils from the start of the **Oligocene epoch** (38–22 millions years B.P.) at several locations in the Old World and the New World. The climate cooled during this time, and there was an expansion of grasslands and a reduction in forests. This change in climate seems to have resulted in the southward movement of primate populations, and we find little evidence of further evolution in North America or Europe. Most of the fossil evidence for anthropoid evolution is found in southern climates in Africa and South America, and parts of eastern Asia (Fleagle 1995).

Most of the Old World evidence comes from an area known as the Fayum beds in Egypt. During the Oligocene, the Fayum was a rich tropical forest, in contrast to much of the area today. Although limited geographically, the Fayum fossil evidence shows that there was an adaptive radiation of anthropoids, the higher primates. The Fayum had a warm and wet climate, with plants similar to those found today in tropical regions of Southeast Asia. Analysis of Fayum fossils is often complicated by the fact that the region appears to have been somewhat unique. Fossil mammals found there are often different from those found in other Oligocene deposits (Fleagle

Eocene epoch The second epoch of the Cenozoic era, dating roughly between 55 and 38 million years B.P., when the first true primates, early prosimians, appeared.

Oligocene epoch The third epoch of the Cenozoic era, dating roughly between 38 and 22 million years B.P., when there was an adaptive radiation of anthropoids.

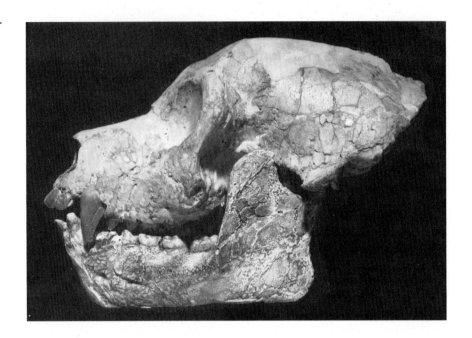

1988). Some evidence shows that all the Fayum primates lived before 31 million years ago (Fleagle et al. 1986).

The Oligocene primates show the continued radiation of anthropoid forms in both the Old World and the New World. The Oligocene anthropoids show continued reduction of the snout and nasal area, indicating greater reliance on vision than on smell. In addition to the postorbital bar shared with all primates, the Oligocene anthropoids have a fully enclosed eye socket, characteristic of modern anthropoids. All of the Oligocene anthropoids were small and arboreal and were generalized quadrupeds; none show signs of specialized locomotion. Their diet appears to have consisted primarily of fruit supplemented with insects and leaves.

The smaller eye orbits of many early anthropoids suggests that these forms were diurnal (Figure 9.5). The transition from a nocturnal lifestyle to a diurnal lifestyle was extremely important in the later evolution of the anthropoids. Given variation in the daily schedule of living creatures, we can imagine a situation in which some ancestral primates began feeding during daylight hours. As this new environmental niche was exploited, natural selection would act to favor individuals that possessed the abilities needed for such a way of life, such as improved vision. Daylight living also offers increased opportunities for social interactions because animals can see one another at greater distances. As a result, we would expect the development of larger social groups and an increase in social behaviors.

EVOLUTION OF THE NEW WORLD MONKEYS   What about the New World monkeys? The earliest fossil record of New World monkeys dates back roughly 30 million years. Most of this evidence consists of fragmentary dental remains. Many of these fossils resemble living New World monkeys. Other forms have unusual features, such as narrow jaws and protruding incisors, and do not appear to have any living counterparts.

Where did the New World monkeys come from? Decades ago, it was thought that New World and Old World monkeys represented a good example of parallel evolution from prosimians. However, current evidence points to enough similarities between the two groups of monkeys to make it more reasonable to assume a single origin for anthropoids somewhere in the Old World. How did the New World monkeys get to the New World? By this time, continental drift had resulted in the separation of the Old and New Worlds.

One explanation is that anthropoids reached South America by "rafting." No, this does not mean that these early primates built rafts and sailed to South America! Ocean storms often rip up clumps of land and trees near the shore, which are then pulled out into the ocean. Sometimes these trees contain helpless animals. Often they drown, but occasionally they will be washed up on an island or continent.

Present geological evidence supports this rafting hypothesis, with some researchers advocating that the monkeys rafted from North America to South America, and others suggesting they rafted from Africa to South America. At present, the evidence supports an African origin for three reasons. First, no suitable early anthropoid ancestors have been discovered in North America. Second, there is evidence of other animals (rats) rafting from Africa (Fleagle 1995). Third, New World fossil evidence points to a close similarity with African anthropoids (Flynn et al. 1995).

EVOLUTION OF THE MIOCENE APES

Continued evolution of the Old World anthropoids led to two major branches, one line leading to the modern Old World monkeys and the other line leading to the modern hominoids (apes and humans). The oldest evidence for fossil apes is based primarily on dental evidence and comes from Old World sites dating to the **Miocene epoch** (22 to 5 million years B.P.). Most Miocene mammals are fairly modern in form, and roughly half of all modern mammals were present during this time. South America and Australia were isolated due to continental drift. The land mass of **Eurasia** (a term given to the combined land masses of Europe and Asia) and Africa joined during part of the Miocene, roughly 16–17 million years ago.

▲▲

Miocene epoch The fourth epoch of the Cenozoic era, dating between 22 and 5 mil- lion years B.P., when there was great diversity in apes.

Eurasia The combined land masses of Europe and Asia.

The early and middle Miocene (before 16 million years B.P.) was a time of heavy tropical forests, particularly in Africa. Subsequently, the climate became cooler and drier, and there was an increase in open grasslands and mixed environments consisting of open woodlands, bushlands, and savannas.

The Diversity of Miocene Apes

Looking at modern primates, it is apparent that there are more genera and species of monkeys than there are of apes. Monkeys are more diverse than apes. During the Miocene epoch, however, just the reverse was true—apes were incredibly diverse until the past 5 to 10 million years. Since that time, the number of ape species has been declining. This decline is evident when we consider the diversity of fossil Miocene apes now known. Table 9.2 lists the known genera of Miocene apes, which have been found on three continents. There were 23 different genera, many with more than one species. Compare that to the few apes alive today (see Chapter 7). In addition,

■ TABLE 9.2
Genera of Miocene Apes

	DATE			
REGION	EARLY MIOCENE		MIDDLE MIOCENE		LATE MIOCENE
Africa	Dendropithecus Limnopithecus Micropithecus Proconsul Rangwapithecus Simiolus Turkanapithecus	Afropithecus Nyanzapithecus	Otavapithecus	Kenyapithecus	
Asia	Dionysopithecus Platydontopithecus				Gigantopithecus Laccopithecus Lufengpithecus Sivapithecus
Europe			Crouzelia	Dryopithecus Pliopithecus	Ouranopithecus Oreopithecus Sivapithecus

Note that *Sivapithecus* is represented in both Asia and Europe. *Gigantopithecus* is also found in Asia in more recent times, perhaps as little as 500,000 years ago. *Ouranopithecus* is sometimes referred to as *Graecopithecus*.

Sources: Fleagle (1988), Conroy et al. (1992), de Bonis and Koufos (1993)

The Giant Ape

One of the most interesting Miocene apes found so far is *Gigantopithecus*, which literally means "giant ape." The remains of *Gigantopithecus* have been found in Asia—China, India, and Vietnam—dating back as far as 9 million years B.P. (Ciochon et al. 1990). The Chinese specimens may be as recent as 500,000 years B.P., meaning that this ape lived at the same time as our ancestral species *Homo erectus* (discussed in Chapter 11).

Although it sounds strange, *Gigantopithecus* was first found in a drugstore! Throughout much of Asia, fossil teeth and bones are ground into powder and used in various potions that are said to have healing properties. The teeth are often called "dragon's teeth" and are sold in apothecary shops. In 1935, the anthropologist Ralph von Koenigswald discovered huge teeth in one such store, and later named it *Gigantopithecus*. Since then, additional teeth and jaws have been recovered from fossil sites.

The major characteristic of *Gigantopithecus* is that it had huge molar and premolar teeth set in a massive jaw. Another interesting feature is that while the canine teeth are large, they are not that large relative to the rest of the teeth. The *relatively* smaller canines, and

(Illustrations from *Gigantopithecus*, by E. L. Simons and P .C. Ettel. Copyright © 1970 by *Scientific American*, Inc. All rights reserved)

the thick enamel on the molar teeth, suggested to some that *Gigantopithecus* might be related to humans, who have the same characteristics. We now realize that Miocene ape evolution is a lot more complicated than we once thought. *Gigantopithecus* is in some ways similar to *Sivapithecus*, and probably represents a side branch in Asian ape evolution.

The large teeth and jaws have always captured people's imaginations. Based on the size of the teeth, some have suggested that *Gigantopithecus* might have stood over 9 feet tall! However, there are wide differences among species in the relationship between tooth size and body size, and it is more likely that *Gigantopithecus* was around 6 feet tall (which is still pretty big!). Until we find more of the body, we will not know for sure.

The large molars, thick molar enamel, small canines, and large jaws all suggest an ape that was well adapted for a diet consisting of items that were very hard to chew. In fact, the tips of the canines are worn down in a manner consistent with heavy chewing.

Some have suggested that *Gigantopithecus* is somehow related to the mythical "Abominable Snowman," presumably because of its geographic location and possible size. There is no support for this idea (nor for the existence of the Snowman). What *Gigantopithecus* really shows us is yet another example of the diversity of Miocene apes.

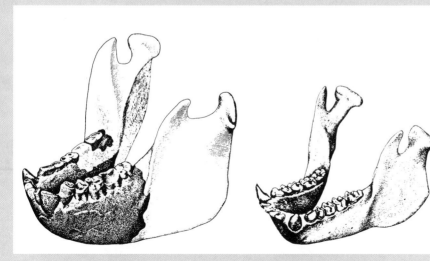

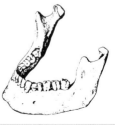

Comparison of the lower jaws of Gigantopithecus (left), a modern gorilla (middle), and a modern human (right). Gigantopithecus has the largest overall size, but relatively small canines compared to the gorilla.

remember that the list in Table 9.2 is incomplete—we find new fossils, and often new genera and species, all the time. In fact, this list is likely to be out of date by the time you look at it!

Why have apes declined and monkeys flourished since the Miocene? One possibility is the slow reproduction rate of modern apes. If Miocene apes had been as nurturing of their offspring as modern apes are, then they may have reproduced too slowly and died out. This problem would have been exacerbated by environmental changes over time.

For the purpose of reconstructing the evolution of the apes, this past diversity creates a problem. Given that there were more species in the past than are alive today, this means that many fossil species have no living descendants. Decades ago, when the fossil record was less complete, it was tempting to identify any newly discovered fossil ape as the Miocene ancestor of one of the living apes, such as the chimpanzee or gorilla (Fleagle 1995). Today, we have evidence of greater diversity in the past, but we now realize that evolution often produces initial diversity followed by later extinction of many branches (as discussed in Chapter 4). It therefore becomes more difficult to find the ancestors of modern apes. We can certainly recognize fossil apes in a general sense, and see general evolutionary trends, but it is much more difficult to arrange the known fossils into a definitive evolutionary tree.

The Fossil Evidence

In general, the identification of the Miocene forms listed in Table 9.2 as *ape* is based on dental and cranial features. In most cases, much less is known about the **postcranial** skeleton (the skeleton below the skull), and such evidence as does exist shows characteristics different from those of modern apes. Overall, it appears that the postcranial structure of Miocene apes was

■ FIGURE 9.6
Reconstructed skeleton of *Proconsul*. (Redrawn from Fleagle, *Primate Adaptation and Evolution,* 1988, with permission, Academic Press, Inc.)

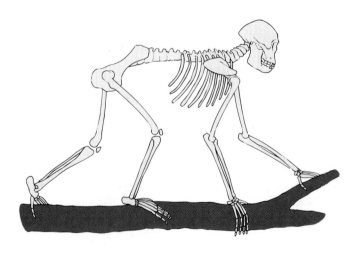

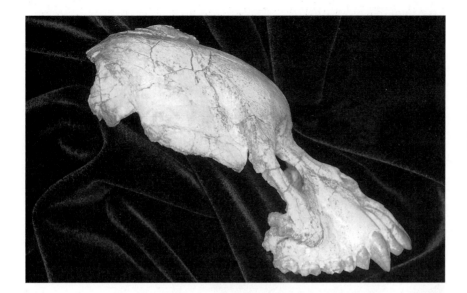

■ **FIGURE 9.7**
Side view of the skull of
Proconsul heseloni, the
smallest of several species of
Proconsul. (Courtesy of Milford
Wolpoff, University of Michigan)

often more generalized than that of modern apes, whose particular adaptations (e.g., knuckle walking) may be more recent. In light of the great diversity of Miocene apes, only a few selected forms are discussed here. Keep in mind that many other forms existed.

PROCONSUL   One form of early Miocene ape that appears to have evolutionary significance is the genus **Proconsul,** which lived in Africa between 23 and 17 million years B.P. Specimens placed in this genus show considerable variation, particularly in overall size, making assignment to specific species somewhat difficult. The skeletal structure of *Proconsul* shows a mixture of monkey and ape features (Figure 9.6). Like modern apes, *Proconsul* did not have a tail (Ward et al. 1991). The limb proportions, however, are more like that of a monkey than an ape, with limbs of roughly the same size. In a modern ape, the front limbs are generally longer than the rear limbs, reflecting knuckle walking. The arms and hands of *Proconsul* are monkeylike, but the shoulders and elbows are more like those of apes. Analyses of the limb structure suggest that *Proconsul* was an unspecialized quadruped that lived in the trees and ate fruit (Pilbeam 1984; Walker and Teaford 1989).

The skull of a typical *Proconsul* specimen (Figure 9.7) is more like that of an ape in that it is large relative to overall body size. The teeth also demonstrate that these forms were hominoid. They possessed Y-5 molars and had large protruding canines (Figure 9.8). The shape of the lower premolar is like that of modern apes, with a single dominant cusp rather than two more or

▲▲▲

postcranial Referring to that part of the skeleton below the skull.

Proconsul A genus of fossil apes that lived in Africa between 23 and 17 million years B.P. and that shows a number of monkey characteristics.

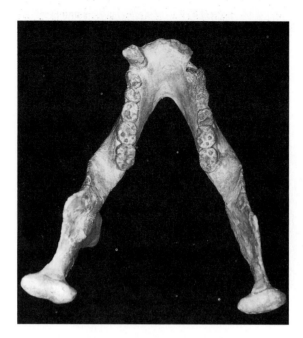

■ **FIGURE 9.8**
The lower jaw of a specimen of *Proconsul nyanzae,* a medium-sized species of *Proconsul.* Note in particular the large canine tooth.
(Courtesy of Milford Wolpoff, University of Michigan)

less equal-sized cusps, as found in humans. In apes, the single large cusp rubs against, and sharpens, the upper canine tooth. Ape jaws also have noticeable gaps (called **diastema**) next to the canine teeth, which allow the jaws to close. Imagine the problem you would have if your canines were long and protruding and you did not have a gap between the teeth in the opposite jaw for them to fit into. You would not be able to close your mouth or chew! *Proconsul* also had a thin layer of enamel on the molar teeth, similar to that found on the teeth of modern African apes. By contrast, humans and orangutans have thick molar enamel.

Overall, the teeth and jaws of *Proconsul* are similar enough to those of modern African apes that they were once thought to be direct ancestors of the chimpanzee and gorilla. Today we realize that the situation is more complex than this. Environmental reconstructions show that *Proconsul* lived in the Miocene forests and primarily ate fruits. The mixture of monkey and ape traits points to them as typical of a transition form from early generalized anthropoid to what we think of as an ape. Though definitely not identical to a modern ape, their overall structure is more like that of an ape than a monkey; hence we refer to them as an early form of hominoid.

Proconsul was adapted to forest living and was a successful group for millions of years. As the climate cooled and became drier in certain regions during the Miocene, their habitat shrank. As competition for dwindling resources increased, other apes developed that were more successful in dealing with the new environments.

SIVAPITHECUS The genus *Sivapithecus* lived in Asia and Europe between 14 and 7 million years B.P. The genus name means "Siva's ape," after the Indian deity Siva (pronounced "SHE-va"). Like *Proconsul, Sivapithecus* was a diverse genus ranging in size and geographic distribution. Because of this variation, it is not clear exactly how many species actually existed. Estimates suggest as many as six different species (Kelly 1988; Conroy 1990).

A major distinguishing feature of *Sivapithecus* lies in the jaws and teeth. First, the molars are relatively large and low-cusped and have thick enamel. Second, the jaws are relatively massive but do not protrude forward as much as in other apes. Third, in many forms the canines are relatively smaller than those in other apes and do not protrude as much. These features are all probably related to a change in diet from soft fruits to foods that are harder to chew, such as nuts, seeds, and hard fruits. This change in diet seems to be associated with the fact that the climate was on average cooler and drier, leading to a change in available foods. It is interesting that, on average, *Siva-pithecus* and other apes with thick molar enamel appear in the fossil record after the thin-enameled forms (such as *Proconsul*) as the climate changed. The upper and lower jaws of a *Sivapithecus* specimen are shown in Figure 9.9.

Thicker enamel represents an adaptation to a diet that is difficult to chew. Think about it: What takes more chewing, a piece of orange or a nut? Given the wear on teeth, harder enamel is more adaptive for heavy chewing and grinding between the back teeth. Larger molars would also be adaptive for heavier chewing. The shorter and more massive jaw relates to diet as well because more power can be applied between the back teeth when the jaw is tucked further under the face. Smaller canines have also been thought to relate to such a diet. Large canines, it has been hypothesized, hinder certain kinds of chewing. When you chew a hard object such as a nut, your jaw does not simply move up and down. Instead, your lower jaw also moves side to side and your chewing pattern is more circular than up and down. Large canines would make the circular motion more difficult. Therefore, smaller canines are seen as an adaptation to a hard diet because they allow more suc-cessful rotary chewing. According to another hypothesis, because larger molars take up more room in the jaw, leaving less room for the canines, the crowd-ing of the teeth leads to dental problems and is therefore selected against.

For a long time all we knew about *Sivapithecus* and other related forms came from remains of teeth and jaws. Based on only this information, many anthropologists felt that some of these forms were actually hominid. After all, humans have the same basic complex of dental traits: larger molars, thicker molar enamel, less-protruding jaws, and smaller canines. Recent finds, reviewed later, indicate that this idea was not correct. *Sivapithecus* was not a hominid.

▲▲

diastema A gap next to the canine tooth that allows space for the canine on the opposing jaw.

Sivapithecus A genus of fossil ape found in Asia and Europe dating between 14 and 7 million years B.P.,

probably an ancestor of the modern-day orangutan.

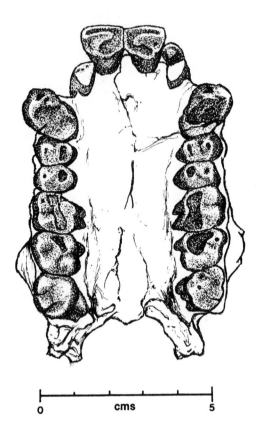

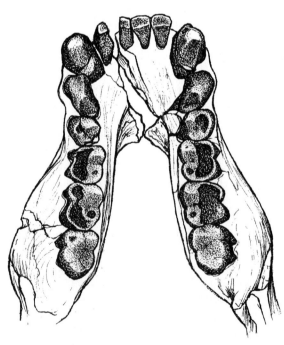

■ FIGURE 9.9
Upper and lower jaws of a *Sivapithecus* specimen from Pakistan. (From Clark Spencer Larsen, Robert M. Matter, and Daniel L. Gebo, *Human Origins: The Fossil Record*, Second Edition, p. 37. Copyright © 1991, 1985 by Waveland Press, Inc., Prospect Heights, Illinois. Reprinted with permission from the publisher)

■ FIGURE 9.10
Side view of *Sivapithecus* specimen from Pakistan. (From Clark Spencer Larsen, Robert M. Matter, and Daniel L. Gebo, *Human Origins: The Fossil Record,* Second Edition, p. 36. Copyright © 1991, 1985 by Waveland Press, Inc., Prospect Heights, Illinois. Reprinted with permission from the publisher)

In what type of environment did *Sivapithecus* live? Initially it was assumed that the dietary specializations found in their teeth meant that this group lived in open grasslands. Seeds, nuts, and other hard objects associated with thick molar enamel and massive chewing were thought to be found in such terrestrial environments (Jolly 1970). A survey of diets and dental characteristics of living primates has shown that these dental characteristics are found in both terrestrial and tree-living primates (Kay 1981). Environmental data suggest, however, that *Sivapithecus* lived more often in a mosaic of mixed woodland, grassland, and forest regions. Our reconstructions of *Sivapithecus* are hampered by the fact that we know very little about their form of locomotion. The few postcranial bones found suggest a generalized skeleton and locomotion (Pilbeam et al. 1977; Rose 1986).

In the 1970s and early 1980s, a number of *Sivapithecus* specimens were found with rather complete skulls, offering us for the first time a glimpse at something other than jaws and teeth. One of these specimens (Figure 9.10) was discovered by David Pilbeam in 1980 during excavations in Miocene deposits in Pakistan (Pilbeam 1982). Its general appearance is extremely similar to a modern orangutan, as shown in Figure 9.11.

The overall shape and orientation of the two skulls is very similar and quite unlike that of either the chimpanzee or gorilla. The eye orbit of the *Sivapithecus* skull is oval in shape and the two eyes are close together, both features found in the orangutan. The unique triangular appearance of an orangutan's nasal region is also found in *Sivapithecus*. Other similarities include the shape and size of the incisor teeth. Note the difference in size between the middle two incisor teeth and the outer two in both specimens.

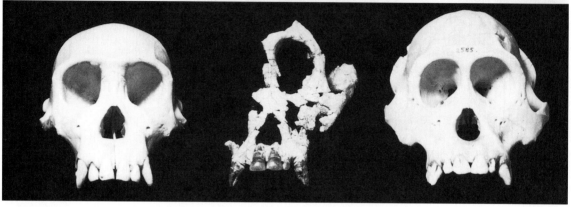

■ FIGURE 9.11
Side views (*top*) and frontal
views (*bottom*) comparing the
Sivapithecus specimen GSP
15000 (*center*) with a modern
chimpanzee (*left*) and a
modern orangutan (*right*).
(Peabody Museum, Harvard
University)

In addition, remember that the thick molar enamel found in sivapithecines and in humans is also found in orangutans. Since Pilbeam's discovery, additional *Sivapithecus* skulls showing the same features have been found in various sites in Asia.

Not every species of *Sivapithecus* exhibits all of these features. Specimens in China, for example, share certain features of the incisor teeth and jaw shape with the Pakistani specimen shown in Figures 9.10 and 9.11. However, the shape of the eye orbits and the distance between the eyes is different. This variation suggests that there were a number of Asian species of *Sivapithecus*, one of which appears ancestral to the modern-day orangutan.

Genetic Evidence

In addition to fossil evidence, our interpretations of Miocene ape evolution must also take genetic evidence from the living apes into account. Since the 1960s, a comparison of the genetics of living organisms using a set of methods known as **molecular dating** has shed new light on hominoid evolution.

In Chapter 7 you read about how scientists use molecular information to judge the relative relationship between living hominoids. These methods provide some idea of which primates are most closely related. If certain assumptions are made, these methods can be used to provide an estimate of the date at which two species split from a common ancestor. When two

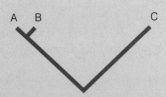

The diagram shows the genetic relationship between three hypothetical species (A, B, and C). Let us assume that the genetic distances between these species have been measured and are:

Distance between species A and species B = 2
Distance between species A and species C = 20
Distance between species B and species C = 20

Based on these data:

The distance between A and B is one-tenth the distance between A and C (2/20 = 1/10)

The distance between A and B is one-tenth the distance between B and C (2/20 = 1/10)

Therefore, the date that species A and B diverged is one-tenth the date that species C diverged from the common ancestor of A and B. If we know from fossil evidence that species C diverged at 40 million years B.P., then species A and B diverged at 4 million years B.P. (40 × 1/10 = 4).

■ **FIGURE 9.12**
Hypothetical example of molecular dating.

species separate, mutations occur and neutral mutations accumulate in each line independently. If the rate of accumulation is constant in both lines, then a comparison of molecular differences in living forms will provide us with a relative idea of how long the two species have been separated.

Imagine three species, A, B, and C, where molecular evidence indicates that A and B are more closely related to each other than either is to C. We would hypothesize that initially species C split off from a common ancestor of all three, followed by a split of species A and B later on. Suppose we then determine through molecular comparisons that the difference between A and B is one-tenth of the difference between either A or B and species C. This evidence suggests that the date of divergence of A and B was one-tenth that of the date of divergence between their common ancestor and species C. Now suppose that we know from fossil evidence that species C split off 40 million years B.P. We can then infer that species A and B split from a common ancestor at 4 million years B.P., because 4 million years is one-tenth of 40 million years. Here we have taken the molecular differences between species and have used it as a "molecular clock," with our clock calibrated using the fossil record (Figure 9.12).

Molecular dating rests on two major assumptions. First, we assume that our calibration date is correct. As more fossil evidence accumulates, we might have to change our estimate of the date at which species C first split off. The second, more critical, assumption is that neutral mutations do accumulate at the same rate in different lines. There are methods for testing this

▲▲▲▲▲▲▲▲▲▲▲▲▲▲▲▲▲▲▲▲▲▲▲▲▲▲▲▲▲

molecular dating
Estimating the sequence and timing of divergent evolutionary lines by applying methods of genetic analysis.

assumption, and it does appear to hold true for some molecular estimates (Cronin 1983).

Constancy in rates of mutation might seem inconceivable, given that mutations occur at random. But remember basic probability. If you flip a coin 10 times, you will not expect to get five heads and five tails. If you flip the coin 10 million times, however, you expect to get results closer to the expected 50:50 ratio. Given millions of generations, the random nature of mutations also seems constant.

The first use of molecular dating was by Sarich and Wilson (1967), who looked at differences in albumin protein and found that the difference between humans and the African apes was one-sixth that found between either and the Old World monkeys. Using the then-established estimate of 30 million years for the separation of Old World monkeys, they computed that humans and the African apes had shared a common ancestor 5 million years ago. At that time most paleoanthropologists thought a date of 15 to 20 million years was more likely and disagreed strongly with Sarich and Wilson's estimate.

Since that time, a great deal of research has been done on molecular dating and its assumptions. Some researchers disputed the idea of constancy in mutation fixation rates and proposed nonlinear models in their place. Other proteins have been analyzed. Additional fossil material was found, and new interpretations of older data were made. Most paleoanthropologists now accept a much more recent split of humans and apes than was the consensus several decades ago.

Different methods of analysis give different estimates from molecular dating. For example, Cronin (1983) computed a split of human and chimpanzee at roughly 5 million years ago, with the orangutan splitting off at roughly 10 million years ago. Arguing that the data should be interpreted using nonlinear rates of change, Gingerich (1985) computed an average date of 9 million years for the chimpanzee and 16 million years for the orangutan. The controversy still continues, but the predominant view from molecular dating is that humans and the African apes split sometime between 7 and 5 million years B.P. There is continuing debate about the specific pattern of splitting among the African apes (see the following section).

Conclusions

By the early 1960s, anthropologists felt that they had reconstructed the general evolutionary tree of the living hominoids and had suitable fossil species identified as the ancestors of modern species. The preliminary dental evidence suggested a number of fossil apes dating back 20 to 15 million years B.P., some big and some smaller. Given the ape features of the teeth, the fossils were thought to represent the ancestors of gorillas (big) and chimpanzees (small). In addition, some apes showed small canines (Figure 9.13), a characteristic felt to be uniquely human, and therefore evidence of the first hominids.

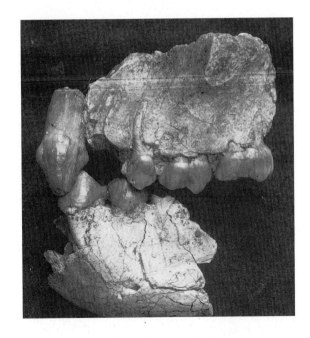

■ FIGURE 9.13
Jaw fragments of *Kenya-pithecus*. Note the small canine teeth. (Courtesy of Dr. Alan Walker, The Johns Hopkins University School of Medicine)

We now realize that these initial conclusions were premature. The Miocene apes were much more diverse than we once thought. The postcranial remains of these early forms (e.g., *Proconsul*) showed us that the earliest Miocene apes were quite primitive in many features. This evidence, combined with insights from molecular dating, led to our current observation of a much later divergence of modern hominoids. Instead of an ape–human split some 20 to 15 million years B.P., we now suggest an earlier date of 7 to 5 million years B.P.

The genetic evidence, combined with anatomical studies of living hominoids, allows us to reconstruct a general evolutionary "tree" of the great apes and humans. Orangutans split off from a common ancestor first, followed by a later split between the African apes and humans. The specific pattern of the African ape–human split is still being debated, as shown in Figure 9.14. Some favor the gorilla splitting off first, followed by a split between the chimpanzee-bonobo line and the human line (Figure 9.14a). Others favor an initial split of an African ape line and a human line, followed by subsequent splits of the gorilla and chimpanzee-bonobo lines (Figure 9.14b). At present, neither genetic nor anatomical evidence is able to definitively choose between these hypotheses.

Regardless of the fine details of the tree, the basics provide us with a framework for assessing the evolutionary significance of the Miocene fossil apes. Estimates from molecular dating add the needed time element to Figure 9.14. Once we know the pattern (the "tree"), we can then determine where on the tree we should place a given fossil species. This would be straightforward enough if the actual evolutionary tree were as simple as shown in Figure 9.14. As we have seen, however, there were more ape species living during the Miocene than are alive today (Figure 9.15). This means that any given fossil species might *not* lie on the tree of Figure 9.14, but rather be a member of a now-extinct side branch of ape evolution. In fact, given the

■ FIGURE 9.14
Alternate models of hominoid
evolution showing the
evolutionary relationships
between the great apes and
humans. These two models
are similar, differing only in
the exact relationship between
the African apes and humans.
(a) The gorilla splits off first
and the chimpanzee-bonobo
and human lines have a more
recent common ancestor.
(b) The common ancestor of
the African apes and humans
splits off first, and the gorilla
and chimpanzee-bonobo lines
have a more recent common
ancestor. Anatomical and
genetic data have been used
to support both of these
positions, but at present we
lack a definitive answer.

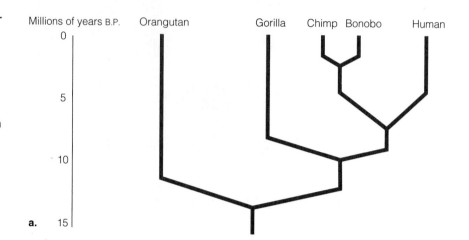

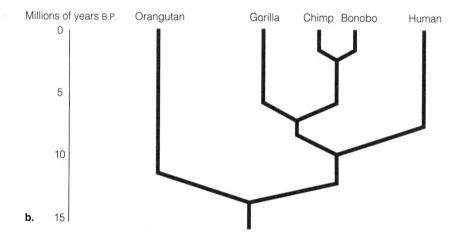

large number of ape species in the past, the odds are that any given species
will probably represent an extinct branch, and *not* a direct ancestor of a
modern hominoid.

   We can be more definite for some parts of the tree than for others.
Based on primitive morphology, the mix of monkey and ape features, and
the date, it seems reasonable to suggest that *Proconsul* (or something similar
to it) was the common ancestor of the great apes and humans. This position
would place *Proconsul* at the base of Figure 9.14—a common ancestor of the
orangutan, African ape, and human lines.

   The part of the tree for which there is the most evidence is the line leading to the orangutan. Because of its close dental and cranial similarity with
modern orangutans, a species of *Sivapithecus* seems to be a reasonable ancestor. The dates for *Sivapithecus* also agree with estimates of the divergence of

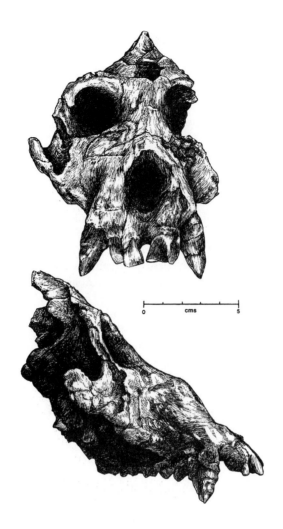

■ **FIGURE 9.15**
Another example of the diversity of Miocene apes—the genus *Afropithecus*. This specimen dates to roughly 17 million years B.P. In some respects, it is similar to both *Proconsul* and to later apes such as *Sivapithecus,* but in other details (such as facial profile) it is quite different. It may represent a common ancestor of African and Asian apes or may be a side branch in ape evolution. (From Clark Spencer Larsen, Robert M. Matter, and Daniel L. Gebo, *Human Origins: The Fossil Record,* Second Edition, p. 27. Copyright © 1991, 1985 by Waveland Press, Inc., Prospect Heights, Illinois. Reprinted with permission from the publisher)

the orangutan line based on molecular dating. As noted, the best candidate for an orangutan ancestor is the Pakistan species of *Sivapithecus* because it is most similar to modern orangutans.

What of the African ape–human line? Here, we cannot be as definitive. A number of potential candidates for the common ancestor of the African apes and humans have been suggested. These include *Kenyapithecus* (Figure 9.13), *Ouranopithecus* (de Bonis and Koufos 1993), and *Dryopithecus* (Begun 1994). We lack sufficient evidence, however, to determine which of these (if any) is the most reasonable common ancestor of African apes and humans. This does not mean we have no evidence; instead, it means we cannot choose between the alternatives at present. In addition, we must keep in mind that the Miocene fossil record continues to unfold as each year brings new discoveries.

SUMMARY

Following the extinction of the dinosaurs 65 million years ago, early mammal forms spread out into new environments. Some early insectivores began to adapt more and more to life in the trees, developing grasping hands and binocular stereoscopic vision. These changes may have begun in response to the needs of insect predation and were later used to exploit additional food resources in a three-dimensional environment. The origin of primates began with the primatelike mammals of the Paleocene epoch and the ancient prosimians of the Eocene. Primitive anthropoids evolved from a group of Eocene primates. The early Oligocene anthropoids ultimately gave rise to the separate lines of Old World monkeys and hominoids.

The Miocene epoch is characterized by two major adaptive radiations. In the early Miocene, primitive hominoid forms appeared in Africa. These forms, placed in the genus *Proconsul*, were similar in some ways to later apes, but were also monkeylike in a number of features. They had jaws and teeth like those of later apes and lacked a tail. Their postcranial skeleton was generalized and primitive in a number of features. They had thin molar enamel.

During the middle Miocene, several new genera of apes evolved. They had relatively large molars and thick molar enamel. These dental changes correspond to changing climatic patterns and available food resources, specifically the need to process food that was harder to chew. These thick-enameled apes appear to be the ancestor of present-day great apes and humans, although the specific evolutionary relationships between Miocene species and modern species are not clear at present. One species of the genus *Sivapithecus* appears to be the ancestor of the orangutan, based on close similarity of dental and facial traits.

We are not able to identify precisely the common ancestor of the African apes and humans. Evidence from molecular dating supports a fairly recent split, roughly 7 to 5 million years B.P. Although several genera of fossil apes could be a common ancestor (or related to a common ancestor), we cannot be definitive at this time. What is clear, however, is that there was extensive diversity in apes during the Miocene.

SUPPLEMENTAL READINGS

Conroy, G. C. 1990. *Primate Evolution*. New York: W. W. Norton.

Fleagle, J. G. 1988. *Primate Adaptation and Evolution*. San Diego: Academic Press.

These two texts are excellent sources for information on primate evolution.

Lewin, R. 1987. *Bones of Contention: Controversies in the Search for Human Origins*. New York: Simon & Schuster. A lively summary of controversies in human evolution. Chapters 5 and 6 deal with human origins, Miocene hominoids, and molecular dating.

PART THREE

Human Evolution

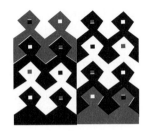

Human Origins

CHAPTER **10**

 How old are human beings? This is one question anthropologists are frequently asked. It seems simple enough, but in fact we have no simple answer. It depends on how we define human beings. If we limit our question to humans who are more or less anatomically similar to modern humans, the answer may be more than 100,000 years old. If we include all the fossils placed in our species, old- and modern-looking, the answer is roughly 400,000 years old. If we focus on all members of our genus (*Homo*), including forms placed in other species, the answer is 2.5 million years old. If we are interested only in hominids, regardless of genus or species, the answer is over 4.4 million years old.

Past human evolution was not a one-step process. Humans did not emerge instantaneously from an apelike ancestor. What we are, biologically and culturally, is the product of many different evolutionary changes occurring at different times. Here we will focus on the origin of the first hominids and their relationship to later hominid forms, including ourselves.

This chapter examines the fossil record for human evolution from the time of the oldest known hominids through the beginnings of the evolution of the genus *Homo*. Most of the oldest known hominids are classified in the genera *Ardipithecus* and *Australopithecus*, characterized primarily by their small brains, large faces and teeth, and bipedal locomotion.

OVERVIEW OF HUMAN EVOLUTION

Before getting into the details of the biology and behavior of the first hominids, we will look briefly at an overview of the story of human evolution. A most succinct discussion of the main events goes something like this: "Over four million years ago, the first hominids appeared. They had apelike teeth and ape-sized brains but walked on two legs. By 2.5 million years ago, the human line had split. One line developed big back teeth for chewing, and they became extinct about one million years ago. The other line evolved larger brains, smaller teeth and faces, and started using stone tools. Ultimately, those large-brained forms evolved into us."

The most important concept we learn from this overview is that bipedalism evolved well *before* larger brains. Through most of this chapter, we look at the evidence for the origins of bipedalism and larger brains, and examine possible hypotheses.

Let's look at the story of human evolution now in somewhat more detail (consult Figure 10.1 for a graphic representation of this review). As discussed in the last chapter, our best estimates suggest that the hominid line split from the African ape line between 7 and 5 million years B.P. Our earliest definite evidence of hominids is a species known as *Ardipithecus ramidus* that lived 4.4 million years ago in Africa and seems to have been a side branch in human evolution. By 4.2 million years B.P., we see the first members of the genus *Australopithecus*, which walked upright and had a small ape-sized brain and relatively large teeth and face. From the neck up, they were more apelike than humanlike, but the fact that they had the unique derived characteristics associated with bipedalism means that they were hominids. They foraged for food, primarily fruit, in the woodlands and savanna. Roughly 3 to 2.5 million years B.P., perhaps in response to climatic cooling, at least two lines of hominids evolved from a species of *Australopithecus*. One line led to the robust australopithecines, which evolved larger back teeth and huge, powerful jaws—both adaptations to a diet that was hard to chew, such as seeds, nuts, and hard-skinned fruits.

The other line of hominid adapted to environmental change by relying more and more on learned behavior. By 2.5 million years B.P., we see the first evidence of the genus *Homo*, characterized by a larger brain and the use of stone tools. The first such species was *Homo habilis*, which had a brain roughly half the size of modern humans and still retained a fairly large face and teeth. *Homo habilis* seems to have used the stone tools for scavenging animal flesh. By 1.8 million years B.P., another species appeared—*Homo erectus*, which had an even larger brain (about three-fourths the size of a modern

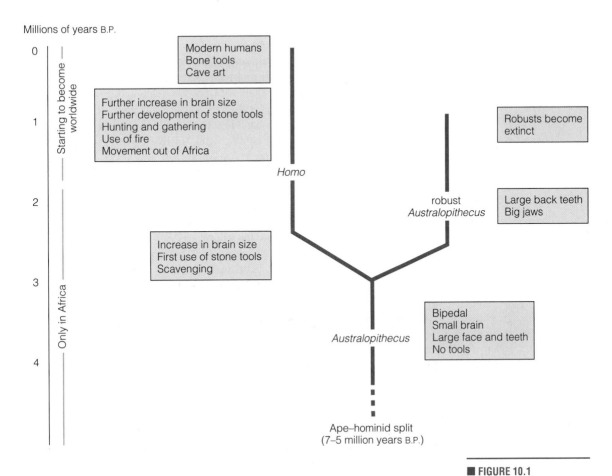

Millions of years B.P.

Modern humans
Bone tools
Cave art

Further increase in brain size
Further development of stone tools
Hunting and gathering
Use of fire
Movement out of Africa

Robusts become
extinct

Homo

robust
Australopithecus

Large back teeth
Big jaws

Increase in brain size
First use of stone tools
Scavenging

Bipedal
Small brain
Large face and teeth
No tools

Australopithecus

Ape–hominid split
(7–5 million years B.P.)

Starting to become worldwide

Only in Africa

■ FIGURE 10.1
Simplified summary of
hominid evolution.

human), was a hunter and gatherer, and used fire. Between 1 and 1.7 million years B.P., *Homo erectus* became the first hominid to move outside of Africa, reaching Indonesia, China, and perhaps parts of Europe. Stone tool technology became more sophisticated with *Homo erectus*.

Brain size increased again starting at around 400,000 years ago, when we see the first evidence for hominids that are similar enough to modern humans to classify as *Homo sapiens*. These hominids had a large brain, but still had a rather large face and a less well-rounded skull compared to modern humans. Anthropologists are still debating whether these forms represent a different species (or two), but they are generally given the label of "archaic *Homo sapiens*" to contrast them with "modern *Homo sapiens*," such as ourselves. Modern *Homo sapiens* apparently originated in Africa over 100,000 years ago, and the relationship between these moderns and preexisting archaic groups (including the famous Neandertals) is still controversial.

Roughly 50,000 years ago a "creative explosion" of culture took place, associated with new technologies, such as bone tools, and new behaviors, such as cave art. Modern humans dispersed even farther across the globe, reaching Australia by 50,000 years ago, and the New World by 15,000 years ago. Starting 12,000 years ago, human populations in several different places developed agriculture, and the human species began to increase in number. Cities and state-level societies began about 8,000 years ago. Subsequent cultural developments took place at an ever-increasing pace. The Industrial Revolution began only 250 years ago. The use of electricity as a power source became common in many parts of the world only a century ago. Finally, it has been less than 50 years since the exploration and utilization of outer space began.

This brief review shows one thing very clearly—what we are today as modern humans did not come about all at the same time, but at different times over millions of years. Thus, we should not speak of a single human *origin*, but rather of multiple human origin*s*.

In the remainder of this chapter, and in the next two chapters, we will flesh out this rough sketch with additional details.

THE FIRST HOMINIDS

To date, all fossil hominids have been placed into three genera: *Ardipithecus*, *Australopithecus*, and *Homo*. The first hominids comprise one species of *Ardipithecus* and six species of *Australopithecus*. All of the early hominids had relatively large teeth and faces and walked upright. In many ways, they might be thought of as bipedal apes. They had small **cranial capacities,** a measure of the interior volume of the brain case, measured in cubic centimeters (cc). They were definitely hominid (after the split from the African apes) because they possess certain derived features of the teeth and skeleton (including bipedalism) that are found only in hominids. However, they also retained a number of primitive ape characteristics, so we should not equate them directly with "humans." To do so implies that their biology and behavior were in many ways similar to our own.

Although we share certain characteristics with the early hominids, we are different in many ways. For example, we have not found any evidence that the early hominids made tools. It is possible, and perhaps even likely, that some of them used simple wood tools, but because wood decomposes quickly, we have no direct knowledge. Some researchers have suggested that at least some early hominids *could* have made tools because their hand bones reflect a certain level of manual dexterity (Susman 1988). However, we find no definite evidence of stone tools (which last for millions of years) having been made by any hominid other than the first members of the genus *Homo*.

All of the first hominids have been found dating between 4.4 and 1 million years B.P. This time period includes portions of the **Pliocene epoch** (5 to 1.8 million years B.P.) and the **Pleistocene epoch** (1.8 to 0.01 million years B.P.). The time period of the first hominids and early *Homo* is often called the **Plio-Pleistocene.**

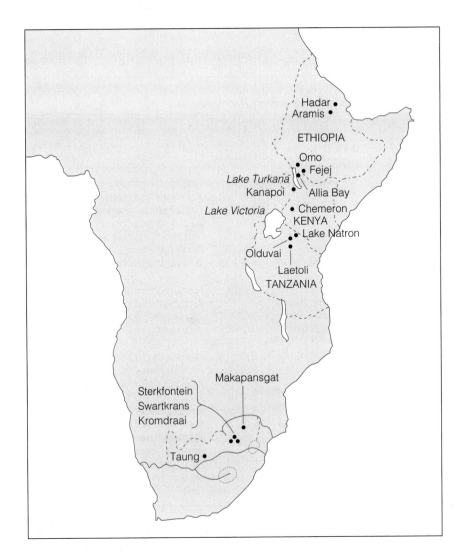

■ **FIGURE 10.2**
Location of some of the major sites in Africa where *Australopithecus* and *Homo habilis* specimens have been found.

The first hominids have all been found only in Africa. Neither *Ardipithecus* nor *Australopithecus* has ever been found outside of Africa. This finding supports Darwin's early idea that Africa was the birthplace of hominids. It also means that the first hominids were limited to a specific environment—tropical grasslands for the most part. Not until later in the fossil record (Chapters 11 and 12) do we see evidence for hominids moving outside of Africa. Figure 10.2 shows the location of the major sites of the

cranial capacity A measurement of the interior volume of the brain case, used as an approximate estimate of brain size.

Pliocene epoch The fifth epoch of the Cenozoic era, dating from 5 to 1.8 million years B.P., when hominids appeared.

Pleistocene epoch The sixth epoch of the Cenozoic era, dating from 1.8 to 0.01 million years B.P., marked by the continued evolution of the genus *Homo*.

Plio-Pleistocene The time frame of the first hominids and early *Homo* from 4.4 to 1 million years B.P.).

■ TABLE 10.1
List of Major Fossil Sites for *Ardipithecus* and *Australopithecus*

Country	*Locality*	*Age (millions of years B.P.)*	*Species*	*Figure Number(s) in Text*
Ethiopia	Aramis	4.4	*Ardipithecus ramidus*	
Kenya	Allia Bay	4.1	*Australopithecus anamensis*	
Kenya	Kanapoi	4.2–3.9	*Australopithecus anamensis*	
Kenya	East Turkana	4.0+	*Australopithecus afarensis*	
Ethiopia	Fejej	3.6+	*Australopithecus afarensis?*	
Tanzania	Laetoli	3.8–3.6	*Australopithecus afarensis*	10.6
Ethiopia	Hadar	3.5–2.9	*Australopithecus afarensis*	10.3,10.4, 10.7
Ethiopia	Omo	3.0–2.6	*Australopithecus afarensis?*	
Kenya	West Turkana	2.5	*Australopithecus aethiopicus*	10.13
Republic of South Africa	Makapansgat	3.0?	*Australopithecus africanus*	
Republic of South Africa	Sterkfontein	3.0?–2.5	*Australopithecus africanus*	10.14, 10.15
Republic of South Africa	Taung	2.5?	*Australopithecus africanus*	
Republic of South Africa	Swartkrans	2.0?–1.5	*Australopithecus robustus*	10.9, 10.11
Republic of South Africa	Kromdraii	2.0?	*Australopithecus robustus*	
Ethiopia	Omo	2.5–1.2	*Australopithecus boisei*	
Tanzania	Olduvai Gorge	1.8	*Australopithecus boisei*	
Kenya	Lake Baringo	2.0–1.5	*Australopithecus boisei*	
Tanzania	Lake Natron	1.5	*Australopithecus boisei*	10.8
Kenya	East Turkana	1.5	*Australopithecus boisei*	10.10

Sources: Klein (1989); Fleagle et al. (1991); Larsen et al. (1991); Leakey et al. (1995); Coffing et al. (1994); White et al. (1994, 1995)

hominid species discussed in this chapter, and Table 10.1 lists some of these sites. Note that there have been two major areas of discovery: South Africa and East Africa. The South African sites were discovered first. However, the geology of South Africa and the nature of fossilization in that area have made chronometric dating difficult. As a result, for many years we were not sure exactly how old the first hominids were. Sites in East Africa have since been discovered, and their dates have been determined by chronometric dating; extensive volcanic activity in East Africa during the time of the first hominids allows us to use potassium-argon and argon-argon dating methods at these sites.

Early Species

The early hominids, prior to 3 million years B.P., can be categorized roughly as species with many primitive traits. Remember that "primitive" refers in a biological sense to the possession of traits from earlier ancestors. In this case, the first hominids are considered primitive in many ways because they still retain a number of ape characteristics that are not found in later hominids. From an evolutionary perspective this makes perfect sense. After the African ape and hominid lines split, each line would have retained, for some time, primitive characteristics of their common ancestor. Among the earliest hominids, such characteristics include large canine teeth, apelike configurations of the teeth and skull, and ape-sized brains. The earliest hominids also had certain derived characteristics, primarily the development of bipedalism. However, even here, the earliest hominids still possessed some primitive features.

Three species of early hominids existed before 3 million years B.P. Of these, the best known is the youngest—*Australopithecus afarensis*, which lived between 4 and 3 million years B.P. The other two early hominid species have only been announced in recent years (1994 and 1995). Because less is known of them at this time, most of the information in this section of the chapter is based on *Australopithecus afarensis*. However, these other known early hominid species are reviewed first in order to present the information in chronological order.

ARDIPITHECUS RAMIDUS   In 1994, Tim White and his colleagues Gen Suwa and Berhane Asfaw named a new species to accommodate fossil remains that they had uncovered over the previous two years at the site of Aramis in Ethiopia. These remains are highly fragmentary and represent 17 different individuals. Most of the remains are dental, and they essentially show apelike features, such as relatively large canines. Certain features, however, are hominid, such as the canines being more like incisors in structure. The fragmentary crania remains are also apelike and show many primitive characteristics, although there is a suggestion that the location of the **foramen magnum** (the large hole in the base of the skull where the spinal cord enters) may reflect bipedalism. Additional fossils will be needed to confirm this. The Aramis site has been dated to 4.4 million years B.P. (WoldeGabriel et al. 1994), making *Ardipithecus ramidus* at present the oldest known hominid species (but see Kappelman and Fleagle [1995] and WoldeGabriel et al. [1995] for some debate on the exact date).

Based on these remains, White et al. (1994) first assigned these fossils to the genus *Australopithecus*, which includes all other early hominid species other than the genus *Homo*. After further analysis, however, they decided that the Aramis remains are sufficiently different from other early hominid remains to justify placing them in a different genus, and in 1995 they created the name **Ardipithecus ramidus** (White et al. 1995). *Ardi* means "floor" in

foramen magnum The large opening at the base of the skull where the spinal cord enters.

Ardipithecus ramidus The oldest known hominid, dating to 4.4 million years B.P. in

Africa, and very primitive. This species may represent a side branch in early human

evolution, and not be a direct ancestor of later hominids.

the local Afar language, and *ramid* means "root." The genus and species name thus reflects the apelike anatomy of these finds—this was a species that lived close to the initial "root" or "floor" of the human family tree.

Given that *Ardipithecus* is the oldest known hominid, does that mean that it is the ancestor of all later hominids, including ourselves? Not necessarily. In years past, there was an unfortunate tendency to assume that every fossil hominid species was a stage along a single evolutionary line running from the initial split from apes to modern humans. We now realize that human evolution was not a simple single line, but rather more like a "bush," with many side branches. Although *Ardipithecus* has yet to be widely studied among the anthropological community (as of this writing), preliminary analyses suggest that it might be a side branch of early hominid (Leakey et al. 1995).

THE GENUS AUSTRALOPITHECUS   Apart from *Ardipithecus*, all other fossil hominid species have been assigned to the genus *Homo* or the genus **Australopithecus**. The genus name *Australopithecus* translates as "southern ape," so named because the first specimen was found in southern Africa and was regarded as having a number of ape characteristics. Perhaps a better name could be coined now, but scientists have agreed to an international system of naming genera and species, in which the first name given takes precedence. (Although some confusion and inconsistency does still exist in the naming of fossil species, without such a code there would be even more.)

Scientists generally recognize six different species of *Australopithecus*. A general term, **australopithecines,** is used to refer to all members of the genus *Australopithecus*. Two species of *Australopithecus* have been discovered that are relatively primitive: *Australopithecus anamensis* and *Australopithecus afarensis*.

AUSTRALOPITHECUS ANAMENSIS   A likely candidate for the oldest hominid species directly in the line of later human evolution was announced by Meave Leakey and colleagues in 1995 (Leakey et al. 1995). This species, named **Australopithecus anamensis,** has been found at the African sites of Kanapoi and Allia Bay, both off Lake Turkana in Kenya (see Figure 10.2). The species name is based on the word for lake ("anam") in the Turkana language. *A. anamensis* (the A. is shorthand for the genus name *Australopithecus*) has been dated to 4.2 to 3.9 million years B.P. based on the argon-argon dating method.

A total of 21 specimens has been recovered thus far from the two sites. The fossil evidence consists primarily of dental remains, but also includes skull fragments and pieces of both upper arm bone and a lower leg bone. The leg bone is particularly instructive because it shows bipedalism. The teeth, jaws, and skull fragments all show primitive apelike characteristics, such as large canine teeth and a small ear hole. Estimates of weight, based on statistical relationships known to exist between body size and bone measurements, suggest individuals weighing roughly 47 to 58 kg (104–128 lb).

Thus, *A. anamensis* reflects a mix of features that are primitive (and ape-like) and derived (bipedalism), further evidence that human features did not evolve all at once. Although these fossils are newly described and have not yet been subject to many comparative analyses, it appears that *A. anamensis* may be the oldest known species directly in line with later hominids (including ourselves). The anatomy and dating of *A. anamensis* suggests that it was a direct ancestor of another, and better known, primitive early hominid species: *Australopithecus afarensis.*

AUSTRALOPITHECUS AFARENSIS   *Australopithecus afarensis* lived in East Africa between 4 and 3 million years B.P. Much of our data on this species comes from Donald Johanson's field work in the early 1970s at the site of Hadar, Ethiopia (see Figure 10.2). The fossils collected by Johanson and colleagues date between 3.5 and 2.9 million years B.P. Additional fossils collected by Mary Leakey at the site of Laetoli, Tanzania, date back to 3.75 million years B.P. Johanson and colleagues (1978) noted the close similarity between the Hadar and Laetoli finds and placed them together in different species from all other known australopithecines—*Australopithecus afarensis.* The species name, *afarensis*, comes from the Afar region where the Hadar site is located. Discoveries in southern Ethiopia may date back more than 4 million years B.P. (Fleagle et al. 1991).

A. afarensis is another primitive australopithecine. It is more apelike in certain characteristics, such as the cranial features (Figure 10.3), than later australopithecine species. Nonetheless, it is definitely hominid, for it possesses the human form of bipedalism. The most dramatic find showing bipedalism is the fossil nicknamed "Lucy," a 40 percent complete skeleton of an adult female (Figure 10.4). We know she was an adult because her third molar teeth had fully erupted, an event that occurs in young adulthood in hominids. We also know she was a female because her pelvis is fairly intact. Determining the sex of a fossil is best done by examination of the pelvis (Figure 10.5). Females have a wider and more rounded pelvic opening. Such comparisons show that Lucy was a female.

▲▲▲

Australopithecus A genus of fossil hominid that lived in Africa between 4.2 and 1 million years B.P., characterized by bipedal locomotion, small brain size, large face, and large teeth.

australopithecines All species in the genus *Australopithecus.*

Australopithecus anamensis The oldest known austalopithecine, dating to 4.2 to 3.9 million years B.P. in East Africa. It was a biped but had many primitive apelike features of the skull and teeth. It may represent the ancestor of all later hominids.

Australopithecus afarensis A primitive australopithecine, dating between 4 and 3 million years B.P. and found in East Africa.

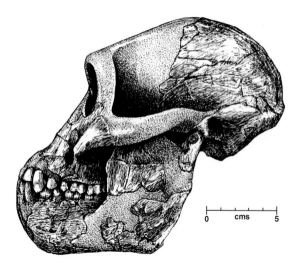

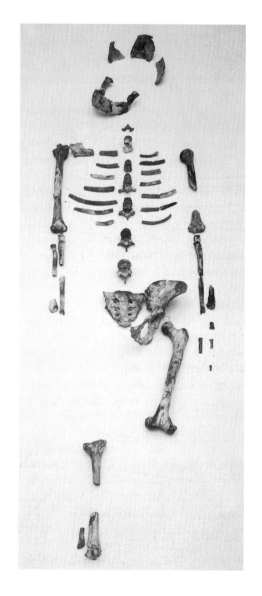

■ FIGURE 10.3
Side view of a reconstructed
Australopithecus afarensis
skull. (From Clark Spencer
Larsen, Robert M. Matter, and
Daniel L. Gebo, *Human Origins:
The Fossil Record,* 2d ed., p.51.
Copyright © 1991,1985 by
Waveland Press, Inc., Prospect
Heights, Illinois)

■ FIGURE 10.4
The skeletal remains of
"Lucy," a 40 percent complete
specimen of *Australopithecus
afarensis.* (John Reader/
Science Photo Library/ Photo
Researchers, Inc.)

■ FIGURE 10.5
Comparison of the pelvic
anatomy of modern human
males and females. (From
*Human Antiquity: An Introduction
to Physical Anthropology and
Archaeology,* 2d ed., by Kenneth
Feder and Michael Park, Fig. 7.17.
Copyright © 1993 by Mayfield
Publishing Company)

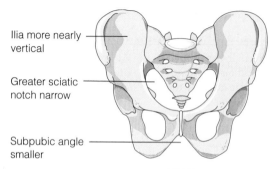

Ilia more nearly
vertical

Greater sciatic
notch narrow

Subpubic angle
smaller

MALE

Ilia splayed
outward

Greater sciatic
notch wide

Subpubic angle
larger

FEMALE

■ FIGURE 10.6
Fossil footprints at the Laetoli
site. (John Reader/ Science Photo
Library/ Photo Researchers, Inc.)

Although an adult, Lucy was small. She was a little over a meter tall (about 3 ft 3 in.) and weighed roughly 27 kg (60 lb) (McHenry 1992). Her pelvic bones and femur show bipedal locomotion. In addition to Lucy, other fossils from Hadar show bipedalism, including a knee joint. Also, fossil footprints have been found at the site of Laetoli dating back to 3.75 million years B.P. (Figure 10.6). These prints show the bipedal characteristics of a nondivergent big toe, heel strike, and a well-developed arch.

All this evidence shows that A. *afarensis* was bipedal. Because bipedal locomotion is unique to humans among living primates, we classify A. *afarensis* as a hominid. Nevertheless, although A. *afarensis* was bipedal, opinion differs on *how* bipedal it was. Some have noted certain ape tendencies in the postcranial material, such as relatively long arms and curved toe bones.

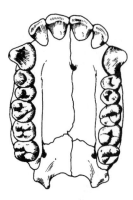
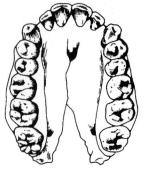
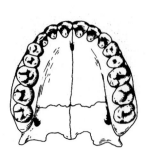

Chimpanzee
upper jaw

Australopithecus afarensis
upper jaw

Modern human
upper jaw

■ FIGURE 10.7

Comparison of the teeth and upper jaws of a modern chimpanzee, *Australopithecus afarensis*, and a modern human. In most features, the teeth and jaws of *Australopithecus afarensis* are intermediate between those of modern apes and modern humans (see text).

These data suggest that despite its bipedalism, *A. afarensis* was not completely modern and did not walk in exactly the same way we do. The evidence also suggests that *A. afarensis* had considerable climbing ability (Stern and Susman 1983).

Cranial material for *A. afarensis* consists of a number of fragments and a fairly complete skull of an adult male. These remains show a small brain, a large protruding face, and a number of primitive cranial features (Kimbel et al. 1994). The brain size of *A. afarensis* ranges between 400 and 500 cc. (Blumenberg 1985). Overall, the skull of *A. afarensis* resembles that of a small ape (see Figure 10.3).

The teeth of *A. afarensis* show a number of characteristics intermediate between those of apes and humans. The teeth of modern apes and humans can be easily distinguished (Figure 10.7). The canines of modern apes are large and project past the surface of the other teeth, whereas modern humans have small, nonprojecting canine teeth. The canine teeth of *A. afarensis* are intermediate; they are larger and more projecting than modern humans, but smaller than most modern apes. An ape's upper jaw has a diastema (gap) between the canine and the adjacent incisor. This space is needed for the large lower canine to fit into when an ape closes its jaw. Modern humans do not have a diastema. The jaws of *A. afarensis* show a small diastema, larger than that of modern humans but smaller than that of modern apes. The lower first premolar of a modern ape is pointed with one cusp, whereas the lower premolar of a modern human has two cusps ("bicuspid"). The lower premolar teeth of *A. afarensis* show two cusps, but one cusp is more developed than the other—an intermediate condition. The orientation of the cusps to the jaw is like that of an ape. Indeed, most features of the jaws and teeth of *A. afarensis* show a state intermediate between that of ape and human.

What can we tell about the behavior of *A. afarensis*? No evidence for stone tool manufacture has been found with *A. afarensis*. As discussed earlier, this does not mean that they may not have been using tools made of perishable materials, such as wooden digging sticks. Analyses of dental remains show a wide range of variation in size, which suggests extensive sexual dimorphism. If our observations on living primates can be applied, such sexual dimorphism suggests a polygynous social structure (one adult male and several adult females). Such inferences, however, may not always be appropriate in dealing with a form unlike any living primate. The discovery of fossils from 13 individuals at one Hadar site, representing males and females of all ages, has led Johanson to suggest that they were a family group that all perished in a short period of time, perhaps because of a flash flood (Johanson and Edey 1981). Another possibility is that the fossils of all these individuals were together because of animal scavenging or some other factor that could result in the deposition of bones from different individuals at one site.

In summary, *A. afarensis* shows a number of primitive features in its jaws, teeth, skull, and postcranial skeleton. These features often show an intermediate condition between those found in apes and humans. Because *A. afarensis* was bipedal, it is a hominid, but its primitive features suggest it was not far from the split between ape and hominid evolutionary lines. This hypothesis is supported by molecular evidence (Chapter 9), which suggests a relatively recent ape–human split, roughly five to seven million years ago.

Later Australopithecines

Our best current evidence suggests that by 3 million years B.P., some *A. afarensis* populations had evolved into two or more different evolutionary lines, including several species of *Australopithecus* and the first members of the genus *Homo*.

ROBUST AUSTRALOPITHECINES   Environmental reconstructions show us that climatic factors, such as temperature and rainfall, have varied in the past. In East Africa temperatures dropped roughly 2.5 million years ago, leading to a reduction in woodlands and an increase in open grasslands. Along with this change came an increase in the number of species of certain mammals, such as antelopes, that adapted to this new environment (Vrba 1985). There is also evidence of two or more hominid lines appearing at this time, presumably as a consequence of the same set of ecological changes. One of these new hominid lines consists of three species that are collectively referred to as the **robust australopithecines.** (The name comes from the fact that their back teeth, jaws, and face are all very large and robust compared to those of other hominids.) These robust species lived in Africa between 1 and 2.5 million years ago, at which time they became extinct.

One of the key characteristics of the robust australopithecines is their large back teeth and relatively small front teeth. Apart from size, the overall structure of the teeth is quite human: the canines are nonprojecting, there is no diastema, and the lower premolar has two cusps. In terms of size, however, the robust australopithecines are quite different from modern humans.

robust australopithecines Australopithecines with large back teeth, cheekbones, and faces, among other anatomical adaptions to heavy chewing. The robust australopithecines lived in Africa between 2.5 and 1 million years B.P. Three species are generally recognized: *A. aethiopicus, A. robustus,* and *A. boisei.*

■ FIGURE 10.8
Lower jaw of a robust
australopithecine
(*Australopithecus boisei*) from
the Lake Natron site, Tanzania.
Note the small front teeth
(incisors and canines) and
the massive back teeth
(premolars and molars).
(From Clark Spencer Larsen,
Robert M. Matter, and Daniel L.
Gebo, *Human Origins: The Fossil
Record,* Second Edition, p. 67
(bottom). Copyright © 1991, 1985
by Waveland Press, Inc., Prospect
Heights, Illinois. Reprinted with
permission from the publisher)

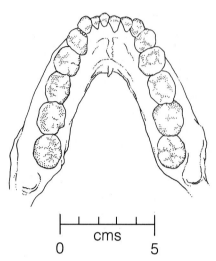

■ FIGURE 10.9
Lower jaw of a robust
australopithecine
(*Australopithecus robustus*),
specimen SK 23, Swartkrans,
Republic of South Africa.
Because of distortion, the
rows of the jaw are closer
than they should be. Note the
small front teeth and the large
back teeth. (Transvaal Museum)

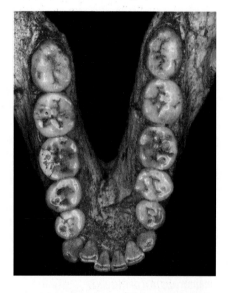

■ FIGURE 10.10
Side, top, and frontal views of
a robust australopithecine
(*Australopithecus boisei*),
skull, specimen KNM-ER 406,
from Lake Turkana, Kenya. (©
The National Museums of Kenya)

■ FIGURE 10.11
Skull of a robust
australopithecine
(*Australopithecus robustus*),
specimen SK 48, Swartkrans,
Republic of South Africa.
(Transvaal Museum)

■ FIGURE 10.11
Skull of a robust
australopithecine
(*Australopithecus robustus*),
specimen SK 48, Swartkrans,
Republic of South Africa.
(Transvaal Museum)

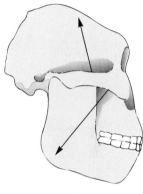

■ FIGURE 10.12
Skull of a robust
australopithecine, with arrows
indicating the action of
chewing muscles: (*top*)
temporalis, (*bottom*)
masseter.

The front teeth are small, both in absolute size and in relationship to the rest of the teeth. The back teeth (premolars and molars) are huge, over four times the size of modern humans in some cases (see Figures 10.8 and 10.9). Note how massive the jaws are and how large the back teeth are, especially in relationship to the front teeth. Also note that the premolars are larger side to side than front to back. These features all show a large surface area for the back teeth, indicating heavy chewing.

The skulls of robust australopithecines also reflect heavy chewing (Figures 10.10 and 10.11). These skulls show massive dished-in faces, large flaring cheek bones, and a bony crest running down the top. All of these features are related to large jaws and back teeth and powerful chewing muscles. As shown in Figure 10.12, two muscles are responsible for closing the mouth during chewing. One, the masseter, runs from the back portion of the jaw to the forward portion of the **zygomatic arch** (the bone on the side of the skull connecting the zygomatic and temporal bones). The zygomatic arch and facial skeleton anchor this muscle. In hominids with large jaws and masseter muscles, the face and zygomatic arch need to be massive to withstand the force generated during chewing. The other muscle, the temporalis, runs from the jaw up under the zygomatic arch and attaches to the sides and top of the skull. The larger this muscle is, the more the zygomatic arch must flare out from the side of the skull. To anchor the temporalis muscle on the sides and top of the skull, a ridge of bone develops down the center of the skull (called a **sagittal crest**). All these cranial and facial features indicate powerful chewing activity.

▲▲

zygomatic arch The bone on the side of the skull connecting the zygomatic and temporal bones and that anchors muscles used in chewing.

sagittal crest A ridge of bone running down the center of the top of the skull that serves to anchor chewing muscles.

■ FIGURE 10.13
Specimen KNM-WT 17000
from Lake Turkana, Kenya,
also known as the "Black
Skull" because of the color of
mineral staining. This skull is
dated to 2.5 million years B.P.
It is a robust australopithecine
that has been classified as
Australopithecus aethiopicus
by some, and as an early
example of *Australopithecus
boisei* by others. It shows a
mixture of specialized robust
features (e.g., the sagittal
crest) and primitive features
(e.g., the forward jutting of
the jaw). This mix links
Australopithecus afarensis
and the later robust
australopithecines. (A. Walker
© The National Museums of Kenya)

Despite the name "robust," the robust australopithecines were not that
large in terms of overall body size, with estimated height being roughly 4 to
5 feet. On average, males weighed about 45 kg (roughly 100 lb) and females
weighed about 33 kg (73 lb) (McHenry 1992). As with all australopithecines,
brain size was small, averaging roughly 500 cc, with a range of 410 to 530 cc
(Aiello and Dunbar 1993).

Three species of robust australopithecine are generally recognized. The
oldest at 2.5 million years B.P. is **Australopithecus aethiopicus,** which is very
robust but also shows a number of primitive cranial traits that link it with
Australopithecus afarensis (Figure 10.13). The later two species, **Australopithecus robustus** and **Australopithecus boisei,** differ in terms of geography and
size. *A. robustus* is found in South Africa and *A. boisei* is found in East
Africa. Of the two, *A. boisei* is the most robust.

What factors led to the changes from early *Australopithecus* to robust
australopithecines? Because the major changes are in the teeth, jaws, and
chewing characteristics, a different diet seems a likely answer. As the environment became drier, vegetation and fruit would be relatively harder to
chew (Vrba 1985). Larger back teeth and more powerful chewing muscles
would provide the ability to process this altered food efficiently and would
be selected for. Their diet is thought to have consisted of small, hard-to-
chew objects, such as seeds, nuts, and hard fruits. Such objects require heavy
chewing and large teeth.

Regardless of the specific adaptations of the robust australopithecines,
they became extinct by roughly 1 million years B.P. Their extinction could

■ FIGURE 10.14
Skull of *Australopithecus
africanus,* specimen STS 5,
Sterkfontein, Republic of
South Africa. (Transvaal
Museum)

■ FIGURE 10.15
Lower jaw of *Australopithecus
africanus,* specimen STS 52b,
Sterkfontein, Republic of
South Africa. The teeth are
larger than in modern
humans, but the relative
proportions of front and back
teeth are more similar to
those of modern humans than
those of the robust australopithecines are. (From Clark
Spencer Larsen, Robert M. Matter,
and Daniel L. Gebo, *Human
Origins: The Fossil Record,*
Second Edition, p. 59. Copyright
© 1991, 1985 by Waveland Press,
Inc., Prospect Heights, Illinois.
Reprinted with permission from
the publisher)

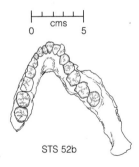

STS 52b

relate to environmental change, because another episode of climatic cooling took place during this time. In any case, they are not our ancestors, but merely "cousins" who are no longer alive.

AUSTRALOPITHECUS AFRICANUS Australopithecine specimens found in South Africa dating between 3 and 2 million years B.P. have been placed in the species **Australopithecus africanus** (named after Africa). A. africanus had reduced canines, large faces, and an average brain size of roughly 450 cc (Aiello and Dunbar 1993). A skull of A. africanus is shown in Figure 10.14. Like other australopithecines, it had a small brain and a large face. The face is not as massive as the robust forms, however, and there is no sagittal crest. A lower jaw of A. africanus is shown in Figure 10.15. Compared to the robust forms, the front teeth are not as small relative to the back teeth. In overall size, however, the back teeth are still larger than those of modern humans.

▲▲▲

*Australopithecus
aethiopicus* The oldest
robust australopithecine,
dating to 2.5 million
years B.P. in East Africa.
Some view this as an
early example of *A.
boisei.* It combines
derived features seen
in other robust

australopithecines with
primitive features seen
in *A. afarensis.*

*Australopithecus
robustus* A robust
species of australo-
pithecine, dating
between 2 and 1 million
years B.P. and found in
South Africa.

Australopithecus boisei
The most robust of
the australopithecines,
dating between 2 and 1
million years B.P. and
found in East Africa.

*Australopithecus
africanus* A species of
australopithecine dating
between 3 and 2 million
years B.P. and found in
South Africa.

Like the robust species, *A. africanus* is considered a descendant of *A. afarensis*. Some anthropologists view *A. africanus* as a likely candidate for an ancestor to the genus *Homo*, whereas others consider it a side branch of hominid evolution (see Figure 10.22 later in the chapter).

HOMO HABILIS

Thus far, we have a scenario whereby *A. anamensis* evolved into *A. afarensis*, which in turn gave rise to the robust australopithecines and *A. africanus*. At the same time the robust forms first appeared, another line of hominid evolution evolved—the genus **Homo.** The oldest known species in this genus is **Homo habilis,** which differs from the australopithecines in having a larger brain, smaller teeth, and a definite association with stone tools. Table 10.2 lists some of the major sites in Africa where *H. habilis* has been discovered.

Starting in the 1930s, Louis and Mary Leakey conducted fieldwork at the site of Olduvai Gorge in Tanzania. Among their early finds were the remains of the then oldest known stone tools, dating back to throughout the Pleistocene. For many years the Leakeys searched Olduvai Gorge looking for the maker of these tools. In 1960, they found a jaw, two cranial fragments, and several postcranial remains dating to 1.75 million years B.P. These finds represented a hominid with smaller teeth and a larger brain than that of any of the australopithecines found up to that time. Continued work led to the discovery of several more specimens, and in 1964 Leakey and colleagues proposed a new species based on this material: *Homo habilis* (Leakey et al. 1964). The species, whose name literally translates as "able man," was named for its association with manufactured stone tools. Since that time, additional fossils and stone tools have been found elsewhere in East and South Africa. *Homo habilis* has been dated to 2.5 to 1.5 million years B.P.

■ TABLE 10.2
List of Major Fossil Sites for *Homo habilis*

COUNTRY	LOCALITY	AGE (MILLIONS OF YEARS B.P.)	FIGURE NUMBER(S) IN TEXT
Kenya	Chemeron	2.4	
Republic of South Africa	Sterkfontein	2.0–1.5	
Republic of South Africa	Swartkrans	2.0–1.5	
Tanzania	Olduvai Gorge	2.0–1.5	10.17, 10.20
Kenya	East Turkana	1.8	10.18, 10.19

Sources: Larsen et al. (1991); Hill et al. (1992)

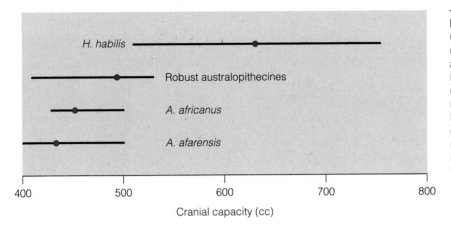

■ FIGURE 10.16
Comparison of the cranial
capacities of *Australopithecus*
and *Homo habilis*. The dots
indicate the average cranial
capacity (in cubic centi-
meters) for each group. The
lines indicate the range
of cranial capacity from
minimum to maximum.
(*Source of data:* Aiello and Dunbar
1993)

General Physical Characteristics

The major distinguishing feature of *Homo habilis*, compared to the australopithecines, is its larger brain size. The teeth and postcranial skeleton also
show differences.

BRAIN SIZE The most noticeable difference between *H. habilis* and the australopithecines is the larger average brain size of *H. habilis*. The average cranial capacity of *H. habilis* is roughly 630 cc, which is 40 percent larger than
the average cranial capacity of *A. africanus*. Figure 10.15 compares the average and range in cranial capacity for *Australopithecus* and *H. habilis*. There is
very little overlap, and the higher cranial capacity of *H. habilis* is obvious.

Figure 10.16 also shows that the range in cranial capacity for *H. habilis* is
rather high, ranging from a minimum of 509 cc to a maximum of 752 cc
(Aiello and Dunbar 1993). Some anthropologists have suggested that this
large range is evidence that two different species are being lumped together
in the fossils we call *H. habilis* (e.g., Stringer 1986). Others disagree, and note
that such a range is not that large if, as some suggest, *H. habilis* was a highly
sexually dimorphic species (Miller 1991). If this is the case, then the large
range in cranial capacity might reflect smaller females and larger males. Based
on the presence or absence of other anatomical features, Wood (1992)

▲▲

Homo A genus of
hominid with three
recognized species
(*Homo habilis, Homo
erectus,* and *Homo
sapiens*), dating to

2.5 million years B.P.
and characterized by
large brain size and
dependence on culture
as a means of adaption.

Homo habilis The oldest
known species in the
genus *Homo,* dating
between 2.5 and 1.5
million years B.P. and
found in Africa, sim-

ilar in appearance to
australopithecines but
with a larger cranial
capacity.

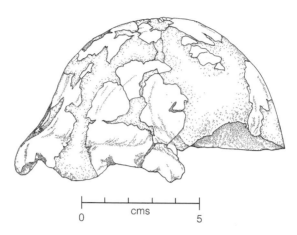

0   cms   5

■ **FIGURE 10.17**
Skull of *Homo habilis,*
specimen OH 16, Olduvai
Gorge, Tanzania. Although
this skull is small compared
to that of a modern human,
its cranial capacity (638 cc)
marks it as much larger than
the australopithecine skull.
(Figure from *Atlas of Human
Evolution,* Second Edition by
C. Loring Brace and Harry Nelson,
copyright © 1979 by Holt,Rinehart
and Winston, Inc., reprinted by
permission of the publisher)

argues that what we call *H. Habilis* is actually two or more species of early *Homo.* Although most anthropologists consider *H. habilis* a single species, the issue is not yet resolved.

A skull assigned to *H. habilis* is shown in Figure 10.17. This specimen (OH 16), dating to 1.7 million years B.P. was discovered at Olduvai Gorge. The specimen consists of a reconstructed skull cap. Its estimated cranial

■ **FIGURE 10.18**
Frontal and side views of
Homo habilis, specimen KNM-
ER 1470, Lake Turkana,
Kenya. (© The National
Museums of Kenya)

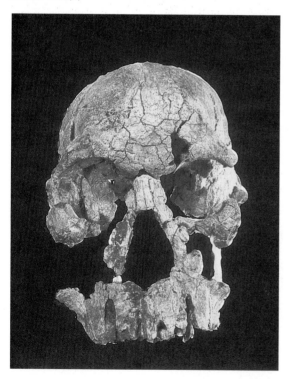
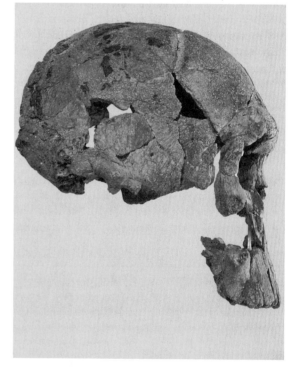

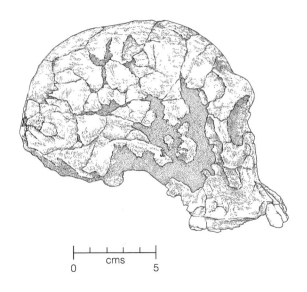

cms
0   5

capacity is 638 cc. Another example of *H. habilis*, ER 1470, is shown in Figure 10.18. This specimen was discovered on the eastern shore of Lake Turkana in Kenya, and is dated to 1.9 million years B.P. Its cranial capacity is 752 cc, and it has a rather well-rounded brain case compared to that of the australopithecines. Figure 10.19 shows specimen ER 1813, also from Lake Turkana. Dating to 1.8 million years B.P., this specimen has the smallest cranial capacity (509 cc) of any specimen yet assigned to *H. habilis*. It is the contrast of this specimen with that of ER 1470 (see Figure 10.18) that has led a number of anthropologists to question the validity of putting all of these specimens into a single species. Interestingly, although ER 1813 has a smaller brain size than ER 1470, it is more like modern humans in certain facial features.

Evidence exists that the brains of *H. habilis* were structurally different from those of the australopithecines, in addition to being larger. Falk (1983) investigated an **endocast** (a cast of the interior brain case) of one *H. habilis* specimen and found fissures in the area of the frontal lobes similar to those of modern humans but different from those of apes and australopithecines. This pattern seems to be associated with the development of brain structures linked to language abilities.

TEETH The teeth of *H. habilis* are in general smaller than those of most australopithecine species but larger than those of modern humans. In particular, the back teeth are not as large relative to the front teeth as they are in the australopithecines (Figure 10.20). The shape of the premolars of *H. habilis* is more similar to that of modern humans; they are more elongated than the premolars of the robust australopithecines.

THE SKELETON For many years little was known about the postcranial skeleton of *H. habilis*. The few fossil remains were isolated parts. In 1986, a partial adult skeleton assigned to *H. habilis* was discovered (Johanson et al. 1987).

endocast A cast of the interior of the brain case used in analyzing brain size and structure.

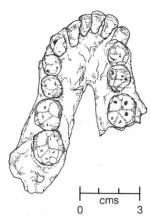

```
     ├──┼──┼──┤
        cms
     0           3
```

■ **FIGURE 10.20**
Lower jaw of *Homo habilis*
specimen OH 7, Olduvai
Gorge, Tanzania.
(Figure from *Atlas of Human
Evolution,* Second Edition by
C. Loring Brace and Harry
Nelson, copyright © 1979 by
Holt, Rinehart and Winston, Inc.,
reprinted by permission of the
publisher)

Preliminary analysis suggests this skeleton is similar to that of *A. afarensis,*
with small size and relatively long arms. Johanson and colleagues assigned
this specimen to *H. habilis* on the basis of fragmentary cranial and dental
remains; other anthropologists argue that it might be an australopithecine
(Falk 1992). Until further discoveries, with more definitive cranial remains,
are found, the nature of the postcranial skeleton of *H. habilis* remains
unclear.

Behavior

What can we say about the behavior of *H. habilis?* The increase in brain size
and changes in brain structure suggest some associated behavioral evolution
compared to the australopithecines. When *H. habilis* was first described,
there was a tendency to ascribe a variety of modern human behaviors to it,
including use of shelter, manufacture of stone tools, and coordinated hunting. Recent work has suggested that the behavior of *H. habilis* was not like
that of modern hunting-gathering societies. Certain behaviors, such as stone
tool manufacture, did take place.

STONE TOOL TECHNOLOGY   The earliest known stone tools date to 2.5 million
years B.P. Many of these stone tools have been found in association with fossil remains of *H. habilis.*

The stone tool culture of *H. habilis,* referred to as the **Oldowan tradition,** consists of relatively simple chopping tools. Two examples of Oldowan
tools are shown in Figure 10.21. These tools were made by striking several
flakes off a rounded stone to give it a rough cutting edge. They are normally
made from materials such as lava and quartz. The stone was held steady and
was then struck with another stone at the right angle to remove a flake of
stone. Several strikes often produced a rough edge capable of cutting through
animal flesh or other objects that hominids could not tear themselves. The
chipped-off flakes could also be used as small cutting tools. This type of tool
manufacture sounds extremely easy but actually involves a great deal of skill,
as anthropologists attempting to duplicate these tools have found out.
Proper tool manufacture requires skill in finding the right materials and
using the right amount of force. Mistakes could ruin a tool and injure a
hominid's hand.

These simple chopping tools can be used for a wide variety of purposes.
Significantly, they can cut through bone and muscle. Because hominids do
not have claws or sharp teeth, these tools would provide the only means to
eat an animal. The tools could also be used to sharpen sticks, which then
could be used for weapons or digging. Hides could be scraped for a number
of uses. These stone tools represent the modification of environmental materials to meet needs that could not otherwise be met. Of course, just finding the tools with *H. habilis* is not enough to demonstrate exactly how they
used them.

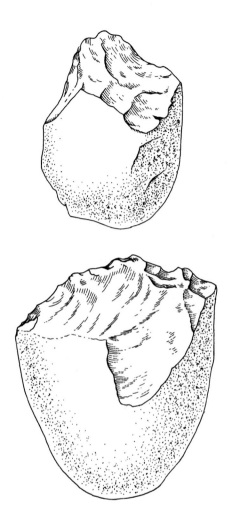

■ FIGURE 10.21
Oldowan tools. (From *The Old Stone Age* by F. Bordes, 1968. Reprinted with permission of the publisher, Weidenfeld and Nicolson, Ltd.)

Until recently, the emphasis on archaeological investigations of *H. habilis* had been on the stone cores produced by flaking. The small flakes, often found in great abundance, were felt to be nothing more than waste material. Analysis of the scratch marks on these flakes, however, shows that they were often used for a variety of tasks, including sawing wood, cutting meat, and cutting grass stems (Klein 1989). Archaeologists analyze these scratches by comparing them to those produced under experimental conditions.

HUNTING OR SCAVENGING?   The older interpretation that *H. habilis* was a hunter has given way to a new interpretation that it was a scavenger. This hypothesis is based on analyses of the stone tools and the distribution of animal bones found alongside these tools. Much of this research is based on *H. habilis* sites at Olduvai Gorge, where both the animal bones and the stone tools had

▲▲▲▲▲▲▲▲▲▲▲▲▲▲▲▲▲▲▲▲▲▲▲▲▲▲▲▲▲▲▲

Oldowan tradition The stone tool culture of *Homo habilis.*

been brought to these sites from farther away. To complicate matters, there is extensive evidence of carnivore activity at these sites. One interpretation is that *H. habilis* was responsible for the tools, and the carnivores were responsible for the animal carcasses. In this view, *H. habilis* would bring tools to carnivore dens to scavenge from the remains. However, it seems unlikely that early hominids would bring stone tools to carnivore dens because of the danger (Potts 1984). Another interpretation is that *H. habilis* was responsible for bringing both carcasses and tools to these sites, and carnivores frequented these sites to scavenge meat.

Electron-scanning microscopes have been used to investigate the cut patterns on stone tools to distinguish marks made by tool use from other factors, such as erosion. These analyses show that the Oldowan tools were used for cutting; many animal bones show the characteristic grooves left by stone tools. Many of these bones, however, also show tooth marks from carnivores. In some cases, the tool marks overlap the tooth punctures, showing that stone tools were used on an animal *after* it had been gnawed on by carnivores. Other bones show the opposite pattern. The dead animals were a source of food for both *H. habilis* and carnivores.

The available evidence suggests that *H. habilis* was a scavenger. Over half the cut marks left by stone tools are found on bones with little meat, such as the lower legs. This suggests that *H. habilis* was taking what was left over from carnivores. Also, there is no evidence of complete carcasses of larger animals brought to the Olduvai sites, only portions—and these are most often the bones left over by carnivores (Wolpoff 1980; Potts 1984). In addition, the animal bones are not completely processed and considerable meat and marrow was often left over. This type of behavior is strikingly different from that of modern hunters, who utilize the entire remains of an animal.

Though it is likely that *H. habilis* did hunt occasionally, perhaps in a manner similar to living chimpanzees, the available evidence does not support the idea that it was an organized hunter. Instead, *H. habilis* appears to have been a scavenger of meat from dead and dying animals. Though this might not sound like our idea of a "noble ancestor," the act of scavenging did expand the food resources of early hominids.

HOME BASES?   The association of stone tools with *H. habilis* suggested to many anthropologists a wide variety of cultural behaviors. Given stone tools, these hominids could hunt game and bring portions back to feed others. This interpretation further suggests the presence of social groups, with division of labor in which some individuals brought meat back to others. The stone tools are often found at sites with many animal bones, usually broken into smaller pieces. This association suggests that these sites were **home bases,** campsites where hunted animals were brought, processed, and distributed to the members of the group. Presumably others would gather fruit and vegetation and bring them back to the home base.

The idea that these sites were home bases for *H. habilis* was widely accepted until recently. Because modern hunters and gatherers have home sites, it seemed reasonable to assume that any collection of stone tools and animal remains in the archaeological record was evidence of home bases. Other interpretations of these sites are possible, however. As discussed, *H. habilis* was most likely a scavenger rather than a hunter. Is it still possible to consider the sites where scavenged carcasses were brought to be home bases?

The evidence of carnivore activity at the Olduvai sites suggests that these were not home bases. Teeth marks left on hominid bones show that *H. habilis* was often prey to large carnivores. It seems unlikely that early hominids would camp near a carnivore den! Also, much of the scavenging seems to have been done hastily, as though the hominids were trying to finish what they were doing and get away as quickly as possible.

The archaeological evidence shows that *H. habilis* was the first step in future cultural evolution. Though the stone tools were crude and most likely used for scavenging, they marked the beginning of an adaptive pattern that relied more and more on technological advances and increased problem solving. From this point on, the mainstream of human evolution consists of further associated changes in both biology and cultural behaviors. The rest of this story is told in the next two chapters. Before ending this discussion of Plio-Pleistocene hominids, though, we must answer one more general question—when and how did *H. habilis* evolve from the australopithecines?

EVOLUTIONARY TRENDS

Given the diversity in early hominids, what conclusions can we reach regarding evolutionary relationships, evolutionary trends, and possible reasons for the major changes seen during this period of time? It is useful to synthesize the material covered thus far before proceeding to these questions. Table 10.3 provides a summary of the distribution, anatomy, and behavior of the australopithecines and *H. habilis*.

Evolutionary Relationships

The first step in synthesis is to take all of our information and use it to reconstruct a "family tree" so that we can see what, when, and where various events took place in early hominid evolution. Once we have the broad outline of a "tree" in place, we can then move on to the question of Why?

HISTORICAL OVERVIEW Before considering the *current* fossil evidence, we examine the history of past interpretations. The study of the historical development of any scientific discipline is important for a number of reasons.

▲▲▲▲▲▲▲▲▲▲▲▲▲▲▲▲▲▲▲▲▲▲▲▲▲▲▲▲▲

home base Campsite where hunters brought back food for sharing with other members of their group.

■ TABLE 10.3
Summary of Plio-Pleistocene Hominids

SPECIES	DATES (MILLIONS OF YEARS B.P.)	LOCOMOTION	CRANIAL CAPACITY	CRANIAL AND DENTAL CHARACTERISTICS	CULTURE
Ardipithecus ramidus	4.4	Suggested to be bipedal, but not definite	?	Fragmentary but very apelike	No stone tools
Australopithecus anamensis	4.2–3.9	Bipedal	?	Primitive apelike features in both skull and teeth	No stone tools
Australopithecus afarensis	4.0–3.0	Bipedal; some apelike features suggesting considerable climbing ability	Range: 400–500 cc Mean: 433 cc	Large face; primitive apelike features in both skull and teeth	No stone tools
Robust australopithecines (three species)	2.5–1.0	Bipedal	Range: 410–530 cc Mean: 494 cc	Large face and cheekbones; often show sagittal crest on top of skull; large back teeth and relatively small front teeth	No stone tools
Australopithecus africanus	3.0–2.0	Bipedal	Range: 428–500 cc Mean: 452 cc	Large face but slightly higher crania than *A. afarensis;* teeth are human in shape and proportion but larger than modern humans'	No stone tools
Homo habilis	2.5–1.5	Bipedal	Range: 509–752 cc Mean: 632 cc	Larger brain, but still smaller than later species (Chapters 11–12); smaller face than *Australopithecus* but still protruding; smaller teeth than *Australopithecus*	Simple stone tools; scavenging of animals

Source for cranial capacity data: Aiello and Dunbar (1993)

Because science is an ongoing, cumulative process, its current state always partially reflects past ideas and hypotheses. Even after hypotheses have been rejected, they may still continue to influence thinking in a field. Scientists do not work in a vacuum but are rather part of a larger culture, and current intellectual philosophies and trends can have an impact on the formulation of hypotheses and the interpretation of data.

It is also important to remember that our current knowledge is incomplete—not the final answer. It is not uncommon to read newspaper headlines such as "Fossil Discovery Overturns Previous Ideas About Human Origins." The impression that many people get from such headlines is that anthropologists know little about their subject, or else they would not have gotten things wrong. This impression ties in with a common belief that science produces ultimate truth and that mistakes in interpretation are tragic and indicative of serious trouble within a discipline. However, this is not how science works. Ideas are not simply accepted on faith, but are tested. If shown wrong, they are rejected and alternative hypotheses are constructed.

Many hypotheses in the study of human evolution have been tested and rejected. Others have stood the test of time, perhaps in modified form. Some examples from the study of human evolution show how ideas have been tested, as new evidence has accumulated and new analyses have been conducted. When the first species of *Australopithecus* (*A. africanus*) was announced in 1925, for example, it went against then-current thinking that the first step in human evolution was the origin of a larger brain, followed by bipedalism. *Australopithecus* showed just the reverse—bipedalism had come before the increase in brain size. Although it took time and additional evidence, ultimately the entire scientific community was convinced that the old "brain first" model was incorrect.

For many decades during the middle of the twentieth century, little was known about early hominid variation. One early debate focused on whether only a single hominid species was living, at any one time, or whether two or more hominid species were living at the same time. The **single species hypothesis** postulated that only one hominid species was living at any one time, and that the pattern of human evolution was essentially in a straight line, from *A. africanus* to the genus *Homo*. As more species were discovered, though, this view became harder and harder to defend—there was simply too much variation at any time to lump all specimens under a single species. Eventually, the single species hypothesis was rejected. Today, anthropologists debate exactly *how many* species lived at any one time—but they are in complete agreement that at certain times two or more hominid species existed.

Many different variations on the basic material are presented in this chapter. For example, some anthropologists would split *H. habilis* into two species. Others recognize as many as four robust species. Others claim that some species can be lumped together, such as the different robust species. Although debate on these issues is often intense, there is agreement on the basics. There are many variations on an early hominid "family tree," but there is agreement on the general scenario outlined at the beginning of this chapter: early, small-brained bipedal hominids were the base for two major evolutionary directions—a line that resulted in larger teeth, well adapted for chewing, and a line that resulted in a larger brain and a reliance on tools and culture for survival.

A TENTATIVE FAMILY TREE   Figure 10.22 presents a tentative family tree based on the fossil evidence to date. The newly discovered species *Ardipithecus ramidus* is near the base of the tree and the initial split of apes and hominids, but it does not lead to any later known hominid species. The species *Australopithecus anamensis* seems a likely candidate for the ancestor of Lucy and her

▲▲▲▲▲▲▲▲▲▲▲▲▲▲▲▲▲▲▲▲▲▲▲▲▲▲▲▲▲

single species hypothesis A model of Plio-Pleistocene hominid evolution, no longer accepted, that stated that only one species of hominid was present at any one time.

■ **FIGURE 10.22**
Tentative family tree of
hominid evolution. The dotted
lines indicate relationships
that are less certain. Some
questions concern the
placement of *Australopithecus
africanus*. Some view *A.
africanus* as a species linking
A. afarensis and *Homo
habilis*. Others view it as a
separate hominid line. There
is also some debate regarding
the placement of the South
African robust form, *A.
robustus*. Was it a descendant
of the first robust species, or
does it represent the parallel
evolution of a robust species
from *A. africanus?* Other
debates concern the number
of recognized species: Should
there be three, two, or one
robust species? Does *H.
habilis* represent one or two
species? Despite these
debates, the basic model of at
least two lines (one robust
and one of the genus *Homo*)
is agreed upon by most.

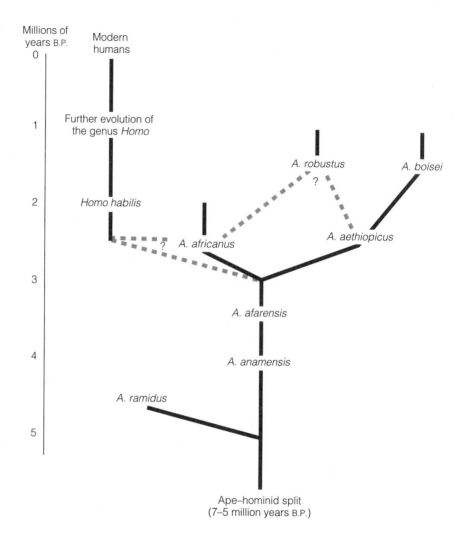

kind—the species *Australopithecus afarensis*. By 2.5 million years B.P., this
basal line led in two different directions. The first robust australopithecine
(*Australopithecus aethiopicus*) shares a number of features with *A. afarensis*
and the later robust forms and probably links them. The other hominid line,
characterized by an increase in brain size and the development of a stone
tool technology, is first represented by *Homo habilis*. There is much debate
about where *Australopithecus africanus* fits in, as shown by the dotted lines.
Was it an intermediate species between *A. afarensis* and *H. habilis*, or was it a
side branch of hominid evolution that ultimately became extinct? Another
question is whether the South African robust species, *Australopithecus robustus*, was a descendant of *A. aethiopicus* or whether it represents the parallel

The Piltdown Hoax

One of the main points made in this chapter is that characteristics of modern humans did not all appear at the same time. In particular, we know from the fossil record that bipedalism started at least 1.5 to 2 million years before we see any significant increase in brain size or the origin of stone tools. This finding is based on the fossil and archaeological records.

Early ideas about human origins suggested just the reverse—that brain size evolved first. Because there were few fossils to show otherwise at that time, this hypothesis could not then be rejected and was quite popular. The model predicted that the fossil record would ultimately show that, of all modern human characteristics, large brain size would be the oldest. Of course, today we have sufficient information to reject this hypothesis altogether. At the beginning of the twentieth century, however, we did not.

In fact, fossil evidence *was* found to support the antiquity of the large human brain. Between 1911 and 1915, hominid fossils were discovered at Piltdown, England, alongside stone tools and the fossils of prehistoric animals such as mastodons. A primary specimen ("Piltdown Man") consisted of a large skull and an apelike jaw. The teeth, however, were worn flat, more closely resembling the condition of human teeth. The specimen showed a mixture of ape and human traits and had a modern human brain size. It offered clear proof that large brains came first in human origins.

Because of Piltdown, any fossil that had human characteristics but did not have the large brain were rejected, for a time, as possible human ancestors. Indeed, this was part of the reluctance of scientists to accept *Australopithecus* as a hominid. The first australopithecine specimen was discovered by Raymond Dart in 1924. The specimen consisted of the face, teeth, and cranial fragments (including a cast of the brain case) of a young child. Dart named the specimen *Australopithecus africanus*. Based on cranial evidence relating to the angle at which the spinal cord enters the skull, he claimed it was an upright walker. The brain size was apelike, as was the protruding face. The teeth, however, were more like those of humans, particularly in having small canines. Here was another specimen that had a mixture of ape and human traits,

but that suggested the large brain evolved *after* bipedalism and humanlike teeth. At the time, more people tended to support Piltdown (in fairness, some of their criticisms of *Australopithecus*, including the difficulty in interpreting remains of children, were valid).

Some scientists, however, were more skeptical about Piltdown Man. And, eventually, continuing investigation showed that the find was a fake. In 1953, a fluorine analysis (see Chapter 5) confirmed that the jaw bones and skull bones did not come from the same time period. Closer inspection showed that the skull was that of a modern human and the jaw that of an orangutan. The teeth had been filed down, and all of the bones had been chemically treated to simulate age. To this day, no one knows exactly who was responsible for the hoax, although a number of suspects had both motive and opportunity.

The story of Piltdown Man is often offered up as evidence that anthropologists (and other scientists) often do not know what they are talking about. After all, look how easily they were fooled. This criticism misses the point altogether. Science and scientists make mistakes, and sometimes commit outright fraud. It is ridiculous to expect otherwise. Science does not represent truth per se, but rather a means of arriving at the truth. When Piltdown was discovered, scientific investigation did not stop. Instead, scientists kept looking at the evidence, questioning it and various assumptions, and devising new ways of testing. As a result, the hoax was uncovered. This is how science is supposed to work.

Side view of Piltdown Man. The dark-colored areas and the back part of the lower jaw were found; the rest was reconstructed. This find, which confirmed the then-popular notion that early humans had large brains and apelike jaws, was a hoax; the remains of a modern human and an orangutan were placed together at the Piltdown site.

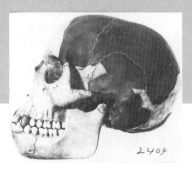

evolution of a robust form from *A. africanus*. Although these questions are of considerable importance to professionals in the field, the *exact* answers do not alter the basic patterns described here.

Looking over this suggested family tree (and remembering that there are lots of variations on the specifics of the tree), two big questions emerge. Why did bipedalism evolve? Why did brain size increase in *H. habilis* (and not in the robust australopithecines)?

The Origin of Bipedalism

The australopithecine fossils show us that of all the unique traits used to define hominids (Chapter 8), bipedalism is the oldest. Therefore, any model of hominid origins must consider the origin of bipedalism. Ever since Darwin's time, scientists have proposed hypotheses for the evolutionary advantage of bipedalism. The anatomical changes are known, and it would probably not take major genetic changes to bring them about. The critical question is *why* bipedalism would be selected for. Walking on two legs is often less efficient than walking on four legs. Four-legged animals can run faster and maintain their balance more easily than two-legged animals. Why, then, did bipedalism evolve in hominids?

THE TOOL USE MODEL   For many decades, the **tool use model,** which postulated that bipedalism, small canines, and large brains were all linked to the use of tools in adapting to the environment, was the accepted explanation for the origin of those characteristics. This idea was first suggested by Charles Darwin and was later expanded by a number of anthropologists such as Washburn (1960). The basis of the model is that **feedback** has occurred among the different hominid adaptations. In other words, one factor influences (and is influenced by) all other factors. This model views hominid characteristics as a complex of interrelated traits that evolved simultaneously.

The use of tools as an adaptive strategy requires learning and intelligence. This is seen in studies of modern chimpanzees, who occasionally use tools and pass these skills on to the young. The tool use model of hominid origins states that tool use shifted from being an optional strategy to an essential strategy, presumably as the environment changed. As tool use became more and more important, selection would take place for enhanced learning abilities, intelligence, and relatively larger brains. As larger brains evolved along with longer periods of infant dependency, tools would become even more important for survival. Thus, tool use affected brain size increase, which in turn affected tool use. This model does not rely on a single cause and single event, but rather on two components (tool use and brain size) that affect each other.

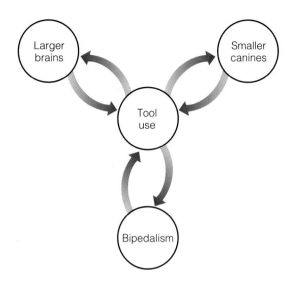

■ **FIGURE 10.23**
The tool use model of hominid origins. According to this model, larger brains, smaller canines, bipedalism, and tool use all developed at the same time. This model is now rejected because we know that bipedalism evolved well before the increase in brain size.

The tool use model also explains the evolution of other hominid characteristics. Upright walking would be advantageous for carrying tools. Freeing the hands would also allow carrying of food, and tools would be useful in obtaining food. Bipedalism would also allow weapons to be carried to fend off predators. Continued bipedalism would lead to even greater reliance on tools. If tools (e.g., sticks and stones) were used for defense, then large canines would no longer be necessary for defense and could become smaller (this is a somewhat weak point of the model because it assumes that when a structure is no longer needed it reduces in size). The more tools were used for defense, the more selection for bipedalism and larger brains took place.

The tool use model is a specific hypothesis that was tested using the fossil record (Figure 10.23). If, as the model suggests, the four major hominid characteristics evolved at the same time, then the fossil record should show a gradual change from a form with large canines, small brain, no bipedalism, and no tools to a form with small canines, large brain, bipedalism, and tools. For much of the twentieth century, this model was supported by then-available fossil evidence. During the last two decades, however, newer

tool use model A model of hominid origins, no longer accepted, that stated that bipedalism, large brains, and small canines all evolved simultaneously during hominid evolution as a consequence of increased reliance on tool use.

feedback When one factor influences, and is influenced by, other factors in a system.

evidence has led to the rejection of the tool use model as traditionally stated. As we saw earlier in this chapter, bipedalism evolved *before* the increase in brain size. Hominid evolution is mosaic, and we must separate the initial development of bipedalism from its ultimate function in later humans. Bipedalism allows tool use, but it did not evolve because of this characteristic.

Why study the tool use model if it is wrong? First, certain aspects of the model, such as the relationship between brain size and tool use, are still useful. Second, the tool use model provides an excellent example of the ways in which evolutionary models may be tested. Remember that a hypothesis, to be scientific, must be testable.

Many other models have served to explain the origin of bipedalism. Some of the major ideas are outlined below. It is important to stress that perhaps no one single factor was responsible; the origin of bipedalism might have been due to two or more of these factors.

PREDATOR AVOIDANCE   Whenever hominids left the woodlands and moved on to the savanna, they were in danger of being hunted by larger carnivores. Four-legged mammals, such as the lion, can move faster than humans over short distances. Walking on two legs would seem to be a disadvantage. In terms of avoiding predators, however, the characteristic shows possible advantages. Some writers have suggested that standing on two legs would allow hominids to see over the savanna and spot potential predators. This is true, but it did not necessarily require the full bipedal adaptations seen in humans. If the only thing needed is the ability to stand up occasionally and scan the surrounding area, any modern ape could do as well. Day (1986) suggests that bipedalism combined with tree-climbing abilities would have been very useful in avoiding predators. It is interesting to note that a number of anthropologists have claimed considerable climbing ability for the earliest hominids.

REPRODUCTIVE SUCCESS   Natural selection operates on traits that increase the probability of survival. One way of ensuring increased survival is to increase the number of children or increase the amount of care and protection given to each child. Bipedalism frees the hands, allowing more efficient transportation of babies and greater ease in transporting food.

Owen Lovejoy (1981) has expanded on the idea that bipedalism results in increased reproductive success. His basic premise is that bipedalism evolved as a means of having more offspring and providing better care for them. Lovejoy believes that overlapping births (a characteristic of modern humans) was made possible through bipedalism. When the hands are free to carry food and babies, more than one infant can be cared for at a time (assuming a sedentary population). Overlapping births would therefore result in greater fertility and population growth because a hominid mother would not have to wait until one infant was grown before having another.

Lovejoy argues that caring for infants would reduce the mobility of mothers. How, then, would they obtain food? Lovejoy thinks that monogamous pair bonding developed between males and females so that the more mobile males would bring food back to mothers and infants. In exchange, the males received sex. So that sex would be more frequently available to males, females lost the estrus cycle, becoming continuously sexually receptive. Lovejoy's model therefore also explains the origin of the loss of estrus in hominids.

Though logically consistent, Lovejoy's model has a number of problems. The most serious is that sexual behavior leaves no traces in the fossil record, and even inferences made about social structure are difficult. Some have criticized Lovejoy's model because monogamy is relatively rare among hominoids. When we attempt to infer the behavior of early hominids based on modern apes and humans, we are on shaky ground. We have no living primates that approximate the earliest ancestors (essentially bipedal apes). Monogamy *could* have been possible. The real question is: How can we test this hypothesis? If anything, the fossil evidence of the earliest hominids argues against monogamy because the early hominids had considerable sexual dimorphism—a feature most often found in polygynous species.

Lovejoy's model has also been criticized for its basic premise that hominids show greater reproductive success than apes because of overlapping births. Because we cannot obtain measures of fertility from fossil remains, all these arguments have focused on fertility measures from living apes and humans. Some have questioned this assumption (e.g., Allen et al. 1982; Harley 1982), but Lovejoy (1982) has presented countering arguments.

In spite of its problems, Lovejoy's model remains useful in its effort to link bipedalism with increased fertility and/or survival. The monogamy argument and the assumption that females were dependent on males are the additional points many find problematic. Other types of social structure, however, could also account for the basic link between bipedalism and reproductive success. Cann and Wilson (1982) think that the advantages bipedalism provides to mothers is sufficient without invoking the pair-bonding argument. Their idea is attractive because it focuses on the all-important mother–infant bond found in all primate societies. Bipedalism would be useful regardless of the specific type of social structure. Allen and colleagues (1982) note that the most efficient social structure would revolve around a group of related females who could share child care and food procurement. This female kinship group is a social structure found in many primate species, including chimpanzees, and offers an attractive base for the model.

FOOD ACQUISITION Along with avoiding predators and supporting reproduction, the other major potential selective factor in survival resulting from bipedalism is obtaining food. Having free hands allows a human to carry more food, which would be particularly advantageous in situations such as

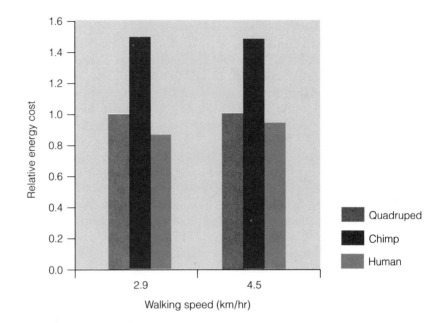

The relative energy cost of movement for chimpanzees and humans compared with a quadruped of similar size (set equal to 1.0 in this graph). The knuckle-walking chimpanzee uses more energy for movement (values > 1) and the bipedal human uses less (< 1). These comparisons have been made at two speeds: 2.9 km per hour (the normal speed of a chimpanzee) and 4.5 km per hour (the normal speed of a human). These results show that bipedalism is more energy-efficient at normal walking speeds. (*Source of data:* Rodman and McHenry 1980)

an open woodland or savanna environment, where food was widely distributed. Also, bipedalism is more energy-efficient in traveling long distances in search of food. Energy efficiency refers to the amount of energy expended relative to the task performed. In terms of movement, increased energy efficiency means using less energy to move about looking for and gathering food.

Though human bipedalism is less efficient than ape locomotion in the act of running, the opposite is true at normal walking speeds. Rodman and McHenry (1980) looked at the energy efficiency of bipedal humans and knuckle-walking chimpanzees at normal walking speeds. The results, shown in Figure 10.24, indicate that bipedalism is more energy-efficient at speeds of both 2.9 km per hour (the normal speed of a chimpanzee) and 4.5 km per hour (the normal speed of a human).

In a changing environment such as that found at the end of the Miocene, food resources would be scattered. The ability to move long distances in search of food would be an advantageous trait, and the shift to a hominid form of bipedalism would provide this ability.

TEMPERATURE REGULATION   Wheeler (1991b) has suggested recently that bipedalism might be related to temperature regulation among early hominids. Overheating and water loss are considerable threats, particularly to organisms exposed to extensive sunlight on the savanna. Based on laboratory experiments, Wheeler found that standing upright reduces the amount of direct solar radiation that strikes the body. Further, the higher wind speed and lower temperature felt by an animal off the ground would increase the rate of heat dissipation and effective evaporation of sweat. According to Wheeler, bipedalism might have been extremely adaptive for early hominoids venturing into the savanna in search of food.

Of course, it is possible (and perhaps likely) that more than one of the factors listed above played a role in the origin of bipedalism. Many of these are interrelated in an organism's survival. For example, the ability to walk long distances efficiently would enhance food gathering and infant care. As another example, improved temperature regulation would allow a hominid to forage at higher temperatures and to go further distances without having to consume as much water or food (Wheeler 1991a). This increased food-gathering ability would also benefit infants.

Given what we know about prehominid locomotion, the shift to bipedalism is reasonable because it involves relatively minor genetic and anatomical changes. Bipedalism is an adaptation that occurred in a changing environment to provide increased survival and reproduction. This change was the first step in human evolution (pun intended).

The Increase in Brain Size

The fossil record suggests that *H. habilis* led to the later species *H. erectus* and *H. sapiens*. The major evolutionary changes along our branch of human evolution have been an increase in brain size, a reduction in the size of the face and teeth, and an increase in cultural adaptations. *H. habilis* shows the beginnings of both large brains and stone tool technology. Although it is reasonable to link larger brains with intelligence and cultural adaptations, the origin of larger brains is more difficult to explain. Any model requires explanation of a genetic mechanism for larger brains as well as the selective advantages of such larger brains.

The genetic basis for larger brains in *H. habilis* and later hominid species most likely lies in the regulation of prenatal and postnatal brain growth. Primates in general show rapid rates of prenatal brain growth. Because primates require larger brains early in life, such rapid rates are necessary. Following birth, the usual primate pattern is for the size of the brain to double during the growth process. Modern humans are different in having more rapid rates of postnatal brain growth, so that our adult brain size is roughly four times that at birth.

NEOTENY   Our large brains can be explained by the process of **neoteny,** which is the retention of juvenile characteristics into adulthood (Gould 1977). This process is best explained by looking at the differences between an infant chimpanzee and an adult chimpanzee, then comparing these differences to those found between infant and adult humans. Figure 10.25 shows an infant and an adult chimpanzee. With its large rounded skull and relatively small face, the infant looks very similar to an infant human. The adult chimpanzee

neoteny The retention of juvenile characteristics in adulthood.

is different, with a relatively small brain and a large, protruding face. An adult human, however, looks very similar to an infant human. In other words, the shape and relative proportions of brain and face do not change much in humans. Infant apes have relatively large brains because of rapid rates of prenatal brain growth. After birth, however, the rate of brain growth slows down and the face continues to grow. The end result is an adult ape with a relatively small brain. In humans the rapid rate of prenatal brain growth is extended into infancy. Our brains continue to enlarge as our bodies grow. We retain the infant characteristic of a large, well-rounded skull.

Changes in the timing and rates of brain and facial growth can explain the major physical differences between ourselves and apes. Such changes could be the result of a small number of regulatory genes, helping to explain why we look so different from apes but yet have so much of our DNA sequences in common (Gould 1977). The increase in cranial capacity of *H. habilis* could be a consequence of selection for some initial mutations leading to neoteny. This idea assumes that larger brains and greater intelligence are adaptive. Are they?

ADVANTAGES AND DISADVANTAGES OF LARGER BRAINS   The benefits of larger brains and greater mental abilities are obvious. They allow greater behavioral flexibility in adaptation through cultural transmission from one generation to the next. Large brains also have a cost, however. The extension of fetal growth rates into infancy means that offspring will be born extremely helpless and require greater parental care, which in turn requires greater reliability of food, more protection, and social structures capable of assisting others. Also, rapid fetal brain growth requires greater maternal energy, which in turn also requires adequate food and environmental stability. Martin (1981) has shown that a lack of adequate maternal energy limits fetal brain growth.

Selection for larger brains requires that the advantages of larger brains outweigh the disadvantages. In a population that does not have adequate maternal energy or postnatal parental care, such genes would be selected against. On the other hand, if conditions existed in which adequate maternal energy and postnatal care were available, then more helpless infants with greater rates of brain growth would be selected for. The increase in brain size, intelligence, and cultural adaptations would then provide the basis for additional selection for larger brains. Increased cranial capacity and cultural adaptations are linked in a feedback loop; an increase in cultural adaptations allows further brain growth, which then allows further cultural adaptations.

THE RADIATOR THEORY   If larger brains have an overall advantage, then why didn't they develop among the robust australopithecines? Dean Falk (1990, 1992) has proposed a model of brain evolution in hominids that focuses on heat stress as a constraint on the development of larger brains. Quite simply, large brains in large heads must shed quite a bit of heat. This is particularly a problem if a large-brained hominid is spending a great deal of its time in hot

■ **FIGURE 10.25**
An infant and adult chimpanzee. (From *Human Antiquity: An Introduction to Physical Anthropology and Archeology*, 2d ed., by Kenneth Feder and Michael Park, Fig. 8.8. Copyright © 1993 by Mayfield Publishing Company)

climates such as equatorial Africa. How does the brain cool itself? During heat stress, blood that is cooled by evaporation flows from the skin into the brain case. In modern humans, blood circulates through a network of veins that also allows blood to drain from the brain into the rest of the body. One of Falk's interesting findings was that although some early hominids had this type of drainage system, others had a different one, whereby blood circulated through enlarged sinuses in the occipital and mastoid regions of the skull. Falk suggests that this other drainage system is not as effective in cooling the brain.

It turns out that the robust australopithecines (and the A. afarensis fossils from Hadar) had the less efficient system. Skulls of A. africanus and H. habilis showed a higher frequency of specific foramina (openings in the skull) characteristic of the more effective system. Therefore, it seems that the robust australopithecines did not have a system that would allow a larger brain—they would not have been able to handle the heat stress.

Why didn't the robust australopithecines evolve such a system? Again, evolution works on what variation already exists. For whatever reason (it may have been random, such as genetic drift), the robust australopithecines had a biological constraint that would have limited any increase in brain size. Their drainage system could only handle the heat stress of a smaller brain. Other hominids, such as A. africanus, had a system that *allowed* them to evolve larger brains. Once again, any evolutionary change must be viewed in terms of both costs and benefits. For the robust australopithecines, the costs outweighed the benefits, so they did not evolve larger brains.

SUMMARY

The first hominids belong to the genera *Ardipithecus* and *Australopithecus*, all of which lived in Africa, dating back as far as 4.4 million years B.P. Early hominids were bipedal, with small brains, large faces, and large teeth. Early species had many primitive characteristics in terms of both teeth and the skeleton. By 2.5 million years B.P., there were at least two major lines of hominids. One line, the robust australopithecines, had large back teeth, large jaws, and large chewing muscles. The robust species were well adapted for chewing hard foods, such as seeds, nuts, and hard-skinned fruits. Although successful for some time, they ultimately became extinct roughly 1 million years B.P.

The other line of hominid evolution shows an increase in brain size (although still roughly only half the size of a modern human) and the development of a stone tool technology. These hominids, generally referred to as *Homo habilis* (although there might be more than one species), lived in Africa from roughly 2.5 to 1.5 million years B.P. The archaeological evidence suggests that H. habilis was a scavenger. The ability to make and use stone tools, along with increased brain size, marks the beginnings of the genus *Homo*. The genus's continued evolution is discussed in the next two chapters.

SUPPLEMENTAL READINGS

Falk, D. 1992. *Braindance.* New York: Henry Holt. This well-written and lively book provides an interesting discussion of ideas regarding the evolution of hominid brains, including a review of the "radiator theory."

Johanson, D., and Edey, M. 1981. *Lucy: The Beginning of Humankind.* New York: Simon & Schuster. The story of the senior author's discovery and interpretation of "Lucy" and other specimens of *Australopithecus afarensis.* Somewhat out of date but still interesting.

Lewin, R. 1987. *Bones of Contention: Controversies in the Search for Human Origins.* New York: Simon & Schuster. An excellent account of several controversial subjects in human origins. Chapters 3, 4, and 7–12 focus on Plio-Pleistocene evolution.

Morell, V. 1995. *Ancestral Passions: The Leakey Family and the Quest for Humankind's Beginnings.* New York: Simon & Schuster. A detailed and fascinating history of the lives and discoveries of Louis, Mary, and Richard Leakey, and their impact on the field of human origins.

Schick, K. D., and Toth, N. 1993. *Making Silent Stones Speak: Human Evolution and the Dawn of Technology.* New York: Simon & Schuster. A review of stone tool technology and its relationship to human origins and evolution, including excellent descriptions of how stone tools are made and used.

The Evolution
of the Genus Homo

CHAPTER **11**

Three species are generally recognized in the genus *Homo*: *Homo habilis*, *Homo erectus*, and *Homo sapiens*. The evolution of the genus *Homo* involved an increase in brain size, a reduction in the size of the face and teeth, and increased sophistication of stone tool technologies and other cultural adaptations.

Despite this seemingly simple picture, many questions still remain about the specific nature of hominid evolution during the last 1.8 million years. How and why did one species evolve into the next? Were these events true speciations (cladogenesis) or continuations of basic trends over time within a single line (anagenesis)? Has hominid evolution been punctuated or gradual? There are also many questions about behavioral changes. When did hominids first use fire? When did they begin hunting large animals, and why? What types of social organizations existed in the past? What does past evolution tell us about our species today? This chapter looks at the major biological and cultural changes associated with the evolution of *Homo erectus* and early *Homo sapiens*.

Location of major *Homo erectus* sites in Africa and Asia.

HOMO ERECTUS

The species name **Homo erectus** literally means "upright walking human." This may sound odd, given the fact that earlier species also walked upright. When the first specimens of *H. erectus* were found in the late nineteenth century, they were thought to represent the oldest evidence of bipedalism. Originally, the species was called "*Pithecanthropus erectus*" (upright walking ape-man). Later the genus name *Homo* was assigned because of the similar adaptations of this early hominid species with our species: larger brains and a reliance on culture.

This section of the chapter reviews the currently known biological and behavioral evidence for *Homo erectus*. We will also look at evolutionary trends within *Homo erectus* and its relationship with earlier (*Homo habilis*) and later (*Homo sapiens*) hominids.

■ TABLE 11.1
List of Some Major Fossil Sites for *Homo erectus* in Africa and Asia

GEOGRAPHIC REGION	COUNTRY	SITE/SPECIMEN	AGE (MILLIONS OF YEARS B.P.)	FIGURE NUMBER(S) IN TEXT
East Africa	Kenya	East Turkana	1.8–1.3	11.4
		West Turkana	1.6	11.10
	Tanzania	Olduvai Gorge	1.2–0.7	
South Africa	Republic of South Africa	Swartkrans	1.7–0.9	
North Africa	Algeria	Ternifine	0.7	11.9
	Morocco	Salé	0.2	
Southeast Asia	Indonesia	Sangiran	1.7*	11.6
		Trinil	0.9?	
		Sambungmachan	0.4	
		Ngandong	0.2	
East Asia	China	Lantian	0.8	
		Zhoukoudian	0.5–0.2	11.5
		Hexian	0.25	

The range of dates for Olduvai Gorge indicates a series of different levels, the youngest dating to 0.7 million and the oldest dating to 1.2 million years B.P.

*See text.

Source: Klein (1989); Larsen et al. (1991); Swisher et al. (1994)

Distribution in Time and Space

The distribution of *H. erectus* sites is shown in Figure 11.1 and a list of the major fossil sites is given in Table 11.1. The most important feature of the spatial distribution of *H. erectus* is the species' move out of Africa; it is the first hominid species to do so. Current evidence points to an African origin for *H. erectus*, followed by movement of some populations into Asia (Indonesia and China). As discussed below, it is still not clear to what extent *H. erectus* lived in Europe, if it did so at all.

    H. erectus fossils have been dated to be as old as 1.8 million years B.P. and as recent as 0.2 million years (200,000 years) B.P., and possibly younger. There appears to be some overlap in time with later *H. habilis*. (Remember from Chapter 10 that *H. habilis* fossils have been dated to be as recent as 1.5 million years B.P.) This type of overlap may reflect uncertainties about dating or species identification, or it may simply reflect a common form of evolutionary change—"parent" species frequently survive for some time after the appearance of a new "daughter" species. In this case, we suggest that *some* population(s) of *H. habilis* evolved into *H. erectus*, but not all of them. That is, some *H. habilis* populations may have persisted for a short time after the initial origin of *H. erectus*. In any event, the oldest fossil remains of *H. erectus*

▲▲▲▲▲▲▲▲▲▲▲▲▲▲▲▲▲▲▲▲▲▲▲▲▲▲▲▲▲

Homo erectus A species of genus *Homo* that lived between 1.8 and 0.2 million years B.P., first appearing in Africa and later spreading to Asia (and possibly Europe).

are found in East Africa, and suggest a rather rapid evolution from *H. habilis* (that is, rapid in an evolutionary sense—within 100,000 to 200,000 years).

For many years, researchers believed that Asian *H. erectus* was much younger than African *H. erectus*. Until recently, they dated the African populations back to 1.8 million years B.P. and the oldest Asian populations (in Indonesia) at roughly 1 million years B.P. Given these dates, it appeared that *H. erectus* had remained in Africa for 800,000 years before some groups moved out to Asia. However, recent evidence, based on argon-argon dating, has caused a reassessment of this scenario. The new evidence dates *H. erectus* to 1.7 million years B.P. in Indonesia (Swisher et al. 1994). This new date suggests that some *H. erectus* populations moved out of Africa into Asia soon after the initial species origin. As we will see later, this may have implications for African-Asian differences in culture.

The evidence for possible European settlement by *H. erectus* is less clear. Most of the possible European sites are archaeological; they provide tools but few fossils. Although the tools at these sites are typical of *H. erectus*, similar tools have been found with early *Homo sapiens* as well. Thus, the tools alone do not tell us whether the sites were occupied by *H. erectus* or early *H. sapiens*.

The few European fossils that have been found are mostly dental remains whose origins are not altogether clear. Some recent evidence, however, suggests that the *fringes* of Europe may have been occupied by *H. erectus*. A lower jaw in the Georgian region of the former Soviet Union has been assigned to *H. erectus*, and has been tentatively dated between 1.8 and 1.6 million years B.P. (Gabunia and Vekja 1995).

Some biological differences have been found between African and Asian populations of *H. erectus*. Given the large geographical distance between the two populations, such differences are not surprising. Although anthropologists have interpreted these differences as indicating two separate species, most evidence to date points to a single species (Kramer 1993).

H. erectus was around for 1.6 million years. This is a long time for a hominid species. Such longevity suggests that *H. erectus* was a well-adapted species. Even though it is in many ways intermediate in appearance between *H. habilis* and *H. sapiens*, we should not regard it as a transitional form. *H. erectus* was not simply a species in the process of becoming us; rather, it was a long-lived, highly successful life form. We need to examine the biological and cultural adaptations of *H. erectus* to understand its evolutionary success.

General Physical Characteristics

The following section focuses on the physical characteristics of *Homo erectus*, specifically those of the skull, teeth, and postcranial skeleton.

BRAIN SIZE   The most obvious characteristic of *H. erectus*, compared to earlier forms such as *H. habilis*, is its larger brain size (Figures 11.2 and 11.3). The

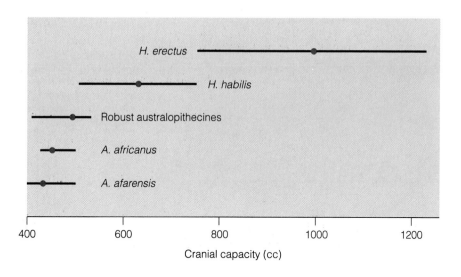

FIGURE 11.2
Comparison of the cranial capacities of *Australo-pithecus, Homo habilis,* and *Homo erectus.* The dots indicate the average cranial capacity (in cubic centimeters) for each group. The lines indicate the range of cranial capacity from minimum to maximum. (*Source of data:* Aiello and Dunbar 1993)

average cranial capacity of *H. erectus* is roughly 1,000 cc, which is approximately 75 percent that of a modern human. On average, the brain size of *H. erectus* is almost 60 percent larger than that of *H. habilis*. Figure 11.3 shows that the brain size of *H. erectus* increased somewhat over time, particularly after 700,000 years B.P. (Leigh 1992).

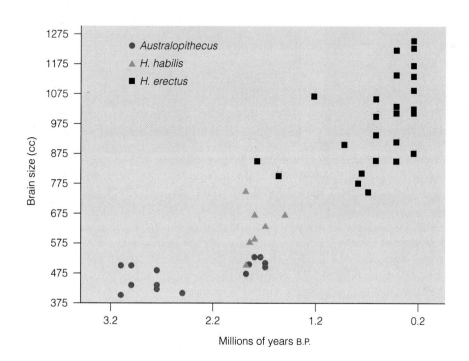

FIGURE 11.3
Plot of cranial capacities of fossil specimens over time for *Australopithecus, Homo habilis,* and *Homo erectus.* (*Source of data:* Aiello and Dunbar 1993)

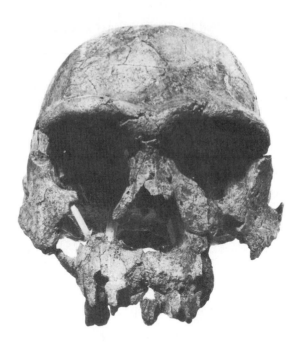

■ **FIGURE 11.4**
Homo erectus skull, specimen KNM-ER 3733, Lake Turkana, Kenya. Dated at 1.8 million years B.P., this is one of the oldest known specimens of *Homo erectus*. (© The National Museums of Kenya)

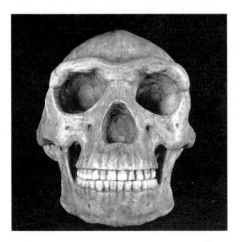

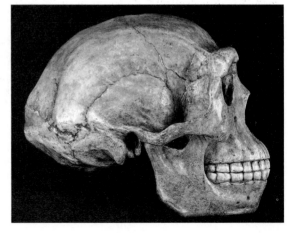

■ **FIGURE 11.5**
Frontal and side views of *Homo erectus* from the site of Zhoukoudian, China. The specimens from this site are sometimes referred to as "Peking Man" in older literature. (Neg. No. 315446, 315447. Courtesy Department of Library Services, American Museum of Natural History)

CRANIAL AND DENTAL CHARACTERISTICS One of the earliest *H. erectus* skulls, from Lake Turkana, Africa, is shown in Figure 11.4. Examples of Asian *H. erectus* are shown in Figure 11.5 (China) and Figure 11.6 (Indonesia). Overall, the brain case of *H. erectus* is larger than that of *H. habilis*, but it is still smaller than that of modern *H. sapiens*. The skull is lower and the face still protrudes more than in modern humans. Neck muscles attach to a ridge of bone along the back side of the skull. The development of this bony ridge shows that *H. erectus* had powerful neck muscles.

Figure 11.7 shows a *H. erectus* skull and a *H. sapiens* skull from a top view. The frontal region of the skull is still rather narrow (**postorbital constriction**), suggesting lesser development in the frontal and temporal lobes of

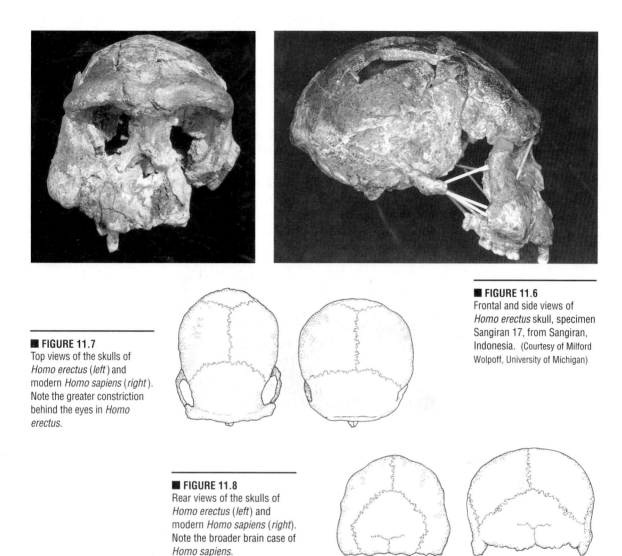

■ FIGURE 11.7
Top views of the skulls of
Homo erectus (*left*) and
modern *Homo sapiens* (*right*).
Note the greater constriction
behind the eyes in *Homo
erectus*.

■ FIGURE 11.8
Rear views of the skulls of
Homo erectus (*left*) and
modern *Homo sapiens* (*right*).
Note the broader brain case of
Homo sapiens.

the brain relative to modern humans. This implies that the intellectual abilities of *H. erectus* were not as great as in modern humans. The best evidence for the mental aptitude of *H. erectus*, however, comes from the archaeological record, discussed later. Figure 11.8 shows a *H. erectus* skull and a *H. sapiens* skull from the rear view. Note that the brain case of *H. erectus* is much broader toward the bottom of the skull.

The jaws and teeth of *H. erectus* are still large compared to those of modern humans but smaller than those of earlier hominids (Figure 11.9). In particular, the size of the back teeth of *H. erectus* decreased relative to those of the Plio-Pleistocene hominids. The front teeth are larger than in modern humans, possibly indicating that they were used as tools for holding objects

▲▲▲▲▲▲▲▲▲▲▲▲▲▲▲▲▲▲▲▲▲▲▲▲▲▲▲▲▲

postorbital constriction
The narrowness of the
skull behind the eye
orbits, a characteristic of
early hominids.

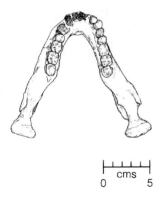

■ FIGURE 11.9
Lower jaw of *Homo erectus,*
specimen Ternifine 3,
Ternifine, Algeria, 700,000
years B.P. (From Clark Spencer
Larsen, Robert M. Matter, and
Daniel L. Gebo, *Human Origins:
The Fossil Record,* Second
Edition, p. 94 (top). Copyright ©
1991, 1985 by Waveland Press,
Inc., Prospect Heights, Illinois.
Reprinted with permission from
the publisher)

(Wolpoff 1980). Electron-scanning-microscopic analysis shows that the wear patterns on *H. erectus* teeth are characteristic of extensive meat eating.

The face of *H. erectus* protrudes, but not as much as in earlier hominids. One noticeable characteristic of the *H. erectus* face is the development of large ridges of bone above the eye orbits (**brow ridges**). These brow ridges are not apparent in *H. habilis* and are much smaller in archaic and modern *H. sapiens.* The appearance and subsequent loss of large brow ridges in humans is an evolutionary reversal that makes sense in terms of the overall pattern of cranial and dental evolution. Changes in diet reduced the amount of force needed for the back teeth, and increased use of the incisors as tools led to an increase in the force exerted at the front of the jaw. Changes in overall brain and face size produced differences in the orientation of neck and chewing muscles. The crest at the back of the skull indicates the attachment of strong neck muscles. On the face, the various forces exerted by chewing and neck muscles meet above the eyes. The brow ridges of *H. erectus* are a structural adaptation to strengthen the face at this critical juncture (Wolpoff 1980).

THE POSTCRANIAL SKELETON   The first specimen of *H. erectus* was discovered by Eugene Dubois in Java in 1891. This find consisted of the upper portion of a skull and a femur. Most scientists in the late nineteenth century would have been hesitant to include the skull cap in our genus, for the then-current view was that all human ancestors had large brains. Any fossil with a smaller brain was excluded from our ancestry. The femur that Dubois found, however, was virtually the same as that of a modern human. Because the two bones were found together, Dubois reasoned that upright walking had developed before the completion of a modern human skull. Though this statement now seems perfectly reasonable, it was controversial at the time.

Dubois's find shows again the mosaic nature of human evolution. The femur is similar to that of modern humans, indicating bipedalism. The smaller brain case, however, along with other features of the skull cap, does not resemble modern humans. We now see Dubois's find as a good example of the differences between *H. erectus* and modern humans; the *major* differences are in the skull and not in the postcranial skeleton.

For many years, the postcranial evidence for *H. erectus* was limited to portions of individuals—a femur here or a pelvic bone there. In 1984, this situation changed with the discovery of a nearly complete *H. erectus* skeleton at Lake Turkana dating back to 1.6 million years B.P. (Brown et al. 1985). This skeleton (Figure 11.10) is that of a young male. The pattern of dental eruption suggests he was about 12 years old when he died. This age estimate depends on the extent to which his growth patterns were similar to those of modern humans; some have suggested he might have been younger. One of the most striking features of this extremely complete skeleton is that he was tall; had he lived to adulthood, he might have been 6 feet tall, well above the height of many modern human populations! Also, note that the body proportions are very similar to those of modern humans, and different from those of earlier hominids, which had slightly longer arms.

This *H. erectus* find also provides us with valuable information about the evolution of brain size in early human evolution. Portions of the pelvis are narrow relative to those of modern humans. Because little sexual dimorphism is apparent in certain pelvic dimensions, Brown and colleagues (1985) feel that some measurements taken from this specimen can apply to both males and females. Their analysis leads to the suggestion that *H. erectus* females could not have given birth to very large-brained babies. To reach the relatively large brain sizes shown by *H. erectus*, the rate of brain growth must have continued to increase after birth. Had *H. erectus* shown the typical primate pattern of the brain size simply doubling after birth, they would not have had as large brains as they did. It seems that the modern human pattern of extensive postnatal brain growth had begun.

Cultural Behavior

Given the change in brain size from *H. habilis* to *H. erectus*, it is no surprise that corresponding changes took place in cultural adaptations. The stone tool technology of *H. erectus* was more sophisticated and specialized than that of *H. habilis*. Although not all agree, most anthropologists suggest that *H. erectus* was a skilled cooperative hunter. Some populations of *H. erectus* used caves for shelter and others, perhaps, made their own temporary shelters when caves were not available. *H. erectus* also used fire for cooking and warmth, although it is not clear whether they made fire or relied instead on natural fire.

STONE TOOL TECHNOLOGY In general, the stone tool technology of *H. erectus* was more diverse and sophisticated than the simple Oldowan tool technology used by *H. habilis*. This cultural change did not, however, take place immediately with the origin of *H. erectus*. That is, these biological and cultural changes did not occur simultaneously. Initially, early *H. erectus* in Africa made tools similar to but somewhat more sophisticated than Oldowan tools (often called "Evolved Oldowan"). Starting 1.4 million years B.P., however, *H. erectus* developed a new type of stone tool technology referred to as the **Acheulian tradition**. Acheulian tools are found in Africa and Europe.

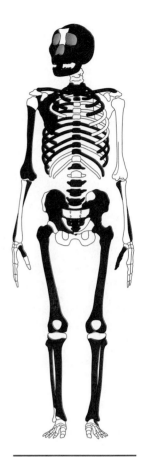

■ **FIGURE 11.10**
Homo erectus skeleton, specimen KNM-WT 15000, Lake Turkana, Kenya. This skeleton of a 12-year-old boy, dated to 1.6 million years B.P., is the most complete specimen of *Homo erectus* yet found. The shaded areas are the bones that were found.

brow ridges The large ridges of bone above the eye orbits, most noticeable in *Homo erectus* and archaic *Homo sapiens*.

Acheulian tradition The stone tool technology associated with some groups of *Homo erectus*.

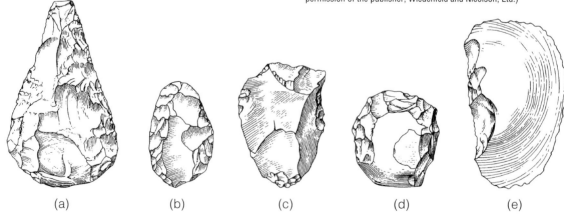

(a)   (b)   (c)   (d)   (e)

Acheulian tools are **bifaces;** the stone is worked on both sides. These tools are flatter and have straighter, sharper sides than Oldowan tools. The change in manufacture produced a more efficient tool. To produce a biface tool, smaller flakes must be removed than is necessary to produce an Oldowan chopping tool, a process that requires greater skill. One method of flake removal involves the use of some softer material, such as wood or antler, instead of another stone. Softer materials absorb much of the shock in flake removal, allowing more precise control over flaking.

The basic Acheulian tool is the hand axe (Figure 11.11), which could be used for a variety of purposes, including meat preparation. Other tools were made for different purposes. Scrapers were used for cleaning animal flesh, and cleavers were used for breaking animal bones during butchery (Figure 11.12).

The use of individual tools for different purposes marks an important step in the cultural evolution of hominids. Increased specialization allows more efficient tool use and also requires greater mental sophistication in tool design and manufacture.

Not all *H. erectus* populations made Acheulian tools. At sites in China, the tools used by *H. erectus* are somewhat different. The Chinese sites contain many of the smaller tools characteristic of the Acheulian, but not hand axes. Instead, there are large chopping tools that were manufactured differently (see Figure 11.12d and 11.12e). Geographically, the Acheulian and chopping tool cultures are distinct.

This cultural difference has always puzzled anthropologists. How could two populations so biologically similar give rise to distinct cultures? One possibility has to do with natural resources. Pope (1989) has suggested bamboo was frequently used as a raw material in Asia. Bamboo is a convenient natural and renewable resource from which a variety of tools can be made, including knives, spear points, and containers. If tools like these were made from bamboo, then stone tools would have been used only for tasks such as cutting wood. Pope's hypothesis is supportable if the distribution of bamboo in the past reflects his hypothesis; unfortunately, however, the hypothesis cannot be tested directly because bamboo tools are not preserved over time.

Another possible reason for these cultural differences relates to the revised dates for the Indonesian sites at 1.7 million years B.P., which is earlier than the initial invention of Acheulian tools (at 1.4 million years B.P.). If *H. erectus* had arrived in Indonesia by this date, it means that some *H. Erectus* had left Africa *before* Acheulian tools were invented.

HUNTING AND GATHERING   Recent evidence suggests that *H. habilis* was a scavenger instead of a hunter, but the fossil and archaeological records show that *H. erectus* was definitely a hunter of small and large game. The earliest evidence of hunting dates from Olduvai Gorge (Figure 11.13) 1.5 million years B.P. The bones of animals found at these sites differ in several ways from those at earlier *H. habilis* sites. All of the bones from larger animals are

biface Stone tool with both sides worked, producing greater symmetry and efficiency.

■ FIGURE 11.13
Olduvai Gorge, Tanzania.
Homo erectus fossils and
Acheulian hand axes have
been found at this site, as
well as other hominid fossils
and tools. (Bildarchiv Okapia
© 1989/ Science Source/ Photo
Researchers, Inc.)

found, suggesting a single butchering site, rather than fragmentary scavenging. The bones are also more fragmented, showing greater use of the animal carcass (Wolpoff 1980). The complete use of animal carcasses matches the pattern found with modern hunting-and-gathering groups and is different from that expected from scavenging. The increased variety of stone tools for butchering also supports the idea that *H. erectus* was a hunter, as does dental evidence, which shows a significant amount of meat in the diet.

One of the best known *H. erectus* sites with evidence of hunting is Zhoukoudian, China. Here *H. erectus* populations lived intermittently in caves between roughly 460,000 and 230,000 years B.P. The caves were used as living sites and are littered with animal bones, remnants of fire, tools and tool scraps, and fossilized hominid feces. In addition, parts of the remains of over 40 *H. erectus* individuals have been found at the Zhoukoudian caves. This site has long been known as the place of "Peking Man," named after the nearby city of Beijing (Peking), China.

The Zhoukoudian caves show evidence of two major cultural adaptations of *H. erectus*: fire and hunting. There are large hearths in the caves, some with ash as deep as 7 ft. Fire was important in the northern environments for warmth, light, and chasing off predators. Fire was also used to cook animal flesh. Charred bones found in the cave represent a number of animal species, including wild pigs and water buffalo. Deer bones are the most numerous and represent the major prey for *H. erectus* in this region.

The bones and stones at different sites show that hunting was an important source of food. Was it the only source? Gathering of vegetables, fruits, nuts, and other foods was surely just as important to the survival of *H. erectus*. In modern hunting-gathering societies, up to 75 percent of the total caloric intake of a group comes from gathering. In the past, anthropologists have tended to focus more on hunting than on gathering. This focus was in part a consequence of the nature of the archaeological record (bones and stones preserve more easily than do vegetables or wooden containers).

Another factor was male bias, unfortunately common in many scientific fields. Modern hunting-gathering societies show a clear division of labor by sex—men are generally the hunters and women the gatherers. The early interpretation of (mostly male) anthropologists focused on what was considered the more "important" and "difficult" task of male hunting. This interpretation influenced other hypotheses on prehistoric human behavior. Males were assumed to be the hunters because they had the necessary strength. However, although males are generally stronger than females, this slight difference would not have mattered in hunting. Not even the strongest male today can knock down an elephant by himself! Hunting requires skill and stealth more than strength. The important distinction between hunting and gathering is that the former activity requires greater mobility, and moving around may not be conducive to successful human pregnancy or nursing. Gathering can be performed in a local area, whereas hunting requires traveling long distances over many days. Also, the crying of infants would make hunting difficult.

Because gathering accounts for the majority of calories, we could also argue for a female-centered view: instead of "man the hunter" we could have "woman the gatherer." Both of these ideas, however, miss the main feature of hunting-and-gathering society—food sharing. Hunting and gathering were equally important activities, and the survival and geographic expansion of *H. erectus* depended on both. The division of labor and food sharing of hunter-gatherers show close and cooperative social structures. We cannot observe *H. erectus* society firsthand, of course. Using what we know from the archaeological record and from modern hunting-gathering societies, however, we can safely infer the existence of small social groups banded together for mutual benefit.

FIRE   The movement of *H. erectus* into East Asia shows the importance of cultural adaptations. Hominids are tropical primates, and expansion into colder climates required an appropriate level of technology. Fire was an important source of warmth, light, and cooking. In addition, fire can be used for tool manufacture. The tip of a wooden spear can be placed in a fire for a short period to harden the point. We can also speculate that fire allowed social interactions and teaching after dark.

Evidence for controlled fire comes from the cave hearths at Zhoukoudian and other *H. erectus* sites. The earliest known use of controlled fire dates to almost 1 million years B.P. (Pfeiffer 1985), although recent evidence from South Africa suggests a possible earlier date of up to 1.5 million years B.P. There are older sites with evidence of fire, but it is not clear whether these represent controlled use of fire. Because fires occur in nature, we cannot merely look for ash and charcoal. We must look for small areas of ash, usually less than a meter in diameter, as evidence of campfires.

Although we know that *H. erectus* used fire, we do not know if they made it. The earliest evidence of fire starters, only 15,000 years old, consists of a ball of iron pyrites with deep grooves left by repeated striking. Even if *H. erectus* could not make fire, however, and had to rely on nature, they could, nevertheless, keep fires smoldering for long periods of time at campsites.

Regardless of how *H. erectus* obtained fire, its use marks an important step in human cultural evolution. Making and using fire represent the controlled exploitation of an energy source. Because we rely on many other sources of controlled energy today, we tend to overlook the vital importance of fire as an energy source.

ARCHAIC *HOMO SAPIENS*

At the simplest level, the fossil record shows the evolution of *H. erectus* into *H. sapiens*. Closer examination, however, shows this statement to be a bit too simplistic, masking variation across time and space. As we have seen, some populations of *H. erectus* survived until roughly 200,000 years ago. Elsewhere in the Old World, however, we see fossils that are different from *H. erectus* appear roughly 400,000 years ago. Many anthropologists classify these non-*erectus* fossils as early *H. sapiens*, in large part because they are clearly not *H. erectus* and they had larger brains. However, they are not the same as modern *H. sapiens*, thus creating a problem in naming and classification. What do we call them?

There are several solutions to this problem, each reflecting a different view of hominid macroevolution. Some anthropologists suggest that we are simply seeing a transition in morphology over time, and that it is not useful to break up this continuous evolutionary line into distinct species. According to this view, the change from what we call *H. erectus* into *H. sapiens* is a good example of anagenesis, the transformation of a single species over time (refer back to Chapter 4). Here, species names are to a large extent arbitrary. Another school of thought sees the change from *H. erectus* to modern *H. sapiens* as an example of cladogenesis, the formation of one or more new species from a previous species. Here, the fossils are not viewed as transitional, but as a separate species (or several species) lying in time between *H. erectus* and ourselves.

Although there is some growing support for the identification of distinct intermediate species between *H. erectus* and ourselves (Tattersall 1995), most anthropologists prefer to label these hominids as *H. sapiens*, in large part because their brain size is roughly the same as that of modern *H. sapiens*. To reflect the differences that exist between *H. erectus* and *H. sapiens*, these anthropologists add the label "archaic." Thus, they contrast **archaic Homo sapiens** with **anatomically modern Homo sapiens.** The adjectives "archaic" and "modern" are not proper taxonomic labels, but they serve a crude purpose in showing that the two groups are similar yet different. This is not a perfect solution, however, and the category of archaic *H. sapiens* has become somewhat of a grab bag in recent years (Rightmire 1992; Tattersall 1995). For the remainder of this chapter, we use the "archaic" versus "modern" contrast in spite of its problems.

Analysis of archaic *H. sapiens* is confusing because of the wide range of variation within this general group in space and time. Some characteristics are found throughout the group, whereas others are specific to certain regions. As with modern humans, archaic *H. sapiens* showed distinct regional differences.

Distribution in Time and Space

Archaic *H. sapiens* has been found at a number of sites in Africa, Europe, and Asia (Figure 11.14) dating, for the most part, between roughly 400,000 and 35,000 years B.P. This time range is conservative—recent discoveries from the Atapuerca site in Spain suggest that members of the genus *Homo* might date back as far as 780,000 years B.P. (Carbonell et al. 1995; Parés and Pérez-González 1995). Although these remains are not those of *H. erectus*, it is not clear whether they are an early group of archaic *H. sapiens* or a different species altogether.

Given the large number of sites and specimens, it is useful to look more closely at patterns of regional variation. Some of the better-known regions include sub-Saharan Africa, North Asia, South Asia, and Southeast Asia and Australia (often lumped together as "Australasia"). Table 11.2 lists a

▲▲▲

archaic Homo sapiens An earlier variant of *Homo sapiens*, found	at dates ranging from over 400,000 to 35,000 years B.P.	**anatomically modern Homo sapiens** Modern *Homo sapiens* dating to	roughly the past 100,000 years.

Map of some archaic *Homo sapiens* sites.

number of the major sites of archaic *H. sapiens*. Note the heavy concentration of sites in Europe. In the past, scientists tended to focus most of their efforts on these sites. Now it is generally recognized that human evolution needs to be studied on a *global* level.

Because of this interest in European fossils, particular emphasis in the past was placed on a regional population known as the **Neandertals.** The word *Neandertal* is simply the German for "Neander Valley," the site where one of the first specimens was discovered. The Neandertals lived in the regions surrounding the Mediterranean, including Western Europe, Central and Eastern Europe, and the Middle East. Neandertal remains have been found dating between roughly 125,000 to 35,000 years B.P. Earlier literature often used the term *Neandertal* to refer to *all* archaic *H. sapiens* populations, but now we confine the term to a specific region and time period.

■ **TABLE 11.2**
List of Some Major Fossil Sites for Archaic *Homo sapiens*

GEOGRAPHIC REGION	COUNTRY	SITE/SPECIMEN	AGE (THOUSANDS OF YEARS B.P.)	FIGURE NUMBER(S) IN TEXT
Africa	Tanzania	Lake Ndutu	350	
	Ethiopia	Bodo	500–200	
	Zambia	Kabwe	150–125	11.18
North Africa	Morocco	Jebel Irhoud	127–87	
Asia	India	Narmada	730–150	
	China	Yinkou	263	
		Dali	200–150	11.19
		Maba	140–119	
Europe	France	Arago	400–200	
		La Chapelle (N)	56–47	11.21
		La Quina (N)	55–40	
		La Ferrassie (N)	50–40	11.20
		Le Moustier (N)	40	
		St. Césaire (N)	36	
	Greece	Petralona	300–200	11.17
	England	Swanscombe	250–200	
	Germany	Steinheim	250–200	
		Neandertal (N)	70–35	
	Croatia	Krapina (N)	70	
	Gibraltar	Forbe's Quarry (N)	70–45	
	Italy	Saccapastore (N)	60	
		Mt. Circeo (N)	60–40	
	Hungary	Vértesszölös	225–185	
Middle East	Israel	Kebara (N)	64–60	
		Tabun (N)	120	11.22
		Amud (N)	50–42	
	Iraq	Shanidar (N)	51–47	11.23

N = Neandertal

This table is not meant to be complete; many other specimens of archaic *Homo sapiens* have been found.

Source: Klein (1989); Kennedy et al. (1991); Larsen et al. (1991); Stringer and Gamble (1993)

Physical Characteristics

Archaic brain size is compared to that of other fossil hominids in Figure 11.15. Figure 11.16 shows the brain size of archaic *H. sapiens* compared to other hominids when plotted over time. Both archaic and modern *H. sapiens* have large brains of roughly equal size. The average cranial capacity of modern humans is roughly 1,350 cc (Beals et al. 1984); the average archaic brain size was 1,370 cc (Aiello and Dunbar 1993). The archaic sample masks some

▲▲▲▲▲▲▲▲▲▲▲▲▲▲▲▲▲▲▲▲▲▲▲▲▲▲▲▲▲

Neandertals A regional population of archaic *Homo sapiens* found in Europe and the Middle East, dating between roughly 125,000 to 35,000 years B.P.

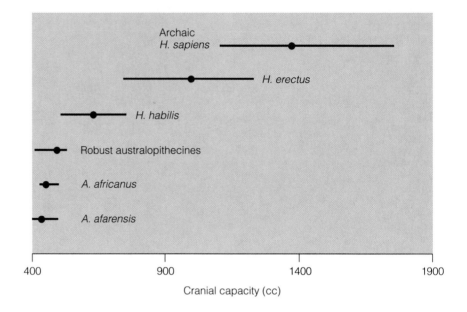

important variation. The earliest archaics generally have smaller cranial
capacities, showing that an increase in brain size has taken place during the
past 200,000 years. In fact, the rate of change between 200,000 years B.P. and
45,000 years B.P. was extremely rapid (Godfrey and Jacobs 1981). During the
past 45,000 years, however, brain size has not increased at all. In fact, a slight

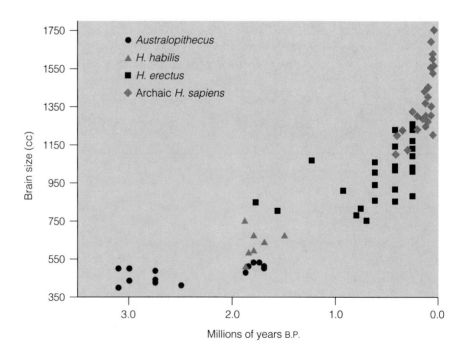

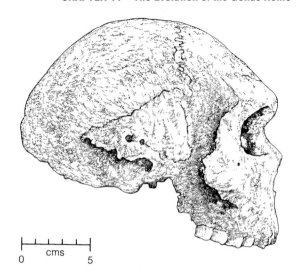

■ **FIGURE 11.17**
The Petralona skull, Greece.
An example of an early archaic
Homo sapiens from Europe.
(From Clark Spencer Larsen,
Robert M. Matter, and Daniel L.
Gebo, *Human Origins: The Fossil
Record,* Second Edition, p. 112.
Copyright © 1991, 1985 by
Waveland Press, Inc., Prospect
Heights, Illinois. Reprinted with
permission from the publisher)

cms
0   5

decrease in average brain size has occurred, reflecting a general decrease in skeletal size (Henneberg 1988).

Because both archaic and anatomically modern *H. sapiens* have large brains, brain size cannot be used to distinguish between the two groups. The morphology of the skulls of these two groups, however, is on average different. Archaic *H. sapiens* has a low skull with a sloping forehead, whereas anatomically modern *H. sapiens* has a high skull and a vertical forehead. Also, the face and teeth of archaic *H. sapiens* are larger than those in modern *H. sapiens*. Specimens of archaic *H. sapiens* rarely have a chin, something found in modern *H. sapiens*. The postcranial skeleton of many (not all) archaic *H. sapiens* specimens is very similar to modern forms. In general, the bones of archaic *H. sapiens* are thicker and show greater musculature.

REGIONAL VARIATION   An example of an early archaic *H. sapiens* is shown in Figure 11.17. This skull, from Petralona, Greece, dates to between 300,000 and 200,000 years B.P. Its cranial capacity (1,230 cc) places it at the upper range of later *H. erectus* or the lower range of archaic *H. sapiens*. Another example of an archaic specimen is the skull shown in Figure 11.18, which was discovered in Zambia, Africa, and dates to roughly 150,000 to 125,000 years B.P. The large brain size (1,285 cc) is readily apparent. The face is rather large and so are the brow ridges. The shape of the skull shows typical archaic features: a sloping forehead and a low skull.

Another example of an archaic *H. sapiens* skull (Figure 11.19) is from the site at Dali, China, and dates to between 200,000 and 150,000 years B.P. The cranial capacity is on the low end of the range for *H. sapiens* (1,120 cc) and the brow ridges are large. The skull is low and has a sloping forehead, both typical archaic features. The Dali skull also illustrates regional variation. As in many archaic North Asian specimens, the face is smaller and flatter than in other regions of the world. These traits, among others, are also found in earlier and later North Asian specimens (Thorne and Wolpoff 1992).

■ **FIGURE 11.18**
The Broken Hill skull, Kabwe,
Zambia. An example of early
archaic *Homo sapiens* from
Africa. (Neg. no. 410816.
Courtesy Department of Library
Services, American Museum of
Natural History)

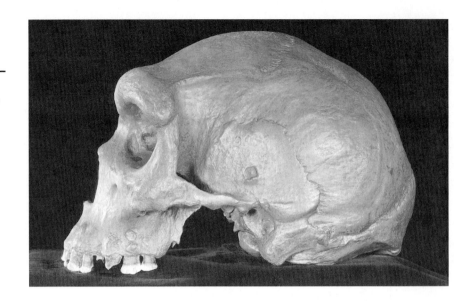

■ **FIGURE 11.18**
The Broken Hill skull, Kabwe,
Zambia. An example of early
archaic *Homo sapiens* from
Africa. (Neg. no. 410816.
Courtesy Department of Library
Services, American Museum of
Natural History)

■ **FIGURE 11.19**
The Dali skull, Dali County,
People's Republic of China.
An example of archaic *Homo
sapiens* from Asia. (From Clark
Spencer Larsen, Robert M. Matter,
and Daniel L. Gebo, *Human
Origins: The Fossil Record*,
Second Edition, p. 119. Copyright
© 1991, 1985 by Waveland Press,
Inc., Prospect Heights, Illinois.
Reprinted with permission from
the publisher)

```
|--|--|--|--|--|
0        cms        5
```

THE NEANDERTALS Of all the regional populations of archaic *H. sapiens*, the
best known is the Neandertals. Many of the Neandertals lived during the
time of the **Würm glaciation.** The Pleistocene epoch witnessed alternating
periods of glaciation and interglacials as the earth's climate changed. In the
Northern Hemisphere large sections of land were covered with advancing
ice sheets during glaciations, which receded during interglacial periods. Earlier views on glaciation held that four major glaciations, or "ice ages," took
place during the Pleistocene. It is now recognized that the climate changed
much more frequently, perhaps as many as 17 times, in this period. Even
during times typically characterized as "ice ages," the temperature and
southern advancement of ice varied considerably. In any case, the Neandertals lived during times when the climate was cooler in their habitat. They did
not live right on the ice, but the reduction in average temperature surely had

Neandertals: Names and Images

The name *Neandertal* comes from the site in the Neander Valley in Germany where Neandertals were first found. In German, *tal* means "valley." Hence, *Neandertal* means "Neander Valley." You may be more familiar with an alternative spelling ("Neanderthal") and an alternative pronunciation (emphasizing the "THAL" sound). However, the *h* is silent in German, so that *thal* is actually pronounced "tal." Because of this characteristic of German pronunciation, many (although not all) anthropologists simply drop the *h* in the spelling as well.

The very mention of Neandertals usually invokes a number of images and preconceptions. You may, for example, conjure up one of many images of the Neandertals as crude and simple subhumans with limited intelligence that walk bent over. These images have become such a part of our popular culture that a typical dictionary definition includes "Neandertal" as an adjective meaning "suggesting primitive man in appearance or behavior (*Neandertal* ferocity)" and "extremely old-fashioned or out-of-date," as well as a noun meaning "a rugged or uncouth person" (*Webster's Third International Dictionary*).

Why do Neandertals have such a bad reputation? As discussed in this chapter, Neandertals are viewed by most anthropologists as a regional population of archaic *Homo sapiens*. The distinctive appearance of Neandertals is often acknowledged by scientists who refer to them as a different subspecies of humans—

that is, *Homo sapiens neanderthalensis*, as opposed to modern humans, who are classified in the subspecies *Homo sapiens sapiens*. Some anthropologists argue that Neandertals are sufficiently different to be placed in a different species altogether—*Homo neanderthalensis* (note that the *h* remains in the species and subspecies names, as per international agreement). Regardless of classification, however, we know that Neandertals had large brains, walked upright, and possessed a sophisticated culture including stone tools, hunting, use of fire, and cave burial.

Part of the image problem comes from an inaccurate reconstruction of a Neandertal skeleton in the early 1900s. Because of certain physical features, such as curved thigh bones, scientists of the time believed that Neandertals did not walk completely upright, moving about bent over instead. It was discovered later that the curved bones and other features were simply a reflection of the poor health, including severe arthritis, of that particular Neandertal. Other features once taken to indicate mental inferiority, such as large brow ridges, are now recognized as biomechanical in nature. Even though the scientific interpretation has changed, the popular images of Neandertals remain to this day. More information on the history of Neandertals, including further discussion of their image, can be found in Trinkaus and Shipman (1992) and Stringer and Gamble (1993).

---

an effect on their environments, especially in Western Europe. The ability of the Neandertals to survive in these conditions is proof of their cultural adaptations, which included hunting, shelter, and use of fire.

Neandertals had the typical archaic features of sloping forehead, low skull, lack of chin, and large brow ridges. They also possessed several unique characteristics that tend not to be found in other regions (or to be found at a much lower frequency).

The Neandertals had very large brains, averaging 1,465 cc (Aiello and Dunbar 1993). The males had larger average cranial capacities because of their larger body size. In fact, relative to body size, the Neandertals may have had slightly larger brain sizes than many modern human populations. According to a review by Holloway (1985), the structural organization of Neandertal brains, as assessed from endocasts, is no different from that of modern humans.

▲▲▲▲▲▲▲▲▲▲▲▲▲▲▲▲▲▲▲▲▲▲▲▲▲▲▲▲▲

Würm glaciation One of the times of intense climatic cooling ("ice ages") during the Pleistocene epoch.

■ **FIGURE 11.20**
Frontal and side views of La
Ferrassie skull, a Neandertal
from France. (Courtesy of
Milford Wolpoff, University of
Michigan)

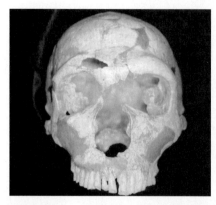
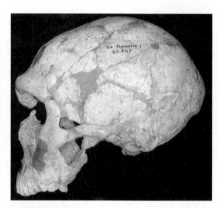
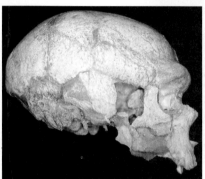
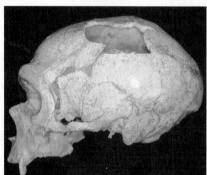

■ **FIGURE 11.21**
Two side views of La Chapelle
skull, a Neandertal from
France. (Courtesy of Milford
Wolpoff, University of Michigan)

Neandertals differ from other archaic *H. sapiens* populations in several features. Figures 11.20 and 11.21 show two skulls of Western European Neandertals, both from sites in France between 50,000 and 40,000 years B.P.

Neandertal faces are generally long and protrude more than in other archaic populations. The nasal region is large, suggesting large noses, and the sinus cavities to the side of the nose expand outward. The large nasal and midfacial areas on Neandertal skulls have often been interpreted as some type of adaptation to a cold climate. However, Rak (1986) interprets the large faces of Neandertals in terms of the biomechanics of the skull. He suggests that the Neandertal face acted to withstand stresses brought about by the use of relatively large front teeth. The front teeth of Neandertals are large in relation to their back teeth and often show considerable wear, suggesting their use as tools. Spencer and Demes (1993) also suggest that Neandertal morphology was to a large extent shaped by the use of the front teeth.

Many Neandertal specimens have a large crest of bone running from behind the ear toward the back of the skull. The back of the skull is rather puffed out (a feature called an **occipital bun**). The occipital bun is caused by relatively late posterior brain growth (Trinkaus and LeMay 1982). Though this feature is most common in Neandertals, it is also found in other archaic and modern *H. sapiens* populations.

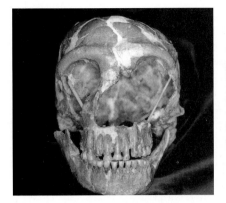

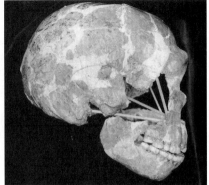

■ **FIGURE 11.22**
Frontal and side views of
Neandertal skull from Tabun,
Israel. (Courtesy of Milford
Wolpoff, University of Michigan)

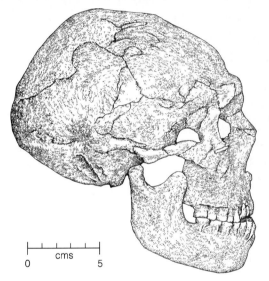

cms
0   5

■ **FIGURE 11.23**
Shanidar I skull, Iraq.
(From Clark Spencer Larsen,
Robert M. Matter, and Daniel L.
Gebo, *Human Origins: The Fossil
Record,* Second Edition, p. 128.
Copyright © 1991, 1985 by
Waveland Press, Inc., Prospect
Heights, Illinois. Reprinted with
permission from the publisher)

There is also variation within Neandertals. Figures 11.22 and 11.23 show
the skulls of two Middle Eastern Neandertals. Though they possess the general characteristics of Neandertals, they are not as morphologically extreme.
The skulls are a bit more well rounded than most Western European Neandertal skulls. The differences between the two skulls may reflect some aspect
of local adaptation to their environments.

Neandertal postcranial remains show essentially modern bipedalism,
but also a few differences compared with other *H. sapiens* populations.
Neandertals were relatively short and stocky. The limb bone segments farthest from the body (lower arm and lower leg) are relatively short, most
likely reflecting cold adaptation (Trinkaus 1981). The limb and shoulder
bones are more rugged than those of modern humans. The areas of muscle
attachment show that the Neandertals were very strong. It has been suggested that Neandertal hands were not as capable of fine manipulation as

▲▲▲▲▲▲▲▲▲▲▲▲▲▲▲▲▲▲▲▲▲▲▲▲▲▲▲▲▲

occipital bun The
protruding of the rear
region of the skull, a
feature often found in
Neandertals.

modern human hands are, or had at least different patterns of manipulation (Stoner and Trinkaus 1981).

The pelvic bones are also rather robust compared to those of modern humans, with the exception of the upper portion of the pubis (at the front of the pelvis), which is actually thinner and longer than in modern humans. The uniqueness of the Neandertal pelvis seems to reflect a biomechanical function (Rak and Arensburg 1987). Evidence also shows that Neandertals had a smaller pelvic outlet, which may have meant more difficult childbirth than in modern *H. sapiens* (Tague 1992).

Cultural Behavior

Archaic *H. sapiens* were hunters and gatherers, exploiting a wide variety of natural resources. Remains of animal bones at their sites show that they hunted both small game and large, including bears, mammoths, and rhinoceroses. In some areas it appears that archaic *H. sapiens* hunted year round; in others they apparently migrated along with animal herds.

STONE TOOL TECHNOLOGY   The stone tools of archaic *H. sapiens* represent an advancement over the Acheulian and chopping tool traditions of *H. erectus*. Much of the evidence for stone tool manufacture comes from Neandertal sites, where the stone tool tradition is known as the **Mousterian.** Similar tools found in other regions where archaic *H. sapiens* lived are sometimes referred to as Mousterian or Mousterianlike, as well as by other names (for example, in Africa, the term *Middle Stone Age* is frequently used). In this chapter, the term *Mousterian* is used in a general sense to refer to the basic patterns of tool manufacture among archaic *H. sapiens*. However, as with *H. erectus*, there is often considerable variation from region to region, reflecting availability of local resources and cultural differences in toolmaking.

The key feature of the Mousterian tradition is the use of a prepared-core technique in tool manufacture. As Figure 11.24 shows, a flint nodule is first chipped around the edges. Small flakes are then removed from the top surface of the core. In the final step, the core is struck precisely at one end.

The use of the prepared-core technique, which produces sharp and symmetric tools (Figure 11.25), tells us two important things about archaic *H. sapiens*. First, they were capable of precise toolmaking, which implies an excellent knowledge of flaking methods and the structural characteristics of stone. Second, they were able to visualize the final tool early in production. Not until the last step does the shape of the finished tool become apparent. Such manufacture is a process quite different from simply chipping away at a stone until a tool is finished.

Archaeological evidence shows considerable variation in the types of Mousterian tools. Archaic *H. sapiens* used different tools for different purposes to a greater extent than *H. erectus* did. Sites also show variation in the frequency of Mousterian tools, once again indicating regional differences.

■ **FIGURE 11.24**
Manufacture of a Mousterian tool, using the prepared-core method. First, the core is shaped by removing small flakes from the sides and top (a–d). Then the finished tool is removed from the core (e). (From *Archaeology: Discovering Our Past*, 2d ed., by Robert Sharer and Wendy Ashmore, Fig. 10.3. Copyright © 1993 by Mayfield Publishing Company)

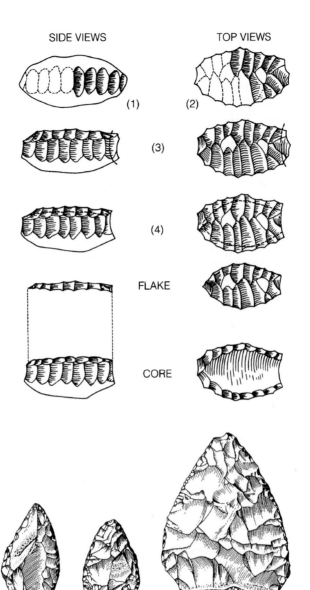

SIDE VIEWS   TOP VIEWS

(1)   (2)

(3)

(4)

FLAKE

CORE

(a)   (b)   (c)   (d)   (e)

■ **FIGURE 11.25**
Examples of Mousterian tools: (a) scraper, (b) point, (c) scraper, (d) point, (e) hand axe. (From *The Old Stone Age* by F. Bordes, 1968. Reprinted with permission of the publisher, Weidenfeld and Nicolson, Ltd.)

SYMBOLIC BEHAVIOR Archaeological evidence suggests that archaic *H. sapiens* may have been capable of symbolic thought, perhaps even holding beliefs in the supernatural. Archaic *H. sapiens* (specifically, some Neandertals) were the first hominids to bury their dead deliberately. Evidence of burial comes from a number of European and Middle Eastern sites, where dead persons' bones have been arranged carefully in graves, often in association with tools, food, and flowers.

▲▲▲▲▲▲▲▲▲▲▲▲▲▲▲▲▲▲▲▲▲▲▲▲▲▲▲▲▲▲▲

Mousterian tradition
The stone tool technology of the Neandertals.

The intentional burial of the dead has suggested a ritualistic purpose to some researchers. At a site in Belgium, fires had been lit above two buried bodies. One interpretation of this is that archaic *H. sapiens* believed the fires would counteract the "coldness" of death. At the Shanidar Cave site in Iraq, flowers had been placed all over the bodies, an event that was reconstructed based on the presence of fossil pollen in the graves.

Such evidence suggests the evolution of symbolic expressions and the possibility of supernatural beliefs. This standard interpretation, however, is changing. The flexed positions of many of the dead might not reflect intentional posing but rather be a consequence of digging the smallest possible graves. In addition, although the Shanidar burial is still considered one of the best examples of symbolic behavior, it is possible the pollen was introduced by rodents burrowing into the grave *after* burial.

The physical condition of fossil remains offers another window on the behavior of archaic *H. sapiens*. By looking at bone fractures, condition of teeth, and other features, we can get a good idea of the age and health status of early humans. Many archaic *H. sapiens* remains are of elderly individuals with numerous medical problems. Some of the elderly had lost all of their teeth, many had arthritis, and one had lost part of his arm. By looking for signs of healing or infection, we can tell that many of these elderly individuals did not die from these afflictions. How, then, did they survive, in particular, if they had lost all of their teeth? Survival of many of the elderly and impaired archaic *H. sapiens* suggests that others cared for them. This implies not only compassion as a social value but also the existence of a social system that allowed for the sharing of food and of resources.

This perspective may be based more on our interpretive biases, however, than on reality. Dettwyler (1991) questions the traditional view of the elderly and disabled as nonproductive members of a group who must be cared for. Drawing on cross-cultural studies, she notes that physically disabled individuals in many societies still frequently make important contributions.

LANGUAGE CAPABILITY   Did archaic *H. sapiens* have language? Lieberman and Crelin (1971), who reconstructed the vocal anatomy of Neandertals, concluded they were incapable of vocalizing certain vowel sounds. The implication was that archaic *H. sapiens* did not possess as wide a range of sounds as modern humans and perhaps had limited language abilities. This hypothesis was criticized, however, because of differences of opinion on vocal anatomy reconstruction. The lack of direct fossil evidence at the heart of the debate was ultimately furnished with the discovery of the first hyoid bone for archaic *H. sapiens*, a bone lying in the neck that can be used to provide information on the structure of the respiratory tract. That this specimen is almost identical in size and shape to the hyoid bone of modern humans indicates that there were no differences in vocal ability between archaics and moderns (Arensberg et al. 1990). Indeed, no evidence exists from brain anatomy to show that archaic *H. sapiens* lacked speech centers (Holloway 1985).

SUMMARY

Following the initial appearance of the genus *Homo* (*H. habilis*), the record of human biological and cultural evolution shows an increase in brain size and complexity, reduction in the size of the face and teeth, and an increasing reliance on cultural adaptations.

The species *Homo erectus* appears to have evolved rapidly from some populations of *H. habilis* in East Africa by 1.8 million years B.P. *H. erectus* had an increased cranial capacity and exhibited a variety of new cultural adaptations, including greater sophistication in stone tool technology, hunting and gathering, and the use of fire. These adaptations allowed *H. erectus* to expand out of Africa into Asia, and possibly into parts of Europe as well. Although it has long been thought that *H. erectus* reached southeast Asia by one million years ago, new evidence suggests that this movement may have happened as early as 1.7 million years B.P. *H. erectus* continued in parts of Africa and Asia until roughly 200,000 years ago.

Fossils showing an increased brain size begin to appear in the fossil record dating roughly 400,000 years B.P. By 200,000 years B.P., the average brain size of this group of hominids is roughly the same as that in modern humans. Although debate continues over whether these hominids should be assigned to a separate species, current usage is to refer to them as "archaic" *H. sapiens*, as compared to ourselves (modern *H. sapiens*). These terms are an attempt to acknowledge differences between earlier forms and ourselves (primarily larger faces and brow ridges, a sloping forehead, a less well-rounded skull, and no chin), but at the same time to recognize the similarity (large brains). One of the best known populations of archaic *H. sapiens* are the Neandertals, found in Europe and the Middle East from 125,000 to 35,000 years B.P. Neandertals are distinctive in having large noses and mid-facial structures, perhaps reflecting climatic adaptation. Contrary to popular thought, the Neandertals had a sophisticated stone tool technology, buried their dead, and adapted to harsh climates.

SUPPLEMENTAL READINGS

Klein, R. G. 1989. *The Human Career: Human Biological and Cultural Origins.* Chicago: University of Chicago Press. An excellent summary of human evolution, with particular attention to the biology and culture of *H. erectus* and *H. sapiens*.

Stringer, C., and Gamble, C. 1993. *In Search of the Neanderthals: Solving the Puzzle of Human Origins.* New York: Thames and Hudson. An excellent and up-to-date review of Neandertal (and other archaics') biology and culture, as well as the history of debates over modern human origins.

Trinkaus, E., and Shipman, P. 1992. *The Neandertals: Changing the Image of Mankind.* New York: Knopf. An excellent historical review of the history of Neandertal discoveries and interpretations.

CHAPTER **12**

The Origin of Modern Humans

 Starting over 100,000 years ago, populations of archaic *Homo sapiens* evolved into what we refer to as anatomically modern *Homo sapiens*. This is the name by which we refer to ourselves today, as well as the name by which we classify our early ancestors, who possessed certain physical characteristics unlike those of archaic *H. sapiens*: a more well-rounded skull and a noticeable chin. The overall brain size of these ancestors had changed little from that of later archaic *H. sapiens*. The evolution of archaic to modern *H. sapiens* is a subject of considerable debate today among anthropologists.

At the heart of this debate is a series of basic questions. What is the nature of this change? When and where did it occur? Did the change occur in only one place, or was it widespread? Why did it occur? What cultural changes took place, and how are they related to the biological changes? In short, our questions concern the recent (100,000+ years) history of the human species.

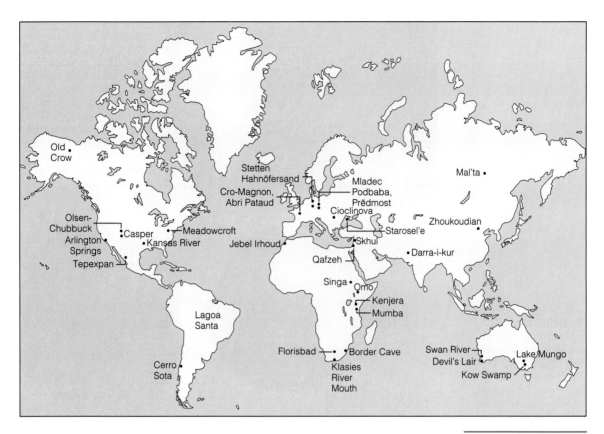

■ FIGURE 12.1
Location of some anatomically modern *H. sapiens* sites.

ANATOMICALLY MODERN *HOMO SAPIENS*

Human evolution did not end with archaic *H. sapiens*. By 35,000 years B.P., all fossil humans are anatomically modern in form. Though it is clear that archaic *H. sapiens* evolved into anatomically modern *H. sapiens*, the exact nature of this evolution is less certain. This section deals with the biological and cultural characteristics of anatomically modern *H. sapiens*, followed by consideration of the nature of their evolution.

Distribution in Time and Space

Anatomically modern *H. sapiens* are found in many sites across both the Old World and the New World (Figure 12.1). Although only modern *H. sapiens* has been found dating within the past 35,000 years, we now have growing evidence that this form is actually much older than once thought.

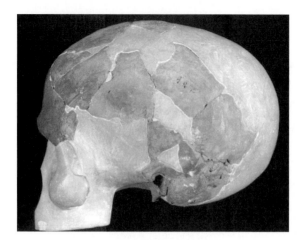

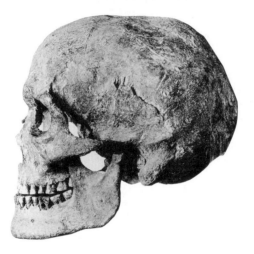

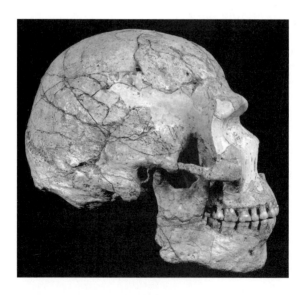

Cranial remains from the Border Cave site in southeast Africa are fragmentary but show typical anatomically modern features (Figure 12.2). The dating for this site is not definite but could range between 115,000 and 90,000 years B.P. Modern humans may have occupied the Klasies River Mouth, South Africa, at least as early as 90,000 years B.P. (Grün et al. 1990). Other African sites also provide evidence of an early appearance of anatomically modern *H. sapiens*: Omo, Ethiopia (roughly 130,000 years B.P.) and Laetoli (perhaps 120,000 years B.P.). There is also evidence of an early occurrence of anatomically modern *H. sapiens* in the Middle East, with both the Qafzeh and Skhul sites in Israel dating to 92,000 years B.P. (Grün et al. 1991). Although some argument about these dates continues, it is becoming increasingly certain that modern *H. sapiens* existed *before* the youngest known archaic forms.

Physical Characteristics

Figure 12.3 shows a skull from one of the more famous anatomically modern sites—Cro-Magnon, France, dating between 27,000 and 23,000 years B.P. This skull shows many of the characteristics of anatomically modern *H. sapiens*. It is high and well rounded. There is no occipital bun; the back of the skull is rounded instead. The forehead rises vertically above the eye orbits and does not slope, as in archaic *H. sapiens*. The brow ridges are small, the face does not protrude very much, and a strong chin is evident.

Another example of anatomically modern *H. sapiens* is shown in Figure 12.4, a skull from the Skhul site at Mt. Carmel, Israel. This skull also has a high, well-rounded shape without an occipital bun and with a small chin. Compared to the Cro-Magnon skull, the brow ridges are larger and the face protrudes slightly. The differences between the Skhul and Cro-Magnon skulls are typical of variation within a species, particularly when we consider that they existed at different times in separate places. Other specimens also show similarities and differences when compared to one another. The skull in Figure 12.5 (Combe Capelle, France, 35,000 to 30,000 years B.P.) is high and well rounded, but the face protrudes slightly, and the chin is rather weak. The recent skull from Five Knolls, England (3,500 to 1,500 years B.P.) is high and well rounded, has small brow ridges and face, and a small chin (Figure 12.6). There is clearly variation within both archaic and anatomically modern forms of *H. sapiens*. This variation makes evolutionary relationships difficult to assess.

Cultural Behavior

Discussing the cultural adaptations of anatomically modern *H. sapiens* is difficult because they include prehistoric technologies as well as more recent developments, such as agriculture, generation of electricity, the internal

328

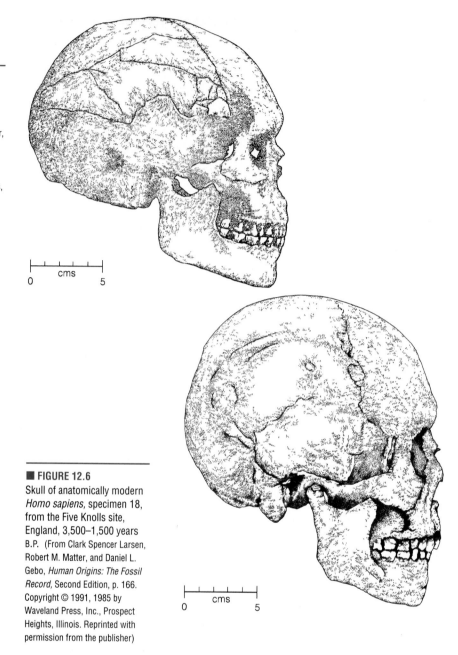

■ **FIGURE 12.5**
The Combe Capelle skull,
anatomically modern *Homo
sapiens,* France. (From Clark
Spencer Larsen, Robert M. Matter,
and Daniel L. Gebo, *Human
Origins: The Fossil Record,*
Second Edition, p. 16. Copyright
© 1991, 1985 by Waveland Press,
Inc., Prospect Heights, Illinois.
Reprinted with permission from
the publisher)

0 cms 5

■ **FIGURE 12.6**
Skull of anatomically modern
Homo sapiens, specimen 18,
from the Five Knolls site,
England, 3,500–1,500 years
B.P. (From Clark Spencer Larsen,
Robert M. Matter, and Daniel L.
Gebo, *Human Origins: The Fossil
Record,* Second Edition, p. 166.
Copyright © 1991, 1985 by
Waveland Press, Inc., Prospect
Heights, Illinois. Reprinted with
permission from the publisher)

0 cms 5

combustion engine, and nuclear energy. So that we may provide a comparison with the culture of the archaic forms, this section is limited to prehistory before the development of agriculture (roughly 12,000 years B.P.).

TOOL TECHNOLOGIES There is so much variation in the stone tool technologies of anatomically modern *H. sapiens* that it is impossible to define a single tradition. For the sake of discussion, the types of stone tool industries are

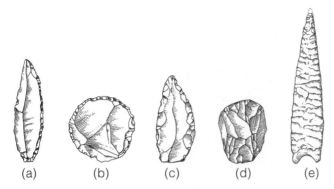

(a)   (b)   (c)   (d)   (e)

■ FIGURE 12.7
Examples of Upper Paleolithic stone tools: (a) knife, (b) scraper, (c) point, (d) scraper, (e) point. Tools *a, b,* and *c* are from the Perigordian culture; tool *d* is from the Aurignacian culture; tool *e* is from the Solutrean culture. (From *The Old Stone Age* by F. Bordes, 1968. Reprinted with permission of the publisher, Weidenfield and Nicolson, Ltd.)

often lumped together under the term **Upper Paleolithic** (which means "Upper Old Stone Age"). **Lower Paleolithic** consists of the stone tool traditions of *H. habilis* and *H. erectus,* and **Middle Paleolithic** includes the stone tool traditions of archaic *H. sapiens.* Even though we use a single label to describe common features of Upper Paleolithic tool industries, do not be misled into thinking all traditions were the same. Variation, both within and among sites, is even greater in the Upper Paleolithic than in earlier cultures. This variation demonstrates the increasing sophistication and specialization of stone tools.

Figure 12.7 shows some examples of Upper Paleolithic stone tools. These tools are much more precisely made than the stone tools of earlier hominids, and are also quite a bit more diverse in function and styles. One notable characteristic of the Upper Paleolithic is the development of **blades,** stone tools defined as being at least twice as long as wide (Figure 12.8). Blade tools are made by removing long, narrow flakes off a prepared core. The core is struck by a piece of antler or bone, which in turn is struck by a stone. That is, the core is not hit directly by the hammerstone; rather, the force of the blow is applied through the antler. This method allows very thin and sharp blade tools to be made (Figure 12.9).

Upper Paleolithic tools were also used to make tools out of other resources, such as bone. A small stone tool called a **burin** has an extremely sharp edge that is used to cut, whittle, and engrave bone. Bone was used to make needles, awls, points, knives, and harpoons, as well as art objects. Bone tools and art objects first appear with modern *H. sapiens*; they are not found

▲▲▲

Upper Paleolithic The Upper Old Stone Age; also refers to the stone tool technologies of anatomically modern *Homo sapiens.*

Lower Paleolithic The Lower Old Stone Age; also refers to the stone tool technologies of *Homo habilis* and *Homo erectus.*

Middle Paleolithic The Middle Old Stone Age; also refers to the stone tool technologies of archaic *Homo sapiens.*

blade A stone tool characteristic of the Upper Paleolithic, defined as being at least twice as long as it is wide.

burin A stone tool with a sharp edge that is used to cut and engrave bone

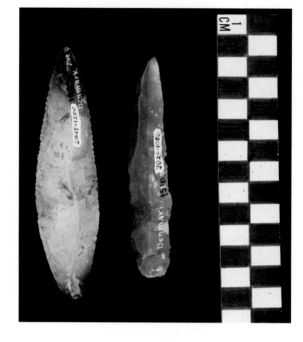

■ FIGURE 12.8

Example of a flint blade tool. (From *Human Antiquity: An Introduction to Physical Anthropology and Archaeology,* 2nd ed., by Kenneth Feder and Michael Park, Fig. 12.14. Copyright © 1993 by Mayfield Publishing Company.)

Direction of force

Striking platform

Core

Blade

■ FIGURE 12.9

Method of blade tool manufacture. A striking platform is formed and a blade tool can then be made by flaking off a long vertical piece from the side. (From *Discovering Anthropology* by Daniel R. Gross, Fig. 7.10. Copyright © 1993 by Mayfield Publishing Company)

■ FIGURE 12.10

Reconstruction of a hut at the Mal'ta site in Russia. This site dates to 18,000 years B.P. (From *Human Antiquity: An Introduction to Physical Anthropology and Archaeology,* 2nd ed., by Kenneth Feder and Michael Park, Fig. 12.16. Copyright © 1993 by Mayfield Publishing Company)

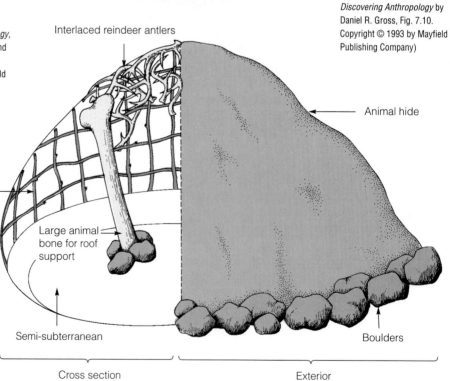

Interlaced reindeer antlers

Animal hide

Wood framing

Large animal bone for roof support

Semi-subterranean

Boulders

Cross section
Interior

Exterior

■ FIGURE 12.11
Cave painting of a running horse from Lascaux Cave, France. (Museum of Man, Paris; photographer F. Windels)

in the culture of earlier hominids. For years, it appeared that bone tools were fairly recent, dating back roughly 40,000 years. Recent work in Zaire, however, has produced a much earlier age of 90,000 years (Brooks et al. 1995; Yellen et al. 1995).

SHELTER   As with archaic *H. sapiens*, modern *H. sapiens* lived in caves and rock shelters where available. The archaeological evidence also shows definite evidence of manufactured shelter—huts made of wood, animal bone, and animal hides. Although much of this material decomposes, we can still find evidence of support structures. One example of hut building comes from the 18,000-year-old site of Mal'ta in south-central Russia (Figure 12.10). This hut is particularly interesting because people used mammoth ribs and leg bones for structural support. Other sites, such as the 15,000-year-old site of Mezhirich in the Ukraine, contain evidence of shelters built almost entirely from mammoth bones.

CAVE ART   Another form of symbolic behavior appears with modern *H. sapiens*—cave art. Cave art dates back over 30,000 years (although most is not this old) and has been found in Europe, Africa, and Australia. Some of the best-known cave art, primarily paintings of large game animals and hunting, comes from sites in Europe (Figures 12.11 and 12.12). These paintings are anatomically correct and are well executed. Painting is a human activity that

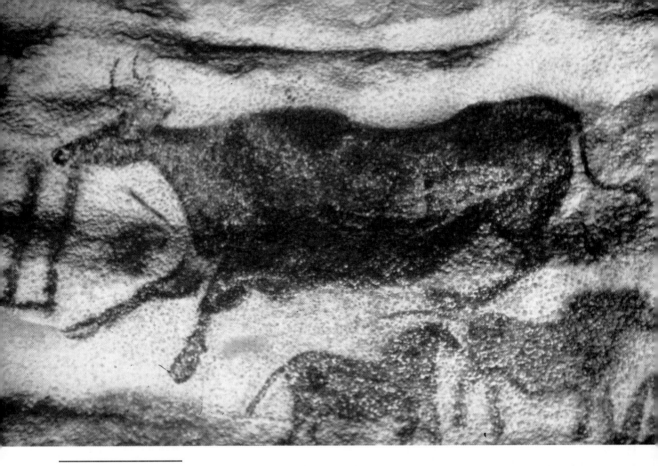

■ **FIGURE 12.12**
Cave painting of a cow from Lascaux cave, France. (Mario Ruspoli: Caisse Nationale Des Monuments Historiques et Des Sites)

is spiritually rewarding but has no apparent function in day-to-day existence. Why, then, did early humans paint images on the walls of caves? Several interpretations have been offered, including sympathetic magic (capturing the image of an animal may have been felt to improve hunters' chances of actually killing it). Other interpretations focus on cultural symbolism (e.g., male–female images) or a means of communicating ideas and images. We will never know exactly *why* early humans made these paintings. What is clear, however, is that they did something that serves a symbolic purpose. Although we cannot know the reason for these behaviors, the art shows us that humans by this time had developed a need to express themselves symbolically. To these early moderns, life was not just eating and surviving—something else was important to them as well.

OTHER EVIDENCE OF ART Cave paintings are not the only form of art associated with early modern *H. sapiens*. We also find evidence of engravings, beads and pendants, and ceramic sculpture. One of the best-known examples is the "Venus" figurines found throughout parts of Europe. These figures are pregnant females with exaggerated breasts and buttocks (Figure 12.13). Although these figurines are often interpreted as fertility symbols (fertility would have been a critical factor to survival), we are not sure of their exact meaning or function. However, as with cave paintings, the Venus figurines show us that symbolism was fully a part of the life of early modern *H. sapiens*.

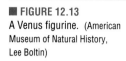

■ **FIGURE 12.13**
A Venus figurine. (American Museum of Natural History, Lee Boltin)

GEOGRAPHIC EXPANSION The archaeological evidence shows that humans became more and more successful in adapting to their environments, and consequently populations grew and expanded.

By 50,000 years B.P., populations of anatomically modern *H. sapiens* had reached Australia (Roberts et al. 1990). During times of glaciation, the sea levels drop, extending the land mass of the continents. The drop in sea level had allowed earlier populations of hominids to reach Southeast Asia, but Australia was not then connected to the Asian continent. For humans to reach Australia, they had to cross many kilometers of sea. The only way they could do this was by some sort of raft or boat.

Anatomically modern *H. sapiens* also moved into the New World. The number of such movements, and their dates, are a continuing source of controversy (Rogers et al. 1992). All agree, however, that humans were living in the New World by 12,000 years B.P. Some argue that these dates are the earliest, whereas others cite newer evidence and reanalysis of previous finds indicating a much earlier initial occupation—perhaps 30,000 to 20,000 years B.P.

Genetic evidence shows a close relationship between modern Native Americans and modern northeast Asians. Archaeological evidence also demonstrates an Asian origin for the first migrants to the New World. The most commonly suggested route is across the Bering land bridge. During periods of glaciation the sea levels fell, exposing a stretch of land connecting Asia and North America. This "land bridge" was almost 2,100 kilometers (roughly 1,300 miles) wide (Figure 12.14). It did not appear or disappear suddenly

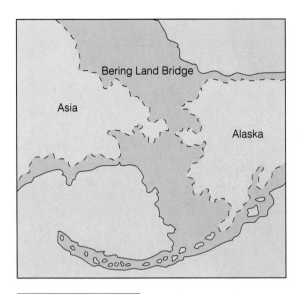

■ FIGURE 12.14
The Bering Land Bridge.
Today the former Soviet Union
and Alaska are separated by
water. During the "Ice Ages,"
water was trapped in glaciers,
producing a drop in the sea
level that exposed the land
area known as the Bering
Land Bridge. This "bridge"
connecting North America and
Asia was actually 2,100 km
wide!

■ TABLE 12.1
Oldest Known Dates for Selected Cultural Traits

	DATE (THOUSANDS OF YEARS B.P.)
Art	40
Bone tools	90
Blade tools	100+?
Ceramics	25
Body Ornamentation	40
Built hearths	50
Storage pits	40
Cave burials	80
Open site burials	40
Huts	50–40
Long-distance exchange of raw materials	60–40
Sea voyaging	55

Source: Stringer and Gamble (1993); Yellen et al. (1995)

but instead developed over thousands of years as the sea levels dropped. Groups of humans following game herds moved across this region and eventually moved down into North, Central, and South America.

SUMMARY OF THE CULTURE OF EARLY MODERN H. SAPIENS   Many cultural changes took place in the past 100,000 years. Table 12.1 lists the earliest known dates for selected cultural behaviors. Note that many of these first appear roughly 40,000 to 60,000 years ago, a time period characterized as a "creative explosion" by some anthropologists. What is the cause of this rapid cultural change? Is it tied to the biological changes associated with the modern *H. sapiens?* To discuss these questions, we must first consider what we know about *where* and *when* modern humans first appeared.

THE ORIGIN OF ANATOMICALLY MODERN *HOMO SAPIENS*

When, where, and how did anatomically modern *H. sapiens* evolve from archaic *H. sapiens?* The general trend indicated by the fossil record is clear; some archaic populations evolved into the more modern forms. The specific questions are harder to answer. Did *all* populations of archaics evolve into modern forms? If so, did this occur at the same time in different places? Or did only a few archaic populations evolve into modern forms and then expand out to replace, or interbreed, with the remaining archaic forms? If so, where and when did the transition to anatomically modern *H. sapiens* first take place? Finally, does our use of such terms as *archaic* and *modern* obscure variation over time and space? We use these categories as a useful sorting device, but we may be in danger of obscuring reality by pigeonholing all human fossil remains into two groups.

Early Models

Many models have been proposed to answer these questions. Past analyses have been complicated by the fact that the best-known samples of archaic *H. sapiens* were the western European Neandertals, which in many ways are the most unique of all the archaic populations. The distinctiveness of the Neandertals had given rise to various interpretations of the origin of anatomically modern *H. sapiens*. In the early part of this century, it was common to view Neandertals as a side branch of human evolution, perhaps even a different species. At that time the fossil record suggested a 5,000-year "gap" between the last Neandertals and the first modern humans. Such a gap was felt to be too short in duration for the evolutionary changes needed for a transition from Neandertals into modern humans. Another explanation was that the modern forms evolved elsewhere, then invaded and wiped out the Neandertals (see Brace [1964] for a thorough discussion of early views on Neandertal evolution).

This simple model is no longer accepted. For one thing, we now have evidence of overlap in dates for archaic and anatomically modern *H. sapiens*. The major problem with the invasion hypothesis is that it was strongly influenced by previous interpretations of the extent of differences between archaic and modern forms. This early idea emphasized the differences between these forms and tended to ignore their similarities.

An alternative, first proposed by Hrdlicka and later supported by Brace, was the Neandertal phase hypothesis. Here Neandertals represented a stage through which all populations of *H. sapiens* evolved. The problem with this model is that according to the definition of Neandertal given earlier, we find evidence of Neandertals only from regions around the Mediterranean.

Current Models and Debates

Here, we examine two hypotheses for the evolution of modern *H. sapiens*: the multiregional model and the recent African origin model. Numerous variants exist of both of these, including some intermediate models that combine aspects of both. In this section, we examine these two versions to see how well they fit available evidence.

MULTIREGIONAL MODEL   The **multiregional model** views what we call "archaic" and "modern" *Homo sapiens* as part of an evolving single species. The heart of the model states that the evolution from archaic to modern took place throughout the Old World. By 1 million years B.P. (or earlier), *H. erectus* had

▲▲▲▲▲▲▲▲▲▲▲▲▲▲▲▲▲▲▲▲▲▲▲▲▲▲▲▲▲

multiregional model
The hypothesis that modern humans evolved throughout the Old World as a single species after the first dispersion of *Homo erectus* out of Africa.

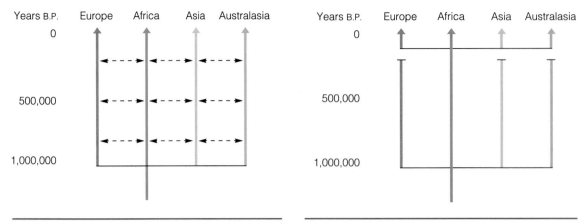

■ **FIGURE 12.15**
The multiregional model of the origin of modern *H. sapiens*. *Homo erectus* appears first in Africa and then spreads throughout the Old World. This species evolves into modern *H. sapiens* as part of a worldwide transition. The horizontal lines indicate gene flow, which maintains all regional populations as part of a single evolving species.

■ **FIGURE 12.16**
The recent African origin model. *Homo erectus* appears first in Africa and then spreads throughout the Old World, evolving over time into what are called "archaic *H. sapiens*." Modern *H. sapiens* evolves in Africa between 200,000 and 100,000 years B.P., and then spreads throughout the Old World, replacing preexisting archaic groups. In some versions of this model there is some mixture with archaic populations.

moved out of Africa across parts of the Old World. Over time, these populations grew to differ from one another because of genetic drift and selection to different environments. Gene flow continued between regions, however, so that all regional populations remained part of a single species. Changes that occurred in one region were thus shared with populations in other regions. Through a balance between the evolutionary forces, all regional populations changed from archaic to modern form, although not necessarily at the same time. Because of the balance, these regional populations also retained some differences over time (Thorne and Wolpoff 1992; Wolpoff et al. 1994).

According to the multiregional evolution model, the ancestors of modern Europeans were archaic Europeans, with a certain amount of gene flow from the rest of the world. Likewise, the ancestors of modern Africans were archaic Africans with some gene flow from the rest of the world. According to strict proponents of the model, the transition from archaic to modern *H. sapiens* did not occur first in any one place, but rather throughout the entire species over time.

Consider the patterns of human biological variation seen among humans today. We are clearly all one species, but it is also obvious that different regions are distinctive from one another. The multiregional model extends this pattern into the past—a single evolving species with local variations. There is a balance between drift and selection on one hand and gene flow on the other, such that just enough gene flow acts to maintain a single species, but not enough occurs so that regional differences are wiped out. A schematic drawing of the multiregional evolution model is shown in Figure 12.15.

THE RECENT AFRICAN ORIGIN MODEL   According to the **recent African origin model,** the transition from archaic to modern *H. sapiens* took place in Africa between 200,000 and 150,000 years B.P. Some moderns then left Africa by 100,000 years B.P., replacing earlier archaic populations throughout the rest of the Old World (Cann et al. 1987; Stringer and Andrews 1988; Stringer 1994). Little, if any, mixture with archaics took place outside of Africa, and in some versions of this model, the new moderns are considered a distinct species. The actual replacement is often considered a result of some evolutionary advantage held by modern *H. sapiens,* so that over time moderns became more and more numerous and archaic populations ultimately died out (Figure 12.16).

If true, then the recent African origin model implies that all modern humans today share common ancestors in Africa dating no more than 200,000 years B.P. The ancestors of modern Europeans, for example, are considered to have been African. Some variants of this model include a possible mix with archaic populations, but consider it minimal (e.g., Bräuer 1992). To complicate matters further, some advocates of the multiregional model allow for possible major evolutionary changes to stem primarily from Africa. At this point, versions of the two models look very similar. The key difference is that the recent African origin model postulates less (if any) mix with archaics.

The Fossil Evidence

Which model, or models, does the fossil evidence support? It is important to realize that each model makes certain predictions that, in theory, can be tested using the fossil evidence available on archaic and modern *H. sapiens.* Predictions are made regarding the biological relationships between archaic and modern forms within each region, and the relationships between regions.

The recent African origin model predicts that anatomically modern fossils in all regions will be more similar to earlier fossils in Africa than to earlier fossils in other regions. For example, European moderns should be more similar to earlier Africans than to earlier Europeans. Outside of Africa, there should be more or less abrupt changes over time, corresponding to the influx of African-based populations. A further prediction of the model is that anatomically modern *H. sapiens* will appear first in Africa, and later in other regions.

▲▲▲

recent African origin model The hypothesis that modern humans evolved in Africa between 200,000 and 100,000 years B.P., and then spread throughout the Old World replacing preexisting archaic *H. sapiens* populations.

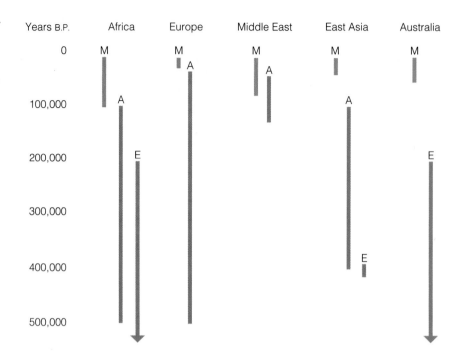

■ FIGURE 12.17
Approximate distribution of
fossil hominids over the past
500,000 years. E = *H. erectus,*
A = archaic *H. sapiens,*
M = modern *H. sapiens.*

The multiregional model makes a different set of predictions, proposing that archaic and modern forms within each region are similar, displaying continuity over time. Because of this **regional continuity,** European archaics should share unique features with European moderns, Asian archaics should share unique features with Asian moderns, and so on.

A first step in answering our question is to examine the spatial and temporal distribution of the fossils. This may seem relatively simple, but in practice it is not. Differing interpretations of fossil morphology, disagreement about whether physical features are primitive or derived, and debates over the dating of sites all complicate the process. In addition, we must always deal with the fact that the fossil record is incomplete, and our range of dates for any given region may be an underestimate. Figure 12.17 presents the distribution of *H. erectus,* archaic *H. sapiens,* and modern *H. sapiens* according to one interpretation of the evidence (Stringer and Gamble 1993). The oldest known evidence for modern *H. sapiens* (at present) is from Africa (although the Middle East is very close in time). Modern *H. sapiens* appears later in other geographic regions, and latest in Europe.

Does the earlier appearance of modern *H. sapiens* in Africa support the recent African origin model? Yes, but it does not reject the multiregional model, which can incorporate an initial evolution of modern morphology in one region, followed by a spread through gene flow to other regions. The earlier appearance of modern *H. sapiens* in Africa is consistent with some versions of the multiregional model (Wolpoff et al 1994b).

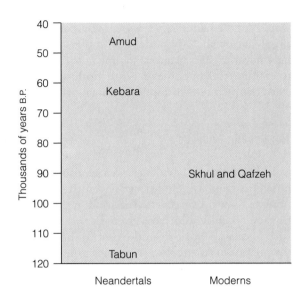

■ **FIGURE 12.18**
Middle Eastern sites
containing Neandertal and
modern humans based on
the most recent dates. If
these dates are confirmed,
it appears that different
populations occupied the
Middle East at different times.

What about regional continuity? The evidence for this is strongest in Australasia (Kramer 1991), and has been suggested for parts of Europe as well (Smith et al. 1989b; Thorne and Wolpoff 1992). In some cases, there is a tendency for moderns to resemble archaics within the same region, although this continuity is still strongly debated. Many researchers feel the case for regional continuity is weak for western Europe and the Middle East. Overall, the fossil evidence can be used to support both models to various extents. Perhaps what we are seeing is something combining aspects of both models: an initial African influence combined with mixture outside of Africa.

The Middle East is particularly interesting, because our current dates show a pattern of occupation by archaics followed by moderns, followed again by archaics (Figure 12.18). To some, the existence of both archaics and moderns in the Middle East is a result of how we "label" fossils; by pigeonholing the fossils into different categories, are we obscuring variation and creating a false impression? Most anthropologists acknowledge the crude nature of the labels "archaic" and "modern," but also point to distinct physical differences. If we are dealing with distinct populations (some claim different species), then what explains their coexistence? One solution has been offered by archaeologist Ofer Bar-Yosef (1994), who suggests that the Middle East has repeatedly served as a refuge for different populations during times of environmental change. During warmer times, the Neandertals may have moved north and west into Europe, and African moderns may have moved into the Middle East. When the climate cooled, the Neandertals could have moved south into the Middle East, and the moderns in the Middle East could have moved back into Africa. If this model is correct, then we

▲▲▲▲▲▲▲▲▲▲▲▲▲▲▲▲▲▲▲▲▲▲▲▲▲▲▲▲

regional continuity
The appearance of
similar traits within a
geographic region over
time.

would get the pattern that we see: occupation of the Middle East at different times by archaics (Neandertals) and moderns. The two populations may have never existed at the same time in the Middle East. More work is needed to confirm this hypothesis, but if nothing else it demonstrates how complicated the picture is of modern human origins.

The Genetic Evidence

In addition to fossil evidence, we can also examine the questions of modern human origins using information on the genetics of living people. We can observe patterns of genetic variation in the present day, and ask what evolutionary model could have given rise to these observed patterns. Whereas with fossils we work from the past to the present, this approach starts with the present in an effort to reconstruct the past. We view the patterns of contemporary genetic variation as reflections of the past.

PATTERNS OF GENETIC VARIATION   We can examine differences within and between living human populations using a variety of data, including blood groups and other genetic markers, DNA sequences, measures of the face and skull, and other measures of variation (see Chapter 13). Another source of information that has been widely used is a form of DNA known as **mitochondrial DNA.** Almost all of our DNA is contained in the chromosomes within the nucleus of our cells (see Chapter 2). Mitochondrial DNA (mtDNA) is an exception—it consists of a small amount of DNA that is contained in the mitochondria, a part of the cell outside the nucleus that is involved in energy production.

For most traits, *both* parents contribute genetically to the child. For mtDNA, however, *only* the female contributes genetically, because female sex cells contain mitochondria, whereas male sex cells consist only of the nucleus. In other words, mtDNA is inherited only through the mother. Your mtDNA came only from your mother, who obtained it from her mother, and so on. You inherit the rest of your DNA from both parents, who inherited from two parents, and so on. For most traits, the number of ancestors doubles every generation you go back: two parents, four grandparents, eight great-grandparents, and so on. For mtDNA, you only have one ancestor in any given generation. This property allows patterns of genetic relationship to be reconstructed without the complication of the gene shuffling that occurs every generation for the rest of your DNA.

Based on genetic evidence to date, several conclusions have been reached regarding the nature of our species' current biological variation. Compared to many other species, we are not that diverse. Genetic studies show, for example, that we are fairly limited in our total genetic diversity when compared to that of the great apes (e.g., Ruvolo et al. 1994). This finding can be explained in two ways. First, our species has been more mobile than many other organisms, such that differences between geographic regions are less

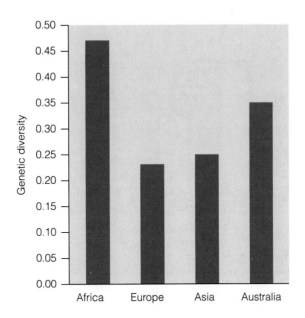

■ FIGURE 12.19
Diversity of mitochondrial DNA in several populations. Africa shows the greatest diversity, a finding that could indicate that modern humans arose first in Africa and/or that the average population size in Africa in the past was greater than that in other regions. (*Source of data:* Cann et al. 1987)

than they would be if we were more isolated. Second, our limited diversity may reflect a relatively recent common origin, which supports the recent African origin model.

Another finding used to support the recent African origin model is the greater diversity, for certain data, shown by African populations than by populations in other regions (Cann et al. 1987; Relethford and Harpending 1994). This greater diversity has been used to argue for a recent African origin under the assumption that the oldest population will accumulate the most mutations over a long period of time, and therefore be more genetically diverse (Figure 12.19).

A third finding of genetic studies focuses on the degree of genetic relationship between different geographic regions. Analysis of individual mitochondrial DNA shows an interesting pattern—the human species today forms two clusters reflecting similarity of mtDNA. One cluster consists only of people with African ancestry and the other cluster consists of people of different ancestries, African and non-African. This finding has been interpreted as reflecting population history: an initial origin of modern humans in Africa followed by a subsequent split of non-African populations. These findings were initially viewed as strong evidence for the recent African origin model (Cann et al. 1987; Vigilant et al. 1991). Subsequent work, however, showed flaws in the analysis: some data supported an African origin, others did not (Hedges et al. 1992; Templeton 1992).

Despite these flawed mtDNA analyses, a similar pattern emerges when we look at genetic similarity among populations based on a variety of other genetic data (Cavalli-Sforza et al. 1994). These analyses consistently show the greatest genetic similarity among non-African populations (Figure 12.20).

▲▲▲▲▲▲▲▲▲▲▲▲▲▲▲▲▲▲▲▲▲▲▲▲▲▲▲▲

mitochondrial DNA
The DNA inside the mitochondria of cells, inherited only through the mother.

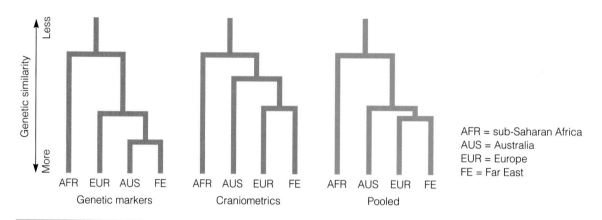

AFR = sub-Saharan Africa
AUS = Australia
EUR = Europe
FE = Far East

■ **FIGURE 12.20**

Genetic distances between major geographic regions. The diagrams are based on the analysis of genetic markers (e.g., blood groups, serum proteins), craniometric measures, and a "pooled" sample that combines genetic markers and craniometrics. These distances have been adjusted for the finding of a larger population size in Africa. All three diagrams show that the greatest genetic distances among humans today are between sub-Saharan Africans and other regions. Such patterns have been taken to support the recent African origin model, but might also reflect differences in population size and migration. (*Source:* Relethford and Harpending 1995).

That is, populations outside of Africa are closer genetically than any are to populations within Africa. Again, this pattern has most often been interpreted as support for the recent African origin model.

POPULATION SIZE AND MODERN HUMAN ORIGINS Although genetic analyses generally provide results that are consistent with the recent African origin model, the analyses can be interpreted in other ways. Looking at patterns of variation, Relethford and Harpending (1994) found that the average population size of Africa was probably larger than that in other regions over the past 100,000 years or so. This larger African population can explain many of the patterns of genetic variation. Larger populations, for example, are expected to show greater genetic diversity because there is less effect of genetic drift. Differences in population size can also explain the genetic distinctiveness of African populations. The genetic data may therefore be telling us nothing about origins, but instead be simply reflecting a larger African population in the past (Relethford 1996b).

Population size is also important when considering mitochondrial DNA variation. Initially, the mtDNA evidence was used to support the view that *all* mtDNA in our species today comes from a single woman who lived in Africa some 200,000 years B.P. (often referred to as "Eve"). Of course, a single female ancestor for mtDNA does *not* mean that *all* of our genetic ancestry comes from only one woman in the distant past. Remember that mtDNA is inherited only through the mother. Some females could have produced only sons, in which case their mtDNA would not be passed on, although they still contributed the rest of their DNA to the next generation (this is analogous to inheriting a last name—you generally get the last name from only one parent, although you obviously inherit genetically from both).

Henry Harpending and colleagues (1993) note that variation in mitochondrial DNA shows us that the human species at the time of "Eve" was very small in number. Their work, and that of others, provides estimates that the *entire* human species some 200,000 to 100,000 years B.P. consisted of perhaps only 10,000 adults or fewer (Rogers and Jorde 1995). This finding provides some indirect support for the recent African origin model. That such a small number of people could have been spread out over three continents as required by the multiregional model seems unlikely. The small species size suggests that most humans at that time were in one area—Africa. This finding does not rule out the possibility of some mixture outside of Africa.

A PREHISTORIC POPULATION EXPLOSION?   The pattern of human mitochondrial DNA variation tells us even more about ancient population size. Rogers and Harpending (1992) found that mtDNA variation showed evidence that the human species was initially very small in number, but then grew rapidly at some point in the past, perhaps increasing by several hundredfold or more. Mitochondrial DNA data from around the world suggest that this population explosion took place roughly 60,000 to 40,000 years B.P. (Sherry et al. 1994). This date is particularly interesting since it corresponds to the timing of the "creative explosion" claimed by some archaeologists (refer back to Table 12.1). These rapid cultural changes may be related to a rapid growth in the human population at this time. Preliminary analysis also suggests that populations in Africa may have expanded in size before other Old World populations. Of course, much of this work is still somewhat tentative, and needs to be investigated further.

Consensus?

What is the bottom line? Although the fossil data, and particularly the genetic data, lend more support to some version of the recent African origin model, the issue is not yet decided, and, in the tradition of science, we can expect continued analysis and debate. At present, there is some consensus that modern humans arose fairly recently in Africa, but the issue of the genetic involvement in other regions is still not settled. More extensive mixture may have occurred in some regions (such as Australasia) but less in others (Europe). In this sense, the origin of modern humans may have involved several, but not all, regions.

Why Did Modern Humans Evolve?

The alternative models for the origin of modern humans are fascinating to debate, but we don't want to lose track of a basic fact that all agree on: only modern human fossils have been found within the past 35,000 years or so. In addition to explaining the timing and nature of the transition from archaics to moderns, we must also ask ourselves why this transition occurred in the first place. The available evidence suggests that anatomically modern *H. sapiens* had some evolutionary advantage over archaic *H. sapiens*. But what was this advantage?

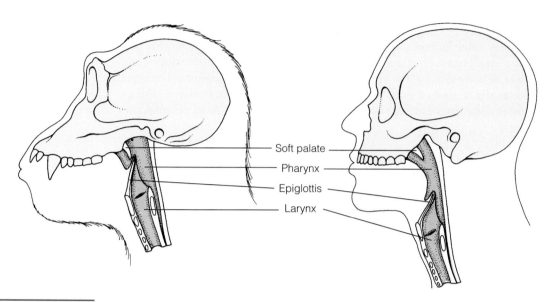

■ **FIGURE 12.21**
The vocal anatomy of a
chimpanzee (*left*) and a
modern human (*right*). In
apes, the larynx is higher in
the throat. In humans, it is
lower, allowing a greater
number of sounds, but
increasing the possibility of
choking on food.   (Redrawn and
reprinted by permission of the
Smithsonian Institution Press
from Roger Lewin: *In the Age of
Mankind: A Smithsonian Book of
Human Evolution,* 1989: 181,
Smithsonian Institution Press)

LANGUAGE AND MODERN HUMAN ORIGINS   It has often been suggested that the development of human language capabilities marks the origin of modern *H. sapiens.* Cranial changes are seen to relate to changes in language ability, with a claim that modern *H. sapiens* was linguistically superior to the archaics. This view is tempting when evidence for the increased symbolic and technological achievements of modern *H. sapiens* is also considered. Can cranial changes and these cultural achievements be related? It is possible—but the basic problem remains that these cultural changes took place well after the initial *biological* changes associated with modern *H. sapiens.* Of course, cave art, bone tools, and other achievements may actually be older than we think, an idea supported to some extent by the new dating of bone tools in Africa. However, basing a model on what has *not* been found is not a good idea. We must always deal with the known fossil and archaeological records and be willing to make appropriate revisions when we make new discoveries.

How can we date the origin of language? This question is central to any discussion of differences in language ability between archaics and moderns. One approach is to examine the fossil evidence of vocal anatomy. Striking differences exist between the vocal tract of a modern human and an ape. The **larynx** is part of the respiratory system that contains the vocal chords for speech. Apes, like other mammals, have their larynx high in the throat. Humans, however, have the larynx further down in the throat, a position that allows the throat to serve as a resonating chamber capable of a greater number of sounds (Figure 12.21). Humans can make a wider number of sounds, and do it faster, than apes. We pay a price for this adaptation, though—unlike apes, we cannot breathe and eat at the same time, and we are in far greater danger of choking to death. Human infants still have the larynx high in the throat and *can* breathe and swallow at the same time. By early childhood, however, the larynx has descended into the throat and they are no longer capable of this.

The position of the larynx represents a clear-cut anatomical difference between humans and apes, and, as such, larynx position can help in assessing the language abilities of any fossil hominid. Unfortunately, the throat, like all soft tissue, decomposes and we cannot recover it. We can get clues about the positioning of the larynx, however, by looking at the base of a cranium. Note that in Figure 12.21 the lower profile of the ape skull is fairly straight, whereas in the modern human it is flexed. The degree of this flexion is directly related to the position of the larynx. Given this relationship, what do the fossils tell us? Laitman and colleagues (1979) investigated the crania of a number of fossil hominids and concluded that, whereas *Australopithecus* had the ape pattern, the crania of many archaic *H. sapiens* are more similar to modern-day humans. The Neandertals had a pattern that was between those of a modern subadult and modern adult human, suggesting that their language abilities may have been somewhat different. Other reconstructions and interpretations are possible (Houghton 1993; Schepartz 1993); some suggest there was little difference in language ability between any of the archaics and modern humans. Schepartz (1993) argues instead that complex language began with the initial origin of the genus *Homo*.

Another source of information on language origins is the archaeological record. Some argue that complex language is of more recent origin; these researchers feel that complex language developed as a result of the "creative explosion" of 40,000 to 60,000 years ago. Others argue that the evidence for a sudden "explosion" is weak, and that the archaeological record shows that cultural abilities developed more gradually (e.g., Schepartz 1993). This latter group feels that, by focusing on the more recent cultural innovations, such as bone tools and cave art, we are ignoring significant earlier innovations, such as complex stone tool manufacture and burial of the dead. Could such things be possible without some language abilities? Although it seems unlikely, the possibility exists nevertheless that some enhancement of language ability coincided with the origin of modern *H. sapiens*. We have too few data at present to answer these questions.

TECHNOLOGY AND BIOLOGICAL CHANGE If changes in language abilities are not the reason for the origin of modern *H. sapiens*, what else might have been involved? Technological changes have also been suggested as mechanisms for the change from archaic to modern forms. This view holds that many of the structural characteristics of archaic *H. sapiens* were the result of stresses generated by the use of their front teeth as tools. The large size and wear patterns of the incisor teeth of archaics (especially Neandertals) support the notion that these teeth were used for a variety of purposes. The stresses generated by heavy use of the front teeth can also be used to explain the large face, large neck muscles, and other features of archaic skulls. Once technological adaptations had developed sufficiently, these physical adaptations were no longer necessary and would not be selected for. Smaller teeth and

▲▲▲▲▲▲▲▲▲▲▲▲▲▲▲▲▲▲▲▲▲▲▲▲▲▲▲▲▲▲
larynx Part of the vocal anatomy in the throat.

The Iceman

Our understanding of ancient times comes from reconstructions based on the fossil and archaeological records, supplemented by evidence from past environments. Although new methods and techniques for analysis have aided our ability to reconstruct the past, we are nevertheless dealing only with bits and pieces of what actually once existed.

Occasionally, though, we come across more detailed evidence. On September 19, 1991, hikers in the glacial mountains between Austria and Italy stumbled upon the body of a man. This is not unusual—bodies are often found in this region, the result of accidents while climbing or hiking in the mountains. Initial investigation, however, showed that this was a naturally occurring mummy (mummification occurs when a corpse is cut off from oxygen). How did the corpse remain so well preserved? The man died in a shallow depression in the ground, and the advancing glacier moved over him, preserving him in a mummified state without carrying his body downhill. In 1991, the ice had receded, and the body was exposed. Because of his discovery in the glacier, he is known today as "The Iceman."

The body became of greater interest because of several items found with it, including a flint knife and an axe. The axe consisted of a wooden shaft attached to what appeared to be a bronze axe head. The bronze implied that the axe and the body dated to the European Bronze Age, roughly 4,000 years B.P. Closer analysis of the axe head showed, however, that it was not bronze (which is a mixture of copper and tin), but almost entirely pure copper. Use of copper is known to be even older than 4,000 B.P. The greater age was confirmed by carbon-14 dating of the body, which placed it at 5,250 B.P.

Research continues on the Iceman, but preliminary study has revealed much about his life and death. Marks have been found on the body that might possibly be tattoos. In addition to the knife and the axe, he had a bow, arrows, and a leather quiver. Remains of his clothes show that they were made of fur, and boots have also been found. He also had two lumps of fungus connected by a leather strap. At first, it was thought that the fungus might have been used as tinder for starting fires. The fungus has now been identified as a species that is know to have antibiotic properties, so we might be seeing some evidence of ancient medicine.

How did the Iceman die? We are not sure although there are several clues. Based on some berries found with the body (which grow only during one season), he appears to have died in late summer or autumn. Climatic reconstruction shows that the nights would have been quite cold. Combined with the high altitude of the find, current thinking is that the Iceman died from exhaustion and dehydration.

For further information, see Sjøvold (1992).

faces might then be advantageous, because smaller structures require correspondingly less energy for growth and maintenance (Smith et al. 1989a). Similar arguments can be made to explain the reduction in body size and musculature (e.g., Frayer 1984). Once cultural behaviors took the place of larger teeth, faces, and bones, then smaller structures actually became more adaptive.

Calcagno and Gibson (1988) present evidence that larger teeth can be nonadaptive. They cite clinical evidence from contemporary human populations that show that large teeth can have many disadvantages. Larger teeth are more susceptible to dental decay, due to crowding of teeth, and periodontal disease. In earlier prehistoric times, the advantages of larger teeth as tools may have outweighed the disadvantages. When cultural change led to more efficient tools, however, these advantages diminished, and selection would then have been *against* large teeth.

Once again, evolution is best seen in terms of the overall balance between costs and benefits. Human evolution is particularly interesting because human behaviors frequently affect this balance. In the past, as new technologies and behaviors arose, they changed the balance between cost and benefit. At some point in the past, for example, the less rugged and less muscular modern morphology may have shifted from being a disadvantage to being an advantage. The origin of modern *H. sapiens* may itself reflect this type of process. If so, we would expect the kind of "lag" between cultural and biological change that we see in the fossil record. Biological changes allow further cultural changes, which in turn allow further biological changes. Each change shifts the balance.

RECENT BIOLOGICAL AND CULTURAL EVOLUTION IN *HOMO SAPIENS*

Human evolution did not end with the origin of modern *H. sapiens*. Biologically, we have continued to change in subtle ways even over the past 10,000 to 20,000 years or so. Cranial capacity has declined somewhat (Henneberg 1988), probably a reflection of a general decrease in size and ruggedness as discussed in the last section. Teeth have also become somewhat smaller (Brace et al. 1987), most likely reflecting the changing costs and benefits of larger teeth.

Within the very recent past (10,000–15,000 years), the major changes in human evolution have been cultural. One major change in human existence—the invention of agriculture—began roughly 12,000 years ago. Up to this point, humans had been exclusively hunters and gatherers. Agriculture changed the entire ecological equation for human beings. Humans began manipulating the environment to increase the availability of food through the domestication of plants and animals. Many explanations are offered as to why agriculture developed, including that it was a solution to the increased population size that had resulted from more efficient hunting and gathering. In any case, the effects of agriculture were and continue to be quite dramatic—the human population grew and continues to do so today (see Chapter 17).

Agriculture did not have a single origin but rather developed independently in many parts of both the Old World and the New World. Over the next several thousand years, the use of agriculture became increasingly dominant around the world (Figure 12.22). Today, there are very few hunters and gatherers left. Our current focus on agriculture often blinds us to the reality that we have changed so much culturally in so short a time. Biologically, we are still hunters and gatherers.

Cultural change continued at an even faster rate following the origin of agriculture and rapid population growth. Cities and state-level societies developed. Exploration brought the inhabitants of the Old World and New

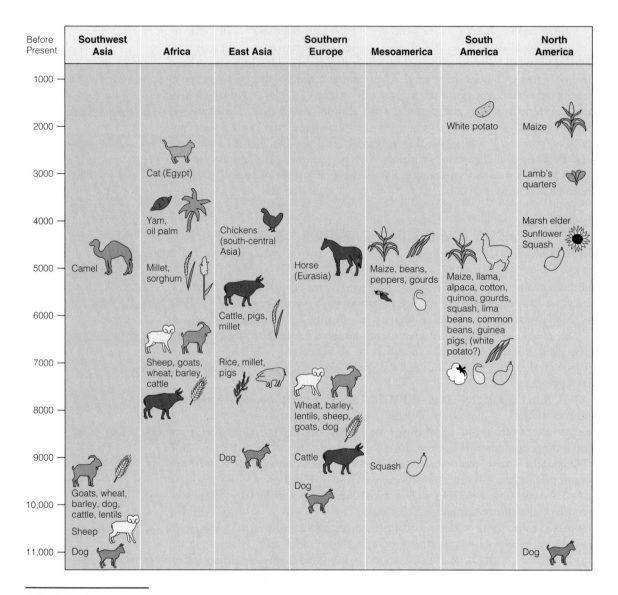

Before Present

	Southwest Asia	Africa	East Asia	Southern Europe	Mesoamerica	South America	North America

- 1000
- 2000 — White potato (South America); Maize (North America)
- 3000 — Cat (Egypt); Lamb's quarters (North America)
- 4000 — Yam, oil palm (Africa); Chickens (south-central Asia); Marsh elder, Sunflower, Squash (North America)
- 5000 — Camel (Southwest Asia); Millet, sorghum (Africa); Horse (Eurasia); Maize, beans, peppers, gourds (Mesoamerica); Maize, llama, alpaca, cotton, quinoa, gourds, squash, lima beans, common beans, guinea pigs, (white potato?) (South America)
- 6000 — Cattle, pigs, millet (East Asia)
- 7000 — Sheep, goats, wheat, barley, cattle (Africa); Rice, millet, pigs (East Asia)
- 8000 — Wheat, barley, lentils, sheep, goats, dog (Southern Europe)
- 9000 — Dog (East Asia); Cattle (Southern Europe); Squash (Mesoamerica)
- Dog (Southern Europe)
- 10,000 — Goats, wheat, barley, dog, cattle, lentils (Southwest Asia); Sheep
- 11,000 — Dog (Southwest Asia); Dog (North America)

FIGURE 12.22

Chronological outline of the origins of domestication and agriculture. (From *Human Antiquity: An Introduction to Physical Anthropology and Archaeology,* 2nd ed., by Kenneth Feder and Michael Park, Fig. 14.1. Copyright © 1993 by Mayfield Publishing Company)

World back into contact, and industrialization spread rapidly. Today, only 12,000 years after the time our ancestors survived by hunting and gathering, we are able to explore and live in every environment on earth, and beyond (Figure 12.23). However one feels about the rapid cultural changes of *H. sapiens*, these changes can be viewed as a continuation of the basic adaptations of culture and learning that have been apparent for at least the past 2.5 million years of human evolution.

■ FIGURE 12.23
The space shuttle is one feature of our species' continuing exploration and utilization of new environments. (Courtesy of NASA)

SUMMARY

Among other features, anatomically modern *Homo sapiens* is characterized by a higher, more well-rounded skull and a smaller face than most archaics, and by the presence of a noticeable chin. Modern *H. sapiens* is best known from fossil records dating over the past 35,000 years. There is growing evidence, however, that these humans appeared first over 100,000 years B.P. in Africa and by 100,000 to 90,000 years B.P. in the Middle East. By 50,000 years B.P., the culture of *H. sapiens* had begun to change rapidly; the use of more sophisticated stone tools (especially blade tools) and bone tools spread, burials of the dead became more elaborate, and art appeared. Modern humans colonized Australia by 50,000 years B.P., and the New World by at least 15,000 years B.P.

There is continuing controversy regarding the origin of anatomically modern humans. The multiregional model hypothesizes that the transition from *H. erectus* to archaic *H. sapiens* to modern *H. sapiens* occurred throughout the Old World. According to this model, the evolution of modern humans took place within a widespread species across several continents.

Gene flow is considered here to be sufficient to have maintained a single species of human after the initial dispersal of *H. erectus* from Africa. Conversely, the recent African origin model hypothesizes that the evolution of modern humans occurred in one place—Africa, between 200,000 and 100,000 years B.P.—and that modern humans then spread outward across the world, replacing preexisting archaic populations. There are variants of each model, including the possibility of a primary African origin combined with mixture with archaic populations. Fossil and genetic data have been used to examine these hypotheses. There is still considerable debate about *why* modern humans first evolved.

Human evolution did not end after the initial appearance of modern humans. Although there have been some biological changes during our recent past, most of our species' evolution during the past 10,000 years has been cultural. Perhaps the single most important event was the development of agriculture, which changed our entire way of life. Predicting the specifics of future human evolution is problematic, but it does appear clear that our future will involve more and more cultural change, which occurs at a far greater rate than biological evolution. This does not mean that biological evolution has stopped, but rather that our fate is becoming increasingly affected by cultural change.

SUPPLEMENTAL READINGS

Klein, R. G. 1989. *The Human Career: Human Biological and Cultural Origins*. Chicago: University of Chicago Press. Although somewhat dated in spots, this remains one of the single best summaries of the fossil and archaeological record of human evolution, with considerable attention to the evolution of modern humans.

Stringer, C., and C. Gamble. 1993. *In Search of the Neanderthals: Solving the Puzzle of Human Origins*. New York: Thames and Hudson. This book provides an excellent review of the fossil, archeological, and genetic evidence supporting a recent African origin.

Thorn, A. G., and M. H. Wolpoff. April 1992. The multiregional evolution of humans. *Scientific American* 266(4): 76–83. A nontechnical review of the multiregional model and its supporting evidence.

Wilson, A. C., and R. L. Cann. April 1992. The recent African genesis of humans. *Scientific American* 266(4): 68–73. Appearing in the same issue as the Thorne and Wolpoff article, this paper provides a nontechnical review of some of the genetic evidence supporting a recent African origin model although recent work has questioned their interpretations.

PART FOUR

Human Variation

*The Study
of Human Variation*

CHAPTER **13**

 Every day we encounter human biological diversity (Figure 13.1), but we seldom speak of what we see in evolutionary terms. On a day-to-day basis, most people think about variation in terms of the widely used, but imprecise, word *race*. People are often surprised to learn that anthropologists today look at variation in terms of evolutionary forces, and are not concerned (except in an historical sense) with race or racial classifications. Race is a descriptive concept and not an analytic tool. At best, it provides a crude and often misleading label for variation, and explains nothing.

However, because the concept of race is so ingrained in society and structures many of our ideas on variation, we need to review exactly what race is and is not. Throughout much of this chapter, then, we review the concept of race and then examine the evolutionary alternative. As we shall see, the evolutionary forces discussed in Chapter 3 form the basis for our understanding of the patterns and causes of human biological variation.

■ **FIGURE 13.1**
Human biological diversity in
external physical traits.
(*Top left,* © Bachman/The Image
Works; *top right,* © A. Carey/The
Image Works; *center left,* © John
Moss/Photo Researchers, Inc.;
center right, © Renee Lynn/Photo
Researchers, Inc.; *bottom left,* ©
Bachman/Photo Researchers, Inc.;
bottom right, © David Young-
Wolff/PhotoEdit)

MEASURING HUMAN VARIATION

Exactly *what* are we talking about? Whether we approach human variation from a racial perspective or an evolutionary perspective, we need to know what we mean by "human variation." Variation, of course, means the differences that exist among people and populations. We are all aware of biological variation—some people are taller, or darker, or have differently shaped skulls. We also know from Chapters 2 and 3 that people frequently have different blood groups, or other varying aspects of their biochemical makeup. Is the measure of human variation simply a matter of examining how different people look? Although we frequently do just that in our daily lives, simple observation is not adequate for scientific analysis. First of all, it is too subjective. Looking at people and rating them as "tall" versus "short," or "dark" versus "light," is too fraught with problems of observer bias to be much use. Second, our mental categories of variation (e.g., "light" versus "dark") do not acknowledge that traits such as human skin color do not come in three or four groups but are instead continuous. Third, much of the genetic variation that exists is invisible to our eyes—you cannot tell a person's blood group by looking at him or her.

Many different measures and methods have been devised to assess biological variation, and new methods are being developed all the time. A few of these methods are reviewed here briefly.

Biochemical Variation

First we examine "simple" genetic traits—those that are not affected by the environment during a person's life and that reflect a simple relationship between genotype and phenotype. These traits reflect differences in biochemistry, such as blood types.

BLOOD TYPES One of the most common genetic measures used in studies of human variation is a person's blood type, such as the ABO blood type and the MN blood type discussed in Chapter 2. These are only a couple of the blood type systems that have been discovered; others include the Rhesus, Diego, Duffy, and Kell blood group systems, to name only a few. Different blood group systems are identified by the types of molecules present on the surface of the red blood cells. Each blood group system has a particular antibody–antigen reaction that can be used to identify the different blood groups. **Antibodies** are substances that react to foreign substances invading the blood steam (**antigens**). This antibody–antigen reaction (clumping of red blood cells) allows us to classify different blood groups.

▲▲

antibody A substance that reacts to other substances invading the body (antigens).

antigen A substance invading the body that stimulates the production of antibodies.

■ TABLE 13.1
Determining a Person's ABO Blood Type

	Antigen(s) Present in Blood	Reaction with Antibody	
Blood type		anti-A	anti-B
A	A	Yes	No
B	B	No	Yes
AB	A and B	Yes	Yes
O	None	No	No

As an example, consider the ABO blood group discussed in Chapter 2. Remember that this system has three alleles (*A*, *B*, and *O*), where *A* and *B* are codominant and *O* is recessive. There are four different phenotypes: type A (genotypes *AA* and *AO*), type B (genotypes *BB* and *BO*), type O (genotype *OO*), and type AB (genotype *AB*). There are two antibodies that react to specific antigens. One of these, anti-A, reacts to A-type molecules (in people with blood type A). The other, anti-B, reacts to B-type molecules (in people with blood type B). Because each blood type has a different combination of A and B antigens (Table 13.1), these reactions allow us to find out which of the four ABO blood types a person has. For example, people with type A blood have the A antigen but not the B. Suppose we take a sample of a person's blood and find that the blood clumps when exposed to anti-A antibodies but not when exposed to anti-B antibodies. This means the person has A antigens but not B antigens, and therefore has type A blood. The same basic method (although sometimes more complex) is used for determining the phenotypes of other blood group systems.

OTHER GENETIC TRAITS   In addition to red blood cell groups, genetic analyses have been done on many populations for red blood cell enzymes and proteins and for proteins in blood serum (the fluid part of the blood). One method used for detecting variants of such traits is **electrophoresis.** With this method, blood samples are placed on a gel that is electrically charged. Proteins move along the flow of electrons from negative to positive, and some proteins move at faster rates. This difference in movement allows us to determine a person's genotype.

Another set of methods focuses on DNA, including DNA sequences. Some of these were discussed in Chapter 7. Some types of DNA analysis can be performed now with small samples of hair, a method well suited to many anthropological studies (Figure 13.2).

One method of DNA analysis focuses on **restriction fragment length polymorphisms (RFLPs).** Certain enzymes produced by different species of

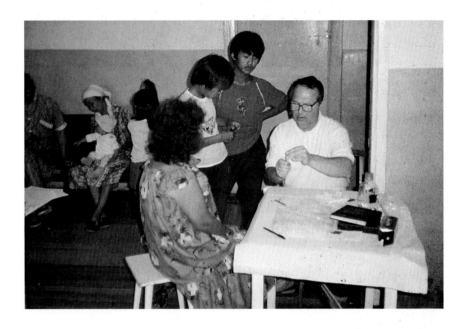

bacteria, known as *restriction enzymes*, bind to sections of DNA and cut the DNA sequence at a given point. A difference in a person's DNA sequence will change the location where it is cut, and hence change the length of the DNA fragment (White and Lalouel 1988). Differences in the *length* of DNA sequences provide us with yet another measure of human variation.

Complex Trait Variation

Many of the traits of interest in studying human variation are complex traits—those that are frequently affected by growth and the environment and that reflect a much more complicated relationship between genotype and phenotype.

ANTHROPOMETRICS Measurements of the human body, including the head and the face, are known as **anthropometrics.** Two of the most commonly used anthropometric measures are height and weight (Figure 13.3). Other measurements of the body include the length of limbs and limb segments and the width of the body at different places, such as the shoulders and the hips. There are many measurements of the skull, such as the length, width, and

electrophoresis A laboratory method that uses electric current to separate proteins, allowing genotype to be determined.

restriction fragment length polymorphism (RFLP) A genetic trait defined in terms of

the length of DNA fragments produced through cutting by certain enzymes.

anthropometrics Measurements of the human body, skull, and face.

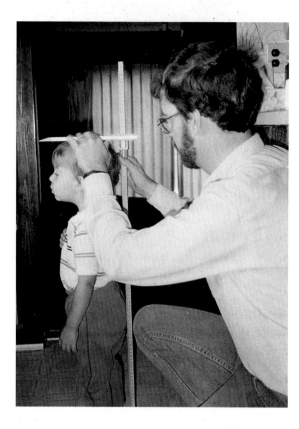

■ FIGURE 13.3
The author measures his son's stature. Stature and weight are two of the most common anthropometric measures.

height of the head, the relative width of the head at different points, and the size of the nose. Anthropometrics are applied to skeletal data as well as to living people.

SKIN COLOR   In the past, skin color was often measured by comparing a person's skin to a set of standardized tiles. This method is too subjective and inaccurate, and the more common method today involves the use of a reflectance spectrophotometer—a device that measures the percentage of light reflected back from a given source at different wavelengths. To minimize the effects of tanning, we measure skin color on the inside of the upper arm, which is generally not as exposed to the sun as other parts of the body. The more light that is bounced back off the skin, the lighter the person is. Instead of trying to shove people into categories such as "light" or "dark," we can measure skin color precisely.

OTHER MEASURES   Measures of the size of the teeth are known as **odontometrics.** From a cast made of a person's upper and lower jaws, researchers can measure the length and width of each tooth. Fingerprints are also useful in studying human variation; these measures are called **dermatoglyphics.** They include classification of different types of prints as well as counts of the number of ridge lines on each digit. In addition to all these measures (and others), anthropologists often measure a variety of physiologic traits, such as blood pressure, heart rate, and aerobic functioning.

THE RACIAL APPROACH TO VARIATION

Given measure after measure of human variation, how do we make sense of it all? Although we focus today on evolutionary forces, the dominant perspective in the past, as noted earlier, was one of race and racial classification. This approach is also used by most people today in their daily exposure to human variation. A problem here is that we use words like *race* without defining them. What do phrases like the "white race," the "Japanese race," and the "Jewish race" mean to you? They are extremely confusing because the term *race* is used to stand for a variety of factors such as skin color, national origin, and religion. Sometimes we use the term in a biological sense, sometimes in a social sense.

The definition of race is no mere academic issue. Race is discussed daily in the newspapers and other media. Race has been used to justify discrimination and persecution of people as well as to grant favored status. Statistics on race are gathered by local, state, federal, and international organizations. Economic and political decisions are often based on race.

Obviously, race is an important concept in our lives. But what exactly is it? How many races are there? What are the differences between races?

The Biological Concept of Race

From a biological standpoint, a **race** is generally defined as "a division of a species that differs from other divisions by the frequency with which certain hereditary traits appear among its members" (Brues 1977:1). Race in this definition has two characteristics. First, it is a group of populations that share some biological characteristics. Second, these populations differ from other groups of populations according to these characteristics. The concept of race seeks to fill the void between the single "human race" and the thousands of local human populations. Race is meant to provide a classification of biologically similar populations.

▲▲▲

odontometrics
Measurements of the size of teeth.

dermatoglyphics
Measurements of finger and palm prints.

race A group of populations sharing certain traits that make them distinct from other groups of populations.

The concept of race is difficult to apply to patterns of human variation.

The race concept works better biologically with some organisms than with others. For organisms that are isolated from one another in different environments, the race concept often provides a usable, though rough, means of summarizing biological variation. For other organisms, such as humans, the concept has less utility. Humans inhabit a wide number of environments and move between them frequently. The high degree of gene flow among human populations, compared to that of many other organisms, means that clear-cut boundaries among groups of populations are difficult to establish.

The race concept presents a number of problems that are outlined in the next section. Given these problems, race and racial classifications provide only a crude tool for description, one with little utility for today's biologist or anthropologist, when sophisticated statistical methods and computers allow us to analyze patterns of biological variation more precisely than ever before. Indeed, some authors have suggested that we drop the entire concept for it has little use biologically (Livingstone 1964).

Problems with the Concept of Race

What is wrong with classifying people into races? After all, we can do it accurately. Or can we?

THE NUMBER OF HUMAN RACES   A major problem with the race concept is that scientists have never agreed on the number of human races. How many can you name, or see? Some have suggested that there are three human races: Europeans, Africans, and Asians (often referred to by the archaic terms "Caucasoid," "Negroid," and "Mongoloid," which are almost never used in scientific research today). But many populations do not fit neatly into these three basic categories. What about native Australians (aborigines)? As shown in Figure 13.4, these are dark-skinned people who frequently have curly or wavy hair that is sometimes blond and who have abundant facial hair. On the basis of skin color, we might be tempted to label these people as African, but on the basis of hair and facial shape they might be classified as European. One approach has been to create a fourth category, the "Australoid" race.

As we travel around the world, however, we find more and more populations that do not fit a three- or four-race system. As a result, some authors have added races to their list. There has never been clear consensus on the actual number, though. In 1758, for example, Linnaeus described four major human races in his classification of humans. Since that time, different authors have suggested four, five, and nine major races, among other numbers. During the twentieth century, hierarchies of races have been suggested. That is, a varying number of major races can be subdivided into minor races, which are further subdivided into even smaller races. Some anthropologists have divided "primary races" into "primary subraces" (Hooten 1946).

■ **FIGURE 13.4**
An Australian aborigine with
dark skin and curly hair.
(Neg. no. 330831. Photo by A. P.
Elkin. Courtesy Department of
Library Services, American
Museum of Natural History)

Others have suggested subdividing major "geographic races" into "local races," which are further subdivided into "microraces" (Garn 1965). Additional populations that are the result of **admixture,** such as African Americans, are often referred to as "composite races." In each case there has been little agreement on the number of races or subraces.

Two points emerge from a study of the history of attempts to classify and apply the race concept to human populations. First, the lack of agreement among different researchers indicates that the entire concept of race is arbitrary as it applies to humans. If clearly discernible races existed, their number should have long since been determined without argument. How useful is a classification system when there is so much disagreement about the number of units? Second, something is being described here, although in a crude manner. All racial classifications, for example, note the wide range in skin color among human populations and note further an association with geography. The native peoples of Africa tend to have darker skin than those of northern Europe. The geographic distribution of many traits, such as skin color, is well known. Then why doesn't the race concept work well when describing biological variation?

THE NATURE OF CONTINUOUS VARIATION Biological variation is real; the order we impose on this variation by using the concept of race is not. Race is a product of human minds, not of nature. One reason race fails to describe

▲▲▲▲▲▲▲▲▲▲▲▲▲▲▲▲▲▲▲▲▲▲▲▲▲▲▲▲▲▲▲

admixture The interbreeding of individuals from two or more populations.

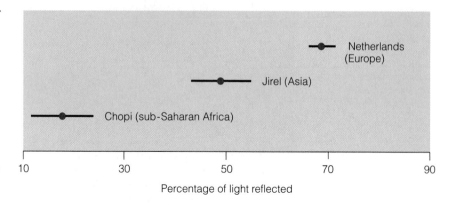

■ FIGURE 13.5
Variation in skin color in three selected human populations (males). Dots indicate the mean skin reflectance measured at a wavelength of 685 nanometers; lines indicate 1 standard deviation on each side of the mean. Compare this with Figure 13.6, which shows more populations. The discontinuity in skin color shown here disappears when more of humanity is sampled. (*All data from published literature*)

variation accurately is that much variation is continuous, whereas race is a discrete unit. In other words, we must reduce variation into a few small categories.

Consider human height as an example. Most of us cannot describe a person's height to the nearest centimeter without actually measuring that person. When we look at someone, we are unlikely to know *exactly* how tall that person is. We would not, however, describe everyone as the same height simply because we do not know the exact values. Instead, we use relative terms such as "short," "medium," and "tall." Often our definitions of these categories do not always agree with other people's (many people call anyone shorter than themselves "short" regardless of their actual height.) Also, some people might add categories, such as "medium tall" or "very short." In any case, these categories have some limited use. When we say that a basketball player is "tall," most people know roughly how tall we mean. But are these categories real? When we forget that these are only convenient crude levels for classification, we can fall into the trap of thinking that they have a reality of their own. Do you actually think all people fall into one of three categories—"short," "medium," or "tall"? Height is a continuous trait that can have an infinite number of values within a certain range.

The same problem applies to races. Many racial classifications in Western societies use skin color as a major distinguishing feature. The races correspond to different measures of skin color—"white," "yellow," "red," "brown," and "black," for example. We know, however, that skin color does not fall into 5, or even 50, different categories. Skin color is a continuous variable. This means that any attempt to divide the continuous range into discrete units (races) is going to be arbitrary.

Figure 13.5 shows the average skin reflectance for three samples of males—one from sub-Saharan Africa (Chopi), one from Asia (Jirels), and one from Europe (the Netherlands). For each sample, the dot represents the average value and the lines represent 1 standard deviation below and above the average. (A standard deviation is a statistical measure of variation.

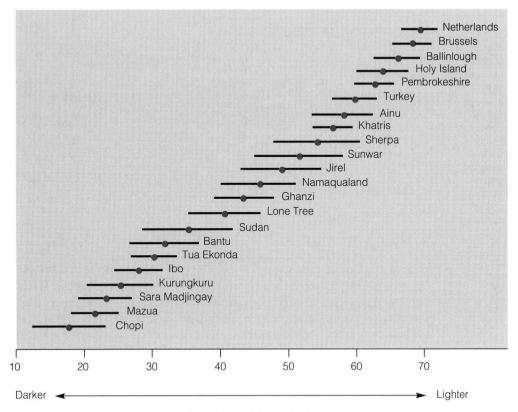

Darker ← ────────────────────────────────→ Lighter

Percentage of light reflected

Roughly 68 percent of the cases in each sample lie between the ends of the lines drawn in the figure. Each sample contains some individuals who are lighter or darker.) These three samples are quite distinct from one another. There is no overlap in skin color, and it would be very easy to classify a given person into one of the three groups based on his skin color. Isn't this an accurate reflection of three distinct races?

No. The appearance of three distinct races is a biased reflection because humanity is made up of more than simply these three populations. When we add more populations to the picture, the interpretation changes. Figure 13.6 shows the average skin reflectance and standard deviations for 22 male samples from Africa, Asia, and Europe. Note that there are no longer discrete boundaries that can be used to identify different races. The ranges in skin reflectance overlap one another. In other words, on the basis of skin color, it is not possible to tell where one "race" ends and another starts. We can identify the extremes, but there are no discrete clusters.

Despite these arguments, many people are still convinced that human races are easily identifiable. After all, they say, you can walk down any city

■ FIGURE 13.6
Variation in skin color in 22 human populations (males). Dots indicate the mean skin reflectance measured at a wavelength of 685 nanometers; lines indicate 1 standard deviation on each side of the mean. (*All data from published literature*)

■ **FIGURE 13.7**
Original settlement of the United States from the perspective of skin color. From the continuous range of skin color in the human species, the majority of earliest settlers were from the two extreme ends—dark-colored West Coast Africans and light-colored Western Europeans. This differential settlement gives rise to the seeming existence of two distinct races in the United States based on skin color.

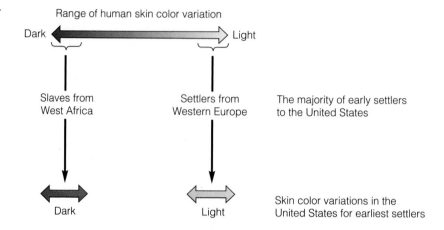

street in the United States and point out who is "white" and who is "black" (ignoring for the moment those people who are difficult to classify). Under such circumstances, race is easily identifiable (or is it?). This may be true in a limited area, such as a street in a medium-sized American city, but it does not hold true when we look at the world in general. Races seem distinct in certain situations because disproportionate numbers of peoples from different geographic regions are present. We do not find equal representation of all human populations on most U.S. city streets. For example, we tend to see far fewer Australian aborigines than we see people of predominantly European or African ancestry.

In short, the overall composition of the U.S. population tends to give us a distorted view of the total variation in the world. The majority of early settlers in the United States came from Western Europe, one of the regions in the world whose human populations show the lightest skin color. During the next few centuries, many slaves were brought from West Africa, one of the regions where human skin color is darkest. The result has been a disproportionate representation of the range of skin color. More people in the United States have either very light or very dark skin than any shade in between (Figure 13.7). On the other hand, a tour through other parts of the world will soon give you a different picture. Many of the people in the world are neither so dark nor so light.

Not all biological traits show continuous variation. Blood group phenotypes, for example, are discrete traits. We do not, however, often find situations in which all members of one race have one phenotype and all members of another race have a different phenotype. Some genetic markers are useful in separating populations in certain geographic areas, but many such traits show patterns of variation that are not well described by racial classification. For example, the frequency of the *a* allele for the Diego blood group is moderately high in native South American populations, ranging up to 0.32. In both Africa and Europe, however, the frequency is 0 (Roychoudhury and Nei 1988). This allele is useful in separating South America from other regions but does not separate Africa and Europe—two regions typically assigned to different races. In addition, there are populations in South America that have a near-zero allele frequency. If we used the Diego blood group, we would have to assign these South American populations to a mixed European/African race!

Another example of a discrete trait is eye form. The so-called "slanted" eyes of Asians are caused in part by a fold of skin at the inner corner of the eye. (This shape is also related to the size and projection of the root of the nose.) This eye shape is found in many Asian populations, and to a less extent in other groups as well. At first this trait might seem like a good "racial" trait because its presence allows us to separate populations of Asian ancestry from other groups. It does not, however, separate other groups, such as those of African or European ancestry.

CORRESPONDENCE OF DIFFERENT TRAITS If race were to be a useful biological concept, the classifications would have to work for a number of independent traits. A classification developed from skin color would also need to show the same racial pattern in other traits, such as head shape, nasal shape, and hair color. If each trait produces a different set of races, then the race concept is not very useful as a description of overall biological similarity. In fact, racial classifications vary according to the biological trait used.

High frequencies of the sickle cell allele are found not only in populations belonging to "African races," but also in parts of Europe and India. Any racial classification based on high or low frequencies of the sickle cell allele in a population would not produce the same distribution as skin color. Another example is the frequency of lactase deficiency. Some populations in Africa, because of their dependence on dairy farming, have low frequencies of lactase deficiency, similar to rates found in European populations (lactase deficiency is discussed in the next chapter).

Using different traits often results in different groupings of populations. For examples such as sickle cell and lactase deficiency, we expect this to be the case because the variation in a trait is related to natural selection, which will operate differently in diverse environments. In using racial classifications, however, we often find that as we add more traits the situation becomes even more complex. The fact that traits show different distributions argues against the utility of the race concept for describing human variation.

With the proper choice of variables, however, we can find combinations that are useful in looking at the relationships between populations on a worldwide basis. By examining a number of traits presumed neutral in terms of natural selection, we try to come up with an average pattern that reflects the tendency of gene flow and genetic drift to affect all loci to the same extent. Often we find clusters of populations that agree in a limited sense

Genetics, Race, and IQ

Perhaps the most controversial topic in the study of human variation is the question of the relationship of genetics, race, and intelligence. What is intelligence? Are IQ tests an accurate measure of intelligence? Are IQ scores due to genetic inheritance or environmental factors, or both? Are there "racial" differences in IQ scores? If so, do they reflect genetics or environment, or both?

Over time, as observations were collected that showed "racial" differences in intelligence test scores, several researchers argued that this difference is at least partially due to genetic differences between the races. A common line of argument goes as follows:

1. IQ scores are a measure of intelligence.
2. Differences in IQ scores are partly due to genetic differences.
3. The races have different average IQ scores.
4. Because races are by definition genetically different, then the racial differences in IQ scores are genetic.

It is worthwhile to examine briefly each of these claims.

What is IQ? It stands for "intelligence quotient" and is a measure derived by dividing a person's "mental age" by her or his chronological age, and is designed so that the average score for a reference population is 100. The IQ test was developed in France by Alfred Binet, who sought a means by which to identify children with learning disabilities. The purpose of the test was not to measure intelligence per se, but rather to identify those children who would most likely require special education. The test was not meant to provide a ranking of intelligence among the rest of the students. That is, someone with an IQ score of 120 was not to be considered inherently "better" or "smarter" than someone with a score of 110.

Is intelligence a single "thing" that can be measured accurately by an IQ test? Although some argue that IQ is a fair measure of intelligence (Herrnstein and Murray 1994), others note that there are many different types of intelligence, some of which may not be assessed as well by conventional IQ tests (Bodmer and Cavalli-Sforza 1976; Hunt 1995). There is an unfortunate tendency to assume that intelligence is a single thing, measurable with a single test (Gould 1981).

These problems change the questions somewhat. Instead of looking at genetic and environmental factors affecting intelligence, what we are really doing is looking at genetic and environmental factors affecting IQ test scores, which might not be the same thing. In terms of IQ, there is evidence for a strong

with geography. That is, we can identify some separation between sub-Saharan African populations, European populations, Middle Eastern populations, and so on. This is expected, given the close relationship of geographic distance and gene flow in human populations. Sub-Saharan African populations should be more similar to each other, on average, than they are to European populations. We can identify large geographic regions that have a *rough* correspondence with the usual definitions of race. But how useful are these labels for describing variation? To answer that, we must look closely at the difference between variation *within* a population and variation *between* populations.

VARIATION BETWEEN AND WITHIN GROUPS Racial classifications represent a form of **typology,** a set of discrete groupings. Instead of looking at the continuous range of variation, populations are placed into different races. The major problem with the usual application of the race concept and its emphasis on typology is the assumption that most of the variation that exists in the human species is *between* races. Variation *within* races is considered to be

inherited component (Bouchard et al. 1990) and strong environmental components, including diet, education, social class, and health, among others (Gould 1981).

The third point in the list is that there are "racial" differences in IQ test scores. In the United States, for example, European Americans tend to score, on average, roughly 15 points higher than African Americans. Asian Americans tend to score, on average, several points higher than European Americans. However, is this what we mean by a "racial" difference? Categories such as "European American," "African American," and "Asian American" are broad groupings based on ethnicity and national origin, but are not by any stretch of the imagination homogeneous populations. People within any of these broad ancestral groupings can come from a wide variety of countries and environments. Does it make sense to talk about a "European-American race"? Problems arise when we take our labels as accurate reflections for the true nature of biological variation.

Putting aside for the moment the utility of even looking at IQ by "race," the largest problem is point 4 in the list. We assume that *any* group differences of a trait that has a genetic basis *must* be genetic in nature. However, we also know of genetic traits that do *not* vary across humanity. Some traits vary among groups,

and some do not. We have no way of knowing beforehand whether IQ test performance will be one way or the other. The answer requires testing. The other problem with analysis is that we also know that different groups have different environmental conditions (e.g., education, income, and others) that affect performance on IQ tests. To date, the bulk of the evidence supports an environmental explanation of "racial" difference in IQ test scores (Loehlin et al. 1975; Gould 1981; Woodward 1992). Direct tests have also been made of the hypothesis that group differences are genetic. If this were true, then IQ test scores among African Americans should vary proportionately according to the degree of European admixture; those with greater European ancestry should score higher. An analysis of this hypothesis, however, showed no relationship between amount of European component and IQ scores (Scarr and Weinberg 1978).

The entire debate over "race" and IQ is obviously influenced by political, economic, and social ideologies. From a scientific viewpoint, much of the debate is flawed because of overreliance on the biological race concept.

less. This is apparent when using group stereotypes (e.g., "they are short," or "they have broad heads"). Such statements provide information about the *average* in a group, but not about its variation. For example, consider the statement that adult males in the United States tend to be taller than adult females in the United States. No one can argue with this statement of averages. However, does it imply that *all* males are taller than *all* females? Of course not. There is variation within both sexes and a great deal of overlap.

The problem with the race concept, then, is that it acknowledges little overlap in genetic characteristics; in other words, the concept sees most variation as being between the races and not within the races. This is interesting because our observations show that the truth is actually completely different—there is much more variation *within* differently identified races than exists *between* them. This finding was first quantified by Lewontin (1972), who examined the actual levels of genetic variation between and within seven designated "races": Africans, Europeans, Asians, Native Americans, South Asians, Oceanians, and Australian aborigines. Lewontin looked at variation for a number of loci. Lewontin found that 94 percent of the total

▲▲▲▲▲▲▲▲▲▲▲▲▲▲▲▲▲▲▲▲▲▲▲▲▲▲▲▲

typology A set of discrete groupings in classification that emphasize average tendencies and ignore variation within groups.

variation occurred *within* races and only 6 percent occurred *between* races. Since his initial study, similar results have been found consistently using different loci, different racial groupings, and larger samples. In general, studies of simple genetic traits show that roughly 10 percent of the total genetic variation of the human species occurs between races. A recent study on cranial and facial characteristics produced the same number (Relethford 1994). The bottom line is that race explains only about 10 percent of human genetic diversity. This low number doesn't say much about race as an accurate description of human variation—it ignores most of the variation.

WHAT USE IS THE RACE CONCEPT?   Acknowledging the many problems associated with using race to explain human variation, does the concept have any use? In the scientific study of human variation, the answer is little, if any. It is a descriptive tool, not an analytic one. If we examine the biological characteristics of a population and then assign the population to a given race, all we have accomplished is to label some observed phenomenon. We have not explained the causes of variation, nor why some groups are similar to, or different from, others. The name explains nothing. The race concept does not ask or answer any interesting questions.

Until the 1950s, much of biological anthropology was devoted to racial description and classification. Most sciences go through a descriptive phase, followed later by an explanatory phase in which hypotheses are proposed and tested. Indeed, at least until the work of Charles Darwin, much of biology was basically a descriptive science. Today biological anthropologists rarely treat race as a concept. It has no utility for explanation, and its value for description is limited.

In contemporary society, however, race is still a common category. In this context the term has more a social connotation than a biological one. In state and federal government reports, "race" identifies some aspect of geographic origin and ethnic identity. For example, "black" refers to African or African-American descent. "Hispanic" refers to Spanish speakers but actually encompasses a wide variety of peoples from Mexicans to Bolivians. Such classifications have their use, particularly in defining groups of people who have suffered social inequities, but they are not without their own problems. Classification into discrete groups always means that we obscure the subtle gradations of human variation.

Human variation is best analyzed using an approach that focuses on microevolutionary forces and uses individuals or local populations as the unit of analysis. This approach, aided by modern statistical and computer methods, allows better description than the race concept, avoids the problems of classification, and provides a focus for *explanation*.

In any case, we should not confuse social and biological categories, nor draw biological inferences from social identity. Race as a concept has little utility for analyzing human biological variation. Although we still distinguish "social" races, the term tends to generate misunderstanding even when used in this sense.

THE EVOLUTIONARY APPROACH TO VARIATION

When dealing with human biological variation, we need methods to describe and analyze patterns that we observe. As noted in the last section, the race concept is at best a crude description of variation, and it provides nothing in terms of explanation. The alternative approach stressed by biological anthropologists for the past 30 years or so is an evolutionary one. Here we look at the pattern of biological variation in terms of the evolutionary forces: mutation, selection, gene flow, and genetic drift.

Different methods are used to analyze human variation depending on the specific questions being asked. Are we interested in the history of a set of populations? If so, we want to consider factors such as gene flow, which in turn might be related to patterns of marriage, migration, and changes in population size. In such cases, we would want as much information from as many different traits as possible in order to obtain some measure of overall genetic similarity. Or, are we interested in the patterns of variation of a specific trait, such as the ABO blood group or skin color? In that case, we would focus on that specific trait.

Given this contrast, we can draw a distinction between **univariate analysis** (one trait at a time) and **multivariate analysis** (many traits at one time). The difference in these approaches relates to the goals of a given study, and whether the focus is on the forces of gene flow and genetic drift on the one hand, or natural selection on the other.

The basic starting point is that gene flow and genetic drift are expected to affect *all* loci to the same degree, whereas natural selection is expected to affect each locus differently. For example, if you move from one population to another and have offspring in your new population, all of your genetic material moves with you: gene flow should affect all loci the same. Likewise, the *average* effect of genetic drift is expected to be the same for all loci. Natural selection, however, should affect each locus differently—unless, of course, the loci are both related to the same selective force.

As a result, we tend to study natural selection one locus or trait at a time, unless we are looking at related traits. If we wish to study the effects of genetic drift and gene flow, we try to sample as many loci or traits as possible with the goal of getting the best estimate of overall effect. Of course, any study must consider *all* of the evolutionary forces. The univariate and

▲▲▲

univariate analysis
The analysis of human biological variation focusing on a single trait at a time.

multivariate analysis
The analysis of human biological variation

that considers the interrelationships of several traits at a time.

multivariate approaches together often provide us with information regarding a number of these evolutionary forces.

An example of the multivariate approach is Workman and colleagues' (1963) study of allele frequencies of African Americans in Claxton, Georgia. Table 13.2 lists the frequencies of eight alleles from seven loci for the African-American and European-American populations of Claxton and those of the West Coast of Africa (a presumed source of many ancestors for the Claxton African Americans). In all cases, the allele frequencies for the Claxton African Americans lie between those of West Coast Africans and the Claxton European Americans. In most cases, the allele frequencies of the Claxton African Americans are more similar to those of West Coast Africans. This is expected, given the predominately African ancestry of the Claxton African-American population. European gene flow, however, has caused the Claxton African-American allele frequencies to move further away from the West African frequencies. This example shows how admixture of Europeans has occurred in the African-American population of Claxton.

Is gene flow the only factor operating on the Claxton African-American allele frequencies? If so, then the relative position of the Claxton African Americans should be the same for all alleles because gene flow is expected to have the same effect on all loci. Figure 13.8 plots their relative positions for the eight alleles. Most of the Claxton African-American allele frequencies plot in a similar location, as expected from gene flow. The allele frequencies for G6PD deficiency and the sickle cell allele (S) are quite different. They do not fit the pattern of the other alleles, which suggests that natural selection has been operating on those loci.

■ TABLE 13.2
Allele Frequencies of African-American and European-American Populations in Claxton, Georgia

Locus	Allele	West Coast African	Claxton African Americans	Claxton European Americans
Rhesus	d	0.211	0.230	0.358
ABO	A	0.148	0.158	0.246
ABO	B	0.151	0.129	0.050
MN	M	0.476	0.485	0.508
Duffy	Fy a	0.000	0.046	0.422
P	P	0.780	0.757	0.526
Hemoglobin	S	0.110	0.043	0.000
G6PD	GD⁻	0.195	0.118	0.000

Source: Workman et al. (1963:451)

West
Coast
Africans

Claxton
European
Americans

■ **FIGURE 13.8**
The relative genetic position
of the African-American
population in Claxton,
Georgia, as compared to
the European-American
population of Claxton and to
West Coast Africans. Eight
alleles are shown here (see
Table 13.2). Six of the alleles
cluster together, suggesting
the common effect of gene
flow. Two alleles, from the
hemoglobin and G6PD loci,
show a different relative
position, suggesting the effect
of natural selection (see text).

The Analysis of Gene Flow and Genetic Drift

A number of methods are used to examine the joint effect of gene flow and genetic drift on patterns of human variation. Two of the more common approaches are discussed here.

GENETIC DISTANCE ANALYSIS   When comparing a number of biological traits across populations, we frequently compute a summary measure known as a **genetic distance.** This is an average measure of relatedness between groups based on a number of traits (i.e., a multivariate approach). Quite simply, the larger the genetic distance, the *less* similar two populations are to each other. For example, imagine that you have investigated a number of traits for three groups, called A, B, and C. You compute one of a number of genetic distance measures and obtain the following distances (don't worry about the units of measure; most distance measures are relative):

Distance between A and B = 9

Distance between A and C = 16

Distance between B and C = 25

Interpretation of these results is fairly straightforward. Populations A and B have the smallest distance, so they are the *most* similar to each other. Population C is the most distant and so is the least similar genetically. Further analysis would require additional data on the history and location of these groups to determine *why* population C is the most different. If, for example, you also knew that population C was on the other side of a mountain from populations A and B, then it would seem reasonable to assume that the mountain acted as a barrier to gene flow and caused population C's genetic dissimilarity.

Interpretation is difficult when more than three populations are being considered. For that reason, we often take the genetic distance measures and use them to construct what is known as a **genetic distance map,** a picture

genetic distance An average measure of relatedness between populations based on a number of traits.

genetic distance map
A picture showing the genetic relationships between populations,

based on genetic distance measures.

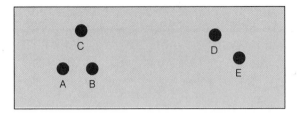

FIGURE 13.9
Example of a genetic distance map for five hypothetical populations (A, B, C, D, E). The closer populations are genetically, the closer they plot near each other on the map.

showing the genetic relationships between groups. These maps are easy to interpret—the closer two populations are on the map, the closer they are genetically. An example of a genetic distance map is shown in Figure 13.9, which shows five hypothetical populations (A, B, C, D, E). It is clear that populations A, B, and C are all similar to one another genetically, as is population D to population E. The most striking feature is that populations D and E are quite distant genetically from the other three populations. Additional data would be needed to determine why. Are D and E separated geographically from the other three populations? This would be easy to check: simply compare the genetic distance map with a geographic distance map. Other hypotheses, such as differences in religion or other cultural variables, could also be tested using a comparative approach. Several examples of genetic distance maps from actual studies will be presented in Chapter 14.

DEMOGRAPHIC MEASURES   Much information regarding the effect of genetic drift and gene flow can be extracted from analysis of demographic measures, especially population size and migration. These measures can be used to estimate the likely effect of genetic drift and gene flow by means of a variety of complex mathematical methods. If information is available for genetic traits, then these estimates can be compared with observed reality. This type of comparison allows us to test various assumptions of models and to determine the relative effect of gene flow and genetic drift. When genetic traits are not available, the analysis of demographic measures still provides us with an idea of the relative magnitude of genetic change *likely* under certain conditions.

The relationship between demographic measures and microevolution is relatively straightforward. Because the magnitude of genetic drift is related to population size (the smaller the population, the greater the effect of drift), a knowledge of population size can give us an estimate of the effects of genetic drift. Much gene flow is related to migration, so an analysis of marriage records and other vital statistical data can provide us with an idea of the relative magnitude of gene flow. Using appropriate models, scientists can consider the effects of gene flow and genetic drift simultaneously to predict genetic distances and then compare them with actual genetic distances. This approach also gives us an opportunity to study demographic shifts in histor-ical populations—groups for which we have no genetic data but do have demographic information.

The Analysis of Natural Selection

The analysis of natural selection in human populations is complex. Rather than set up laboratory experiments, most of the time we must rely on com-parisons of situations existing in nature. Consider the following hypotheti-cal situation. You are interested in testing the hypothesis that mammalian body size is related to temperature. If you were dealing with laboratory ani-mals such as mice, you would set up an experiment in which you would expose different groups of mice to different ambient temperatures and then determine what change, if any, takes place from one generation to the next. But what if you were interested in testing this hypothesis on elephants? It is unlikely you would be able to overcome the large number of practical diffi-culties involved in such a project. Where would you get enough space? How many elephants would you need? Could you obtain these elephants? Finally, you would also have to deal with the problem of a long generation length.

If you were interested in humans, the whole laboratory approach would be immoral and illegal in many societies, as well as impractical. Does this mean that the hypotheses cannot be tested? No, because you could examine a natural experiment. You would collect data on body size and temperature from human populations across the world to determine if a relationship in fact existed. Your study could be improved by trying to control for other effects. For example, you would not want to select an undernourished popu-lation from Africa and a well-nourished population from northern Europe because the differences in body size could be the result of both temperature and nutrition. Careful choice of samples in this type of natural experiment is critical. Though research on human populations is extremely difficult, the challenge is also part of the appeal for many biological anthropologists.

There are several approaches to measuring natural selection in human populations. The most direct method involves comparing measures of sur-vival and reproduction (fitness) among individuals with different genotypes. Another method is to look at regional or worldwide variation in a trait to determine if it has any relationship with climate or other environmental fac-tors. A third method is to look at the potential for natural selection by using measures of births and deaths from demographic data.

INDIVIDUAL GENETIC ASSOCIATIONS   Because natural selection refers to the process in which individuals with certain genetic characteristics are more likely to survive or reproduce, we want to determine whether individuals with certain genotypes have a greater probability of surviving or reproducing. If you were interested in looking at the potential effects of natural selection on the

MN blood group system, you would want to separate your sample into groups of individuals with the same genotype (MM, MN, or NN). You would then attempt to determine if there were any differences in mortality or fertility among these groups. For instance, do individuals with one genotype live longer than those with other genotypes? Is there any relationship between genotype and the individual's history of disease? Do individuals with certain genotypes have more surviving children than those with other genotypes? Are individuals with one genotype more likely to be sterile than others?

These questions, and others, can be answered in principle by looking at the associations among some measure of health, survival, or fertility and different genotypes. Suppose you were interested in whether or not different MN genotypes have different susceptibilities to diseases. You could select a group, determine its MN genotypes, and monitor its members for the rest of their lives to track their disease histories. Alternatively, you could select a group of individuals having had a given disease and compare their MN genotypes with those of a random sample of people who have not had the disease.

ENVIRONMENTAL CORRESPONDENCE   One way of looking for the effects of natural selection is to analyze patterns of variation over a large geographic region. Given that natural selection is related to environmental variation, differences among locations might reflect changes in environment and in genotype. The goal is to determine the level of correspondence between some aspect or aspects of the physical environment and a genotype. To test the idea that climate is related to body size, you would look at the distribution of body size and see how well it matches the distribution of climatic variables. Again, proper selection of your samples is necessary to ensure that you do not measure some other factor affecting biological variation. This method has other potential problems, such as the fact that migration can affect the level of correspondence. For example, if you were looking at the relationship of skin color and latitude, you would not want to include African Americans or European Americans in your analysis because they are relatively recent migrants to the United States.

DEMOGRAPHIC MEASURES   Natural selection operates on differences in mortality and fertility, both of which may be measured from demographic records. The death rate of a population is a measure of the proportion of deaths occurring within a given period of time. The birth rate measures fertility within a population. These measures can provide an idea of the overall potential for natural selection. They do not tell us what specific effect natural selection will have on a particular set of loci. These measures are also so highly dependent on cultural variation that we cannot always extrapolate to genetic factors. For example, two populations may show different disease rates. Even though it might be tempting to suggest that the difference in disease patterns is due to genetic differences, we must first control for other sources of this variation, cultural and environmental.

Nonetheless, demographic measures do provide us with some information about the potential for natural selection to operate (Crow 1958). With proper controls and research strategies, such measures can even be used to test biological hypotheses in the absence of any direct biological data. A good example of this approach is Meindl and Swedlund's (1977) study of mortality in the populations of Deerfield and Greenfield in historical Massachusetts. Historical data indicated that both populations experienced epidemics of childhood dysentery, a serious disease, between 1802 and 1803. Meindl and Swedlund used death records to determine the effect of these epidemics on the mortality of those who survived the disease. They found that the individuals who survived the disease actually lived longer than those who were not exposed to it. They concluded that the greater longevity of those individuals reflected, in part, genetic differences. One possible interpretation is that those who survived had genetic characteristics that gave them greater resistance to dysentery; this is natural selection in action. Another possibility is that those exposed to the disease developed stronger immune systems as a response. Such augmented resistance is a physiological response, although there is most likely also a genetic component involved. Though such demographic analyses cannot provide any definite answers regarding natural selection, they do provide useful supplements to traditional genetic analysis.

PROBLEMS IN ANALYSIS   Some problems are common to any study of natural selection in human populations, regardless of the specific methods of study. The methods described here can demonstrate a relationship between some measure of fitness and some environmental factor. Correlation does not necessarily imply causation, however. We still need to document the link among genetics, environment, and the action of natural selection.

For example, a high degree of association between a specific blood group genotype and a given disease is suggestive but not conclusive. To complete the analysis, it is necessary to look at the specific biochemical nature of the blood group genotype. What changes in biological structure are related to this genotype, and how do these changes relate to the specific disease? A knowledge of the biochemical nature of the blood groups is required to answer these questions.

Another potential problem is that whatever association we detect may not have been present in the past. It is also possible that natural selection operated on a specific allele in the past but no longer does so. Certain blood group genotypes, for example, are associated with susceptibility to the disease smallpox. Today, smallpox has been eradicated as the result of intensive health care and immunization programs. In the past, however, smallpox was devastating. Thus, smallpox may have been a factor in the natural selection of certain blood types in the past, but it is not at present.

We have an unfortunate tendency to view natural selection in terms of *major* differences between different genotypes. Natural selection is often looked at as an all-or-none phenomenon—one individual survives and another does not. In reality, natural selection often operates on very small differences between different genotypes. One genotype may have only a slight advantage—1 or 2 percent, or even lower—relative to another.

If natural selection works with small differences, then how can substantial change result? The key to understanding this problem is to realize that small changes can have large impacts over a long period of time. Like compound interest in a bank account, the effects of even small levels of natural selection can add up over long periods. Of course, such low amounts of natural selection may be difficult to detect in a single generation. Imagine a population of organisms where the average body weight is 10 kg (22 lb). Suppose there is a small amount of selection for those individuals with larger body sizes. Each generation, the average body size would increase in the population as a result of natural selection. Suppose the change is only one-tenth of 1 percent. The change in the first generation would be only from 10 kg to 10.001 kg, which is not noticeable. If this selection continues for 1,000 generations, however, the average body size would be over 27 kg (almost 60 lb). Also, remember that 1,000 generations is a very short time in evolution. Of course, change is not likely to occur in a steady, uniform manner. This hypothetical example, which is very simple, does show the cumulative nature of natural selection over long periods of time.

Slight differences in survival and reproduction, then, can add up over time. Slow change over time, however, poses a problem for our analyses of natural selection. If differences are slight, we may not be able to detect them in a short period of time, or we might require extremely large samples. Other evolutionary forces, such as drift and gene flow, would also alter the degree of change from one generation to the next. In many studies of human populations we find that gene flow "swamps" the effect of natural selection. This does not mean that we cannot study natural selection; it merely shows us one of the potential problems we must take into account.

SUMMARY

The study of human variation looks at the patterns and causes of biological diversity among living human beings. Human variation has been studied using a racial approach and an evolutionary approach. The biological concept of race emphasizes differences between groups and deemphasizes variation within groups. In the past, race was used as a crude means by which to describe patterns of human variation. A major problem in using race as a concept is that distinct "races" take on a reality of their own in people's minds. The race concept has limited use in analyses of biological variation, however, particularly for widespread species such as human beings. The race

concept uses arbitrary classifications of predominately continuous variation, does not account for patterns of variation among different traits, and
does not account for variation within groups. These problems aside, the race
concept is further limited because it is purely descriptive and offers no
explanation of variation.

The evolutionary approach looks at biological variation in terms of the
evolutionary forces of mutation, natural selection, gene flow, and genetic
drift. The focus of microevolutionary studies depends on the specific problem being analyzed. If the purpose is to look at average patterns reflecting
gene flow and genetic drift, then many traits are analyzed at the same time
(multivariate) because these two evolutionary forces affect all loci the same.
If the purpose is to look at natural selection, then one trait is analyzed at a
time (univariate) in order to find correlations with survival and/or reproduction. The microevolutionary approach is somewhat difficult to use for humans,
as compared to laboratory animals, because there are no controls. Nonetheless, various methods have been developed to extract as much information
as possible from patterns of human biological diversity.

SUPPLEMENTAL READINGS

Gould, S. J. 1981. *The Mismeasure of Man.* New York: W. W. Norton. An
    excellent review of the historical controversies regarding intelligence
    tests, which also addresses problems with the race concept.

Harrison, G. A., J. M. Tanner, D. R. Pilbeam, and P. T. Baker. 1988. *Human
    Biology: An Introduction to Human Evolution, Variation, Growth, and
    Adaptability.* 3d ed. Oxford: Oxford University Press.

Molnar, S. 1992. *Human Variation: Races, Types, and Ethnic Groups.* 3d ed.
    Englewood Cliffs, NJ: Prentice-Hall. This book and the preceding one by
    Harrison et al. (1988) provide information on patterns of human biolog-
    ical variation and the different approaches to their study.

Shipman, P. 1994. *The Evolution of Racism: Human Differences and the Use
    and Abuse of Science.* New York: Simon & Schuster. This book (as well
    as Marks' listed in Chapter 2) look at the race concept historically.

CHAPTER **14**

Human Microevolution

In this chapter, we examine several case studies of human microevolution in order to illustrate the different evolutionary approaches discussed in Chapter 13. The first part of this chapter deals with studies that look primarily at the joint effects of gene flow and genetic drift. The remainder of the chapter looks at several studies focusing on natural selection.

CASE STUDIES OF GENE FLOW AND GENETIC DRIFT

Many studies of human microevolution are concerned with population history. How are different populations related? Did they have different histories in terms of settlement or contact with other groups? Do invaders leave traces of their genes behind? Were populations always the same size, or did some grow and expand, while others shrank or became isolated? These are but a few of the types of questions that are dealt with when using biological data to answer questions of human history. The worldwide studies of human genetic variation that were used in Chapter 12 to examine questions of modern human origins are an example of this type of approach.

When we look at the biological history of human populations, we are looking at the joint effects of gene flow and genetic drift. Any past migrations, invasions, or contacts between peoples ultimately involves gene flow, so we can analyze gene flow in such a way as to reconstruct these past events. Because the history of human populations also involves changes in population size, we must also consider the effect of genetic drift. Looking at gene flow and genetic drift at the same time can be somewhat tricky. Imagine, for example, that you find two small, isolated populations that appear rather genetically distinct. Is this distinctiveness due to cultural or geographical isolation (low gene flow), or might it be due to the small size of the populations and the increased effect of genetic drift?

We must also remember that any attempt to reconstruct population history must involve as many traits as possible in order to get the best chance of seeing average patterns. In other words, we must use the multivariate approach discussed in Chapter 13. Again, the reason we do this is because gene flow and genetic drift are expected to have the same effect on *all* traits.

Three case studies are presented here to illustrate how we can analyze past patterns of gene flow and genetic drift. The first focuses on variation on a local level—small tribes in South America. The second looks at patterns of variation on a regional level—Irish counties. The third deals with variation across several continents—the genetic relationship of Jewish and non-Jewish populations.

Social Organization and Genetics of South American Indians of the Rain Forest

A number of genetic studies have been carried out on the tribal populations living in the rain forests of South America. Studies of these populations have allowed investigation into the ways in which the social structure of small tribes contributes to genetic diversity. Of course, the small size of the populations and their general isolated nature act to increase the likelihood of genetic drift. What makes these studies so fascinating is the specific social and political structures that act in certain ways to increase drift and in other ways to counter it.

Many of these populations have a fission-fusion structure. As populations grow, the limits of the environment are soon reached. Political factions develop, creating unrest within the local villages resulting from too many people in one place. When populations become too large, they will often fission into separate groups. Some of these separate groups will be too small to remain viable villages, and smaller groups may then undergo fusion to form a large group (Figure 14.1).

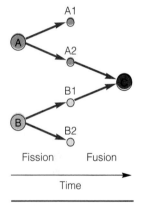

Fission   Fusion

Time

■ FIGURE 14.1
Fission-fusion social structure. Fissioning is the splitting of a population into two or more smaller populations. Fusioning is the merging of two or more populations into a larger population. Circles in this figure indicate the relative sizes of each population: populations A and B both split into two smaller populations; populations A2 and B1 then merge to form a larger population, C.

The Biological History of the Ancient Egyptians

The ancient Egyptians have long been a source of fascination. Egyptian civilization dates back roughly 5,000 years, and is best known because of its many pyramids. There have been many debates over the origin of the ancient Egyptians. Some argue that this population is distinctly related to Europeans, while others favor a sub-Saharan origin. Still others suggest that the ancient Egyptians did not come from any one specific group but rather represent an in-place evolution in northeastern Africa, with contact with other populations.

The origin of the ancient Egyptians has been argued on the basis of archaeology and other clues. Here, we examine what inferences can be made from patterns of biological variation. One example is given. Genetic distances were computed among 13 samples of ancient skulls—three populations each from sub-Saharan Africa, Europe, the Far East, and Australia, and a sample from the ancient Egyptians (26th–30th dynasties, dating between 2550 and 2150 years B.P.). The data consisted of 57 measurements of the skull and face, provided by Dr. W. W. Howells (Howells 1973, 1989). These data were used to estimate genetic distances (Relethford and Blangero 1990).

Different patterns of genetic distances would result depending on which historical hypothesis was correct. If, for example, the ancient Egyptians came primarily from Europe, then they should be most similar to European populations. If they came from sub-Saharan Africa, then they should be most similar to sub-Saharan African populations. If, however, the ancient Egyptians were not the result of primary movement from one region or another, then their biological relationships would be somewhere intermediate between other geographic regions.

The figure here shows the results very clearly. The ancient Egyptian sample does not cluster with either Europeans or sub-Saharan Africans. More extensive analyses have shown similar results (Brace et al. 1993)—the ancient Egyptians are Egyptian. Their biological affinities reflect their geographic position more than anything else. The fact that Egypt is part of the African continent does not mean that they are closer to other African populations than to non-African groups.

This analysis reveals an important feature of human variation. If we ignore Egypt for the moment, we can see four recognizable clusters—Europe, sub-Saharan Africa, the Far East, and Australia. The clear separation of these clusters seems to argue strongly for four distinct "races." Or does it? By adding Egypt to the analysis, we see the problem of inferring race from widespread geographic samples; other populations fall in between, thus forcing us to add a fifth "race." Of course, if we add still other groups, we have to continually increase our number of races. Our image of distinct races often results from not using a full sampling of humanity.

The formation of new, smaller villages from old (fission) is expected to lead to increased opportunity for genetic drift. The merging of smaller villages to form large ones (fusion) acts to some extent to counter the effects of genetic drift. Adding to this complex situation is the fact that all villages practice **exogamy** (finding a mate in another group) to some extent. Exogamous marriage results in gene flow between villages, which also acts to counter the effects of genetic drift.

Village fissioning is a form of the founder effect and is expected to lead to group differences because of genetic drift. The amount of genetic drift can be predicted and then compared to observed allele frequencies to test the hypothesis that genetic variation is being affected by drift. Following up on pioneering work by James Neel, Peter Smouse and colleagues (1982) performed extensive analyses on a number of genetic systems for several tribal

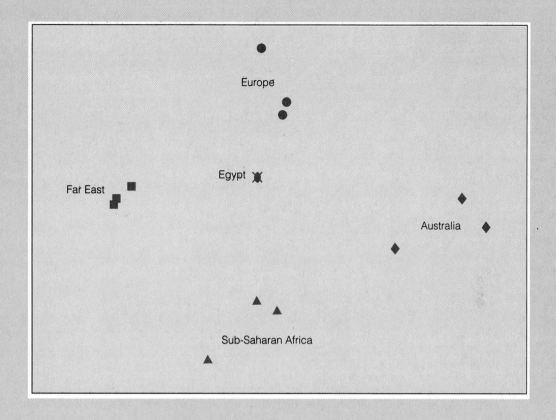

populations, such as the Yanomamo (Figure 14.2), and found the observed level of genetic differences between groups exceeded the level expected under random genetic drift. Closer analysis has shown that the village fissions were not random. Rather, many fissions take place along kinship lines. Instead of a random group of individuals forming a new village, often a group of related individuals does so. This nonrandom splitting actually enhances the effects of genetic drift because new villages are less likely to have an equal representation of alleles from the original population. Thus, the individual pattern of village fissioning adds to the effect of genetic drift.

Complicating matters further, mating practices add to the process of genetic drift in these populations. The marriage system in these societies is characterized by multiple wives for each man. Differences in local political power mean that some men have more wives than others and therefore

▲▲▲▲▲▲▲▲▲▲▲▲▲▲▲▲▲▲▲▲▲▲▲▲▲▲▲▲▲
exogamy The tendency to choose mates from outside the local population.

■ FIGURE 14.2
The Yanomamo Indians of the
South American rain forest.
(Courtesy of Napoleon A.
Chagnon)

contribute in greater frequencies to the next generation. Though the entire analysis of Smouse and colleagues is too lengthy to discuss here, it should be clear that the complexity of human populations can affect genetic drift in many ways.

The Vikings and Irish Population History

From the perspective of biological variation, the population history of Ireland is fascinating because of the numerous possibilities for gene flow in the island's past ("Ireland" refers here to the entire island, which is currently made up of two countries—the Republic of Ireland and Northern Ireland). In the past, Ireland has seen many different invasions and settlements from England, Scotland, Wales, and Scandinavia. What was the impact of these different sources of gene flow?

Relethford and Crawford (1995) investigated the patterns of biological variation among Irish populations using ten anthropometric measures of the

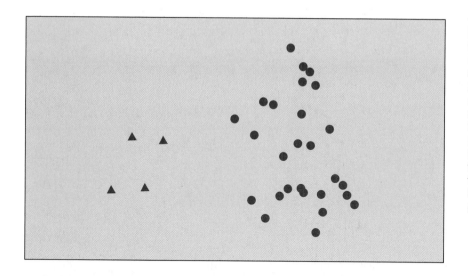

■ FIGURE 14.3
Genetic distance map of 31 Irish counties based on head and facial measurements of Irish adult males. The four counties indicated by diamonds are clearly separate from the remaining Irish counties (indicated by circles). As discussed in the test, these four counties lie in the Irish midlands and have a history of Viking contact. (Relethford and Crawford 1995)

head and face. With appropriate methods, anthropometric data can be used to derive genetic distances (Relethford and Blangero 1990). These data were originally collected during the 1930s on over 7,000 Irish adult men. Relethford and Crawford used the data to look at genetic distances between 31 Irish counties (political units). The genetic distance map is shown in Figure 14.3. The most obvious pattern of this map is the separation of four counties (marked as diamonds on the figure). These four counties are all located in the midlands of Ireland. Their common distance from all other Irish counties suggests some unique aspect of population history, reflecting gene flow and/or genetic drift.

What could be responsible for this difference? One possibility is gene flow from Viking invasion and settlement. Irish history reveals that the Vikings first came into contact with Ireland in A.D. 794 and continued through the early thirteenth century. Although some Viking settlements were on the coast, there were a number of substantial Viking movements into the Irish midlands. At least one of these incursions involved as many as 12,000 men, which would be expected to have a noticeable genetic impact. Relethford and Crawford (1995) suggest that the distinctiveness of the Irish midlands reflects this Viking influence, and that Viking settlements along the Irish coast had less impact because the genetic makeup of later migrants from England and Wales overrode any Viking influence.

If the Viking hypothesis is correct, then we should also see the Irish midlands, of all Ireland, to be the most genetically similar to the Scandinavian countries from which the Vikings originated (Norway and Denmark). Relethford and Crawford compared different regions of Ireland with data from several other European countries, including Norway and Denmark. The results, shown in Figure 14.4, show that the Irish midlands sample is

■ FIGURE 14.4
Genetic distance map comparing six regions of Ireland with data from Denmark, Norway, and England. The genetic distances were based on head and facial measurements. The Irish midlands are closest to Norway and Denmark, whose populations represent the source of Viking invaders to Ireland. This analysis supports the hypothesis of Viking gene flow. (Relethford and Crawford 1995)

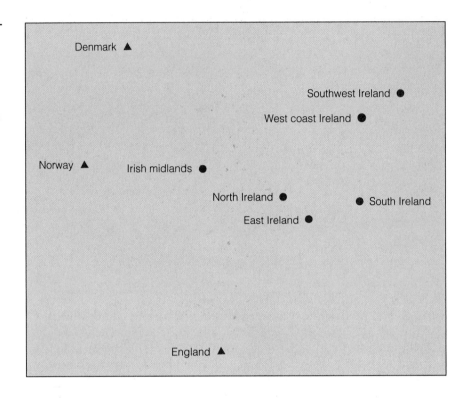

indeed genetically closest to the Scandinavian samples. Based on this comparative analysis and other information, Relethford and Crawford concluded that the Viking hypothesis was confirmed.

Genetic Relationships of Jewish and Non-Jewish Populations

The Jewish Diaspora resulted in Jews spreading throughout much of the world. Given religious and ethnic differences, often combined with discrimination in their new lands, many Jews remained culturally isolated. Based on microevolutionary theory, we would expect there to be genetic isolation as well. However, we know historically that intermarriage between Jews and non-Jews has often occurred, although at different rates in different times and places. What are the present-day genetic relationships between Jewish and non-Jewish populations? How much gene flow has there been between groups in the past? Are Jewish populations throughout the world more similar to each other, or more similar to their non-Jewish neighbors? Has genetic drift further complicated the picture, because many Jewish populations were small in size to begin with?

A number of studies have looked at these questions, often with mixed results. In a recent study, Relethford (1996) reexamined the questions using

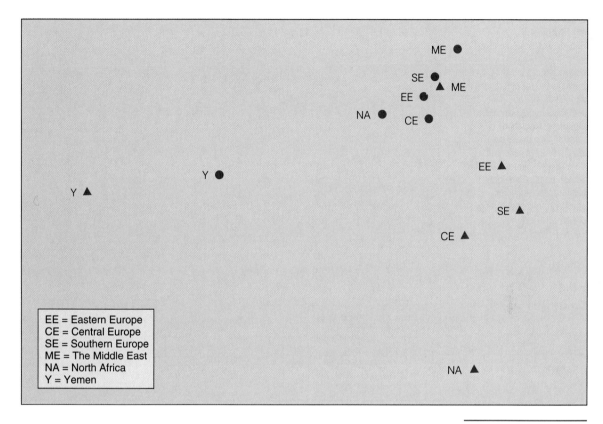

EE = Eastern Europe
CE = Central Europe
SE = Southern Europe
ME = The Middle East
NA = North Africa
Y = Yemen

■ FIGURE 14.5
Genetic distance map of six Jewish and six non-Jewish populations based on seven genetic loci. The dots indicate Jewish populations and the diamonds indicate their non-Jewish neighbors. (Relethford 1996, using data from Kobyliansky et al. 1982) The most genetically different populations are from the country of Yemen, whose small size had led to considerable genetic drift (compare with Figure 14.6).

data on seven genetic marker loci. These data, published originally by Kobyliansky and colleagues (1982), consist of allele frequencies for both Jewish and non-Jewish populations in six geographic regions: eastern Europe, central Europe, southern Europe, the Middle East, North Africa, and Yemen (the latter being representative of isolated groups). Figure 14.5 presents the genetic distance map for these 12 samples.

The first, and most obvious, feature of this genetic distance map is the separation of the two samples from Yemen from the other samples. This fits in with our knowledge of the isolated nature of the small Yemenite populations. Second, all of the remaining Jewish populations cluster together, supporting the hypothesis that the cultural isolation between Jewish and non-Jewish neighbors has had a genetic impact.

Although it is tempting to see the genetic distance map as reflecting cultural barriers to gene flow, the distinctive position of the two Yemenite samples suggests that genetic drift has complicated the basic picture. In addition, we have historical data showing that all other Jewish populations were considerably smaller than the non-Jewish populations, which means that their position on the distance map might also be affected by genetic drift. The

Genetic distance map using the same data and populations as in Figure 14.5 but adjusted for differences in population size and genetic drift. This figure provides a picture of population relationships that is not obscured by genetic drift. Compared to Figure 14.5, the Jewish populations (dots) cluster closer together, showing a recent common ancestry.

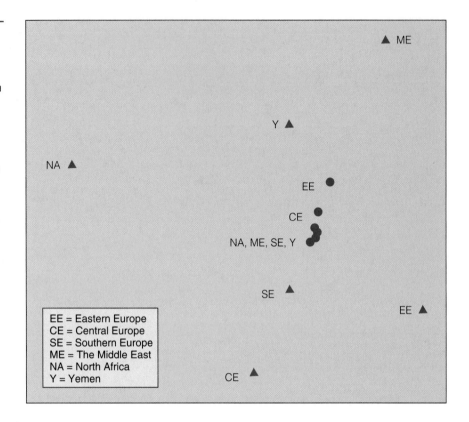

basic problem is trying to unravel the dual influences of gene flow and genetic drift in order to reconstruct history.

A new method of genetic distance analysis, developed by Relethford (1996), deals with this problem. Figure 14.6 shows the results of applying this method to the same genetic data as were used for Figure 14.5. There are two basic results. First, the non-Jewish populations (indicated by diamonds in Figure 14.6) are separated approximately to the degree that you would expect based on geographic location—the three European samples are separate from the samples from the Middle East, North Africa, and Yemen. Second, all the Jewish samples, including the Yemenite sample, form a tight cluster. Because the method used to construct Figure 14.6 controls for genetic drift, the historical connection among the geographically dispersed Jewish populations is much clearer than it is in Figure 14.5. The lower level of genetic differences among the Jewish samples (as compared to the non-Jewish samples) is expected based on the history of post-Diaspora Jews. The samples show greater similarity because they have been separate for a fairly short period of time in evolutionary terms. In conclusion, we see that Jewish populations tend to be more genetically similar to other Jewish populations

 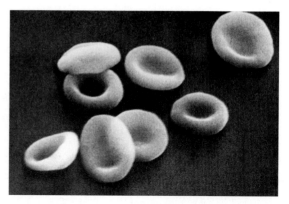

■ FIGURE 14.7
Sickle cell anemia. The blood cells on the left are twisted and deformed compared to the shape of normal red blood cells on the right. (© AP/Wide World Photos)

than to their non-Jewish neighbors, and that this similarity reflects a recent common historical origin. Genetic drift (reflected in Figure 14.5) obscures these basic findings to some extent.

CASE STUDIES OF NATURAL SELECTION

This section provides several examples of natural selection in human populations. Because natural selection operates differently on different loci, the focus will be on individual loci or traits rather than on specific populations.

Hemoglobin, Sickle Cell, and Malaria

Perhaps the best-known example of natural selection operating on a discrete genetic trait is the relationship of hemoglobin variants to malaria. One of the proteins in red blood cells is hemoglobin, which functions to transport oxygen to body tissues (see Chapter 2). The normal structure of the beta chain of hemoglobin is coded for by an allele usually called hemoglobin A. In many human populations, the A allele is the only one present, and as a result everyone has the AA, or normal adult hemoglobin, genotype.

HEMOGLOBIN VARIANTS   Many hemoglobin variants are produced by the mutation of an A allele to another form. The most widely studied mutations include hemoglobin S, C, and E. The S allele is also known as the sickle cell allele. A person who has two S alleles (genotype SS) has **sickle cell anemia,** a condition whereby the structure of the red blood cells is altered and oxygen transport is severely impaired (Figure 14.7). Roughly, only 15 percent of those with genotype SS survive to adulthood. An estimated 100,000 deaths per year throughout the world are from sickle cell anemia.

▲▲▲▲▲▲▲▲▲▲▲▲▲▲▲▲▲▲▲▲▲▲▲▲▲▲▲▲▲

sickle cell anemia A genetic disease occurring in a person homozygous for the sickle cell allele, which alters the structure of red blood cells.

■ **FIGURE 14.8**
Distribution of the sickle
cell allele in the Old World.
Compare high-frequency
areas with the high-frequency
areas of malaria in
Figure 14.9.

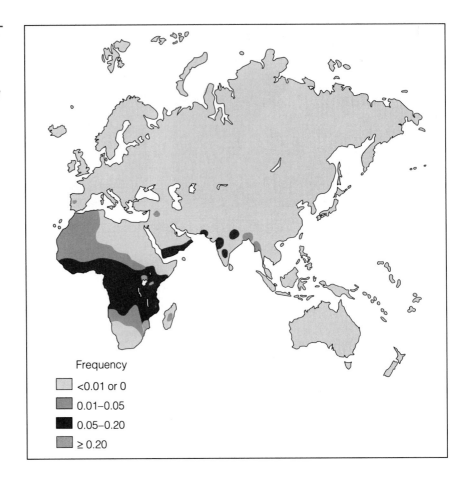

Frequency

☐ <0.01 or 0

☐ 0.01–0.05

■ 0.05–0.20

☐ ≥ 0.20

If the S allele is harmful in homozygotes, we expect natural selection to eliminate S alleles from the population in such a way that the frequency of S should be relatively low. Mutation introduces the S allele, but natural selection eliminates it. Indeed, in many parts of the world the frequency of S is extremely low, fitting the model of mutation balanced by selection. In a number of populations, however, the frequency of S is much higher—often up to 10 to 20 percent. Such high frequencies seem paradoxical, given the harmful effect of the S allele in the homozygous genotype. Why does S reach such high frequencies? Genetic drift might seem likely, except for the definite association of geography and higher frequencies of S. That is, higher frequencies of S occur only in certain environments. Genetic drift is random and influenced by population size, not environment. If genetic drift were responsible for the high frequencies of S, we would expect to see high frequencies in isolated groups in many different environments.

DISTRIBUTION OF THE SICKLE CELL ALLELE AND MALARIA   The distribution of the sickle cell allele is related to the prevalence of a certain form of malaria. Malaria is

■ **FIGURE 14.9**
Regions where falciparum
malaria is common.

an **infectious disease**—that is, a disease caused by the introduction into the body of an organic foreign substance, such as a virus or parasite (a disease that is not caused by an organic foreign substance is a **noninfectious disease**). Malaria is caused by a parasite that enters an organism's body, and four different species of the malarial parasite can affect humans. Malaria remains one of the major infectious diseases in the world today. In the late 1970s, as many as 120 million people in the world had some form of malaria (Encyclopaedia Britannica 1988).

The Old World shows a striking correspondence between higher frequencies of the S allele (Figure 14.8) and the prevalence of malaria caused by the parasite *Plasmodium falciparum* (Figure 14.9). This parasite is spread through the bites of certain species of mosquitoes. Except for blood transfusions, humans cannot give malaria to one another directly. Those areas with frequent cases of malaria, such as Central Africa, also have the highest frequencies

▲▲▲

infectious disease
A disease caused by
the introduction of

an organic foreign
substance into the body.

noninfectious disease
A disease caused by
factors other than

the introduction of
an organic foreign
substance into the body.

of the sickle cell allele. The falciparum form of malaria, the most serious of all forms of malaria, is often fatal.

The strong geographic correspondence suggests that sickle cell anemia and malaria are both related to the high frequencies of the S allele. Further experimental work has confirmed this hypothesis. Because the S allele affects the structure of the red blood cells, it makes the blood an inhospitable place for the malaria parasite.

In a malarial environment, people who are heterozygous (genotype AS) actually have an advantage. The presence of one S allele does not give the person sickle cell anemia, but it does change the blood cells sufficiently so that the malaria parasite does not have as serious an effect. Overall, the heterozygote has the greatest fitness in a malarial environment. As discussed in Chapter 3, this is a case of balancing selection, in which selection occurs for the heterozygote (AS) and against both homozygotes (AA from malaria and SS from sickle cell anemia).

In addition to greater survival of the heterozygote in malarial environments, it has also been suggested that women with genotype AS have greater fertility. If so, then is selection for the heterozygote in environments with malaria a function of differential mortality, differential fertility, or both? Madrigal (1989) studied this problem by examining the hemoglobin genotype and reproductive histories of women in Limon, Costa Rica. She found that there was no difference between AA and AS women for a number of measures of differential fertility (family size, number of pregnancies, number of live births, and number of spontaneous abortions).

If the effects of sickle cell anemia and malaria were equal, then we would expect the frequencies of the normal allele (A) and the sickle cell allele (S) ultimately to reach equal frequencies. The two diseases, however, are not equal in their effects. Sickle cell anemia is much worse. The balance between these two diseases is such that the maximum fitness of an entire population occurs when the frequency of S is somewhere between 10 and 20 percent.

An analysis of one African population suggests that for every 100 people with AS who survive to adulthood, 88 people with AA survive and only 14 of those with SS (Bodmer and Cavalli-Sforza 1976). Clearly, the relationship between hemoglobin, sickle cell anemia, and malaria represents a very strong case of natural selection. Instead of a difference in survival between genotypes of only several percent, the differences are quite striking. Such differences can lead to major changes in allele frequencies in a very short period of time. To illustrate the rapidity of such change, Figure 14.10 shows a hypothetical example of changes in the frequency of the sickle cell allele. In this example, the initial frequency of S from mutation was set equal to a reasonable estimate of 0.00001. The fitness values mentioned earlier were used to examine the kind of change in the frequency of S that could take place. Because the initial allele frequency is low, there is little change for the first 40 generations or so. (Of course, if the initial allele frequency were

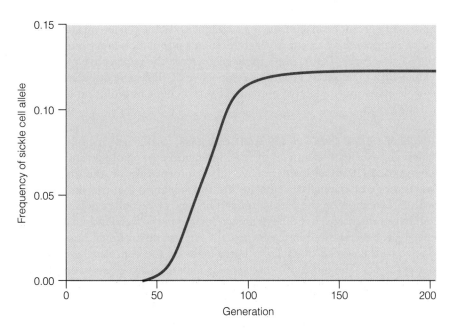

Reconstruction of past changes in sickle cell allele frequency in malarial Africa. This simulation assumes an initial allele frequency of 0.00001 caused by mutation. Relative fitness values are assumed constant over time: AA = 88%, AS = 100%, SS = 14%. The first 40 generations would show little change because the initial allele frequency was so low. After 40 generations, the allele frequency would increase rapidly, reaching an equilibrium after roughly 100 generations.

higher, the rate of change would be greater; a higher initial frequency could occur due to genetic drift or the initial occurrence of the mutation in a small population.) As the frequency of S increases, change takes place more rapidly because there are more people with the AS genotype to be selected for. After 100 generations, there is little change in the frequency of the S allele because it has reached an equilibrium based on the balance between the effects of sickle cell anemia and malaria. In this example, the sickle cell allele would reach an equilibrium frequency of 0.122. Of course, this simple illustration does not take other evolutionary forces into account, but it does show how quickly allele frequencies can change under strong natural selection.

The sickle cell example clearly shows the importance of the specific environment on the process of natural selection. In a nonmalarial environment, the AS genotype has no advantage, and the AA genotype has the greatest evolutionary fitness. In such cases, the frequency of the S allele is very low, approaching zero. In a malarial environment, however, the situation is different, and the heterozygote has the advantage. Clearly, we cannot label the S allele as intrinsically "good" or "bad"; it depends on circumstances.

The example of sickle cell also shows that evolution has a price. The equilibrium is one in which the fitness for the entire population is at a maximum. The cost of the adaptation, however, is an increased proportion of individuals with sickle cell anemia because the frequency of S has increased. People with the heterozygous genotype AS have the greatest fitness, but they also carry the S allele. When two people with the AS genotype mate, they have a 25 percent chance of having a child with sickle cell anemia (in the previous example, 1.5 percent of all children in a population is expected to have the SS genotype). This is not advantageous from the perspective of the individual with the disease. From the perspective of the entire population, however, it is the most adaptive outcome. Every benefit in evolution is likely to carry a price.

EFFECTS OF CULTURE CHANGE ON SICKLE CELL FREQUENCY   Sickle cell anemia also provides an excellent example of the interaction of biology and culture. Livingstone (1958) and others have taken information on the distribution and ecology of the malaria parasite and the mosquito that transmit it, along with information on the prehistory and history of certain regions in Africa, and have presented a hypothesis about changes in the frequency of the sickle cell allele. Several thousand years ago, the African environment was not conducive to the spread of malaria. Large areas of the continent consisted of dense forests. The mosquito that spreads malaria thrives best in ample sunlight and pools of stagnant water. Neither condition then existed in the African forests. The extensive foliage prevented much sunlight from reaching the floor of the forest. In addition, the forest environment was very absorbent, so water did not tend to accumulate in pools. In other words, the environment was not conducive to large populations of mosquitoes. Consequently, the malaria parasite did not have a hospitable environment, either.

This situation changed several thousand years ago when prehistoric African populations brought horticulture into the area. **Horticulture** is a form of farming employing only simple hand tools. As the land was cleared for crops, the entire ecology shifted. Without the many trees, it was easier for sunlight to reach the land surface. Continued use of the land changed the soil chemistry, allowing pools of water to accumulate. Both changes led to an environment ideal for the growth and spread of mosquito populations, and therefore the spread of the malaria parasite. The growth of the human population also provided more hosts for the mosquitoes to feed on, thus increasing the spread of malaria.

Before the development of horticulture in Africa, the frequency of the sickle cell allele was probably low, as it is in nonmalarial environments today. When the incidence of malaria increased, it became evolutionarily advantageous to have the heterozygote AS genotype because those who had it would have greater resistance to malaria without suffering the effects of sickle cell anemia. As shown earlier, this change could have taken place in a short period of time, roughly 100 generations, because of the large differences in fitness among hemoglobin genotypes. The initial introduction of the sickle cell allele, through mutation or gene flow, was followed by a rapid change, reaching an equilibrium point in which the fitness of the entire human population was at a maximum. Research suggests that the sickle cell mutation occurred several times in Africa (Labie et al. 1986), although Livingstone (1989) has argued for a one-time origin.

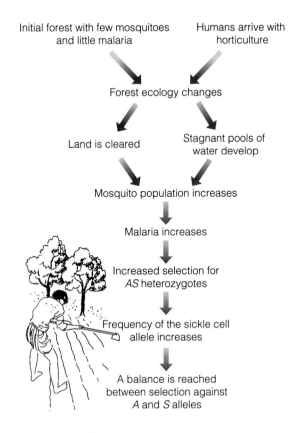

■ FIGURE 14.11
Sequence of cultural and environmental changes leading to changes in the frequency of the sickle cell allele in malarial Africa.

This scenario shows that human cultural adaptations (horticulture) can affect the ecology of other organisms (the mosquito and malaria parasite), which can then cause genetic change in the human population (an increase in the frequency of the sickle cell allele). This sequence of events is summarized in Figure 14.11.

Of course, we cannot observe these events directly because they occurred in the past. Nonetheless, all available evidence supports this hypothesis. We know the physiological differences between different hemoglobin types. We also know that low frequencies of S occur in nonmalarial environments and higher frequencies occur where there is malaria. Archaeological evidence shows when and where the spread of horticulture took place in Africa. From studies of modern-day agriculture, we also know that malaria spreads quickly following the clearing of land. Taking all this information together, we find the scenario for changes in the frequency of the sickle cell allele in Africa is most reasonable.

The study of human history also provides another example of the evolution of the sickle cell allele. In African-American populations, the frequency of S ranges from 0.02 to 0.06, which is higher than the frequency in

▲▲▲▲▲▲▲▲▲▲▲▲▲▲▲▲▲▲▲▲▲▲▲▲▲▲▲▲▲

horticulture A form of farming in which only simple hand tools are used.

European Americans (essentially zero), but less than that in malarial regions of Africa (Workman et al. 1963). The biological history of African Americans explains part of this difference; some degree of European admixture has taken place. This admixture would have the effect of reducing the frequency of S in African Americans. Extensive calculations have shown, however, that admixture is not the only factor operating. Researchers found that if admixture alone were operating, then the frequency of S in African Americans should be higher than it actually is. Another reason that the frequencies of the sickle cell allele are lower in African Americans than in West Africans is that natural selection has been operating to remove the S allele from the population. In general, malaria has not been epidemic in the United States. The slaves brought into the United States came from areas in Africa with high frequencies of malaria and the sickle cell allele. When they arrived in the United States, there was no longer the same evolutionary advantage for high frequencies of S because there was less malaria. As a result, the frequency of S has been reduced through natural selection, along with European admixture.

Sickle cell anemia is a health problem among modern African Americans. During the 1960s there was a tendency to label sickle cell anemia as a "black disease." The reason for higher levels of sickle cell anemia among African Americans has nothing to do with skin color but is rather the result of their ancestors coming from a malarial environment with high frequencies of the S allele. Sickle cell anemia is not confined to dark-skinned populations in Africa. High frequencies of S are also found in malarial environments in parts of Europe, India, and South Asia.

OTHER RELATIONSHIPS WITH MALARIA   A number of other genetic loci appear to have been affected by natural selection from malaria. Two different alleles of the hemoglobin locus, C and E, appear in high frequencies in certain malarial environments. Several inherited biochemical disorders, collectively known as thalassemia, are also related to malaria. These disorders do not directly affect the structure of the adult hemoglobin molecule but do interfere with its production. Another genetic trait, G6PD deficiency, leads to a deficiency of a certain enzyme and also appears to confer some resistance to malaria. It is not surprising to find a number of loci related to malaria because it is a severe disease, and any trait that alters the blood sufficiently to confer resistance to the parasite might be selected for over time.

Blood Groups and Natural Selection

The relationship between the sickle cell allele and malaria is the most well-studied example of natural selection for a discrete genetic trait in human populations. It is often frustrating that the situation is not as clear for other traits. The differences in fitness between different genotypes is often much less than that seen for the hemoglobin locus. Also, we often find evidence of multiple relationships between genetic traits and natural selection. It is often difficult to determine which factor is the most important or which was initially responsible for the evolution of a trait.

The human blood groups have been the subject of many investigations of natural selection. There are many different blood groups, defined on the basis of the type of molecules present on the surface of the red blood cells. Some blood groups are associated with different antibodies that react to various substances invading the blood stream (foreign antigens). Two blood groups—MN and ABO—have already been mentioned in previous chapters. Other red blood cell groups include Rhesus, Diego, Duffy, Lutheran, Lewis, and Xg, to name but a few. Some of these blood groups appear to be neutral in terms of natural selection, or perhaps we just have not been able to detect any effects. Also, some may have been selected for or against in the past, but not at present. Others are definitely related to natural selection, but in ways that are difficult to discern.

RHESUS BLOOD GROUP The Rhesus blood group (also called the Rh blood group) has a complicated mode of genetic inheritance involving three linked loci called C, D, and E. One locus, D, is particularly important in terms of natural selection. This locus has two alleles, *D* and *d*, where *D* is dominant. Individuals with genotypes *DD* or *Dd* are called *Rh positive*, and those with genotype *dd* are called *Rh negative*. Those with Rh positive blood have certain antigens in their red blood cells (D), and those with Rh negative blood can produce an opposing antibody (anti-D). In terms of blood chemistry, anti-D antibodies can destroy red blood cells with D molecules on their surface.

Selection occurs for the Rhesus blood group through **Rhesus incompatibility,** a condition in which a pregnant woman and her fetus have incompatible Rhesus blood groups. Rhesus incompatibility occurs when an Rh negative mother has an Rh positive fetus. Normally, the circulatory systems of mother and fetus are separate, but some blood may leak across the placenta in both directions or enter the mother's bloodstream at the time of delivery. The fetus's blood carries D molecules. When these molecules enter the mother's bloodstream, the mother's immune system produces anti-D antibodies to destroy the red blood cells carrying these "invaders." Once produced, the antibodies can leak back across a placenta to destroy blood cells of a fetus. The destruction of fetal blood cells leads to a form of anemia that can be fatal (Figure 14.12). Interestingly, Rhesus incompatibility is generally not a problem for the first Rh positive fetus born to the mother. The antibodies need time to be produced, and the first Rh positive infant's blood is rarely affected.

Today, Rhesus incompatibility is less of a problem than it once was because we can check blood types and use various techniques to control its effects. In the past, and even in many parts of the world today, this anemia

▲▲▲▲▲▲▲▲▲▲▲▲▲▲▲▲▲▲▲▲▲▲▲▲▲▲▲▲▲

Rhesus incompatibility
A condition in which a pregnant woman and her fetus have incompatible Rhesus blood group phenotypes.

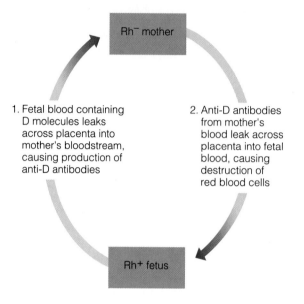

1. Fetal blood containing D molecules leaks across placenta into mother's bloodstream, causing production of anti-D antibodies

2. Anti-D antibodies from mother's blood leak across placenta into fetal blood, causing destruction of red blood cells

■ **FIGURE 14.12**
Sequence of events in Rhesus incompatibility between an Rh⁻ mother and an Rh⁺ fetus. Because it normally takes time to produce anti-D antibodies, the first Rh⁺ fetus is not affected. Subsequent Rh⁺ fetuses, however, are affected.

often resulted in death. From an evolutionary standpoint, this is selection against the heterozygote. An Rh negative mother has genotype *dd*, which means that the fetus will receive a *d* allele from her. A fetus with a *d* allele from the mother requires a *D* allele from the father to be Rh positive. The fetus will then have the heterozygous genotype *Dd*. We also know that the father of a heterozygous fetus is RH positive because that is the only way he could contribute a *D* allele to the fetus. Table 14.1 lists all possible matings between a man and woman according to their genotypes.

Selection against the heterozygote eliminates both alleles from the population in equal amounts. Given enough time, such selection will result in the loss of the initially less common allele (unless the initial allele frequencies were 0.5). For Rhesus incompatibility, there is selection against some heterozygous fetuses, and we should see the total elimination of one allele or the other. The *D* allele is more common in human populations today, so we should ultimately see the elimination of the rarer *d* allele if we can assume no other factors are operating on the evolution of this blood group system. A number of human populations, such as Pacific Islanders and Native Americans, appear to have had no *d* alleles before admixture with European groups. The frequency of the *d* allele is higher in other parts of the world.

One possible explanation for high frequencies of the *d* allele is that it is *gradually* being eliminated and ultimately will have a frequency of zero. The fact that different populations have different frequencies of the *d* allele, however, suggests that factors such as genetic drift and gene flow may also be responsible for the observed pattern of Rhesus blood groups. The possibility exists as well that incompatibility is not the only factor involved in nat-

■ **TABLE 14.1**
Possible Rhesus-incompatible Matings

MOTHER		FATHER		
GENOTYPE	PHENOTYPE	GENOTYPE	PHENOTYPE	INCOMPATIBLE MATING
DD	Rh⁺	DD	Rh⁺	No
DD	Rh⁺	Dd	Rh⁺	No
DD	Rh⁺	dd	Rh⁻	No
Dd	Rh⁺	DD	Rh⁺	No
Dd	Rh⁺	Dd	Rh⁺	No
Dd	Rh⁺	dd	Rh⁻	No
dd	Rh⁻	DD	Rh⁺	Yes, 100%
dd	Rh⁻	Dd	Rh⁺	Yes, 50%
dd	Rh⁻	dd	Rh⁻	No

ural selection for or against Rhesus genotypes. For example, Gloria-Bottini and colleagues (1992) have found that the infants of diabetic mothers heterozygous at the Rhesus C locus have a lower incidence of hypoglycemia than other infants. This suggests selection *for* a heterozygote. In addition, glucose intolerance was less severe among women who were homozygous for the *e* allele at the E locus (selection against a dominant allele). There is also evidence that selection at the Rhesus loci is affected by the presence or absence of other blood groups, as discussed later in this section.

ABO BLOOD GROUP The ABO blood group is the most widely studied simple genetic trait in human populations. As shown in Chapters 2 and 13, there are three different alleles (A, B, O) in this group: A and B are codominant and O is recessive. There are four possible phenotypes: type A (genotypes *AA* and *AO*), type B (genotypes *BB* and *BO*), type O (genotype *OO*, and type AB (genotype *AB*).

Worldwide, the O allele is the most common, the A allele is next most frequent, and the B allele is the least common. The allele frequencies of all human populations fall within certain limits. The frequency of the O allele ranges from 0.4 to 1.0, the frequency of the A allele ranges from 0 to 0.55, and the frequency of the B allele ranges from 0 to 0.3 (Brues 1977). These allele frequencies are too high to be explained by mutation alone (because mutation occurs at low rates). Gene flow, genetic drift, and natural selection must be considered as possible explanations.

If the evolution of the ABO blood group system were totally the result of drift and gene flow, we would expect to see a wider range of allele frequencies. For example, we expect to see populations with frequencies such as A = 0.8, B = 0.1, and O = 0.1. Of the hundreds of human populations studied for the ABO blood group to date, however, none is in this range. The

■ TABLE 14.2
ABO Blood Group Phenotypes and Antibodies

GENOTYPES	PHENOTYPE	ANTIGENS	ANTIBODIES
AA AO	A	A	anti-B
BB BO	B	B	anti-A
AB	AB	A, B	none
OO	O	none	anti-A, anti-B

fact that the allele frequencies fall within a certain range suggests that natural selection has been operating to keep the frequencies for the entire species within certain limits.

One possible clue to the effects of natural selection on the ABO blood groups is that certain antibodies are associated with different blood groups. Recall from Chapter 13 that there are two antibodies in the ABO system: anti-A and anti-B. Unlike the Rhesus system, the ABO antibodies are present throughout an individual's life. The anti-A antibody reacts to destroy A-type molecules, and the anti-B antibody reacts to destroy B-type molecules. There is no antibody for O. People with blood type A have the anti-B antibody, people with blood type B have the anti-A antibody, people with blood type O have both, and people with blood type AB have neither (Table 14.2). The fact that individuals with different ABO blood types have different antibodies has important implications for blood transfusions. If you have blood type A, you must not receive a blood transfusion from someone with blood type B. If you do, your anti-B antibodies will attack and destroy the incoming B molecules, with very harmful effects. Of course, any transfusion must also take into account other factors, such as Rhesus blood type.

The fact that different blood types have different antibodies also has implications for natural selection and susceptibility to different diseases. If you have blood type A, and hence anti-B antibodies, your immune system will tend to fight off any microorganisms that are biochemically similar to type B molecules. For example, the microorganism that causes venereal syphilis is biochemically similar to A molecules. Therefore, people with blood types B and O will have greater resistance to syphilis because they have the anti-A antibodies. People with blood types A and AB will not have this resistance because they lack the anti-A antibodies. It has been suggested that a link exists between various ABO blood types and a number of infectious diseases, such as smallpox, typhoid, influenza, bubonic plague, and others. Many of these diseases were indeed serious in the past, and differential resistance could be a possible factor in explaining the range of allele frequencies for the ABO system. More work, however, needs to be done to substantiate these claims.

In any case, the action of natural selection is complex because of the wide variety of different disease microorganisms and their relationships to ABO blood types. It has been suggested that each blood type is more susceptible than others to certain diseases. For example, type A seems more susceptible to smallpox, type B seems more susceptible to infantile diarrhea, and type O seems more susceptible to bubonic plague. If these theories are verified, it seems that the frequencies of the ABO alleles are subject to a variety of different types of selection. This makes analysis extremely difficult.

The distribution of the ABO alleles is to some extent consistent with selection and infectious disease. India, for example, is a region with a high frequency of the *B* allele (Roychoudhury and Nei 1988). India also has a history of frequent epidemics of both smallpox and bubonic plague. Because blood type O is more susceptible to plague, O alleles would be removed from the population. Because type A is more susceptible to smallpox, A and O alleles would be removed from the population. The net result would be a relatively higher frequency of the *B* alleles—precisely what is found in India.

ABO blood types also appear to be related to noninfectious diseases. Some hospital studies have suggested that people with blood type O have a greater chance of getting duodenal and stomach ulcers (this might be related to antibodies because recent work has confirmed that some ulcers are actually infectious in nature, being caused by bacteria). People with blood type A have a greater chance of getting certain forms of cancer. The differences between the phenotypes appear strong, but we do not understand the reasons for these associations. In any case, it is unclear what evolutionary importance these associations have. Most of the noninfectious diseases have severe effects late in life and therefore should not be subject to natural selection because they usually occur after an individual's reproductive life is over. Some people, however, do acquire these diseases early enough in life so that at least the possibility exists that natural selection could be operating through differential survival to noninfectious diseases. We must demonstrate, however, that such selection did (or does) in fact take place, and not merely that it is possible.

Natural selection may also be operating on ABO blood groups as a consequence of incompatibility between mother and fetus. As with the Rhesus blood group, incompatible matings will often lead to the destruction of red blood cells in the fetus. Most often, ABO incompatibility will lead to spontaneous abortion early in prenatal life. Incompatibility occurs when the mother's blood has an antibody corresponding to the type of molecule present in the fetus's blood. An example of incompatibility is a woman with blood type A whose fetus is blood type AB. The woman's blood contains anti-B antibody, which reacts with the B molecules present in the fetus's blood. All possible types of incompatibility between mother and fetus are listed in Table 14.3. Note that in each case the genotype of the fetus is heterozygous. This suggests selection against some heterozygotes.

To make matters more complicated, it turns out that ABO incompatibility affects Rhesus incompatibility. To be incompatible for both is less

■ TABLE 14.3
ABO Blood Group Maternal-Fetal Incompatibilities

MOTHER'S GENOTYPE	INCOMPATIBLE FETAL GENOTYPES
AA	AB
AO	AB, BO
BB	AB
BO	AB, AO
AB	None
OO	AO, BO

severe than to be incompatible for either one alone! The reason for this effect is not known, but it appears that ABO incompatibility prevents the build-up of anti-D antibodies when Rhesus incompatibility is present. As the fetal red blood cells enter the mother's bloodstream, the ABO incompatibility destroys them before they can stimulate the production of anti-D. This effect shows how complicated the effects of natural selection can be, and how important it is to look at the entire organism and not just at isolated genetic traits.

There seems to be little doubt that natural selection has affected allele frequencies for the ABO blood group system. Studies have shown the relationship among blood type and incompatibility, infectious disease, and noninfectious disease. It does not appear likely that any one of these factors is solely responsible for the observed allele frequency range in human beings. It is also possible that there are other factors of which we are unaware. A further complication is that we generally have data on ABO phenotypes and not on genotypes. Our blood tests can tell us if someone is blood type A, but they cannot tell us if that person has the AA or AO genotype. Simply because we cannot tell the difference, however, does not mean that natural selection does not affect these genotypes in different ways. As we develop more sophisticated methods of genetic analysis, we may be able to look more closely at the relationship between selection and genotype for the ABO system.

Lactase Deficiency

As shown in the sickle cell example, cultural variation can affect genetic variation. **Lactase deficiency** is another example of a genetic trait that is influenced by cultural factors. As mammals, human infants receive nourishment from mother's milk. Infants have an enzyme, lactase, that allows milk sugar, lactose, to be digested. In most human populations, the manufacture of the lactase enzyme is "turned off" by four years of age as it is in most mammals after infancy. A person who has a deficiency of this enzyme as a child or adult will not be able to digest milk efficiently and can develop severe cramps, diarrhea, and other intestinal problems if he or she consumes it. The genetics of adult lactase deficiency are not fully understood, but it may be caused by a recessive allele. The environment may also exert some influence because individuals who are lactase-deficient may be able to build up some ability to digest milk over time. Though lactase deficiency is probably not a "simple" discrete trait, the available evidence does suggest a relatively simple mode of inheritance.

Most human populations have high frequencies of lactase deficiency, but some populations do not. The enzyme continues to be produced throughout life, and these people can continue to digest milk sugar. Interestingly, a clear relationship exists between the frequency of lactase deficiency

■ **TABLE 14.4**
Frequencies of Lactase Deficiency in Some Human Populations

POPULATION		PERCENTAGE OF LACTASE DEFICIENCY
African ancestry	African Americans	70–77
	Ibos	99
	Bantus	90
	Fulani	22
	Yoruba	99
	Baganda	94
Asian ancestry	Asian Americans	95–100
	Thailand	97–100
	Eskimos	72–88
	Native Americans	58–67
European ancestry	European Americans	2–19
	Finland	18
	Switzerland	12
	Sweden	4

Sources: Lerner and Libby (1976:327); Molnar (1992:124)

in a population and whether or not the population is involved in dairy farming. Table 14.4 lists the frequency of lactase deficiency in a number of populations of African, Asian, and European ancestry. In general, the lowest frequency is found in populations of European ancestry with a known history of dairy farming. The highest frequency of lactase deficiency occurs in populations of African and Asian ancestry that did not practice dairy farming. Populations that rely extensively on cheese products generally do not conform to this pattern, probably reflecting the fact that the lactose is broken down in the process of cheese making. The digestion of cheese is not accomplished by the lactase enzyme but by certain intestinal enzymes and bacteria.

The correspondence of low frequencies of lactase deficiency and dairy farming suggests that the ability to digest milk later in life is selected for in environments where milk is a major source of nutrition. This circumstance suggests that humans originally had very high frequencies of lactase deficiency and that as populations grew to rely more and more on milk in their diet after infancy, natural selection acted to decrease the proportion of those with lactase deficiency. After all, we would expect higher survival and reproduction in those individuals best able to utilize available nutrition. An examination of some discrepancies in the usual pattern of frequencies in Table 14.4 supports this hypothesis. Many African populations, such as the Ibos and Bantus, are known horticultural populations that do not practice dairy

▲▲▲▲▲▲▲▲▲▲▲▲▲▲▲▲▲▲▲▲▲▲▲▲▲▲▲▲▲
lactase deficiency A condition in which an older child or adult lacks the ability to produce the lactase enzyme needed to digest milk sugar.

farming. The Fulani, however, are a group of African nomadic cattle herders who rely extensively on milk in their diet. The percentage of lactase deficiency among the Fulani is low (22 percent) and similar to the percentage found in European populations. African Americans have high rates of lactase deficiency, but much lower than those populations found in West Africa from whom they are descended. The reduction in the frequency of lactase deficiency among African Americans may represent European admixture, physiological adaptation to milk diets, and/or some degree of natural selection.

Lactase deficiency provides a good example of rapid natural selection in human populations. Dairy agriculture is less than 12,000 years old, and the observed differences among dairy- and nondairy-producing economies must have arisen since then. The study of lactase deficiency also helps us understand something about policy decisions in the modern world. In the United States, which has a large dairy economy, milk is regarded as an essential part of daily nutrition. We think of milk as intrinsically good and in the past have sent milk to peoples in underdeveloped countries in the belief that what is good for us must be good for them. It was soon realized, however, that many of these people were lactase-deficient and the milk was not useful to them. In fact, it was often harmful. We should always consider differences in biology, culture, and environment in formulating policy decisions.

Skin Color

Human skin color is a complex trait. Several studies have shown that skin color is a polygenic trait although it is not clear how many loci might be involved (Byard 1981). Skin color has a strong genetic component (Williams-Blangero and Blangero 1992) and is affected by the environment, such as the amount of direct sunlight.

THE BIOLOGY OF SKIN COLOR   Skin color is caused by three pigments. One pigment, *melanin*, is responsible for the majority of variation in lightness and darkness in skin color. Melanin is a brown pigment secreted by cells in the bottom layer of the skin. All human populations appear to have the same number of melanin-producing cells. Variation in the darkness of the skin depends on how many cells actually produce melanin and how they cluster together (Szabo 1967). The more they cluster, the darker the skin color.

Another pigment affecting skin color is *hemoglobin*, which gives oxygenated blood cells their red color. Light-skinned people have little melanin near the surface of the skin and so the red color shows through. Because of this effect, "white" people are actually "pink." A third pigment is *carotene*, a yellowish pigment obtained from certain foods. A person who eats these foods in sufficient amounts may notice a yellowish tinge to the skin. Carotene, however, is *not* responsible for the yellowish hue of many Asian popula-

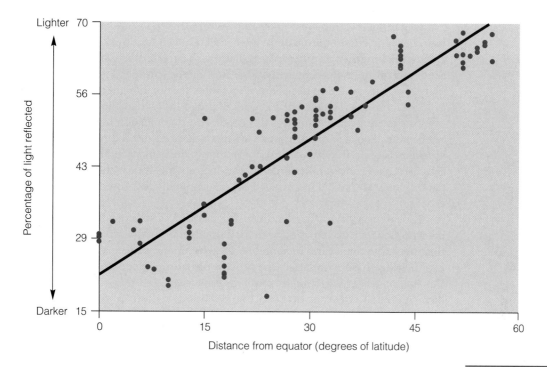

tions. Their coloring is caused instead by a thickening of the outer layer of the skin.

Skin color is also affected to a certain extent by sex and age. In general, males are darker than females, probably because of differential effects of sex hormones on melanin production. Age also produces variation. The skin darkens somewhat during adolescence, particularly in females.

THE DISTRIBUTION OF SKIN COLOR   The worldwide distribution of human skin color among native populations shows a striking correspondence with latitude. Figure 14.13 shows the relationship between skin color and distance from the equator for 93 male samples from the Old World. Native populations closer to the equator tend to be the darkest, while those farther from the equator tend to be the lightest. Note that there are no discrete breaks. Skin color shows a continuous distribution, and not separation into "light," "medium," and "dark" races. The distribution of skin color and latitude corresponds to the amount of ultraviolet radiation received at the earth's surface. Because of the way sunlight strikes the earth, ultraviolet radiation is strongest at the equator and diminishes in strength as we move away from the equator. It is even more diminished where cloud cover is extensive.

SKIN CANCER, SUNBURN, AND ULTRAVIOLET RADIATION   What are the biological effects of ultraviolet radiation? This radiation causes the skin to tan—that is, to

■ **FIGURE 14.13**
Geographic distribution of human skin color for 93 human Old World populations (males). Circles indicate the mean skin reflectance measured at a wavelength of 685 nanometers plotted against the distance, in degrees of latitude, from the equator. The solid line indicates the best-fitting linear curve relating skin reflectance and latitude. (*All data from published literature*)

produce more melanin. Too much exposure burns the skin, leading to infection. In sufficient amounts, ultraviolet radiation can lead to skin cancer. The greater the intensity of ultraviolet radiation, the greater the risk for skin cancer at any given level of pigmentation. Among the European-American population of the United States, skin cancer rates are much higher in Texas than in Massachusetts (Damon 1977). Dark-skinned individuals have lower rates of skin cancer because the heavy concentration of melanin near the surface of the skin blocks some of the ultraviolet radiation. Accordingly, the correspondence of latitude and skin color may reflect, in part, the differential effects of skin cancer. Ultraviolet radiation is strongest near the equator, and dark skin is advantageous in such an environment to protect against skin cancer.

Researchers have argued against skin cancer as a selective factor, suggesting that skin cancer, like many cancers, affects mostly older individuals past their reproductive years. If someone dies from skin cancer after reproducing, their death does not affect the process of natural selection. According to this line of reasoning, some researchers have suggested that skin cancer has had a minimal effect, at best, on the evolution of human skin color (e.g., Blum 1961).

The problem with this argument is that the evidence does not support it. Robins (1991) points out that all albinos studied in Nigeria and Tanzania either had skin cancer or precancerous skin lesions by 20 years of age. People are normally dark skinned in these countries, and the albinos, because of a rare genetic condition, would be particularly susceptible to the harmful effects of ultraviolet radiation. From an evolutionary standpoint, the important finding is that skin cancers and precancerous conditions occur *early* in life, contrary to the opinion that they are generally found among the elderly. In addition, only 6 percent of Nigerian albinos are in the age range of 31 to 60 years, compared to 20 percent of nonalbinos. This indicates that fewer albinos survive their younger years. Thus, skin cancer could have been a powerful selective agent, particularly among early humans who had limited protection from the sun.

Sunburn could also have been an important factor in natural selection. Severe sunburn can lead to infection and can interfere with the body's ability to sweat efficiently. Dark skin could protect from these effects, and thus be selected for.

Natural selection related to skin cancer and sunburn may be part of the answer to the question of worldwide skin color variation, but it is not the entire answer. Even though there is less ultraviolet radiation farther away from the equator and light-skinned people would have less risk for skin cancer and sunburn, this does not explain *why* light skin evolved in such regions. The model only shows that light skin *could* evolve. Skin cancer and sunburn help explain dark skin near the equator but do not explain light skin farther away from the equator.

THE VITAMIN D HYPOTHESIS   A more subtle effect of ultraviolet radiation is the synthesis of vitamin D, a nutrient needed by humans for proper bone growth. Today we may receive vitamin D either through vitamin supplements or through the injection of vitamin D into our milk. Both of these dietary modifications are relatively recent human inventions, however. Formerly, humans had to obtain their vitamin D through diet or from stimulation of the synthesis of certain chemical compounds by ultraviolet radiation. Some foods, such as fish oils, are high in vitamin D but are not found in all environments. For most human populations in the past the major source of vitamin D was the sun.

Because vitamin D synthesis depends on ultraviolet radiation, it seems reasonable to assume that more of it will be produced near the equator, where ultraviolet radiation is strongest. It has been suggested that too much or too little of the vitamin is harmful to the human body. An excess of vitamin D can lead to vitamin poisoning, cause calcification of soft tissues, and interfere with proper kidney functioning, while a lack of it can lead to poor bone development and maintenance, including diseases, such as rickets, that lead to deformed bones. Such health hazards can affect fertility as well as mortality. One frequent consequence of childhood rickets is the deformation of a woman's pelvic bones, which can hinder or prevent successful childbirth. In one U.S. study, only 2 percent of European-American women had such pelvic deformities as compared to 15 percent of African-American women (Molnar 1992). This difference presumably relates to skin color; darker women are unable to absorb enough vitamin D for healthy bone growth.

The idea that vitamin D intake must lie in a certain range, without excess or deficit, is at the core of the vitamin D hypothesis of skin color evolution (Loomis 1967). According to this hypothesis, in regions close to the equator, where ultraviolet radiation is the greatest, darker skin serves to block the harmful effects of excessive vitamin D production. In areas farther away, dark skin blocks too much of the sun's rays, which leads to insufficiency of vitamin D. Natural selection thus produced a change toward lighter skin color, that would be adaptive in such environments.

The vitamin D hypothesis thus explains the entire distribution of human skin color, showing the adaptive significance of both dark skin and light skin in different environments. Although logical, some investigations have suggested that this model is *not* correct. Holick and colleagues (1981) have shown that vitamin D synthesis reaches a maximum level during continued exposure to ultraviolet radiation. A light-skinned person's prolonged exposure to ultraviolet radiation will *not* lead to toxic vitamin D levels.

Though the vitamin D hypothesis does not hold up as an explanation for dark skin near the equator, can it still be used to explain the occurrence of light skin farther away from the equator? Robins (1991) listed a number of reasons why the vitamin D hypothesis fails here as well. First, rickets is a disease associated with recent urbanization. It is essentially absent in rural areas, and there is little evidence of rickets in the fossil record of our ancestors (who lived in rural, not urban, conditions). Second, although dark skin is not as effective as light skin in synthesizing vitamin D, it is still effective enough for production and maintenance of proper vitamin D levels. Laboratory studies have shown that African Americans can produce their maximum quota of vitamin D in three hours. Though this is not as fast as for European Americans (30 minutes), it is still effective enough for proper health except under conditions of modern urbanization, such as smog and tall buildings that cut down on exposure. Studies have also determined that dark-skinned peoples could produce and maintain sufficient vitamin D in northern climates even with only their heads, necks, and hands exposed to ultraviolet radiation. This is an important point because in cold climates less of the body would be exposed. In sum, the relationship between rickets and limited vitamin D appears confined to recent urban areas and is also associated with lower social class (the poor have less money for milk). For conditions typical of our ancestors, dark skin would *not* be at a disadvantage in terms of limited vitamin D production.

SKIN COLOR AND COLD INJURY   The vitamin D hypothesis, as just noted, does not hold true when explaining the distribution of human skin color, and we must look for other answers. One possibility for the occurrence of light skin at distances away from the equator is cold injury. Reviewing a wide range of data, Post and colleagues (1975) noted that, in cold climates, dark-skinned individuals are at greater risk for frostbite than light-skinned individuals. Data reporting this difference are available on soldiers in World Wars I and II, the Korean War, and those stationed in Alaska during the late 1950s. For example, during the Korean War, African-American soldiers were over four times more likely to get frostbite than European-American soldiers. Closer analysis of the data from the Korean War shows that this difference persists even after controlling for other sociological and health factors.

These observations suggest that in the colder northern climates darker skin is more prone to cold injury than lighter skin, a hypothesis supported by laboratory experiments on piebald guinea pigs (having both light and dark skin). Cold injury could be induced more frequently and more severely in the darker-skinned animals.

Existing evidence allows a model for the evolution of light skin in northern climates to be developed. Because the fossil record shows the first human ancestors evolved in or near equatorial Africa, it seems likely they had darker skin. As human ancestors left the continent, they moved into different environments, including colder climates in the north. Once there, selection pressure for dark skin was reduced because there was less ultraviolet radiation and less risk of skin cancer and sunburn. Lighter skin, however, would be advantageous because those individuals would be at less risk for cold injury. Today, many of these problems can be eliminated with cultural adaptations, such as clothing and shelter. In earlier times, however, the direct effect of the physical environment was more intense.

At present, the evidence supports skin cancer and sunburn as selective factors for dark skin in equatorial regions. Farther away from the equator, there is less of an advantage for dark skin, and more of an advantage for light skin, the former being more vulnerable to severe cold injury. Further study will be needed to strengthen support for both of these ideas and to explore the possibility that other factors affect skin color variation. Recent observations that ultraviolet radiation affects functioning of the immune system (Robins 1991) are also worth investigating.

SUMMARY

Case studies of human microevolution presented in this chapter illustrate some of the methods and results of studies dealing with an evolutionary approach to contemporary human biological variation. The case studies of gene flow and genetic drift emphasize how factors such as social structure, population size, migration patterns, cultural barriers, and history all affect the genetic relationships among human populations.

Several examples of natural selection in human populations are reviewed. Perhaps the best-documented example is the relationship between hemoglobin alleles and two selective forces: sickle cell anemia and malaria. In environments where malaria is common, selection has led to an increase in the sickle cell allele because the heterozygotes are the most fit—they show greater resistance to malaria but do not suffer from the adverse effects of sickle cell anemia. Studies of blood groups and other genetic markers also suggest a role for natural selection in human variation. Skin color is another example of a trait that shows a strong environmental correlation, in this case with latitude. This distribution, combined with other evidence, suggests that dark skin is selected for near the equator primarily to protect against the harmful effects of excess ultraviolet radiation (skin cancer and sunburn). The reasons why light skin evolved farther from the equator is not known, although there is strong evidence for some relationship between skin color, temperature, and the likelihood of frostbite.

SUPPLEMENTAL READINGS

In addition to the readings suggested for Chapter 13, other sources are:

Cavalli-Sforza, L. L., P. Menozzi, and A. Piazza. 1994. *The History and Geography of Human Genes*. Princeton: Princeton University Press.

Crawford, M. H., and J. H. Mielke, eds. 1982. *Current Developments in Anthropological Genetics.* Vol. 2. *Ecology and Population Structure.* New York: Plenum Press. This book and the preceding one by Cavalli-Sforza et al. (1994) are somewhat detailed, but provide many examples of the use of genetic distance analysis to unravel the effects of gene flow and genetic drift on human biological variation.

Robins, A. H. 1991. *Biological Perspectives on Human Pigmentation.* Cambridge: Cambridge University Press. An excellent review of the biology, variation, and evolution of human skin color. The final chapter on the evolution of human skin color is the best to date.

Human Adaptation

CHAPTER **15**

 As discussed in Chapter 1, adaptation is the successful interaction of a population with its environment. Thus far, adaptation has been discussed in terms of genetic adaptation—that is, natural selection. In this chapter, we examine a broader perspective. Central to the study of adaptation is the concept of **stress,** broadly defined as any factor that interferes with the normal limits of operation of an organism. Organisms maintain these limits through an ability known as **homeostasis.** As ways of dealing with the stresses that alter your body's functioning, adaptations restore homeostasis. For example, within normal limits, your body maintains a relatively constant body temperature. When you stand outside in a cold wind you may shiver. This is your body's way of adapting to cold stress. You might also choose to put on a heavy jacket.

As human beings, we can adapt both biologically and culturally. It is important to note, however, that our biocultural nature can work against us. In adapting to stresses culturally, we can introduce other stresses as a result of our behavior. Pollution, for example, is a consequence of cultural change and has negatively impacted our physical environment in numerous ways.

▲▲▲▲▲▲▲▲▲▲▲▲▲▲▲▲▲▲▲▲▲▲▲▲▲▲▲▲▲

stress Any factor that interferes with the normal limits of operation of an organism.

homeostasis In a physiologic sense, the maintenance of normal limits of body functioning.

409

Key to the interaction between human biology and culture, human adaptation operates on a number of levels—physiologic, developmental, genetic, and cultural—all of which are interrelated, for better or for worse. Thus the countering of a biological stress such as disease by the cultural adaptation of medicine can lower the death rate for human populations but also can increase population size, which in turn can lead to further stresses, such as food shortages and environmental degradation.

This chapter examines two specific examples of stress and adaptation: one involving climate and one, high altitude. Throughout this chapter, it is important to remember that not all biological and cultural traits are necessarily adaptive.

TYPES OF ADAPTATION

How do humans adapt? What are the different ways we have to cope with the stresses of the physical and cultural environments?

PHYSIOLOGIC, GENETIC, AND CULTURAL ADAPTATION

Besides genetic and cultural adaptation, humans are capable of three other forms of adaptation that are physiologic in nature: acclimation, acclimatization, and developmental acclimatization. **Acclimation** refers to short-term changes that occur very quickly after exposure to a stress, such as sweating when you are hot. **Acclimatization** refers to physiologic changes that take longer, from days to months, such as an increase in red blood cell production after moving to a high-altitude environment. When a change occurs during the physical growth of any organism, it is known as **developmental acclimatization.** An example (covered later in the chapter) is the increase in chest size that occurs when growing up at high altitudes. The ability of organisms to respond physiologically or developmentally to environmental stresses is often referred to as **plasticity.**

Adaptation to Ultraviolet Radiation

A focus on ultraviolet radiation is a useful way of coming to grips with some of the basic concepts of adaptation. As mentioned in Chapter 14, excessive ultraviolet radiation can lead to severe sunburn and skin cancer and may even interfere with the proper functioning of the immune system. How have humans adapted, or attempted to adapt, to this stress?

Short-term exposure to ultraviolet radiation results in darkening of the skin, or tanning, which can take two different forms. *Immediate tanning* darkens the skin within 1 to 2 hours, and fades away during the first 24 hours after exposure. *Delayed tanning* is a more gradual process caused by repeated exposure. Delayed tanning begins within 2 to 3 days of initial exposure and reaches a maximum after 19 days. The effects of delayed tanning can last as much as 9.5 months (Robins 1991). From a physiologic perspective, tanning is a response to skin cell damage. Delayed tanning is an adaptive response, whereby darkening of the skin provides some protection against further damage. Immediate tanning does not appear to be effective in this respect.

Tanning is not the only form of adaptation to ultraviolet radiation. There is strong evidence that in equatorial regions dark skin evolved in response to the stress of excessive levels of ultraviolet radiation (Chapter 14). Individuals with darker skin were more likely to survive and therefore more likely to pass on the genes for darker skin to the next generation. In other words, natural selection occurred as a result of genetic adaptation.

Cultural adaptations can also deal with exposure to ultraviolet radiation. If your occupation or leisure activity increases your risk of exposure, you can wear protective clothing, such as hats or long-sleeved garments, or apply chemical sunscreens. Changes in the hours you work or play outdoors can also help minimize exposure. With the growing concern about skin cancer in the United States, increasing numbers of people are turning to behaviors that provide protection from ultraviolet radiation, or at least minimize exposure.

CLIMATE AND HUMAN ADAPTATION

Though originally tropical primates, we humans have managed to expand into virtually every environment on our planet. Such expansion has been possible largely because of multiple adaptations to the range of temperatures around the world.

Physiologic Responses to Temperature Stress

As warm-blooded creatures, humans have the ability to maintain a constant body temperature. This homeostatic quality works well only under certain limits.

acclimation Short-term physiologic responses to a stress, usually within minutes or hours.	**acclimatization** Long-term physiologic responses to a stress, usually taking from days to months.	**developmental acclimatization** Changes in organ or body structure that occur during the physical growth of any organism.	**plasticity** The ability of an organism to respond physiologically or developmentally to environmental stress.

Cold Nights in Tierra del Fuego

Tierra del Fuego is an archipelago off the southern tip of South America. A native population, the Alacaluf Indians, are a small population that has attracted attention because of their ability to handle cold stress. Charles Darwin had written of poor shelter and of observing naked natives sleeping on the ground (Hutchinson et al. 1902).

The Alacaluf live in an environment with moderate and chronic cold stress. The minimum temperature ranges from about 32° F in the winter to 45° F in the summer. The maximum temperature ranges from about 42° F in the winter to 56° F in the summer. Their environment is also humid and windy, both of which compound the cold stress.

Many studies have shown that among people who are not cold-adapted, the skin temperature decreases over time (during a cold night). The Alacaluf show the same decrease, but start with a higher skin temperature, so that the temperature of their extremities remains about 4° to 5° F higher than that of non-adapted people. Their higher extremity temperature is also apparent by looking at the results of short-term immersion in very cold water (41° F). After 30 minutes, the Alacaluf subjects did not show any discomfort. The Alacaluf Indians also have high metabolic rates, and these rates are maintained throughout the nights, so that heat production also remains higher than that of non-adapted people. Both the higher extremity temperature and higher metabolic rates appear to be developmental in origin, occurring as a consequence of growing up in this environment.

Similar responses have been noted in other populations under conditions of chronic cold stress. Not all populations, however, have adapted to cold in the same way. In environments with more moderate cold stress, natives tend to have lower metabolic rates and less heat production, which results in lower peripheral temperatures and a high cold tolerance. As is typical of adaptation in general, there are multiple responses to a similar stress (Frisancho 1993).

COLD STRESS When you are cold, your body is losing heat too rapidly. One response is to increase heat production temporarily through shivering, which also increases your metabolic rate. This response is not very efficient and is costly in terms of energy. A more efficient physiologic response to cold stress is minimization of heat loss through alternate constriction and dilation of blood vessels. **Vasoconstriction,** the narrowing of blood vessels, reduces blood flow and heat loss. **Vasodilation,** the opening of the blood vessels, serves to increase blood flow and heat loss.

When a person is first subjected to cold stress, vasoconstriction acts to minimize the loss of heat from the body to the extremities (i.e., the hands, feet, and face). As a result, skin temperature drops. This response becomes dangerous, however, if it continues too long. Should this start to happen, vasodilation begins, causing blood and heat to flow from the interior of the body to the extremities. The increased blood flow prevents damage to the extremities, but now the body is losing heat again! Neither vasoconstriction nor vasodilation by itself provides an effective physiologic response to cold stress. *Both* must operate, back and forth, to maintain a balance between heat loss and damage to the extremities.

An interesting phenomenon occurs after initial exposure to cold stress. The cycles of alternating vasoconstriction and vasodilation, accompanied by alternating cycles of cold and warm skin temperatures, begin to level out, becoming more frequent and less extreme. Skin temperature changes more

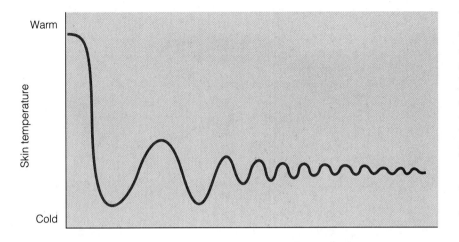

Warm

Skin temperature

Cold

■ **FIGURE 15.1**
The Lewis hunting phenom-
enon. Initial exposure of
a finger into ice water
produces a decrease in skin
temperature, caused by
vasoconstriction. After a
while, this response gives way
to vasodilation, which causes
skin temperature to increase.
The cycles continue over time
but become more frequent
and less extreme, thus
providing more efficient
adaptation. (Modified after
Frisancho [1979:45])

quickly, but the increases and decreases are not as great. This pattern, called
the *Lewis hunting phenomenon*, demonstrates how effective is the body's
ability to adapt. The smaller and more frequent cycles are more efficient
(Figure 15.1).

HEAT STRESS   When experiencing heat stress, your body is not removing heat
quickly enough. There are four ways in which heat is lost from the body,
three of which can also increase heat (Frisancho 1979). *Radiation* is heat flow
from objects in the form of electromagnetic radiation. The body removes
heat through radiation but also picks up heat radiated by other objects. *Convection* refers to the removal or gain of heat through air molecules. Heat
flows from a warm object to a cooler object. *Conduction* is heat exchange
through physical contact with another object, such as the ground or clothes.
Conduction generally accounts for a very small proportion of heat exchange.
Evaporation is the loss of heat through the conversion of water to vapor.
In the process of sweat evaporation, heat energy is consumed. Evaporation
is the only one of these four mechanisms that results in heat loss without
heat gain.

The amount of heat loss through these mechanisms varies according to
both temperature and humidity. As the temperature increases, the only way
your body can cope is to increase the amount of evaporation (your body
can't amplify any of the other three mechanisms). As a result, evaporation is
the most effective mechanism for heat removal in excessively hot temperatures. Figure 15.2 shows the relative percentage of heat loss due to radiation,
convection, and evaporation for a nude human in a room with little air

▲▲▲

vasoconstriction The
narrowing of blood

vessels, which reduces
blood flow and heat loss.

vasodilation The
opening of the blood

vessels, which increases
blood flow and heat loss.

■ **FIGURE 15.2**
Heat loss due to radiation, convection, and evaporation at different temperatures, for a nude human in a room with little air movement. The temperatures are: comfortable = 25° C, or 77° F, warm = 30° C, or 86° F, hot = 35° C, or 95° F. Note that evaporation accounts for 90 percent of heat loss at hot temperatures. (Data from Frisancho [1979:16])

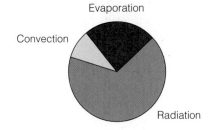

Comfortable

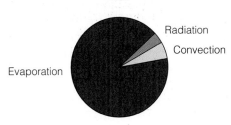

Warm

Hot

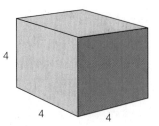

■ **FIGURE 15.3**
Geometric representation of Bergmann's rule relating body size and heat loss. The larger cube has a larger volume (heat production) and a larger surface area (heat loss). The larger cube also has a smaller surface area/volume ratio, however, indicating that it would lose heat less rapidly and therefore be adaptive in colder climates.

Surface area = 24
Volume = 8
Surface area/volume = 3

Surface area = 96
Volume = 64
Surface area/volume = 1.5

movement. At comfortable temperatures, most heat is lost through radiation, and evaporation accounts for only 23 percent of the total lost. At hot temperatures (35° C = 95° F), evaporation accounts for 90 percent. Vasodilation is also important in heat loss. The opening of the blood vessels internal heat to the outside skin. The heat can then be transferred to the environment through radiation, convection, and evaporation.

Evaporation has its drawbacks. The removal of too much water from the body can be harmful or even fatal. The efficiency of evaporation is also affected by humidity. In humid environments, evaporation is less efficient, making heat loss more difficult under hot and humid conditions than under hot and dry conditions.

Climate and Morphological Variation

Differences in physiologic responses and certain morphological variations, most notably the size and shape of the body and head, affect people's ability to handle temperature stress. Nose size and shape are related to humidity.

THE BERGMANN AND ALLEN RULES Human populations in colder climates tend to be heavier than those in hotter climates. This does not mean that all people in cold climates are heavy and all people in hot climates are light. Every human group contains a variety of small and large people. Some of this variation is caused by factors such as diet. However, a strong relationship of *average* body size and temperature does exist among indigenous human populations (Roberts 1978).

A nineteenth-century English zoologist, Carl Bergmann, noted the relationship between body size and temperature in a number of mammal species. Bergmann explained his findings in terms of mammalian physiology and principles of heat loss. **Bergmann's rule** states that if two mammals have similar shapes but different sizes, the smaller animal will lose heat more rapidly and will therefore be better adapted to warmer climates, where the ability to lose heat is advantageous. Larger mammals lose heat more slowly and are therefore better adapted to colder climates.

The reason for these relationships is that heat production is a function of the total volume of a mammal, whereas heat loss is a function of total surface area. Consider two hypothetical mammals whose body shape is that of a cube. Imagine that one cube is 2 cm long and the other is 4 cm long in each dimension (Figure 15.3). As a measure of heat production, we can compute the volume of each cube (volume = length × width × height). The volume of the 2-cm cube is 8 cm³; that of the 4-cm cube is 64 cm³. The larger cube can produce more heat because of its greater volume. The greater the volume of a mammal, the greater the heat produced.

As a measure of heat loss, we can compute the surface area of each cube. The surface area of each side is length times width. There are six sides

▲▲▲▲▲▲▲▲▲▲▲▲▲▲▲▲▲▲▲▲▲▲▲▲▲▲▲▲

Bergmann's rule
(1) Among mammals of similar shape, the larger mammal loses heat less rapidly than the smaller mammal, and (2) among mammals of similar size, the mammal with a linear shape will lose heat more rapidly than the mammal with a nonlinear shape.

■ **FIGURE 15.4**
Geometric representation of Bergmann's rule relating body shape and heat loss. The cube has a lower surface area/volume ratio than the rectangular block and would therefore lose heat less rapidly.

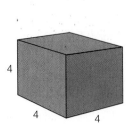

Surface area = 96
Volume = 64
Surface area/volume = 1.5

Surface area = 112
Volume = 64
Surface area/volume = 1.75

to a cube, so we multiply our result by 6. The surface area of the 2-cm cube is 24 cm^2; that of the 4-cm cube is 96 cm^2. With the greater surface area, the larger cube seems to produce more heat and to lose it at a greater rate. The relevant factor in heat loss in mammals, however, is the ratio of surface area to volume—that is, the rate of heat loss relative to the amount of surface area. The surface area/volume ratio is 24/8 = 3 for the smaller cube, and 96/64 = 1.5 for the larger cube. Therefore, the larger cube loses heat at a slower rate relative to heat production. In cold climates, the larger cube would be at an advantage because it loses heat less quickly. In hot climates, the reverse would be true; hot climates would favor the smaller cube, with its quicker rate of heat loss.

Another aspect of Bergmann's rule involves the shape of an object and its relationship to heat production and loss. Figure 15.4 shows two objects with the same volume but different shapes. The first object is a 4-cm cube with a volume of 64 cm^3, a surface area of 96 cm^2, and a surface area/volume ratio of 1.5. The second object is a rectangular block 2 cm wide, 4 cm deep, and 8 cm high. The volume of this block is also 64 cm^3. The surface area is 112 cm^2 and the surface area/volume ratio is 112/64 = 1.75. Even though both objects produce the same amount of heat as measured by their volumes, the rectangular block loses heat more quickly. Linear objects such as the block would be at an advantage in hot climates, whereas less linear objects, such as the cube, would be at an advantage in cold climates. Accordingly, Bergmann's rule predicts that mammals in hot climates will have linear body shapes and mammals in cold climates will have less linear body shapes. Another zoologist, J. Allen, applied these principles to body limbs and other appendages. **Allen's rule** predicts that mammals in cold climates should have shorter, bulkier limbs, whereas mammals in hot climates should have longer, narrower ones.

BODY SIZE AND SHAPE   Do the Bergmann and Allen rules hold for human body size and shape? Figure 15.5 shows !Kung men from Africa and an Inuit (Eskimo). Note the thinness and length of the tribesman's body and limbs.

■ FIGURE 15.5
!A Kung man (*top*) and Inuits
(*bottom*) illustrate the
relationship among body size,
body shape, and climate
predicted by the Bergmann
and Allen rules. (Richard
Lee/Anthro-Photo)

▲▲

Allen's rule Mammals
in cold climates tend to
have short, bulky limbs,
allowing less loss of
body heat; mammals in
hot climates tend to
have long, slender limbs,
allowing greater loss of
body heat.

Those of the Inuit are shorter and bulkier. These physiques do in fact conform to Bergmann's and Allen's predictions. Analysis of data from many human populations has found the rules to be accurate in describing the *average* trends among populations. Again, don't forget that extensive variation exists within populations. Also, some populations are exceptions to the general rule. African pygmies, for example, are short and have short limbs, yet they live in a hot climate. The pygmy's short size appears to be due to a hormonal deficiency (Shea and Gomez 1988).

The Bergmann and Allen rules apply to adult human body size and shape. Are these average patterns the result of natural selection (i.e., genetic adaptation) or changes in size and shape during the growth process (i.e., developmental acclimatization)? Do infants born elsewhere who move into an environment attain the same adult size and shape as native-born infants? If so, this suggests a direct influence of the environment on growth. If not, then the growth pattern leading to a certain adult size and shape may be genetic in nature and determined by natural selection. If the growth pattern is entirely genetic, then we may expect to see the same ultimate size and shape regardless of environment. That is, an infant born in a cold climate but raised in a hot climate would still show the characteristic size and shape of humans born in cold climates. Of course, if *both* environmental and genetic factors are responsible for adult size and shape, then the expected pattern is more complex. Unraveling the potential genetic and climatic effects is a difficult process because other contributing influences, such as nutrition, also vary with climate.

The evidence to date suggests that both genetic and environmental factors influence the relationship among climate, growth, body size, and shape. When children grow up in a climate different from that of their ancestors, they tend to grow in ways the indigenous children do (Malina 1975; Roberts 1978). This finding supports the idea that environment directly influences the growth process. The relationship between growth and climate in such children, however, is not as strong as it is among indigenous children. Therefore, long-term genetic adaptation is also responsible for the association of size, shape, and climate observed in adults. Natural selection leads to changes in growth potential that are further modified by environmental factors. It appears that climate can alter the growth patterns of all children, although those with certain genetic predispositions may show greater response.

The principles of the Bergmann and Allen rules have also been extended to analysis of the fossil record. The *Homo erectus* skeleton from Kenya (Figure 11.10 in Chapter 11) shows the linear physique expected in a hot climate (Ruff 1993). The date of this fossil (1.6 million years B.P.) shows that climatic adaptation has a long history in our evolution.

CRANIAL SIZE AND SHAPE The size and shape of the human head has long been of interest to anthropologists. In past times the shape of the head was the focus of studies of racial classification. In the nineteenth century, the Swedish anatomist Anders Retzius developed a measure of cranial shape called the

a   b

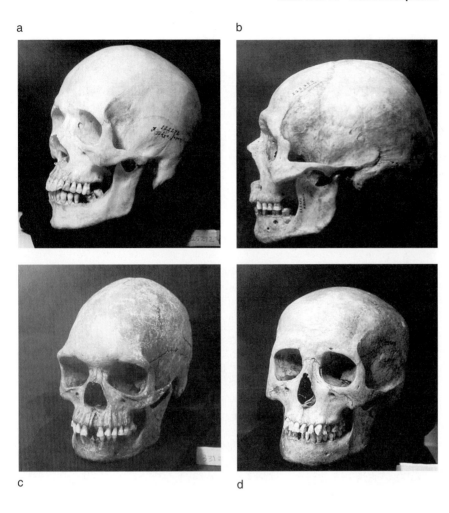

c   d

■ **FIGURE 15.6**
Variation in cranial shape:
(a) Japanese, (b) North
Dakotan Native American,
(c) Australian aborigine,
(d) Lapp. (Courtesy of Alice
Brues, University of Colorado at
Boulder)

cephalic index. This index is derived from two measurements: the total length of the head and its maximum width. To compute the index, you simply divide the width of the head by the length of the head and multiply the result by 100. For example, if a person has a head length of 182 mm and a head width of 158 mm, the cephalic index is $(158/182) \times 100 = 86.8$. That is, the person's head width is almost 87 percent of head length. Among human populations today, the cephalic index ranges from roughly 70 to 90 percent.

There is considerable variation in cranial shape among human populations (Figure 15.6). At first, cranial shape was felt to be a measurement capable of determining racial groupings. For example, African skulls were found to have lower cephalic indices than European skulls. Further study showed *rough* agreement but also produced many examples of overlap and similar values in different populations. For example, both Germans and Koreans have average cephalic indices of roughly 83 percent. Likewise, both African pygmies and Greenland Eskimos have average cephalic indices of roughly 77 percent (Harrison et al. 1988). These values do not correspond to any racial

▲▲▲▲▲▲▲▲▲▲▲▲▲▲▲▲▲▲▲▲▲▲▲▲▲▲▲▲▲▲▲

cephalic index A
measure of cranial shape
defined as the maximum
width of the head
divided by the total
length of the head.

■ **FIGURE 15.7**
Forms of human shelter such
as this igloo and this Pueblo
house reflect adaptation to
a wide range of climatic
conditions. (*Top*, © UPI/The
Bettmann Archive; *bottom*,
National Anthropological Archives,
neg. no. 1846, Smithsonian
Institution)

classification; they represent *averages* for each population. There is also considerable variation *within* each population.

As more data were obtained and compared geographically, a different pattern emerged—a correspondence was found to exist between cranial shape and climate. Beals (1972) examined the cephalic index and climate for 339 populations from all over the world. He found a direct relationship: populations in colder climates tend to have wider skulls relative to length than those in hot climates. In particular, he found the average cephalic index for populations that experienced winter frost to be higher than for those in tropical environments.

This correspondence makes sense in terms of the Bergmann and Allen rules. The shape of the upper part of the skull is related to heat loss. Rounded heads (those with a high cephalic index) lose heat slowly and therefore are at an advantage in cold climates. Narrow heads lose heat more quickly and are therefore at an advantage in hot climates. It appears that as human populations moved into colder climates, natural selection led to a change in the relative proportions of the skull. Beals and colleagues (1983) have extended this analysis to fossil human crania over the past 1.5 million years and found similar results.

NASAL SIZE AND SHAPE   The shape of the nasal opening in the skull is another morphological variation that has a strong relationship to climate. The **nasal index** is the width of the nasal opening divided by the height of the nasal opening, multiplied by 100. Typical values of the nasal index range from roughly 60 to 104 percent (Molnar 1992). Stereotypic racial views associate wide noses (large nasal indices) with African peoples. Although it is true that some African populations have very wide noses, others have long, narrow noses.

Numerous studies have found positive associations between the average nasal index of populations and average temperature. Populations in cold climates tend to have narrow noses; those in hot climates tend to have wide noses. Relationships have also been found between average nasal index and average humidity. Populations in dry climates tend to have narrow noses; those in humid climates tend to have wide noses (Franciscus and Long 1991). The mucous membranes of the nose serve to warm and moisten incoming air. High, narrow noses can warm air to a greater extent than low, wide noses and therefore may be more adaptive in cold climates. High, narrow noses also have a greater internal surface area with which to moisten air and are thus more adaptive in dry climates.

Cultural Adaptations

In Western societies we tend to take cultural adaptations to temperature stress for granted. Housing, insulated clothing, heaters, air conditioners, and other technologies are all around us. How do people in other cultures adapt to excessive cold or heat?

COLD STRESS   The Inuit, or Eskimo people, of the Arctic have realized effective cultural adaptations to cold stress, most notably in their clothing and shelter. It is not enough just to wear a lot of clothes to stay warm; if you work hard you tend to overheat. The Inuit wear layered clothing, trapping air between layers to act as an insulator. Outer layers can be removed if a person overheats. Also, the Inuit design their clothing with multiple flaps that can be opened, to prevent buildup of sweat while working.

While out hunting or fishing, the Inuit frequently construct temporary snow shelters, or igloos, that are quite efficient protection from the cold. The ice is an excellent insulator, and its reflective surface helps retain heat (Figure 15.7). More permanent shelters also provide ample protection from

nasal index A measure of the shape of the nasal opening, defined as the width of the nasal opening divided by the height.

the cold. Inuit houses have an underground entry, which is curved to reduce incoming wind. Inside, the main living area lies at a higher level than the fireplace; this architectural feature serves to increase heat and minimize drafts (Moran 1982).

Not all cold-weather housing is as effective as the types constructed by the Inuit. Among the Quechua Indians of the Peruvian highlands, the temperature inside temporary houses is often not much warmer than it is outside. However, these shelters do provide protection against rain and to some extent the cold. The bedding used by the Quechua is their most effective protection against heat loss (Frisancho 1979).

HEAT STRESS   Human populations live in environments that are dry and hot (i.e., deserts) and that are humid and hot (i.e., tropical rain forests). Moran (1982) has summarized some basic principles of clothing and shelter that are used in desert environments, where the objectives are fourfold: to reduce heat production, to reduce heat gain from radiation, to reduce heat gain from conduction, and to increase evaporation. Clothing is important because it protects from both solar radiation and hot winds. Typical desert clothing is light and loose, thus allowing circulation of air to increase evaporation. The air between the clothing and the body also provides excellent insulation.

Shelters are frequently built compactly to minimize the surface area exposed to the sun. Light colors on the outside help reflect heat. Doors and windows are kept closed during the day to keep the interior cool. Building

■ **FIGURE 15.8**

The relationship between barometric pressure and altitude. Barometric pressure decreases as altitude increases, causing a decrease in the percentage of arterial oxygen saturation (see Figure 15.10). (*Source of data:* Frisancho [1979:104])

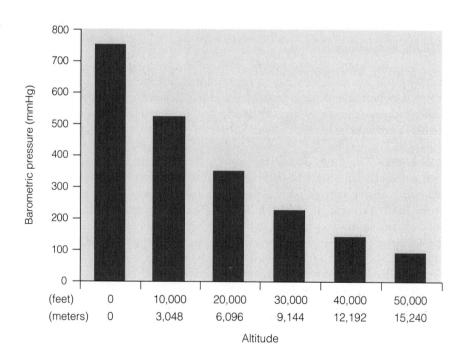

Altitude

materials are also adaptive. Adobe, for example, is efficient in absorbing heat during the day and radiating it at night (see Figure 15.7); nighttime temperatures may drop precipitously in desert environments.

Heat stress in tropical environments is often a problem because the extreme humidity greatly reduces the efficiency of evaporation through sweating. Cultural adaptations to tropical environments are similar throughout the world. Clothing is minimal, helping increase the potential for evaporation. In some cultures, shelters are built in an open design, without walls, to augment cooling during the day; in others, shelters are built closed to increase warmth at night. The combination of high heat and humidity obviously affects daily routines. Generally people start work early in the day, taking long midday breaks to keep from overheating.

In sum, humans have adapted to a number of environments that produce temperature stress. Humans have managed to adapt to extremes of hot and cold through physiologic changes, long-term genetic adaptations, and adaptive behaviors, particularly those manifested in clothing and shelter technology and in the pace of daily life.

HIGH-ALTITUDE ADAPTATION

Some human populations have lived for long periods of time at elevations of over 2,500 meters or roughly 8,200 ft. An estimated 25 million people currently live between 2,500 and 5,000 meters (Harrison et al. 1988).

High-Altitude Stresses

High-altitude environments produce several stresses, including oxygen starvation, cold, and sometimes poor nutrition. Studies of high-altitude populations have provided us insight into how humans cope with multiple stresses.

HYPOXIA   Oxygen starvation, or **hypoxia,** is more common at high altitudes because of the relationship of barometric pressure and altitude. Although the percentage of oxygen in the atmosphere is relatively constant up to almost 70 miles above the earth, barometric pressure decreases quickly with altitude (Figure 15.8). Because air is less compressed at high altitudes, its oxygen content is less concentrated and less oxygen is thus available to the hemoglobin in the blood. The percentage of arterial oxygen saturation decreases rapidly with altitude (Figure 15.9). For persons at rest, hypoxia generally occurs above 3,000 meters; for active persons, it can occur as low as 2,000 meters (Frisancho 1979).

OTHER STRESSES   Because the air is thinner at high altitudes, the concentration of ultraviolet radiation is greater and the air itself offers less protection against it. The thinner air also causes considerable heat loss from the atmo-

▲▲▲▲▲▲▲▲▲▲▲▲▲▲▲▲▲▲▲▲▲▲▲▲▲▲▲▲▲▲

hypoxia Oxygen starvation: occurs frequently at high altitudes.

■ **FIGURE 15.9**
The relationship between
arterial oxygen saturation
and altitude. (*Source of data:*
Frisancho [1979:104])

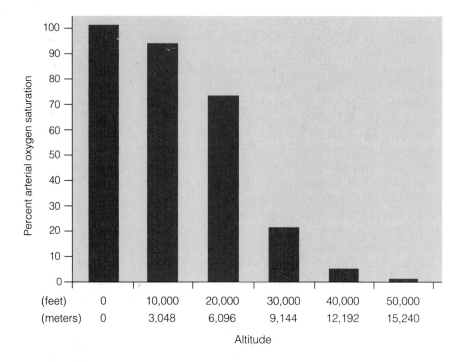

sphere, resulting in cold stress. In many high-altitude environments conditions are also extremely dry because of mountain winds and low humidity. In addition, hypoxia affects plants and animals; for lack of oxygen, trees cannot grow above 4,000 meters. The limited availability of plants and animals means that nutritional stress is likely in many high-altitude environments.

Numerous studies have compared the physiology and morphology of high-altitude and low-altitude populations. Early research tended to attribute any differences to the effects of hypoxia on the human body. More recent studies have shown that other stresses of high altitude are significant factors as well (Frisancho 1990). When dealing with human adaptation, it is best to consider the effect and interaction of *multiple* stresses.

Physiologic Responses to Hypoxia

People who live at low altitudes experience several physiologic changes when they enter a high-altitude environment. Some of these happen immediately; others occur over several months to a year. Such physiologic responses help to maintain sufficient oxygen levels. Respiration increases initially but returns to normal after a few days. Red blood cell production increases for roughly three months. The weight of the right ventricle of the heart is greater than

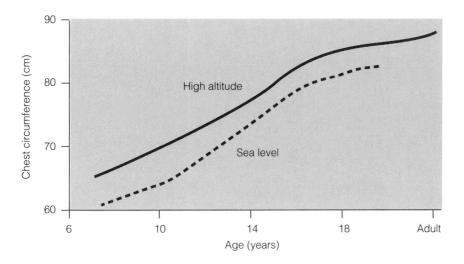

■ **FIGURE 15.10**
Distance curves for chest
circumference for high-
altitude and low-altitude
Peruvian Indian populations.
At all ages, the high-altitude
population has the greatest
chest circumference.
(Courtesy A. F. Frisancho)

the weight of the left ventricle in individuals that have grown up at high altitudes. Other changes include possible hyperventilation and higher hemoglobin concentration in the blood. In addition to these adaptive responses, loss of appetite and weight loss are common. Memory and sensory abilities may be affected, and hypoxia may influence hormone levels.

The physiologic differences between high-altitude and low-altitude natives are primarily acquired during the growth process. Studies of children who were born at low altitudes but moved into high altitudes during childhood clearly substantiate this phenomenon. In terms of aerobic capacity, for example, the younger the age of migration, the higher the aerobic capacity (Frisancho 1979). In other words, the longer a child lives in a high-altitude environment, the greater the developmental response to that environment. Age at migration has no effect on the aerobic capacity of adults, however, further indicating that most physiologic changes are the result of developmental acclimatization.

Physical Growth in High-Altitude Populations

Studies conducted by Paul Baker and his colleagues of high-altitude and low-altitude Indian populations in Peru found two peculiarities in growth. Chest dimensions and lung volume were greater at all ages in the high-altitude group (Figure 15.10), and high-altitude populations were also shorter at most ages than low-altitude populations (Figure 15.11) (Frisancho and Baker 1970). The shorter stature is related to delayed maturation, whereas the increase in chest size is due to growth acceleration during childhood.

Initially, the researchers interpreted both patterns of physical growth as direct developmental responses to hypoxia and cold stress at high altitude.

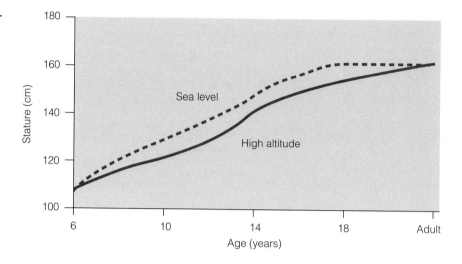

Distance curve for stature for high-altitude and low-altitude Peruvian Indian populations. At most ages, the low-altitude population is taller. (Courtesy A. R. Frisancho)

Larger chests and larger lung volumes relative to body size would be better able to provide sufficient oxygen levels. More energy devoted to the growth of oxygen transport systems, however, would leave less energy available for growth in other organ systems, especially the skeletal and muscle systems. Compounded by cold stress at high altitudes, this energy deficit would lead to an increase in basal metabolic rates and further reduction in energy available for body growth. As discussed later, this view is now being questioned.

Studies in high-altitude environments around the world show a similar pattern of growth in chest dimensions, although the extent of growth varies. Migrants to high-altitude populations also show an increase in chest dimensions, particularly among those that migrate at an early age. Increased growth of oxygen transport systems appears to be a developmental response to hypoxia.

Are the developmental changes in chest and lung growth in high-altitude populations genetic in nature? Were they shaped by natural selection? Most research to date assigns a relatively minor role to genetic factors. A recent study examined high-altitude and low-altitude populations of European ancestry in Bolivia (Greska 1990). Because these groups do not have a long history of residence at high altitude, they would not possess any genetic predisposition for high-altitude adaptations. The study showed there was an increased capacity of the oxygen transport system in these populations at high altitude even though they were not of high-altitude ancestry. The observed changes were instead direct effects of a chronic hypoxic stress.

The delayed maturation and small stature of the Peruvians have not been found in all studies of growth in high-altitude populations. As a result, some researchers have questioned the initial premise that hypoxia and cold stress have necessarily led to these characteristics, suggesting instead that other causal factors might be at work. A study undertaken in Peru has in fact shown that nutrition has had a major influence on stature (Leonard et al. 1990). Though high altitude may play a role in nutritional stress in the Peruvian highlands, income levels and access to land are of greater consequence. Also, other high-altitude populations, such as those found in Ethiopia, have a higher standard of living and do not show the growth deficits observed in Peru. Thus, it appears that although increased chest growth is a functional adaptation to hypoxia, the smaller body size is not necessarily related to high altitude. These results amply illustrate the complexity in assessing the relative value of stresses in any given environment.

SUMMARY

Studies of adaptation focus on the many ways in which organisms respond to environmental stresses. Human adaptation is particularly interesting because humans not only adapt both biologically and culturally but also must deal with stresses from their physical and cultural environments. Biological adaptation includes physiologic responses and genetic adaptation (natural selection). Cultural adaptation includes aspects of technology, economics, and social structure. In any study of human adaptation, we must look at multiple stresses and multiple adaptive (or nonadaptive) mechanisms.

Many studies of human adaptation have focused on cold and heat stress. Though as mammals humans have the capacity for maintenance of body temperature, they must still cope with extremes in temperature. Physiologic responses of the human body to temperature stress include changes in peripheral blood flow and evaporation. Studies have shown that general relationships exist worldwide between body size and shape and temperature. These observed trends agree with the predictions of the Bergmann and Allen rules. In hot climates, small body size and linear body shape maximize heat loss. In cold climates, large body size and less linear body shape minimize heat loss. Cranial studies show that worldwide the shape of the skull also varies predictably, according to the principles of differential heat loss and the Bergmann and Allen rules. Although some of these biological features are the result of genetic adaptation, studies of children have revealed that response to temperature stress can affect growth. Cultural adaptations, especially those involving clothing, shelter, and physical activity, are also important in climatic adaptation.

Over 25 million people around the world live at high altitudes. The major stresses of a high-altitude population are hypoxia (oxygen shortage) and cold stress. Many physiologic changes have been documented in high-altitude peoples, including short-term responses and long-term increases in the size of the lungs and other components of the oxygen transport system. These changes are caused by hypoxic stress during the growth period, and their degree of change is related to the time spent living at high altitudes: the longer one has lived there as a child, the more adapted one is. Early studies of high-altitude populations also noted small body size that, along with delayed maturation, could be due to insufficient energy levels for body growth because of hypoxia and cold stress. More recent studies have shown this is not always the case, because some high-altitude groups do not show this growth deficit. Instead, variation in diet appears to be the key factor.

SUPPLEMENTAL READINGS

Frisancho, A. R. 1993. *Human Adaptation and Accommodation.* Ann Arbor: University of Michigan Press. This text is a thorough review of adaptation studies, focusing on physiologic adaptation.

Moran, E. F. 1982. *Human Adaptability: An Introduction to Ecological Anthropology.* Boulder, CO: Westview Press. This general text provides another review of human adaptation but focuses more on cultural adaptations.

The Evolution of Human Health and Disease

CHAPTER **16**

One of the most recent and rapid changes in human biology has been in human disease patterns. In the last 100 years, the major causes of death in developed regions of the world have shifted from infectious diseases to noninfectious diseases (remember that infectious diseases are those caused primarily by microorganisms). Some infectious diseases, such as smallpox, have been eradicated. Others have been reduced, although certain infectious diseases, such as malaria and schistosomiasis, continue to take their toll in tropical environments. In developed nations, the incidence of noninfectious diseases, such as diabetes, has risen.

These changes are the consequence of cultural innovations. Improvements in public health and sanitation have accounted for the major reduction in the spread of many infectious microorganisms. Advances in medical technology, such as the use of immunizations and antibiotics, have also reduced the risk for many infectious diseases. In addition, changes in health care systems have increased the availability of medical care to a larger proportion of the population.

This chapter takes an evolutionary perspective on human health and disease. Instead of focusing on health and disease solely from the viewpoint of the present, anthropologists take a broader view, being interested in *all* humans, past and present. This is not simply a matter of academic interest; a growing number of medical researchers and physicians are now incorporating an evolutionary perspective into their work (Nesse and Williams 1994). Such a focus is particularly important because we live in a time of rapid cultural and technological change. Much of what we are biologically has evolved under extremely different conditions. Because our culture changes much more rapidly than our genetics, we must always keep in mind potential problems that can result. Also, an evolutionary perspective is vital to understanding infectious diseases—those caused by microorganisms *that are also evolving*. As discussed later in this chapter, a number of scientists fear that we will be unable to keep up with the rapid evolution of these microorganisms, which has in recent years led to an increasing number of antibiotic-resistant strains.

THE STUDY OF EPIDEMIOLOGY

The study of human disease patterns and their causes is known as **epidemiology.** Epidemiology is an interdisciplinary field that focuses on the analysis of rates of diseases in human populations.

Types of Diseases

As discussed in Chapter 14, diseases can be classified as infectious or noninfectious. Infectious diseases are caused by the introduction of organic matter, such as a virus, bacteria, or a parasite, into the body. Infectious diseases can also be classified as *communicable* or *noncommunicable*, depending on whether the disease can be transmitted directly from one person to another. Malaria, for example, is an infectious disease caused by a parasite. It is not, however, a communicable disease because it cannot be passed from one human to another, except by means of a blood transfusion. Malaria is transmitted instead through the bites of mosquitoes carrying the malarial parasite. Measles, another infectious disease, is communicable because it can be transmitted from one human to another. Diabetes, by contrast, is a noninfectious disease that is caused by a variety of genetic and environmental factors.

The factors responsible for the spread of a disease through a population are different for infectious and noninfectious diseases. Because infectious diseases are spread through microorganisms, we need to look at the evolution and ecology of these microorganisms as well as those of humans. Environmental factors such as temperature, humidity, and sunlight can all affect the size of the microorganism population, which in turn affects disease rates.

The type of microorganism and the mode of transmission are also important factors. Viruses, bacteria, and parasites, for example, all act in different ways. Some infectious diseases spread very quickly in human populations because they are transmitted through respiration. Others, including a number of sexually transmitted diseases, are spread only through personal contact.

Noninfectious diseases reflect multiple causes, genetic and environmental. An individual's genotype may give increased resistance or susceptibility to a noninfectious disease, but the phenotype depends on many environmental factors. Noninsulin-dependent diabetes, for example, is affected not only by genetic predisposition but also by sex, age, diet, and lifestyle. Noninfectious diseases are generally more difficult than infectious diseases to analyze because multiple factors affect their occurrence.

Rates of Diseases

Epidemiological research looks at the rates of incidence and prevalence of both infectious and noninfectious diseases in populations over time and space. Rates are proportions of population size. The **incidence rate** is the rate of new cases of a disease that develop within a given population in a given period of time. Incidence rates are also used to describe the proportion of deaths in a population within a given period. For example, an annual incidence rate for spinal cord injury of 4 per 100,000 means that 4 out of every 100,000 people will have a spinal cord injury each year. The **prevalence rate** is the rate of the total number of cases, old and new, within a given population within a given period. For example, a prevalence rate for spinal cord injury of 90 per 100,000 means that 90 out of 100,000 people now living have a spinal cord injury, regardless of when they incurred it.

Several terms are used to describe the overall magnitude of disease rates. An **epidemic** pattern is one in which new cases of a disease spread quickly. An **endemic** pattern is a low but constant rate; a few cases are always present, but no major spread occurs. A **pandemic** pattern is an epidemic that takes place over large geographic ranges, such as the major bubonic plague

epidemiology The study of patterns of human disease and their causes.

incidence rate The rate of new cases of a disease developing in a population in a specified period of time.

prevalence rate The rate of total cases of a disease, old and new, in a population in a specified period of time.

epidemic A pattern of disease rate when new cases of a disease spread rapidly through a population.

endemic A pattern of disease rate when new cases of a disease occur at a relatively constant but low rate over time.

pandemic An epidemic that occurs over a large geographic range.

■ TABLE 16.1
Cholera: An Example of a Current Pandemic

Year	Occurrence of Epidemic
1961	Indonesia (first outbreak)
1963	Bangladesh
1964	India
1965	Former Soviet Union
1970	Africa
1990	Parts of Europe
1991	South America

Source: Dixon and McBride (1992)

pandemics during the Middle Ages that spread throughout Europe. Another example is the 1918 influenza pandemic. Pandemics are not just something that happened in the past; pandemics occur today as well. Currently, the world is experiencing a cholera pandemic that began in 1961, and epidemic spread of the disease has now reached four continents (Table 16.1).

Causes of Diseases

Incidence and prevalence rates are analyzed to determine their relationship with space and time. Geographic patterns of disease rates can provide clues about factors responsible for the disease. One example of geographic patterning occurs in those areas showing high rates of malaria. As discussed in Chapter 14, the highest rates of malaria are found in environments conducive to the mosquitoes that spread malaria.

Geographic analysis can also help determine which populations are in greatest need of health care services. It can help as well in predicting the future spread of a disease. As an example of this approach, let us look at the current geographic range of Lyme disease in the northeastern United States. Lyme disease, which is spread by the deer tick, was first found in parts of Long Island, New York, and Westchester County, New York, and in Connecticut. Analysis of the geographic range of Lyme disease cases shows that the deer tick population is spreading widely into other parts of the United States. Such forecasting allows public health officials to have adequate time for public education and other preventive measures. Careful prediction also allows physicians and other health personnel to become aware of the symptoms and treatments of a spreading disease.

Epidemiology also looks at changing disease rates over time. An increase in disease rates in a population may indicate the start of an epidemic. Changes over time can also be used to evaluate changes in disease prevention or environmental changes. Epidemiologists also investigate short-term changes in disease rates to determine the influence of seasonal change on disease risk. For example, the incidence of mumps cases generally increases during the winter and decreases in the summer. Because mumps is an infectious disease that spreads through personal contact, it seems likely that the close crowding of people in winter months, particularly in schools, increases the probability of contact with an infected person (Lilienfeld and Lilienfeld 1980).

Determining the timing of disease outbreaks can also be useful in assessing potential causes. For example, during the late 1980s, there was a rapid increase in cases of a disease known as Rift Valley Fever in towns along the Senegal River in Senegal, West Africa. The outbreak coincides to some extent with the development of a dam downstream from these towns. This suggests a potential connection between dam operations and increased rates of Rift Valley Fever. Perhaps the increased amount of standing water because of the dam has resulted in an increased mosquito population, which in turn has spread the disease (Walsh 1988).

Individual characteristics are also an important focus of epidemiological research. These include age, sex, ethnicity, physiologic state, hygiene, and occupation, among others (Lilienfeld and Lilienfeld 1980). For example, a person's behavior can affect the probability of contact with an infectious microorganism. People with many sexual partners have a higher risk, all other factors being equal, of acquiring a sexually transmitted disease. U.S. military personnel who served in the Vietnam War had a higher risk of contracting malaria than those at home because malaria-carrying mosquitoes were common in Vietnam.

Individual characteristics also play a role in determining the risk of acquiring a noninfectious disease. A diet high in protein and saturated fat can increase risk of hypertension, heart disease, and diabetes. Increased exposure to sunlight, either through recreation or occupation, can increase the risk for skin cancer. Working in a chemical plant may also increase the risk for certain types of cancers.

The search for causal factors in disease risk becomes even more complicated when we consider the fact that many factors are interrelated. Suppose, for example, that you find higher rates of skin cancer among male construction workers than among female factory workers. Is this difference the result of biological factors? Or is it caused by the circumstances of occupation? Perhaps comparison of men's and women's rates of skin cancer in outdoor occupations could shed light on this problem. Other factors might still be uncontrolled for, however, such as the fact that in Western societies it is acceptable for men, but not for women, to remove their shirts during work. This is a purely hypothetical example, but it does show potential complications in trying to analyze disease risk.

Anthropology and Epidemiology

Epidemiology is not a subfield of anthropology. Rather, anthropology is only one of many disciplines concerned with epidemiological questions. What, then, are the unique characteristics of anthropology in epidemiological research?

MEDICAL ANTHROPOLOGY   The study of disease in an anthropological context is often described as the field of *medical anthropology*. In the simplest sense, medical anthropology looks at health and disease as a component of the entire human experience. Using a holistic approach, a medical anthropologist is interested in determining the relationship among disease rates, diagnosis, treatment, and other cultural and environmental components in a society. Possible questions include: How do differences in social class affect health care and relative disease risk? How do a culture's religious beliefs

434

■ FIGURE 16.1
A !Kung healer transmitting healing power to a woman. Such beliefs can often have therapeutic effects. (Irven DeVore/Anthro-Photo)

■ FIGURE 16.2
Anthropologist Michael Park examining a prehistoric human skull. (Courtesy Michael Park, Central Connecticut State University)

influence its health care? What are the differences in diseases between hunting-gathering and agricultural societies? Instead of focusing on the biochemical level, medical anthropologists view health and disease as part of a much larger system.

Medical anthropology also relies on the comparative approach. By looking at cultures in different environments, we may find clues to causes of disease and their prevention. Medical anthropologists are also interested in how cultures diagnose and treat disease (Figure 16.1). This interest is not merely academic; many methods used today in Western medicine have their origins in other cultures. Acupuncture is a good example of this. We also use many drugs developed by other cultures, such as the South American tree extract known as curare, used to relax muscles during anesthesia.

BIOMEDICAL ANTHROPOLOGY The field of anthropology includes two distinct approaches to health and disease. Some cultural anthropologists focus more on systems of health care and less on biological factors. These medical anthropologists are interested in the ways in which members of a culture classify diseases and how they attempt cures. Other anthropologists focus on the biological side of health and disease, looking at genetic and environmental factors that affect risk for specific diseases. Though many medical anthropological studies combine both cultural and biological interests, biological

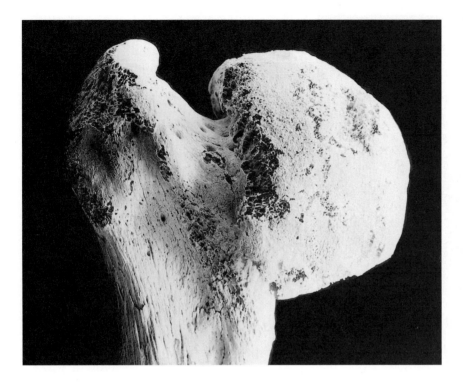

■ **FIGURE 16.3**
Osteoarthritis in a prehistoric Peruvian. The head of the femur is deformed. (Field Museum of Natural History, Chicago, neg. no. 74749B)

anthropologists have shown a growing tendency to pursue what is often called *biomedical anthropology.*

PALEOPATHOLOGY Anthropologists often obtain data on health, disease, and death from ancient populations using the methods of **paleopathology,** the study of ancient disease. Paleopathology not only gives us a glimpse into conditions in ancient populations, it also contributes to our evolutionary perspective on disease. By looking at populations in different environments over time, we may be able to gain insights into the long-term relationship of human biology, culture, and disease. An example is the use of paleopathology to document changing patterns of disease and health that took place during the transition from hunting and gathering to agriculture during human evolution, discussed later in this chapter (Cohen and Armelagos 1984; Cohen 1989).

The primary source of paleopathological information is skeletal remains. Inspection of bones (Figure 16.2) is augmented with X-rays, chemical analysis, and other methods. Such studies can tell us something of an individual's history of health and disease, and often the age and cause of death. Diseases such as osteoarthritis may affect bones directly (Figure 16.3). Other diseases, such as syphilis and tuberculosis, may leave indications of their effects on the skeletal system (Figure 16.4). Physical traumas due to injuries or violence

▲▲▲▲▲▲▲▲▲▲▲▲▲▲▲▲▲▲▲▲▲▲▲▲▲▲▲▲

paleopathology The study of disease in prehistoric populations based on analysis of skeletal remains and archaeological evidence.

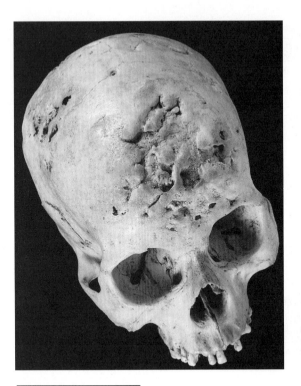

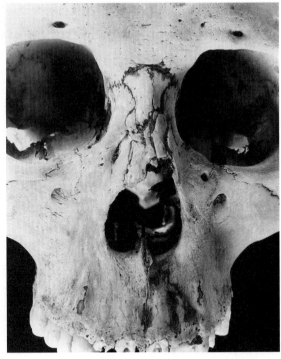

■ **FIGURE 16.4**
The skull of a prehistoric
Eskimo who suffered from
syphilis. The marks on the top
of the skull are typical of a
long-term syphilitic infection.
(© Hrdlicka Paleopathology
Collection, Courtesy San Diego
Museum of Man)

■ **FIGURE 16.5**
Nasal fracture in a prehistoric
Peruvian. The affected area
shows signs of healing,
indicating that this individual
survived the initial trauma.
(© Hrdlicka Paleopathology
Collection, Courtesy San Diego
Museum of Man)

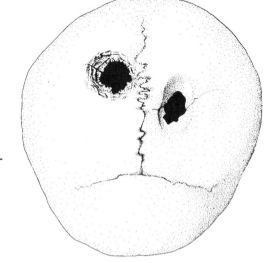

■ **FIGURE 16.6**
Top view of a prehistoric
Mexican who had two
trephinations. The hole on the
right side healed, but the hole
on the left side became
infected.

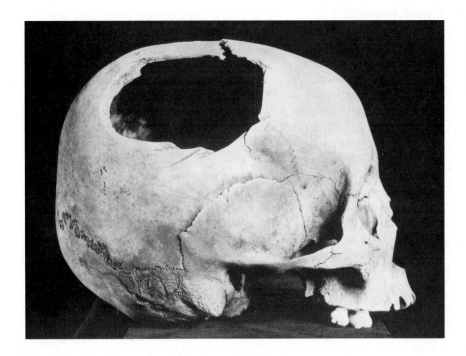

■ FIGURE 16.7
A massive trephination in a prehistoric Peruvian. (Field Museum of Natural History, Chicago, neg. no. 74689)

often leave detectable fractures. Signs of healing or infection tell us the long-term effects of such traumas (Figure 16.5).

Paleopathology also provides information on health care and medical knowledge. One interesting finding is that early humans practiced surgery. One of the most common forms of skeletal surgery is **trephination,** the removal of a section of bone from the skull. The reasons for ancient trephi-nation are unknown, but they may have included relieving cranial pressure following a blow to the head, as a cure for headaches, or to release various "demons" thought to be responsible for a variety of ailments. Ancient trephinations were performed using flint tools to scrape or cut through the bone. Sometimes large pieces of bone were removed by making a series of cuts in the skull around a central region and then lifting off that portion (Wilkinson 1975). Figure 16.6 shows the skull of a prehistoric Mexican who had two separate trephinations, one of which shows signs of healing and the other which reveals infection. It is possible that infection from the second trephination killed this person. Trephination has been a common practice among many peoples, past and present. Despite the dangers, many individu-als survived the operation. Some even survived multiple and massive trephinations (Figure 16.7). In one study of trephination in Peru, it is esti-mated that up to 75 percent of the subjects recovered from the operation (Wood 1979).

▲▲▲▲▲▲▲▲▲▲▲▲▲▲▲▲▲▲▲▲▲▲▲▲▲▲▲▲▲

trephination Surgery involving the removal of a section of bone from the skull.

FORENSIC ANTHROPOLOGY   Many of the techniques of paleopathology are also useful to another area of anthropological interest—forensic anthropology. Forensic anthropologists carry out much of their work as consultants to various law enforcement agencies. For example, Dr. Douglas Ubelaker, who works at the National Museum of Natural History at the Smithsonian Institution, is a consultant to the Federal Bureau of Investigation. In his book *Bones: A Forensic Detective's Casebook* (1992), co-authored with Henry Scammell, he describes the methods of forensic anthropology, illustrating their use in homicide and missing-persons investigations.

In medical terms, forensics is the identification of dead people. For example, a plane crash or other catastrophe may leave few remains, and forensic analysis can be used to identify the dead. Dental remains can be compared to dental records (teeth and jaws preserve well under such conditions and many people have unique dental records). Another area of interest is the discovery of skeletal remains. Who was the person whose bones were found? Can these bones be linked to a list of missing persons?

If sufficient remains exist, such as the pelvis, the sex of the individual may be determined. Analyzing the teeth and skeletal bones provides estimates for the age at death. The presence of skeletal fractures or breaks may often provide information on cause of death or may be used in comparison with medical records.

Even when an entire skeleton is not available, clues about sex, age, and physical appearance can be found. If, for example, only a single long bone (such as the femur) is found, an estimate can still be made of a person's height. This is possible because there is a strong relationship between leg length and height, allowing the use of statistical estimation methods.

These are only a few of the examples in which experts in human skeletal anatomy can offer assistance in identifying the dead.

THE EVOLUTION OF HUMAN DISEASE

A unique contribution of anthropology to epidemiological research has been its investigation into the evolution of human diseases. A shift began roughly 12,000 years ago from hunting and gathering to agriculture. During the past several centuries, further changes have led to the development and spread of large industrial societies. What effects have these rapid shifts, and related environmental and cultural changes, produced on patterns of human health and disease? Part of this question can be answered by looking at contemporary populations at different levels of subsistence. We can also examine the fossil and archaeological record to infer changes in the patterns of disease. This section focuses on general trends in disease across three different levels of subsistence: hunting-gathering, agriculture, and industrialization.

Disease in Hunting-Gathering Societies

Given that humans relied exclusively on hunting and gathering until the relatively recent development of agriculture, a large part of our genetic makeup resulted from adaptations to a hunting-gathering way of life. This fact has powerful implications for the analysis of disease. How do these adaptations affect our response to disease under very different environmental circumstances?

INFECTIOUS DISEASE   The two most common types of infectious diseases in hunting-gathering populations are caused by parasites and **zoonoses** (diseases transmitted from other animals to humans). Parasitic diseases may reflect the long-term evolutionary adaptation of different parasites to human beings. Among hunting-gathering societies, these parasites include lice and pinworms. The zoonoses are introduced through insect bites, animal wounds, and ingestion of contaminated meat. The diseases include sleeping sickness, tetanus, and schistosomiasis (Armelagos and Dewey 1970). The prevalence of various parasitic and zoonotic diseases varies among different hunting-gathering environments. The disease microorganisms found in arctic or temperate environments are generally not found in tropical environments.

In general, hunting-gathering populations do not experience epidemics of infectious disease. This is because of two ecological factors associated with a hunting-gathering way of life: small population size and nomadism (Figure 16.8). Hunters and gatherers live in small groups of roughly 25 to 50 people that interact occasionally with other small groups in their region. Under such conditions, infectious diseases do not spread. There are not enough people to become infected to keep the disease going at high rates. Without more people to infect, the disease microorganisms die. This does not apply to chronic infectious diseases, whose microorganisms can stay alive long enough to infect people coming into the group. Certain diseases caused by parasitic worms fall into this category. In such cases, the prevalence rate of infectious diseases is low. Most infectious diseases in hunting-gathering societies are endemic rather than epidemic (McElroy and Townsend 1989).

The nomadic lifestyle of hunting-gathering groups also reduces risk to certain infectious diseases. The microorganisms infecting humans may not survive in new environments. Other aspects of the hunting-gathering way of life also reduce the chance of epidemics. Given a small, mobile population, there are few problems with sanitation or contamination of the water supply.

NONINFECTIOUS DISEASE   The noninfectious diseases common in industrial societies, such as heart disease, cancer, diabetes, and hypertension, are rare in

▲▲▲▲▲▲▲▲▲▲▲▲▲▲▲▲▲▲▲▲▲▲▲▲▲▲▲▲▲▲▲

zoonose A disease transmitted directly from animals to humans.

!Kung women gathering
vegetables. The small size and
nomadic nature of hunting-
gathering populations mean
that infectious disease is
endemic, not epidemic.
(M. Shostak/Anthro-Photo)

hunting-gathering societies. Part of the reason for low rates of such noninfectious "Western diseases" may be the diet and lifestyle of hunters and gatherers, but the primary reason may be simply the fact that fewer individuals among hunters and gatherers are likely to live long enough to develop these diseases.

The nutrition of hunting-gathering populations is varied and provides a well-balanced diet. Perhaps this diet, along with greater levels of exercise, accounts for the lack of cardiovascular problems in such societies. The major nutritional problem in hunting-gathering societies is the scarcity of food during hard times, such as drought. To some extent, hunting-gathering populations have adapted to occasional fluctuations in food supply through reduced rates of growth and smaller body sizes. In any case, the rate of malnutrition and starvation in most hunting-gathering groups is usually very low (Dunn 1968).

The reduced rate of noninfectious diseases in hunting-gathering populations, particularly those diseases that occur in old age, reflects the low life expectancy at birth in these groups (**life expectancy at birth** is a measure of the average length of life). Many noninfectious diseases require long periods of time for full development. Life expectancy at birth is low in hunting-gathering populations—roughly 20 to 40 years (Cohen 1989). These low life expectancies at birth reflect high infant mortality. If many people die early in life, the median age at death will be lowered. Keep in mind that life expectancy at birth is an average length of life. A value of 20 to 40 reflects a large number of infant and child deaths that brings the average down, and does *not* mean that people only lived 20 to 40 years total. Some live much longer; it is the *average* that is 20 to 40 years.

OTHER CAUSES OF DEATH   Apart from endemic infectious disease, what else accounts for the major causes of death in hunting-gathering societies? Injury deaths are one factor. In most environments, death could result from burns and hunting injuries. In arctic hunting-gathering populations, death could also result from drowning and exposure to cold. In some hunting-gathering populations, injuries are the major cause of death (Dunn 1968). For females, an additional factor in low life expectancy is death during childbirth.

Dunn (1968) has also listed a number of types of what he calls "social mortality" in hunting-gathering populations. These are deaths related to cultural behaviors such as infanticide (the killing of newborn children), geronticide (the killing of old people), sacrifice, and warfare. Infanticide and geronticide have been recorded for a number of hunting-gathering populations in past times and have often been interpreted as mechanisms of population size regulation.

▲▲

life expectancy at birth
A measure of the aver-

age length of life for a
newborn child.

Agriculture and Disease

The pattern of human disease is quite different in agricultural societies (both slash-and-burn and intensive agriculture). Agriculture allows larger population size and requires a nonnomadic life. The increased population size and lack of mobility has certain implications for the spread of disease.

INFECTIOUS DISEASE   Large populations of susceptible individuals allow the spread of short-lived microorganisms. Such conditions exist in agricultural populations because of increased population size and the increased probability of coming into contact with someone with the disease. As a result, agricultural populations have often shown epidemics of diseases such as smallpox, measles, mumps, and chicken pox (note that smallpox is no longer a factor; it has been eliminated worldwide, although it was quite a problem in the past). The size of a population needed for an epidemic varies according to disease. Some infectious diseases require larger population sizes for rapid spread.

Sedentary life increases the spread of infectious disease in other ways. Large populations living continuously in the same area can accumulate sewage. Poor sanitation and contamination of the water supply increases the chance for disease epidemics.

Agricultural practices also cause ecological changes, making certain infectious diseases more likely. The introduction of domesticated animals adds to waste accumulation and provides the opportunity for further exposure to diseases carried by animals. Cultivation of the land can also increase the probability of contact with insects carrying disease microorganisms.

The use of feces for fertilization can also have an impact on rates of infectious disease. In addition to contamination from handling these waste products, the food grown in these fertilizers can become contaminated. This problem was so acute in South Korea that steps had to be taken to reduce the use of feces as fertilizer (Cockburn 1971). Also, irrigation can lead to an increase in the spread of infectious disease. One of the major problems in tropical agricultural societies is the increased snail population that lives in irrigation canals and carries schistosomiasis. Irrigation can pass infectious microorganisms from one population to the next (Figure 16.9).

NUTRITIONAL DISEASE   Although agriculture provides populations with the ability to feed more people, this way of life does not guarantee an improvement in nutrition. Extensive investment in a single food crop, such as rice or corn, may provide too limited a diet for many people, and certain nutritional deficiency diseases can result. For example, populations relying extensively on corn as a major food source may show an increase in pellagra (a disease caused by a deficiency in the vitamin niacin) as well as protein deficiency. Dependency on rice is often associated with protein and vitamin deficiencies

■ FIGURE 16.9
Chinese farmers planting rice. The larger size and sedentary nature of agricultural populations contribute to epidemics of infectious disease. (Courtesy Kenneth Feder and Michael Park, Central Connecticut State University)

(McElroy and Townsend 1989). Perhaps the greatest problem of reliance on a single crop is that if that crop fails, starvation can result. The population becomes so dependent on a major crop for all of its food that if a drought or plague wipes it out, not enough food is left for all the people.

An agricultural diet can also lead to dental problems. The increased amount of starches in an agriculturalist's diet, combined with an increase in dirt and grit in the food, can lead to an increase in dental wear and cavities. Such changes are readily apparent in many paleopathological studies (Cohen 1989), showing once more that the advent of agriculture did not mean improved health. On the contrary, such studies have demonstrated that the transition to agriculture was often associated with increases in infectious disease, nutritional deficiencies, and nutritional stress. As with biological evolution, cultural changes have both benefits and costs. Nothing is free.

Urbanization and Disease

Following the origin and spread of agriculture, a number of human populations became urbanized. An urban area is defined in terms of large population size and density as well as a population with occupational specialization that produces a variety of economic goods and services provided to surrounding areas. We can subdivide cities into preindustrial and industrial. Each type of city has its own associated health problems.

DISEASE IN PREINDUSTRIAL CITIES   Preindustrial cities date back to several thousand years B.P. Such cities often developed as market or administrative centers for a region, and their increased population size and density provided ample opportunity for epidemics of infectious disease. In addition, a number of early cities had inadequate sewage disposal and contaminated water, both major factors increasing the spread of epidemics. To feed large numbers of people, food had to be brought in from the surrounding countryside and stored inside the city. In Europe during the Middle Ages, grain was often stored inside the house. Rats and other vermin had easy access to these foods, and their populations increased, furthering the spread of disease. In preindustrial cities located in dry parts of the world, grain was stored in ceramic containers, which limited the access of vermin.

Perhaps the best-known example of an epidemic disease in preindustrial cities is the Black Death in Europe during the fourteenth century. The Black Death is another name for the infectious disease bubonic plague. Caused by a bacterium, the disease affects field rodents, among whom it is spread by fleas. With the development of large urban areas and the corresponding large indoor rat populations, the disease spread to rats in the cities. The rats' fleas then infected humans. The spread of bubonic plague during this time was pandemic, affecting populations throughout Europe. It is estimated that up to 20 million Europeans died from bubonic plague between 1346 and 1352 (McEvedy 1988). The ecological changes accompanying the development of urbanization in Europe provided an opportunity for the rapid spread of fleas, rats, and the disease. Bubonic plague is still around today, including in the American southwest, although treatment by antibiotics has kept the incidence rate low.

DISEASE IN INDUSTRIAL CITIES   Industrialization, which began several centuries ago, accelerated population growth in urban areas. Technological changes allowed more efficient methods of agriculture and provided the means to support more people than in previous eras. The increased growth of urban areas was accompanied initially by further spread of infectious diseases. As industrialization continued, however, the rate of infectious disease declined and the rate of noninfectious disease increased. This shift in disease patterns was accompanied by a reduction in mortality, especially infant mortality, and an increase in life expectancy. In evolutionary terms, all of these changes are very recent.

Culture Contact

With the rise of European exploration in the 1500s, previously separate human populations came into contact with one another. In addition to the vast cultural, economic, and political problems resulting from such contact, infectious diseases could now spread into populations that had no prior immune experience. The results were generally devastating.

The epidemiologic effects of culture contact have been documented for a number of populations, particularly Native Americans and Pacific islanders. Many infectious diseases, such as smallpox, measles, and mumps, were introduced into the New World at this time, leading to massive loss of life in many populations (McNeill 1977; Cohen 1989). A recent review suggests that the actual impact of infectious disease varied across populations—some were hit much harder than others at different times (Larsen 1994). The flow of disease seems to have been primarily in one direction, from the Old World to the New World. One possible exception are treponemal diseases, including venereal syphilis. Venereal syphilis (spread by sexual contact) increased rapidly in Europe after 1500, a date that coincides with the contact between New World and Old World populations. Following European settlement in the Americas, it was also noted that many Native Americans had syphilis. Did the disease evolve in Europe and then spread to the Americas? Or, did it first appear in the New World and then spread to Europe? Evidence from paleopathology shows that cases of venereal syphilis occurred in the New World *before* European contact. This evidence rules out the hypothesis that venereal syphilis came from Europe; it appears to have evolved in the New World prior to European contact (Baker and Armelagos 1988).

The Epidemiologic Transition

The shift from infectious diseases to noninfectious diseases as the primary cause of death is a feature of the **epidemiologic transition** model, developed by Omran (1977).

THE NATURE OF THE EPIDEMIOLOGIC TRANSITION   According to Omran's model, a pretransition population has high death rates, particularly because of epidemics of childhood infectious diseases. As a culture's medical technologies, public health, and sanitation improve, epidemics become less frequent and less intense. Following the transition, the primary cause of death is not infec-

▲▲▲▲▲▲▲▲▲▲▲▲▲▲▲▲▲▲▲▲▲▲▲▲▲▲▲▲▲▲

epidemiologic transition The change in disease patterns in which there is a decline in infectious diseases and an increase in noninfectious diseases.

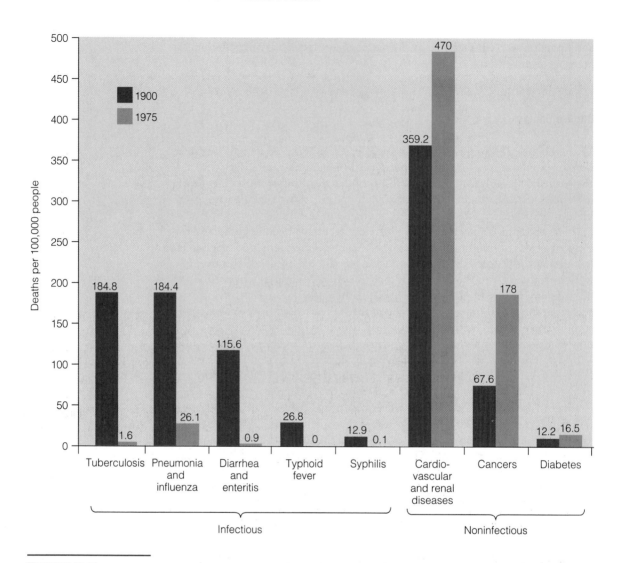

■ **FIGURE 16.10**
Death rates for selected
diseases in the United States
in 1900 and 1975. Note the
decrease in infectious disease
deaths and the increase in
noninfectious disease deaths.
(*Source of data:* Molnar
[1983:219])

tious diseases but degenerative noninfectious diseases. This shift in disease patterns is also accompanied by an increase in life expectancy at birth.

Figure 16.10 presents death rates per 100,000 people in the United States in 1900 and 1975 for several selected diseases. Note the tremendous decline in the death rates for infectious diseases such as tuberculosis and pneumonia but the increase in death rates from cardiovascular diseases, cancers, and diabetes. In addition, the total number of deaths per year per 100,000 of the population has decreased from 1622 in 1900 to 890 in 1975. A large proportion of this decrease has been a consequence of the reduction of infant mortality (death during the first year of life). In 1900, the infant mortality rate was 162 deaths per 1,000 live births. By 1975, the infant mortality rate had dropped to 14 deaths per 1,000 live births (Molnar 1983).

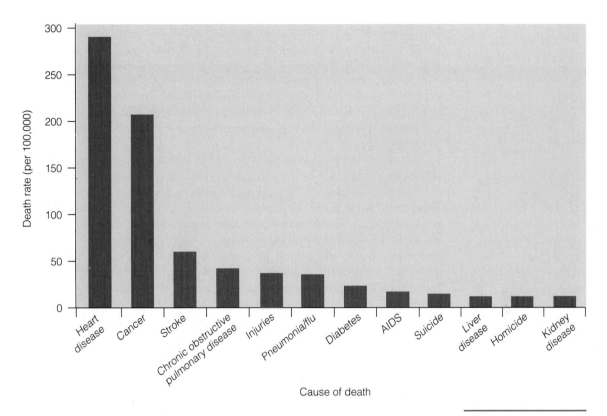

■ **FIGURE 16.11**
The 12 leading causes of
death in the United States in
1994. The death rate is the
number of deaths per year per
100,000 people. (*Source of
data:* Haub [1995])

Thus, there has been a decrease in infectious disease and an increase in noninfectious disease in those societies that have undergone the epidemiologic transition. For the United States, this has resulted in our current pattern of the leading causes of death, shown for 1994 in Figure 16.11. The two major causes of death are heart disease and cancer, followed by stroke, chronic obstructive pulmonary disease, and injuries. Only 2 of the top 12 causes of death in the United States, pneumonia/influenza and AIDS, are infectious diseases.

The epidemiologic transition has also affected life expectancy in developed societies. In the United States in 1900, life expectancy at birth was 49 years. In the United States in 1994, life expectancy had risen to 75.7 years (Haub 1995). Although high, it is not the highest in the world; in 1990, the United States had the sixteenth highest life expectancy at birth in the world (Haub 1992). Not everyone has the same life expectancy at birth. In the United States, females have a higher life expectancy at birth (79 years) than males (72 years), and that for European Americans is higher than that for African Americans (Haub 1995).

The increase in life expectancy is not confined to developed societies. Other groups undergoing modernization and the epidemiologic transition have also shown an increase, such as the residents of the modernizing population of American Samoa. From 1950 to 1980, life expectancy at birth increased 10 years for males and 18 years for females (Crews 1989).

A controversial topic today is the extent to which life expectancy can be expected to increase in developed societies. Based on statistical analysis of death rates, Olshansky and colleagues (1990) argue that even with major reductions in chronic disease, life expectancy at birth will not increase past 85 years of age.

In the United States, the last century has seen a reduction in infant mortality, a reduction in infectious diseases as the cause of death, an increase in noninfectious diseases as the cause of death, and an overall increase in life expectancy at birth. There appears to have been no overall change in the total life span of humans, however. **Life span** is the measure of maximum longevity. Discounting Biblical accounts of Methuselah and other unsubstantiated claims, there have been no verified claims of humans living past 120 years. Changes in medicine and health care have increased life expectancy, but they have not, as yet, increased the human life span. This means that more and more people are likely to reach the limit of life, a phenomenon with far-reaching implications that will be discussed in the next chapter.

■ FIGURE 16.12
Changes in the death rate in New York City during the nineteenth and twentieth centuries. (*Source:* Omran [1977:12]. Courtesy of the Population Reference Bureau, Inc., Washington, D.C.)

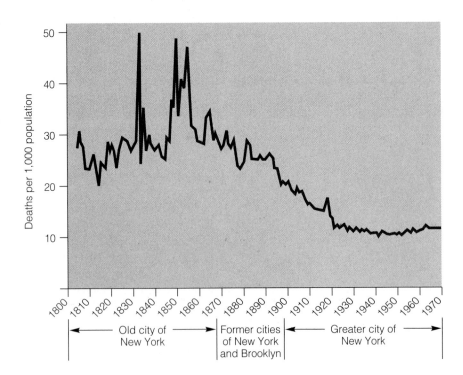

What has caused these rapid changes in disease rates and life expectancy? Cultural changes in industrial societies have often resulted in average improvements in health care, public sanitation, and water quality. These factors aid in reducing the spread and effect of infectious diseases, particularly in infancy. As a result, more people are likely to live to older ages—long enough, therefore, to develop the long-term noninfectious diseases, such as cancer. These diseases often require lengthy periods of time to reach a debilitating stage. A person who dies in early life from an infectious disease will obviously not have had sufficient time to develop noninfectious disorders.

Other contributing factors are changes in the physical environment brought about by urbanization and industrialization. Industrial pollution of the air and water can lead to increased levels of cancer and other noninfectious diseases. Technological and social changes have also led to the increased abundance of drugs such as alcohol and tobacco, which increase disease. Widespread use of infant formula, rather than breast feeding, in poor countries contributes greatly to infant and childhood health problems. Factors such as stress, lifestyle, crowding, and noise levels also appear to play a role in the disease process.

STUDIES OF THE EPIDEMIOLOGIC TRANSITION   The relationship between cultural change and disease rates emerges clearly in specific case studies of the epidemiologic transition. Omran (1977) looked at overall death rates in his study of the epidemiologic transition in New York City. Figure 16.12 shows the changing overall death rate in New York City over time. Before the 1860s, the overall death rate was high and had frequent spikes, primarily because of epidemics of cholera. Following the mid-1860s, both the overall death rate and the intensity of epidemics declined. This decrease corresponds with the establishment of the Health Department. After the 1920s, the spread of better sanitation and water supplies along with an improvement in drugs and health care and the introduction of pasteurized milk caused the death rates to decline even more.

Another study of the epidemiologic transition has been carried out on a smaller scale. Levison and colleagues (1981) analyzed census and burial data from the town of Manti, Utah, from 1849 to 1977. Their study focused on changes in disease patterns as the town changed from a frontier population (1849–1889) to a transitional rural agricultural population (1890–1929) to a modern agricultural community (1930–1977). Census data showed that the life expectancy at birth increased over time, and the major causes of death changed. Table 16.2 lists the five leading causes of death for the three periods. Infectious and parasitic diseases dropped from the primary cause of death in the initial frontier stage to the third cause of death during the transitional stage; it was not among the top five causes of death in the modern stage. Another major shift took place in circulatory diseases, which were not

life span A measure of the maximum length of life recorded for a species.

■ TABLE 16.2
The Five Leading Causes of Death in Manti, Utah, from 1849 to 1977

1849–1889	1890–1929	1930–1977
1. Infectious and parasitic diseases	Respiratory diseases	Circulatory system diseases
2. Respiratory diseases	Circulatory system diseases	Injuries
3. Congenital abnormalities	Infectious and parasitic diseases	Cancers
4. Digestive system diseases	Congenital abnormalities	Respiratory diseases
5. Injuries, genitourinary system diseases, and nervous system diseases (tied)	Digestive system diseases	Congenital abnormalities

Source: Levison et al. (1981:90)

among the top five causes of death in the frontier stage but rose to the second place in the transitional stage and the primary cause of death in the modern stage. By the modern stage, cancers had also risen to become the third cause of death. The changes in disease patterns were associated with improved sanitation, elimination of dependence on contaminated water supplies, and the adoption of newer medical techniques. The type of pattern shown in the Manti study parallels those found in other studies of the epidemiologic transition.

Not all human populations today have experienced the epidemiologic transition. In many Third World nations death rates, especially among infants and children, remain high. Inadequate health care, poor sanitation, contaminated water, poor nutrition, and warfare continue to produce high levels of mortality. These populational differences show up most clearly in rates of infant mortality. Worldwide, 8 percent of all children die in the first year of life. In a few nations, such as Japan, this rate is as low as 1 percent, whereas in some Asian and African nations it is as high as 20 percent (Teitelbaum 1988).

Secular Changes in Human Growth

The epidemiologic transition affects more than disease and death rates; its effects have also been observed in studies of child growth. During the past century, many industrialized nations have shown several secular changes in

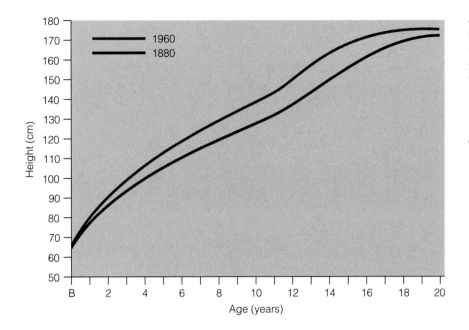

■ **FIGURE 16.13**
Secular change in European-
American males in North
America. At all ages the males
living in 1960 have greater
height than those who lived
in 1880. (From *Growth and
Development* by Robert M. Malina
© 1975, publisher Burgess Publishing Company, Min-
neapolis, MN)

child growth. A **secular change** is simply a change in the pattern of growth
across generations.

TYPES OF SECULAR CHANGES   Three basic secular changes have been observed
over the past century: (1) an increase in height, (2) an increase in weight, and
(3) a decrease in the age of sexual maturation. Children in many Westernized
nations are today taller and heavier than children the same age a century or
so ago. Figure 16.13 shows the average distance curve for height of North
American males of European ancestry in 1880 and 1960. There is no noticeable difference in body length at birth. Note, however, that at all postnatal
ages the 1960 males are consistently taller than the 1880 males. This difference is most noticeable during adolescence. Comparison of distance curves
for weight show the same pattern.

Another secular change is a decrease in the age of maturation. This is
most apparent in a specific measure of human development—the **age at
menarche,** the age at which a female experiences her first menstrual period.
Figure 16.14 plots the average age at menarche for the United States and

▲▲

secular change A
change in the average
pattern of growth in

a population over
different generations.

age at menarche The
age at which a female
experiences her first
menstrual period.

■ FIGURE 16.14
Secular change in age at
menarche (the age of the
female's first menstrual
period) in the United States
and several European
countries. (From *Growth and
Development* by Robert M. Malina
© 1975, publisher Burgess
Publishing Company,
Minneapolis, MN)

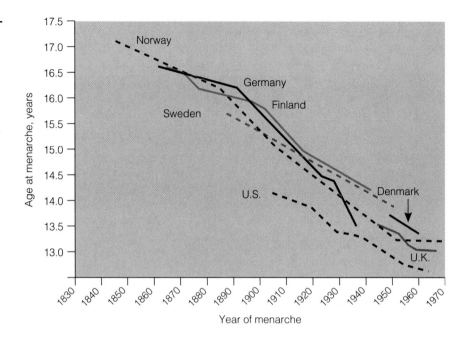

several European industrial nations over time. The general trend is one of earlier biological maturation.

CAUSES OF SECULAR CHANGE   The basic secular changes observed in industrialized nations during the past century reflect environmental change. There is no evidence that genetic potential has changed in such a short period of time; rather, environmental changes have allowed more people to reach their genetic potential for growth. These trends, however, should not be projected indefinitely into the future! Some data suggest that the secular changes in height, weight, and age at menarche have slowed down or stopped in some countries (Eveleth and Tanner 1990). Future environmental improvements could allow more and more children to reach their genetic potential for growth, but we should not expect average heights of 8 feet or more in another 100 years!

Many environmental factors have been suggested as responsible for these secular changes, including improved nutrition, reduction of childhood infectious disease, improved availability of health care, improved standard of living, and reduction of family size. Many of these factors are interrelated, making precise identification of causes difficult.

Malina (1979) notes that improved nutrition has often been cited as a primary cause of the observed secular changes. Though availability of nutritional intake has improved for many people, especially during infancy, Malina does not think it is solely responsible for secular changes. Many factors have operated together to produce the secular changes. Malina does suggest that one of the most important factors was an improvement in health conditions, resulting in the reduction in childhood infectious disease. Thus, the epidemiologic transition appears to be related to secular changes in human growth as well.

Some Contemporary Issues

The evolution of human health and disease did not end with the epidemiologic transition—it continues today. Cultural influences on disease continue to change, as does the environment and even the organisms responsible for infectious disease. Although even a review of all contemporary health problems is beyond the scope of an introductory text, several brief examples are given to illustrate *some* of our species' current health issues.

THE *"NEW WORLD SYNDROME"*   Kenneth Weiss and colleagues (1984) have applied the label **New World syndrome** to a set of noninfectious diseases that appear in elevated frequencies among Native Americans and groups with substantial Native-American admixture. These diseases include noninsulin-dependent diabetes (Figure 16.15), gallstones, gall bladder cancer, and increased obesity. Rates for these diseases tend to be highest in Native-American populations. Among admixed populations, such as Mexicans and Mexican Americans, the disease rates vary with the amount of Native-American admixture. In other words, the more Native-American ancestry a person has, the greater the risk of developing these diseases, other factors being equal. In addition, all these diseases tend to run in families.

These three characteristics point to genetic susceptibility to the diseases among Native-American peoples. Noninfectious diseases, however, are affected not only by genetic predispositions but also by environmental factors. In the case of the New World syndrome, rates of these diseases have increased dramatically since World War II. To understand this increase, we need to look not only at genetic factors but also at changing environmental conditions.

Weiss and colleagues argue there is strong evidence that genetic susceptibilities to the New World syndrome diseases existed in the earliest inhabitants of the Americas. If such genetic predispositions are unique among New World populations, then there must have been rapid genetic change since the initial occupation of the Americas by migrants from Asia. Weiss and colleagues think that the genes that currently predispose individuals to the New World syndrome were originally advantageous. Today, however, these same genetic factors are generally disadvantageous. Weiss and colleagues therefore ask the question: "What kind of gene has disadvantage now but advantage among northern hunter-gatherers?" (1984:171). They suggest that the relationship of all diseases in the syndrome to nutrient utilization provides a possible answer: these genes conferred changes in metabolism,

▲▲▲▲▲▲▲▲▲▲▲▲▲▲▲▲▲▲▲▲▲▲▲▲▲▲▲▲▲▲

New World syndrome
A set of noninfectious diseases that appears in elevated frequencies in persons of Native-American ancestry.

■ FIGURE 16.15
Prevalence rates (percent)
for noninsulin-dependent
diabetes in selected samples
from the United States,
and grouped by ethnicity:
European Americans, Mexican
Americans, and Native
Americans. Native Americans
have the highest prevalence
rates, followed by Mexican
Americans (who have con-
siderable Native-American
ancestry). (*Source of data:*
Weiss et al. [1984], using samples
that consist of adults 25 years
or older).

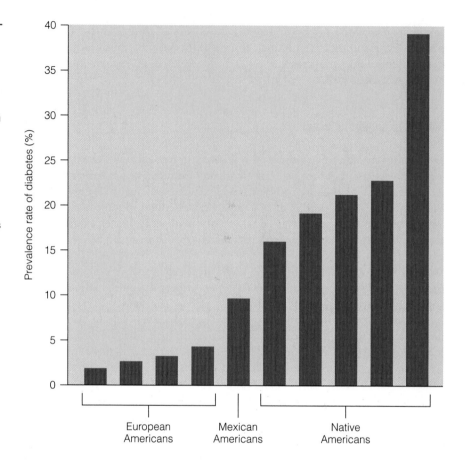

allowing more efficient use of food resources and fat storage. Given the importance of fat resources in hunting-gathering populations, particularly during pregnancy and nursing, such genes would be advantageous in an environment characterized by frequent food shortages.

Today, however, these same genetic factors are proving disadvantageous to individuals with Native-American ancestry. The reason may lie in the continued "westernization" of these populations and the associated changes in diet. An increase in carbohydrates and fats in the diet will result in greater fat storage, leading to obesity and increased risk for other noninfectious disorders. Populations without Native-American ancestry have also shown increases in certain noninfectious diseases because of changes in culture and lifestyle. Native Americans and related populations, however, show even greater increases because of their additional genetic susceptibility.

AIDS   At present, **acquired immune deficiency syndrome (AIDS)** is a growing medical problem in many parts of the world. This disease results in the breakdown of the body's immune defense system, ultimately leading to

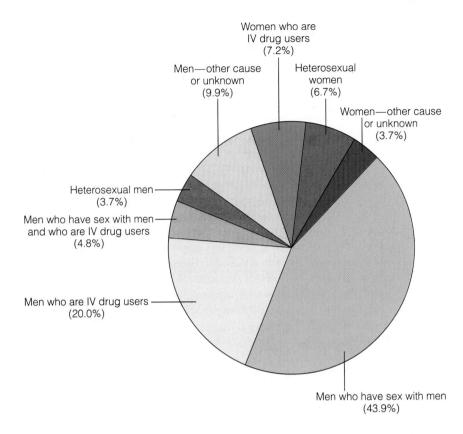

Women who are
IV drug users
(7.2%)

Men—other cause
or unknown
(9.9%)

Heterosexual
women
(6.7%)

Women—other cause
or unknown
(3.7%)

Heterosexual men
(3.7%)

Men who have sex with men
and who are IV drug users
(4.8%)

Men who are IV drug users
(20.0%)

Men who have sex with men
(43.9%)

■ FIGURE 16.16
Risk factors of new cases
of AIDS in the United States
in 1994. (*Source of data:*
Centers for Disease Control and
Prevention, 1995)

death. Research has linked AIDS to infection from HIV (human immuno-deficiency virus). The origin of HIV is unclear, but it may have started as a zoonosis. The virus is transmitted through sexual intercourse, particularly anal intercourse. AIDS is also transmitted by transfusions of contaminated blood and by sharing of contaminated needles among drug users. The disease can also be transmitted from an infected pregnant woman to her fetus.

From 1981 through the end of 1994, over 440,000 cases of AIDS have been reported in the United States, based on the revised diagnostic criteria of 1993. Of these cases, over 270,000 had died by the end of 1994. Analysis of new cases diagnosed in 1994 shows that the vast majority of adult or adolescent cases were male (82 percent). Analysis of risk factors among male and female adults and adolescents (Figure 16.16) shows the primary risk group is men who have had sex with another man (44 percent), followed by male intravenous drug users (20 percent). The next largest category is women who are IV drug users (7 percent), followed by women who obtained AIDS through heterosexual contact (slightly less than 7 percent) and finally, men who obtained AIDS through heterosexual contact (slightly less than 4 percent) (Centers for Disease Control and Prevention 1995).

In other parts of the world the epidemiologic pattern of AIDS risk is different. In much of Africa, for example, the primary spread of AIDS is

▲▲▲▲▲▲▲▲▲▲▲▲▲▲▲▲▲▲▲▲▲▲▲▲▲▲▲▲▲

**acquired immune
deficiency syndrome
(AIDS)** A fatal viral
disease that results in
the breakdown of the
body's immune defense
system.

through heterosexual contact (McGrath 1990). Although some feel that the AIDS epidemic is slowing down in the United States, the epidemic in Africa is still increasing, with indication of an increase in Asia as well. As of 1993, an estimated 12 million people worldwide had the HIV virus (Cowley 1993).

Even though AIDS is a recent disease, it has already had major effects on American culture. The threat of such a deadly disease has led to proposed quarantines, increased discrimination against homosexuals, and the burning of houses of AIDS-infected children. Perhaps the greatest change, however, has been a reduction in sexual activity with multiple partners or with partners whose backgrounds are not known.

In sum, the current spread of AIDS shows us a clear example of how a disease can affect society both biologically and culturally. This is not a new phenomenon. During the Middle Ages, the Black Death continued to have a profound effect on culture long after the epidemics were over. Images of death and despair endured in the arts and in literature.

By studying diseases such as AIDS and the Black Death, medical anthropologists not only contribute to an understanding of the spread of diseases but also show us the relationships between disease and society. We cannot view health and disease as an isolated segment of our total lives. They affect all aspects of living.

PROTEIN-CALORIE MALNUTRITION   Low quantity and quality of nutrition is a major problem in the world today, affecting millions of infants and children. Undernutrition, particularly during infancy, can have severe effects. Not only is the physical growth stunted, but mental retardation may also result. Without an adequate diet, infants and children are more susceptible to infectious disease. Severe undernutrition is highly prevalent in Third World nations, where poor nutrition is often associated with overpopulation, poverty, inadequate sewage disposal, contaminated water, high rates of infectious disease, and economic and political conflicts.

A number of nutritional problems, collectively known as **protein-calorie malnutrition,** results from an inadequate amount of proteins and/or calories in the diet. Protein-calorie malnutrition is the most serious nutritional problem on the planet. Its various forms have different physical symptoms, but all stem from the basic problems of an inadequate diet and have the same ultimate effects, ranging from growth retardation to death.

The most severe types of protein-calorie malnutrition are **kwashiorkor** (a severe deficiency in proteins but not calories) and **marasmus** (severe deficiencies in both proteins and calories). Kwashiorkor occurs most often in infants and young children who are weaned from their mother's breast onto a diet lacking in proteins. The infant suffers growth retardation, muscle wasting, and lowered resistance to disease. One of the symptoms of kwashiorkor is the swelling of the body (Figure 16.17). Marasmus is also most prevalent during infancy and similarly leads to growth retardation, muscle wasting, and death. A child suffering from marasmus typically looks emaciated (Figure 16.18). The devastating effects of protein-calorie malnutrition should

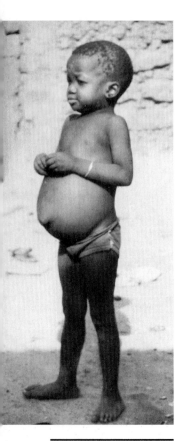

■ **FIGURE 16.17**
Child with kwashiorkor in Mali, West Africa. (Courtesy Katherine Dettwyler)

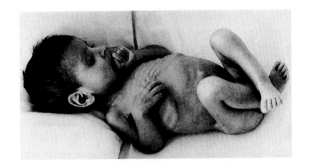

■ **FIGURE 16.18**
A child with marasmus, a
severe protein and calorie
deficiency. (World Health
Organization photo by A. Isaza)

not be underestimated; between 5 and 45 percent of children in some developing nations suffer from one of these nutritional diseases.

Although the physical appearance of children with kwashiorkor and marasmus differs, both suffer from an inadequate diet. Population pressure and poverty certainly play a major role in much of protein-calorie malnutrition, but they are not the only factors that come into play. Some researchers, such as anthropologist Katherine Dettwyler, have argued that cultural beliefs regarding nutrition are at least as important. Such beliefs include stressing quantity over quality, postponing the age at which children eat solid foods, and other practices that compromise proper nutrition. Thus, the elimination of protein-calorie malnutrition will require more than an attack on population growth and the reduction of disease; it will also require nutritional education (Dettwyler 1994).

SUMMARY

Epidemiology, the study of disease patterns, is an interdisciplinary field that draws on the knowledge of a variety of biological, physical, and social sciences. Anthropology contributes to an understanding of epidemiology by bringing comparative, evolutionary, and holistic perspectives to the study of health and disease. Within biological anthropology, many researchers are interested in the relationship among genetics, environment, culture, and the biological manifestations of a disease.

Anthropology's comparative approach allows us to look at the relationship of health and disease to cultural as well as biological evolution. Hunting-gathering populations have different patterns of disease than do agricultural or industrialized populations. Ecological differences account for

▲▲

protein-calorie malnutrition A group of nutritional diseases resulting from inadequate amounts of protein and/or calories.

kwashiorkor An extreme form of protein-calorie malnutrition resulting from a severe deficiency in proteins but not calories.

marasmus An extreme form of protein-calorie malnutrition resulting from severe deficiencies in both proteins and calories.

The Coming Plague?

In May 1995, the world focused much of its attention on Zaire, in Africa, where there was an outbreak of a frequently fatal disease: Ebola. Although the Ebola virus was only discovered in 1976, previous epidemics had killed hundreds of people in Zaire and Uganda. The Ebola virus is very mysterious; its origin is still unknown and it is not clear what factors precipitate epidemics (Cowley et al. 1995).

What makes this recent outbreak alarming is that it is not the only case of a recent epidemic of an infectious disease. There have been a number of newly identified infectious diseases within the past few decades, including the HIV virus that causes AIDS. Other examples include Lyme disease, the Kyasanur Forest virus, the O'nyong-nyong virus, hepatitis C and E viruses, Legionnaire's disease, toxic-shock syndrome, and cat-scratch fever, among others. There have also been new variants of old diseases, such as a new type of cholera bacterium and strains of tuberculosis that are antibiotic-resistant (Levins et al. 1994; Karlen 1995).

The continued outbreak of new infectious diseases, and the reemergence of old ones, has caused scientists to reevaluate the historic nature of the epidemiologic transition. In 1975, it was written that virtually all infectious diseases had been eliminated in the Western world (Levins et al. 1994). Smallpox was eliminated worldwide in 1977, and tuberculosis and polio were close behind. It was perhaps natural for many to feel optimistic regarding these changes, and to project the epidemiologic transition into the future, where all infectious diseases had been conquered.

The situation now looks much more complex. It is unlikely that infectious diseases will be eliminated. The microorganisms responsible for such diseases continue to evolve, often resulting in new and devastating epidemics. In addition, we have to keep in mind that human culture continually modifies the environment, such that old diseases often get a new opportunity for growth, or evolve themselves to adapt to the new environment. Rates of tuberculosis, for example, have risen in past years in some locations after a long period of steady decline. It seems that the tuberculosis bacterium has evolved a resistance to the traditional antibiotics used to control it. What this means is that we must now seek new antibiotics, which in turn will likely lead to new antibiotic-resistant strains of tuberculosis. Because microorganisms evolve faster than humans, we might find ourselves in an eternal struggle to catch up.

Any time the environment changes, there is an opportunity for the emergence of new infectious diseases. New technologies often lend themselves to the development of infectious disease by creating microenvironments conducive to bacterial spread. Air-conditioning, for example, is implicated in the origin and spread of Legionnaire's disease. New environments are also created by rapid deforestation and conversion of land for agriculture and industrialization. In addition, this continued conversion of remote and isolated habitats allows previously rare microorganisms to come into contact with the human species. Another problem is that continued pollution increases the mutation rate of microorganisms in addition to interfering with ecosystems (Levins et al. 1994). Also, we live in a world where it is easier than ever for an infectious disease to spread across nations and continents. New forms of travel (such as the airplane) and international commerce allow quick contact between human groups, including those that have no prior immune experience (Levins et al. 1994; Karlen 1995).

The continued emergence of infectious diseases, particularly those that are antibiotic-resistant and often fatal, has led many to suggest that our problems with infectious disease are far from over, and indeed may soon rise again. One current example is a book entitled The Coming Plague (1994) by Laurie Garrett, who warns of these problems and others. Will we soon see the emergence of worldwide pandemics equivalent in mortality to the Black Death of the Middle Ages or the 1918 influenza pandemic, both of which killed millions of people? Will we someday look back on the latter half of the twentieth century as a "golden age," where epidemic infectious diseases were temporarily controlled by drugs before the microorganisms evolved beyond them? Although the future is unknown, it is now clear to all that predictions about the elimination of infectious disease were premature. We will always have to deal with infectious disease, and the nature of the threat will change over time as the microorganisms continue to evolve and as we continue to change our environment. We win many battles, but we cannot give up even for a moment in the fight against infectious disease.

much of this difference. In hunting-gathering populations, the group size is too small to sustain large epidemics; the major causes of death are from accidents and infections from animals. In agricultural societies, population size is larger, the group is sedentary, and there are often problems in sewage disposal and water supply; all these factors result in increased epidemics of infectious disease.

Industrialized nations have gone through an "epidemiologic transition": the primary causes of death have shifted again, from infectious to noninfectious diseases. The epidemiologic transition was brought about by a variety of factors, perhaps the most significant of which were the development of clean water and the proper disposal of sewage. This change in disease patterns has had other effects as well. Life expectancy at birth has increased, primarily because of the elimination or reduction of childhood infectious diseases. There have also been several secular changes in human growth, with children being taller and heavier at any given age, and reaching sexual maturity more quickly. These changes also relate to the reduction of infectious disease. The reduction in infectious diseases means more of us live to older ages, and as a consequence we are more likely to develop chronic noninfectious diseases. This shift also means that we must expand our views regarding the control of disease. For a century we have thought of solving infectious disease problems by means of an antibiotic or vaccination when in fact improved hygiene is at least as important. The noninfectious diseases, such as diabetes and heart disease, do not have a single cause. As such, we can no longer count on the development of a "magic bullet" (i.e., a single cure) in our search to cure disease. Genetic, environmental, dietary, and other factors affect the relative risk for these diseases. We can modify these factors, but to what extent is still not clear.

SUPPLEMENTAL READINGS

Cohen, M. N. 1989. *Health and the Rise of Civilization.* New Haven: Yale University Press. An excellent review of epidemiologic changes in the human species prior to industrialization, with particular attention to the transition from hunting and gathering to agriculture.

Karlen, A. 1995. *Man and Microbes: Disease and Plagues in History and Modern Times.* New York: G. P. Putnam. A review of the history of infectious disease in the human species, including some discussion of the future.

Lilienfeld, A., and D. E. Lilienfeld, 1980. *Foundations of Epidemiology.* 2d ed. New York: Oxford University Press. A well-written introduction to the field of epidemiologic research with many examples.

McElroy, A., and P. K. Townsend, 1989. *Medical Anthropology in Ecological Perspective.* 2d ed. Boulder, CO: Westview Press. An excellent introduction to the different approaches of medical anthropology, providing many case studies.

CHAPTER 17

The Demographic Evolution of Human Populations

The interrelationship of biology and culture in human populations is perhaps most clearly visible in demographic patterns. **Demography** is the study of the size, composition, and distribution of human populations. Like epidemiology, demography is an interdisciplinary subject. Demography is studied by anthropologists, biologists, geographers, historians, economists, sociologists, and others.

As with the study of human health and disease, anthropology brings to demography comparative, evolutionary, and holistic perspectives. Anthropologists do not focus only on demographic processes within a single society, such as the United States. We examine all types of societies, from hunter-gatherers, to agricultural, to industrialized nations. We also look at demographic processes in an evolutionary context, seeking to understand demographic shifts in the evolution of our species. Using a holistic perspective, we link demographic processes with patterns of biological and cultural variation.

THE STUDY OF DEMOGRAPHY

Demographic studies focus on the measurement of three characteristics: fertility, mortality, and migration.

Demographic Measures

In literate human populations the demographic measures of fertility, mortality, and migration are often revealed in census records and similar data. Birth records, for example, provide data for computing different measures of fertility. Death records provide information for determining the rate of deaths, the age at death, and the cause of death. In societies where written records are not kept, anthropologists gather demographic data from interviews.

FERTILITY   The measure of fertility provides us with information on the rate of actual births in a population. When we count birth records or interview people to find out how many children they have had, we are measuring the **fertility** of a population. On the other hand, we are also sometimes interested in measurements of **fecundity,** or the number of individuals capable of having children. Measurements of fertility and fecundity are not always the same; people that are capable of having children do not necessarily have them.

The analysis of fertility is particularly interesting to biological anthropologists because fertility reflects both biological and cultural variation. Some individuals may have more children than others because of biological differences in fertility. An example of reduced fertility, discussed in Chapter 14, reflected incompatibilities in blood types. In addition, some individuals may have more, or fewer, children for cultural reasons. For example, economic factors play a role in determining fertility. Many North American middle- and upper-class couples are deliberately having fewer children today. Part of the reason is that many people postpone having their first child for a number of years to finish an education or become established in a career.

Biology and culture can interrelate to affect fertility. One example of this is fertility control among the !Kung San, a group of hunters and gatherers who live in the Kalahari Desert in southern Africa (the "!" preceding their name indicates a clicking sound made in their language). Even though

---

demography The study of the size, composition, and distribution of human populations.

fertility Actual reproduction: the number of births per individual.

fecundity Potential reproduction: the number of people capable of having children.

the !Kung do not use modern contraceptive devices, their fertility rates are not high. The spacing between births is rather high, 44 months on average (Potts 1988), which acts to keep overall fertility lower than if the birth interval were shorter. Why is the time between births so long? A major factor is breast feeding. When a woman nurses her child, hormonal changes take place that reduce the probability of ovulation (Wood 1994). Because !Kung women nurse for several years, the average interval between births increases. Although breast feeding is not a recommended means of contraception for many societies (where much more effective means are available), it does have an average statistical effect on the fertility rates of the entire population.

!Kung fertility is also affected by the frequency pattern of nursing, one quite different from that often practiced in Western societies. Among the !Kung, breast feeding may occur as frequently as every 15 minutes but for only a minute or so. According to Peter Ellison, the frequency of nursing is the important component that acts to reduce the probability of ovulation among the !Kung (Ackerman 1987).

Although fertility is affected by both biological and cultural factors, changes in fertility also affect the biology and culture of a population. For example, an increase in the number of births in a population may lead to an increase in population size. Larger populations require more food, are less affected by genetic drift, and are more likely to experience epidemics of infectious disease. Such changes can, in turn, further affect fertility. The relationship between fertility and biological and cultural variation in populations can best be described in terms of a feedback loop. Fertility is affected by, and causes effects on, biology and culture.

MORTALITY   The measure of **mortality** is the measurement of death. Like fertility, mortality can be influenced by biological and cultural factors. The age at death and the cause of death may relate to biological factors, such as susceptibility to certain diseases. Culture can also affect the timing and cause of death. Differences in social class may affect quality of health care. Warfare may increase the probability of early death, as will hazardous employment. A long history of drug use or poor nutrition also affects the probability of death.

As discussed in the last chapter, measures of life expectancy at birth can tell us something about the average age of death and, by extension, about the average health of individuals in a population. Life expectancy is most often determined from a **life table,** a compilation of the number of deaths for different age groups in a population. Both demographers and the life insurance industry use these records, which could more accurately be called "death tables" because they provide a measure of the probability of dying by a given age. The data in life tables can be used to compute the life expectancy of individuals at different ages. One measure, discussed in the last chapter, is life expectancy at birth. This measure provides a good index of overall mortality and health in a population.

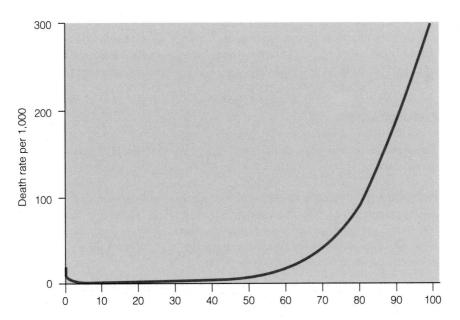

■ FIGURE 17.1
Mortality rates in the United States in 1970 as a function of age. This figure shows the typical mortality curve for human populations. Death rates decrease rapidly after the first year of life and increase again among the elderly. (*Source of data:* Fries and Crapo [1981:146])

A given life expectancy does not mean everyone will live to that age. It is only an average. Many people die before their original life expectancy and many live beyond it. As an average measure, however, life expectancy does tell us something about the net patterns of mortality in a population. If, for example, 40 percent of a population dies in the first year of life, the overall life expectancy at birth for the population will be low. Reduction of the number of infant deaths will lead to an increase in average life expectancy at birth.

Mortality rates are strongly related to age. Plotting death rates against age gives a characteristics curve, as shown in Figure 17.1 for the United States in 1970. Death rates drop quickly after the first year of life, remaining relatively low and constant through midadulthood. Death rates increase rapidly with age among the elderly. The *exact* shape of the curve will vary from one population to another. In underdeveloped nations, for example, infant mortality will be higher. The overall shape of the curve is basically the same in all human populations (Gage 1989).

MIGRATION   **Migration** is the movement of people, normally for long periods of time, from one location (village, city, state, country) to another. As with

mortality Death.

life table A table that provides an estimate of the probability that an individual will die by a certain age, used to estimate life expectancy.

migration The movement of individuals from one population to another.

fertility and mortality, migration is affected by biological and cultural factors and in turn has an effect on biology and culture. Examples of the relationship of migration to biology and culture have been discussed in Chapters 3 and 14 in the context of gene flow.

Population Growth

The overall size of a population results from the net effects of fertility, mortality, and migration.

COMPONENTS OF POPULATION GROWTH   Births increase the population size and deaths decrease the population size. Migration can either increase or decrease the population size, depending on whether more people move into a population (increase) or leave the population (decrease). The amount a population can grow, or reduce, is expressed as

Change in population size = births – deaths ± migrants

If we ignore the effect of migration for a moment, the change in population size because of **natural increase** is the number of births minus the number of deaths. If more people are born than die in a certain period of time, then the population grows. If the number of deaths exceeds the number of births, the population size declines.

Under ideal conditions, human populations may grow at an exponential rate. There is a limit, however, to growth in any population, dictated by available land and food resources. This limit, called the **carrying capacity,** can change, given certain ecological or technological changes. For example, the development of agriculture resulted in a dramatic increase in the carrying capacity of land for human populations. The ability to extract more food resources from a given amount of land allowed larger populations.

CASE STUDY: IRISH POPULATION GROWTH   Examination of historical patterns of population growth in Ireland provides an example of the ways in which fertility, mortality, and migration relate to ecological and cultural changes. Figure 17.2 shows the total population of the Republic of Ireland from 1687 through 1966. After 1700, the population increased rapidly, reaching a peak during the 1840s. The population then declined rapidly until 1900, after which time little overall change in population size took place.

The traditional explanation for the rapid increase of Ireland's population is the introduction of the potato during the early 1700s. The decline after the 1840s is usually associated with the Great Famine (1846–1851), at which time the repeated failure of the potato crop led to large numbers of deaths and migrations. The full story of Irish population growth is a bit more complicated, involving agriculture, marriage patterns, and land inheritance.

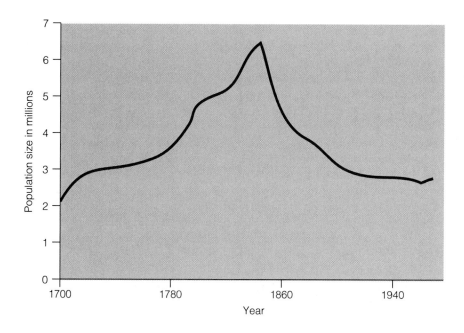

■ FIGURE 17.2
Population growth in the
Republic of Ireland from 1687
to 1966. (*Source of data:* 1687–
1791 [Connell 1950], 1821–1966
[Kennedy 1973])

Before the 1700s, agriculture in Ireland had been severely limited because of hilly terrain and large sections of bog. As a result, the carrying
capacity of the population was limited. Though fertility among the largely
Catholic population of Ireland had been moderately high per married person, many people did not marry, and marriages were usually late. Marriages
were most often arranged by the parents of the bride and groom as part of
an economic contract. A common prerequisite for marriage in rural areas
was for the groom to have land and the bride to have a dowry. Most men
acquired land through inheritance, often late in life because of the father's
delay in passing the land on to a son. Because the agricultural output of the
land was low, in most cases only one son could inherit the land. The other
sons tended to leave or had to remain unmarried (Arensberg and Kimball
1968). In either case, overall population growth was kept in check by the fact
that few men and women married. Given the religious rules on premarital
and extramarital sex, almost all births resulted from marriages. A limit on
the number of marriages meant a limit on fertility and population growth.

The introduction of the potato changed these patterns. Potatoes can
grow in a wide variety of environments and provide ample nutrition. An

natural increase
Number of births minus
number of deaths.

carrying capacity The
maximum population
size capable of being

supported in a given
environment.

increased emphasis on the potato allowed more efficient use of the land. Now fathers could subdivide their land and pass it on to more than one son. Some of the land was also relinquished earlier (Connell 1950). As a result, marriages became more frequent and occurred at an earlier age, which led to many more births and population growth. This situation continued for several generations, and more and more sons required more and more land. Family plots were repeatedly subdivided until families were living on extremely small portions.

The introduction of the potato, combined with cultural views on large family size, led to rapid population growth in Ireland. It also resulted in a precarious ecology. Failures in the potato crop had serious consequences. The potato crop was often destroyed by blight, and the Great Famine saw five continuous years of blight with no relief. Compounding the problem was the fact that the potato crop was used not only for food but also to pay rent to English landlords. During the Great Famine, roughly 1.5 million people died and 1 million left the country (Woodham-Smith 1962). Following the Great Famine, the system returned to an earlier pattern of delayed marriage, less frequent marriage, and fewer subdivisions of the land.

The Irish example shows how changing patterns of fertility and mortality had resulted in rapid changes in population size. Migration also played an important role in the regulation of population size. Even before the Great Famine, large numbers of people had left Ireland for economic opportunities in England or the United States. These early migrants were often able to

■ **FIGURE 17.3**
The age-sex structure of developing regions of the world in 1984. (*Source:* Bouvier [1984:12]. Courtesy of the Population Reference Bureau, Inc., Washington, D.C., and United Nations, *Demographic Indicators of Countries: Estimates and Projections as Assessed in 1980* [New York: 1982], pp. 61 and 63, data for 1985)

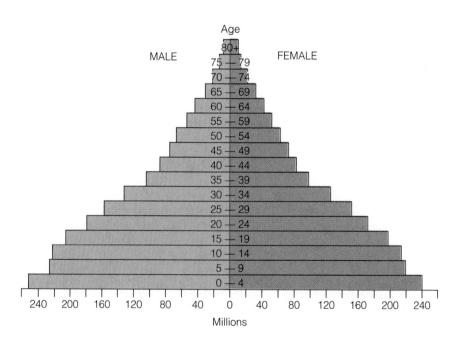

provide aid to families during the Great Famine, thus allowing them to leave the country. Migration out of Ireland became very frequent during the nineteenth and twentieth centuries. In fact, the rate of natural increase (births minus deaths) since the late nineteenth century has been positive. If natural increase is positive, then the population grows. If people had not moved out of the country, then the population would have gotten larger (Aalen 1963).

The Age-Sex Structure of Populations

Demographers also study the composition of populations. Who makes up the population, in terms of sex, age, ethnicity, occupation, and religion, among other characteristics? Most demographic studies focus special attention on the number of males and females per age group in a population— that is, on the **age-sex structure** of a population. A device known as a **population pyramid** is the best way to describe a population's age-sex structure at a particular point in time. The population pyramid is a graph showing the numbers of both sexes at different age groups.

DEVELOPING NATIONS   Figure 17.3 shows the age-sex structure of developing regions of the world in 1984 (those where industrial development is fairly recent, such as Mexico, Cuba, and Taiwan). The bottom axis of the graph shows the number of males on the left and the number of females on the right. The vertical axis represents different age groups, from 0 to 4 years of age in the first group, to 80-plus years of age in the top group. The population pyramid allows a succinct display of basic demographic patterns. It is obvious that infants and children greatly outnumber young adults or the elderly.

   The age-sex structure of developing nations illustrates the nature of fertility and mortality in these populations. High fertility results in the large numbers of people in young age groups. The pyramid shape results from the fact that fewer people live to the next age group. Developing nations typically have high fertility rates, combined with a reduction in mortality, leading to high rates of population growth.

DEVELOPED NATIONS   The age-sex structure of a developed nation, such as the United States or Sweden is quite different. Figure 17.4 shows the age-sex structure of the developed regions of the world in 1984. This population

▲▲

age-sex structure A measure of the composition of a population in terms of	the numbers of males and females at different ages.	**population pyramid** A diagram of the age-sex structure.

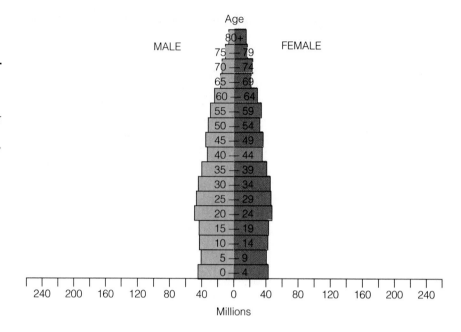

■ **FIGURE 17.4**
The age-sex structure of developed regions of the world in 1984. (*Source:* Bouvier [1984:12]. Courtesy of the Population Reference Bureau, Inc., Washington, D.C., and United Nations, *Demographic Indicators of Countries: Estimates and Projections as Assessed in 1980* [New York: 1982], pp. 61 and 63, data for 1985)

pyramid is more rectangular in shape. The largest section of the population is not infants and young children but young adults. This shape results from a reduction in infant mortality combined with lower fertility. Fewer people are born, making the lower age groups smaller. Because more people live longer, the older age groups stay fairly numerous. The many biological and cultural implications of this change in the age-sex structure from developing nations to developed nations will be discussed later.

DEMOGRAPHY AND THE MODERN WORLD

Today's world is constantly changing. Advances in communications technologies bring the peoples of the world in closer contact with one another. The average life expectancy in developed nations continues to increase. More and more, the economic systems of many nations are becoming interconnected. Many demographic changes are taking place as well, acting as both cause and effect of social, political, and economic changes. Several of the major changes in the world's demography are discussed here.

The Demographic Transition

The demographic changes that have taken place in many industrialized nations over the past century have been described by demographic transition theory. Though how applicable this theory is for all populations is still being debated, it does serve as a convenient summary of basic demographic trends that have occurred in a number of societies.

Demographic transition theory states that as a population becomes more economically developed, a reduction in death rates will take place first, followed by a reduction in fertility rates. Three stages are usually identified in this model (Swedlund and Armelagos 1976). Stage 1 populations are those of undeveloped areas with high mortality and high fertility rates. Because the high number of births is balanced by the high number of deaths, the overall population size remains more or less stable. The age-sex structure of a stage 1 population resembles a true pyramid with a very wide base and a very narrow apex. The broad base, corresponding to infants and young children, is a product of the high fertility. In a stage 1 population, the majority consists of very young people, many of whom will not live to grow older.

Stage 2 populations are found in developing regions where demographic and economic factors are changing rapidly. A stage 2 population is characterized by high fertility and lowered mortality. The transition to lowered mortality, especially in childhood, is a consequence of improvements in heath care and medical technologies. Because the fertility rate remains high, there are more births than deaths. As a result, the population grows in size. The age-sex structure still resembles a pyramid, but with the top portion becoming wider as more people survive to older ages (see Figure 17.3). The base of the pyramid is still broad because fertility rates are high.

Stage 3 populations are found in developed regions and are characterized by low rates of fertility and mortality. Because of technological, social, economic, and educational changes, people in developed regions have more of an opportunity to control family size. As is often the case, the fertility rate declines. Because the rates of births and deaths are both low such populations may show little growth. The age-sex structure becomes more and more rectangular as the base decreases (see Figure 17.4). Some nations, such as Sweden, show this pattern clearly. Others, such as the United States, are still in the process of becoming a stage 3 population.

The demographic transition model has several problems. Mortality and fertility rates represent a continuous range and cannot easily be separated into "low" and "high" phases. Situations unique to certain populations, such as the Baby Boom in the United States, may result in fluctuating rates of fertility (see the Special Topic box). Also, it is not clear to what extent stage 1 has been characteristic of most human history (Swedlund and Armelagos 1976). In spite of these problems and others, the model does provide a rough summary of the types of average changes found accompanying economic and industrial development.

World Population Growth

The total human population of the world has increased throughout human evolution, especially during the past several centuries. Estimates of prehistoric population size are crude, but they do provide us with an idea of the

▲▲▲▲▲▲▲▲▲▲▲▲▲▲▲▲▲▲▲▲▲▲▲▲▲▲▲▲▲

demographic transition theory A model of demographic change that states that as a population becomes economically developed, a reduction in death rates (leading to population growth) will take place first, followed by a reduction in birth rates.

The Baby Boom

A classic example of how changing social and economic factors affect population growth is the "Baby Boom" in the history of the United States. In general, although the population of the United States has continually risen since the first Federal Census of 1790, the *rate* of increase has generally declined. The accompanying figure shows this clearly by plotting the percentage change in population size every decade from 1790 through the most recent Census of 1990. There is a general trend for the percentage of growth to decline; in some cases, such as time periods corresponding to the Civil War and the Great Depression, this reduction has been even more noticeable.

The exception to this general rule was the temporary increase in the *rate* of population growth that occurred following World War II. Examination of demographic records shows that this increase was due to an increase in the fertility rate. The "Baby Boom" is the name given to the increase in the number of births between 1946 and 1964. Several social and economic factors account for the Baby Boom. It was not simply that men returning from the war made up for lost time with their wives. Such an effect often accompanies the end of a war, but the Baby Boom lasted much longer.

The economic growth of the United States continued to increase rapidly following World War II. As economic growth increases, so does the demand for labor. This demand is often met by new immigrants into a population. In the United States, however, restrictive laws had reduced the number of immigrants. The pool of available labor was also reduced by the fact that there had been fewer births during the 1920s and 1930s. Thus, fewer men were available to meet the increased demand. Women tended to be locked out of many occupations because of sexual bias. Though it is true that women took the place of men in the workforce during the war, afterwards the preference for women to remain at home raising children prevailed.

The relative lack of available labor meant that young men returned from the war often had excellent opportunities for employment. A good income meant that men could afford to marry and raise a family earlier than they could under lesser conditions. The economic conditions prevailing after World War II meant that a couple could have several children without lowering their standard of living (Weeks 1981). People married earlier and the spacing between births was shorter than in previous times, both of which contributed to an increase in the birth rate. Of course, not everyone married or had larger families or even shared in economic growth. On average, however, these changes were sufficient to affect the birth rate, and therefore the rate of population growth.

After 1958, the fertility rates in the United States began to decline. By the mid-1960s the Baby Boom was over. From this point on, changing economic conditions and greater educational and economic opportunities contributed to delayed marriage and childbirth as well as the desire for smaller families. By

extent of population growth. For example, the total world population 50,000 years B.P. was most likely to be in the neighborhood of 1.3 million people. By 10,000 years B.P., the estimated population was 6 million people (Weiss 1984). These low numbers are consistent with what we know about hunting-and-gathering cultures and their carrying capacities.

Following the development and spread of agriculture, the population of the world increased more and more rapidly. The major acceleration came following the Industrial Revolution (roughly 1750). Since this time, the world's population has increased at an exponential rate to the present size (Figure 17.5). Between 1750 and 1950, the world's population tripled in size. Between 1950 and 1990, the world's population increased from 2.5 billion to 5.3 billion—an increase of 112 percent (Horiuchi 1992). The world popula-

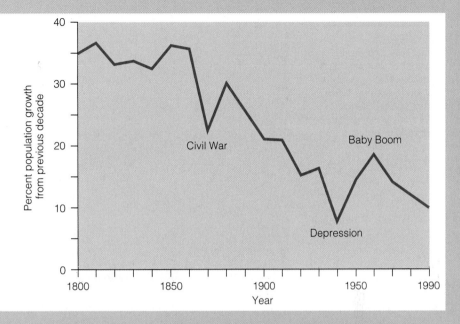

Changes in the rate of population growth in the United States from 1790 to 1990. The percentage of increase in population size from the previous decade is plotted against year. Note the reversal of the downward trend during the Baby Boom years.

the mid-1980s, the average number of children per couple was less than replacement (that is, less than two children on average per couple). Of course, the United States continues to grow because so many women were born during the Baby Boom. Even if the average number of children per women is less than two, the sheer number of women will continue to lead to increased population growth for a short time. In fact, the total number of births in the United States rose starting in 1977 and peaked in 1990 (Gabriel 1995).

This short burst of births is often referred to as the "Baby Boomlet," brought about by the fact that so many of the original Baby Boomers were now in their child-bearing years. Thus, the Baby Boom continues to affect fertility levels and population growth a generation later.

(Source of data: U.S. Department of Commerce 1991)

tion was estimated to be 5,607,000,000 people in mid-1994. The current rate of growth is an increase of roughly 245,000 people per day, reflecting an estimated 386,000 births and 141,000 deaths each day (Haub 1995).

The projected world population in the year 2000 is over 6 billion, and over 8 billion by the year 2050 (Haub 1992). Such projections are difficult to compute, relying on extrapolation of current trends. It is possible to be overly optimistic or pessimistic when evaluating trends. Bouvier (1984) believes that by the year 2034 the actual rate of world population growth will begin to diminish. This estimate is based on the continued transition to developed nations, an increase in the efforts to control fertility in developing nations, and a continued increase in life expectancy throughout the world. Regardless of the specific estimate, the current trend is toward continued

■ FIGURE 17.5
World population growth
since the origin of agriculture.
(From *Population: An Introduction
to Concepts and Issues*, Second
Edition, by John R. Weeks ©
1978 by Wadsworth Publishing
Company)

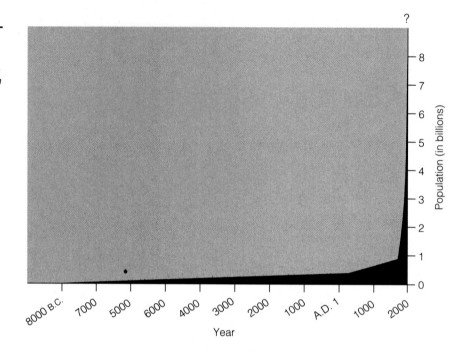

population growth. Many people are concerned with a probable lack of resources, such as food and energy. Others feel less concerned and believe new technologies will help bridge the gap between population size and resources. Many developing nations today are making efforts to control fertility, such as providing increased awareness of birth control. The effectiveness of such measures varies depending on the political, economic, social, and religious nature of specific nations.

The overall rate of world population growth masks a number of important trends within specific nations. Today, rapid population growth is most often a problem for the developing nations and less of a problem for developed nations. In fact, the populations in some developed nations may have problems associated with too little growth.

Variation in population growth among nations will most probably lead to major shifts in the world's demographic profile. One way of seeing this effect is to look at the 10 largest urban areas in the world in 1990 along with the projected 10 largest in the future. Table 17.1 lists the 10 largest urban areas of the world in 1990 along with a projection for the year 2034. In 1990, the three largest were Tokyo, New York City (metropolitan area), and Seoul. It is estimated that by the year 2034 the three largest urban areas will be Mexico City, Shanghai, and Beijing. By 2034, the only currently developed nation likely to be in the top 10 is Japan; the United States will not even make this list.

■ TABLE 17.1
The 10 Largest Urban Areas in the World: 1990 and Estimated for 2034

RANK	1990	2034 ESTIMATE
1	Tokyo, Japan	Mexico City, Mexico
2	New York City metropolitan area, U.S.A.	Shanghai, China
3	Seoul, South Korea	Beijing, China
4	São Paulo, Brazil	São Paulo, Brazil
5	Osaka, Japan	Bombay, India
6	Mexico City, Mexico	Dacca, Bangladesh
7	Los Angeles, U.S.A.	Calcutta, India
8	Shanghai, China	Jakarta, Indonesia
9	Bombay, India	Madras, India
10	London, U.K.	Tokyo, Japan

Source: Bouvier (1984); Haub (1992)

Implications of Changing Age Structure

The transition to developed nations with low rates of fertility and mortality will lead to many changes in culture. The age-sex structure of such nations continues to show a shrinking base and a widening apex. As fewer people are born and as people live longer, the age-sex structure of developed nations will continue to resemble a rectangle. Figure 17.6 shows the estimated population pyramid of western Germany in the year 2034, based on current trends and expected economic changes. Bouvier (1984) presented this figure as typical of a Western European developed nation that is expected to become more of a service and information-based economy and less a manufacturing-based economy. Figure 17.6 shows that the elderly will make up the majority of such a population.

We can expect many cultural changes to accompany such a shift to an older population. Many of these shifts are apparent today in North America. For example, if we assume current average ages for retirement, it is clear that there will be fewer people of working age in the future. Such a shift might be seen as having both advantages and disadvantages. A smaller labor pool might mean better economic opportunities for working-age people. On the other hand, we may also expect greater taxation to help provide for the well-being of the retired portion of the population.

Many questions are being asked by those concerned with social and economic shifts. For example, how well will our Social Security system function when more people are drawing from it? What changes need to be made in the insurance industries? How can we provide adequate health and other care to an aging population?

Economic shifts can also be examined. Perhaps one of the best examples of the effects of changing age structure is in our system of higher

■ **FIGURE 17.6**

Estimated age-sex structure
of Germany in 2034.
(Projection based on the former
nation of West Germany prior to
German unification.) (*Source:*
Bouvier [1984:26])

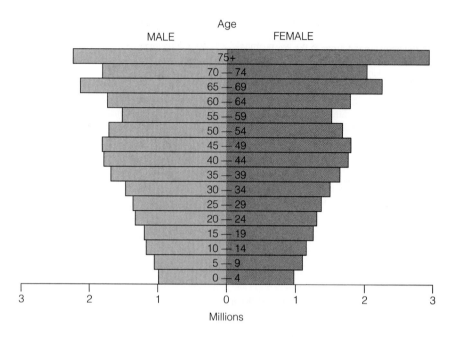

education. During the 1960s and early 1970s, as more and more Baby Boom
children reached college age, the demand for colleges and universities
increased. This demand was accompanied by an increased desire for a college education, in part because of a changing economy and the value of a
college degree in earning potential. As college enrollments increased, more
schools were built, and more faculty and staff were hired. By the mid-1970s,
the effects of the Baby Boom were over, and enrollments began to diminish
at many institutions. How, then, can we afford to maintain our colleges?
Increases in tuition and taxes are remedies, but they are generally not very
popular. Should schools be closed? If so, what happens to the local economies,
which are often highly dependent on these schools? What about the future?
If we cut back on programs now, will we need to start them up again in a
few years?

Business provides another example of these far-reaching changes. Sound
business practice dictates the gearing of products to specific age groups. As
the numbers in different age groups change, so does demand for specific
products. In the entertainment industry, for example, teenagers have been,
and still are, major consumers of tapes and compact discs. As our population ages, however, there will be more demand for tapes and CDs from the
growing middle-aged population. Today this is apparent in the Baby Boomers'
demands for "oldies," music from the time they were teenagers. What type
of changes will occur in this industry and others in the future as a consequence of the changing age structure?

These questions have no easy answers. Awareness of the problems and
their connection to a variety of economic, social, and political factors is a

start in the right direction. Today's world is marked by an unusually high level of change. A society's successful integration of demographic change requires analysis of current trends and, above all, a basic acknowledgment that, for good or ill, these changes are indeed taking place.

SUMMARY

Demography is the study of the size, composition, and distribution of populations. The focus of demography is on the processes of fertility, mortality, and migration. All these processes are affected by cultural and biological factors and have their own effect in turn on cultural and biological variation. Population growth reflects the balance between fertility, mortality, and migration. In general, a situation of more births than deaths leads to population growth.

Patterns of fertility and mortality also affect the age distribution of a population. Populations with high fertility and mortality rates have more infants and young children than any other age group. As populations undergo economic development, the mortality rates drop, leading to both population growth and an increase in the proportion of older people. Developed nations, where fertility and mortality rates are low, show a reduction in the number of young people and an increase in the number of older people.

Patterns of fertility and mortality are affected extensively by cultural change. In today's world, the total population continues to increase, particularly among the Third World nations. In the United States, population growth continues but at a slower rate than in the recent past. Changes in demographic structure will lead in the near future to strikingly different distributions of the world's population, both by nation and age group.

SUPPLEMENTAL READINGS

Scientific American, ed. 1974. *The Human Population.* San Francisco: W. H. Freeman. Both this book, consisting of articles from the magazine, and the Weeks text provide a good introduction to the study of demography.

Swedlund, A. C., and G. J. Armelagos. 1976. *Demographic Anthropology.* Dubuque, Iowa: Wm. C. Brown. This book, unfortunately no longer in print, provides a general review of demography from an anthropological perspective—in particular, the use of paleontological data in reconstructing demographic processes.

Weeks, J. R. 1981. *Population: An Introduction to Concepts and Issues.* 2d ed. Belmont, Calif.: Wadsworth.

Epilogue:
The Future of
Our Species

This book has focused on human biological variation and evolution, past and present. What about the future? Can biological anthropology, or indeed any science, make predictions about the future of our species? What possible directions will our biological and cultural evolution take?

One thing is for certain—we continue to evolve both biologically and culturally and will do so in the future. Human evolution is increasingly complex because of our biocultural nature. Much of our adaptive nature is culturally based. We can adapt to a situation more quickly through cultural evolution than through biological evolution. Theoretically, we can also direct our cultural evolution. We can focus our efforts on solutions to specific problems, such as finding a vaccine for AIDS or developing ways to further reduce dental decay. Biological evolution, however, has no inherent direction. Natural selection works on existing variation, not on what we might desire or need.

Our success with cultural adaptations should not lead us to conclude that we do not continue to evolve biologically. Regardless of our triumphs in the field of medicine, many incurable diseases still carry on the process of natural selection. Biological variation still takes place in potential and realized fertility. Perhaps as many as a third to half of all human conceptions fail to produce live births. We still live in a world in which up to 50 percent of the children have an inadequate diet. Even if all inhabitants of the world were raised to an adequate standard of living tomorrow, we would still be subject to natural selection and biological evolution. The fact that we are cultural organisms does not detract from the fact that we are also biological organisms. Scholars in various fields throughout history have argued about whether humans and human behavior should be studied biologically, as products of nature, or culturally, as products of nurture. Both sides were wrong. Humans must be studied as *both* biological and cultural organisms.

Given that we will continue to evolve, *how* will we evolve? This question cannot be answered. Evolution has many random elements that cannot be predicted. Also, the biocultural nature of humans makes prediction even harder. The incredible rate of cultural and technological change in the past century was not predicted. What kinds of cultural evolution are possible in the next hundred years? We may be able to forecast some short-term changes, but we know nothing about the cultural capabilities of our species hundreds or thousands of years in the future.

Another problem is that our own viewpoint can influence our predictions. An optimistic view might focus on the success of past cultural adaptations and the rate of acquisition of knowledge and then develop a scenario including increased standard of living for all, cheap energy sources, and an elevated life expectancy. A pessimistic view might consider all the horrors of the past and present, and project a grim future. A pessimist might envisage widespread famine, overcrowding, pollution, disease, and warfare. Most likely, any possible future will be neither pie-in-the-sky nor doom, but a combination of positive and negative changes. If the study of evolution tells us one thing, it is that every change has potential costs and benefits. We need to temper our optimism and pessimism with a sense of balance.

In any consideration of the future, we must acknowledge change as basic to life. Many people find it tempting to suggest we would be better off living a "simpler" life. Others argue that we should stop trying to deal with our problems and let nature take its course or that we should trust in the acts of God. This is unacceptable—indeed our understanding of human evolution argues for the reverse. Our adaptive pattern has been one of learning and problem solving. More than that, this is our primate heritage. Our biology has allowed us to develop the basic mammalian patterns of learned behavior to a high degree. We have the capability for rational thought, for reason, and for learning. Even if many of our cultural inventions have led to suffering and pain, our *potential* for good is immense. In any case, we must continue along the path of learning and intelligence; it is our very nature. Good or bad, the capabilities of the human mind and spirit may be infinite.

Mathematical Population Genetics

Population genetics was discussed in Chapter 3 with a minimum of mathematical formulae. This appendix is intended for those wishing to obtain an elementary understanding of the mathematical basis of population genetics. Additional sources, such as Crow and Kimura (1970), Cavalli-Sforza and Bodmer (1971), Spiess (1977), and Hartl (1988), are recommended for further information.

The formulae presented here are limited to a simple genetic case—a single locus with two possible alleles, A and a. Following convention, the symbol p is used to denote the frequency of the A allele, and the symbol q is used to denote the frequency of the a allele. Because there are only two alleles, $p + q = 1$. For this simple case, there are three genotypes: AA, Aa, and aa.

HARDY-WEINBERG EQUILIBRIUM

The Hardy-Weinberg equilibrium model, discussed briefly in Chapter 3, states that: (1) under random mating, the expected genotype frequencies are $AA = p^2$, $Aa = 2pq$, and $aa = q^2$, and (2) under certain conditions, the allele frequencies p and q will remain constant from one generation to the next.

There are a number of ways to demonstrate the first conclusion of the Hardy-Weinberg model. Perhaps the simplest proof rests on the fact that p and q represent probabilities. If the frequency of the A allele is p, then the probability of drawing an A allele from the entire gene pool is equal to p. To obtain the AA genotype in the next generation, it is necessary to have an A allele from both parents. Assuming that the allele frequencies are the same in both sexes, the probability of getting an A allele from one parent is p, and the probability of getting an A allele from the other parent is also p. The probability of *both* these events happening is the product of these probabilities, or $p \times p = p^2$. The same method can be used to determine the probability of getting the aa genotype ($q \times q = q^2$).

Getting an Aa genotype in the next generation requires one parent contributing the A allele (probability $= p$) and the other parent contributing the a allele (probability $= q$). The joint probability is $p \times q = pq$. It is also possible, however, that the order may be reversed. The first parent could contribute the a allele and the second parent could contribute the A allele. The joint probability of this happening is also equal to pq. The overall probability of having the Aa genotype is therefore $pq + pq = 2pq$.

The reasoning behind the Hardy-Weinberg model is summarized as follows:

Genotype of child	Allele from parent 1	2	Probability	
AA	A	A	$p \times p = p^2$	
Aa	A	a	$p \times q = pq$	
	or			$pq + pq = 2pq$
	a	A	$q \times p = pq$	
aa	a	a	$q \times q = q^2$	

Also note that the sum of genotype frequencies ($p^2 + 2pq + q^2$) is equal to 1.

The second part of the Hardy-Weinberg model states that, in the absence of evolutionary forces, the allele frequencies will remain the same from one generation to the next. This may be easily demonstrated by using the genotype frequencies in a given generation to predict the allele frequencies in the next generations. Allele frequencies are easily derived from genotype frequencies. In the present example, the frequency of allele A is computed as the frequency of genotype AA plus *half* the frequency of genotype Aa (we only wish to count the A alleles that make up half the total number of alleles in heterozygotes). The frequency of the A allele in the next generation, designated p', is therefore equal to

p' = frequency of AA + (frequency of Aa/2)

which is equal to

$$p' = p^2 + \frac{2pq}{2}$$

The 2s cancel out, giving

$$p' = p^2 + pq$$

Factoring p from the equation gives

$$p' = p(p + q)$$

Now, because the quantity $(p + q)$ is equal to 1 by definition, the equation becomes

$$p' = p$$

The fact that the allele frequency in the next generation (p') is equal to the initial allele frequency (p) shows that, given certain assumptions, there will be no change in the allele frequency over time. Therefore, when we *do* see a change in allele frequency over time, we know that one of the assumptions of the Hardy-Weinberg model has been violated. Because the model assumes no evolution has taken place, the fact that the model does not fit means this assumption is incorrect and therefore that a change in allele frequency (evolution) has taken place.

INBREEDING

Inbreeding does not change allele frequencies, but it does change genotype frequencies. The genotype frequencies predicted by Hardy-Weinberg require the assumption that mating is random and that there is no inbreeding. The inbreeding coefficient, F, is a measure of the probability that a homozygous genotype is the result of common ancestry of the parents. For example, the inbreeding coefficient for offspring born to first cousins is $F = 0.0625$. This value indicates the *additional* probability of the child having a homozygous genotype because the parents were first cousins. Inbreeding coefficients are most often computed from genealogical data, although with certain assumptions they may also be estimated from frequencies of last names and from allele frequencies (in certain cases).

At the populational level, there is also a probability of having a homozygous genotype due to random mating (p^2 or q^2, depending on the genotype). Inbreeding increases this probability. Under inbreeding, the genotype frequencies are

AA: $p^2 + pqF$

Aa: $2pq(1 - F)$

aa: $q^2 + pqF$

Thus, inbreeding increases the frequency of homozygotes (AA and aa) and decreases the frequency of heterozygotes. As an example, consider a population where $p = 0.5$ and $q = 0.5$. Under random mating ($F = 0$), the genotype frequencies are: AA = 0.25, Aa = 0.50, and aa = 0.25. If the population had an inbreeding coefficient of $F = 0.05$, these frequencies would be: AA = 0.2625, Aa = 0.4750, and aa = 0.2625.

It is easy to see why inbreeding does not change allele frequencies. Given the genotype frequencies expected under inbreeding, we can compute the frequency of the A allele in the next generation as

$$p' = \text{frequency of AA} + \left(\text{frequency of } \frac{Aa}{2} \right)$$

Substituting the formulae for AA and Aa given earlier, this equation becomes

$$p' = p^2 + pqF + \frac{2pq(1 - F)}{2}$$

The 2s in the equation cancel out. When the remaining terms are multiplied out, the equation becomes

$$p' = p^2 + pqF + pq - pqF$$

After subtracting pqF from pqF, the equation then becomes

$$p' = p^2 + pq$$

Factoring the p in the equation gives

$$p' + p(p + q)$$

Because $p + q = 1$, the allele frequency in the next generation is

$$p' = p$$

Thus, the allele frequency does not change from one generation to the next under inbreeding.

MUTATION

Mutation involves the change from one allele into another. For the simple case given here, let us assume that allele a is the mutant form. The mutation rate, usually denoted as u, is the proportion of A alleles that mutates into a alleles in a single generation. The value u therefore represents the probability of any A allele mutating into the a allele. Models also exist to deal with backward mutation (a into A), but these are not presented here because the rate of back mutations is usually very low.

How can mutation change the allele frequency in a population over time? To answer that, assume that mutation is the only force acting to change allele frequencies. The frequency of allele a in the next generation (q') depends on the current frequency of a alleles (q), the frequency of A alleles that have not mutated ($p = 1 - q$), and the rate of mutation (u). The frequency of the a allele in the next generation, q', is therefore equal to

$$q' = q + u(1 - q)$$

The first part of this equation represents the initial frequency of a alleles (q), and the second part represents the expected increase in a alleles due to mutation of A alleles.

As an example, assume that the initial allele frequencies are $p = 1.0$ and $q = 0.0$, and that the mutation rate is $u = 0.0001$. The allele frequencies in the next generation are

$$q' = 0 + 0.0001\,(1 - 0)$$

$$= 0.0001$$

$$p' = 1 - q' = 0.9999$$

If we carry this to an additional generation, the allele frequencies in the second generation (q'' and p'') are

$$q'' = 0.0001 + 0.0001(1 - 0.0001)$$

$$= 0.0001 + 0.00009999$$

$$= 0.00019999$$

$$p'' = 1 - q'' = 0.9980001$$

Continued mutation, in the absence of any other evolutionary forces, will lead to an increase in q and a decrease in p. For example, after 50 generations of mutation the allele frequencies in the example here are $p = 0.99501223$ and $q = 0.00498777$.

The mutation model presented here is simplified and does not take into consideration back mutation, changes in mutation rates over time, or any of the other evolutionary forces. It does, however, illustrate how mutation will lead to a cumulative increase in the frequency of the mutant allele. These examples also show that such increases are relatively low, even over many generations. Of course, evolution is not caused only by mutation. Other evolutionary forces act to increase, or decrease, the allele frequencies.

NATURAL SELECTION

Natural selection is modeled mathematically by assigning a fitness value to each genotype. Fitness is defined as the probability that an individual will survive to reproductive age. The actual proportion of individuals surviving is known as *absolute fitness*. Mathematically, the effects of natural selection are easier to model if relative fitness is used; here the absolute fitness values are converted such that the largest absolute fitness equals 1.

As an example, consider absolute fitness values of $AA = 0.8$, $Aa = 0.8$, and $aa = 0.4$. These numbers mean that 80 percent of those with the AA genotype survived, 80 percent of those with the Aa genotype survived, and 40 percent of those with the aa genotype survived. Because the largest absolute fitness is 0.8, relative fitness values are obtained by dividing each fitness by 0.8. Thus, the relative fitness values are $AA = 1.0$, $Aa = 1.0$, and $aa = 0.5$. The genotype aa has a fitness value of 0.5 relative to the most fit genotypes (AA and Aa). As another example, consider the following absolute fitness values: $AA = 0.7$, $Aa = 0.9$, and $aa = 0.3$. The relative fitness values are $AA = 0.7/0.9 = 0.778$, $Aa = 0.9/0.9 = 1.0$, and $aa = 0.3/0.9 = 0.333$.

The symbol w is used to designate relative fitness. Here w_{AA} is the relative fitness of genotype AA, w_{Aa} is the relative fitness of genotype Aa, and w_{aa} is the relative fitness of genotype aa. The effect of natural selection can now be determined by looking at the genotype frequencies before and after selection. The genotype frequencies before selection are obtained from the Hardy-Weinberg model: $AA = p^2$, $Aa = 2pq$, and $aa = q^2$. The genotype frequencies after selection are obtained by multiplying the genotype frequencies before selection by the respective relative fitness values. After selection, the genotype frequencies are therefore

$$AA = w_{AA}\,p^2$$

$$Aa = 2w_{Aa}\,pq$$

$$aa = w_{aa}\,q^2$$

The frequency of the A allele after selection is then computed by adding the frequency of genotype AA to half the frequency of genotype Aa and dividing this figure by the sum of all genotype frequencies after selection. That is,

$$p' = (w_{AA}\,p^2 + (2w_{Aa}\,pq/2)) / (w_{AA}\,p^2 + 2w_{Aa}\,pq + w_{aa}q^2)$$

$$= (w_{AA}\,p^2 + w_{Aa}\,pq) / (w_{AA}\,p^2 + 2w_{Aa}\,pq + w_{aa}\,q^2)$$

As an example, consider a population with initial allele frequencies of $p = 0.8$ and $q = 0.2$. Assume relative fitness values for each genotype as $AA = 1.0$, $Aa = 1.0$, and $aa = 0.5$. In this example, there is partial selection against the homozygous genotype aa. Logically, we expect that such selection will lead to a reduction in the frequency of the a allele and an increase in the frequency of the A allele.

Using Hardy-Weinberg, the expected genotype frequencies before selection are

AA: $p^2 = (0.8)^2 = 0.64$

Aa: $2pq = 2(0.8)(0.2) = 0.32$

aa: $q^2 = (0.2)^2 = 0.04$

Using the relative fitness values, the relative proportion of each genotype after selection is

AA: $w_{AA}\, p^2 = (1)(0.8)^2 = 0.64$

Aa: $2w_{Aa}\, pq = 2(1)(0.8)(0.2) = 0.32$

aa: $w_{aa}\, q^2 = (0.5)(0.2)^2 = 0.02$

The frequency of the A allele after selection is computed as

$p' = (0.64 + (0.32/2)) / (0.64 + 0.32 + 0.02)$

$= (0.64 + 0.16) / (0.64 + 0.32 + 0.02)$

$= 0.8 / 0.98$

$= 0.8163$

Also, the frequency of the a allele after selection is

$q' = 1 - p' = 0.1837$

The entire process can be repeated for additional generations. To extend the analysis another generation, use the new values of $p = 0.8163$ and $q = 0.1837$. After an additional generation of selection, the allele frequencies will be $p = 0.8303$ and $q = 0.1697$. If you continue this process, the frequency of A keeps increasing, and the frequency of a keeps decreasing.

Some forms of natural selection can be represented using simplified formulae. For example, complete selection against recessive homozygotes involves relative fitness values of $AA = 1.0$, $Aa = 1.0$, and $aa = 0.0$. Given these values, the frequency of the A allele after one generation of selection is

$p' = (w_{AA}\, p^2 + w_{Aa}\, pq) / (w_{AA}\, p^2 + 2w_{Aa}\, pq + w_{aa}q^2)$

$= ((1)p^2 + (1)pq) / ((1)p^2 + 2(1)pq + (0)q^2)$

$= (p^2 + pq) / (p^2 + 2pq)$

$= (p(p + q)) / (p(p + q + q))$

$$= (p + q) \ / \ (p + q + q)$$

$$= 1 \ / \ (1 + q)$$

$$= 1 \ / \ (1 + (1 - p))$$

$$= 1 \ / \ (2 - p)$$

which is a much easier formula to work with. Other forms of natural selection also have simplified formulae and are listed in the references given at the beginning of this appendix.

As an example, assume initial frequencies of $p = 0.5$ and $q = 0.5$. The frequency of the A allele in the next five generations of natural selection would be 0.6667, 0.7500, 0.8000, 0.8333, and 0.8571.

GENETIC DRIFT

The process of genetic drift is random. As a result, we cannot predict the exact allele frequencies resulting from a generation of genetic drift. We can, however, describe the probability of obtaining a given allele frequency caused by genetic drift. For example, assume a population of six people (and hence 12 alleles at each locus) with initial allele frequencies of $p = 0.5$ and $q = 0.5$. A generation of genetic drift could result in the frequency of the A allele ranging from $0/12 = 0.0$ to $12/12 = 1.0$. Other possible allele frequency values are $1/12 = 0.083$, $2/12 = 0.167$, $3/12 = 0.250$, $4/12 = 0.333$, $5/12 = 0.417$, $6/12 = 0.500$, $7/12 = 0.583$, $8/12 = 0.667$, $9/12 = 0.750$, $10/12 = 0.833$, $11/12 = 0.917$.

The frequency of the A allele depends on how many A alleles are represented in the next generation (which can range from 0 to 12). Because genetic drift is a random process, we cannot tell how many A alleles will be represented in the next generation. We can, however, compute the probability of each of these events occurring. We would expect, for example, that getting 6 A alleles is more likely than getting 12 A alleles (just as we would expect it to be more likely that we get 6 heads rather than 12 heads or 1 if we flipped a coin 12 times). The exact formula used is a bit complex and is not presented here (see Hartl 1988:70). Using this formula, the probability of getting 6 A alleles in the next generation (and an allele frequency of $6/12 = 0.5$) is 0.223. Therefore, the probability of getting *some* change in allele frequency (some number *other* than 6 A alleles) is $1 - 0.223 = 0.777$. Mathematical investigation also shows that smaller populations are more likely to experience genetic drift than larger populations.

GENE FLOW

The process of gene flow is best described mathematically by considering allele frequencies in two populations, 1 and 2. The allele frequencies of population 1 are denoted p_1 and q_1, and the allele frequencies of population 2 are denoted p_2 and q_2. What happens when gene flow takes place between these two populations? Assume that populations 1 and 2 mix together at rate m. The term m is a measure of the proportion of migrants moving from one population into the other. For simplicity, further assume that the rate of migration from population 1 into population 2 is the same as the rate of migration from population 2 into population 1.

The frequency of the A allele in population 1 after one generation of gene flow is then expressed as

$$(1 - m)p_1 + mp_2$$

The first part of the righthand side of the equation shows the contribution to allele frequency from the proportion of individuals who stayed in population 1 $(1 - m)$. The second part of the righthand side of the equation shows the contribution to allele frequency caused by the proportion of individuals migrating from population 2 (m). Likewise, the frequency of allele A in population 2 after one generation of gene flow is

$$mp_1 + (1 - m)p_2$$

As an example, assume initial allele frequencies in population 1 are $p_1 = 0.7$ and $q_1 = 0.3$, and that initial allele frequencies in population 2 are $p_2 = 0.2$ and $q_2 = 0.8$. Further assume a rate of gene flow of $m = 0.3$. After one generation of gene flow, the frequencies of the A allele are

$$(1 - 0.3)(0.7) + (0.3)(0.2) = 0.49 + 0.06 = 0.55$$

for population 1, and

$$(0.3)(0.7) + (1 - 0.3)(0.2) = 0.21 + 0.14 = 0.35$$

for population 2. Thus, the frequency of the A allele has made populations 1 and 2 more similar as a result of gene flow. An additional generation of gene flow at the same rate would result in allele frequencies of

$$(1 - 0.3)(0.55) + (0.3)(0.35) = 0.385 + 0.105 = 0.49$$

for population 1, and

$$(0.3)(0.55) + (1 - 0.3)(0.35) = 0.165 + 0.245 = 0.41$$

for population 2. The two populations continue to become more similar genetically. Another generation of gene flow would result in allele frequencies of 0.466 for population 1 and 0.434 for population 2. After only a few more generations of gene flow, the allele frequencies of the two populations would be essentially equal.

SUMMARY

The formulae presented here represent a simplified view of mathematical population genetics. Each model ignores the effects of other evolutionary forces, although they can easily be extended to consider simultaneous effects. These models also deal only with a simple situation of one locus with two alleles. More complicated analyses require more sophisticated mathematical methods that are best performed on a computer. Nonetheless, these formulae do demonstrate the basic nuts and bolts of population genetic theory.

Taxonomy
of Living
Primates

The chart that begins on the next page lists representatives of all living primate groups. As discussed in Chapter 7, there are alternative classifications, especially the strepsirhine-haplorhine subdivision and the different schemes for classifying hominoids. The taxonomy listed here is a "traditional" one, used more widely than any other.

Each primate suborder is broken down to the level of the genus, and the number of species within each genus is also given. The overall taxonomy is from Fleagle (1988), excepting the breakdown within the hylobatids, which is from Bramblett (1994). The number of species within each genus and the common names are from Bramblett (1994).

ORDER: PRIMATES
SUBORDER: PROSIMII

Infraorder	Superfamily	Family	Subfamily	Genus	Number of Species	Common Name
Lemuriformes	Lemuroidea	Indriidae		Indris	1	Indrid
				Propithecus	2	Sifaka
				Avahi	1	Woolly lemur
		Daubentoniidae		Daubentonia	1	Aye-aye
		Lepilemuridae		Lepilemur	1	Lepilemur
		Lemuridae		Hapalemur	3	Gentle lemur
				Lemur	6	Lemur
				Varecia	1	Ruffed lemur
	Lorisoidea	Cheirogaleidae		Microcebus	2	Mouse lemur
				Mirza	1	Coquerel's mouse lemur
				Cheirogaleus	2	Dwarf lemur
				Allocebus	1	Hairy-eared dwarf lemur
				Phaner	1	Fork-marked lemur
		Galagidae		Galagoides	4	Bush baby
				Euoticus	2	Needle-clawed bush baby
				Galago	3	Bush baby
				Otolemur	2	Greater bush baby
		Lorisidae		Periodicticus	1	Potto
				Arctocebus	1	Angwantibo
				Nycticebus	2	Slow loris
				Loris	1	Slender loris
Tarsiiformes		Tarsiidae		Tarsius	3	Tarsier

ORDER: PRIMATES
SUBORDER: ANTHROPOIDEA

INFRAORDER	*SUPERFAMILY*	*FAMILY*	*SUBFAMILY*	*GENUS*	*NUMBER OF SPECIES*	*COMMON NAME*
Platyrrhini	Ceboidea	Callitricidae	Callitrichinae	Cebuella	1	Pygmy marmoset
				Callithrix	3	Marmoset
				Saguinus	11	Tamarin
				Leontopithecus	1	Lion tamarin
				Callimico	1	Goeldi's marmoset
		Cebidae	Cebinae	Saimiri	2	Squirrel monkey
				Cebus	4	Capuchin
			Aotinae	Aotus	1	Owl monkey
				Callicebus	3	Titi
		Atelidae	Pitheciinae	Pithecia	3	Saki
				Chiropotes	2	Bearded saki
				Cacajao	3	Uakari
			Atelinae	Alouatta	6	Howler monkey
				Lagothrix	2	Woolly monkey
				Brachyteles	1	Woolly spider monkey
				Ateles	4	Spider monkey

| | | | | | ORDER: PRIMATES SUBORDER: ANTHROPOIDEA | |
INFRAORDER	SUPERFAMILY	FAMILY	SUBFAMILY	GENUS	NUMBER OF SPECIES	COMMON NAME
Catarrhini	Cercopithecoidea	Cercopithecidae	Cercopithecinae	*Allenopithecus*	1	Swamp guenon
				Erythrocebus	1	Patas
				Miopithecus	1	Talapoin guenon
				Cercopithecus	17	Guenon
				Macaca	19	Macaque
				Cercocebus	4	Mangabey
				Papio	5	Baboon
				Mandrillus	2	Mandrill
				Theropithecus	1	Gelada baboon
			Colobinae	*Procolobus*	1	Olive colobus
				Piliocolobus	2	Red colobus
				Colobus	4	Colobus
				Presbytis	16	Langur
				Simias	1	Pig-tailed langur
				Nasalis	1	Proboscis monkey
				Pygathrix	1	Douc langur
				Rhinopithecus	2	Snub-nosed monkey

			ORDER: PRIMATES			
			SUBORDER: ANTHROPOIDEA			
INFRAORDER	*SUPERFAMILY*	*FAMILY*	*SUBFAMILY*	*GENUS*	*NUMBER OF SPECIES*	*COMMON NAME*
	Hominoidea	Hylobatidae		*Hylobates*	6	Gibbon
				Symphalangus	1	Siamang
		Pongidae		*Pongo*	1	Orangutan
				Gorilla	1	Gorilla
				Pan	2	Chimpanzee
						Bonobo
		Hominidae		*Homo*	1	Human

Conversion Factors

Conversion Factors for Common Measures Used in the Text

TO CONVERT	INTO	MULTIPLY BY
Centimeters	Inches	0.3937
Cubic centimeters	Cubic inches	0.06102
Cubic inches	Cubic centimeters	16.39
Feet	Meters	0.3048
Grams	Ounces	0.03527
Inches	Centimeters	2.54
Inches	Millimeters	25.4
Kilograms	Pounds	2.205
Kilometers	Miles	0.6214
Kilometers	Yards	1,094
Meters	Feet	3.281
Meters	Yards	1,094
Miles	Kilometers	1.609
Millimeters	Inches	0.03937
Ounces	Grams	28.349527
Pounds	Kilograms	0.4536
Yards	Kilometers	9.144×10^{-4}
Yards	Meters	0.9144

Source: Frisancho (1993)

Temperature conversion:

From Celsius to Fahrenheit: $(C° \times 1.8) + 32$

From Fahrenheit to Celsius: $(F° - 32) / 1.8$

Comparative Primate Skeletal Anatomy

APPENDIX 4

 This appendix provides a general background in comparative primate anatomy by showing the skeletons of three primates—a modern human, an ape (gorilla), and an Old World monkey (baboon). In addition to noting the differences between these species, you should also note the similarities, particularly in terms of the homology of the skeletons (see Chapter 6 for a review of the principle of homology).

■ **FIGURE 1**

The human skeleton is made up of 206 bones on average (not all of which are shown here). Of these, 29 bones are found in the crania, 27 are found in *each* hand, and 26 are found in *each* foot. Note the homology between the human skeleton and the skeleton of the gorilla (Figure 2) and the baboon (Figure 3). Also note differences in certain anatomical structures, such as the pelvis, that reflect human bipedalism (discussed in Chapter 8).

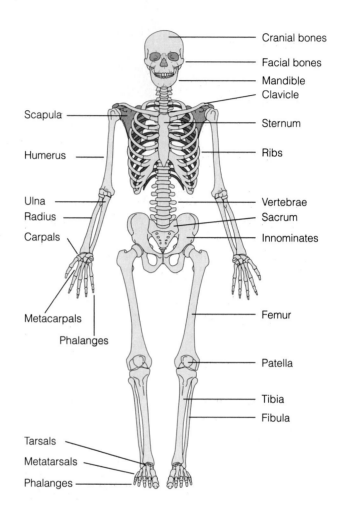

Cranial bones
Facial bones
Mandible
Clavicle
Scapula
Sternum
Humerus
Ribs
Ulna
Vertebrae
Radius
Sacrum
Carpals
Innominates
Metacarpals
Phalanges
Femur
Patella
Tibia
Fibula
Tarsals
Metatarsals
Phalanges

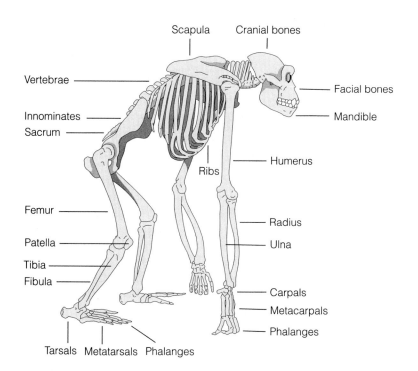

Scapula   Cranial bones

Vertebrae

Innominates
Sacrum

Facial bones

Mandible

Humerus

Ribs

Femur

Patella

Tibia

Fibula

Radius

Ulna

Carpals

Metacarpals

Phalanges

Tarsals   Metatarsals   Phalanges

■ **FIGURE 2**
Skeleton of a gorilla, one of the African apes (discussed in Chapter 7) shown in the typical knuckle-walking mode of locomotion. Note the longer arms and shorter legs when compared with the human (Figure 1) and the baboon (Figure 3).

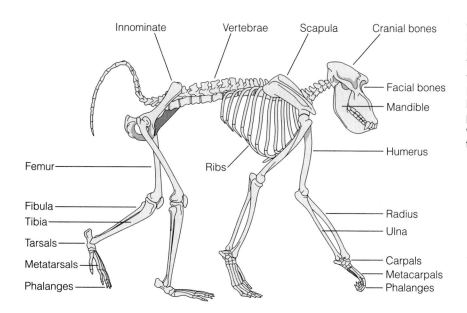

Innominate   Vertebrae   Scapula   Cranial bones

Facial bones

Mandible

Humerus

Femur

Ribs

Fibula

Tibia

Tarsals

Metatarsals

Phalanges

Radius

Ulna

Carpals

Metacarpals

Phalanges

■ **FIGURE 3**
Skeleton of a baboon, an Old World monkey, shown in the typical quadrupedal mode of locomotion. Note the similar length of the arms and legs, particularly when compared with the human (Figure 1) and the gorilla (Figure 3).

Glossary

acclimation. Short-term physiologic responses to a stress, usually occurring within minutes or hours.

acclimatization. Long-term physiologic responses to a stress, usually taking from days to months.

Acheulian tradition. The stone tool technology associated with some populations of *Homo erectus.* Many of these tools were constructed using a biface method.

acquired characteristics. Lamarck's hypothesis that traits change in response to environmental demands and are passed on to offspring.

acquired immune deficiency syndrome (AIDS). A fatal disease that results in the breakdown of the body's immune defense system.

adaptation. The process of successful interaction between a population and an environment. Cultural or biological traits that offer an advantage in a given environment are adaptations.

adaptive radiation. The formation of many new species following the availability of new environments or the development of a new adaptation.

age at menarche. The age at which a human female experiences her first menstrual period.

age-sex structure. A measure of the composition of a population in terms of the numbers of males and females at different ages.

allele. The alternative forms of a gene that occur at a given locus. Some genes have only one allele, some have two, and some have many alternative forms. Alleles occur in pairs, one on each chromosome.

Allen's rule. States that mammals in cold climates tend to have shorter and bulkier limbs, allowing less loss of body heat, whereas mammals in hot climates tend to have long, slender limbs, allowing greater loss of body heat.

allometry. The study of the change in proportion of various body parts as a consequence of their growth at different rates.

anagenesis. The transformation of a single species over time.

analogous trait. Physical trait that has a similar function in two species but a different structure. The wings of a bird and those of a flying insect are an example of an analogous trait; both perform the same function but have different structures.

anatomically modern *Homo sapiens*. The modern form of the human species, which dates back 100,000 years or more.

Anthropoidea (anthropoids). The suborder of primates consisting of monkeys, apes, and humans.

anthropological archaeology. The subfield of anthropology that focuses on cultural variation in prehistoric (and some historic) populations through an analysis of the culture's remains.

anthropology. The science that investigates human biological and cultural variation and evolution.

anthropometrics. Measurements of the human body, skull, and face.

antibody. A substance that reacts to other substances invading the body (antigens).

antigen. A substance invading the body that stimulates the production of antibodies.

arboreal. Living in trees.

archaic *Homo sapiens*. An earlier variant of *Homo sapiens*, found at dates ranging from over 400,000 to 35,000 years B.P. Archaic forms had roughly the same brain size as modern humans but a different-shaped skull, including a sloping forehead and lower cranial height.

***Ardipithecus ramidus*.** The oldest known hominid, dating to 4.4 million years B.P. in Africa, and very primitive. This species may represent a side branch in early human evolution, and not be a direct ancestor of later hominids.

argon-argon dating. A chronometric dating method based on the half-life of radioactive argon that can be used with very small samples.

assortative mating. Mating between phenotypically similar individuals: for example, between two people with the same hair color.

australopithecine. A general term used to refer to any species in the genus *Australopithecus*.

***Australopithecus*.** A genus of fossil hominid that lived in Africa between 4.2 and 1 million years B.P., characterized by bipedal locomotion, small brain size, large face, and large teeth.

***Australopithecus aethiopicus*.** The oldest known robust australopithecine, dating to 2.5 million years B.P. in East Africa. Some view this species as an early example of *A. boisei*. It combines derived features seen in other robust australopithecines (e.g., large cheek bones, sagittal crest) with primitive features seen in *A. afarensis* (e.g., protruding face, apelike features of the base of the cranium).

***Australopithecus afarensis*.** A primitive australopithecine, dating between 4 and 3 million years B.P. and found in East Africa. The teeth and postcranial skeleton show a number of primitive and apelike features.

***Australopithecus africanus*.** A species of australopithecine dating between 3 and 2 million years B.P. and found in South Africa. The teeth and skull of this species are not as large as those of the robust australopithecines.

***Australopithecus anamensis*.** The oldest known australopithecine, dating to 4.2 to 3.9 million years B.P. in East Africa. It was a biped but had many primitive apelike features of the skull and teeth. It may represent the ancestor of all later hominids.

***Australopithecus boisei*.** The most robust of the australopithecines, dating between 2 and 1 million years B.P. and found in East Africa. This species has extremely large back teeth and a large supporting facial and cranial structure, indicating large chewing muscles.

***Australopithecus robustus*.** A robust species of australopithecine, dating between 2 and 1 million years B.P. and found in South Africa. This species has large back teeth, although not as large on average as *Australopithecus boisei*.

balancing selection. Selection for the heterozygote and against the homozygotes (the heterozygote is most fit). Allele frequencies move toward an equilibrium defined by the fitness values of the two homozygotes.

bases. Chemical units that make up part of the DNA molecule. There are four bases (adenine, thymine, guanine, cytosine). The sequence of bases in the DNA molecule specifies genetic instructions.

Bergmann's rule. States that (1) among mammals of similar shape, the larger mammal loses heat less rapidly than the smaller mammal, and (2) among mammals of similar size, the mammal with a linear shape will lose heat more rapidly than the mammal with a nonlinear shape.

biface. Stone tool with both sides worked. The result is a more symmetric and efficient tool.

bilateral symmetry. Symmetry in which the right and left sides of the body are approximately mirror images, a characteristic of vertebrates.

binocular stereoscopic vision. Overlapping fields of vision (binocular), with both sides of the brain receiving images from both eyes (stereoscopic). Binocular stereoscopic vision provides depth perception.

biocultural approach. A method of studying humans that looks at the interaction between biology and culture in evolutionary adaptation.

biological anthropology. The subfield of anthropology formerly referred to as physical anthropology that focuses on the biological evolution of humans and human ancestors, the relationship of humans to other organisms, and patterns of biological variation within and among human populations.

bipedalism. Moving about on two legs. Unlike the movement of other bipedal animals such as kangaroos, human bipedalism is further characterized by a striding motion.

blade. A stone tool characteristic of the Upper Paleolithic, defined as being at least twice as long as it is wide. Blade tools were made using an efficient and precise method.

B.P. Abbreviation for "Before Present," the internationally accepted form of designating past dates. The "Present" has been set arbitrarily at the year 1950. A date of 75,000 years B.P. thus means 75,000 years before the year 1950.

brachiation. A method of movement that uses the arms to swing from branch to branch. Gibbons and siamangs are true brachiators.

breeding population. A group of organisms that tend to choose mates from within the group.

brow ridge. The large ridge of bone above the eye orbit. Brow ridges are most noticeable in *Homo erectus* and archaic *Homo sapiens*.

burin. A stone tool with a sharp edge that is used to cut and engrave bone.

canine. One of four types of teeth found in mammals. The canine teeth are located in the front of the jaw behind the incisors. Mammals normally use these teeth for puncturing and defense. Unlike most mammals, humans have small canine teeth that function like incisors.

carbon-14 dating. A chronometric dating method based on the half-life of carbon-14. This method can be applied to organic remains such as charcoal dating back over the past 50,000 years or so.

carrying capacity. The maximum population size capable of being supported in a given environment.

catastrophism. The hypothesis that patterns of evolutionary change observed in the fossil records can be explained by repeated catastrophes followed by repopulation from other areas by different organisms.

Cenozoic era. The third and most recent geologic era of the Phanerozoic eon, dating roughly to the past 65 million years, also known as the "Age of Mammals." The first primates appeared during the Cenozoic era.

cephalic index. A measure of cranial shape defined as the total length of a skull divided by the maximum width of the skull.

cerebrum. The area of the forebrain that consists of the outermost layer of brain cells. The cerebrum is associated with memory, learning, and intelligence.

Chordata. A vertebrate phylum consisting of organisms that possess a notochord at some period during their life.

chromosomes. Long strands of DNA sequences.

chronometric dating. Method of dating fossils or sites that provides an estimate of the specific date (subject to probabilistic limits).

cladistics. A school of thought that stresses evolutionary relationships between organisms in forming biological classifications. Organisms are grouped together on the basis of the number of derived traits they share.

cladogenesis. The formation of one or more new species from another over time.

codominant. Pertaining to two alleles, when both alleles affect the phenotype of a heterozygous genotype and neither is dominant over the other.

comparative approach. A method used by anthropologists that compares populations to determine common and unique behaviors or biological traits.

continental drift. The movement of continental land masses on top of a partially molten layer of the earth's mantle. Because of continental drift, the relative location of the continents has changed over time.

convergent evolution. Independent evolution of similar adaptations in rather distinct evolutionary lines. For example, the development of flight in birds and certain insects is an example of convergent evolution.

cranial capacity. A measurement of the interior volume of the brain case, used as an approximate estimate of brain size.

crossing over. The result of segments of DNA switching between pairs of chromosomes. Crossing over is an exception to linkage.

cultural anthropology. The subfield of anthropology that focuses on variations in cultural behaviors among human populations.

culture. Behavior that is learned and socially transmitted rather than instinctual and genetically transmitted.

cusp. A raised area on the chewing surface of a tooth.

demographic transition theory. A model of demographic change that states that as a population becomes economically developed, there will first be a reduction in death rates (leading to population growth), followed by a reduction in birth rates.

demography. The study of the size, composition, and distribution of populations.

dendrochronology. A chronometric dating method based on the fact that trees in dry climates tend to accumulate one growth ring per year. The width of the rings varies according to climate, and a sample can be compared with a master chart of tree rings over the past 10,000 years.

dental formula. A shorthand method of describing the number of each type of tooth in half of one jaw of a mammal. The dental formula consists of four numbers: I-C-PM-M, where I is the number of incisors, C is the number of canines, PM is the number of premolars, and M is the number of molars. When a mammal has a different number of teeth in the upper and lower jaws, two dental formulae are used.

derived trait. A trait that has changed from an ancestral state. For example, the large human brain is a derived trait relative to the common ancestor of humans and apes.

dermatoglyphics. Measurements of finger and palm prints, including classification of type and counts of ridges.

developmental acclimatization. Changes in organ or body structure that occur during the physical growth of any organism.

diastema. A gap next to the canine teeth that allows space for the canine on the opposing jaw.

directional selection. Selection against one extreme in a continuous trait and/or selection for the other extreme.

distance curve. A measure of size over time—as, for example, a person's height at different ages.

diurnal. Active during the day.

diversifying selection. Selection for the extremes in a continuous trait and against the average value.

DNA. Deoxyribonucleic acid. The molecule that provides the genetic code for biological structures and the means to translate this code.

dominance hierarchy. The ranking system within a society that indicates those individuals who are dominant in social behaviors.

dominant allele. An allele that masks the effect of the other allele (which is recessive) in a heterozygous genotype.

electron spin resonance. A chronometric dating method that estimates dates from observation of radioactive atoms trapped in the calcite crystals present in a number of materials, such as bones and shells. This method is useful for dating sites back to roughly one million years.

electrophoresis. A laboratory method that uses electric current to separate proteins, allowing genotypes to be determined.

embryo. The stage of prenatal life lasting from roughly two to eight weeks following conception, characterized by structural development.

endemic. Pertaining to disease, when new cases occur at a relatively constant but low rate over time.

endocast. A cast of the interior of the brain case, used in the analysis of brain size and structure.

Eocene epoch. The second epoch of the Cenozoic era, dating roughly between 55 and 38 million years B.P. The first true primates, early prosimians, appeared during this epoch.

eon. The major subdivision of geologic time.

epidemic. Pertaining to disease, when new cases spread rapidly through a population.

epidemiologic transition. The change in disease patterns, seen in many developed regions of the world, in which there is a decline in infectious diseases and an increase in noninfectious diseases.

epidemiology. The study of patterns of human diseases and their causes.

era. Subdivision of a geological eon.

estrus. A time during the month when females are sexually receptive (also known as "heat). Among primates, human and orangutan females lack an estrus period.

Eurasia. The combined land masses of Europe and Asia.

evolution. The transformation of species of organic life over long periods of time. Anthropologists study both the cultural and biological evolution of the human species.

evolutionary forces. The mechanisms that can cause changes in allele frequencies from one generation to the next. The four evolutionary forces are: mutation, natural selection, genetic drift, and gene flow.

exogamy. The tendency to choose mates from outside the local population.

exon. A section of DNA that codes for the amino acids that make up proteins. It is contrasted with an intron, which is a section of DNA that does not code for amino acids making up a protein.

faunal correlation. A relative dating method in which sites can be assigned an approximate age based on the similarity of animal remains with other dated sites.

fecundity. Potential reproduction, often defined as the number of people capable of having children.

feedback. A situation in which one factor in a system influences, and is influenced by, other factors in the system.

fertility. Actual reproduction—the number of births per individual.

fetus. The stage of prenatal growth from roughly eight weeks following conception until birth, characterized by further development and rapid growth.

fission-fusion. A form of population structure in which a group breaks into smaller populations (fission) and may then later combine with other populations to form a larger group (fusion).

fission-track dating. A chronometric dating method based on the number of tracks made across volcanic rock as uranium decays into lead.

fitness. The probability of survival and reproduction of an organism. Fitness is generally measured in terms of the different genotypes for a given locus.

foramen magnum. The large opening at the base of the skull where the spinal cord enters.

founder effect. A type of genetic drift caused by the formation of a new population by a small number of individuals. The small size of the sample can cause marked deviations in allele frequencies from the original population.

gene. A section of DNA that has an identifiable structure or function.

gene flow. A mechanism for evolutionary change resulting from the movement of genes from one population to another. Gene flow introduces new genes into a population and also acts to make populations more similar genetically to one another.

generalized structure. A biological structure adapted to a wide range of conditions and used in very general ways. For example, the grasping hands of humans are generalized structures allowing climbing, food gathering, toolmaking, and a variety of other functions.

genetic distance. An average measure of relatedness between populations based on a number of traits. Genetic distances are used for understanding effects of genetic drift and gene flow, which should affect all loci to the same extent.

genetic distance map. A picture that shows the genetic relationships between populations, based on genetic distance measures.

genetic drift. A mechanism for evolutionary change resulting from the random fluctuations of gene frequencies from one generation to the next, or from any form of random sampling of a larger gene pool.

genotype. For a given locus, the genetic endowment of an individual from the two alleles present.

genus. A taxonomic category designating groups of species with similar adaptations.

gradualism. A model of macroevolutionary change whereby evolutionary changes occur at a slow, steady rate over time.

grooming. The handling and cleaning of another individual's fur or hair. In primates, grooming serves as a form of communication that soothes and provides reassurance.

half-life. The average length of time it takes for half of a radioactive substance to decay into another form.

Haplorhini (haplorhines). One of two suborders of primates suggested to replace the prosimian/anthropoid suborders (the other is the strepsirhines). Haplorhines are primates without a moist nose (tarsiers, monkeys, apes, and humans).

Hardy-Weinberg equilibrium. A mathematical model demonstrating that, in the absence of evolutionary forces, allele frequencies remain constant from one generation to the next.

hemoglobin. The molecule in blood cells that transports oxygen.

heritability. The proportion of total variance in a trait attributable to genetic variation. This measure is not always the same; the actual value depends on the degree of environmental variation in any population.

heterozygous. Pertaining to the two alleles at a given locus being different.

holistic. Refers to the viewpoint that all aspects of existence are interrelated and important in understanding human variation and evolution.

home base. Campsite where hunters brought back food for sharing with other members of their group.

homeobox gene. One of a group of regulatory genes that encode a sequence of 60 amino acids that regulate embryonic development. Homeobox genes subdivide from head to tail a developing embryo into different regions, which then form limbs and other structures. These genes are similar in many organisms, such as insects, mice, and humans.

homeostasis. In a physiologic sense, the maintenance of normal limits of body functioning.

home range. The size of the geographic area that is normally occupied and used by a social group.

hominid. Humans and humanlike ancestors. Hominids are defined by a number of unique derived traits, particularly bipedalism.

hominoid. A group of anthropoids consisting of apes and humans. Hominoids have a shoulder structure adapted for climbing and hanging, lack a tail, are generally larger than monkeys, and have the largest brain size: body size ratio among primates.

Homo. A genus of hominid with three recognized species (*Homo erectus, Homo habilis,* and *Homo sapiens*), dating from 2.5 million years

B.P. The major characteristic of *Homo* is a large brain size and dependence on culture as a means of adaptation.

Homo erectus. A species of the genus *Homo* that lived between 1.8 and 0.2 million years B.P. *Homo erectus* first appeared in Africa and later spread to Asia (and possibly Europe). *Homo erectus* had a larger brain size than *Homo habilis* but not as large as *Homo sapiens*.

Homo habilis. The oldest known species in the genus *Homo*, dating between 2.5 and 1.5 million years B.P. and found in Africa. In overall appearance, this species is similar to the australopithecines but has a larger cranial capacity (an average of roughly 630 cc, with a range of 509 to 752 cc).

homoiotherm. Organism capable of maintaining a constant body temperature under most circumstances. Mammals are homoiotherms.

homologous trait. Physical trait in two species that has a similar structure but may or may not show a similar function. The arm bones in humans and whales are an example of homologous structure; the bones are the same, but they are used for different functions.

homozygous. Pertaining to both alleles at a given locus being identical.

horticulture. A form of farming in which only simple hand tools are used.

hypothesis. An explanation of observed facts. To be scientific, a hypothesis must be testable.

hypoxia. Oxygen starvation. Hypoxia occurs frequently at high altitudes.

inbreeding. Mating between biologically related individuals.

incidence rate. The rate of new cases of a disease developing in a population in a specified period of time.

incisor. One of four types of teeth found in mammals. The incisors are the flat front teeth used for cutting, slicing, and gnawing food.

infanticide. The killing of infants.

infectious disease. A disease caused by the introduction of an organic foreign substance into the body. Such substances include viruses and parasites.

insectivore. An order of mammals adapted to insect eating.

intron. A section of DNA that does not code for the amino acids that make up proteins. It is contrasted with an exon, which is a section of DNA that does code for amino acids making up a protein.

kin selection. A concept used in sociobiological explanations of altruism. Sacrificial behaviors, for example, can be selected for if they increase the probability of survival of close relatives.

knuckle walking. A form of movement used by chimpanzees and gorillas that is characterized by all four limbs touching the ground, with the weight of the arms resting on the knuckles of the hands.

kwashiorkor. An extreme form of protein-calorie malnutrition, resulting from a severe deficiency in proteins but not calories.

lactase deficiency. A condition in which an older child or adult lacks the ability to produce the lactase enzyme needed to digest milk sugar.

larynx. Part of the vocal anatomy in the throat.

lemur. A prosimian found today on the island of Madagascar. Lemurs include both nocturnal and diurnal species.

life expectancy at birth. A measure of the average length of life for a newborn child.

life span. A measure of the maximum length of life recorded for a species. In humans, this measure is currently 120 years.

life table. A table that provides an estimate of the probability of an individual dying by a certain age. Life table analysis is used to estimate life expectancy.

linguistic anthropology. The subfield of anthropology that focuses on the nature of human language, the relationship of language to culture, and the languages of nonliterate peoples.

linkage. The situation in which alleles on the same chromosome are inherited together.

locus. The specific location of a gene on a chromosome. (Plural *loci.*)

loris. Nocturnal prosimian found today in Asia and Africa.

Lower Paleolithic. The Lower Old Stone Age. A general term used to refer collectively to the stone tool technologies of *Homo habilis* and *Homo erectus.*

macroevolution. Long-term evolutionary change. The study of macroevolution focuses on biological evolution over many generations and on the origin of higher taxonomic categories, such as species.

major genes. Genes that have the primary effect on the phenotypic distribution of a complex trait. Additional variation can be due to smaller effects from other loci and/or environmental influences.

marasmus. An extreme form of protein-calorie malnutrition resulting from severe deficiencies in both proteins and calories.

mass extinction. Many species becoming extinct at roughly the same time.

meiosis. The creation of sex cells by replication of chromosomes followed by cell division. Each sex cell than contains 50 percent of an individual's chromosomes (one from each pair).

Mendelian genetics. The branch of genetics concerned with patterns and processes of inheritance. This field was named after Gregor Mendel, the first scientist to work out many of these principles.

Mendel's Law of Independent Assortment. The segregation of any pair of chromosomes does not affect the probability of segregation for other pairs of chromosomes.

Mendel's Law of Segregation. Sex cells contain one of each pair of alleles.

Mesozoic era. The second geologic era of the Phanerozoic eon, dating roughly between 245 and 65 million years B.P., also known as the "Age of Reptiles." The first mammals and birds also appeared during the Mesozoic era.

messenger RNA. The form of RNA that transports the genetic instructions from the DNA molecule to the site of protein synthesis.

microevolution. Short-term evolutionary change. The study of microevolution focuses on changes in allele frequencies from one generation to the next.

Middle Paleolithic. The Middle Old Stone Age. A general term used to refer collectively to the stone tool technologies of archaic *Homo sapiens.*

migration. The movement of individuals from one population to another. Migration may be short-term or long-term, and may or may not have genetic effects.

Miocene epoch. The fourth epoch of the Cenozoic era, dating roughly between 22 and 5 million years B.P. The first apes evolved during the Miocene.

mitochondrial DNA. A small amount of DNA that is located in the mitochondria of cells. Mitochondrial DNA is inherited only through the mother.

mitosis. The process of replication of chromosomes in body cells. Each cell produces two identical copies.

molar. One of four types of teeth found in mammals. The molars are back teeth used for crushing and grinding food.

molecular dating. The application of methods of genetic analysis to estimate the sequence and timing of divergent evolutionary lines.

monogamous family group. Social structure in which the primary social group consists of an adult male, an adult female, and their immature offspring.

monogamy. An exclusive sexual bond between an adult male and an adult female for a long period of time.

monosymy. A condition in which only one chromosome rather than a pair is present in body cells.

morphology. The physical structure of organisms.

mortality. Death. Mortality, fertility, and migration are the three prime measures of population size.

mosaic evolution. The concept that major evolutionary changes tend to take place in stages, not all at once. Human evolution shows a mosaic pattern in the fact that small canine teeth, large brains, and tool use did not all evolve at the same time.

Mousterian tradition. The stone tool technology of the Neandertals, characterized by the careful preparation of a stone core from which finished flakes can be removed.

multimale/multifemale group. A type of social structure in which the primary social group is made up of several adult males, several adult females, and their offspring.

multiregional model. The hypothesis that modern humans evolved throughout the Old World as a single species after the first dispersion of *Homo erectus* out of Africa. According to this view, the transition from *Homo erectus* to archaic *Homo sapiens* to modern *Homo sapiens* occurred within a single evolutionary line throughout the Old World.

multivariate analysis. The analysis of human biological variation that takes into consideration the interrelationship of several traits at a time.

mutation. A mechanism for evolutionary change resulting from a random change in the genetic code. Mutation is the ultimate source of all genetic variation. Mutations must occur in sex cells to cause evolutionary change.

nasal index. A measure of the shape of the nasal opening, defined as the width of the nasal opening divided by the height.

natural increase. The change in population size expected because of fertility and mortality but not migration. Natural increase is the number of births minus the number of deaths.

natural selection. A mechanism for evolutionary change resulting from the differential survival and reproduction organisms because of their biological characteristics.

Neandertal. Member of a regional population of archaic *Homo sapiens* found in Europe and the Middle East, dating between roughly 125,000 to 35,000 years B.P. The relationship between Neandertals and later *Homo sapiens* populations in these regions is still being debated.

neoteny. The retention of juvenile characteristics into adulthood. The rounded skull and large brain of humans are examples of neoteny.

New World syndrome. A set of noninfectious diseases that appear in elevated frequencies in individuals with Native-American ancestry.

nocturnal. Active during the night.

noninfectious disease. A disease caused by factors other than the introduction of an organic foreign substance into the body (e.g., age, nutrition).

nonrandom mating. Patterns of mate choice, other than total random mating, that influence the distributions of genotype and phenotype frequencies. Nonrandom mating does not lead to changes in allele frequencies.

notochord. A flexible internal rod that runs along the back of an animal. Animals possessing a notochord at some period in their life are known as chordates.

occipital bun. A slight protrusion of the rear region of the skull, a feature often found in Neandertals.

odontometrics. Measurements of the size of teeth.

Oldowan tradition. The stone tool culture of *Homo habilis.* Oldowan tools are often simple tools made by removing several flakes from a stone. The flakes removed could also be used as cutting tools.

Oligocene epoch. The third epoch of the Cenozoic era, dating roughly between 38 and 22 million years B.P.., when there was an adaptive radiation of anthropoids.

orthogenesis. A discredited idea that evolution would continue in a given direction because of some vaguely defined nonphysical "force."

Paleocene epoch. The first epoch of the Cenozoic era, dating roughly between 65 and 55 million years B.P. The primatelike mammals lived during the Paleocene.

paleoecology. The study of ancient environments.

paleomagnetic reversal. A method of dating sites based on the fact that the earth's magnetic pole has shifted back and forth from the north to the south in the past at irregular intervals.

paleopathology. The study of disease in prehistoric populations based on analysis of skeletal remains and archaeological evidence.

paleospecies. Species identified from fossil remains based on their physical similarities and differences relative to other species.

Paleozoic era. The first geologic era of the Phanerozoic eon, dating roughly between 545 and 245 million years B.P. The first vertebrates appeared during this era, including the reptiles and mammallike reptiles.

palynology. The study of fossil pollen. Palynology allows prehistoric plant species to be identified.

pandemic. An epidemic that occurs over a large geographic range.

parallel evolution. Independent evolution of similar evolutionary adaptations in closely related species.

parental investment. A concept used in sociobiological models that describes parental behaviors that increase the probability that offspring will survive.

period. Subdivision of a geologic era.

Phanerozoic eon. The past 545 million years.

phenetics. A school of thought that stresses the overall physical similarities among organisms in forming biological classifications.

phenotype. The observable appearance of a given genotype in the organism. The phenotype is determined by the relationship of the two alleles at a given locus, the number of loci, and often environmental influences as well.

placenta. An organ that develops inside a pregnant placental mammal. It provides the fetus with oxygen and food and helps filter out harmful substances.

plasticity. The ability of an organism to respond physiologically or developmentally to environmental stress.

pleiotropy. A single allele having multiple effects on an organism.

Pleistocene epoch. The sixth epoch of the Cenozoic era, dating from 1.8 to 0.01 million years B.P.. The major event in human evolution was the continued development of the genus *Homo*.

Pliocene epoch. The fifth epoch of the Cenozic era, dating from 5 to 1.8 million years B.P. The major event in human evolution was the origin of the hominid.

Plio-Pleistocene. A term used to describe the time of the early hominids (from 4.4 to 1 million years B.P.).

polyandrous group. A rare type of primate social structure, consisting of a small number of adult males, one reproductively active adult female, and their offspring. Other adult females may belong to the group but are not reproductively active.

polyandry. In humans, a form of marriage in which a wife has several husbands. In more general terms, it refers to an adult female having several mates.

polygamy. In general terms, it refers to having more than one mate.

polygenic. Refers to a trait that is affected by two or more loci. Complex traits, such as skin color and height, are polygenic.

polygyny. In humans, a form of marriage in which a husband has several wives. In more general terms, it refers to an adult male having several mates.

polymorphism. A discrete genetic trait, such as a blood group, in which there are at least two alleles at a locus having frequencies greater than 0.01.

population pyramid. A graphic illustration of the age-sex structure of a population.

postcranial. Referring to that part of the skeleton below the skull.

postnatal. Referring to the period of life from birth until death.

postorbital bar. The bony ring that separates the eye orbit from the back of the skull. The postorbital bar is a primate characteristic.

postorbital constriction. The narrowness of the skull behind the eye orbits. Early hominids, such as *Homo habilis* and *Homo erectus*, show considerable postorbital constriction, particularly when compared to modern humans.

potassium-argon dating. A chronometric dating method based on the half-life of radioactive potassium (which decays into argon gas). This method can be used to date volcanic rock older than 100,000 years.

Precambrian eon. The eon from the earth's beginning (4.6 billion years B.P.) until 545 million years B.P. During this eon, life originated and single-celled and simple multicelled organisms first evolved.

prehensile. Capable of grasping. Primates have prehensile hands and feet, and some primates (certain New World monkeys) have prehensile tails.

premolar. One of four types of teeth found in mammals. The premolars are back teeth used for crushing and grinding food.

prenatal. Referring to the period of life from conception until birth.

prevalence rate. The proportion of total cases of a disease, old and new, in a population during a specified period of time.

primate. A member of an order of mammals that has a complex of characteristics related to an initial adaptation to life in the trees (even though many modern primates now live on the ground), including binocular stereoscopic vision and grasping hands. The primates are the prosimians, monkeys, apes, and humans.

primitive trait. In biological terms, a trait that has not changed from an ancestral state. The five digits of the human hand and foot are primitive traits inherited from earlier vertebrate ancestors.

Proconsul. A genus of fossil apes that lived in Africa between 23 and 17 million years B.P.

Though classified as apes, this genus also shows a number of monkey characteristics. It most probably represents one of the first forms to evolve following the divergence of the monkey and ape lines.

Prosimii (prosimians). The suborder of primates that are biologically primitive compared to anthropoids.

protein-calorie malnutrition. A group of nutritional diseases resulting from inadequate amounts of protein and/or calories. Protein-calorie malnutrition is a severe problem in developing regions today.

punctuated equilibrium. A model of macroevolutionary change in which long periods of little evolutionary change (stasis) are followed by relatively short periods of rapid evolutionary change.

quadrupedal. A form of movement in which all four limbs are of equal size and make contact with the ground, and the spine is roughly parallel to the ground. Monkeys are typical quadrupedal primates.

race. In terms of biological variation, a group of populations sharing certain traits that make them distinct from other groups of populations. In practice, the concept of race is very difficult to apply to patterns of human variation.

recent African origin model. The hypothesis that modern humans evolved in a local region of Africa between 200,000 and 100,000 years B.P., and then spread throughout the rest of the Old World. Most variants of this model suggest that the expanding moderns replaced preexisting archaic populations, although some suggest there might have been a small amount of mixture with archaic populations.

recessive allele. An allele whose effect is masked by the other allele (which is dominant) in a heterozygous genotype.

regional continuity. The appearance of similar traits within a geographic region over time. Regional continuity means that certain traits specific to a given geographic area will be present over long periods of time.

regulatory gene. Gene that codes for the regulation of biological processes such as growth and development.

relative dating. Comparative method of dating fossils and sites that provides an estimate of the older find but not a specific date.

reproductive isolation. The genetic isolation of populations that can render them incapable of producing fertile offspring.

restriction fragment length polymorphism (RFLP). A genetic trait defined in terms of the length of DNA fragments produced through cutting by certain enzymes.

Rhesus incompatibility. A condition in which a pregnant woman and her fetus have incompatible Rhesus blood group phenotypes: the woman has the Rhesus negative phenotype and the fetus has the Rhesus positive phenotype.

RNA. Ribonucleic acid. The molecule that functions to carry out the instructions for protein synthesis specified by the DNA molecule.

robust australopithecines. Australopithecines with large back teeth, cheekbones, and faces, among other anatomical adaptations to heavy chewing. The robust australopithecines lived in Africa between 2.5 and 1 million years B.P. Three species are generally recognized: *A. aethiopicus* (East Africa, 2.5 million years B.P.), *A. robustus* (South Africa, 2–1 million years B.P.), and *A. boisei* (East Africa, 2–1 million years B.P.).

sagittal crest. A ridge of bone running down the center of the top of the skull that serves to anchor chewing muscles. Sagittal crests are found in some australopithecines.

savanna. An environment consisting of open grasslands. Food resources tend to be spread out over large areas.

secular change. A change in the average pattern of growth in a population over different generations.

sensitive period of growth. Times during the life cycle when catch-up growth is not possible.

sexual dimorphism. In terms of body size, the average difference in size between adult males and adult females. Primate species with sexual dimorphism in body size are characterized by adult males being, on average, larger than adult females.

sickle cell allele. An allele of the hemoglobin locus. If two such alleles are present, the individual has sickle cell anemia.

sickle cell anemia. A genetic disease that occurs in a person homozygous for the sickle cell allele; the altered structure of red blood cells leads to greatly reduced fitness.

single species hypothesis. A model of Plio-Pleistocene hominid evolution developed in the 1960s that stated that only one species of hominid existed at any one time. Later fossil discoveries led to the rejection of this model.

Sivapithecus. A genus of fossil ape found in Asia and Europe dating between 14 and 7 million years B.P. On the basis of cranial and dental remains, one of the Asian species of *Sivapithecus* appears to be an ancestor of the modern-day orangutan.

social structure. The composition of a social group and the way it is organized, including size, age structure, and number of each sex in the group.

sociobiology. A discipline concerned with evolutionary explanations of social behavior, focusing on the role of natural selection.

socioecology. The study of social structure and organization in relationship to environmental factors.

solitary group. The smallest primate social group, consisting of the mother and her dependent offspring.

specialized structure. A biological structure adapted to a narrow range of conditions and used in very specific ways. For example, the hooves of horses are specialized structures allowing movement over flat terrain.

speciation. The origin of a new species.

species. A taxonomic category designating a group of populations whose members can interbreed naturally and produce fertile offspring.

species selection. A process of selection in which some species are more likely to survive and/or develop into new species. Species selection is essentially the differential survival and reproduction of species.

stabilizing selection. Selection against extreme values, small or large, in a continuous trait.

stasis. Little or no evolutionary change occurring over a long period of time.

stratigraphy. A relative dating method based on the fact that older remains are found deeper in the earth (under the right conditions). This method makes use of the fact that a cumulative buildup of the earth's surface takes place over time.

Strepsirhini (strepsirhines). One of two suborders of primates suggested to replace the prosimian/anthropoid suborders (the other is the haplorhines). Strepsirhines are primates that have a moist nose (lemurs and lorises).

stress. Any factor that interferes with the normal limits of operation of an organism.

structural gene. Gene that codes for the production of proteins.

suspensory climbing. The ability to raise the arms above the head and hang on branches and to climb in this position. Hominoids are suspensory climbers.

taphonomy. The study of what happens to plants and animals after they die. Taphonomy helps in determining reasons for the distribution and condition of fossils.

tarsier. Nocturnal prosimian found today in Indonesia. Unlike other prosimians, tarsiers lack a moist nose.

taxonomy. A formal classification of organisms. The term also applies to the science of classification.

terrestrial. Living on the ground.

territory. A home range that is actively defended.

theory. A set of hypotheses that have been tested repeatedly and that have not been rejected. This term is sometimes used in a different sense in social science literature.

therapsid. An early group of reptiles also known as the mammallike reptiles. Therapsids were the ancestors of later mammals.

thermoluminescence. A chronometric dating method that uses the fact that certain heated objects accumulate trapped electrons over time, which allows the date when the object was initially heated to be determined.

tool use model. A now-rejected model of hominid origins that stated that bipedalism, large brains, and small canines all evolved simultaneously during hominid-evolution as a consequence of increased reliance on tool use.

transfer RNA. A free-floating molecule that is attracted to a strand of messenger RNA, resulting in the synthesis of a protein chain.

trephination. Surgery involving the removal of a section of bone from the skull.

trisomy. A condition in which three chromosomes rather than a pair occur. Down syndrome is caused by trisomy by the addition of an extra chromosome to the 21st chromosome pair.

typology. A set of discrete groupings in classification. Typologies emphasize average tendencies and ignore variation within groups. Racial classifications are a form of typology.

uni-male group. Social structure in which the primary social group consists of a single adult male, several adult females, and their offspring.

univariate analysis. The analysis of human biological variation focusing on a single trait at a time.

Upper Paleolithic. The Upper Old Stone Age. A general term used to collectively refer to the stone tool technologies of anatomically modern *Homo sapiens*.

variation. The differences that exist among individuals or populations. Anthropologists study both cultural and biological variation.

vasoconstriction. The narrowing of blood vessels, which reduces blood flow and heat loss.

vasodilation. The opening of the blood vessels, which increases blood flow and heat loss.

velocity curve. A measure of the rates of change in growth over time.

Vertebrata. A subphylum of the phylum Chordata, defined by the presence of an internal, segmented spinal column and bilateral symmetry.

visual predation model. The model of primate origins that hypothesizes that stereoscopic vision and grasping hands first evolved as adaptations for hunting insects along branches.

Würm glaciation. One of the times of glaciation ("ice ages") during the Pleistocene epoch.

zoonose. Disease that is transmitted directly from animals to humans.

zygomatic arch. The bone on the side of the skull that connects the zygomatic and temporal bones. This bone serves to anchor muscles used in chewing.

zygote. A fertilized egg.

References

Aalen, F. H. A. 1963. A review of recent Irish population trends. *Population Studies* 17:73–78.

Ackerman, S. 1987. American Scientist interviews: Peter Ellison. *American Scientist* 75:622–27.

Aiello, L. L., and R. Dunbar. 1993. Neocortex size, group size, and the evolution of language. *Current Anthropology* 34:184–93.

Allen, L. L., P. S. Bridges, D. L. Evon, K. R. Rosenberg, M. D. Russell, L. A. Schepartz, V. J. Vitzthum, and M. H. Wolpoff. 1982. Demography and human origins. *American Anthropologist* 84:888–96.

Alvarez, W., L. W. Alvarez, F. Asaro, and H. V. Michel. 1980. Extraterrestrial cause for a Cretaceous-Tertiary extinction. *Science* 208:1095–1108.

Anderson, C. M. 1992. Male investment under changing conditions among Chacma baboons at Suikerbosrand. *American Journal of Physical Anthropology* 87:479–96.

Arensberg, B., L. A. Schepartz, A. M. Tillier, B. Vandermeersch, and Y. Rak. 1990. A reappraisal of the anatomical basis for speech in Middle Paleolithic hominids. *American Journal of Physical Anthropology* 83:137–46.

Arensberg, C. M., and S. T. Kimball. 1968. *Family and Community in Ireland*. 2d ed. Harvard University Press: Cambridge.

Armelagos, G. J., and J. R. Dewey. 1970. Evolutionary response to human infectious diseases. *BioScience* 157:638–44.

Armstrong, E. 1983. Relative brain size and metabolism in mammals. *Science* 220:1302–4.

Baker, B. J., and G. J. Armelagos. 1988. The origin and antiquity of syphilis: Paleopathological diagnosis and interpretation. *Current Anthropology* 29:703–37.

Bakker, R. T. 1986. *The Dinosaur Heresies*. New York: William Morrow.

Bar-Yosef, O. 1994. The contributions of southwest Asia to the study of the origins of modern humans. In *Origins of Anatomically Modern Humans*, ed. M. H. Nitecki and D. V. Nitecki, pp. 23–66. New York: Plenum Press.

Beals, K. L. 1972. Head form and climatic stress. *American Journal of Physical Anthropology* 37:85–92.

Beals, K. L., C. L. Smith, and S. M. Dodd. 1983. Climate and the evolution of brachycephalization. *American Journal of Physical Anthropology* 62:425–37.

Beals, K. L., C. L. Smith, and S. M. Dodd. 1984. Brain size, cranial morphology, climate and time machines. *Current Anthropology* 25:301–30.

Begun, D. R. 1994. Relations among the great apes and humans: New interpretations based on the fossil great ape *Dryopithecus*. *Yearbook of Physical Anthropology* 37:11–63.

Bittles, A. H., W. M. Mason, J. Greene, and N. A. Rao. 1991. Reproductive behavior and health in consanguineous marriages. *Science* 252:789–94.

Blum, H. F. 1961. Does the melanin pigment of human skin have adaptive value? *Quarterly Review of Biology* 36:50–63.

Blumenberg, B. 1985. Population characteristics of extinct hominid endocranial volume. *American Journal of Physical Anthropology* 68:269–79.

Bodmer, W. F., and L. L. Cavalli-Sforza. 1976. *Genetics, Evolution, and Man*. San Francisco: W. H. Freeman.

Bogin, B. A. 1988. *Patterns of Human Growth*. Cambridge: Cambridge University Press.

———. 1995. Growth and development: Recent evolutionary and biocultural research. In *Biological Anthropology: The State of the Science*, ed. N. T. Boaz and L. D. Wolfe, pp. 49–70. Bend, Ore.: International Institute for Human Evolutionary Research.

Bouchard, T. J., D. T. Lykken, M. McGue, N. L. Segal, and A. Tellegen. 1990. Sources of human psychological differences: The Minnesota study of twins reared apart. *Science* 250:223–28.

Bouvier, L. F. 1984. Planet Earth 1984–2034: A demographic vision. *Population Bulletin* 39(1).

Brace, C. L. 1964. The fate of the "classic" Neandertals: A consideration of hominid catastrophism. *Current Anthropology* 5:3–43.

Brace, C. L., K. R. Rosenberg, and K. D. Hunt. 1987. Gradual change in human tooth size in the Late Pleistocene and Post-Pleistocene. *Evolution* 41:705–20.

Brace, C. L., D. P. Tracer, L. A. Yaroch, J. Robb, K. Brandt, and R. Nelson. 1993. Clines and clusters versus "race:" A test in ancient Egypt and the case of a death on the Nile. *Yearbook of Physical Anthropology* 36:1–31.

Bramblett, C. A. 1976. *Patterns of Primate Behavior.* Palo Alto, Calif.: Mayfield.

———. 1994. *Patterns of Primate Behavior.* 2d ed. Prospect Heights, Ill.: Waveland.

Bräuer, G. 1992. Africa's place in the evolution of *Homo sapiens.* In *Continuity or Replacement: Controversies in Homo sapiens Evolution,* ed. G. Bräuer and F. H. Smith, pp. 83–98. Netherlands: A. A. Balkema.

Brooks, A. S., D. M. Helgren, J. S. Cramer, A. Franklin, W. Hornyak, J. M. Keating, R. G. Klein, W. J. Rink, H. Schwarcz, J. N. L. Smith, K. Stewart, N. E. Todd, J. Verniers, and J. E. Yellen. 1995. Dating and context of three Middle Stone Age sites with bone points in the Upper Semliki Valley, Zaire. *Science* 268:548–53.

Brown, F., J. Harris, R. Leakey, and A. Walker. 1985. Early *Homo erectus* skeleton from west Lake Turkana, Kenya. *Nature* 316:788–92.

Brues, A. M. 1977. *People and Races.* New York: Macmillan.

Buss, D. M. 1985. Human mate selection. *American Scientist* 73:47–51.

Byard, P. J. 1981. Quantitative genetics of human skin color. *Yearbook of Physical Anthropology* 24:123–37.

Cabana, T., P. Jolicoeur, and J. Michaud. 1993. Prenatal and postnatal growth and allometry of stature, head circumference, and brain weight in Québec children. *American Journal of Human Biology* 5:93–99.

Calcagno, J. M., and K. R. Gibson. 1988. Human dental reduction: Natural selection or the probable mutation effect. *American Journal of Physical Anthropology* 77:505–17.

Campbell, B. G. 1985. *Human Evolution.* 3d ed. New York: Aldine.

Cann, R. L., M. Stoneking, and A. C. Wilson. 1987. Mitochondrial DNA and human evolution. *Nature* 325:31–36.

Cann, R. L., and A. C. Wilson. 1982. Models of human evolution. *Science* 217:303–4.

Carbonell, E., J. M. Bermúdez de Castro, J. L. Arsuaga, J. C. Díez, A. Rosas, G. Cuenca-Bescós, R. Sala, M. Mosquera, and X. P. Rodrígue. 1995. Lower Pleistocene hominids and artifacts from Atapuerca-TD6 (Spain). *Science* 269:826–30.

Carpenter, C. R. 1965. The howlers of Barro Colorado Island. In *Primate Behavior: Field Studies of Monkeys and Apes,* ed. I. DeVore, pp. 250–91. New York: Holt, Rinehart, and Winston.

Carroll, S. B., S. D. Weatherbee, and J. A. Langeland. 1995. Homeotic genes and the regulation and evolution of insect wing number. *Nature* 375:58–61.

Cartmill, M. 1974. Rethinking primate origins. *Science* 184:436–43.

———. 1982. Basic primatology and prosimian evolution. In *A History of American Physical Anthropology 1930–1980,* ed. F. Spencer, pp. 147–86. New York: Academic Press.

———. 1992. New views on primate origins. *Evolutionary Anthropology* 1:105–11.

Cavalli-Sforza, L. L., and W. F. Bodmer. 1971. *The Genetics of Human Populations.* San Francisco: W. H. Freeman.

Cavalli-Sforza, L. L., P. Menozzi, and A. Piazza. 1994. *The History and Geography of Human Genes.* Princeton: Princeton University Press.

Centers for Disease Control and Prevention. 1995. HIV/AIDS Surveillance Report, 1994:6 (no. 2). Atlanta: Centers for Disease Control and Prevention.

Cheney, D. L., and R. W. Wrangham. 1987. Predation. In *Primate Societies,* ed. B. B. Smuts, D. L. Cheney, R. M. Seyfarth, R. W. Wrangham, and T. T. Struhsaker, pp. 227–39. Chicago: University of Chicago Press.

Ciochon, R., J. Olsen, and J. James. 1990. *Other Origins: The Search for the Giant Ape in Human Prehistory.* New York: Bantam Books.

Clark, G. A. 1988. Some thoughts on the Black Skull: An archeologist's assessment of WT-17000 (*A. boisei*) and systematics in human paleontology. *American Anthropologist* 90:357–71.

Cockburn, T. A. 1971. Infectious diseases in ancient populations. *Current Anthropology* 12:45–62.

Coffing, K., C. Feibel, M. Leakey, and A. Walker. 1994. Four-million-year-old hominids from East Lake Turkana, Kenya. *American Journal of Physical Anthropology* 93:55–65.

Cohen, M. N. 1989. *Health and the Rise of Civilization.* New Haven: Yale University Press.

Cohen, M. N. and G. J. Armelagos. 1984. *Paleopathology at the Origins of Agriculture.* New York: Academic Press.

Connell, K. H. 1950. *The Population of Ireland 1750–1845.* Oxford: Clarendon Press.

Conroy, G. C. 1990. *Primate Evolution.* New York: W. W. Norton.

Conroy, G. C., M. Pickford, B. Senut, J. Van Couvering, and P. Mein. 1992. *Otavipithecus namibiensis,* first Myocene Hominoid from southern Africa. *Nature* 356:144–48.

Cowen, R. 1995. *History of Life.* 2d ed. Boston: Blackwell.

Cowley, G. 1993. The future of AIDS. *Newsweek,* March 22, 1993. Reprinted in *Annual Editions: Physical Anthropology 95/96,* ed. E. Angeloni, pp. 35–41. Guilford, Conn.: Dushkin.

Cowley, G., J. Contreras, A. Rogers, J. Lach, C. Dickey, and S. Raghavan. 1995. Outbreak of fear. *Newsweek,* May 22, 1995.

Coyne, J. A. 1992. Genetics and speciation. *Nature* 355:511–15.

Cracraft, J. 1983. Cladistic analysis and vicariance biogeography. *American Scientist* 71:273–81.

Crews, D. E. 1989. Cause-specific mortality, life expectancy, and debilitation in aging Polynesians. *American Journal of Human Biology* 1:347–53.

Crockett, C. M. and J. F. Eisenberg. 1987. Howlers: Variations in group size and demography. In *Primate Societies,* ed. B. B. Smuts, D. L. Cheney, R. M. Seyfarth, R. W. Wrangham, and T. T. Struhsaker, pp. 54–68. Chicago: University of Chicago Press.

Cronin, J. E. 1983. Apes, humans and molecular clocks: A reappraisal. In *New Interpretations of Ape and Human Ancestry,* ed. R. L. Ciochon and R. S. Corruccini, pp. 115–36. New York: Plenum Press.

Crook, J. H., and J. S. Gartlan. 1966. Evolution of primate societies. *Nature* 210:1200–3.

Crow, J. F. 1958. Some possibilities for measuring selection intensities in man. *Human Biology* 30:1–13.

Crow, J. F., and M. Kimura. 1970. *An Introduction to Population Genetics Theory.* Minneapolis, Minn.: Burgess.

Damon, A. 1977. *Human Biology and Ecology.* New York: W. W. Norton.

Day, M. H. 1986. Bipedalism: Pressures, origins and modes. In *Major Topics in Primate and Human Evolution,* ed. B. Wood, L. Martin, and P. Andrews, pp. 188–202. Cambridge: Cambridge University Press.

de Bonis, L., and G. D. Koufos. 1993. Our ancestor's ancestor: *Ouranopithecus* is a Greek link in human ancestry. *Evolutionary Anthropology* 3:75–83.

Denham, W. W. 1971. Energy relations and some basic properties of primate social organization. *American Anthropologist* 73:77–95.

De Robertis, E. M., G. Oliver, and C. V. E. Wright. 1990. Homeobox genes and the vertebrate body plan. *Scientific American* 263(1): 46–52.

Dettwyler, K. A. 1991. Can paleopathology provide evidence for "compassion"? *American Journal of Physical Anthropology* 84:375–84.

———. 1994. *Dancing Skeletons: Life and Death in West Africa.* Prospect Heights, Ill.: Waveland.

DeVore, I. 1963. A comparison of the ecology and behavior of monkeys and apes. In *Classification and Human Evolution,* ed. S. L. Washburn, pp. 301–9. Chicago: Aldine.

de Waal, F. B. M. 1995. Bonobo sex and society. *Scientific American,* March 1995. 82–88.

Dixon, B., and G. W. McBride. 1992. Health and disease. *Encyclopaedia Britannica Book of the Year, 1992,* pp. 172–76. Chicago: Encyclopaedia Britannica.

Dunn, F. L. 1968. Epidemiological factors: Health and disease among hunter-gatherers. In *Man the Hunter,* ed. R. B. Lee and I. DeVore, pp. 221–28. Chicago: Aldine.

Eaton, G. G. 1976. The social order of Japanese macaques. *Scientific American* 235(4): 96–106.

Eldredge, N. 1985. *Time Frames: The Rethinking of Darwinian Evolution and the Theory of Punctuated Equilibria.* New York: Simon & Schuster.

Eldredge, N., and S. J. Gould. 1972. Punctuated equilibria: An alternative to phyletic gradualism. In *Models in Paleobiology,* ed. T. J. M. Schopf, pp. 82–115. San Francisco: Freeman, Cooper.

Encyclopaedia Britannica. 1988. *Encyclopaedia Britannica Book of the Year, 1988.* Chicago: Encyclopaedia Britannica.

Ereshefsky, M., ed. 1992. *The Units of Evolution: Essays on the Nature of Species.* Cambridge: MIT Press.

Erlich, H. A., D. Gelfand, and J. J. Sninsky. 1991. Recent advances in the polymerase chain reaction. *Science* 252:1643–51.

Eveleth, P. B., and J. M. Tanner. 1990. *Worldwide Variation in Human Growth.* 2d ed. Cambridge: Cambridge University Press.

Falk, D. 1983. Cerebral cortices of East African early hominids. *Science* 221:1072–74.

———. 1990. Brain evolution in *Homo:* The radiator theory. *Behavioral and Brain Sciences* 13:333–81.

———. 1992. *Braindance.* New York: Henry Holt.

Fedigan, L. M. 1983. Dominance and reproductive success in primates. *Yearbook of Physical Anthropology* 26:91–129.

Fisher, H. 1992. *Anatomy of Love: A Natural History of Mating, Marriage, and Why We Stray.* New York: Ballantine.

Fleagle, J. G. 1988. *Primate Adaptation and Evolution.* San Diego: Academic Press.

———. 1995. The origin and radiation of anthropoid primates. In *Biological Anthropology: The State of the Science,* ed. N. T. Boaz and L. D. Wolfe, pp. 1–21. Bend, Ore.: International Institute for Human Evolutionary Research.

Fleagle, J. G., T. M. Brown, J. D. Obradovich, and E. L. Simons. 1986. Age of the earliest African anthropoids. *Science* 234:1247–49.

Fleagle, J. G., D. T. Rasmussen, S. Yirga, T. M. Brown, and F. E. Grine. 1991. New hominid fossils from Fejej, Southern Ethiopia. *Journal of Human Evolution* 21:145–52.

Flynn, J. J., A. R. Wyss, R. Charrier, and C. C. Swisher. 1995. An early Miocene anthropoid skull from the Chilean Andes. *Nature* 373:603–7.

Fossey, D. 1983. *Gorillas in the Mist.* Boston: Houghton Mifflin.

Fox, R. C., G. P. Youzwyshyn, and D. W. Krause. 1992. Post-Jurassic mammal-like reptile from the Paleocene. *Nature* 358:233–35.

Franciscus, R. G., and J. C. Long. 1991. Variation in human nasal height and breadth. *American Journal of Physical Anthropology* 85:419–27.

Frayer, D. W. 1984. Biological and cultural change in the European Late Pleistocene and Early Holocene. In *The Origins of Modern Humans: A World Survey of the Fossil Evidence,* ed. F. H. Smith and F. Spencer, pp. 211–50. New York: Alan R. Liss.

Friedlaender, J. S. 1975. *Patterns of Human Variation.* Cambridge: Harvard University Press.

Fries, J. F., and L. M. Crapo. 1981. *Vitality and Aging.* San Francisco: W. H. Freeman.

Frisancho, A. R. 1979. *Human Adaptation: A Functional Interpretation.* St. Louis: C. V. Mosby.

———. 1990. Introduction: Comparative high-altitude adaptation. *American Journal of Human Biology* 2:599–601.

———. 1993. *Human Adaptation and Accommodation.* Ann Arbor: University of Michigan Press.

Frisancho, A. R., and P. T. Baker. 1970. Altitude and growth: A study of the patterns of physical growth of a high altitude Peruvian Quechua population. *American Journal of Physical Anthropology* 32:279–92.

Futuyma, D. J. 1983. *Science on Trial: The Case for Evolution.* New York: Pantheon Books.

———. 1986. *Evolutionary Biology.* 2d ed. Sunderland, Mass.: Sinauer.

———. 1988. *Sturm und Drang* and the evolutionary synthesis. *Evolution* 42:217–26.

Gabriel, T. 1995. A generation's heritage: After the boom, a boomlet. *New York Times,* February 12, 1995.

Gabunia, L., and A. Vekja. 1995. A Plio-Pleistocene hominid from Dmanisi, East Georgia, Caucasus. *Nature* 373:509–12.

Gage, T. B. 1989. Bio-mathematical approaches to the study of human variation in mortality. *Yearbook of Physical Anthropology* 32:185–214.

Galdikas, B. M. F., and J. W. Wood. 1990. Birth spacing patterns in humans and apes. *American Journal of Physical Anthropology* 83:185–91.

Garn, S. M. 1965. *Human Races.* 2d ed. Springfield, Ill.: Charles C. Thomas.

Garrett, L. 1994. *The Coming Plague: Newly Emerging Diseases in a World out of Balance.* New York: Farrar, Straus and Giroux.

Gingerich, P. D. 1985. Nonlinear molecular clocks and ape-human divergence times. In *Hominid Evolution: Past, Present and Future,* ed. P. V. Tobias, pp. 411–16. New York: Alan R. Liss.

———. 1986. *Plesiadapis* and the delineation of the order Primates. In *Major Topics in Primate and Human Evolution,* ed. B. Wood, L. Martin and P. Andrews, pp. 32–46. Cambridge: Cambridge University Press.

Gingerich, P. D., B. H. Smith, and E. L. Simons. 1990. Hind limbs of Eocene *Basilosaurus*: Evidence of feet in whales. *Science* 249:154–57.

Glass, H. B. 1953. The genetics of the Dunkers. *Scientific American* 189(2): 76–81.

Gloria-Bottini, F., G. Gerlini, A. Amante, R. Pascone, and E. Bottini. 1992. Diabetic pregnancy: Evidence of selection on the Rh blood group system. *Human Biology* 64:81–87.

Godfrey, L., and K. H. Jacobs. 1981. Gradual, autocatalytic and punctuational models of hominid brain evolution: A cautionary tale. *Journal of Human Evolution* 10:255–72.

Godinot, M., and M. Mahboubi. 1992. Earliest known simian primate found in Algeria. *Nature* 357:324–26.

Goodall, J. 1986. *The Chimpanzees of Gombe: Patterns of Behavior*. Cambridge: Harvard University Press.

Gould, S. J. 1977. *Ontogeny and Phylogeny*. Cambridge: Harvard University Press.

———. 1981. *The Mismeasure of Man*. New York: W. W. Norton.

———. 1983. *Hen's Teeth and Horse's Toes*. New York: W. W. Norton.

———. 1987. *An Urchin in the Storm*. New York: W. W. Norton.

———. 1989. *Wonderful Life: The Burgess Shale and the Nature of History*. New York: W. W. Norton.

———. 1991. *Bully for Brontosaurus*. New York: W. W. Norton.

Gould, S. J., and N. Eldredge. 1977. Punctuated equilibria: The tempo and mode of evolution reconsidered. *Paleobiology* 3:115–51.

Gould, S. J., and R. C. Lewontin. 1979. The spandrels of San Marco and the Panglossian paradigm: A critique of the adaptationist programme. *Proceedings of the Royal Society of London* (Series B), 205:581–98.

Grant, P. R. 1991. Natural selection and Darwin's finches. *Scientific American* 265(4): 82–87.

Grant, V. 1985. *The Evolutionary Process: A Critical Review of Evolutionary Theory*. New York: Columbia University Press.

Greska, L. P. 1990. Developmental responses to high-altitude hypoxia in Bolivian children of European ancestry: A test of the developmental adaptation hypothesis. *American Journal of Human Biology* 2:603–12.

Grün, R. 1993. Electron spin resonance dating in paleoanthropology. *Evolutionary Anthropology* 2:172–81.

Grün, R., C. B. Stringer, and H. P. Schwartz. 1991. ESR dating of teeth from Garrod's Tabun cave collection. *Journal of Human Evolution* 20:231–48.

Hagelberg, E. 1994. Ancient DNA studies. *Evolutionary Anthropology* 2:199–207.

Harcourt, A. H., P. H. Harvey, S. G. Larson, and R. V. Short. 1981. Testis weight, body weight, and breeding system in primates. *Nature* 293:55–57.

Harley, D. 1982. Models of human evolution. *Science* 217:296.

Harlow, H. F. 1959. Love in infant monkeys. *Scientific American* 200(6): 68–74.

Harlow, H. F., and M. K. Harlow. 1962. Social deprivation in monkeys. *Scientific American* 207(5): 136–46.

Harpending, H., A. Rogers, and P. Draper. 1987. Human sociobiology. *Yearbook of Physical Anthropology* 30: 127–50.

Harpending, H. C., S. T. Sherry, A. R. Rogers, and M. Stoneking. 1993. Genetic structure of ancient human populations. *Current Anthropology* 34:483–96.

Harris, M. 1987. *Cultural Anthropology*, 2d ed. New York: Harper & Row.

Harrison, G. A., J. M. Tanner, D. R. Pilbeam, and P. T. Baker. 1988. *Human Biology: An Introduction to Human Evolution, Variation, Growth, and Adaptability*. 3d ed. Oxford: Oxford University Press.

Hartl, D. L. 1988. *A Primer of Population Genetics*. 2d ed. Sunderland, Mass.: Sinauer.

Harvey, P. H., R. D. Martin, and T. H. Clutton-Brock. 1987. Life histories in comparative perspective. In *Primate Societies*, ed. B. B. Smuts, D. L. Cheney, R. M. Seyfarth, R. W. Wrangham, and T. T. Struhsaker, pp. 181–96. Chicago: University of Chicago Press.

Harvey, P. H., and M. D. Pagel. 1991. *The Comparative Method in Evolutionary Biology*. Oxford: Oxford University Press.

Haub, C. V. 1992. Populations and population movements. *Encyclopaedia Britannica Book of the Year, 1992*, pp. 250–52. Chicago: Encyclopaedia Britannica.

———. 1995. Populations and population movements. *Encyclopaedia Britannica Book of the Year, 1995*, pp. 255–57. Chicago: Encyclopaedia Britanica.

Hedges, S. B., S. Kumar, K. Tamura and M. Stoneking. 1992. Human origins and analysis of mitochondrial DNA sequences. *Science* 255:737–39.

Henneberg, M. 1988. Decrease of human skull size in the Holocene. *Human Biology* 60:395–405.

Herrnstein, R. J., and C. Murray. 1994. *The Bell Curve: Intelligence and Class Structure in American Life.* New York: The Free Press.

Hill, A., S. Ward, A. Deino, G. Curtis, and R. Drake. 1992. Earliest *Homo. Nature* 355:719–22.

Holick, M. F., J. A. MacLaughlin, and S. H. Doppelt. 1981. Regulation of cutaneous previtamin D_3 photosynthesis in man: Skin pigment is not an essential regulator. *Science* 211:590–93.

Holloway, R. L. 1985. The poor brain of *Homo sapiens neanderthalensis*: See what you please. In *Ancestors: The Hard Evidence,* ed. E. Delson, pp. 319–24. New York: Alan R. Liss.

Hooton, E. A. 1946. *Up from the Ape.* New York: Macmillan.

Horiuchi, S. 1992. Stagnation in the decline of the world population growth rate during the 1980s. *Science* 257:761–65.

Horr, D. A. 1972. The Borneo orangutan. *Borneo Research Bulletin* 4(2): 46–50.

Houghton, P. 1993. Neandertal supralaryngeal vocal tract. *American Journal of Physical Anthropology* 90:139–46.

Howells, W. W. 1973. *Cranial Variation in Man: A Study by Multivariate Analysis of Patterns of Difference Among Recent Human Populations.* Papers of the Peabody Museum. Vol. 67. Cambridge: Harvard University.

———. 1989. *Skull Shapes and the Map: Craniometric Analyses in the Dispersion of Modern Homo.* Papers of the Peabody Museum. Vol. 79. Cambridge: Harvard University.

Hrdy, S. B. 1977. *The Langurs of Abu.* Cambridge: Harvard University Press.

Hrdy, S. B., C. Janson, and C. van Schaik. 1995. Infanticide: Let's not throw the baby out with the bath water. *Evolutionary Anthropology* 3:151–54.

Hunt, E. 1995. The role of intelligence in modern society. *American Scientist* 83:356–68.

Hutchinson, H. N., J. W. Gregory, and R. Lydekker. 1902. *The Living Races of Mankind.* New York: D. Appleton.

Jensen, A. R. 1969. How much can we boost IQ and scholastic achievement? *Harvard Educational Review* 33:1–123.

Johanson, D. C., and M. A. Edey. 1981. *Lucy: The Beginnings of Humankind.* New York: Simon & Schuster.

Johanson, D. C., F. T. Masau, G. G. Eck, T. D. White, R. C. Walter, W. H. Kimbel, B. Asfaw, P. Manega, P. Ndessokia, and G. Suwa. 1987. New partial skeleton of *Homo habilis* from Olduvai Gorge, Tanzania. *Nature* 327:205–9.

Johanson, D. C., and T. D. White. 1979. A systematic assessment of early African hominids. *Science* 203:321–30.

Johanson, D. C., T. D. White, and Y. Coppens. 1978. A new species of the genus *Australopithecus* (Primates: Hominidae) from the Pliocene of Eastern Africa. *Kirtlandia* 28:1–14.

Johnston, F. E., and R. M. Malina. 1966. Age changes in the composition of the upper arm in Philadelphia children. *Human Biology* 38:1–21.

Jolly, A. 1972. *The Evolution of Primate Behavior.* New York: Macmillan.

———. 1985. *The Evolution of Primate Behavior.* 2d ed. New York: Macmillan.

Jolly, C. J. 1970. The seed eaters: A new model of hominid differentiation based on a baboon analogy. *Man* 5:5–26.

Kappelman, J., and J. G. Fleagle. 1995. Age of early hominids. *Nature* 376:558–59.

Karlen, A. 1995. *Man and Microbes: Disease and Plagues in History and Modern Times.* New York: G. P. Putnam.

Karn, M. N., and L. S. Penrose. 1951. Birth weight and gestation time in relation to maternal age, parity, and infant survival. *Annals of Eugenics* 15:206–33.

Kay, R. F. 1981. The nut-crackers: A new theory of the adaptations of the Ramapithecinae. *American Journal of Physical Anthropology* 55:151–56.

Kelly, J. 1988. A new large species of *Sivapithecus* from the Siwaliks of Pakistan. *Journal of Human Evolution* 17:305–24.

Kennedy, K. A. R. 1976. *Human Variation in Space and Time.* Dubuque, Iowa: Wm. C. Brown.

Kennedy, K. A. R., A. Sonakia, J. Chiment, and K. K. Verma. 1991. Is the Narmada hominid an Indian *Homo erectus? American Journal of Physical Anthropology* 86:475–96.

Kennedy, R. E., Jr. 1973. *The Irish: Emigration, Marriage, and Fertility.* Berkeley: University of California Press.

Kimbel, W. H., D. C. Johanson, and Y. Rak. 1994. The first skull and other new discoveries of *Australo-*

pithecus afarensis at Hadar, Ethiopia. *Nature* 368:449–51.

King, M. C., and A. C. Wilson. 1975. Evolution at two levels: Molecular similarities and biological differences between humans and chimpanzees. *Science* 188:107–16.

Kitcher, P. 1982. *Abusing Science: The Case Against Creationism.* Cambridge: MIT Press.

Klein, R. G. 1989. *The Human Career: Human Biological and Cultural Origins.* Chicago: University of Chicago Press.

Kobyliansky, E., S. Micle, M. Goldschmidt-Nathan, B. Arensberg, and H. Nathan. 1982. Jewish populations of the world: Genetic likeness and differences. *Annals of Human Biology* 9:1–34.

Kollar, E. J., and C. Fisher. 1980. Tooth induction in chick epithelium: Expression of quiescent genes for enamel synthesis. *Science* 207:993–95.

Kramer, A. 1991. Modern human origins in Australasia: Replacement or evolution? *American Journal of Physical Anthropology* 86:455–73.

———. 1993. Human taxonomic diversity in the Pleistocene: Does *Homo erectus* represent multiple hominid species? *American Journal of Physical Anthropology* 91:161–71.

Labie, D., J. Pagnier, H. Wajcman, M. E. Fabry, and R. L. Nagel. 1986. The genetic origin of the variability of the phenotypic expression of the Hb S gene. In *Genetic Variation and its Maintenance*, ed. D. F. Roberts and G. F. DeStefano, pp. 149–156. Cambridge: Cambridge University Press.

Laitman, J. T., R. C. Heimbuch, and E. S. Crelin. 1979. The basicranium of fossil hominids as an indicator of their upper respiratory systems. *American Journal of Physical Anthropology* 51:15–34.

Larsen, C. S. 1994. In the wake of Columbus: Native population biology in the postcontact Americas. *Yearbook of Physical Anthropology* 37:109–54.

Larsen, C. S., R. M. Matter, and D. L. Gebo. 1991. *Human Origins: The Fossil Record.* 2d edition. Prospect Heights, Ill.: Waveland.

Leakey, L. S. B., P. V. Tobias, and J. R. Napier. 1964. A new species of the genus *Homo* from Olduvai Gorge. *Nature* 202:7–10.

Leakey, M. G., C. S. Feibel, I. McDougall, and A. Walker. 1995. New four-million-year-old hominid species from Kanapoi and Allia Bay, Kenya. *Nature* 376:565–71.

Leigh, S. R. 1992. Cranial capacity evolution in *Homo erectus* and early *Homo sapiens. American Journal of Physical Anthropology* 87:1–13.

Leonard, W. H., T. L. Leatherman, J. W. Carey, and R. B. Thomas. 1990. Contributions of nutrition versus hypoxia to growth in rural Andean populations. *American Journal of Human Biology* 2:613–26.

Lerner, I. M., and W. J. Libby. 1976. *Heredity, Evolution, and Society.* San Francisco: W. H. Freeman.

Leutenegger, W. 1982. Sexual dimorphism in nonhuman primates. In *Sexual Dimorphism in Homo sapiens: A Question of Size*, ed. R. L. Hall, pp. 11–36. New York: Praeger.

Levins, R., T. Awerbuch, U. Brinkman, I. Eckardt, P. Epstein, N. Makhoul, C. A. de Possas, C. Puccia, A. Spielman, and M. E. Wilson. 1994. The emergence of new diseases. *American Scientist* 82:52–60.

Levison, C. H., D. W. Hastings, and J. N. Harrison. 1981. Epidemiologic transition in a frontier town—Manti, Utah: 1849-1977. *American Journal of Physical Anthropology* 56:83–93.

Lewis, D. E., Jr. 1990. Stress, migration, and blood pressure in Kiribati. *American Journal of Human Biology* 2:139–51.

Lewontin, R. C. 1972. The apportionment of human diversity. In *Evolutionary Biology.* Vol. 6, ed. T. Dobzhansky, pp. 381–98. New York: Plenum Press.

Lieberman, P., and E. S. Crelin. 1971. On the speech of Neanderthal. *Linguistic Inquiry* 2:203–22.

Lilienfeld, A. M., and D. E. Lilienfeld. 1980. *Foundations of Epidemiology.* 2d ed. New York: Oxford University Press.

Linden, E. 1981. *Apes, Men, and Language.* Rev. ed. Middlesex, England: Penguin Books.

Livingstone, F. B. 1958. Anthropological implications of sickle cell gene distribution in West Africa. *American Anthropologist* 60:533–62.

———. 1964. On the nonexistence of human races. In *The Concept of Race*, ed. A. Montagu, pp. 46–60. New York: Collier.

———. 1989. Who gave whom hemoglobin S: The use of restriction site haplotype variation for the interpretation of the evolution of the β^s-Globin gene. *American Journal of Human Biology* 1:289–302.

Loehlin, J. C., G. Lindzey, and J. N. Spuhler. 1975. *Race Differences in Intelligence.* San Francisco: W. H. Freeman.

Loomis, W. F. 1967. Skin-pigment regulation of vitamin-D biosynthesis in man. *Science* 157:501–6.

Lovejoy, C. O. 1981. The origin of man. *Science* 211: 341–50.

———. 1982. Models of human evolution. *Science* 217:304–6.

McElroy, A., and P. K. Townsend. 1989. *Medical Anthropology in Ecological Perspective*. 2d ed. Boulder, Colo.: Westview Press.

McEvedy, C. 1988. The bubonic plague. *Scientific American* 258(2): 118–23.

McGrath, J. W. 1990. AIDS in Africa: A bioanthropological perspective. *American Journal of Human Biology* 2:381–96.

McGrew, W. C. 1992. *Chimpanzee Material Culture.* Cambridge: Cambridge University Press.

McHenry, H. M. 1992. How big were the early hominids? *Evolutionary Anthropology* 1:15–20.

McNeill, W. H. 1977. *Plagues and Peoples.* New York: Doubleday.

Madrigal, L. 1989. Hemoglobin genotype, fertility, and the malaria hypothesis. *Human Biology* 61:311–25.

Malina, R. M. 1975. *Growth and Development: The First Twenty Years in Man.* Minneapolis, Minn.: Burgess.

———. 1979. Secular changes in size and maturity: Causes and effects. *Monograph for the Society of Research in Child Development* 44:59–102.

Markham, R., and C. P. Groves. 1990. Brief communication: Weights of wild orangutans. *American Journal of Physical Anthropology* 81:1–3.

Marks, J. 1995. *Human Biodiversity: Genes, Races, and History.* New York: Aldine de Gruyter.

Marks, J., and R. B. Lyles. 1994. Rethinking genes. *Evolutionary Anthropology* 3:139–46.

Martin, R. D. 1981. Relative brain size and basal metabolic rate in terrestrial vertebrates. *Nature* 293:57–60.

Mascia-Lees, F. E., J. H. Relethford, and T. Sorger. 1986. Evolutionary perspectives on permanent breast enlargement in human females. *American Anthropologist* 88:423–28.

Mayr, E. 1982. *The Growth of Biological Thought.* Cambridge: Harvard University Press.

Meindl, R. S., and A. C. Swedlund. 1977. Secular trends in mortality in the Connecticut River Valley, 1700–1850. *Human Biology* 49:389–414.

Miller, J. A. 1991. Does brain size variability provide evidence of multiple species in *Homo habilis*? *American Journal of Physical Anthropology* 84: 385–98.

Mittermeier, R. A., and E. J. Sterling. 1992. Conservation of primates. In *The Cambridge Encyclopedia of Human Evolution,* ed. S. Jones, R. Martin, and D. Pilbeam, pp. 33–36. Cambridge: Cambridge University Press.

Molnar, S. 1983. *Human Variation: Races, Types and Ethnic Groups.* 2d ed. Englewood Cliffs, N.J.: Prentice-Hall.

———. 1992. *Human Variation: Races, Types, and Ethnic Groups.* 3d ed. Englewood Cliffs, N.J.: Prentice-Hall.

Montagu, A., ed. 1984. *Science and Creationism.* Oxford: Oxford University Press.

Moran, E. F. 1982. *Human Adaptability: An Introduction to Ecological Anthropology.* Boulder, Colo.: Westview Press.

Nesse, R. M., and G. C. Williams. 1994. *Why We Get Sick: The New Science of Darwinian Medicine.* New York: Random House.

Oates, J. F. 1987. Food distribution and foraging behavior. In *Primate Societies,* ed. B. B. Smuts, D. L. Cheney, R. M. Seyfarth, R. W. Wrangham, and T. T. Struhsaker, pp. 197–209. Chicago: University of Chicago Press.

Olshansky, S. J., B. A. Carnes, and C. Cassel. 1990. In search of Methuselah: Estimating the upper limit to human longevity. *Science* 250:634–40.

Omran, A. R. 1977. Epidemiologic transition in the United States: The health factor in population change. *Population Bulletin* 32:3–42.

Parés, J. M., and A. Pérez-González. 1995. Paleomagnetic age for fossil hominids at Atapuerca archaeological site, Spain. *Science* 269:830–32.

Pasachoff, J. M. 1979. *Astronomy: From the Earth to the Universe.* Philadelphia: W. B. Saunders.

Passingham, R. 1982. *The Human Primate.* San Francisco: W. H. Freeman.

Pfeiffer, J. E. 1985. *The Emergence of Humankind.* 4th ed. New York: Harper & Row.

Pianka, E. R. 1983. *Evolutionary Ecology.* 3d ed. New York: Harper & Row.

Pilbeam, D. 1982. New hominoid skull material from the Miocene of Pakistan. *Nature* 295:232–34.

———. 1984. The descent of hominoids and hominids. *Scientific American* 250(3): 84–96.

Pilbeam, D., G. E. Meyer, C. Badgley, M. D. Rose, M. H. L. Pickford, A. K. Behrensmeyer, and S. M. Ibrahim Shah. 1977. New hominoid primates from the Siwaliks of Pakistan and their bearing on hominoid evolution. *Nature* 270:689–95.

Pope, G. G. 1989. Bamboo and human evolution. *Natural History*, October: 49–56.

Post, P. W., F. Daniels, Jr., and R. T. Binford, Jr. 1975. Cold injury and the evolution of "white" skin. *Human Biology* 47:65–80.

Potts, M. 1988. Birth control. In *The New Encyclopaedia Britannica*. Vol. 15, pp. 113–20. Chicago: Encyclopaedia Britannica.

Potts, R. 1984. Home bases and early hominids. *American Scientist* 72:338–47.

Rak, Y. 1986. The Neanderthal: A new look at an old face. *Journal of Human Evolution* 15:151–64.

Rak, Y., and B. Arensburg. 1987. Kebara 2 Neanderthal pelvis: First look at a complete inlet. *American Journal of Physical Anthropology* 73:227–31.

Raup, D. M., and J. J. Sepkoski. 1986. Periodic extinction of families and genera. *Science* 231:833–36.

Reader, J. 1986. *The Rise of Life: The First 3.5 Billion Years*. New York: Knopf.

Reid, R. M. 1973. Inbreeding in human populations. In *Methods and Theories of Anthropological Genetics*, ed. M. H. Crawford and P. L. Workman, pp. 83–116. Albuquerque: University of New Mexico Press.

Relethford, J. H. 1992. Cross-cultural analysis of migration rates: Effects of geographic distance and population size. *American Journal of Physical Anthropology* 89:459–66.

———. 1994. Craniometric variation among human populations. *American Journal of Physical Anthropology* 95:53–62.

———. 1995. Genetics and modern human origins. *Evolutionary Anthropology* 4: 53–63.

———. 1996. Genetic drift obscures population history: Problem and solution. *Human Biology* 68: 29–44.

Relethford, J. H., and J. Blangero. 1990. Detection of differential gene flow from patterns of quantitative variation. *Human Biology* 62:5–25.

Relethford, J. H., and M. H. Crawford. 1995. Anthropometric variation and the population history of Ireland. *American Journal of Physical Anthropology* 96:25–38.

Relethford, J. H., and H. C. Harpending. 1994. Craniometric variation, genetic theory, and modern human origins. *American Journal of Physical Anthropology* 95:249–70.

———. 1995. Ancient differences in population size can mimic a recent African origin of modern humans. In *Current Anthropology* 36: 667–74.

Richard, A. F. 1985. *Primates in Nature*. New York: W. H. Freeman.

Rightmire, G. P. 1992. *Homo erectus*: Ancestor or evolutionary side branch? *Evolutionary Anthropology* 1:43–49.

Roberts, D. F. 1968. Genetic effects of population size reduction. *Nature* 220:1084–88.

———. 1978. *Climate and Human Variability*. 2d ed. Menlo Park, Calif.: Benjamin Cummings.

Roberts, R. G., R. Jones, and M. A. Smith. 1990. Thermoluminescence dating of a 50,000-year-old human occupation site in northern Australia. *Nature* 345:153–56.

Robins, A. H. 1991. *Biological Perspectives on Human Pigmentation*. Cambridge: Cambridge University Press.

Rodman, P. S., and H. M. McHenry. 1980. Bioenergetics and the origin of human bipedalism. *American Journal of Physical Anthropology* 52:103–6.

Roebroeks, W. 1994. Updating the earliest occupation of Europe. *Current Anthropology* 35:301–5.

Rogers, A. R., and H. C. Harpending. 1992. Population growth makes waves in the distribution of pairwise genetic differences. *Molecular and Evolutionary Biology* 9:552–69.

Rogers, A. R., and L. B. Jorde. 1995. Genetic evidence on modern human origins. *Human Biology* 67:1–36.

Rogers, R. A., L. A. Rogers, and L. D. Martin. 1992. How the door opened: The peopling of the New World. *Human Biology* 64:281–302.

Rose, M. D. 1986. Further hominoid postcranial specimens from the Late Miocene Nagri formations of Pakistan. *Journal of Human Evolution* 15:333–67.

Rowell, T. E. 1966. Forest-living baboons in Uganda. *Journal of Zoology, London* 149:344–64.

Roychoudhury, A. K., and M. Nei. 1988. *Human Polymorphic Genes: World Distribution*. Oxford: Oxford University Press.

Ruff, C. B. 1993. Climatic adaptation and hominid evolution: The thermoregulatory imperative. *Evolutionary Anthropology* 2:53–60.

Ruse, M. 1987. Biological species: Natural kinds, individuals, or what? *British Journal for the Philosophy of Science* 38:225–42.

Ruvolo, M., D. Pan, S. Zehr, T. Goldberg, T. R. Disotell, and M. von Dornum. 1994. Gene trees and hominoid phylogeny. *Proceedings of the National Academy of Science, USA* 91:8900–4.

Sagan, C. 1977. *The Dragons of Eden: Speculations on the Evolution of Human Intelligence.* New York: Ballantine Books.

Sarich, V. M., and A. C. Wilson. 1967. Immunological time scale for hominoid evolution. *Science* 158:1200–3.

Savage-Rumbaugh, S., and R. Lewin. 1994. *Kanzi: The Ape at the Brink of the Human Mind.* New York: John Wiley & Sons.

Scammon, R. E. 1930. The measurement of the body in childhood. In *The Measurement of Man,* ed. J. A. Harris, C. M. Jackson, D. G. Paterson, and R. E. Scammon, pp. 171–215. Minneapolis: University of Minnesota Press.

Scarr, S., and A. Weinberg. 1978. Attitudes, interests, and IQ. *Human Nature* 1(4): 29–36.

Schepartz, L. A. 1993. Language and modern human origins. *Yearbook of Physical Anthropology* 36:91–126.

Schopf, J. W., ed. 1992. *Major Events in the History of Life.* Boston: Jones and Bartlett.

Schopf, J. W. 1993. Microfossils of the early Archean Apex chert: New evidence of the antiquity of life. *Science* 260:640–46.

Schow, D. J., and J. Frentzen. 1986. *The Outer Limits: The Official Companion.* New York: Ace.

Schwartz, J. H. 1987. *The Red Ape: Orangutan-utans and Human Origins.* Boston: Houghton Mifflin.

Shea, B. T., and A. M. Gomez. 1988. Tooth scaling and evolutionary dwarfism: An investigation of allometry in human pygmies. *American Journal of Physical Anthropology* 77:117–32.

Sheehan, P. M., D. E. Fastovsky, R. G. Hoffman, C. B. Berghaus, and D. L. Gabriel. 1991. Sudden extinction of the dinosaurs: Latest Cretaceous, Upper Great Plains, U.S.A. *Science* 254:835–39.

Sherry, S. T., A. R. Rogers, H. Harpending, H. Soodyall, T. Jenkins, and M. Stoneking. 1994. Mismatch distributions of mtDNA reveal recent human populations expansions. *Human Biology* 66:761–75.

Simons, E. L., and T. Rasmussen. 1994. A whole new world of ancestors: Eocene anthropoids from Africa. *Evolutionary Anthropology* 3:128–39.

Sjøvold, T. 1992. The Stone Age Iceman from the Alps: The find and the current status of investigation. *Evolutionary Anthropology* 1:117–24.

Smith, F. H., A. B. Falsetti, and S. M. Donnelly. 1989a. Modern human origins. *Yearbook of Physical Anthropology* 32:35–68.

Smith, F. H., J. F. Simek, and M. S. Harrill. 1989b. Geographic variation in supraorbital torus reduction during the later Pleistocene (c. 80,000–15,000 B.P.). In *The Human Revolution,* ed. P. Mellars and C. Stringer, pp. 172–93. Princeton: Princeton University Press.

Smouse, P. E. 1982. Genetic architecture of swidden agricultural tribes from the lowland rain forests of South America. In *Current Developments in Anthropological Genetics.* Vol. 2, *Ecology and Population Structure,* ed. M. H. Crawford and J. H. Mielke, pp. 139–78. New York: Plenum Press.

Snowden, C. T. 1990. Language capacities of nonhuman animals. *Yearbook of Physical Anthropology* 33:215–43.

Spencer, M. A., and B. Demes. 1993. Biomechanical analysis of masticatory system configuration in Neandertals and Inuits. *American Journal of Physical Anthropology* 91:1–20.

Spiess, E. B. 1977. *Genes in Populations.* New York: John Wiley.

Stanley, S. M. 1979. *Macroevolution: Pattern and Process.* San Francisco: W. H. Freeman.

———. 1981. *The New Evolutionary Timetable: Fossils, Genes, and the Origin of Species.* New York: Basic Books.

Stebbins, G. L. 1982. *Darwin to DNA, Molecules to Humanity.* San Francisco: W. H. Freeman.

Stern, J. T., Jr., and R. L. Susman. 1983. The locomotor anatomy of *Australopithecus afarensis. American Journal of Physical Anthropology* 60:279–317.

Stone, A. C., and M. Stoneking. 1993. Ancient DNA from a Pre-Columbian Amerindian population. *American Journal of Physical Anthropology* 92:463–71.

Stoner, B. P., and E. Trinkaus. 1981. Getting a grip on the Neandertals: Were they all thumbs? *American Journal of Physical Anthropology* 54:281–82.

Stringer, C. B. 1986. The credibility of *Homo habilis.* In *Major Topics in Primate and Human Evolution,* ed. B. Wood, L. Martin and P. Andrews, pp. 266–94. Cambridge: Cambridge University Press.

———. 1994. Out of Africa—A personal history. In *Origins of Anatomically Modern Humans,* ed. M. H. Nitecki and D. V. Nitecki, pp. 149–72. New York: Plenum Press.

Stringer, C. B., and P. Andrews. 1988. Genetic and fossil evidence for the origin of modern humans. *Science* 239:1263–68.

Stringer, C., and C. Gamble. 1993. *In Search of the Neanderthals: Solving the Puzzle of Human Origins.* New York: Thames and Hudson.

Strum, S. C., and W. Mitchell. 1987. Baboon models and muddles. In *The Evolution of Human Behavior: Primate Models*, ed. W. G. Kinzey, pp. 87–104. Albany, N.Y.: State University of New York Press.

Susman, R. L. 1988. Hand of *Paranthropus robustus* from Member I, Swartkrans: Fossil evidence for tool behavior. *Science* 240:781–84.

Sussman, R. W. 1991. Primate origins and the evolution of angiosperms. *American Journal of Primatology* 23:209–23.

Sussman, R. W., J. M. Cheverud, and T. Q. Bartlett. 1995. Infant killing as an evolutionary strategy: Reality or myth? *Evolutionary Anthropology* 3:149–51.

Sutton, H. E., and R. P. Wagner. 1985. *Genetics: A Human Concern*. New York: Macmillan.

Swedlund, A. C., and G. J. Armelagos. 1976. *Demographic Anthropology*. Dubuque, Iowa: Wm. C. Brown.

Swisher, C. C., G. H. Curtis, T. Jacob, A. G. Getty, A. Suprijo, and Widiasmoro. 1994. Age of the earliest known hominids in Java, Indonesia. *Science* 263:1118–21.

Szabo, G. 1967. The regional anatomy of the human integument with special reference to the distribution of hair follicles, sweat glands and melanocytes. *Philosophical Transactions of the Royal Society of London*. 252B: 447–85.

Tague, R. G. 1992. Sexual dimorphism in the human bony pelvis, with a consideration of the Neandertal pelvis from Kebara Cave, Israel. *American Journal of Physical Anthropology* 88:1–21.

Tattersall, I. 1995. *The Fossil Trail: How We Know What We Think We Know About Human Evolution*. New York: Oxford University Press.

Teitelbaum, M. S. 1988. Population. In *The New Encyclopaedia Britannica*. Vol. 25, pp. 1038–47. Chicago: Encyclopaedia Britannica.

Templeton, A. R. 1992. Human origins and analysis of mitochondrial DNA sequences. *Science* 255:737.

Terrace, H. S. 1979. *Nim: A Chimpanzee Who Learned Sign Language*. New York: Knopf.

Thomas, D. H. 1986. *Refiguring Anthropology: First Principles of Probability and Statistics*. Prospect Heights, Ill.: Waveland Press.

Thorne, A. G., and M. H. Wolpoff. 1992. The multiregional evolution of humans. *Scientific American* 266(4): 76–83.

Tobias, P. V. 1971. *The Brain in Hominid Evolution*. New York: Columbia University Press.

Trinkaus, E. 1981. Neanderthal limb proportions and cold adaptation. In *Aspects of Human Evolution*, ed. C. B. Stringer, pp. 187–224. London: Taylor and Francis.

———. 1990. Cladistics and the hominid fossil record. *American Journal of Physical Anthropology* 83:1–11.

Trinkaus, E., and M. LeMay. 1982. Occipital bunning among later Pleistocene hominids. *American Journal of Physical Anthropology* 57:27–35.

Trinkaus, E., and P. Shipman. 1992. *The Neandertals: Changing the Image of Mankind*. New York: Knopf.

Ubelaker, D., and H. Scammell. 1992. *Bones: A Forensic Detective's Casebook*. New York: HarperCollins.

Underwood, J. H. 1979. *Human Variation and Human Microevolution*. Englewood Cliffs, N.J.: Prentice-Hall.

United States Department of Commerce. 1991. *1990 Census Profile, March 1991*. Washington: U.S. Department of Commerce, Economics and Statistics Administration, Bureau of the Census.

Vigilant, L., M. Stoneking, H. Harpending, K. Hawkes, and A. C. Wilson. 1991. African populations and the evolution of human mitochondrial DNA. *Science* 253:1503–7.

Vrba, E. S. 1985. Ecological and adaptive changes associated with early hominid evolution. In *Ancestors: The Hard Evidence*, ed. E. Delson, pp. 63–71. New York: Alan R. Liss.

Walker, A., and M. Teaford. 1989. The hunt for *Proconsul*. *Scientific American* 260(1): 76–82.

Walsh, J. 1988. Rift Valley Fever rears its head. *Science* 240:1397–99.

Ward, C. V., A. Walker, and M. F. Teaford. 1991. *Proconsul* did not have a tail. *Journal of Human Evolution* 21:215–20.

Washburn, S. L. 1960. Tools and human evolution. *Scientific American* 203:62–75.

Watts, E. S. 1986. Evolution of the human growth curve. In *Human Growth: A Comprehensive Treatise*. Vol. 1, *Developmental Biology, Prenatal Growth*, ed. F. Falkner and J. M. Tanner, pp. 153–66. New York: Plenum Press.

Weeks, J. R. 1981. *Population: An Introduction to Concepts and Issues*. 2d ed. Belmont, Calif.: Wadsworth.

Weiss, K. M. 1984. On the number of members of the genus *Homo* who have ever lived, and some evolutionary implications. *Human Biology* 56:637–49.

Weiss, K. M., R. E. Ferrell, and C. L. Hanis. 1984. A New World syndrome of metabolic diseases with a genetic and evolutionary basis. *Yearbook of Physical Anthropology* 27:153–78.

Wheeler, P. E. 1991a. The influence of bipedalism on the energy and water budgets of early hominids. *Journal of Human Evolution* 21:117–36.

———. 1991b. The thermoregulatory advantage of hominid bipedalism in open equatorial environments: The contribution of increased convective heat loss and cutaneous evaporative cooling. *Journal of Human Evolution* 21:107–15.

White, R., and J. M. Lalouel. 1988. Chromosome mapping with DNA markers. *Scientific American* 258:40–48.

White, T. D., G. Suwa, and B. Asfaw. 1994. *Australopithecus ramidus*, a new species of early hominid from Aramis, Ethiopia. *Nature* 371:306–12.

White, T. D., G. Suwa, and B. Asfaw. 1995. Corrigendum: *Australopithecus ramidus*, a new species of early hominid from Aramis, Ethiopia. *Nature* 375:88.

Wilford, J. N. 1985. *The Riddle of the Dinosaur*. New York: Knopf.

Wilkinson, R. G. 1975. Trephination by drilling in ancient Mexico. *Bulletin of the New York Academy of Medicine* 51(7): 838–50.

Willerman, L., R. Schultz, J. N. Rutledge, and E. D. Bigler. 1991. *In vivo* brain size and intelligence. *Intelligence* 15:223–28.

Williams-Blangero, S., and J. Blangero. 1992. Quantitative genetic analysis of skin reflectance: A multivariate approach. *Human Biology* 64:35–49.

Wilson, E. O. 1980. *Sociobiology: The Abridged Edition*. Cambridge: Harvard University Press.

WoldeGabriel, G., P. Renne, T. D. White, G. Suwa, J. de Heinzelin, W. K. Hart, and G. Heiken. 1995. Age of early hominids. *Nature* 376:559.

WoldeGabriel, G., T. D. White, G. Suwa, P. Renne, J. de Heinzelin, W. K. Hart, and G. Heiken. 1994. Ecological and temporal placement of early Pliocene hominids at Aramis, Ethiopia. *Nature* 371:330–33.

Wolfe, L. D. 1995. Current research in field primatology. In *Biological Anthropology: The State of the Science*, ed. N. T. Boaz and L. D. Wolfe, pp. 149–68. Bend, Ore.: International Institute for Human Evolutionary Research.

Wolpoff, M. H. 1980. *Paleoanthropology*. New York: Knopf.

Wolpoff, M. H., A. G. Thorne, F. H. Smith, D. W. Frayer, and G. G. Pope. 1994. Multiregional evolution: A world-wide source for modern human populations. In *Origins of Anatomically Modern Humans*, ed. M. H. Nitecki and D. V. Nitecki, pp. 175–200. New York: Plenum Press.

Wood, B. 1992. Origin and evolution of the genus *Homo*. *Nature* 355:783–90.

Wood, C. S. 1979. *Human Sickness and Health: A Biocultural View*. Mountain View, Calif.: Mayfield.

Wood, J. W. 1994. *Dynamics of Human Reproduction: Biology, Biometry, Demography*. New York: Aldine de Gruyter.

Woodham-Smith, C. 1962. *The Great Hunger: Ireland 1845–1849*. New York: Harper & Row.

Woodward, V. 1992. *Human Heredity and Society*. St. Paul, Minn.: West.

Workman, P. L., B. S. Blumberg, and A. J. Cooper. 1963. Selection, gene migration and polymorphic stability in a U.S. White and Negro population. *American Journal of Human Genetics* 15:71–84.

Wrangham, R. W. 1987. Evolution of social structure. In *Primate Societies*, ed. B. B. Smuts, D. L. Cheney, R. M. Seyfarth, R. W. Wrangham, and T. T. Struhsaker, pp. 282–96. Chicago: University of Chicago Press.

Wright, P. C. 1992. Primate ecology, rainforest conservation, and economic development: Building a national park in Madagascar. *Evolutionary Anthropology* 1:25–33.

Yellen, J. E., A. S. Brooks, E. Cornelissen, M. J. Mahlman, and K. Stewart. 1995. A Middle Stone Age worked bone industry from Katanda, Upper Semliki Valley, Zaire. *Science* 268:553–56.

Zimmer, C. 1995. Coming onto the land. *Discover*, June 1995:119–27.

Index

molecular genetics, 30–39
monkeys
  apes compared to, 138, 175–176, 183–184, *184*, 193, 242
  dental formulae, 147, 176, 179
  diet, 179, 181, 240
  distribution, 176, 177, 179, 180
  evolution, 138, 176–177, 239–241
  humans compared to, 175–176, 179, 183–184, *184*
  learning in, 155–156, *155*, 159–160
  mother–infant bond in, 157, *157*
  New World. *See* New World monkeys
  Old World. *See* Old World monkeys
  play behavior and socialization, 159–160
  sexual dimorphism, 177, 181
  skeletal structure, 175–176, 183–184, *184*, 193, *497*
  social structure, 177–178, 180–181, *180*, *181–182*
  tail development, 138, 176–177, *176*
  taxonomy of, *171*, 174–175, *175*, *491–492*
  teeth, 183
  vocalizations, 175, 182
  See also anthropoids; *specific species*
monogamous family group, 160, **161**
monogamy
  defined, 158–**159**
  of gibbons, 190
  humans and, 220
  origin of, 291
  paternal care and, 158–159
  sexual dimorphism and, 190
  social group of, 160, 161
  See also breeding; marriage; polygamy
monosomy, **53**
monotremes, 130, 140, *141*
Moran, E. F., 422
morphology, 186, **187**
  See also phenetics
mortality
  and age-sex structure, 467–468
  defined, **463**
  as demographic measure, 462–463, *463*
  epidemiological transition and, *448*, 449–450, *450*
  infant, 441, 446, 450

and life tables, 462
natural selection affected by, 73
population growth and, 464, 466, 469
social, 441
See also death, causes of; demography; life expectancy at birth
mosaic evolution, 236, **237**
mother–infant bond, 156–158, *157*, 291
Mousterian tradition, 320, *321*, **321**
movement. *See* locomotion
mtDNA. *See* mitochondrial *DNA*
multimale/multifemale group, 160–**161**
multiregional model of evolution, **335**–336, *336*, 338–343
multivariate analysis, **369**–370
mummy, the Iceman, 346
mumps, 432, 442
mutation
  advantageous, 52–53
  allele frequencies and, 68–69, 71–72, 87–88, *88*
  defined, 52, **53**
  disadvantageous, 52–53
  the environment and, 52–53, 458
  evolution and, 52–53, 68–69
  mathematical basis of, 483–484
  neutral, 52–53
  overview, 51–53
  radiation and, 52
  rates of, 54–55, 250–252
  reverse, 68–69
  sickle cell. *See* sickle cell allele
  and speciation, 100, 101, 102
  types of, 53–54
  See also evolutionary forces

nasal index, **421**
Native Americans
  climate adaptation by, 412, 416–418, *417*, 419, *420*, 421–422
  culture contact and disease in, 445
  Diego blood group in, 364–365
  genetic relationship to Asians, 333
  high–altitude adaptation, 425–427, *425–526*
  New World syndrome and, 453–454, *454*
  social structures, 379–382, *379*, *382*
  See also specific tribes
natural increase, 464, **465**

natural selection
  allele frequencies and, 68–77, 87, 88, 89, 370
  analysis of, 369, 370, 373–376
    case studies, 387–407
  balancing selection, 76
  and behavior, 164–168
  complex traits and, 76–77, *77*
  cumulative effects, 376
  and Darwin, 18–20
  defined, 20, **21**
  directional selection, 77
  diversifying selection, 77
  against dominant alleles, 72–73
  examples, 20–21, *20*
  and extinction, 104, 106, 107
  for heterozygotes, 73–76, *74–75*
  against homozygotes, 70–76
  mathematical basis of, 484–486
  misconceptions about, 106–110
  against recessive alleles, 70–72, *70–71*
  and speciation, 100, 101
  species selection, 106
  stabilizing selection, 76
  and variation. *See* variation
  See also evolutionary forces
nature vs. nurture. *See* genetics: vs. environment
Neandertals
  burial practices, 321–322
  characteristics, 317–320, *318–319*
  defined, 312, **313,** 316
  distribution, 312, 316
  evolution models and, 335, 339–340
  intelligence, 316
  language capability, 322
  popular image of, 316
  See also Homo sapiens (archaic)
Neel, James, 380
neoteny, **293**–294
New World monkeys
  characteristics, 176–177, *176–177*, 179
  evolution and origins, 240–241
  See also monkeys; *specific species*
New World syndrome, **453**–454, *454*
New York City death rate, 448, 449
nipples, body plan and, 110
nocturnal
  defined, **171**
  monkey species as, 173–174
  prosimians as, 171
  transition to diurnal lifestyle from, 240

noncommunicable disease, defined, 430
noninfectious diseases. *See* diseases (human): noninfectious
nonrandom mating, 67–68, **69,** 90
    assortative, 68, 90
    inbreeding. *See* inbreeding
nose shape, and climate, 421
notochord, 139, **140**
nucleus, 58
nurture vs. nature. *See* genetics: vs. environment
nutritional disease, 442–443, 456–457, *456–457*
nutrition. *See* diet

occipital bun, 318, **319**
odontometrics, 358, **359**
offspring care
    and bipedalism, 290–291
    hominoids, 183
    humans, 143–144, 309
    and hunting, 309
    and increased brain size, 294
    mammals, 143, 149, 165–166
    paternal, 158–159, 166
    primates, 156–160, 165–166
    strategy of, 143
    See also birth interval; social structure
offspring distributions, predicting, 44–45
Oldowan tradition, 280–**281,** *281,* 282, 305, 307
Olduvai Gorge site, 276, 278, 281–282, 283, 307, *308*
Old World monkeys
    characteristics, 179–182
    evolution, 239–240, *240*
    and humans, 179
    New World compared to, 176–177
    See also monkeys; *specific species*
Oligocene epoch, **239**
Omran, A. R., 445, 449
On the Origin of Species by Means of Natural Selection (Darwin), 20, 93
open system, language as, 227
orangutans, 192–194, *192*
    brain size, *207*
    characteristics, 192–193
    distribution, 193
    as endangered, 193
    evolution, 252–255, *254*
    and humans (modern *Homo sapiens*)

genetic distance between, *24,* 186, 187, 193
    physiologic similarities, 193
    language capability, 229
    reproduction, 143, 193
    sexual dimorphism, 192
    Sivapithecus compared with, 249–250, *250*
    social structure, 193–194, 199
    taxonomy, 186–188, *188*
    testes size and social structure, 199
origin of species. *See* speciation
origins. *See* evolution; *specific species*
orthogenesis, **107**–109, *108–109*
osteoarthritis, 435, *435*
Ouranopithecus, 255
oxygen starvation, 422, 423–426, *424–425*

Pacific Islanders
    culture contact and disease in, 445
    marriage patterns, 86, *86*
pair bonding, origin of, 291
paleoanthropology, 11
Paleocene epoch, 234, **235**
paleoecology, **119**
paleomagnetic reversal, **117**
paleopathology, *435–436,* **435**–437, 438
paleospecies, 98, **99**
Paleozoic era, **123**–127
palynology, **119**
pandemic, **431**–432
parallel evolution, 136, **137,** 139
parasitic diseases
    in hunting-gathering societies, 439
    malaria. *See* malaria
parental care. *See* offspring care
parental investment, **165.** *See also* mother–infant bond; offspring care
Park, Michael, *434*
paternal care, in primates, 158–159, 166
PCR (polymerase chain reaction), 36
Peking Man, *302,* 309
pellagra, 442
peppered moths, 20–21, *20*
periods
    defined, 122, **123**
    See also geologic history
Permian period, 126–127, 130
Petralona skull, 315, *315*

Phanerozoic eon, *123,* **123**
phenetics, 138, **139,** 186
phenotypes, **41**–43
physical anthropology. *See* biological anthropology
physical traits
    analogous, 137, *137*
    classification by. *See* taxonomy
    complex
        genetics of, 48–51
        measuring variation of, 357–359, *358*
        natural selection and, 76–77, *77,* 402–407
    continuous, examples, 48, *49,* 362–364
    derived, 137–138
    discrete, 48
    heritability of, 50–51
    homologous, 136–137, *136*
    major gene model, 51
    pleiotropy, 48–50, *49, 50*
    polygenic, 48–50, *49, 50*
    polymorphisms, 69
    primitive, 137–138, 151
    simple
        genetics of, 39–48, *49, 50*
        measuring variation of, 355–357
        natural selection and, 387–402
    See also evolutionary forces; human variation; variation
physiologic adaptation, 410–421, *413–414, 416–417, 419–420,* 423–427, *424–426*
Pilbeam, David, 249, 250
Piltdown Man, 287
placenta, **141**
placental mammals, 130, 141
    See also mammals
plants, 35, 101
plasticity, 410, **411**
platypus, origin of, 130
play behaviors, 160
pleiotropy, 48–50, **49,** 50
Pleistocene epoch, 262, **263,** 316
Pliocene epoch, 262, **263**
Plio–Pleistocene, 262, **263**
polar bodies, 62
polio, 458
pollen, study of fossil, 119
pollution
    disease rates and, 449, 458
    human evolution and, 107
polyandrous group, 160, **161**
polyandry, 160, 220, **221**